MASTERING MODERN PSYCHOLOGICAL TESTING

MASTERING MODERN PSYCHOLOGICAL TESTING

THEORY & METHODS

Cecil R. Reynolds

Texas A&M University

Ronald B. Livingston

University of Texas at Tyler

Boston   Columbus   Indianapolis   New York   San Francisco   Upper Saddle River
Amsterdam   Cape Town   Dubai   London   Madrid   Milan   Munich   Paris   Montreal   Toronto
Delhi   Mexico City   Sao Paulo   Sydney   Hong Kong   Seoul   Singapore   Taipei   Tokyo

Editorial Director: Craig Campanella
Editor in Chief: Jessica Mosher
Executive Editor: Susan Hartman
Editorial Project Manager: Kerri Hart-Morris
Editorial Assistant: Alexandra Mitton
Director of Marketing: Brandy Dawson
Senior Marketing Manager: Nicole Kunzmann
Marketing Assistant: Jessica Warren
Director of Production: Lisa Iarkowski
Associate Managing Editor: Liz Napolitano
Senior Production Project Manager: Pat Torelli

Senior Operations Supervisor: Evelyn Beaton
Operations Specialist: Linda Cox
Media Director: Brian Hyland
Lead Media Project Manager: Pam Weldin
Supplements Editor: Madelyn Schricker
Full-Service Project Management: Element Thomson North America
Composition: Element Thomson North America
Printer/Binder: Edwards Brothers Malloy
Cover Printer: Lehigh-Phoenix Color/Hagerstown
Text Font: 10/12 Times

Credits and acknowledgments borrowed from other sources and reproduced, with permission, in this textbook appear on the appropriate page within text.

Many of the designations by manufacturers and sellers to distinguish their products are claimed as trademarks. Where those designations appear in this book, and the publisher was aware of a trademark claim, the designations have been printed in initial caps or all caps.

Library of Congress Cataloging-in-Publication Data
Reynolds, Cecil R.
    Mastering modern psychological testing : theory & methods / by Cecil R. Reynolds,
    Ronald B. Livingston. — 1st ed.
       p. cm.
    Includes bibliographical references and index.
    ISBN 978-0-205-48350-1 (hardcover)
    1. Psychological tests. 2. Psychology—Research—Methodology. I. Livingston, Ronald B. II. Title.
    BF176.R496 2012
    150.28'7–dc22

                                           2011013504

10 9 8 7 6 5 4 3

ISBN 10:   0-205-48350-X
ISBN 13: 978-0-205-48350-1

*To Julia, a special thank you for being such a great partner
and such a wonderful complement to my life.*

CRR

*To my parents, James (in memoriam) and Ruby Livingston;
my wife, Kimberly Harvey-Livingston;
and children, James, Chesley, and Kyle!*

RBL

CONTENTS

PREFACE

When we meet someone for the first or first few times, we engage inescapably in some form of evaluation. Is the person funny, likable, personable, intelligent, witty, arrogant, rude, or the like? These are just some of the descriptors we might apply to people we meet. This happens in classrooms as well. As university professors, just as other classroom teachers do, we meet new students each year and form impressions about them from our interactions. These impressions are forms of evaluation or assessment of characteristics we observe or determine from our discourse with these new students. When you apply for a job, you are being appraised throughout your interactions with everyone you meet at your desired place of employment. We all do this informally and at times we realize, once we have more experience with someone, that we were in error in our early evaluations. There are times, however, when our evaluations must be far more formal and hopefully more precise. This is ultimately a book about those times and how to make our appraisals more accurate and meaningful.

Psychological and educational testing seems to be ubiquitous in our society, and its presence is growing throughout the world. There is renewed interest even in China, long believed to be the birthplace of psychological and educational testing where what were essentially civil service exams were used thousands of years ago. Tests are useful for many reasons. They are shortcuts to learning things about people that would otherwise take us months or more to know, which also leads us to the conclusion that there is nothing tests tell us about people that we could not learn without tests; it would simply take far longer and, in most instances, be less reliable and influenced by subjective and irrelevant contextual factors. Tests are useful because they also allow us to make accurate predictions and reduce uncertainty. Predictions are never perfect nor does uncertainty go to a value of zero, but to the extent we can reduce uncertainty by using tests, they are useful to us. Tests thus enhance decision making and are especially useful when resources are less than infinite. Consider your time as a resource—it is certainly one that is limited. In choosing a vocation, interest and aptitude tests can assist greatly in predicting areas in which you are most likely to be successful and also enjoy the work of people who are in the same vocation. It might otherwise take some people many years and much trial and error to find the right vocational domain, expending one of their most precious of resources—their time—in an unproductive and likely unenjoyable fashion.

The technology and vocabulary of testing *have* changed much over the last century or so, but its fundamental purposes have remained much the same. Test results reduce uncertainty and allow us to predict and to control events with less error than if we did not have test results. Tests quantify behavior for us in ways that allow us to subject behavior to more sophisticated observation and develop a deeper and more complex understanding of behavior than is possible through other means. Tests are a means of measurement, and the ability to measure something is central to any scientific approach to its study and understanding.

In this book we have attempted to integrate these ideas across the full spectrum of psychological and educational testing. We introduce the vocabulary of the profession and the most basic mathematics of testing early as being fundamental to understanding the field. We use examples frequently and often draw these examples from tests that we have authored or otherwise worked on as consultants. We do so because we have access to far more information about these tests than the typical researcher, and we understand them better because we were involved in their development. This also allows us to comment on practical problems encountered in the development of tests and their use because we have both worked not just as academics, but in the professional practice of psychology. We particularly appreciate the generosity of Pearson Assessments, Pro-Ed, Inc., Psychological Assessment Resources, and Western Psychological Services in allowing us to draw on products we have developed for them over many years as well as the use of material by their other authors. We have also adapted materials such as tables, graphs, and so on from our publications, particularly from our existing psychometric text published by Pearson which focuses more on measurement and assessment in educational settings.

Following the introduction of the basic areas of psychometrics (the study and quantification of psychological testing), we move to areas of testing that represent different approaches to measuring different psychological constructs. Controversies exist in many of these areas and we attempt to deal with these in context in most cases. However, you will find that we devote an entire chapter to the complex issue of cultural biases in testing. There is little that generates more emotional polemics in the profession of psychology than how tests are applied and interpreted across cultures within the United States. Even the lay press takes notice of these issues on occasion and there have been many legal battles in state and federal courts over the use of tests with minority groups. We have chosen to tackle this difficult and demanding area in a full-length chapter emphasizing data-based approaches to the issue.

Examples of existing tests are given throughout the text; however, this is not a book that is designed to prepare students to go out and administer, score, and interpret any specific psychological test. Rather, it is a textbook that gives the foundational core of knowledge of tests, measurement, and assessment constructs, issues, and most basic math to allow students to go forward with an understanding of what constitutes a psychological test, how tests are developed, how they are best used, and how to evaluate their strengths and weaknesses. We do emphasize test development in many places in the text because if one understands the development process and how the psychometric properties of tests are constructed, one has the generalized knowledge to always learn about any test. We felt that if we emphasized specific instruments too much, beyond using them as examples, students would be restricted in their knowledge and ability to generalize to revisions of existing tests and to the many new tests that are published each year. Mastering the fundamentals of psychological testing conceptually builds a better foundation for future understanding.

This book is intended for anyone who wants to develop a deeper understanding of how psychological tests are developed and how they are best used. We presume no prior knowledge of statistics, though such a course may make a section here and there easier to learn. Typically, this text is used in senior-level undergraduate courses in psychology departments or at the master's level in similar departments, including educational psychology, clinical counseling, school psychology, and related programs. Students who are specializing in an area in which they will use psychological tests will benefit greatly from the content of this work.

There are several colleagues we would like to thank for their contributions to the development of this text. First, we want to express our appreciation to Rob Altmann for authoring the chapter on employment and vocational testing and Andrew Schmitt for co-authoring the chapter on neuropsychological assessment. Additionally we want to thank Yossef Ben-Porath, Hale Martin, Kevin McGrew, Daneen Milam, and Victor Willson for sharing their expertise by contributing Special Interest Topics that enhance the scope of this text.

SUPPLEMENTS

Pearson Education is pleased to offer the following supplements to qualified adopters.

Instructor's Manual and Test Bank (0205609147) Prepared by the authors, the instructor's manual is a wonderful tool for classroom preparation and management. Corresponding to the chapters in the text, each of the manual's 18 chapters contains a brief overview of the chapter with suggestions on how to present the material, sample lecture outlines, classrooms activities and discussion topics, ideas for in-class and out-of-class projects, recommended outside readings and related films and videos.

The test bank contains over 1,800 multiple choice, short answer and essay questions, each referencing the relevant page in the text.

Pearson MyTest Computerized Test Bank PEARSON **my test** ☑ **(www.pearsonmytest .com):** The First Edition Test Bank comes with Pearson MyTest, a powerful assessment-generation program that helps instructors easily create and print quizzes and exams. You can do this online, allowing flexibility and the ability to efficiently manage assessments at any time. You can easily access existing questions and edit, create, and store questions using the simple drag-and-drop and Word-like controls. Each question comes with information on its level of difficulty and related page number in the text. For more information, go to www.pearsonmytest.com.

PowerPoint Presentation (0205239145) The PowerPoint Presentation is an exciting interactive tool for use in the classroom. Each chapter pairs key concepts with images from the textbook to reinforce student learning.

MySearchLab (0205699421) MySearchLab is the easiest way to master a writing or research project. Features include round-the-clock access to reliable content for Internet research from a variety of databases, Pearson SourceCheck™, and Autocite. Learning resources, such as step-by-step tutorials and an exclusive online grammar and usage handbook, guide students through the research and writing process.

ACKNOWLEDGMENTS

We would like to acknowledge the Pearson reviewers: Steven Anolik, St. Francis College; Daniel Bishop, Concordia University; Howard Cleavinger, Brigham Young University; Andrea Clements, East Tennessee State University; Anthony DeMarco, William Paterson University; Philip Gasquoine, University of Texas-Pan American; Zandra Gratz, Kean University; Sunde Nesbit, Cal. State-Fresno; Alan Roberts, Indiana University; William Rogers, Grand Valley State University; John Ruscio, The College of New Jersey; Stuart Segal, University of Michigan; Adam Weaver, University of Nebraska-Omaha; and Mark Whatley, Valdosta State University.

We would also here like to acknowledge our mentors. CRR never tires of thanking Alan S. Kaufman for his modeling of scholarship and excellence in teaching about testing; Larry Hartlage for his generosity in sharing with students and his teaching of clinical insight; and, E. Paul Torrance for his support and as a model of humility and brilliance in all things academic. Along the same lines, RBL would like to express his appreciation to Ruth Haak, Earl Jennings, and Cecil Reynolds; mentors and friends that exemplify the highest standards of the profession and have been instrumental in his growth as a psychologist and person. To our families go our sincere expression of gratitude for allowing us the time to pursue such professional projects and the support that is so necessary to our accomplishments.

MASTERING MODERN
PSYCHOLOGICAL TESTING

1

Introduction to Psychological Assessment
Why We Do It and What It Is

Why do I need to learn about testing and assessment?

Learning Objectives

After reading and studying this chapter, students should be able to:

1. Describe major milestones in the history of testing.
2. Define test, measurement, and assessment.
3. Describe and give examples of different types of tests.
4. Describe and give examples of different types of score interpretations.
5. Describe and explain the assumptions underlying psychological assessment.
6. Describe and explain the major applications of psychological assessments.
7. Explain why psychologists use tests.
8. Describe the major participants in the assessment process.
9. Describe some major trends in assessment.

Most psychology students are drawn to the study of psychology because they want to work with and help people, or alternatively to achieve an improved understanding of their own thoughts, feelings, and behaviors. Many of these students aspire to be psychologists or counselors and work in clinical settings. Other psychology students are primarily interested in research and aspire to work at a university or other research institution. However, only a minority of psychology students have a burning desire to specialize in psychological tests and measurement. As a result, we often hear our students ask, "Why do I have to take a course in tests and measurement?" This is a reasonable question, so when we teach test and measurement courses we spend some time explaining to our students why they need to learn about testing and assessment. This is one of the major goals of this chapter. Hopefully we will convince you this is a worthwhile endeavor.

> *Psychological testing and assessment are important in virtually every aspect of professional psychology.*

Psychological testing and assessment are important in virtually every aspect of professional psychology. For those of you interested in clinical, counseling, or school psychology, research has shown assessment is surpassed only by psychotherapy in terms of professional importance (e.g., Norcross, Karg, & Prochaska, 1997; Phelps, Eisman, & Kohout, 1998). However, even this finding does not give full credit to the important role assessment plays in professional practice. As Meyer et al. (2001) observed, unlike psychotherapy, formal assessment is a unique feature of the practice of psychology. That is, whereas a number of other mental health professionals provide psychotherapy (e.g., psychiatrists, counselors, and social workers), psychologists are the only mental health professionals who routinely conduct formal assessments. Special Interest Topic 1.1 provides information about graduate psychology programs that train clinical, counseling, and school psychologists.

The use of psychological tests and other assessments is not limited to clinical or health settings. For example:

- Industrial and organizational psychologists devote a considerable amount of their professional time developing, administering, and interpreting tests. A major aspect of their work is to develop assessments that will help identify prospective employees who possess the skills and characteristics necessary to be successful on the job.
- Research psychologists also need to be proficient in measurement and assessment. Most psychological research, regardless of its focus (e.g., social interactions, child development, psychopathology, or animal behavior) involves measurement and/or assessment. Whether a researcher is concerned with behavioral response time, visual acuity, intelligence, or depressed mood (just to name a few), he or she will need to engage in measurement as part of the research. In fact, all areas of science are very concerned and dependent on measurement. Before one can study any variable in any science, it is necessary to be able to ascertain its existence and measure important characteristics of the variable, construct, or entity.
- Educational psychologists, who focus on the application of psychology in educational settings, are often intricately involved in testing, measurement, and assessment issues. Their involvement ranges from developing and analyzing tests that are used in educational settings to educating teachers about how to develop better classroom assessments.

SPECIAL INTEREST TOPIC 1.1

How Do Clinical, Counseling, and School Psychologists Differ?

In the introductory section of this chapter we discussed the important role that testing and assessment plays in professional psychology. The American Psychological Association accredits professional training programs in the areas of clinical, counseling, and school psychology. Although there are many other types of psychology programs (e.g., social psychology, quantitative psychology, and physiological psychology), most psychologists working with patients or clients are trained in a clinical, counseling, or school psychology program. Some refer to these programs as "practice-oriented" because their graduates are trained to provide psychological health care services. Graduates of doctoral-level clinical, counseling, and school psychology programs typically qualify for equivalent professional benefits, such as professional licensing, independent practice, and eligibility for insurance reimbursement (e.g., Norcross, 2000). However, there are some substantive differences. If you are considering a career in psychology, and you would like to work in applied settings with individuals with emotional or behavioral problems, it is helpful to understand the difference among these training programs.

Before describing how clinical, counseling, and school psychology programs differ, it might be helpful to distinguish between programs that confer a PhD (Doctor of Philosophy) and those that provide a PsyD (Doctor of Psychology). PhD programs provide broad training in both clinical and research applications (i.e., scientist-practitioner model) whereas PsyD programs typically focus primarily on clinical training and place less emphasis on research. There are PhD and PsyD programs in clinical, counseling, and school psychology, and the relative merits of the PhD versus the PsyD are often fiercely debated. We will not delve into this debate at this time, but do encourage you to seek out advice from trusted professors as to which degree is most likely to help you reach your career goals.

At this point, it is probably useful to distinguish between clinical and counseling psychology programs. Historically, clinical psychology programs trained psychologists to work with clients with the more severe forms of psychopathology (e.g., schizophrenia, bipolar disorder, dementia) whereas counseling psychology programs trained psychologists to work with clients with less severe problems (e.g., adjustment disorders, career and educational counseling, couple/marriage counseling). You still see this distinction to some degree, but the differences have diminished over the years. In fact, the American Psychological Association (APA) stopped distinguishing between clinical and counseling psychology internships many years ago. Noting the growing similarity of these programs, Norcross (2000) stated that some notable differences still exist. These include:

- Clinical psychology programs are more abundant and produce more graduates. There are 194 APA-accredited clinical psychology programs and 64 APA-accredited counseling psychology programs.

- In terms of psychological assessment, clinical psychologists tend to use more projective personality assessments whereas counseling psychologists use more career and vocational assessments.

- In terms of theoretical orientation, the majority of both clinical and counseling psychologists favor an eclectic/integrative or cognitive-behavioral approach. However, clinical psychologists are more likely to endorse a psychoanalytic or behavioral orientation, whereas counseling psychologists tends to favor client-centered or humanistic approaches.

- Clinical psychologists are more likely to work in private practice, hospitals, or medical schools, whereas counseling psychologists are more likely to work in university counseling centers and community mental health settings.

- Students entering clinical and counseling programs are similar in terms of GRE scores and undergraduate GPA. However, it is noted that more students with master's degrees enter counseling programs than clinical programs (67% for PhD counseling programs vs. 21% for PhD clinical programs).

(Continued on page 4)

SPECIAL INTEREST TOPIC 1.1 (*Continued*)

In summary, even though clinical and counseling psychology programs have grown in similarity in recent years, some important differences still exist. We will now turn to the field of school psychology. School psychology programs prepare professionals to work with children and adolescents in school settings. Clinical and counseling programs can prepare their graduates to work with children and adolescents; however, this is the focus of school psychology programs. Like clinical and counseling psychologists, school psychologists are trained in psychotherapy and counseling techniques. They also receive extensive training in psychological assessment (cognitive, emotional, and behavioral) and learn to consult with parents and other professionals to promote the school success of their clients. There are currently 57 APA-accredited school psychology training programs.

This discussion has focused on only doctorate-level training programs. There are many more master's-level psychology programs that also prepare students for careers as mental health professionals. Because professional licensing is controlled by the individual states, each state determines the educational and training criteria for licensing, and this is something else one should take into consideration when choosing a graduate school.

You can learn more details about these areas of psychological specialization at the website of the American Psychological Association (http://www.apa.org). The official definitions of each specialty area are housed here as well as other archival documents that describe each specialty in detail that have been accepted by the APA's Commission for the Recognition of Specialties and Proficiencies in Professional Psychology (CRSPPP).

In summary, if you are interested in pursuing a career in psychology, it is likely that you will engage in assessment to some degree, or at least need to understand the outcome of testing and assessment activities. Before delving into contemporary issues in testing and assessment we will briefly examine the history of psychological testing.

BRIEF HISTORY OF TESTING

Anastasi and Urbina (1997) stated that the actual "roots of testing are lost in antiquity" (p. 32). Some writers suggest the first test was actually the famous "Apple Test" given to Eve in the Garden of Eden. However, if one excludes biblical references, testing is usually traced back to the early Chinese. The following section highlights some of the milestones in the history of testing.

Earliest Testing: Circa 2200 BC

The earliest documented use of tests is usually attributed to the Chinese who tested public officials to ensure competence (analogous to contemporary civil service examinations). The Chinese testing program evolved over the centuries and assumed various forms. For example, during the

> *The earliest documented use of tests is usually attributed to the Chinese who tested public officials to ensure competence.*

Han dynasty written exams were included for the first time and covered five major areas: agriculture, civil law, geography, military affairs, and revenue. During the fourth century the program involved three arduous stages requiring the examinees to spend days isolated in small booths composing essays and poems (Gregory, 2004).

Eighteenth- and Nineteenth-Century Testing

CARL FREDERICH GAUSS. Gauss (1777–1855) was a noted German mathematician who also made important contributions in astronomy and the study of magnetism. In the course of tracking star movements he found that his colleagues often came up with slightly different locations. He plotted the frequency of the observed locations systematically and found the observations to take the shape of a curve—the curve we have come to know as the normal curve or normal distribution (also known as the Gaussian curve). He determined that the best estimate of the precise location of the star was the mean of the observations and that each independent observation contained some degree of error. Although Gauss is not typically recognized as a pioneer in testing, we believe his formal recognition of measurement error and its distributional characteristics earns him this recognition.

CIVIL SERVICE EXAMINATIONS. Civil service tests similar to those used in China to select government employees were introduced in European countries in the late 18th and early 19th centuries. In 1883 the U.S. Civil Service Commission started using similar achievement tests to aid selection of government employees (Anastasi & Urbina, 1997).

PHYSICIANS AND PSYCHIATRISTS. In the 19th century physicians and psychiatrists in England and the United States developed classification systems to help classify individuals with mental retardation and other mental problems. For example, in the 1830s the French physician Jean Esquirol was one of the first to distinguish insanity (i.e., emotional disorders) from mental deficiency (i.e., intellectual deficits present from birth). He also believed that mental retardation existed on a continuum from mild to profound and observed that verbal skills were the most reliable way of identifying the degree of mental retardation. In the 1890s Emil Kraepelin and others promoted the use of free-association tests in assessing psychiatric patients. Free-association tests involve the presentation of stimulus words to which the respondent responds "with the first word that comes to mind." Later Sigmund Freud expanded on the technique encouraging patients to express freely any and all thoughts that came to mind in order to identify underlying thoughts and emotions.

BRASS INSTRUMENTS ERA. Early experimental psychologists such as Wilhelm Wundt, Sir Francis Galton, James McKeen Cattell, and Clark Wissler made significant contributions to the development of cognitive ability testing. One of the most important developments of this period was the move toward measuring human abilities using objective procedures that could be easily replicated. These early pioneers used a variety of instruments, often made of brass, to measure simple sensory and motor processes based on the assumption that they were measures of general intelligence (e.g., Gregory, 2004). Some of these early psychologists' contributions were so substantive that they deserve special mention.

Galton is considered the founder of mental tests and measurement and was responsible for the first large-scale systematic collection of data on individual differences.

Sir Francis Galton. Galton is often considered the founder of mental tests and measurement. One of his major accomplishments was the establishment of an anthropometric laboratory at the International Health Exhibition in London in 1884. This laboratory was subsequently moved to a museum where it operated for several years. During this time data were collected including physical (e.g., height, weight, head circumference), sensory (e.g., reaction time, sensory discrimination), and motor measurements (e.g., motor speed, grip strength) on over 17,000 individuals. This represented the first large-scale systematic collection of data on individual differences (Anastasi & Urbina, 1997; Gregory, 2004).

James McKeen Cattell. Cattell shared Galton's belief that relatively simple sensory and motor tests could be used to measure intellectual abilities. Cattell was instrumental in opening psychological laboratories and spreading the growing testing movement in the United States. He is thought to be the first to use the term *mental test* in an article he published in 1890. In addition to his personal professional contributions, he had several students who went on to productive careers in psychology, including E. L. Thorndike, R. S. Woodworth, and E. K. Strong (Anastasi & Urbina, 1997; Gregory, 2004). Galton and Cattell also contributed to the development of testing procedures such as standardized questionnaires and rating scales that later became popular techniques in personality assessment (Anastasi & Urbina, 1997).

Clark Wissler. Wissler was one of Cattell's students whose research largely discredited the work of his famous teacher. Wissler found that the sensory-motor measures commonly being used to assess intelligence had essentially no correlation with academic achievement. He also found that the sensory-motor tests had only weak correlations with one another. These discouraging findings essentially ended the use of the simple sensory-motor measures of intelligence and set the stage for a new approach to intellectual assessment that emphasized more sophisticated higher order mental process. Ironically, there were significant methodological flaws in Wissler's research that prevented him from detecting moderate correlations that actually exist between some sensory-motor tests and intelligence (to learn more about this interesting turn of events, see Fancher, 1985, and Sternberg, 1990). Nevertheless, it would take decades for researchers to discover that they might have dismissed the importance of psychophysical measurements in investigating intelligence, and the stage was set for Alfred Binet's approach to intelligence testing emphasizing higher order mental abilities (Gregory, 2004).

Twentieth-Century Testing

ALFRED BINET—BRING ON INTELLIGENCE TESTING! Binet initially experimented with sensory-motor measurements such as reaction time and sensory acuity, but he became disenchanted with them and pioneered the use of measures of higher order cognitive processes to assess intelligence (Gregory, 2004). In the early 1900s the French government commissioned Binet and his colleague Theodore Simon to develop a test to predict academic performance. The result of their efforts was the first Binet-Simon Scale, released in 1905. The scale contained some sensory-perceptual tests, but the emphasis was on verbal items assessing comprehension, reasoning, judgment, and short-term memory. Binet and Simon achieved their goal and developed a test that was a good predictor of academic success. Subsequent revisions of the Binet-Simon Scale were released in 1908 and 1911. These scales gained wide

The first Binet-Simon Scale was released in 1905 and was the first intelligence test that was a good predictor of academic success.

acceptance in France and were soon translated and standardized in the United States, most successfully by Louis Terman at Stanford University. This resulted in the Stanford-Binet Intelligence Scale, which has been revised numerous times (the fifth revision, SB5, remains in use today). Ironically, Terman's version of the Binet-Simon Scale became even more popular in France and other parts of Europe than the original scale.

ARMY ALPHA AND BETA TESTS. Intelligence testing received another boost in the United States during World War I. The U.S. Army needed a way to assess and classify recruits as suitable for the military and to classify them for jobs in the military. The American Psychological Association (APA) and one of its past presidents, Robert M. Yerkes, developed a task force that devised a series of aptitude tests that came to be known as the Army Alpha and Army Beta—one was verbal (Alpha) and one nonverbal (Beta). Through their efforts and those of the Army in screening recruits literally millions of Americans became familiar with the concept of intelligence testing.

ROBERT WOODWORTH—BRING ON PERSONALITY TESTING! In 1918 Robert Woodworth developed the Woodworth Personal Data Sheet, which is widely considered to be the first formal personality test. The Personal Data Sheet was designed to help collect personal information about military recruits. Much as the development of the Binet scales ushered in the era of intelligence testing, the introduction of the Woodworth Personal Data Sheet ushered in the era of personality assessment.

RORSCHACH INKBLOT TEST. Hermann Rorschach developed the Rorschach inkblots in the 1920s. There has been considerable debate about the psychometric properties of the Rorschach (and other projective techniques), but it continues to be one of the more popular personality assessment techniques in use at the beginning of the 21st century.

COLLEGE ADMISSION TESTS. The College Entrance Examination Board (CEEB) was originally formed to provide colleges and universities with an objective and valid measure of students' academic abilities and to move away from nepotism and legacy in admissions to academic merit. Its efforts resulted in the development of the first Scholastic Aptitude Test (SAT) in 1926 (now called the Scholastic Assessment Test). The American College Testing Program (ACT) was initiated in 1959 and is the major competitor of the SAT. Prior to the advent of these tests, college admissions decisions were highly subjective and strongly influenced by family background and status, so another purpose for the development of these instruments was to make the selection process increasingly objective.

WECHSLER INTELLIGENCE SCALES. Intelligence testing received another boost in the 1930s, when David Wechsler developed an intelligence test that included measures of verbal ability and nonverbal on the same test. Prior to Wechsler, and the Wechsler-Bellevue I, intelligence tests typically assessed verbal or nonverbal intelligence, not both. The Wechsler scales have become the most popular intelligence tests in use today.

MINNESOTA MULTIPHASIC PERSONALITY INVENTORY (MMPI). The MMPI was published in the early 1940s to aid in the diagnosis of psychiatric disorders. It is an objective personality

TABLE 1–1	Milestones in Testing History
Circa 2200 BC	Chinese test public officials
Late 1800s & Early 1900s	Carl Frederich Gauss discovers the normal distribution when evaluating measurement error Civil service exams used in Europe
19th Century	Physicians and psychiatrists assess mental patients with new techniques Brass instruments era—emphasis on measuring sensory and motor abilities Civil service exams initiated in United States in 1883 Early attention to questionnaires and rating scales by Galton and Cattell
1905	Binet-Simon Scale released—ushers in the era of intelligence testing
1917	Army Alpha and Beta released—first group of intelligence tests
1918	Woodworth Personal Data Sheet released—ushers in the era of personality assessment
1920s	Scholastic Aptitude Test (SAT) and Rorshach inkblot test developed—testing expands its influence
1930s	David Wechsler releases the Wechsler-Bellevue I—initiates a series of influential intelligence tests
1940s	The Minnesota Multiphasic Personality Inventory (MMPI) released—destined to become the leading objective personality inventory

test (i.e., can be scored in an objective manner) and has been the subject of a large amount of research. Its second edition, the MMPI-2, continues to be one of the most popular (if not *the* most popular) personality assessments in use today.

Twenty-First-Century Testing

The last 60 years have seen an explosion in terms of test development and use of psychological and educational tests. For example, a recent search of the *Mental Measurements Yearbook* resulted in the identification of over 600 tests listed in the category on personality tests and over 400 in the categories of intelligence and aptitude tests. Many of the chapters in this textbook are devoted to the development and use of different types of tests. Later in this chapter we will examine some current trends in assessment and some factors that we expect will influence the trajectory of assessment practices in the 21st century. We have summarized this time line for you in Table 1–1.

THE LANGUAGE OF ASSESSMENT

We have already used a number of relatively common but somewhat technical terms. Before proceeding it would be helpful to define them for you.

Tests, Measurement, and Assessment

TESTS A test is a device or procedure in which a sample of an individual's behavior is obtained, evaluated, and scored using standardized procedures (American Educational Research

Association [AERA], American Psychological Association [APA], & National Council on Measurement in Education [NCME], 1999). This is a rather broad or general definition, but at this point in our discussion we are best served with this broad definition. Rest assured that we will provide more specific information on different types of tests in due time. Before proceeding we should elaborate on one aspect of our definition of a test: that a test is a sample of behavior. Because a test is only a sample of behavior, it is important that tests reflect a representative sample of the behavior you are interested in. The importance of the concept of a representative sample will become more apparent as we proceed with our study of testing and assessment, and we will touch on it in more detail in later chapters when we address the technical properties of tests.

> *A test is a procedure in which a sample of an individual's behavior is obtained, evaluated, and scored using standardized procedures (AERA et al., 1999).*

Standardized Tests A standardized test is a test that is administered, scored, and interpreted in a standard manner. Most standardized tests are developed by testing professionals or test publishing companies. The goal of standardization is to ensure that testing conditions are as nearly the same as is possible for all individuals taking the test. If this is accomplished, no examinee will have an advantage over another due to variance in administration procedures, and assessment results will be comparable.

> *Measurement is defined as a set of rules for assigning numbers to represent objects, traits, attributes, or behaviors.*

MEASUREMENT Measurement can be defined as a set of rules for assigning numbers to represent objects, traits, attributes, or behaviors. A psychological test is a measuring device, and therefore involves rules (e.g., administration guidelines and scoring criteria) for assigning numbers that represent an individual's performance. In turn, these numbers are interpreted as reflecting characteristics of the test taker. For example, the number of items endorsed in a positive manner (e.g., "True" or "Like Me") on a depression scale might be interpreted as reflecting a client's experience of depressed mood.

ASSESSMENT Assessment is defined as a systematic procedure for collecting information that can be used to make inferences about the characteristics of people or objects (AERA et al., 1999). Assessment should lead to an increased understanding of these characteristics. Tests are obviously one systematic method of collecting information and are therefore one set of tools for assessment. Reviews of historical records, interviews, and observations are also legitimate assessment techniques and all are maximally useful when they are integrated. In fact, assessment typically refers to a process that involves the integration of information obtained from multiple sources using multiple methods. Therefore, assessment is a broader, more comprehensive process than testing.

> *Assessment is defined as any systematic procedure for collecting information that can be used to make inferences about the characteristics of people or objects (AERA et al., 1999).*

In contrasting psychological testing and psychological assessment, Meyer et al. (2001) observed that testing is a relatively straightforward process where a specific test is administered to obtain a specific score. In contrast, psychological assessment integrates multiple scores, typically obtained using multiple tests, with information collected by reviewing records, conducting interviews, and conducting observations. The goal is to develop a better understanding of the client, answer referral questions (e.g., Why is this student doing poorly at school?), and communicate these findings to the appropriate individuals.

McFall and Trent (1999) go a bit further and remind us that the "aim of clinical assessment is to gather data that allow us to reduce uncertainty regarding the probabilities of events" (p. 215). Such an "event" in a clinical setting might be the probability that a patient has depression versus bipolar disorder versus dementia, all of which require treatments. In personnel psychology it might be the probability that an applicant to the police force will be successful completing the police academy, a very expensive training. Test scores are useful in this process to the extent they "allow us to predict or control events with greater accuracy or with less error than we could have done without them" (McFall & Trent, 1999, p. 217). In reference to the previous events, diagnosis and employment selection, tests are useful in the assessment process to the extent they make us more accurate in reaching diagnostic or hiring decisions, respectively. Professionals in all areas make errors; our goal is to minimize these mistakes in number and in magnitude. In psychology, testing and assessment, done properly, are of great benefit to these goals.

Now that we have defined these common terms, with some reluctance we acknowledge that in actual practice many professionals use *testing, measurement,* and *assessment* interchangeably. Recognizing this, Popham (2000) noted that among many professionals *assessment* has become the preferred term. *Measurement* sounds rather rigid and sterile when applied to people and tends to be avoided. *Testing* has its own negative connotations. For example, hardly a week goes by when newspapers don't contain articles about "teaching to the test" or "high-stakes testing," typically with negative connotations. Additionally, when people hear the word *test* they usually think of paper-and-pencil tests. In recent years, as a result of growing dissatisfaction with traditional paper-and-pencil tests, alternative testing procedures have been developed (e.g., performance assessments and portfolios). As a result, *testing* is not seen as particularly descriptive of modern practices. That leaves us with *assessment* as the contemporary popular term.

There are some additional terms that you should be familiar with. *Evaluation* is a term often used when discussing assessment, testing, and measurement-related issues. Evaluation is an activity that involves judging or appraising the value or worth of something. For example, assigning formal grades to students to reflect their academic performance is referred to as summative evaluation. Psychometrics is the science of psychological measurement, and a *psychometrician* is a psychological or educational professional who has specialized in the area of testing, measurement, and assessment. You will likely hear people refer to the psychometric properties of a test, and by this they mean the measurement or statistical characteristics of a test. These measurement characteristics include reliability and validity. **Reliability** refers to the stability, consistency, and relative accuracy of the test scores. On a more theoretical level, reliability refers to the degree to which test scores are free from measurement errors. Scores that are

> **Reliability** *refers to the stability or consistency of test scores.*

relatively free from measurement errors will be stable or consistent (i.e., reliable) and are thus more accurate in estimating some value. **Validity**, in simplest terms, refers to the appropriateness or accuracy of the interpretations of test scores. If test scores are interpreted as reflecting intelligence, do they actually reflect intellectual ability? If test scores are used to predict success on a job, can they accurately predict who will be successful on the job?

> **Validity** *refers to the accuracy of the interpretation of test scores.*

Types of Tests

We defined a *test* as a device or procedure in which a sample of an individual's behavior is obtained, evaluated, and scored using standardized procedures (AERA et al., 1999). You have probably taken a large number of tests in your life, and it is likely that you have noticed that all tests are not alike. For example, people take tests in schools that help determine their grades, a test to obtain a driver's license, interest inventories to help make educational and vocational decisions, admissions tests when applying for college, exams to obtain professional certificates and licenses, and personality tests to gain personal understanding. This brief list is clearly not exhaustive!

Cronbach (1990) noted that tests generally can be classified as measures of either maximum performance or typical response. Maximum performance tests also are referred to as ability tests, but achievement tests are included here as well. On maximum performance tests items may be scored as either "correct" or "incorrect" and examinees are encouraged to demonstrate their very best performance. **Maximum performance tests** are designed to assess the upper limits of the examinee's knowledge and abilities. For example, maximum performance tests can be designed to assess how well a student can perform selected tasks (e.g., 3-digit multiplication) or has mastered a specified content domain (e.g., American history). Intelligence tests and classroom achievement tests are common examples of maximum performance tests. In contrast, typical response tests attempt to measure the typical behavior and characteristics of examinees. Often, typical response tests are referred to as personality tests, and in this context *personality* is used broadly to reflect a host of noncognitive characteristics such as attitudes, behaviors, emotions, and interests (Anastasi & Urbina, 1997). Some individuals reserve the term *test* for maximum performance measures, while using terms such as *scale* or *inventory* when referring to typical response instruments. In this textbook we use the term *test* in its broader sense, applying it to both maximum performance and typical response procedures.

> **Maximum performance tests** *are designed to assess the upper limits of the examinee's knowledge and abilities.*

MAXIMUM PERFORMANCE TESTS. Maximum performance tests are designed to assess the upper limits of the examinee's knowledge and abilities. Within the broad category of maximum performance tests, there are a number of subcategories. First, maximum performance tests are often classified as either achievement tests or aptitude tests. Second, maximum performance tests can be classified as either objective or subjective. Finally, maximum performance tests are often described as either speed or power tests. These distinctions, although not absolute in nature, have

> *Achievement tests measure knowledge and skills in an area in which instruction has been provided (AERA et al., 1999).*

> *Aptitude tests measure cognitive abilities and skills that are accumulated as the result of overall life experiences (AERA et al., 1999).*

a long historical basis and provide some useful descriptive information.

Achievement and Aptitude Tests. Maximum performance tests are often classified as either achievement tests or aptitude tests. **Achievement tests** are designed to assess the knowledge or skills of an individual in a content domain in which he or she has received instruction. In contrast, **aptitude tests** are broader in scope and are designed to measure the cognitive skills, abilities, and knowledge that an individual has accumulated as the result of overall life experiences (AERA et al., 1999). In other words, achievement tests are linked or tied to a specific program of instructional objectives, whereas aptitude tests reflect the cumulative impact of life experiences as a whole. This distinction, however, is not absolute and is actually a matter of degree or emphasis. Most testing experts today conceptualize both achievement and aptitude tests as measures of developed cognitive abilities that can be ordered along a continuum in terms of how closely linked the assessed abilities are to specific learning experiences.

Another distinction between achievement and aptitude tests involves the way their results are used or interpreted. Achievement tests are typically used to measure what has been learned or "achieved" at a specific point in time. In contrast, aptitude tests usually are used to predict future performance or reflect an individual's potential in terms of academic or job performance. However, this distinction is not absolute either. As an example, a test given at the end of high school to assess achievement might also be used to predict success in college. Although we feel it is important to recognize that the distinction between achievement and academic tests is not absolute, we also feel the achievement/aptitude distinction is useful when discussing different types of abilities.

Objective and Subjective Tests. Objectivity typically implies impartiality or the absence of personal bias. Cronbach (1990) stated that the less test scores are influenced by the subjective judgment of the person grading or scoring the test, the more objective the test is. In other words, objectivity refers to the extent that trained examiners who score a test will be in agreement and score responses in the same way. Tests with selected-response items (e.g., multiple-choice, true–false, and matching) that can be scored using a fixed key and that minimize subjectivity in scoring are often referred to as "objective" tests. In contrast, subjective tests are those that rely on the personal judgment of the individual grading the test. For example, essay tests are considered subjective because the person grading the test relies to some extent on his or her own subjective judgment when scoring the essays. Most students are well aware that different teachers might assign different grades to the same essay item. Essays and other test formats that require the person grading the test to employ his or her own personal judgment are often referred to as "subjective" tests. It is common, and desirable, for those developing subjective tests to provide explicit scoring rubrics in an effort to reduce the impact of the subjective judgment of the person scoring the test.

Speed and Power Tests. Maximum performance tests often are categorized as either speed tests or power tests. On a pure **speed test**, performance only reflects differences in the speed of performance. A speed test generally contains items that are relatively easy and has a strict time limit that prevents any examinees from successfully completing all the items. Speed tests are also commonly referred to as "speeded tests." On a pure **power test**, the speed of performance is not an issue. Everyone is given plenty of time to attempt all the items, but the items are ordered according to difficulty, and the test contains some items that are so difficult that no examinee is expected to answer them all. As a result, performance on a power test primarily reflects the difficulty of the items the examinee is able to answer correctly.

> *On* speed tests, *performance reflects differences in the speed of performance.*

> *On* power tests, *performance reflects the difficulty of the items the examinee is able to answer correctly.*

Well-developed speed and power tests are designed so no one will obtain a perfect score. They are designed this way because perfect scores are "indeterminate." That is, if someone obtains a perfect score on a test, the test failed to assess the very upper limits of that person's ability. To access adequately the upper limits of ability, tests need to have what test experts refer to as an "adequate ceiling." That is, the difficulty level of the tests is set so none of the examinees will be able to obtain a perfect score.

As you might expect, this distinction between speed and power tests is also one of degree rather than being absolute. Most often a test is not a pure speed test or a pure power test, but incorporates some combination of the two approaches. For example, the Scholastic Assessment Test (SAT) and Graduate Record Examination (GRE) are considered power tests, but both have time limits. When time limits are set such that 95% or more of examinees will have the opportunity to respond to all items, the test is still considered to be a power test and not a speed test.

TYPICAL RESPONSE TESTS. As noted, **typical response tests** are designed to measure the typical behavior and characteristics of examinees. Typical response tests measure constructs such as personality, behavior, attitudes, or interests. In traditional assessment terminology, *personality* is a general term that broadly encompasses a wide range of emotional, interpersonal, motivational, attitudinal, and other personal characteristics (Anastasi & Urbina, 1997). When describing personality tests, most assessment experts distinguish between objective and projective techniques. Although there are some differences, this distinction largely parallels the separation of maximum performance tests into "objective" or "subjective" tests. These two approaches are described next.

> **Typical response tests** *are designed to measure the typical behavior and characteristics of examinees.*

Objective Personality Tests. As with maximum performance tests, in the context of typical response assessment objectivity also implies impartiality or the absence of personal bias. **Objective personality tests** are those that use selected-response items (e.g., true–false) and are scored in an objective manner. For

> **Objective personality tests** *use items that are not influenced by the subjective judgement of the person scoring the test.*

example, a personality test that includes true–false items such as "I enjoy parties" is considered objective. The test taker simply responds "true" if the statement describes him or her and "false" if it doesn't. By conscientiously using a scoring key, there should be no disagreement among scorers regarding how to score the items.

Projective Personality Tests. **Projective personality tests** typically involve the presentation of unstructured or ambiguous materials that can elicit an almost infinite range of responses from the examinee. For example, the clinician may show the examinee an inkblot and ask: "What might this be?" Instructions to the examinee are minimal, there are essentially no restrictions on the examinee's response, and there is considerable subjectivity when scoring the response. Elaborating on the distinction between objective and projective tests, Reynolds (1998) noted:

> It is primarily the agreement on scoring that differentiates objective from subjective tests. If trained examiners agree on how a particular answer is scored, tests are considered objective; if not, they are considered subjective. Projective is not synonymous with subjective in this context but most projective tests are closer to the subjective than objective end of the continuum of agreement on scoring. (p. 49)

> **Projective personality tests** *involve the presentation of ambiguous material that elicits an almost infinite range of responses. Most projective tests involve subjectivity in scoring.*

What is unique to projective tests is what is referred to as the "projective hypothesis." In brief, the projective hypothesis holds that when an examinee responds to an ambiguous stimulus, he or she responds in a manner that reflects the person's genuine unconscious desires, motives, and drives without interference from the ego or conscious mind (Reynolds, 1998). Projective techniques are extremely popular, but they are the focus of considerable controversy. This controversy focuses on the subjective nature of this approach and the lack of empirical evidence supporting the technical qualities of the instruments. In other words, although the tests are popular there is little evidence that they provide reliable and valid information.

Table 1–2 depicts the major categories of tests we have discussed. Although we have introduced you to the major types of tests, this brief introduction clearly is not exhaustive. Essentially all tests can be classified according to this scheme, but there are other distinctions possible. For example, a common distinction is made between *standardized tests* and *nonstandardized tests*. Standardized tests are professionally developed tests that are administered, scored, and interpreted in a standard manner. The goal of standardization is to make sure that testing conditions are as nearly the same for all the individuals taking the test as is possible. Part of the process of standardizing most tests also involves administering them to a large, representative sample that represents the types of individuals to whom examinees are to be compared. This group, typically referred to as the standardization sample, is used to establish "norms" that facilitate the interpretation of test results. Examples of standardized tests include the Stanford-Binet Intelligence Scale, Fifth Edition (SB5; Roid, 2003), a popular intelligence test, and the Minnesota Multiphasic Personality Inventory, Second Edition (MMPI-2; Butcher, Dahlstrom, Graham, Tellegen, &

TABLE 1–2   Major Categories of Tests

1. Maximum Performance Tests
   a. *Achievement tests:* Assess knowledge and skills in an area in which the examinee has received instruction.
      1. *Speed tests* (e.g., a timed typing test).
      2. *Power tests* (e.g., a spelling test containing words of increasing difficulty).
   b. *Aptitude tests:* Assess knowledge and skills accumulated as the result of overall life experiences.
      1. *Speed tests* (e.g., a timed test where the test taker quickly scans groups of symbols and marks symbols that meet a predetermined criteria).
      2. *Power tests* (e.g., a test of nonverbal reasoning and problem solving that requires the test taker to solve problems of increasing difficulty).
   c. *Objective or subjective tests:* When the scoring of a test does not rely on the subjective judgment of the individual scoring it, it is said to be objective. If the scoring of a test does rely on subjective judgment, it is said to be subjective.
2. Typical Response Tests
   a. *Objective personality tests* (e.g., a test where the test taker answers true–false items referring to the personal beliefs and preferences).
   b. *Projective personality tests* (e.g., a test where the test taker looks at an inkblot and describes what he or she sees).

 Nonstandardized

Kaemmer, 1989), a widely used objective personality test. Nonstandardized tests are those developed in a less formal manner. Administration guidelines may not be explicitly stated and there is often not a standardization sample. The most common type of nonstandardized test is the classroom achievement tests that are administered in large numbers in schools and universities on an almost daily basis.

Finally, it is common to distinguish between individual tests (i.e., tests designed to be administered to one examinee at a time) and group tests (i.e., tests administered to more than one examinee at a time). This is an important distinction that applies to the administration of the test rather than the type of the test. For example, individual aptitude tests and group aptitude tests are both aptitude tests; they simply differ in how they are administered. This is true in the personality domain as well wherein some tests require one-on-one administration but others can be given to groups.

Types of Scores

Almost all tests produce scores that reflect or represent the performance of the individuals taking the tests. There are two fundamental approaches to understanding scores: the norm-referenced approach and the criterion-referenced approach. With **norm-referenced score** interpretations an examinee's performance is compared to the performance of other people, often those in a standardization sample. For example, if you say that a student scored better than 95% of his or her peers, this is a norm-referenced score interpretation. The standardization sample serves as the reference group against which performance is judged.

> **Norm-referenced score** *interpretations compare an examinee's performance to the performance of other people.*

TABLE 1–3	Norm- and Criterion-Referenced Scores	
Type of Score	**Description**	**Example**
Norm-referenced scores	An examinee's performance is compared to that of other people. Interpretation is relative to that of other people.	An examinee earns a percentile rank score of 50, meaning he or she scored better than 50% of the individuals in the standardization sample.
Criterion-referenced scores	An examinee's performance is compared to a specified level of performance. Interpretation is absolute (not relative).	A student correctly answers 50% of the items on a test. On a licensing exam, an examinee obtains a score greater than the cut score and receives a passing score.

With **criterion-referenced score** interpretations, the examinee's performance is not compared to that of other people; instead it is compared to a specified level of performance. With criterion-referenced score interpretations, the emphasis is on what the examinees know or what they can actually do, not their standing relative to other people. One of the most common examples of criterion-referenced scoring is the percentage of correct responses on a classroom examination. For example, if you report that a student correctly answered 95% of the items on a classroom test, this is a criterion-referenced score interpretation. In addition to percentage correct, another type of criterion-referenced interpretation is referred to as mastery testing. Mastery testing involves determining whether the examinee has achieved a specified level of mastery designated by a *cut score*, and performance is usually reported with an all-or-none score such as a pass/fail designation. For example, on a licensing exam for psychologists the cut score might be 70%, and all examinees earning a score of 70% or greater will receive a designation of "pass." Conversely, if an examinee earned a score of 69% he or she would receive a designation of "fail."

> **Criterion-referenced score** *interpretations compare an examinee's performance to a specified level of performance.*

Norm-referenced interpretations are relative (i.e., relative to the performance of other examinees) whereas criterion-referenced interpretations are absolute (i.e., compared to an absolute standard). People often refer to norm-referenced and criterion-referenced tests, but this is not technically correct. The terms *norm-referenced* and *criterion-referenced* actually refer to the interpretation of test scores, not a type of test. Although it is most common for tests to produce either norm-referenced or criterion-referenced scores, it is possible for a test to produce both norm- and criterion-referenced scores. Table 1–3 depicts salient information about norm- and criterion-referenced scores.

ASSUMPTIONS OF PSYCHOLOGICAL ASSESSMENT

Now that we have introduced you to many of the basic concepts of psychological assessment, this is an opportune time to discuss some basic assumptions that underlie psychological assessment. These assumptions were adapted in part from Cohen and Swerdlik (2002) who noted, appropriately, that these assumptions actually represent a simplification of some very complex issues. As you progress through this text you will develop a better understanding of these complex and interrelated issues.

Assumption #1: Psychological Constructs Exist

In assessment terminology, a **construct** is simply the trait or characteristic (i.e., variable) that a test is designed to measure. In psychology we are often interested in measuring a number of constructs, such as a client's intelligence, level of depression, or attitudes. This assumption simply acknowledges that constructs such as "intelligence," "depression," or "attitudes" exist.

> **Constructs** *are the traits or characteristics a test is designed to measure (AERA et al., 1999).*

Assumption #2: Psychological Constructs Can Be Measured

Cronbach (1990) stated that there is an old, often quoted adage among measurement professionals that goes "If a thing exists, it exists in some amount. If it exists in some amount, it can be measured" (p. 34). If we accept the assumption that psychological constructs exist, the next natural question is "Can these constructs be measured?" As you might predict, assessment experts believe psychological and educational constructs can be measured.

Assumption #3: Although We Can Measure Constructs, Our Measurement Is Not Perfect

Assessment experts believe they can measure psychological constructs, but they also acknowledge that the measurement process is not perfect. This is usually framed in terms of measurement error and its effects on the reliability of scores. Some degree of **error** is inherent in all sciences, not just psychology and social sciences, and measurement error reduces the usefulness of measurement. As you will learn, assessment experts make considerable efforts to estimate and minimize the effects of measurement error.

> *Some degree of* **error** *is inherent in all measurement.*

Assumption #4: There Are Different Ways to Measure Any Given Construct

As you will learn in this text, there are multiple approaches to measuring any psychological construct. Consider the example of social anxiety. A client's level of social anxiety can be assessed using a number of different approaches. For example, a psychologist might interview the client and ask about his or her level of anxiety in different social settings. The psychologist might observe the client in a number of different social settings. The psychologist might have individuals familiar with the client complete behavioral rating scales that address symptoms of social anxiety. The psychologist might also administer a number of typical response tests, both objective and projective, to assess the client's level of social anxiety. All of these different assessment procedures can help the psychologist understand the client's experience of social anxiety.

Assumption #5: All Assessment Procedures Have Strengths and Limitations

Acknowledging that there are a number of different approaches to measuring any construct, assessment experts also acknowledge that all assessment procedures have their own specific set of strengths and limitations. One assessment approach might produce highly reliable scores, but not measure some aspects of a construct as well as another approach that produces less reliable scores. As a result, it is important that psychologists understand the specific strengths and weaknesses of the procedures they use. The relatively simple idea that professionals should be aware of the limitations of their assessment procedures and the information obtained from them is a key issue in ethical assessment practice.

> *There are multiple approaches to measuring any given construct, and these different approaches have their own unique strengths and weaknesses.*

Assumption #6: Multiple Sources of Information Should Be Part of the Assessment Process

Given that there are different approaches to measuring any given construct and that each approach has its own strengths and weaknesses, it follows that psychological assessment should incorporate information from different approaches. Important decisions should not be based on the results of a single test or other assessment procedure. For example, when deciding which applicants should be admitted to a college or university, information such as performance on an admissions test (e.g., SAT or ACT), high school grade point average (GPA), letters of recommendation, evidence of extracurricular activities, and a written statement of purpose should be considered. It would be inappropriate to base this decision on any one source of information.

> *Important decisions should not be based on the result of a single test or other assessment procedure.*

Assumption #7: Performance on Tests Can Be Generalized to Non-Test Behaviors

Typically when we give a test we are not interested simply in the individual's performance on the test, but the ability to generalize from test performance to non-test behaviors. For example, it is not an individual's score on the SAT that is in itself important to a college admissions officer, but the fact that the score can be used to help predict performance in college. The same applies to a test designed to detect depression. It is not the client's response to the items on a depression inventory that is of importance, but that the responses to the items on this inventory reflect his or her personal subjective level of depression. This assumption holds that test performance is important, not in-and-of-itself (with some very specialized exceptions), but because of what it tells us about the test taker's standing on the measured construct and the relationship of this standing to other constructs.

> *Information obtained from assessment procedures can help psychologists make better decisions.*

Assumption #8: Assessment Can Provide Information That Helps Psychologists Make Better Professional Decisions

The widespread use of psychological assessments is based on the premise that the information obtained can help psychologists make better decisions. For psychologists working in clinical settings these decisions might include accurately diagnosing a client's disorder and developing and monitoring effective treatment plans. Research psychologists use a variety of tests to collect data and test their scientific hypotheses. Psychologists working in industrial and organizational settings often use tests to help select the most qualified employees. Educational psychologists use tests and other assessments to determine which educational programs are effective and which are not. In these and a multitude of other situations, tests provide valuable information that helps psychologists make better professional decisions. We will elaborate on the many ways assessments help psychologists make better decisions later in this chapter.

> *Psychological assessments are not perfect, but they can provide useful information.*

Assumption #9: Assessments Can Be Conducted in a Fair Manner

Although many critics of testing might argue against this assumption, contemporary assessment experts spend considerable time and energy developing instruments that, when administered and interpreted according to guidelines, are fair and minimize bias. Nevertheless, tests can be used inappropriately, and when they are it discredits or stigmatizes assessment procedures in general. However, in such circumstances the culprit is the person using the test, not the test itself. At times, people criticize assessments because they do not like the results obtained. In many instances, this is akin to "killing the messenger" because tests are not the cause of observed differences among groups for example, they just document them.

Assumption #10: Testing and Assessment Can Benefit Individuals and Society as a Whole

Although many people might initially argue that the elimination of all tests would be a positive event, on closer examination most will agree that tests and other assessment procedures make significant contributions to education and society as a whole. Consider a world without tests. People would be able to present themselves as surgeons without ever having their ability to perform surgery competently assessed. People would be given driver's licenses without having their ability to drive assessed. Airline pilots would be flying commercial jets without having to demonstrate their competence as pilots. All of these examples should give you reasons to consider the value of tests. Although typically not a matter of life-and-death, the use of psychological tests also has important implications that can benefit society. When a psychologist is able to diagnose accurately a client's problem he or she is more likely to develop an effective treatment plan. Accordingly, when a psychologist helps a client better understand his or her personal preferences and career interests, the client is more likely to pursue educational and training activities that lead to a happier life and successful career.

These assumptions are listed in Table 1–4. As we noted, these seemingly simple assumptions represent some complex and controversial issues, and there is considerable debate

TABLE 1–4	Assumptions of Psychological Assessment
1	Psychological constructs exist.
2	Psychological constructs can be measured.
3	Although we can measure constructs, our measurement is not perfect.
4	There are different ways to measure any given construct.
5	All assessment procedures have strengths and limitations.
6	Multiple sources of information should be part of the assessment process.
7	Performance on tests can be generalized to non-test behaviors.
8	Assessment can provide information that helps psychologists make better professional decisions.
9	Assessments can be conducted in a fair manner.
10	Testing and assessment can benefit individuals and society as a whole.

regarding the pros and cons of testing and assessment. Many of the controversies surrounding the use of tests are the results of misunderstandings and the improper use of tests. As we stated in Assumption #3, tests and all other assessment procedures contain some degree of measurement error. Tests are not perfect and they should not be interpreted as if they were perfect. However, this limitation is not limited to psychological measurement; all measurement is subject to error. Chemistry, physics, and engineering all struggle with imperfect, error-laden measurement that is always, to some extent, limiting the advancement of the discipline. An example most of us can relate to involves the medical profession. There is error in medical assessment procedures such as blood pressure tests or tests of blood cholesterol level, but they still provide useful information. The same is true of psychological assessment procedures. They are not perfect, but they still provide useful information. Although you probably will not hear anyone proclaim that there should be a ban on the use of medical tests, you will hear critics of educational and psychological testing call for a ban on, or at least a significant reduction in, the use of tests. Although psychological tests are not perfect (and never will be), testing experts spend considerable time and effort studying the measurement characteristics of tests. This process allows us to determine how accurate and reliable tests are, can provide guidelines for their appropriate interpretation and use, and can result in the development of more accurate assessment procedures (e.g., Friedenberg, 1995).

Assumption #9 suggests that tests can be used in a fair manner. Many people criticize tests, claiming that they are biased, unfair, and discriminatory against certain groups of people. Although it is probably accurate to say that no test is perfectly fair to all examinees, neither is any other approach to selecting, classifying, or evaluating people. The majority of professionally developed tests are carefully constructed and scrutinized to minimize bias, and when used properly actually promote fairness and equality. In fact, it is probably safe to say that well-made tests that are appropriately administered and interpreted are among the most equitable methods of evaluating people. Consider the example of the tests used to help select students for admission to universities. Without tests, admission of-

> *Well-made tests that are appropriately administered and interpreted are among the most equitable methods of evaluating people.*

ficers might make arbitrary decisions based solely on their personal likes and dislikes. In fact, the SAT was developed to increase the objectivity of college admissions, which in the first quarter of the 20th century depended primarily on family status. Research has demonstrated that as the level of subjectivity of any selection process increases, the probability of bias in the process also increases. Nevertheless, the improper use of tests can result in considerable harm to individual test takers, institutions, and society.

WHY USE TESTS?

Because psychological assessment can incorporate a number of procedures in addition to tests (e.g., interviews, observations), it is reasonable to ask, "Why do psychologists use tests so often in their professional practice?" The answer is simple: People are not very good at judging other people objectively, and most "non-test" assessment procedures involve subjective

> *People are not very good at judging other people objectively, and most "non-test" assessment procedures involve subjective judgment.*

judgment. If you are like most people, on more than one occasion your first impression of someone later proved to be totally wrong. Someone who initially seemed aloof and uncaring turns out to be kind and considerate. Someone who initially appeared conscientious and trustworthy ends up letting you down. The undeniable truth is that people are not very good at judging other people in the absence of months and perhaps even years of consistent exposure to them. The reason is that all of us are susceptible to a host of biases and prejudices that undermine our judgment. For example, if someone is initially judged to be outstanding on one trait (or extremely negative on a trait), that single evaluation tends to color our overall impression of the person. As a result, a person who is viewed as physically attractive might also be considered smart, trustworthy, and personable. In contrast, someone who is viewed as physically unattractive might be considered uneducated, lazy, and boring. This is a well-documented cognitive bias that is referred to as the "halo effect." It is by no means the only bias that impairs our ability to accurately judge other people.

    To illustrate the fallibility of our subjective judgments with a clinical example, Dahlstrom (1993) shared a story about one of his clients whose initial diagnosis was significantly impacted by a negative halo effect. When working as an intern, Dr. Dahlstrom had a 15-year-old female client who was described as "Not very attractive, poorly dressed and disheveled, she was silent, withdrawn, and unresponsive to questioning by the psychiatric resident who admitted her. As his preliminary diagnosis he entered into her chart: mental retardation and possible schizophrenia" (p. 2). Dr. Dahlstrom was not convinced that this diagnosis was accurate and coaxed his young client into completing some intelligence tests that did not require verbal responses. Her nonverbal IQ was approximately 115, which is better than about 84% of the population! Clearly the diagnosis of mental retardation was inaccurate. He then had her complete a subjective personality inventory that suggested depression and social introversion, but not schizophrenia. In summary, objective testing quickly revealed that the initial diagnostic impression of mental retardation and schizophrenia, which was based on an interview and observation, was inaccurate. With proper treatment the patient was able to overcome the depressed state and went on to excel as an artist and become an administrator of an art institute. This is a good example of McFall and Trent's

(1999) notation discussed earlier that tests are valuable because they allow us to act with less error than we would act without the information provided by the tests.

Over the years a number of authors (e.g., Meyer et al., 2001) have delineated how formal tests can help psychologists make better clinical and diagnostic decisions. These include:

- Patients are notoriously poor historians and may present biased information. Some clients will attempt to minimize their difficulties in order to appear more competent and/or socially acceptable. This is referred to as "faking good." Other clients, particularly those involved in legal proceedings, may exaggerate their symptoms in hope of gaining a financial reward. This is referred to as "faking bad." These tendencies to misrepresent one's true characteristics are typically referred to as response biases. To address these, many contemporary tests incorporate specific validity scales that are designed to help the clinician detect a response bias.

- Many psychological tests are designed to assess a large number of characteristics or traits, and as a result they may help ensure that important clinical issues are not overlooked. For example, a pediatric behavior rating scale may cover such rare behaviors as "fire-setting" and "cruelty to animals," topics that might be overlooked in a clinical interview.

- Psychological tests typically provide quantitative information that allows more precise measurement of important characteristics. Additionally, many psychological tests are interpreted in such a way that each client is compared to a group of his or her peers. This allows the psychologist to determine how common or unusual a client's responses or performance actually are. For example, based on a clinical interview a skilled clinician might conclude that a client has a deficit in short-term memory. However, the use of a memory test might indicate that the client's performance is two standard deviations below the mean (i.e., below that of 98% of his or her peers). In this case the use of the test confirms the clinician's impression and also helps document how severe the deficit is. Many seasoned clinicians claim they have developed "internal norms" that allow them to judge how extreme a client's complaints or behaviors are. This might be the case if you work with a limited range of patients (e.g., adolescent males), but it would be very difficult for a psychologist to develop internal norms for the wide range of clients one typically sees in modern clinical settings.

- The process and content of clinical interviews and observations often vary considerably from client to client. For example, a clinician might ask one client one set of questions and another client an entirely different set of questions. In contrast, psychological tests have standardized stimuli (i.e., questions or items), administration (e.g., instruction and time limits), and scoring procedures. Because all clients are presented the same stimuli under the same conditions with the same scoring criteria, we can have increased confidence that observed differences are the result of true differences in our clients, not simply differences in the questions they were asked.

- Finally, the use of tests, in addition to interviews and observations, helps ensure that multiple sources of data are included.

According to Dahlstrom (1993), the fallibility of human judgment is one of the main reasons that psychological tests have become increasingly popular over the past century. This does not mean that psychologists should eschew the use of clinical interviews and observations, just that they should use multiple sources of information whenever making professional decisions. When there is consistency in the information we obtain using multiple sources of information (e.g., interviews, observations, tests), then we can have increased confidence in our findings. When the results of different assessment procedures are inconsistent, we must systematically generate and test different hypotheses until we determine what is the most accurate explanation. This process is often complex, requires extensive professional skill, and is the hallmark of psychological assessment when done in a competent, professional manner.

> *The fallibility of human judgment is one of the main reasons that psychological tests have become increasingly popular over the past century.*

We are advocates of a philosophy or model of assessment that incorporates psychometric sophistication, clinical insight, knowledge of psychological theory, and thoughtful reasoning. The goal is to design and conduct an assessment that enhances the client's life (Reynolds & Fletcher-Janzen, 2002). With this model, assessment involves a dynamic evaluation and synthesis of information that is obtained in a reliable and valid manner from multiple sources using multiple procedures. Kaufman (1994) suggested that a psychologist conducting an assessment should assume the role of a "detective" who collects, evaluates, and synthesizes information and integrates that information with a thorough understanding of psychological theories of development, psychopathology, and individual differences. When performed appropriately, psychological assessment is a very demanding and sophisticated process.

COMMON APPLICATIONS OF PSYCHOLOGICAL ASSESSMENTS

Now that we have introduced you to some of the basic terminology, concepts, and assumptions involved in testing and assessment, we will describe some of the major applications of psychological assessment. Tests and other assessments have many uses, but underlying practically all of these uses is the belief that they provide information about important psychological constructs, and that this information can help psychologists and other professionals make better decisions. Below are brief descriptions of prominent applications of assessment procedures.

> *The reason we use tests is the belief that they provide information about important psychological constructs that can help psychologists make better decisions.*

Diagnosis

Diagnosis is implied when a health care professional specifies the nature and/or cause of a disorder, disease, or injury. In psychology and psychiatry, the diagnostic process typically incorporates information obtained using a variety of assessment procedures (e.g., tests, interviews, observations, record reviews) and utilizes the *Diagnostic and Statistical Manual of Mental Disorders* (4th ed., text rev. [*DSM–IV–TR*], American Psychiatric Association, 2000) as the guiding taxonomy. Ideally diagnosis involves more than simply specifying a diagnostic category (e.g., Generalized Anxiety Disorder), but explains the nature of the problem the client is experiencing and guides the development of a treatment plan. As a result, diagnosis is an integral part of effective treatment.

Treatment Planning and Effectiveness

As discussed in the previous section, psychological assessments can provide important information that helps psychologists and other professionals tailor their interventions to meet the specific needs of the individual client. For example, not all clients with dyslexia will exhibit the same pattern of cognitive strengths and weaknesses. Similarly, not all clients with a depressive disorder will present with the same set of symptoms. When developing treatment plans it is important to consider the client's specific needs and develop a program that is most likely to produce the maximum benefit. Repeated testing or measurement of a variable targeted for change can reveal the relative effectiveness (or ineffectiveness) of treatment.

Selection, Placement, and Classification

The terms *selection, placement,* and *classification* are often used interchangeably, but technically they have different meanings. Nitko (2001) states that selection refers to decisions by an individual or institution to either accept or reject an applicant for some position (e.g., hiring employees). With selection decisions, the key factor is that some individuals are "selected" whereas others are "rejected." In contrast, placement decisions involve situations where individuals are assigned to different programs or tracks that are ordered in some way. With placement, all individuals are placed and there are no actual rejections. For example, if all the students in a school are assigned to one of three instructional programs (e.g., remedial, regular, and honors), this is a placement decision. Finally, classification decisions refer to situations in which individuals are assigned to different categories that are not ordered in any way. For example, special education students may be classified as learning disabled, emotionally disturbed, speech impaired, or some other category of disability, but these categories are not ordered in any particular manner, they are simply descriptive. You might have noticed that classification and diagnosis are related procedures. There are, however, some significant differences. Diagnosis is a more elaborate process that goes beyond simple classification. Additionally, when properly executed, diagnosis involves a thorough description and/or explanation of the condition under study.

Self-Understanding

Psychological and educational assessments can provide information that promotes self-understanding and helps individuals plan for their future. For example, there are a number of career assessments designed to help an individual select a college major and/or career that matches their personal interests, preferences, and strengths. There are also tests that help couples considering marriage evaluate their commonalties and differences.

Evaluation

Educators often use a variety of assessment procedures to monitor the academic progress of their students. In schools, probably the most common use of assessments involves assigning grades to students to reflect their academic progress or achievement. This type of evaluation is typically referred to as summative evaluation. In the classroom, summative evaluation typically involves the formal evaluation of student performance, commonly taking the form of a numerical or letter grade (e.g., A, B, C, D, or F). Summative evaluation is often designed to communicate information about student progress, strengths, and weaknesses to parents and other involved adults. Another prominent application of student assessments is to provide feedback to students in order to facilitate or guide their learning. Optimally, students need to know both what they have mastered and what they have not mastered. This type of feedback facilitates and guides learning activities and can help motivate students. It is often frustrating to students to receive a score on an assignment without also receiving feedback about what they can do to improve their performance in the future. This type of evaluation is referred to as formative evaluation. Formative evaluation involves evaluative activities that are aimed at providing feedback to students. Evaluation decisions are not limited to educational settings. For example, industrial-organizational psychologists help develop assessments used to evaluate the performance of employees in work settings. Instructional planning can also be assisted by good assessment results. In educational settings, assessment information can help educators customize curriculum and instruction to take into consideration the individual strengths and weaknesses of their students. For example, one student may possess superior auditory processing abilities while another might possess superior visual processing abilities. Ideally, instruction should be modified to take into account the skills and abilities of each student.

Licensing

Tests and other assessments are used in licensing decisions ranging from who qualifies for a driver's license to who qualifies for a medical license.

Program Evaluation

In addition to providing information about individuals, assessment can also provide information about the quality and usefulness of programs. Cronbach (1990) suggested that in this context, "programs" typically refers to a plan or model for delivering some type of services. For example, job training programs help prepare people for employment. Therefore, it is important to determine if job training programs are actually helping people succeed in the work–force. Programs can be as narrow as the curriculum program implemented by an individual teacher in his or her classroom or as large as a federal program for delivering services to millions of people (e.g., Social Security, Medicaid).

Scientific Method

Tests and other assessments play prominent roles in the scientific process. Regardless of what hypothesis is being tested, measurement is typically involved. Whereas scientists may use commercial tests in their research (e.g., a standardized intelligence test), it is also common for researchers to develop tests that specifically address the hypotheses they are interested in testing.

> *Tests and other assessments impact many aspects of modern life, and whereas tests clearly have their opponents, they are likely to continue to impact our lives for many years to come.*

This brief list of common applications of tests and assessments, summarized in Table 1.5, is clearly not exhaustive. Tests and other assessments impact many aspects of modern life, and even though tests clearly have their opponents, they are likely to continue to impact our lives for many years to come.

TABLE 1–5	Major Applications of Psychological Assessments
Application	**Examples**
Diagnosis	Psychologists often use a variety of assessment procedures to help understand the client's history, identify their current level of functioning, and document the presence of clinical symptoms. These procedures may include a review of historical records, clinical interviews and observations, and formal tests. The information obtained will help the psychologist rule-out competing diagnoses and establish treatment needs.
Treatment planning and effectiveness	Ideally, diagnosis should provide information that allows the clinician to customize the treatment for the individual client. Not all clients with a depressive disorder will present with the same pattern of clinical symptoms, and treatment is optimal when interventions are selected that target specific symptoms. Ongoing assessment can monitor the effectiveness of treatment and indicate if modifications are needed.
Instructional planning	In educational settings, assessment information can help educators customize curriculum and instruction to take into consideration the individual strengths and weaknesses of their students. For example, one student may possess superior auditory processing abilities while another might possess superior visual processing abilities. Ideally, instructions should be modified to take into account the skills and abilities of each student.
Selection	Colleges and universities typically establish admission criteria that help determine which students will be admitted. These criteria often include scores from tests such as the American College Testing (ACT) and the Scholastic Assessment Test (SAT).
Placement	Based on performance on tests and other assessments, students in a school may be assigned to different instructional programs (e.g., remedial, regular, and honors).
Classification	Students in special education may be classified as learning disabled, emotionally disturbed, speech disabled, or some other category of disabling conditions based on the results of an assessment.
Self-understanding	Psychological assessment can help clients enhance their self-understanding in order to make better decisions about educational and career goals. Assessments used in premarriage counseling can help couples identify and address possible areas of conflict before they create problems.
Evaluation	Summative evaluation involves the formal evaluation of performance, often taking the form of a numerical or letter grade (e.g., A, B, C, D, or F). Formative evaluation involves evaluative activities that are aimed at providing feedback based on performance.
Licensing	Many professions require that applicants pass licensing exams in order to be licensed (e.g., physicians, lawyers, psychologists, teachers). Additionally, some fairly common activities such as driving a car require an examination.
Program evaluation	Program evaluation involves the formal evaluation of a service delivery program in order to evaluate its effectiveness. This can range from the effectiveness of a specific curriculum being used in a classroom to the efficiency of a large federal program.
Scientific method	The scientific method involves measurement and the collection of empirical data. Scientists use a wide variety of tests and other assessments in order to test their hypotheses.

PARTICIPANTS IN THE ASSESSMENT PROCESS

There are a large number of individuals who are involved in different aspects of the assessment process. Brief descriptions follow of some the major participants in the assessment process (e.g., AERA et al., 1999).

People Who Develop Tests

Can you guess how many new tests are developed in a given year? Although the exact number is unknown, it is probably much larger than you might imagine. The American Psychological Association (1993) estimated that up to 20,000 new psychological, behavioral, and cognitive tests are developed every year. This number includes tests published by commercial test publishers, tests developed by professionals hoping to have their instruments published, and tests developed by researchers to address specific research questions. However, even

> *The Standards for Educational and Psychological Testing is the most influential and comprehensive set of guidelines for developing and using psychological and educational tests.*

this rather daunting figure does not include the vast number of tests developed by teachers and professors in our schools and universities to assess the achievement or progress of their students. There are minimal standards that all of these tests should meet, whether they are developed by an assessment professional, a graduate student completing a thesis, or a professor assessing the achievement of students in a tests and measurement course. To provide standards for the development and use of psychological and educational tests and other assessment procedures, numerous professional organizations have developed guidelines. The most influential and comprehensive set of guidelines is the *Standards for Educational and Psychological Testing* (which we will refer to as the *Standards*), published by the AERA, APA, and NCME (1999). We have referenced this document numerous times earlier in this chapter, and will do so many more times throughout this text. Special Interest Topic 1.2 illustrates the growing need for test development experts in modern society.

SPECIAL INTEREST TOPIC 1.2

Now Hiring Psychometricians!

On May 5, 2006, the *New York Times* published an article titled "As Test-Taking Grows, Test-Makers Grow Rarer" (Herszenhorn, 2006). The author noted that because federal law requires increased standardized testing of public school students, states and testing companies have to compete for psychometricians to develop assessments and interpret the results. The fact is that there are just not enough psychometricians to go around and salaries are currently running as high as $200,000 a year plus perks. Doctoral programs produce less than 50 graduates a year, and there is such a shortage of psychometricians that agencies are requesting special work visas for foreigners with psychometric training to work in the United States. There is even a movement for the federal government to pay to train 1,000 psychometricians in the next five years. So for those of you who have good quantitative and analytical skills and are looking for a promising career in psychology, consider psychometrics!

People Who Use Tests

The list of people who use tests includes those who select, administer, score, interpret, and use the results of tests and other assessment procedures. Tests are used in a wide range of settings by a wide range of individuals. For example, psychologists and counselors use tests to understand their clients better and to help refine their diagnostic impressions and develop treatment plans. Employers use tests to help select and hire skilled employees. States use tests to determine who will be given driver's licenses. Professional licensing boards use tests to determine who has the knowledge and skills necessary to enter professions ranging from medicine to real estate. Teachers use tests in schools to assess their students' academic progress. This is only a small sampling of the many settings in which tests are used. As with the development of tests, some of the people using these tests are assessment experts whose primary responsibility is administering, scoring, and interpreting tests. However, many of the people using tests are trained in other professional areas, and assessment is not their primary area of training. As with test development, the administration, scoring, and interpretation of tests involves professional and ethical standards and responsibilities.

People Who Take Tests

We have all been in this category at many times in our life. In public school we take an untold number of tests to help our teachers evaluate our academic progress, knowledge, and skills. You probably took the SAT or ACT to gain admission to college. When you graduate from college and are ready to obtain a professional license or certificate you will probably be given another test to evaluate how well prepared you are to enter your selected profession. Although the other participants in the assessment process have professional and ethical responsibilities, test takers have a number of rights. The Joint Committee on Testing Practices (JCTP; 1998) indicated that the most fundamental right test takers have is to be tested with tests that meet high professional standards and that are valid for the intended purposes. Other rights of test takers include the following:

> *The most fundamental right of test takers is to be tested with tests that meet high professional standards and are valid for the intended purpose.*

- Test takers should be given information about the purposes of the testing, how the results will be used, who will receive the results, the availability of information regarding accommodations available for individuals with disabilities or language differences, and any costs associated with the testing.
- Test takers have the right to be treated with courtesy, respect, and impartiality.
- Test takers have the right to have tests administered and interpreted by adequately trained individuals who follow professional ethics codes.
- Test takers have the right to receive information about their test results.
- Test takers have the right to have their test results kept confidential.

The JCTP's "Rights and Responsibilities of Test Takers: Guidelines and Expectations" can be accessed at the APA website (http://www.apa.org).

Other People Involved in the Assessment Process

Although the preceding three categories probably encompass most participants in the assessment process, they are not exhaustive. For example, there are individuals who market and sell assessment products and services, those who teach others about assessment practices, and those who conduct research on assessment procedures and evaluate assessment programs (National Council on Measurement in Education [NCME], 1995).

PSYCHOLOGICAL ASSESSMENT IN THE 21ST CENTURY

The field of psychological assessment is dynamic and continuously evolving. There are some aspects of the profession that have been stable for many years. For example, classical test theory has been around for almost a century and is still very influential today. However, many aspects of psychological assessment are constantly evolving as the result of a number of external and internal factors. Some of these changes are the result of theoretical or technical advances, some reflect philosophical changes within the profession, and some are the result of external societal, economic, and political influences. It is important for assessment professionals to stay informed regarding new developments in the field and to consider them with an open mind. To illustrate some of the developments the profession is dealing with today, we will briefly highlight a few contemporary trends that are likely to continue to impact assessment practices as you enter the teaching profession.

Computerized Adaptive Testing (CAT)

The widespread availability of fairly sophisticated and powerful tabletop computers has had a significant impact on many aspects of our society, and the field of assessment is no exception. One of the most dramatic and innovative uses of computer technology has been the emergence of computerized adaptive testing (CAT). In CAT the test taker is initially given an item that is of medium difficulty. If the test taker correctly responds to that item, the computer selects and administers a slightly more difficult item. If the examinee misses the initial item, the computer selects a somewhat easier item. As the testing proceeds, the computer continues to select items on the basis of the test taker's performance on previous items. CAT continues until a specified level of precision is reached. Research suggests that CAT can produce the same levels of reliability and validity as conventional paper-and-pencil tests, but because it requires the administration of fewer test items, assessment efficiency can be enhanced (e.g., Weiss, 1982, 1985, 1995).

Other Technological Applications Used in Assessment

CAT is not the only innovative application of computer technology in the field of assessment. Some of the most promising applications of technology in assessment involve the use of technology to present problem simulations that cannot be realistically addressed with paper-and-pencil tests. For example, flight-training programs routinely use sophisticated flight simulators to assess the skills of pilots. This technology allows programs to assess how pilots will handle emergency and other low-incidence situations, assessing skills that were previously difficult if not impossible to assess accurately. Another innovative use of technology is the commercially available instrumental music assessment systems that allow students to perform musical pieces and have their performances analyzed and graded in terms of pitch and rhythm. Online versions of these programs allow students to practice at home and have their performance results forwarded to their instructors at school. Although it is difficult to anticipate the many ways technology will change assessment practices in the 21st century, it is safe to say that they will be dramatic and sweeping.

> *Although it is difficult to anticipate the many ways technology will change assessment practices in the 21st century, it is safe to say that they will be dramatic and sweeping.*

"Authentic" Assessments

Although advances in technology are driving some of the current trends in assessment, others are the result of philosophical changes among members of the assessment profession. This is exemplified in the current emphasis on performance assessments and portfolios in educational settings. Performance assessments and portfolios are not new creations, but have been around for many years (e.g., performance assessments have been used in industrial-organizational psychology for decades). However, the use of performance assessments and portfolios in educational settings has increased appreciably in recent years. Traditional testing formats, particularly multiple-choice and other selected-response formats (e.g., true–false, matching) have always had their critics, but their opposition has become more vocal in recent years. Opponents of traditional test formats complain that they emphasize rote memorization and other low-level cognitive skills and largely neglect higher order conceptual and problem-solving skills. To address these and related shortcomings, many assessment experts have promoted the use of more "authentic" or complex-performance assessments, typically in the form of performance assessments and portfolios. Performance assessments require test takers to complete a process or produce a product in a context that closely resembles real-life situations. For example, a graduate student in a clinical psychology program might be required to interview a mock client, select tests and other assessment procedures, provide a diagnosis, and develop a treatment plan. Portfolios, a form of performance assessment, involve the systematic collection of student work products over a specified period of time according to a specific set of guidelines (AERA et al., 1999). Artists, architects, writers, and others have long used portfolios to represent their work, and in the last decade portfolios have become increasingly popular in the assessment of students. Although performance assessments have their own set of strengths and weaknesses, they do represent a significant addition to the assessment options available to teachers.

Health Care Delivery Systems

So far we have described how technological and philosophical developments within the profession have influenced current assessment practices. Other changes are the result of political, societal, and economic influences, and this can be seen in the way managed care is influencing the practice of psychology. Managed care is a generic name for health care systems (e.g., health maintenance organization [HMO] or a preferred provider organization [PPO]) that control expenses by managing programs in which health care professionals accept lowered compensation for their services and patients accept limitations in their choice of health care providers. Managed care systems also limit the services that health care professionals provide, including the number of psychotherapy or counseling sessions a client receives and the types of assessments that can be employed. In

the past it was common for psychologists to use a comprehensive battery of time-consuming tests with their
patients. However, due to managed care's emphasis on
time-limited and problem-focused interventions, current
assessment practices are starting to emphasize the use
of briefer and less expensive behavioral and problem-
oriented assessments (Maruish, 2004). As this text goes
to press the prominent political debate in Washington

> *It is likely that laws will be*
> *implemented that will impact*
> *the delivery of health services,*
> *including psychological*
> *services.*

involves "universal health care." It is unclear what the final results of this debate will be, but it is
likely that laws will be implemented that will impact the delivery of health services, including psychological services—of which diagnostic clinical psychological assessment is a key component.

High-Stakes Assessment

Societal and political forces are also influencing the assessment practices in our public schools.
Although parents and politicians have always closely scrutinized the public schools, over the last
three decades the public demands for increased accountability in the schools have reached an all-
time high. To help ensure that teachers are teaching what they are supposed to be teaching and students are learning what they are supposed to be learning, all 50 states and the District of Columbia
have implemented statewide testing programs (Doherty, 2002). These testing programs are often
referred to as high-stakes testing because they produce results that have direct and substantial consequences for both the students and schools (AERA et al., 1999). Students who do not pass the tests
may not be promoted to the next grade or allowed to graduate. However, the "high-stakes" are not
limited to students. Many states publish "report cards" that reflect the performance of school districts
and individual schools. In some states low-performing schools can be closed, reconstituted, or taken
over by the state, and administrators and teachers can be terminated or replaced (Amrein & Berliner,
2002). Proponents of these testing programs maintain that they ensure that public school students are
acquiring the knowledge and skills necessary to succeed in society. To support their position, they
refer to data showing that national achievement scores have improved since these testing programs
were implemented. Opponents of high-stakes testing programs argue that the tests emphasize rote
learning and generally neglect critical thinking, problem solving, and communication skills. Additionally, these critics feel that too much instructional time is spent "teaching to the test" instead of
teaching the vitally important skills teachers would prefer to focus on (Doherty, 2002).

This debate is likely to continue for the foreseeable future, but in the meantime accountability and the associated testing programs are likely to play a major role in our public schools. In
fact the trend is toward more, rather than less, standardized testing in public schools. For example, the Elementary and Secondary Education Act of 2001 (No Child Left Behind Act) requires
that states test students annually in Grades 3 through 8. Because many states typically administer
standardized achievement tests in only a few of these grades, this new law will require even more
high-stakes testing than is currently in use (Kober, 2002).

This has been a brief and clearly incomplete discussion of some current trends in the
field of assessment. To complicate the situation some of these trends have opposing results. For
example, even though managed care is placing limits on the use of assessments by psychologists
working in many health care settings, the trend toward more high-stakes assessment programs in

the public schools results in the increased use of standardized tests in these settings. Special Interest Topic 1.3 provides a commentary by a respected assessment expert about what she expects to evolve during the next century.

SPECIAL INTEREST TOPIC 1.3

What Does the 21st Century Hold for the Assessment Profession?

Dr. Susan Embretson presented a lecture titled "The Second Century of Ability Testing: Some Predictions and Speculations" at the Educational Testing Service (ETS) in Princeton, New Jersey, in January 2001. In this presentation she started by reviewing the history of ability testing, which dates back approximately 100 years. She noted that by 1930 most of the key psychometric principles were firmly established and that the remainder of the 20th century was largely spent applying and refining those principles. As the profession enters its second century, she predicts changes in the way tests are developed, the way abilities are measured, and the aspects of ability that are measured. A brief summary of some of her key points follows.

The Way Tests Are Developed

Dr. Embretson believes that technological advances will significantly impact the way tests are developed. For example, currently test revision is an expensive and labor-intensive process where tests are revised and re-normed every few years. In the future she anticipates tests will undergo continuous test revisions. As more assessments are administered via computers and data collection is centralized, test developers will be able to try out new items and update normative data on an ongoing basis. Computer-administered tests and centralized data collection will also facilitate automated validity studies and even allow items to be developed through the use of artificial intelligence.

The Way Abilities Are Measured

Based on technological and theoretical advances, Dr. Embretson predicts ability tests will become both shorter and more reliable. She also predicts that there will be a broader conceptualization of test items. For example, ability testing will incorporate more essays and other work-products that had previously been difficult to evaluate in a reliable and economical manner. In recent years computer programs have been developed that can score written essays and graphical problems, and these initial efforts show considerable potential.

The Aspects of Ability That Are Measured

During the 20th century normative interpretations of ability predominated, but Dr. Embretson expects new interpretive models to become increasingly popular. For example, she believes domain-referenced interpretations will emerge where abilities will be interpreted in reference to the cognitive processes and structures that are required to solve the assessment problems or tasks. Instead of focusing almost exclusively on quantitative aspects of performance, future assessments will focus more on the qualitative aspects of test performance. Finally, she believes dynamic testing will become an increasingly important force in ability testing. Dynamic testing measures how responsive the examinee's performance is to changes in conditions as the assessment proceeds.

Although Dr. Embretson expects changes to occur rapidly over the next few decades, she also believes that the basic psychometric principles that have been with us for almost a century will still be important. Therefore, even though some exciting changes are in store for the assessment profession, the basic principles and concepts that are presented in this textbook will continue to be fundamental aspects of the profession.

If you are interested in reading this intriguing paper, it can be accessed at http://www.ets.org/Media/Research/pdf/PICANG7.pdf, or you can purchase a copy for $3.00 by contacting the ETS Policy Information Center, MS-04R, Rosedale Road, Princeton, NJ 651-0001.

Summary

This chapter provides a broad introduction to the field of psychological assessment. We initially briefly reviewed some of the milestones in the history of testing. This began with the use of "civil service" type tests in China as early as 2200 BC and concluded with the development of seminal tests in the 20th century. We then defined some common terms used in the psychological assessment literature, including:

- A test is a procedure in which a sample of an individual's behavior is obtained, evaluated, and scored using standardized procedures.
- Measurement is a set of rules for assigning numbers to represent objects, traits, attributes, or behaviors.
- Assessment is any systematic procedure for collecting information that can be used to make inferences about the characteristics of people or objects.
- Evaluation is an activity that involves judging or appraising the value or worth of something.
- Reliability refers to the stability or consistency of test scores.
- Validity refers to the accuracy of the interpretations of test scores.

Our discussion then turned to a description of different types of tests. Most tests can be classified as either maximum performance or typical response. Maximum performance tests are designed to assess the upper limits of the examinee's knowledge and abilities whereas typical response tests are designed to measure the typical behavior and characteristics of examinees. Maximum performance tests are often classified as achievement tests or aptitude tests. Achievement tests measure knowledge and skills in an area in which the examinee has received instruction. In contrast, aptitude tests measure cognitive abilities and skills that are accumulated as the result of overall life experiences. Maximum performance tests can also be classified as either speed tests or power tests. On pure speed tests performance reflects only differences in the speed of performance whereas on pure power tests performance reflects only the difficulty of the items the examinee is able to answer correctly. In most situations a test is not a measure of pure speed or pure power, but reflects some combination of both approaches. Finally, maximum performance tests are often classified as objective or subjective. When the scoring of a test does not rely on the subjective judgment of person scoring the test it is said to be objective. For example, multiple-choice tests can be scored using a fixed scoring key and are considered objective (multiple-choice tests are often scored by a computer). If the scoring of a test does rely on the subjective judgment of person scoring the test it is said to be subjective. Essay exams are examples of subjective tests.

Typical response tests measure constructs such as personality, behavior, attitudes, or interests, and are often classified as being either objective or projective. Objective tests use selected-response items (e.g., true–false, multiple-choice) that are not influenced by the subjective judgment of the person scoring the test. Projective tests involve the presentation of ambiguous material that can elicit an almost infinite range of responses. Most projective tests involve some subjectivity in scoring, but what is exclusive to projective techniques is the belief that these techniques elicit unconscious material that has not been censored by the conscious mind.

Most tests produce scores that reflect the test takers' performance. Norm-referenced score interpretations compare an examinee's performance to the performance of other people. Criterion-referenced score interpretations compare an examinee's performance to a specified level of performance. Typically tests are designed to produce either norm-referenced or criterion-referenced scores, but it is possible for a test to produce both norm- and criterion-referenced scores.

Next we discussed the basic assumptions that underlie psychological assessment. These include:

- Psychological constructs exist.
- Psychological constructs can be measured.
- Although we can measure constructs, our measurement is not perfect.
- There are different ways to measure any given construct.
- All assessment procedures have strengths and limitations.
- Multiple sources of information should be part of the assessment process.
- Performance on tests can be generalized to non-test behaviors.
- Assessment can provide information that helps psychologists make better professional decisions.
- Assessments can be conducted in a fair manner.
- Testing and assessment can benefit individuals and society as a whole.

We noted that the use of psychological assessments is predicated on the belief that they can provide valuable information that helps psychologists make better decisions. Prominent uses include:

- Diagnosis
- Treatment planning and effectiveness
- Selection, placement, and classification
- Self-understanding
- Evaluation
- Instructional planning
- Licensing
- Program evaluation
- Scientific method

We then described the major participants in the assessment process, including those who develop tests, use tests, and take tests. We concluded this chapter by describing some of the trends in psychological assessment at the beginning of the 21st century. These included the influence of computerized adaptive testing (CAT) and other technological advances, the growing emphasis on authentic assessments, the influence of managed care on assessment practices, and the growing emphasis on high-stakes assessment.

Key Terms and Concepts

Achievement tests, 12
Aptitude tests, 12
Assessment, 9
Construct, 17
Criterion-referenced score, 16
Error, 17

Maximum performance tests, 11
Measurement, 9
Norm-referenced scores, 15
Objective personality tests, 13
Power tests, 13
Projective personality tests, 14

Reliability, 10
Speed tests, 13
Test, 9
Typical response tests, 13
Validity, 11

Recommended Readings

American Educational Research Association, American Psychological Association, & National Council on Measurement in Education. (1999). *Standards for educational and psychological testing.* Washington, DC: American Educational Research Association. In practically every content area this resource is indispensable!

Internet Site of Interest

http://www.apa.org
In addition to general information about the American Psychological Association, this site has information on psychology as a field of study, current reviews, and archival documents such as specialty definitions and practice guidelines. Links to the divisions' websites are provided here as well as applications for student membership.

Chapter Two

The Basic Statistics of Measurement

One does not need to be a statistical wizard to grasp the basic mathematical concepts needed to understand major measurement issues.

Chapter Outline

Learning Objectives

After reading and studying this chapter, students should be able to:

1. Define measurement.
2. Describe the different scales of measurement and give examples.
3. Describe the measures of central tendency and their appropriate use.
4. Describe the measures of variability and their appropriate use.
5. Correctly interpret descriptive statistics.
6. Explain the meaning of correlation coefficients and how they are used.
7. Explain how scatterplots are used to describe the relationships between two variables.
8. Describe major types of correlation coefficients.
9. Distinguish between correlation and causation.
10. Describe how linear regression is used to predict performance.
11. Explain what the standard error of estimate represents and how it can be used to create confidence intervals around predicted scores.

THE ROLE OF MATHEMATICS IN ASSESSMENT

Every semester, when one of us teaches a course in tests and measurement, we inevitably hear a common moan. Students are quick to say they fear this course because they hear it involves "a lot of statistics" and they are not good at math, much less statistics. The truth is you do not have to be a statistical wizard to comprehend the mathematical concepts needed to understand major measurement issues. In fact, Kubiszyn and Borich (2003) estimated that less than 1% of the students in their testing and assessment courses performed poorly entirely because of insufficient math skills. Nevertheless, all measurements in psychology have mathematical properties, and those who use tests and other assessments need to understand the basic mathematical and statistical concepts on which these assessments are predicated. In this chapter we will introduce these mathematical concepts. Generally we will emphasize the development of a conceptual understanding of these issues rather than focusing on mathematical computations. In a few instances we will present mathematical formulas and demonstrate their application, but we will keep the computational aspect to a minimum.

In developing this textbook our guiding principle has been to address only those concepts that psychology students really need to know to select, administer, and interpret assessments in clinical settings. We recognize that most of our students do not desire to become test development experts, but because psychologists use and interpret assessments they need to be competent in their use. In this chapter, we will first discuss scales of measurement and show you how different scales have different properties or characteristics. Next, we will introduce the concept of a collection or distribution of scores and review the different statistics available to describe distributions. We will then introduce the concept of correlation, how it is measured, and what it means. Finally, we will briefly introduce and illustrate the use of linear regression (due to its importance to prediction), the standard error of estimate, and confidence intervals.

SCALES OF MEASUREMENT

What Is Measurement?

We defined **measurement** as a set of rules for assigning numbers to represent objects, traits, attributes, or behaviors. Psychological tests are measuring devices and as such they involve rules (e.g., specific items, administration, and scoring instructions) for assigning numbers to an individual's performance that are interpreted as reflecting characteristics of the individual. For example, the number of items on a depression inventory that a client endorses in a specific manner may be interpreted as reflecting his or her subjective level of depression. Similarly, the number of digits a client can remember and repeat might be interpreted as reflecting his or her short-term auditory memory. As you will learn in this course, there are a vast number of psychological tests available that are designed to measure a vast number of psychological constructs.

> **Measurement** *was defined earlier as a set of rules for assigning numbers to represent objects, traits, attributes, or behaviors.*

When we measure something, the units of measurement have a mathematical property called the scale of measurement. A scale is a system or scheme for assigning values or scores to the characteristic being measured (e.g., Sattler, 1992). Stevens (1946) originally proposed a taxonomy that specified four scales of measurement. These different scales have distinct properties and convey unique types of information. The four scales of measurement are nominal, ordinal, interval, and ratio. The scales form a hierarchy, and as we progress from nominal to ratio scales we are able to perform increasingly sophisticated measurements that capture more detailed information.

Nominal Scales

> **Nominal scales** *classify people or objects into categories, classes, or sets.*

Nominal scales are the simplest of the four scales. **Nominal scales** provide a qualitative system for categorizing people or objects into categories, classes, or sets. In most situations, these categories are mutually exclusive. Gender is an example of a nominal scale that assigns individuals to mutually exclusive categories. Another example is assigning people to categories based on their college academic major (e.g., psychology, biology, chemistry). You may have noticed that in these examples we did not assign numbers to the categories. In some situations we do assign numbers in nominal scales simply to identify or label the categories; however, the categories are not ordered in a meaningful manner. For example, we might use the number one to represent a category of students who list their academic major as psychology, the number two for the academic major of biology, the number three for the academic major of chemistry, and so forth. Notice that no attempt is made to order the categories. Three is not greater than two, and two is not greater than one. The assignment of numbers is completely arbitrary. Another individual might assign a new set of numbers that would be just as useful as ours. In fact, in nominal scales the numbers serve only as names for the categories. We could just as easily call them red, blue, green, or eagles, sparrows, and robins. Because of the arbitrary use of numbers in nominal scales, nominal scales do not actually quantify the variables under examination. Numbers assigned to nominal scales should not be added, subtracted, ranked, or otherwise manipulated. As a result, most common statistical procedures cannot be used with these scales so their usefulness is limited.

Ordinal Scales

> **Ordinal scales** *rank people or objects according to the amount of a characteristic they display or possess.*

Ordinal scale measurement allows you to rank people or objects according to the amount or quantity of a characteristic they display or possess. As a result, ordinal scales enable us to quantify the variables under examination and provide substantially more information than nominal scales. Ranking people according to height from the tallest to the shortest is an example of ordinal measurement. Traditionally the ranking is ordered from the "most" to the "least." In our example the tallest person in the class would receive the rank of 1, the next tallest a rank of 2, and the like. Although ordinal scale measurement provides quantitative information, it does not ensure that the intervals between the ranks are consistent. That is, the difference in height between the person ranked 1 and 2 might be 3 inches while the difference between those ranked 3 and 4 might be 1 inch. Ordinal scales indicate the rank-order position among individuals or objects, but they do not indicate the extent by which they differ. All the ordinal scale tells us then is who is taller, number 5 or number 7; it tells us nothing about how much taller. As a result, these scales are somewhat limited in both the measurement information they provide and the statistical procedures that can be applied. Although you will see it done, it rarely makes sense to add, subtract, multiply, or divide such scores or to find their mean. Nevertheless, the use of these scales is fairly common in many settings. Percentile rank, age equivalents, and grade equivalents are all examples of common ordinal scales.

Interval Scales

Interval scales provide more information than either nominal or ordinal scales. Interval scale measurement allows you to rank people or objects like an ordinal scale, but on a scale with equal units. By equal scale units, we mean the difference between adjacent units on the scale is equivalent. The difference between

> **Interval scales** *rank people or objects like an ordinal scale, but on a scale with equal units.*

scores of 70 and 71 is the same as the difference between scores of 50 and 51 (or 92 and 93; 37 and 38; etc.). Many psychological tests are designed to produce interval-level scores. Let's look at an example of scores for three people on an intelligence test. Assume individual A receives a score of 100, individual B a score of 110, and individual C a score of 120. First, we know that person C scored the highest followed by B, then A. Second, given that the scores are on an interval scale, we also know that the difference between individuals A and B (i.e., 10 points) is equivalent to the difference between B and C (i.e., 10 points). Finally, we know the difference between individuals A and C (i.e., 20 points) is twice as large as the difference between individuals A and B (i.e., 10 points). Interval-level data can be manipulated using common mathematical operations (e.g., addition, subtraction, multiplication, and division), whereas lesser scales (i.e., nominal and ordinal) cannot. A final advantage is that most statistical procedures can be used with interval scale data.

As you can see, interval scales represent a substantial improvement over ordinal scales and provide considerable information. Their one limitation is that interval scales do not have a true zero point. That is, on interval scales a score of zero does not reflect the total absence of the attribute. For example, if an individual were unable to answer any questions correctly on an intelligence test and scored a zero, it would not indicate the complete lack of intelligence, but only that he or she were unable to respond correctly to any questions on this test. (Intelligence tests are designed so no one actually receives a score of zero. We just use this example to illustrate the concept of an arbitrary zero point.) Additionally, ratios are not meaningful with interval scales. For example, even though an IQ of 100 is twice as large as an IQ of 50, it does not mean that the person with a score of 100 is twice as intelligent as the person with a score of 50. For such a statement to be accurate, we would need to have a true zero point.

Despite this limitation, some school districts and agencies continue to use some form of a "percentage discrepancy" between actual and predicted achievement or an IQ. In such a circumstance, the difference between two values, such as an obtained achievement score of say 75, is subtracted from the student's predicted achievement score of 100. The difference score is then used to calculate a percentage of deficiency in the area of academics covered. Various formulas are in use to do this, but simplistically, one might take this difference of 25 points, divide it by 100 (the predicted score), and decide the student has a 25% deficiency in the area in question. Such a percentage is nonsensical, regardless of the formulas used to make the determination because a percentage is a ratio of two numbers—and ratios are uninterpretable in interval scaling because we have no true zero point for reference in interval scaling. Ratio scales are required, as described in the following text.

With behavioral variables such as intelligence or even personality characteristics like friendliness, we do not know where the true zero point lies. With physical characteristics such as height and weight, a zero point is well defined, and we measure beginning at zero and go up. When the zero point is unknown, the only place we can begin measuring accurately is the middle of the distribution. Interval scales are derived by first locating the midpoint of a variable, usually taken to be the mean score of a population or sample, and then measuring outward in each direction, above and below, as far as we can establish scores with reasonable accuracy. We never reach the true bottom or true top of what we are measuring (although a particular test may bottom-out or top-out, the construct continues). Remember that interval scales, the most common scale in psychology and education begin measuring in the middle—the only point we can initially define—and then measure toward the two ends, or tails, of the distribution, never reaching either end (because the normal curve is asymptotic to its axis, meaning it never quite comes into contact with it at either end). In psychology, interval scale scores are most commonly seen in the form of standard scores (there are a number of standard scores used in psychology, which will be discussed in the next chapter).

Ratio Scales

> **Ratio scales** *have the properties of interval scales plus a true zero point.*

Ratio scales have the properties of interval scales plus a true zero point that reflects the complete absence of the characteristic being measured. Miles per hour, length, and weight are all examples of ratio scales. As the name suggests, with these scales we can interpret ratios between scores. For example, 100 miles per hour is twice as fast as 50 miles per hour; 6 feet is twice as long as 3 feet; and 300 pounds is three times as much as 100 pounds. Ratios are not meaningful or interpretable with other scales. As we noted, a person with an IQ of 100 is not twice as intelligent as one with an IQ of 50. Given the enormity of human intelligence, an IQ of 100 may represent only a 1%, 5%, or 10% increase over an IQ of 50. The key point is that absent a ratio scale for intelligence, we cannot know the magnitude of such a difference in absolute terms. This holds in achievement as well: A person with a standardized math achievement test score of 120 does not know "twice as much" as one with a score of 60. With the exception of the percentage of items correct and the measurement of behavioral responses (e.g., reaction time), there are relatively few ratio scales in psychological measurement. Fortunately, we are able to address most of the measurement issues in psychology adequately using interval scales.

Table 2–1 gives examples of common nominal, ordinal, interval, and ratio scales used in psychological measurement. As we noted, there is a hierarchy among the scales with nominal scales being the least sophisticated and providing the least information and ratio scales being the

TABLE 2–1	Common Nominal, Ordinal, Interval, and Ratio Scales	
Scale	**Example**	**Sample Scores**
Nominal	Gender of participant	Female = 1
		Male = 2
	Ethnicity	African American = 1
		White = 2
		Hispanic American = 3
		Native American = 4
		Asian American = 5
	Place of birth	Northeast = 1
		Southeast = 2
		Midwest = 3
		Southwest = 4
		Northwest = 5
		Pacific = 6
Ordinal	Preference for activity	1 = Most preferred
		2 = Intermediate preferred
		3 = Least
	Graduation class rank	1 = Valedictorian
		2 = Salutatorian
		3 = Third rank
		Etc.
	Percentile rank	99th percentile
		98th percentile
		97th percentile
		Etc.
Interval	Intelligence scores	IQ of 100
	Personality test scores	Depression score of 75
	Graduate Record Exam	Verbal score of 550
Ratio	Height in inches	60 inches tall
	Weight in pounds	100 pounds
	Percentage correct on classroom test	100%

most sophisticated and providing the most information. Nominal scales allow you to assign a number to a person that associates that person with a set or category, but other useful quantitative properties are missing. Ordinal scales have all the positive properties of nominal scales with the addition of the ability to rank people according to the amount of a characteristic they possess.

Interval scales have all the positive properties of ordinal scales and also incorporate equal scale units. The inclusion of equal scale units allows one to make relative statements regarding scores (e.g., the difference between a score of 82 and a score of 84 is the same as the difference between a score of 92 and 94). Finally, ratio scales have all the positive properties of an interval scale with the addition of an absolute zero point. The inclusion of an absolute zero point allows us to form meaningful ratios between scores (e.g., a score of 50 reflects twice the amount of the characteristic as a score of 25). Although these scales do form a hierarchy, this does not mean the lower scales are of little or no use. If you want to categorize students according to their academic major, a nominal scale is clearly appropriate. Accordingly, if you simply want to rank people according to height, an ordinal scale would be adequate and appropriate. However, in most measurement situations you want to use the scale that provides the most information.

THE DESCRIPTION OF TEST SCORES

An individual's raw score on a test, taken in isolation, typically provides very little information. For example, if you know that an individual endorsed 50% of the items on a depression inventory in a manner indicating depressive symptoms, you still know very little about that person's level of depression. To interpret or describe test scores meaningfully you need to have a frame of reference. Often the frame of reference is how other people performed on the test (i.e., norm-referenced interpretation). For example, if you knew that in a large representative sample less than 2% of the sample endorsed 50% or more of the items in a manner indicating depressive symptoms, you would likely interpret it as reflecting a high or at least unusual level of depression symptoms. In contrast, if more than 50% of the sample endorsed at least 50% of the items in a manner indicating depressive symptoms, you would likely interpret it as reflecting a normal level of depressive symptoms (unless, of course, your sample was composed mostly of people with a diagnosis of Major Depressive Disorder). The following sections provide information about score distributions and the statistics used to describe them. In the next chapter we will use many of these concepts and procedures to help you learn how to describe and interpret test scores.

Distributions

A **distribution** is simply a set of scores. These can be scores on an intelligence test, scores on a measure of abstract reasoning, or scores on a career interest inventory. We can also have distributions reflecting physical characteristics such as weight, height, or strength. Distributions can be represented in a number of ways, including tables and graphs. Table 2–2 presents scores for 20 students on an exam similar to what might be recorded in a teacher's grade book. Table 2–3 presents an ungrouped frequency distribution of the same 20 scores. Notice that in this example there are only seven possible measurement categories or scores (i.e., 4, 5, 6, 7, 8, 9, and 10). In some situations there are so many possible scores that it is not practical to list each potential score individually. In these situations it is common to use a grouped frequency distribution. In grouped frequency distributions the possible scores are "combined" or "grouped" into class intervals that encompass a range of possible scores. Table 2–4 presents a grouped frequency distribution of 250 hypothetical scores that are grouped into class intervals that incorporate 5 score values.

A distribution is a set of scores.

TABLE 2–2	Distribution of Scores for 20 Students
Student	**Test Score**
Cindy	7
Raul	8
Paula	9
Steven	6
Angela	5
Robert	6
Kim	10
Mario	9
Julie	9
Kareem	9
Karen	8
Paul	4
Teresa	5
Freddie	6
Tammy	7
Shelly	8
Aisha	8
Johnny	7
Jose	8
Randy	5
Mean = 7.3	
Median = 7.5	
Mode = 8	

TABLE 2–3	Ungrouped Frequency Distribution
Score	**Frequency**
10	1
9	4
8	5
7	4
6	3
5	2
4	1

Note: This reflects the same distribution of scores depicted in Table 2–2.

TABLE 2–4 Grouped Frequency Distribution	
Class Interval	**Frequency**
125–129	6
120–124	14
115–119	17
110–114	23
105–109	27
100–104	42
95–99	39
90–94	25
85–89	22
80–84	17
75–79	13
70–74	5

Note: This presents a grouped frequency distribution of 250 hypothetical scores that are grouped into class intervals that incorporate 5 score values.

Frequency graphs are also popular and provide a visual representation of a distribution. When reading a frequency graph, scores are traditionally listed on the horizontal axis (commonly called the *x*-axis) and the frequency of scores is listed on the vertical axis (commonly called the *y*-axis). Figure 2–1 presents a graph of the set of scores listed in Tables 2–2 and 2–3. In examining this figure you see that there was only one score of 10 (reflecting perfect performance) and there was only one score of 4 (reflecting correctly responding to only four questions). Most of the students received scores between 7 and 9. Figure 2–2 presents a graph of a distribution that might reflect a large standardization sample. Examining this figure reveals that the scores tend to accumulate around the middle, with their frequency diminishing as we move further away from the middle.

FIGURE 2–1 Graph of the Test Scores.

FIGURE 2–2 Hypothetical Distribution of Large Standardization Sample.

Low Scores High Scores	Low Scores High Scores
Test Scores	Test Scores

FIGURE 2–3 Negatively Skewed Distribution.   **FIGURE 2–4** Positively Skewed Distribution.

Another characteristic of the distribution depicted in Figure 2–2 is that it is symmetrical. By symmetrical we mean if you divide the distribution into two halves, they will mirror each other. Not all distributions are symmetrical. When a distribution is not symmetrical it is referred to as skewed. Skewed distributions can be either negatively or positively skewed. A negatively skewed distribution is one with few scores at the low end, as illustrated in Figure 2–3; it points toward the *y*- or vertical axis. When a maximal performance test produces scores that are negatively skewed it is probable that the test is too easy because there are many high scores and relatively few low scores. A positively skewed distribution is one with few scores at the high end, as illustrated in Figure 2–4; it points away from the *y*- or vertical axis. If a maximal performance test produces scores that are positively skewed, it is likely that the test is too difficult because there are many low scores and few high scores. Later in this chapter we will talk more about a special type of distribution referred to as the normal or bell-shaped distribution and describe how it is used to help interpret test scores. First, however, we will discuss two important characteristics of distributions and the methods we have for describing them. The first characteristic is central tendency and the second is variability.

Measures of Central Tendency

The scores in many distributions tend to concentrate around a center (hence the term central tendency), and there are three common descriptive statistics used to summarize this tendency. The three measures of central tendency are the mean, median, and mode. These statistics are frequently referenced in mental and in physical measurement and all psychologists should be familiar with them. It is likely that you have heard of all of these statistics, but we will briefly discuss them to ensure that you are familiar with the special characteristics of each.

MEAN. Most people are familiar with the **mean** as the simple arithmetic average. Practically every day you will hear multiple discussions involving the concept of the average amount of some entity. Meteorologists give you information about the average temperature and amount of rain, politicians and economists discuss the average hourly wage, educators talk

*The **mean** is the arithmetic average of a distribution.*

about the grade point average, health professionals talk about the average weight and average life expectancy, and the list goes on. Formally, the mean of a set of scores is defined by the equation:

$$\text{Mean} = \text{Sum of Scores} / \text{Number of Scores}$$

The mean of the test scores listed in Table 2–2 is calculated by summing the 20 scores in the distribution and dividing by 20. This results in a mean of 7.3. Note that the mean is near the middle of the distribution (see Figure 2–1). Although no student obtained a score of 7.3, the mean is useful in providing a sense of the central tendency of the group of scores. The mean of a distribution is typically designated with $\bar{X}$ or M for sample data and *mu* (μ) for a population.

Several important mathematical characteristics of the mean make it useful as a measure of central tendency. First, the mean is meaningful for distributions containing interval and ratio level scores (though it is not applicable for nominal or ordinal scores). Second, the mean of a sample is a good estimate of the mean for the population from which the sample was drawn (assuming you did a good job of drawing a random sample). This is useful when developing tests in which standardization samples are tested and the resulting distribution is believed to reflect characteristics of the entire population of people with whom the examinee or test taker is to be compared (see Special Interest Topic 2.1 for more information on this topic). Another positive characteristic of the mean is that it is essential to the definition and calculation of other descriptive statistics that are useful in the context of measurement.

SPECIAL INTEREST TOPIC 2.1

Population Parameters and Sample Statistics

Although we try to minimize the use of statistical jargon whenever possible, at this point it is useful to highlight the distinction between population parameters and sample statistics. Statisticians differentiate between populations and samples. A population is the complete group of people, objects, or other things of interest. An example of a population is "all of the secondary students in the United States." This is a very large number of students and it would be extremely difficult to study a group this large. Due to these types of constraints researchers often are unable to study entire populations. Instead they study samples. A sample is just a subset of the larger population that is thought to be representative of the population. By studying samples, researchers are able to make generalizations about populations. For example, even though it might not be practical to administer a questionnaire to all secondary students in the United States, it is possible to select a random sample of secondary students and administer the questionnaire to them. If we are careful selecting this sample and it is of sufficient size, the information we garner from the sample may allow us to draw some conclusions about the population.

Now we will address the distinction between parameters and statistics. Population values are referred to as parameters and are typically represented with Greek symbols. For example, statisticians use *mu* (μ) to indicate a population mean and *sigma* (σ) to indicate a population standard deviation. Because it is often not possible to study entire populations, we often don't know population parameters and have to estimate them using statistics. A statistic is a value that is calculated based on a sample. Statistics are typically represented with Roman letters. For example, statisticians use $\bar{X}$ to indicate the sample mean (some statisticians use M to indicate the mean) and SD (or S) to indicate the sample standard deviation. Sample statistics can provide information about the corresponding population parameters. For example, the sample mean ($\bar{X}$) may serve as an estimate of the population mean (μ). Of course the information provided by a sample statistic is only as good as the sample the statistic is based on. Large

(Continued)

representative samples can provide good information whereas small or biased samples provide poor information. Without going into detail about sampling and inferential statistics at this point, we do want to make you aware of the distinction between parameters and statistics. In this and other texts you will see references to both parameters and statistics, and understanding this distinction will help you avoid a misunderstanding. Remember, as a general rule if the value is designated with a Greek symbol it refers to a population parameter, but if it is designated with a Roman letter it is a sample statistic.

An undesirable characteristic of the mean is that it is sensitive to unbalanced extreme scores. By this we mean a score that is either extremely high or extremely low relative to the rest of the scores in the distribution. An extreme score, either very large or very small, tends to "pull" the mean in its direction. This might not be readily apparent, so let's look at an example. In the set of scores 1, 2, 3, 4, 5, and 38, the mean is 8.8. Notice that 8.8 is not near any score that actually occurs in the distribution. The extreme score of 38 pulls the mean in its direction. The tendency for the mean to be affected by extreme scores is particularly problematic when there is a small number of scores. The influence of an extreme score decreases as the total number of scores in the distribution increases. For example, the mean of 1, 1, 1, 1, 2, 2, 2, 2, 3, 3, 3, 3, 4, 4, 4, 4, 5, 5, 5, 5, and 38 is 4.6. In this example the influence of the extreme score is reduced by the presence of a larger number of scores.

MEDIAN. The **median** is the score or potential score (formally referred to as the "point") that divides the distribution in half. In the distribution of scores depicted in Table 2–3, half the scores are 8 or above and half the scores are 7 or below. Therefore, the point that divides the distribution in half is between 8 and 7, or

> *The **median** is the score or potential score that divides a distribution in half.*

7.5. When the number of scores in a distribution is an odd number, the median is simply the score that is in the middle of the distribution. Consider the following set of scores: 9, 8, 7, 6, 5. In this example the median is 7 because two scores fall above it and two fall below it. When the data have been arranged as a grouped frequency distribution, a process referred to as interpolation is used to compute the median. Interpolation is illustrated in practically every basic statistics textbook, but we will not go into detail about the process.

The median can be calculated for distributions containing ratio, interval, or ordinal level scores, but it is not appropriate for nominal level scores. A desirable characteristic of the median is that it is insensitive to extreme scores. For example, in the set of scores 1, 2, 3, 4, 5, and 38, the median is 3.5 (as opposed to a mean of 8.8). The median is a useful and versatile measure of central tendency that is particularly useful for many common descriptive purposes.

MODE. The **mode** of a distribution is the most frequently occurring score. Refer back to Table 2–3 that presents the ungrouped frequency distribution of 20 students on a test. By examining these scores you will see that the most frequently occurring score

> *The **mode** is the most frequently occurring score in a distribution.*

Low Scores   High Scores

Test Scores

FIGURE 2–5 Bimodal Distribution.

is 8. These scores are graphed in Figure 2–1, and by locating the highest point in the graph you are also able to identify the mode (i.e., 8). An advantage of the mode is that it can be used with nominal data (e.g., the most frequent college major selected by students) as well as ordinal, interval, and ratio data (Hays, 1994). However, the mode does have significant limitations as a measure of central tendency. First, some distributions have two scores that are equal in frequency and higher than other scores (see Figure 2–5). This is referred to as a "bimodal" distribution and here the mode is ineffective as a measure of central tendency. Second, the mode is not a stable measure of central tendency, particularly with small samples. For example, in the distribution depicted in Table 2–3, if one student who earned a score 8 had earned a score of either 7 or 9, the mode would have shifted from 8 to 7 or 9. As a result of these limitations, the mode is often of little utility as a measure of central tendency.

CHOOSING BETWEEN THE MEAN, MEDIAN, AND MODE. A natural question is which measure of central tendency is most useful or appropriate? As you might expect, the answer depends on a number of factors. First, as we noted when discussing the mean, it is essential when calculating other useful statistics. For this and other rather technical reasons (see Hays, 1994), the mean has considerable utility as a measure of central tendency. However, for purely descriptive purposes the median is often the most versatile and useful measure of central tendency. When a distribution is skewed, the influence of unbalanced extreme scores on the mean tends to undermine its usefulness. Figure 2–6 illustrates the expected relationship between the mean and the median in skewed distributions. Note that the mean is "pulled" in the direction of the skew. That is, the mean is lower than the median in negatively skewed distributions and higher than the median in positively skewed distributions. To illustrate how the mean can be misleading in skewed distributions, Hopkins (1998) indicated that due to the influence of extremely wealthy individuals, about 60% of the families in the United States have incomes below the national mean. For example, in 2008 the median family income was $50,303 whereas the mean income was $68,424 (http://www.census.gov/). In this situation, the mean is pulled higher by the extremely high income of some individuals (e.g., select actors, athletes, and CEOs) and is somewhat misleading as a measure of central tendency. Finally, if you are dealing with nominal level data, the mode is the only measure of central tendency that provides useful information.

At this point you should have a good understanding of the various measures of central tendency and be able to interpret them in many common applications. However, you might be surprised how often individuals in the popular media demonstrate a fundamental misunderstanding of these measures. See Special Interest Topic 2.2 for a rather humorous example of how a journalist misinterpreted information based on measures of central tendency.

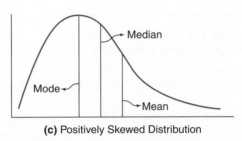

FIGURE 2–6 Relationship Between Mean, Median, and Mode in Normal and Skewed Distributions.

Source: Janda, L. *Psychological Testing: Theory & Applications,* Fig. 2.1 p. 28, ©1998 Allyn & Bacon. Reproduced by permission of Pearson Education, Inc.

SPECIAL INTEREST TOPIC 2.2:

A Public Outrage: Physicians Overcharge Their Patients

Half of all professionals charge above the median fee for their services. Now that you understand the mean, median, and mode you recognize how obvious this statement is. However, a few years back a local newspaper columnist in Texas, apparently unhappy with his physician's bill for some services, conducted an investigation of charges for various medical procedures in the county where he resided. In a somewhat angry column he revealed to the community that "fully half of all physicians surveyed charge above the median fee for their services."

We would like him to know that "fully half" of all professionals, plumbers, electricians, painters, lawn services, hospitals, and everyone else we can think of also charge above the median fee for their services. We wouldn't have it any other way!

Measures of Variability

Two distributions can have the same mean, median, and mode yet differ considerably in the way the scores are distributed around the measures of central tendency. Therefore, it is not sufficient to characterize a set of scores solely by measures of central tendency. Figure 2–7 presents graphs of three distributions with identical means but different degrees of variability. A measure of the dispersion, spread, or variability of a set of scores will help us describe the distribution more fully. We will examine three measures of variability commonly used to describe distributions: range, standard deviation, and variance.

FIGURE 2–7 Three Distributions With Different Degrees of Variability.

Source: Gregory, R. *Psychological Testing: History, Principles, and Applications,* Figs. 3.2 p. 60 ©2000 Allyn & Bacon, Inc. Reproduced by permission of Pearson Education, Inc.

RANGE. The **range** is the distance between the smallest and largest score in a distribution. The range is calculated:

$$\text{Range} = \text{Highest Score} - \text{Lowest Score}$$

> *The **range** is the distance between the smallest and largest score in a distribution.*

For example, in referring back to the distribution of scores listed in Table 2–3 you see that the largest score is 10 and the smallest score is 4. By simply subtracting 4 from 10 you determine the range is 6. The range considers only the two most extreme scores in a distribution and tells us about the limits or extremes of a distribution. However, it does not provide information about how the remaining scores are spread out or dispersed within these limits. We need other descriptive statistics, namely the standard deviation and variance, to provide information about the dispersion or spread of scores within the limits described by the range.

> *The **standard deviation** is a measure of the average distance that scores vary from the mean of the distribution.*

STANDARD DEVIATION. The mean and standard deviation are the most widely used statistics in psychological testing as well as research in the social and behavioral sciences. The **standard deviation** is computed with the following steps:

Step 1. Compute the mean of the distribution.

Step 2. Subtract each score in the distribution from the mean. (This will yield some negative numbers and if you add all of these differences, the sum will be zero. To overcome this, we simply square each difference score because the square of any number is always positive (see step 3).)

Step 3. Square each difference score.

Step 4. Sum all the squared difference scores.

TABLE 2–5	Calculating the Standard Deviation and Variance	
Student Scores	**Difference (Score – Mean)**	**Difference Squared**
7	(7 − 7.3) = −0.3	0.09
8	(8 − 7.3) = 0.7	0.49
9	(9 − 7.3) = 1.7	2.89
6	(6 − 7.3) = −1.3	1.69
7	(7 − 7.3) = −0.3	0.09
6	(6 − 7.3) = −1.3	1.69
10	(10 − 7.3) = 2.7	7.29
8	(8 − 7.3) = 0.7	0.49
5	(5 − 7.3) = −2.3	5.29
9	(9 − 7.3) = 1.7	2.89
9	(9 − 7.3) = 1.7	2.89
9	(9 − 7.3) = 1.7	2.89
8	(8 − 7.3) = 0.7	0.49
4	(4 − 7.3) = −3.3	10.89
5	(5 − 7.3) = −2.3	5.29
6	(6 − 7.3) = −1.3	1.69
7	(7 − 7.3) = −0.3	0.09
8	(8 − 7.3) = 0.7	0.49
8	(8 − 7.3) = 0.7	0.49
7	(7 − 7.3) = −0.3	0.09

Sum = 146

Mean = 7.3

Sum = 48.2

Variance = 48.2/(n)

= 48.2/20

= 2.41

Standard Deviation = $\sqrt{\text{Variance}}$

= $\sqrt{2.41}$

= 1.55

Step 5. Divide this sum by the number of scores to derive the average of the squared deviations from the mean. This value is the variance and is designated by σ^2 (we will return to this value briefly).

Step 6. The standard deviation (σ) is the positive square root of the variance (σ^2). It is the square root because we first squared all the scores before adding them. To now get a true look at the standard distance between key points in the distribution, we have to undo our little trick that eliminated all those negative signs.

SPECIAL INTEREST TOPIC 2.3

Is the Variance Always Larger Than the Standard Deviation?

In this chapter we show that the standard deviation is the positive square root of the variance. For example, if a distribution has a variance of 100, the standard deviation is 10. If the variance is 25 the standard deviation is 5. Can you think of any situations where the variance is not larger than the standard deviation?

It might surprise you but there are situations where the variance is not larger than the standard deviation. If the variance is 1.0, the standard deviation is also 1.0. In the next chapter you will learn about z-scores that have a mean of 0 and a standard deviation of 1.0. It is also possible for the standard deviation to actually be larger than the variance. For example, if the variance is 0.25 the standard deviation is 0.50. Although its not common to find situations where the variance and standard deviation are decimals in psychological and educational assessment, it is good to be aware of the possibility.

These steps are illustrated in Table 2–5 using the scores listed in Table 2–2. This example illustrates the calculation of the population standard deviation designated with the Greek symbol *sigma* (σ). You will also see the standard deviation designated with SD or S. This is appropriate when you are describing the standard deviation of a sample rather than a population (refer back to Special Interest Topic 2.1 for information on the distinction between population parameters and sample statistics).[1]

The standard deviation is a measure of the average distance that scores vary from the mean of the distribution. The larger the standard deviation, the more scores differ from the mean and the more variability there is in the distribution. If scores are widely dispersed or spread around the mean, the standard deviation will be large. If there is relatively little dispersion or spread of scores around the mean, the standard deviation will be small.

VARIANCE. In calculating the standard deviation we actually first calculate the variance σ^2. As illustrated in Table 2–5, the standard deviation is actually the positive square root of the variance. Therefore, the **variance** is also a measure of the variability of scores. The reason the standard deviation is more frequently used when interpreting individual scores is that the variance is in squared units of measurement which complicates interpretation. For example, we can easily interpret weight in pounds, but it is more difficult to interpret and use weight reported in squared pounds. The variance is in squared units, but the standard deviation (i.e., the square root of the variance) is in the same units as the scores and therefore is more easily understood. Although the variance is difficult to apply when describing individual scores, it does have special meaning as a theoretical concept in measurement theory and statistics. For now, simply remember that the variance is a measure of the degree of variability in scores. Special Interest Topic 2.3 examines the relationship between the standard deviation and variance.

> *The* **variance** *is a measure of variability that has special meaning as a theoretical concept in measurement theory and statistics.*

---

[1] The discussion and formulas provided in this chapter are those used in descriptive statistics. In inferential statistics when the population variance is estimated from a sample, the N in the denominator is replaced with $N - 1$.

CHOOSING BETWEEN THE RANGE, STANDARD DEVIATION, AND VARIANCE. As we noted, the range conveys information about the limits of a distribution, but does not tell us how the scores are dispersed within these limits. The standard deviation indicates the average distance that scores vary from the mean of the distribution. The larger the standard deviation, the more variability there is in the distribution. The standard deviation is very useful in describing distributions and will be of particular importance when we turn our attention to the interpretation of scores in the next chapter. The variance is another important and useful measure of variability. Because the variance is expressed in terms of squared measurement units, it is not as useful in interpreting individual scores as is the standard deviation. However, the variance is important as a theoretical concept, and we will return to it when discussing reliability and validity in later chapters.

The Normal Distribution

The normal distribution is a special type of distribution that is very useful when developing and interpreting tests. The normal distribution, which is also referred to as the Gaussian or bell-shaped distribution, is a distribution that characterizes many variables that occur in nature (see Special Interest Topic 2.4 for information on Carl Frederich Gauss, who is credited with discovering the bell-shaped distribution). Gray (1999) indicated that the height of individuals of a given age and gender is an example of a variable that is distributed normally. He noted that numerous genetic and nutritional factors influence an individual's height, and in most cases these various factors average out so that people of a given age and gender tend to be of approximately the same height. This accounts for the peak frequency in the normal distribution. In referring

---

SPECIAL INTEREST TOPIC 2.4

Whence the Normal Curve?

Carl Frederich Gauss (1777–1855) was a noted German mathematician who is generally credited with being one of the founders of modern mathematics. Born in 1777 in Brunswick, he turned his scholarly pursuits toward the field of astronomy around the turn of the century. In the course of tracking star movements and taking other forms of physical survey measurements (at times with instruments of his own invention), he found to his annoyance that students and colleagues who were plotting the location of an object at the same time noted it to be in somewhat different places! He began to plot the frequency of the observed locations systematically and found the observations to take the shape of a curve. He determined that the best estimate of the true location of the object was the mean of the observations and that each independent observation contained some degree of error. These errors formed a curve that was in the shape of a bell. This curve or distribution of error terms has since been demonstrated to occur with a variety of natural phenomena, and indeed has become so commonplace that it is most often known as the "normal curve" or the normal distribution. Of course, you may know it as the bell curve as well due to its shape, and mathematicians and others in the sciences sometimes refer to it as the Gaussian curve after its discoverer and the man who described many of its characteristics. Interestingly, Gauss was a prolific scholar and the Gaussian curve is not the only discovery to bear his name. He did groundbreaking research on magnetism, and the unit of magnetic intensity is called a gauss.

To be fair, some writers (e.g., Osterlind, 2006) credit the discovery of the normal distribution to Abraham de Moivre. They suggest that Abraham de Moivre's studies of probability theory laid the foundation for Gauss's subsequent "discovery" of the normal distribution. Additionally, de Moivre is credited with developing the concept of the standard deviation.

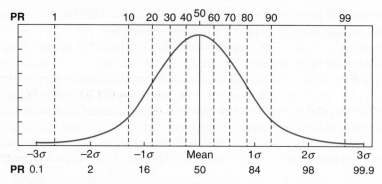

FIGURE 2–8 Normal Distribution With Mean, Standard Deviation, and Percentages.

Source: Janda, L. *Psychological Testing: Theory & Applications,* Fig. 3.1 p. 45, ©1998 Allyn & Bacon. Reproduced by permission of Pearson Education, Inc.

to Figure 2–8 you will see that a large number of scores tend to accumulate or "pile up" around the middle of the distribution. However, for a relatively small number of individuals a unique combination of factors results in them being either much shorter or much taller than the average. This accounts for the distribution trailing off at both the low and high ends, but it never touches the axis or ends. Theoretically, the normal curve ends at a value of infinity so it is known as asymptotic to its axis.

> *The* **normal distribution** *is a symmetrical unimodal distribution in which the mean, median, and mode are all equal.*

Although the previous discussion addressed only observable characteristics of the normal distribution, certain mathematical properties make it particularly useful when interpreting scores. First, the **normal distribution** is a unimodal distribution in which the mean, median, and mode are all equal. It is also symmetrical, meaning that if you divide the distribution into two halves, they will mirror each other. Probably the most useful characteristic of the normal distribution is that predictable proportions of scores occur at specific points in the distribution. Referring to Figure 2–8 you find a normal distribution with the mean and standard deviations (σ) marked. (Figure 2–8 also indicates percentile rank [PR], which will be discussed later.) Because we know that the mean equals the median in a normal distribution, we know that an individual who scores at the mean scored better than 50% of the sample of examinees (remember, earlier we defined the median as the score that divides the distribution in half). Because approximately 34% of the scores fall between the mean and 1 standard deviation above the mean, an individual whose score falls 1 standard deviation above the mean performs at a level exceeding approximately 84% (i.e., 50% + 34%) of the population. A score 2 standard deviations above the mean will be above 98% of the population. Because the distribution is symmetrical, the relationship is the same in the inverse below the mean. A score 1 standard deviation below the mean indicates that the individual exceeds only about 16% (i.e., 50%−34%) of the population on the attribute in question. Approximately two-thirds (i.e., 68%) of the population will score within 1 standard deviation above and below the mean on a normally distributed variable.

We have reproduced in Appendix A a table that allows you to determine what proportion of scores are below any given point in a distribution by specifying standard deviation units. For example, you can use these tables to determine that a score 1.96 SD above the mean exceeds 97.5% of the scores in the distribution whereas a score 1.96 SD below the mean exceeds only 2.5% of the scores. Although we do not feel it is necessary for you to become an expert in using these statistical tables (but the instructor of your statistics course might), we do encourage you to examine Figure 2–8 carefully to ensure you have a good grasp of the basic properties of the normal distribution before proceeding.

Although many variables of importance in psychology such as achievement and intelligence are very close to conforming to the normal distribution, not all psychological and behavioral variables are normally distributed. For example, aggressive behavior and psychotic behavior are two variables of interest to psychologists that are distinctly different from the normal curve in their distributions. Consider physical aggression in children. Most children are not physically aggressive, so on measures of physical aggression, most children tend to pile up at the left side of the distribution (i.e., displaying few aggressive behaviors) whereas those who are only slightly aggressive may score relatively far to the right. Likewise, few people ever experience psychotic symptoms such as hearing voices of people who are not there or seeing things no one else can see. Such variables will each have their own unique distribution, and even though one can, via statistical manipulation, force these score distributions into the shape of a normal curve, it is not always desirable to do so. We will return to this issue later, but at this point it is important to refute the common myth that all human behaviors or attributes conform to the normal curve; clearly they do not!

CORRELATION COEFFICIENTS

Most psychology students are somewhat familiar with the concept of correlation. When people speak of a correlation they are referring to the relationship between two variables. The variables can be physical such as weight and height or psychological such as intelligence and academic achievement. For example, it is reasonable to expect height to demonstrate a relationship with weight. Taller individuals tend to weigh more than shorter individuals. This relationship is not perfect because there are some short individuals who weigh more than taller individuals, but the tendency is for taller people to outweigh shorter people. You might also expect more intelligent people to score higher on tests of academic achievement than less intelligent people, and this is what research indicates. Again, the relationship is not perfect, but as a general rule more intelligent individuals perform better on tests of academic achievement than their less intelligent peers.

Technically, a **correlation coefficient** is a quantitative measure of the linear relationship between two variables. The common correlation coefficient was developed by Karl Pearson (1857–1936) and is designated by the letter r. Correlation coefficients can range from -1.0 to $+1.0$. When interpreting correlation coefficients, there are two parameters to consider. The first parameter is the sign of the coefficient. A positive correlation coefficient indicates that an increase on one variable is associated with an increase on the other variable.

> *A **correlation coefficient** is a quantitative measure of the relationship between two variables.*

For example, height and weight demonstrate a positive correlation with each other. As noted earlier, taller individuals tend to weigh more than shorter individuals. A negative correlation coefficient indicates that an increase on one variable is associated with a decrease on the other variable. For example, because lower scores denote superior performance in the game of golf, there is a negative correlation between the amount of tournament prize money won and a professional's average golf score. Professional golfers with the lowest average scores tend to win the most tournaments.

The second parameter to consider when interpreting correlation coefficients is the magnitude or absolute size of the coefficient. The magnitude of a coefficient indicates the strength of the relationship between two variables. A value of 0 indicates the absence of a relationship between the variables. As coefficients approach a value of 1.0, the strength of the relationship increases. A coefficient of 1.0 (either positive or negative) indicates a perfect correlation, one in which change in one variable is accompanied by a corresponding and proportionate change in the other variable, without exception. Perfect correlation coefficients are rare in psychological measurement, but they might occur in very small samples simply by chance.

There are numerous qualitative and quantitative ways of describing correlation coefficients. A qualitative approach is to describe correlation coefficients as weak, moderate, or strong. Although there are no universally accepted standards for describing the strength of correlations, we offer the following guidelines: <0.30, weak; 0.30–0.70, moderate; and >0.70, strong (these are just guidelines and they should not be applied in a rigid manner). This approach is satisfactory in many situations, but in other contexts it may be more important to determine whether a correlation is "statistically significant," meaning that it is likely not to have value of zero in the population. Statistical significance is determined by both the size of the correlation coefficient and the size of the sample. A discussion of statistical significance would lead us into the realm of inferential statistics and is beyond the scope of this text. However, most introductory statistics texts address this concept in considerable detail and contain tables that allow you to determine whether a correlation coefficient is significant given the size of the sample. In measurement, one typically wants to consider magnitude as well as statistical significance—even weak correlations can be quite useful (see Special Interest Topic 2.5).

Another way of describing correlation coefficients is by squaring it to derive the coefficient of determination (i.e., r^2). The **coefficient of determination** is interpreted as the amount of variance shared by the two variables. In other words, the coefficient of determination reflects the amount of variance in one variable that is predictable from the other variable, and vice versa. This might not be clear so let's look at an example. Assume a correlation between an intelligence test and an achievement test of 0.60 (i.e., $r = 0.60$). By squaring this value we determine the coefficient of determination is 0.36 (i.e., $r^2 = 0.36$). This indicates that 36% of the variance in one variable is predictable from the other variable. Additionally, if you subtract the coefficient of determination from 1.0 (i.e., $1 - r^2$), the result is the amount of variance in one variable that is not predictable from the other variable. This is the *coefficient of nondetermination*. Using our example examining the relationship between intelligence and achievement, we find that 64% of variance in one variable is not predictable from the other variable.

> *The **coefficient of determination** is interpreted as the amount of variance shared by two variables.*

SPECIAL INTEREST TOPIC 2.5

Are Weak Correlations Useless or of No Practical Value?

Suppose you could do the following:

◆ Reduce the number of heart attacks among those at high risk by 8 to 10%.

◆ Reduce the number of citizen complaints against police officers by 8 to 10%.

◆ Reduce the turnover rate in hiring at a large corporation by 8 to 10%.

Do you think any of these actions would be useful or beneficial to the parties involved? The first one is the easiest—of course we would like to reduce heart attacks by any amount and a reduction of 8 to 10% is certainly meaningful, especially if you or a member of your family were among this 8 to 10%! The others are important as well. Certainly hiring police officers who perform their jobs well and abide by the rubric of "serve and protect" is also an important goal. However, it also reduces costs to the public significantly in terms of human outcomes and in terms of dollars and cents—it costs a great deal of money to recruit, train, and employ police officers and even more to investigate complaints against them. Dismissing officers who act inappropriately is an expensive and time-consuming process as well and often means a series of citizens have been mistreated in some way by the offending officers. Job turnover is also a significant expense in the private employment sector. Employers want to hire the right people, people who are competent at the job and who will be happy in their work and remain on the job for as long as possible.

If we look at these effects expressed as a correlation, the value ranges from 0.28 to 0.31. Most people would consider such correlations to be low and complain that they only account for 8 to 10% of the variance in the variable being predicted. Yet in each of the instances mentioned, the observed correlations are in fact very important and tell us what level of effects we can expect to obtain. For heart attacks, this is about the percentage reduction one can expect from taking low-dose aspirin on a daily basis. In the other two cases, these are about the effects we see from using sound psychological tests as a component of the hiring process.

Still, we might question whether such small effects are worth the costs. In making a judgment, we should consider a variety of factors including the costs of doing nothing as well as the cost of the procedure—e. g., whether taking aspirin or taking a psychological test! We also need to ask, is there a better way to accomplish this goal or a way to improve on it?

In the case of hiring decisions, we are always looking to create better employment tests that predict long-term job performance and reduce turnover rates. For some jobs we have tests that perform better than we have discussed above, but in deciding whether a prediction or a correlation is good or useful, we also have to consider how difficult it may be to measure some constructs and the limits of our current knowledge about how variables are in fact related. Some psychological constructs are far more difficult to measure reliably than are others, just as some are far more difficult to predict than are others. In some instances, such as those cited, these so-called weak correlations are quite good and are very practical in terms of saving costs as well as human suffering. On the other hand, if we wanted to predict academic achievement and the test used for prediction only correlated .30, we would likely discard the test as not being very useful since it is relatively easy to find aptitude measures that correlate twice as high (.60) or more with academic outcomes. If we were to develop a test that added to this prediction by another 8 to 10% and was cost-effective in terms of its time and cost of administration, we still might use it due to the incremental validity it would add to the prediction of achievement.

The value of a correlation may also be very important to test validation as well as theory building when it is low in value or considered weak. For example, if we were to build a test to measure intelligence, and it correlated too highly with extraneous variables such as motor speed and fine motor coordination, then we would know that our test was too confounded with other constructs to be a good measure of intelligence. We would prefer that our test of intelligence have weak correlations with motor speed and coordination.

Do not dismiss weak correlations—always view them in the context in which they were derived and the research questions that are trying to be answered. Even a correlational value of zero has something to tell us!

Scatterplots

As noted, a correlation coefficient is a quantitative measure of the linear relationship between two variables. Examining scatterplots may enhance our understanding of the linear relationship between variables. A **scatterplot** is simply a graph that visually displays the relationship between two variables. To create a scatterplot you need to have two scores for each individual. For example, you could graph each individual's weight and height. In the context of psychological testing, you could have scores for research participants on two different measures of cognitive ability. In a scatterplot the *x*-axis represents one variable and the *y*-axis the other variable. Each mark in the scatterplot actually represents two scores, an individual's scores on the *X* variable and the *Y* variable.

> A **scatterplot** *is a graph that visually displays the relationship between two variables.*

Figure 2–9 shows scatterplots for various correlation values. First look at Figure 2–9(a), which shows a hypothetical perfect positive correlation (+1.0). Notice that with a perfect correlation all of the marks will fall on a straight line. Because this is a positive correlation an increase on one variable is associated with a corresponding increase on the other variable. Because it is a perfect correlation, if you know an individual's score on one variable you can predict the score on the other variable with perfect precision. Next examine Figure 2–9(b), which illustrates a perfect negative correlation (−1.0). Being a perfect correlation all the marks fall on a straight line, but because it is a negative correlation an increase on one variable is associated with a corresponding decrease on the other variable. Given a score on one variable, you can still predict the individual's performance on the other variable with perfect precision. Now examine Figure 2–9(c), which illustrates a correlation of 0.0. Here there is not a relationship between the variables. In this situation, knowledge about performance on one variable does not provide any information about the individual's performance on the other variable or enhance prediction.

So far we have examined only the scatterplots of perfect and zero correlation coefficients. Examine Figure 2–9(d), which depicts a correlation of +0.90. Notice that the marks clearly cluster along a straight line. However, they no longer all fall on the line, but rather around the line. As you might expect, in this situation knowledge of performance on one variable helps us predict performance on the other variable, but our ability to predict performance is not perfect as it was with a perfect correlation. Finally examine Figures 2–9(e) and 2–9(f), which illustrate coefficients of 0.60 and 0.30, respectively. As you can see, a correlation of 0.60 is characterized by marks that still cluster along a straight line, but there is more variability around this line than there was with a correlation of 0.90. Accordingly, with a correlation of 0.30 there is still more variability of marks around a straight line. In these situations knowledge of performance on one variable will help us predict performance on the other variable, but as the correlation coefficients decrease so does our ability to predict performance.

> *There are specific correlation coefficients that are appropriate for specific situations.*

Types of Correlation Coefficients

There are specific correlation coefficients that are appropriate for specific situations. The most common coefficient is the Pearson product-moment correlation. The Pearson coefficient is appropriate when the

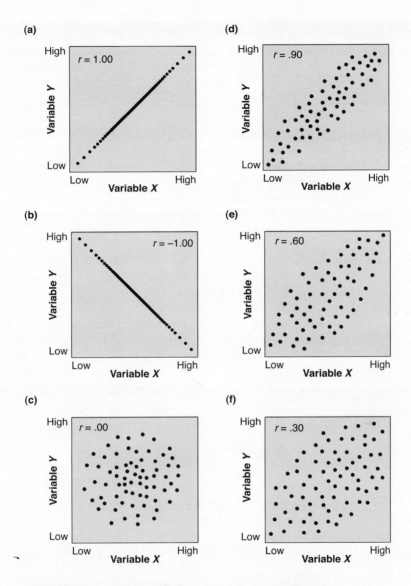

FIGURE 2–9 Scatterplot of Different Correlation Coefficients.

Source: Hopkins, Kenneth, *Educational and Psychological Measurement and Evalutation,* 8th ©1998. Printed and Electronically reproduced by permission of Pearson Education, Inc., Upper Saddle River, New Jersey.

variables being correlated are measured on an interval or ratio scale. Table 2–6 illustrates the calculation of the Pearson correlation coefficient. Although the formula for calculating a Pearson correlation may appear rather intimidating, it is not actually difficult and we encourage you to review this section if you are interested in how these coefficients are calculated (or if your professor wants you to be familiar with the process). Spearman's rank correlation coefficient, another

TABLE 2–6   Calculating a Pearson Correlation Coefficient

There are different formulas for calculating a Pearson correlation coefficient and we will illustrate one of the simpler ones. For this illustration we will use the test scores we have used before as the X variable, and another set of 20 hypothetical scores as the Y variable. The formula is:

$$r_{xy} = \frac{N\Sigma XY - (\Sigma X)(\Sigma X)}{\sqrt{N\Sigma X^2 - (\Sigma X)^2}\sqrt{N\Sigma Y^2 - (\Sigma X)^2}}$$

XY = sum of the XY products
X = sum of X scores
Y = sum of Y scores
X^2 = sum of squared X scores
Y^2 = sum of squared Y scores

Test 1 (X)	X^2	Test 2 (Y)	Y^2	(X)(Y)
7	49	8	64	56
8	64	7	49	56
9	81	10	100	90
6	36	5	25	30
7	49	7	49	49
6	36	6	36	36
10	199	9	81	90
8	64	8	64	64
5	25	5	25	25
9	81	9	81	81
9	81	8	64	72
9	81	7	49	63
8	64	7	49	56
4	16	4	16	16
5	25	6	36	30
6	36	7	49	42
7	49	7	49	49
8	64	9	81	72
8	64	8	64	64
7	49	6	36	42
X = 146	X^2 = 1,114	Y = 143	Y^2 = 1,067	XY = 1,083

$$r_{xy} = \frac{20(1,083) - (140)(143)}{\sqrt{20(1,114) - (146)^2}\sqrt{20(1,067) - (143)^2}}$$

$$\frac{21,660 - 20,878}{\sqrt{22,280 - 21,316}\sqrt{21,340 - 20,449}} = \frac{782}{\sqrt{964}\sqrt{891}}$$

$$\frac{782}{(31.048)(29.849)} = 0.843$$

popular coefficient, is used when the variables are measured on an ordinal scale. The point-biserial correlation coefficient is also widely used in test development when one variable is dichotomous (meaning only two scores are possible, e.g., pass or fail, 0 or 1, etc.) and the other variable is measured on an interval or ratio scale. A common application of the point-biserial correlation is in calculating an item-total test score correlation. Here the dichotomous variable is the score on a single item (e.g., right or wrong) and the variable measured on an interval scale is the total test score. A large item-total correlation is taken as evidence that an item is measuring the same construct as the overall test measures (more on this in later chapters).

Factors That Affect Correlation Coefficients

There are a number of factors that can impact the size of correlation coefficients and need to be considered when interpreting correlation coefficients. In the next section we will briefly discuss two of these factors that are of special concern in the context of psychological measurement.

LINEAR RELATIONSHIP We noted that a correlation coefficient is a quantitative measure of the linear relationship between two variables. It is important to highlight the fact that there is the assumption of a linear relationship between the variables. By linear relationship we mean the relationship is best represented by a straight line. For example, when discussing scatterplots we noted that with a correlation coefficient of 1.0 all of the marks fall on a straight line. Many variables of interest to psychologists do demonstrate linear relationships. The relationship between intelligence and academic achievement is linear. So is the relationship between height and weight. However, not all variables of interest to psychologists demonstrate linear relationships.

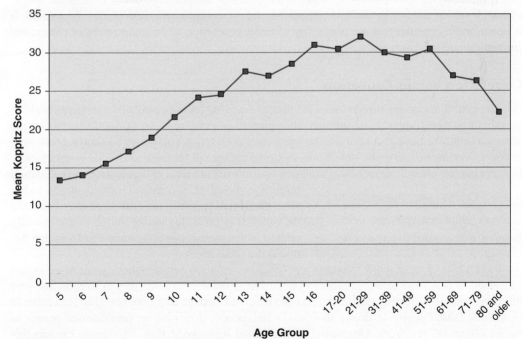

FIGURE 2–10 Curve to fit a Scatterplot of Curvilinear Data.

Source: From Koppitz *Developmental Scoring System for the Bender Gestalt Test*, Second Edition. (KOPPITZ-2) Examiner's Manual by C.R. Reynolds, 2007, Austin: PRO-ED. Used with permission.

If you were to develop a scatterplot reflecting the relationship between visual-motor integration skills and age, you would likely obtain results similar to those in Figure 2–10. As you see, visual-motor integration skills tend to increase with age, peaking in middle-aged individuals and then gradually declining with age. This is an example of a curvilinear relationship. The use of correlation coefficients such as the Pearson or Spearman coefficients would produce spuriously low estimates of the relationship. However, there are special procedures that are appropriate for examining nonlinear relationships. It is usually possible to detect nonlinear relationships by carefully examining scatterplots. This highlights the importance of routinely examining scatterplots prior to analyzing and interpreting the data. It should be noted that nonlinear relationships are not limited to psychomotor variables. For example, Latané (1981) described a number of social psychology studies that found nonlinear relationships between variables.

RANGE RESTRICTION. The values we obtain when calculating coefficients are dependent on characteristics of the sample or group of individuals on which the analyses are based. One characteristic of the sample that can significantly impact the coefficients is the degree of variability in performance (i.e., variance). More precisely, coefficients based on samples with large variances (referred to as heterogeneous samples) will generally produce higher correlation coefficients than those based on samples with small variances (referred to as homogeneous samples). When correlation coefficients are based on a sample with a restricted range of variability, the coefficients may actually underestimate the relationship between the variables. For example, if you calculate a correlation coefficient between two cognitive variables (e.g., short-term memory and vocabulary) among students at a prestigious university, you will receive lower coefficients than if the analyses were based on a more heterogeneous sample (e.g., one that included people with all levels of education, including those that did not complete the 12th grade). As a result, it is important to consider that the possibility of range restriction when interpreting or comparing correlation coefficients.

Correlation Versus Causation

Our discussion of correlation has indicated that when variables are correlated, information about an individual's performance on one variable enhances our ability to predict performance on the other variable. We have also seen that by squaring a correlation coefficient to get the coefficient of determination we can make statements about the amount of variance shared by two variables. In later chapters we will show how correlation coefficients are used in developing and evaluating tests. It is, however, a common misconception to believe that if two variables are correlated one is causing the other. It is possible that the variables are causally related, but it is also possible that a third variable explains the relationship.

> *Correlation analysis does not allow one to establish causality.*

Let's look at an example. Assume we found a correlation between the amount of ice cream consumed in New York and the number of deaths by drowning in Texas. If you were to interpret this correlation as inferring causation, you would either believe that people eating ice cream in New York caused people to drown in Texas or that people drowning in Texas caused people to eat ice cream in New York. Obviously neither would be correct! How would you explain this relationship? The answer is that the seasonal change in temperature accounts for the relationship.

SPECIAL INTEREST TOPIC 2.6

Caution: Drawing Conclusions of Causality

Reynolds (1999) related this historical example of how interpreting a relationship between variables as indicating causality can lead to an erroneous conclusion. In the 1800s a physician noted that a large number of women were dying of "childbed fever" (i.e., puerperal fever) in the prestigious Vienna General Hospital, one of the premier medical facilities of its day. Curiously more women died when they gave birth in the hospital than when the birth was at home. Childbed fever was even less common among women who gave birth in unsanitary conditions on the streets of Vienna. A commission studied this situation and after careful observation concluded that priests who came to the hospital to administer last rites were the cause of the increase in childbed fever in the hospital. The priests were present in the hospital, but were not present if the birth was outside of the hospital. According to the reasoning of the commission, when priests appeared in this ritualistic fashion the women in the hospital were frightened and this stress made them more susceptible to childbed fever.

Eventually, experimental research debunked this explanation and identified what was actually causing the high mortality rate. At that time the doctors who delivered the babies were the same doctors who dissected corpses. The doctors would move from dissecting diseased corpses to delivering babies without washing their hands or taking other sanitary precautions. When hand washing and other antiseptic procedures were implemented, the incidence of childbed fever dropped dramatically.

In summary, it was the transmission of disease from corpses to new mothers that caused childbed fever, not the presence of priests. Although the conclusion of the commission might sound foolish to us now, if you listen carefully to the popular media you are likely to hear contemporary "experts" establishing causality based on observed relationships between variables. However, now you know to be cautious when evaluating this information.

In late spring and summer when it is hot, people in New York consume more ice cream and people in Texas engage in more water-related activities (i.e., swimming, skiing, boating) and consequently drown more frequently. This is a fairly obvious case of a third variable explaining the relationship; however, identifying the third variable is not always so easy. It is fairly common for individuals or groups in the popular media to attribute causation on the basis of a correlation. So the next time you hear on television or read in the newspaper that researchers found a correlation between variable A and variable B, and that this correlation means that A causes B you will not be fooled.

Although correlation analysis does not allow us to establish causality, certain statistical procedures are specifically designed to allow us to infer causality. These procedures are referred to as inferential statistics and are covered in statistical courses. Special Interest Topic 2.6 presents a historical example of when interpreting a relationship between variables as indicating causality resulted in an erroneous conclusion.

LINEAR REGRESSION

In discussing correlation coefficients we mentioned that when variables are correlated, knowledge about performance on one variable can help us predict performance on the other variable. A special mathematical procedure referred to as **linear regression** is designed precisely for this purpose. Linear regression allows you

> Linear regression *is a mathematical procedure that allows you to predict values on one variable given information on another variable.*

to predict values on one variable given information on another variable. For example, if our research shows that indeed X and Y are related, linear regression will allow us to predict the value of Y if we know the value of X. Retaining X and Y as we have used them so far, the general form of our equation would be:

$$Y = a + bX$$

This equation goes by several names. Statisticians are most likely to refer to it as a regression equation. Practitioners of psychology who use the equation to make predictions may refer to it as a prediction equation. However, somewhere around the eighth or ninth grade, in your first algebra class, you were introduced to this expression and told it was the equation of a straight line. You probably even learned to graph this equation and use it to determine a value of Y for any given value of X. What algebra teachers typically do not explain at this level is that they were actually teaching you the statistical concept of regression!

Let's look at an example of how this equation works. For this example, we will let X represent some individual's score on a predictor test (e.g., job screening test) and Y the person's score on a criterion to be measured in the future (e.g., supervisor's performance rating). To determine our actual equation, we would have to test a large number of people with the predictor test (X) and then measure their actual job performance (Y). We then calculate the correlation between the two sets of scores. One reasonable outcome would yield an equation such as this one:

$$Y = 10 + 0.5X$$

In determining the relationship between X and Y, we calculated the value of a to be 10 and the value of b to be 0.5. In your early algebra class, a was referred to as the Y-intercept (the starting point of your line on the y-axis when $X = 0$) and b as the slope of your line. We have graphed this equation for you in Figure 2–11. When $X = 0$, Y is equal to 10 ($Y = 10 + 0.5(0)$), so our line starts on the y-axis at a value of 10. Because our slope is 0.5, for each increase in X, the increase in Y will be half or 0.5 times as much. We can use the equation or the prediction line to estimate or predict the value of Y for any value of X, just as you did in that early algebra class. Nothing has really changed except the names. Instead of the Y-intercept, we typically refer to a from our equation as a constant, since it is always being added to bX in the same amount on every occasion. Instead of "slope," we typically refer to b as a regression coefficient or a beta weight. If you look at Figure 2–11, you can see that for a score of 10 on our predictor test, a score of 15 is predicted for job performance rating. A score of 30 on our predictor test, a 20-point increase, predicts a job performance rating of 25, an increase on Y equal to half the increase in X. These values are the same whether we use our prediction line or use our equation—they are simply differing ways of showing the relationship between X and Y. Table 2–7 presents an example of the calculation of linear regression using the data originally presented in Table 2–6 where we illustrated the calculation of the Pearson correlation coefficient.

Standard Error of Estimate

If we had variables that had perfect correlations with each other (i.e., 1.0), our prediction would be perfect. However, in the real world when we are predicting Y from X, our prediction

FIGURE 2–11 Example of a Graph of the Equation of a Straight Line, also Known as a Regression Line or Prediction Line.

Note: $Y = a + bX$ when $a = 10$ and $b = 0.5$. For example, if X is 30, then $Y = 10 + (0.5)30 = 25$.

is never perfect because perfect correlations among psychological test scores don't exist. As a result, for any one person, we will typically be off somewhat in predicting future criterion performance. Our linear regression model actually is telling us the mean or average score on Y of all the individuals in the research study at each score on X. For example, using the data displayed in Figure 2–11, the mean job performance rating of all employees who had a score of 40 on the predictor test was 30. We know that not all of the employees who earned a 40 on the first test will receive a job performance rating of 30. We use the mean score on Y of all our employees who scored 40 on X as our predicted value for all employees who score 40 on X nevertheless. The mean is used because it results in the smallest amount of error in all our predictions.

In practice, we would also be highly interested in how much error exists in our predictions and this degree of error would be calculated and reported. The standard error of estimate is the statistic that reflects the average amount of error in our predictions and is designated as S_E. Once we know the standard error of estimate in our regression model, we can make statements about how confident we are in predicting Y based on X. For example, if the standard error of estimate is 2 points, we might say that based on John's score of 40 on X, we are 68% confident that his score on Y will be between 38 and 42 and 95% confident that it will fall between 36 and 44. We refer to these intervals as confidence intervals because they reflect a range of scores within which we expect the client's actual score to fall with a specified degree of confidence. The calculation of the standard error of estimate and confidence intervals is illustrated in Table 2–8.

TABLE 2–7   Calculating Linear Regression

The general form for a regression equation is:

$$Y' = a + bX$$

where Y' = predicted score on Y – i.e., criterion

X = score on X variable – i.e., predictor

a = Y-intercept or constant. Calculated as $a = \bar{Y} - (b)\bar{X}$

b = slope or regression coefficient. Calculated as $b = r_{xy}(\sigma_y/\sigma_x)$

Using the X and Y scores presented in Table 2–6, we have:

$\bar{X} = 7.3$

$\bar{Y} = 7.15$

$r_{xy} = 0.84$

$\sigma_y = 1.49$

$\sigma_X = 1.55$

$b = 0.84 (1.49/1.55) = 0.807$

$a = 7.15 - (0.807)7.3 = 1.26$

For example, if an individual received a score of 6 on test $\bar{X}$ (i.e., predictor), the regression equation is:

$Y' = 1.26+0.807(6)$

$Y' = 6.1$

A simple way to check the accuracy of your regression equation is to use $\bar{X}$ as your predictor score and verify that the result is the mean of the Y scores.

$Y' = 1.26 + 0.807(7.3)$

$Y' = 7.15$

The scatterplot shows the regression line for these data.

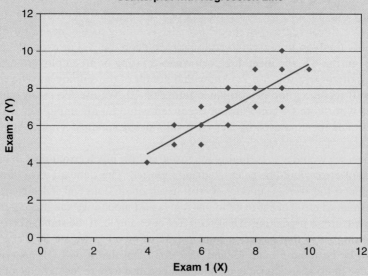

Scatterplot with Regression Line

TABLE 2–8	Calculating the Standard Error of Estimate

The standard error of estimate is designated by S_E and is computed as:

$$S_E = \sigma_y\sqrt{1 - r^2}$$

Work with the data presented in Table 2–7, we have the following results.

$S_E = 1.49 \sqrt{1 - (0.84)^2}$

$S_E = 1.49 \sqrt{0.29}$

$S_E = 1.49 \times 0.54$

$S_E = 0.81$

Based on this, if an individual's predicated score on Y is 7, we are 68% confident their actual score 2 weeks later will be between 6.19 (7 − 0.81) and 7.81 (7 + 0.81). This 68% confidence level is the result of you creating a 1 SD interval around your predicted score. It is rare for people to be satisfied with a 68% confidence interval, and test publishers typically report 90 or 95% confidence intervals (or both). To do this they multiply the S_E by 1.64 for 90% confidence intervals and 1.96 for 95% confidence intervals. These calculations are illustrated as follows:

90% Confidence Interval = $Y' + (1.64)(0.81) = Y' + 1.33$

95% Confidence Interval = $Y' + (1.96)(0.81) = Y' + 1.59$

For our example involving a predicted score on Y of 7, the results are:

90% Confidence Interval = 5.67 to 8.33

95% Confidence Interval = 5.41 to 8.59

Summary

In this chapter we surveyed the basic statistical concepts and procedures essential to understanding psychological measurement. We defined measurement as a set of rules for assigning numbers to represent objects, traits, or other characteristics. Measurement can involve four different scales: nominal, ordinal, interval, and ratio. Each scale has distinct properties which are summarized here:

- Nominal scale: a qualitative system for categorizing people or objects into categories. In nominal scales the categories are not ordered in a meaningful manner and do not convey quantitative information.
- Ordinal scale: a quantitative system that allows you to rank people or objects according to the amount of a characteristic possessed. Ordinal scales provide quantitative information, but they do not ensure that the intervals between the ranks are consistent.
- Interval scale: a system that allows you to rank people or objects like an ordinal scale but with the added advantage of equal scale units. Equal scale units indicate that the intervals between the units or ranks are the same size.
- Ratio scale: a system with all the properties of an interval scale with the added advantage of a true zero point.

These scales form a hierarchy and we are able to perform more sophisticated measurements as we move from nominal to the ratio scales.

We next turned our attention to distributions. A distribution is simply a set of scores, and distributions can be represented in number of ways, including tables and graphs. Descriptive statistics have been developed that help us summarize and describe major characteristics of distributions. For example, measures of central tendency are frequently used to summarize distributions. The major measures of central tendency are:

- Mean: the simple arithmetic average of a distribution. Formally, the mean is defined by the equation:

$$\text{Mean} = \text{Sum of Score} / \text{Number of Scores}$$

- Median: the score or potential score that divides the distribution in half.
- Mode: the most frequently occurring score in the distribution.

Measures of variability (or dispersion) comprise another set of descriptive statistics used to characterize distributions. These measures provide information about the way scores are spread out or dispersed. They include:

- Range: the distance between the smallest and largest score in a distribution.
- Standard deviation: a popular index of the average distance that scores vary from the mean.
- Variance: another measure of the variability of scores, expressed in squared score units. Less useful when interpreting individual scores, but important as a theoretical concept.

We then turned our discussion to correlation coefficients. A correlation coefficient is a quantitative measure of the linear relationship between two variables. We described how correlation coefficients provide information about both the direction and strength of a relationship. The sign of the coefficient (i.e., + or −) indicates the direction of the relationship whereas the magnitude of the coefficient indicates the strength of the relationship. We described the use of scatterplots to illustrate correlations and introduced several types of correlation coefficients that are commonly used in psychological statistics and psychometrics. We cautioned that although correlations are extremely useful in the development and evaluation of tests, they do not imply a causal relationship.

The study of correlation also has important implications in the context of predicting performance on tests and other criteria. The stronger the correlation between two variables the better we can predict performance on one variable given information about performance on the other variable. We briefly introduced the use of linear regression, which is a statistical procedure that allows us to predict performance on one variable (i.e., the criterion) given performance on another variable (i.e., the predictor) when a linear relationship exists. When there is a perfect correlation between two variables (either positive or negative) you can predict performance with perfect precision. Because there are no perfect correlations among psychological variables, our prediction is always less than perfect. We have a statistic called the standard error of estimate that reflects the average amount of error in prediction and allows us to specify a range of scores within which we expect the client's actual score to fall with a specified degree of confidence.

Key Terms and Concepts

Causality, 62
Coefficient of determination, 56
Correlation coefficients, 55
Distribution, 42
Linear regression, 63
Interval scales, 39

Mean, 45
Median, 47
Mode, 47
Nominal scales, 38
Normal distribution, 54
Ordinal scales, 38

Range, 50
Ratio scales, 40
Scatterplots, 58
Standard deviation, 50
Variance, 52

Recommended Readings

Hays, W. (1994). *Statistics* (5th ed.). New York: Harcourt Brace. This is an excellent advanced statistics text. It covers the information discussed in this chapter in greater detail and provides comprehensive coverage of statistics in general.

Nunnally, J. C., & Bernstein, I. H. (1994). *Psychometric theory* (3rd ed.). New York: McGraw-Hill. An excellent advanced psychometric text. Chapters 2 and 4 are particularly relevant to students wanting a more detailed discussion of issues introduced in this chapter.

Reynolds, C. R. (1999). Inferring causality from relational data and designs: Historical and contemporary lessons for research and clinical practice. *The Clinical Neuropsychologist*, 13, 386–395. An entertaining and enlightening discussion of the need for caution when inferring causality from relational data. Contains both historical and contemporary examples, including a lawsuit where hundreds of billions of dollars changed hands.

Internet Sites of Interest

http://www.statistics.com/
The statistics.com site provides access to statistical information ranging from governmental, military, educational, medical, sports and other sources. It has discussion boards that provide forums for discussing statistics and related issues and a section tailored to teachers and students.

http://www.fedstats.gov/
FedStats.com provides easy access to statistics and information from more than 100 U.S. federal agencies.

http://www.ncaa.org
The National Collegiate Athletic Association is great for sports enthusiasts. It provides access to sports statistics ranging from baseball to lacrosse.

http://nces.ed.gov/
This is the site for the National Center for Education Statistics, the primary federal agency responsible for collecting and analyzing data related to education.

http://www.geohive.com/
The GeoHive site contains information on the population and demographics of regions, countries, and cities.

Practice Items

1. Calculate the mean, variance, and standard deviation for the following score distributions. For these exercises, use the formulas listed in Table 2–5 for calculating variance and standard deviation.

Distribution 1	Distribution 2	Distribution 3
10	10	9
10	9	8
9	8	7
9	7	7
8	6	6
8	6	6
8	6	6
7	5	5
7	5	5
7	5	5
7	4	4
6	4	4
5	3	3
4	2	2
4	2	1

2. Calculate the Pearson correlation coefficient for the following pairs of scores.

Sample 1		Sample 2		Sample 3	
Variable *X*	Variable *Y*	Variable *X*	Variable *Y*	Variable *X*	Variable *Y*
9	10	9	10	9	7
10	9	9	9	9	7
9	8	8	8	8	8
8	7	8	7	8	5
9	6	7	5	7	4
5	6	7	5	7	5
3	6	6	4	6	5
7	5	6	3	6	5
5	5	5	4	5	4
4	5	5	5	5	4
7	4	4	4	4	7
3	4	4	3	4	8
5	3	3	2	3	5
6	2	2	3	2	5
5	2	2	2	2	5

Answers can be found in Appendix C.

3

The Meaning
of Test Scores

Scores are the keys to understanding an examinee's performance on tests and other assessments. As a result, thoroughly understanding the meaning of test scores and how they are interpreted is of utmost importance.

Chapter Outline

Learning Objectives

After reading and studying this chapter, students should be able to:

1. Describe raw scores and explain their limitations.
2. Define norm-referenced and criterion-referenced score interpretations and explain their major characteristics.
3. List and explain the important criteria for evaluating standardization data.
4. Describe the normal curve and explain its importance in interpreting test scores.
5. Describe the major types of standard scores.
6. Transform raw scores to standard scores.

7. Define normalized standard scores and describe the major types of normalized standard scores.
8. Define percentile rank and explain its interpretation.
9. Define grade equivalents and explain their limitations.
10. Describe some common applications of criterion-referenced score interpretations.
11. Describe item response theory and the properties of IRT or Rasch-type scores.
12. Read and interpret information on standardization and scores presented in a test manual.

Test scores are a mathematical representation of the performance or ratings of the individuals completing a test. Because test scores are the keys to interpreting and understanding the examinees' performance, their meaning and interpretation are extremely important topics and deserve careful attention. As you will see, there is a wide assortment of scores available for our use and each format has its own unique characteristics. Possibly the simplest type of score is a raw score. A **raw score** is simply the number of items scored or coded in a specific manner such as correct/incorrect, true/false, and so on. For example, the raw score on a classroom math test might be the number of items the student answered correctly. The calculation of raw scores is usually fairly straightforward, but raw scores are often of limited use to those interpreting the test results; they tend to offer very little useful information. Let's say a student's score on a classroom math test is 50. Does a raw score of 50 represent poor, average, or superior performance? The answer to this question depends on a number of factors such as how many items are on the test, how difficult the items are, and the like. For example, if the test contained only 50 items and the student's raw score were 50, the student demonstrated perfect performance. If the test contained 100 items and the

> A **raw score** *is simply the number of items scored or coded in a specific manner such as correct/incorrect, true/false, and so on.*

student's raw score were 50, he or she answered only half of the items correctly. However, we still do not know what that really means. If the test contained 100 extremely difficult items and a raw score of 50 were the highest score in the class, this would likely reflect very good performance. Because raw scores, in most situations, have little interpretative meaning, we need to transform or convert them into another format to facilitate their interpretation and give them greater meaning.

These transformed scores, typically referred to as derived scores, standard scores, or scaled scores, are pivotal in helping us interpret test results. There are a number of different derived scores, but they can usually be classified as either norm-referenced or criterion-referenced. We will begin our discussion of scores and their interpretation by introducing you to these two different approaches to deriving and interpreting test scores (there is actually another score format available based on item response theory, but we will wait until the end of the chapter to discuss it).

NORM-REFERENCED AND CRITERION-REFERENCED SCORE INTERPRETATIONS

To help us understand and interpret test results we need a frame of reference. That is, we need to compare the examinee's performance to "something." Score interpretations can be classified as either norm-referenced or criterion-referenced, and this distinction refers to the "something" to which we compare the examinee's performance. With **norm-referenced score interpretations** the examinee's performance is compared to the performance of other people (a reference group). For example, scores on tests of intelligence are norm-referenced. If you report that an examinee has an IQ of 100 this indicates he or she scored higher than 50% of the people in the standardization or reference sample. This is a norm-referenced interpretation. The examinee's performance is being compared with that of other test takers. Personality tests also typically are reported as norm-referenced scores. For example, it might be reported that an

> With **norm-referenced score interpretations** *the examinee's performance is compared to the performance of other people.*

examinee scored higher than 98% of the standardization sample on some trait such as extroversion or sensation seeking. With all norm-referenced interpretations the examinee's performance is compared to that of others.

With **criterion-referenced score interpretations** the examinee's performance is not compared to that of other people; instead it is compared to a specified level of performance (i.e., a criterion). With criterion-referenced interpretations the emphasis is on what the examinees know or what they can do, not their standing relative to other test takers. Possibly the most common example of a criterion-referenced score is the percentage of correct responses on a classroom examination. If you report that a student correctly answered 85% of the items on a classroom test, this is a criterion-referenced interpretation. Notice that you are not comparing the student's performance to that of other examinees; you are comparing it to a standard, in this case perfect performance on the test.

> *With* **criterion-referenced score** interpretations *the examinee is compared to a specified level of performance.*

Norm-referenced interpretations are relative (i.e., relative to the performance of other examinees) whereas criterion-referenced interpretations are absolute (i.e., compared to an absolute standard). Norm-referenced score interpretations have many applications, and the majority of published standardized tests produce norm-referenced scores. Nevertheless, criterion-referenced tests also have important applications, particularly in educational settings. Although people frequently refer to norm-referenced and criterion-referenced tests, this is not technically accurate. The terms *norm-referenced* and *criterion-referenced* actually refer to the interpretation of test scores. Although it is most common for tests to produce either norm-referenced or criterion-referenced scores, it is actually possible for a test to produce both norm- and criterion-referenced scores. We will come back to this topic later. First, we will discuss norm-referenced and criterion-referenced score interpretations and the types of derived scores associated with each approach.

> *Norm-referenced interpretations are relative whereas criterion-referenced interpretations are absolute.*

Norm-Referenced Interpretations

NORMS AND REFERENCE GROUPS. To understand an examinee's performance on a psychological test, it is often useful to compare their performance to the performance of some preselected group of individuals. Raw scores on a test, such as the number correct, take on special meaning when they are evaluated relative to the performance of a normative or reference group. To accomplish this, when using a norm-referenced approach to interpreting test scores, raw scores on the test are typically converted to derived scores based on information about the performance of a specific normative or reference group. Probably the most important consideration when making norm-referenced interpretations involves the relevance of the group of individuals to whom the examinee's performance is compared. The reference group from which the norms are derived should be representative of the type of individuals expected to take the test or the group to which the examinee is to be compared or referenced. Most often these groups are the same, but they can be different. When you interpret an examinee's performance on a test or other assessment, you should ask yourself, "Are these norms appropriate for this examinee and for this use with this examinee?" For example, it would be reasonable to compare a student's performance on a test of academic achievement to other students of the same age, grade, and educational background. However, it would probably not be particularly useful to compare a student's performance to younger students who had not been exposed to the same curriculum, or to older students who have received additional instruction, training, or experience. For norm-referenced interpretations to be meaningful you need to compare the examinee's performance to that of a relevant reference group or sample. Therefore, the first step in developing good normative data is to define clearly the population for whom the test is designed.

> *Standardization samples should be representative of the type of individuals expected to take the test.*

Once the appropriate reference population has been defined clearly, a random sample is selected and tested. The normative reference group most often used to derive scores is called a national standardization sample. Most test publishers and developers select a national standardization sample using a procedure known as population proportionate stratified random sampling. This means that samples of people are selected in such a way as to ensure that the national population as a whole is proportionately represented on important variables. In the United States, for example, tests are typically standardized using a sampling plan that stratifies the sample by gender, age, education, ethnicity, socioeconomic background, region of residence, and community size based on population statistics provided by the U.S. Census Bureau. If data from the Census Bureau indicate that 1% of the U.S. population consists of African American males in the middle range of socioeconomic status residing in urban centers of the southern region, then 1% of the standardization sample of the test is drawn to meet this same set of characteristics. Once the standardization sample has been selected and tested, tables of derived scores are developed. These tables are based on the performance of the standardization sample and are typically referred to as normative tables or "norms." Because the relevance of the standardization sample is so important when using norm-referenced tests, it is the responsibility of test publishers to provide adequate information about the standardization sample. Additionally, it is the responsibility of every test user to evaluate the adequacy of the sample and the appropriateness of comparing the examinee's score to this particular group. In making this determination, you should consider the following factors:

- Is the standardization sample representative of the examinees with whom you will be using the test? Are demographic characteristics of the sample (e.g., age, race, sex, education, geographic location, etc.) similar to those who will take the test? In lay terms, are you comparing apples to apples and oranges to oranges?
- Is this the correct reference group for this application of this test? For example, if I want to know how Maria's current level of reading skills in English compares to that of the general population of children of the same age and grade in the USA, then a population proportionate stratified random sample of children of the same age and grade would be the appropriate reference group. This would be true even if Maria were a recent immigrant to the United States with limited English proficiency. Some would argue this is an unfair comparison because so few if any such children would be present in the "national standardization sample" and that Maria's reading skills should be evaluated by comparing her to other recently immigrated children with limited English proficiency. The latter comparison is very likely a useful one but so is the former. These two comparisons to different reference groups answer different questions about Maria's reading skills—and that is our point. Comparing Maria's

reading skills to children-at-large describes her progress in learning English relative to all children in the schools. Comparing Maria to other recently immigrated children who are just learning English tells us about her relative progress compared to similar children. Both pieces of information are useful and for these purposes, both samples are appropriate for answering their respective question.

- Is the sample current? Participants in samples from 20 years ago may have responded quite differently from a contemporary sample. Attitudes, beliefs, behaviors, and even cognitive abilities change over time, and to be relevant the normative data need to be current (see Special Interest Topic 3.1 for information on the "Flynn Effect" and how intelligence changes over time).
- Is the sample size large enough to provide stable statistical information? Although there is no magic number, if a test covers a broad age range it is common for standardization samples to exceed 1,000 participants. Otherwise, the number of participants at each age or grade level may be too small to produce stable estimation of means, standard deviations, and the more general distribution of scores. For example, the Wechsler Individual Achievement Test, Second Edition (WIAT-II; Psychological Corporation, 2002) has 3,600 participants in the standardization, with a minimum of 150 at each grade level (i.e., prekindergarten through Grade 12).

> *Normative data need to be current and the samples should be large enough to produce stable statistical information.*

Although a nationally representative sample is the most common type of reference group used by developers of major standardized tests, other reference groups are sometimes selected. For example, the standardized achievement tests used in many school districts provide local normative data that are based on students in individual school districts. This allows school officials and parents to be sure that their students are being compared with students who are comparable on many important variables. Other types of normative data are provided with some standardized tests. For example, the Behavior Assessment System for Children, Second Edition (BASC-2; Reynolds & Kamphaus, 2004) includes normative data based on clinical samples as well as general population norms. These clinical norms are often helpful in refining or narrowing in on a diagnostic impression (see Special Interest Topic 3.2 for an example of how clinical norms are used). Whenever special normative group data are provided, the publisher should describe the normative group thoroughly in the test manual so psychologists can make informed decisions about how appropriate they are for a given examinee and for a given purpose. Different normative or reference samples answer different questions.

A final consideration regarding norm-referenced interpretations is the importance of standardized administration. The normative sample should be administered the test under the same conditions and with the same administrative procedures that will be used in actual practice. Accordingly, when the test is administered in clinical or educational settings, it is important that the test user follow the administrative procedures precisely. For example, if you are administering standardized tests you need to make sure that you are reading the directions verbatim and closely adhering to time limits. It obviously would not be reasonable to compare your examinee's performance on a timed test to the performance of a standardization sample that was given either more or less time to complete the items. (The need to follow standard administration and

SPECIAL INTEREST TOPIC 3.1

The "Flynn Effect"

Research has shown that there were significant increases in IQ during the 20th century. This phenomenon has come to be referred to as the "Flynn Effect" after the primary researcher credited with its discovery, James Flynn. In discussing his research, Flynn (1998) noted:

> Massive IQ gains began in the 19th century, possibly as early as the industrial revolution, and have affected 20 nations, all for whom data exist. No doubt, different nations enjoyed different rates of gains, but the best data do not provide an estimate of the differences. Different kinds of IQ tests show different rates of gains: Culture-reduced tests of fluid intelligence show gains of as much as 20 points per generation (30 years); performance tests show 10–20 points; and verbal tests sometimes show 10 points or below. Tests closest to the content of school-taught subjects, such as arithmetic reasoning, general information, and vocabulary show modest or nil gains. More often than not, gains are similar at all IQ levels. Gains may be age specific, but this has not yet been established and they certainly persist into adulthood. The fact that gains are fully present in young children means that causal factors are present in early childhood but not necessarily that they are more potent in young children than older children or adults. (p. 61)

So what do you think is causing these gains in IQ? When we ask our students, some initially suggest that these increases in IQ reflect the effects of evolution or changes in the gene pool. However, this is not really a plausible explanation because it is happening much too fast. Currently the most widely accepted explanation—and the one Flynn supports—is that changes in our environment that are largely the result of global modernization have increased our ability to deal with abstract concepts, an ability that is reflected to a large degree in contemporary IQ tests. Nevertheless, the underlying reason for the Flynn Effect remains controversial, and even though virtually all researchers accept its existence, there is not universal agreement as to its causes.

Consider the importance of this effect in relation to our discussion of the development of test norms. When we told you that it is important to consider the date of the normative data when evaluating its adequacy we were concerned with factors such as the Flynn Effect. Due to the gradual but consistent increase in IQ, normative data become more demanding as time passes. In other words, an examinee must obtain a higher raw score (i.e., correctly answer more items) each time a test is renormed in order for his or her score to remain the same. Kamphaus (2001) suggested that as a rule-of-thumb, IQ norms increase in difficulty by about 3 points every 10 years (based on a mean of 100 and standard deviation of 15). For example, the same performance on IQ tests normed 10 years apart would result in IQ scores about 3 points apart, with the newer test producing the lower scores. As a result, he recommended that if the normative data for a test is more than 10 years old one should be concerned about the accuracy of the norms. This is a reasonable suggestion, and test publishers are becoming better at providing timely revisions. For example, the Wechsler Intelligence Scale for Children, Revised (WISC-R) was published in 1974, but the next revision, the WISC-III, was not released until 1991—a 17-year interval. The most current revision, the WISC-IV, was released in 2003, only 12 years after its predecessor.

What do you think the social implications of the Flynn Effect might be? The time period in which normative data were collected might well affect whether or not a test taker receives a diagnosis of mental retardation, for example. This has many ramifications for a person's life including receiving disability payments and other forms of public assistance, access to specialized educational and vocational training programs, and in the criminal arena, even whether one can be eligible to receive the death penalty, because persons with mental retardation are fully exempted from such a punishment. What other social implications occur to you?

SPECIAL INTEREST TOPIC 3.2

Using Clinical Norms?

Reynolds and Kamphaus (2004) noted that clinical norms are most useful when an examinee's performance is extreme when compared to the general population. They give the example of a child referred for significant emotional and behavioral problems. Because the referred child's scores are extreme relative to the general population, a profile of his or her scores will indicate the overall degree of the problem, but the profile might appear flat and not help the clinician identify the specific nature of the problem. The figure below illustrates this concept using an example from the Behavior Assessment System for Children, Second Edition. In this figure the child's profile based on the general norms is represented by the bold line. This profile indicates that the child's behavior is extreme, about 4 or more standard deviations above the mean, but it is relatively flat and does not reveal the specific nature of the child's

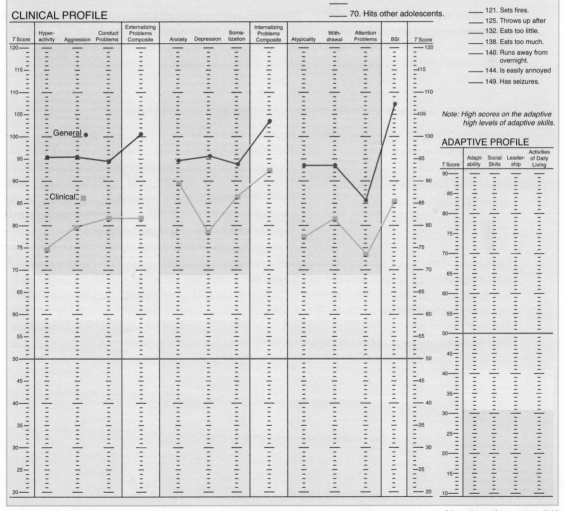

(Continued on page 78)

problem. With this information the clinician knows the child's behavior is deviant, but not what the most salient problems are. The profile based on the clinical norms demonstrates more variability. That is, it is not flat but has peaks and valleys. By examining the profile based on clinical norms you see that the child's most extreme scores reflect internalizing problems (e.g., anxiety and somatization). Clearly the externalizing scores are also elevated (e.g., aggression and conduct problems), but a clinician might decide to initially target the internalizing problems as they appear more prominent.

Source for clinical profile: Behavior Assessment System for Children, Second Edition (BASC-2). Copyright © 2004 NCS Pearson, Inc. Reproduced with permission. All rights reserved. *"BASC"* is a trademark, in the US and/or other countries, of Pearson Education, Inc. or its affiliates(s).

scoring procedures actually applies to all standardized tests, both those with norm-referenced and criterion-referenced interpretations.)

Many types of derived scores or units of measurement may be reported in "norms tables," and the selection of which derived score to employ can influence the interpretation of scores. In Chapter 2 we introduced you to the normal distribution. If you are not confident that you thoroughly understand the material presented on the normal distribution, we encourage you to review it before proceeding to the next section of this chapter.

DERIVED SCORES USED WITH NORM-REFERENCED INTERPRETATIONS

> **Standard scores** *are transformations of raw scores to a desired scale with a predetermined mean and standard deviation.*

Standard Scores. As we have noted, raw scores such as the number of items correct are difficult to work with and interpret. Raw scores therefore typically are transformed to another unit of measurement or derived score. With norm-referenced score interpretations, **standard scores** (sometimes called scaled scores) are often the preferred type of derived score. Transforming raw scores into standard scores involves creating a set of scores with a predetermined mean and standard deviation that remains constant across some preselected variable such as age (termed scaling because we change the underlying metric or rescale the scores). Although we are going to describe a number of different standard score formats, they all share numerous common characteristics. All standard scores use standard deviation units to indicate where an examinee's score is located relative to the mean of the distribution. Often, standard scores are simply linear transformations of raw scores to a desired scale with a predetermined mean and standard deviation. In a linear transformation, the following generic equation is applied to each score:

$$\text{Standard Score} = \overline{X}_{ss} + \text{SD}_{ss} \times \frac{(X_i - \overline{X})}{\text{SD}_x}$$

where X_i = raw score of any individual taking the test i

$\overline{X}$ = mean of the raw scores

SD_x = standard deviation of raw scores

SD_{ss} = desired standard deviation of the derived standard scores

$\overline{X}_{ss}$ = desired mean of the derived or standard scores.

TABLE 3–1	Transforming Raw Scores to Standard Scores

In this chapter we provide the following formula for transforming raw scores to z-scores.

$$z\text{-score} = \frac{X_i - \overline{X}}{SD}$$

where X_i = raw score of any individual i

$\overline{X}$ = mean of the raw scores

SD = standard deviation of the raw scores

Consider the situation where the mean of the raw scores ($\overline{X}$) is 75, the standard deviation of raw scores (SD) is 10, and the individual's raw score is 90.

$$z\text{-score} = \frac{(90 - 75)}{10}$$

$$= 15/10$$

$$= 1.5$$

If you wanted to convert the individual's score to a T-score, you would use the generic formula:

$$\text{Standard Score} = \overline{X}_{ss} + SD_{ss} \times \frac{X_i - \overline{X}}{SD_x}$$

where X_i = raw score of any individual taking the test i

$\overline{X}$ = mean of the raw scores

SD_x = standard deviation of raw scores

SD_{ss} = desired standard deviation of the derived standard scores

$\overline{X}_{ss}$ = desired mean of the derived or standard scores

In this case the calculations are:

$$T\text{-score} = 50 + 10 \times \frac{90 - 75}{10}$$

$$= 50 + 10 \times 1.5$$

$$= 50 + 15$$

$$= 65$$

This transformation is known as a **linear transformation**, and standard scores computed using it retain a direct relationship with the raw scores and the distribution retains its original shape (the importance of this statement will become more evident when we discuss normalized standard scores). Table 3–1 provides an example of how this formula is applied to raw scores to transform them into standard scores.

> *Standard scores calculated using linear transformations retain a direct relationship with raw scores and the distribution retains its original shape.*

As we noted, there are different standard score formats that have common characteristics. They differ in means and standard deviations. Here are brief descriptions of some of the more common standard score formats. This is not an exhaustive list, and it is possible to create a new format with virtually any mean and standard deviation you desire. However, test authors and publishers typically use these common standard score formats because psychologists are most familiar with them.

- *z-scores:* z-scores are the simplest of the standard score formats and indicate how far above or below the mean of the distribution the raw score is in standard deviation units. z-scores are simple to calculate and a simplified equation can be used (equation 2):

$$z\text{-score} = \frac{X_i - \overline{X}}{\text{SD}}$$

where X_i = raw score of any individual i

$\overline{X}$ = mean of the raw scores

SD = standard deviation of the raw scores

> *z-scores are the simplest of the standard scores and indicate how far above or below the mean on the distribution the raw score is in standard deviation units.*

Because z-scores have a mean of 0 and a standard deviation of 1, all scores above the mean will be positive and all scores below the mean will be negative. For example, a z-score of 1.6 is 1.6 standard deviations above the mean (i.e., exceeding 95% of the scores in the distribution) and a score of −1.6 is 1.6 standard deviations below the mean (i.e., exceeding only 5% of the scores in the distribution). As you see, in addition to negative scores, z-scores involve decimals. This results in scores that many find difficult to use and interpret. As a result, few test publishers routinely report z-scores for their tests. However, researchers commonly use z-scores because scores with a mean of 0 and a standard deviation of 1 make statistical formulas easier to calculate.

- **T-*scores:*** T-scores have a mean of 50 and a standard deviation of 10. Relative to z-scores they have the advantage of all scores being positive and without decimals. For example, a score of 66 is 1.6 standard deviation above the mean (i.e., exceeding 95% of the scores in the distribution) and a score of 34 is 1.6 standard deviation below the mean (i.e., exceeding only 5% of the scores in the distribution).

- *IQs:* Most intelligence scales in use today employ a standard score format with a mean of 100 and a standard deviation of 15 (e.g., Kaufman Assessment Battery for Children, Second Edition, Reynolds Intellectual Assessment Scales, Stanford-Binet Intelligence Scale, Fifth Edition, and all current Wechsler scales). Like *T-scores*, this IQ format avoids decimals and negative values. For example, a score of 124 is 1.6 standard deviation above the mean (i.e., exceeding 95% of the scores in the distribution) and a score of 76 is 1.6 standard deviation below the mean (i.e., exceeding only 5% of the scores in the distribution). This format has become very popular and most aptitude and individually administered achievement tests report standard scores with mean of 100 and standard deviation of 15. Special Interest Topic 3.3 provides a historical discussion of how we came to interpret IQs using a mean of 100 and standard deviation of 15.

- *CEEB scores (SAT/GRE):* This format was developed by the College Entrance Examination Board and used with tests including the Scholastic Assessment Test (SAT) and the

SPECIAL INTEREST TOPIC 3.3

Why Do IQ Tests Use a Mean of 100 and Standard Deviation of 15?

When Alfred Binet and Theodore Simon developed the first popular IQ test in the late 1800s, items were scored according to the age at which half the children got the answer correct. This resulted in the concept of a "mental age" for each examinee. This concept of a mental age (MA) gradually progressed to the development of the IQ, which at first was calculated as the ratio of the child's MA to his or her actual or chronological age multiplied by 100 to remove all decimals. The original form for this score, known as the Ratio IQ was:

$$MA/CA \times 100$$

where MA = mental age
        CA = chronological age

This score distribution has a mean fixed at 100 at every age. However, due to the different restrictions on the range of mental age possible at each chronological age (e.g., a 2-year-old can range in MA only 2 years below CA but a 10-year-old can range 10 years below the CA), the standard deviation of the distribution of the ratio IQ changes at every CA! At younger ages it tends to be small and it is typically larger at upper ages. The differences are quite large, often with the standard deviation from large samples varying from 10 to 30! Thus, at one age a Ratio IQ of 110 is one standard deviation above the mean whereas at another age, the same Ratio IQ of 110 is only 0.33 standard deviation above the mean. Across age, the average standard deviation of the now archaic Ratio IQ is about 16. This value was then adopted as *the* standard deviation for the Stanford-Binet IQ tests and was the standard until David Wechsler scaled his first IQ measure in the 1930s to have a standard deviation of 15, which he felt would be easier to work with. Additionally, he selected a standard deviation of 15 to help distinguish his test from the then-dominant Stanford-Binet test. The Stanford-Binet tests have long abandoned the Ratio IQ in favor of a true standard score, but remained tethered to the standard deviation of 16 until the fifth edition of the Stanford-Binet (SB5) was published in 2003. The SB5's new primary author, Gale Roid, converted to the far more popular scale with a mean of 100 and standard deviation of 15.

Graduate Record Examination (GRE). CEEB scores have a mean of 500 and standard deviation of 100. With this format, a score of 660 is 1.6 standard deviation above the mean (i.e., exceeding 95% of the scores in the distribution) and a score of 340 is 1.6 standard deviation below the mean (i.e., exceeding only 5% of the scores in the distribution).

As we noted, standard scores can be set to any desired mean and standard deviation, with the fancy of the test author frequently being the sole determining factor. Fortunately, the few standard score formats we just summarized will account for the majority of standardized tests in education and psychology. Figure 3–1 and Table 3–2 illustrate the relationship between various standard scores formats. If reference groups are comparable, Table 3–2 can also be used to help you equate scores across tests to aid in the comparison of a student's performance on tests of different attributes using different standard scores. Table 3–3 illustrates a simple formula that allows you to convert standard scores from one format to another (e.g., *z*-scores to *T*-scores).

It is important to recognize that not all authors, educators, or clinicians are specific when it comes to reporting or describing scores. That is, they may report "standard scores," but not specify exactly what standard score format they are using. Obviously the format is extremely important. Consider a standard score of 70. If this is a *T*-score it represents a score 2 standard

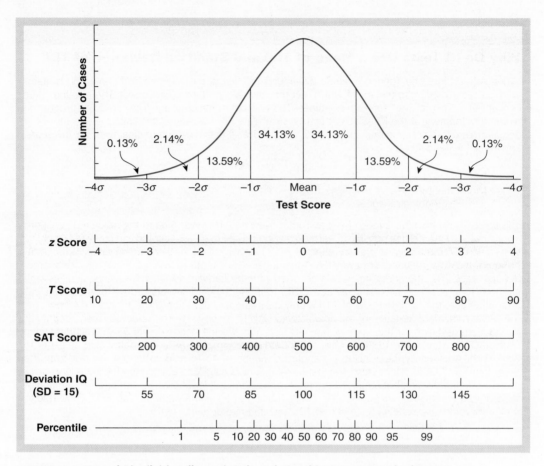

FIGURE 3–1 Normal Distribution Illustrating the Relationship Among Standard Scores.

Source: Janda, L. *Psychological Testing: Theory and Applications*, Fig. 3.2 p. 49, ©1998 Allyn & Bacon. Reproduced by permission of Pearson Education, Inc.

deviations above the mean (exceeding approximately 98% of the scores in the distribution). If it is a Wechsler IQ (or comparable score) it is 2 standard deviation below the mean (exceeding only approximately 2% of the scores in the distribution). Be sure you know what standard score format is being used so you will be able to interpret the scores accurately!

Normalized Standard Scores. Our discussion about standard scores thus far applies primarily to scores from distributions that are normal (or that at least approximate normality) and were computed using a linear transformation. As noted earlier, although it is commonly held that psychological and educational variables are normally distributed, this is not always the case. Many variables such as intelligence, memory skills, and academic achievement will closely approximate the normal distribution when well measured. However, many variables of interest in psychology and education, especially behavioral ones (e.g., aggression, attention, and hyperactivity), may deviate substantially from the normal distribution. As a result it is not unusual for test developers

TABLE 3–2	Relationship of Different Standard Score Formats			
z-Scores $\overline{X} = 0$ SD = 1	T-Scores $\overline{X} = 50$ SD = 10	IQs $\overline{X} = 100$ SD = 15	CEEB Scores $\overline{X} = 500$ SD = 100	Percentile Rank
2.6	76	139	760	>99
2.4	74	136	740	99
2.2	72	133	720	99
2.0	70	130	700	98
1.8	68	127	680	96
1.6	66	124	660	95
1.4	64	121	640	92
1.2	62	118	620	88
1.0	60	115	600	84
0.8	58	112	580	79
0.6	56	109	560	73
0.4	54	106	540	66
0.2	52	103	520	58
0.0	50	100	500	50
−0.2	48	97	480	42
−0.4	46	94	460	34
−0.6	44	91	440	27
−0.8	42	88	420	21
−1.0	40	85	400	16
−1.2	38	82	380	12
−1.4	36	79	360	8
−1.6	34	76	340	5
−1.8	32	73	320	4
−2.0	30	70	300	2
−2.2	28	67	280	1
−2.4	26	64	260	1
−2.6	24	61	240	1

Note: $\overline{X}$ = mean, SD = standard deviation.

to end up with distributions that deviate from normality enough to cause concern. In these situations test developers may elect to develop normalized standard scores.

Normalized standard scores are standard scores based on underlying distributions that were not originally normal, but were transformed into normal distributions. The transformations applied in these situations are often nonlinear transformations. Whereas standard scores calculated with linear transformations retain a direct relationship with the original raw scores and the

TABLE 3–3	Converting Standard Scores From One Format to Another

You can easily convert standard scores from one format to another using the following formula:

$$\text{New Standard Score} = \bar{X}_{ss}2 + SD_{ss}2 \times \frac{(X - \bar{X}_{ss}1)}{SD_{ss}1}$$

where X = original standard score

$\bar{X}_{ss}1$ = mean of original standard score format

$SD_{ss}1$ = standard deviation of original standard score format

$\bar{X}_{ss}2$ = mean new standard score format

$SD_{ss}2$ = mean of new standard score format

For example, consider the situation where you want to convert a z-score of 1.0 to a T-score. The calculations are:

$$T\text{-score} = 50 + 10 \times \frac{1 - 0}{1}$$
$$= 50 + 10 \times (1/1)$$
$$= 50 + 10 \times 1$$
$$= 50 + 10$$
$$= 60$$

If you wanted to convert a T-score of 60 to a CEEB score the calculations are:

$$\text{CEEB score} = 500 + 100 \times \frac{60 - 50}{10}$$
$$= 500 + 100 \times (10/10)$$
$$= 500 + 100 \times 1$$
$$= 500 + 100$$
$$= 600$$

Normalized standard scores *are standard scores based on underlying distributions that were not originally normal, but were transformed into normal distributions.*

distribution retains its original shape, this is not necessarily so with normalized standard scores based on nonlinear transformations. This does not mean that normalized standard scores are undesirable. In situations in which the obtained distribution is not normal because the variable is not normally distributed, normalization is not generally useful and indeed may be misleading. However, in situations in which the obtained distribution is not normal because of sampling error or choice of subjects, normalization can enhance the usefulness and interpretability of the scores. Nevertheless, it is desirable to know what type of scores you are working with and how they were calculated.

In most situations, normalized standard scores are interpreted in a manner similar to other standard scores. In fact, they often look strikingly similar to linear standard scores. For example, they may be reported as normalized z-scores or normalized T-scores and often reported without the prefix "normalized" at all. In this context, they will have the same mean and standard deviation as their counterparts derived with linear transformations. However, there are several types of scores that traditionally have been based on nonlinear transformations and are normalized standard scores. These include:

- **Stanine scores.** Stanine (i.e., standard nine) scores divide the distribution into nine bands (1 through 9). Stanine scores have a mean of 5 and standard deviation of 2. Because stanine scores use only nine values to represent the full range of scores, they are not a particularly precise score format. As a result, some professionals avoid their use. However, certain professionals prefer them because of their imprecision. These professionals are concerned with the imprecision inherent in all psychological measurement and choose stanine scores because they do not misrepresent the precision of measurement (e.g., Popham, 2000). Special Interest Topic 3.4 briefly describes the history of stanine scores.
- **Wechsler scaled scores.** The subtests of the Wechsler Intelligence Scale for Children, Fourth Edition (WISC-IV, Wechsler, 2003) and predecessors are reported as normalized standard scores referred to as scaled scores. Wechsler scaled scores have a mean of 10 and a standard deviation of 3. This transformation was performed so the subtest scores would be comparable, even though their underlying distributions may have deviated from the normal curve and each other.
- **Normal curve equivalent (NCE).** The normal curve equivalent (NCE) is a normalized standard score with a mean of 50 and standard deviation of 21.06. NCE scores range from 1 to 99 and were designed to approximate percentile ranks. However, being normalized standard scores they are equal-interval scores, which is an advantage over percentile ranks which are ordinal-level scores. Because school districts must report NCE scores to meet criteria as part of certain federal education programs, many test publishers report these scores for tests used in educational settings.

SPECIAL INTEREST TOPIC 3.4

The History of Stanine Scores

Stanines have a mean of 5 and a standard deviation of 2. Stanines have a range of 1 to 9 and are a form of standard score. Because they are standardized and have nine possible values, the contrived, contracted name of stanines was given to these scores (*stan*dard *nine*). A stanine is a conversion of the percentile rank that represents a wide range of percentile ranks at each score point. This system was developed by the U.S. Air Force during World War II when a simple score system was needed that could represent scores as a single digit. On older computers, which used cards with holes punched in them for entering data, the use of stanine scores not only saved time by having only one digit to punch, but also increased the speed of the computations made by computers and conserved computer memory. Stanines are now used only occasionally and usually in statistical reporting of aggregated scores (Reynolds, 2002).

> *One of the most popular and easily understood ways to interpret and report a test score is the* percentile rank. *Percentile ranks reflect the percentage of individuals scoring below a given point in a distribution.*

Percentile Rank. One of the most popular and easily understood ways to interpret and report a test score is the **percentile rank**. Like all norm-referenced scores, the percentile rank simply reflects an examinee's performance relative to a specific group. Percentile ranks are interpreted as reflecting the percentage of individuals scoring below a given point in a distribution. For example, a percentile rank of 80 indicates that 80% of the individuals in the standardization sample scored below this score. A percentile rank of 20 indicates that only 20% of the individuals in the standardization sample scored below this score. Percentile ranks range from 1 to 99, and a rank of 50 indicates the median performance (in a perfectly normal distribution it is also the mean score). As you can see, percentile ranks can be explained easily to and understood by individuals without formal training in psychometrics. Whereas standard scores might seem somewhat confusing, a percentile rank might be more understandable. For example, a parent might believe an IQ of 75 is in the average range, generalizing from his or her experience's with classroom tests whereby 70 to 80 is often interpreted as representing average or perhaps "C-level" performance. However, explaining that the child's score exceeded only approximately 5% of the standardization sample or scores of other children at the same age level might clarify the issue. There is one common misunderstanding that may arise when using percentile ranks. When discussing results in terms of percentile rank, it is important to ensure that they are not misinterpreted as "percentage correct"(Kamphaus, 1993). That is, a percentile rank of 60 means that the examinee scored better than 60% of the standardization sample, not that the examinee correctly answered 60% of the items.

Although percentile ranks can be interpreted easily, they do not represent interval-level measurement. That is, percentile ranks are not equal across all parts of a distribution. Percentile ranks are compressed near the middle of the distribution, where there are large numbers of scores, and spread out near the tails where there are relatively few scores (you can see this in Figure 3–1 by examining the line that depicts percentiles). This implies that small differences in percentile ranks near the middle of the distribution might be of little importance, whereas the same difference at the extreme might be substantial. Therefore it is often noted that use of percentile ranks will exaggerate small differences near the mean and obscure large differences near the tails of the distribution. However, because the pattern of inequality is predictable, this can be taken into consideration when interpreting scores and it is not particularly problematic, so long as the user is aware of this particularity of percentile ranks.

There is a distinction you should be aware of: the distinction between percentile rank and percentile. As noted, the percentile rank reflects the percentage of individuals scoring below a given point in a distribution. At times, however, the goal is to identify the point in a distribution at which a specific percentage of scores are less than or equal to a specified score (Hays, 1994). This is typically referred to as *G*th percentile (or the *n*th percentile) where *G* specifies the percentile. For example, saying the 60% percentile is 104 indicates that 60% of the scores are 104 or below. It is a subtle difference, but psychometrics is a precise science, and you should be aware of this distinction.

There are two formats based on percentile ranks that you might come across, most often in educational settings. Some publishers report quartile scores that divide the distribution of percentile ranks into four equal units. The lower 25% receives a quartile score of 1, 26 to 50% a quartile score of 2, 51 to 75% a quartile score of 3, and the upper 25% a quartile score of 4. Similarly, some publishers report decile-based scores, which divide the distribution of percentile ranks into ten equal parts. The lowest decile-based score is 1 and corresponds to scores with percentile ranks between 0 and 10%. The highest decile-based score is 10 and corresponds to scores with percentile ranks between 90 and 100% (e.g., Psychological Corporation, 2002).

Grade Equivalents. **Grade equivalents** are norm-referenced derived scores that attempt to identify the academic "grade level" achieved by the examinee. Although grade equivalents are very popular in some settings and appear to be easy to interpret, they actually need to be interpreted with considerable caution. To understand grade equivalents, it is helpful to be familiar with how they are calculated. When a test is administered to a group of children, the mean raw score is calculated at each grade level and this mean raw score is called the grade equivalent for raw scores of that magnitude. For example, if the mean raw score for beginning third graders on a reading test is 50, then

> **Grade equivalents** *are norm-referenced scores that identify the academic grade level achieved by the examinee. Although grade equivalents are very popular and appear to be easy to interpret, they actually need to be interpreted with considerable caution.*

any examinee earning a score of 50 on the test is assigned a grade equivalent of 3.0 regardless of his or her age. If the mean score for fourth graders is 60, then any examinee earning a score of 60 is assigned a grade equivalent of 4.0. It becomes a little more complicated when raw scores fall between two median grade scores. In these situations intermediate grade equivalents are typically calculated using a procedure referred to as *interpolation*. To illustrate this procedure with a straightforward example, consider a score of 55 on our imaginary reading test. Here, the difference between a grade equivalent of 3.0 (i.e., raw score of 50) and a grade equivalent of 4.0 (i.e., raw score of 60) is divided into 10 equal units to correspond to 10 months of academic instruction. In this example, because the difference is 10 (60 − 50 = 10), each raw scores unit corresponds to one-tenth (i.e., one month) and a raw score of 55 would be assigned a grade equivalent of 3.5. In actual practice interpolation is not always this straightforward. For example, if the difference between a grade equivalent of 3.0 and 4.0 had been 6 points (instead of 10), the calculations would have been somewhat more complicated.

Much has been written about the limitations of grade equivalents, and the following list highlights some major concerns summarized from several sources (Anastasi & Urbina, 1997; Popham, 2000; Psychological Corporation, 2002; Reynolds, 1998).

- The use of interpolation to calculate intermediate grade equivalents assumes that academic skills are achieved at a constant rate and that there is no gain or loss during the summer vacation. This tenuous assumption is probably not accurate in many situations.
- Grade equivalents are not comparable across tests or even subtests of the same battery of tests. For example, grade equivalents of 6.0 on a test of reading comprehension and a test

of math calculation do not indicate that the examinee has the same level of proficiency in the two academic areas. Additionally, there can be substantial differences between the examinee's percentile ranks on the two tests.

- Grade equivalents reflect an ordinal-level scale of measurement, not an interval scale. As discussed in the previous chapter, ordinal-level scales do not have equal scale units across the scale. For example, the difference between grade equivalents of 3.0 and 4.0 is not necessarily the same as the difference between grade equivalents of 5.0 and 6.0. Statistically, one should not add, subtract, multiply, or divide such scores because their underlying metrics are different. It is like multiplying feet by meters—you can multiply 3 feet by 3 meters and get 9, but what does it mean?

- There is not a predictable relationship between grade equivalents and percentile ranks. For example, examinees may have a higher grade equivalent on a test of reading comprehension than of math calculations, but their percentile rank and thus their skill relative to age peers on the math test may actually be higher. For example, a student in grade 10.0 may have a grade equivalent of 8.0 on a reading test and 8.0 on a math test, but the percentile rank for the reading score could easily be 30 and for the math score 5, indicating very different levels of potential academic problems in these content areas.

- A common misperception is that children should receive instruction at the level suggested by their grade equivalents. Parents may ask: "Johnny is only in the fourth grade but has a grade equivalent of 6.5 in math. Doesn't that mean he is ready for sixth-grade math instruction?" The answer is clearly no! Although Johnny correctly answered the same number of items as an average sixth grader, this does not indicate that he has mastered the necessary prerequisites to succeed in math at the sixth-grade level.

- Unfortunately, grade equivalents tend to become standards of performance. For example, lawmakers might decide that all students entering the sixth grade should achieve grade equivalents of 6.0 or better on a standardized reading test. If you will recall how grade equivalents are calculated, you will see how ridiculous this is. Because the mean raw score at each grade level is designated the grade equivalent, 50% of the standardization sample scored below the grade equivalent. As a result, it would be expected that a large number of students with average reading skills would enter the sixth grade with grade equivalents below 6.0. It is a law of mathematics that not everyone can score above the average!

> *We recommend that you avoid using grade equivalents.*

As the result of these and other limitations, we recommend that you avoid using grade equivalents. Age equivalents are another derived score format that indicates the age, typically in years and months, at which a raw score is the mean or median. Age equivalents have the same limitations as grade equivalents, and we again recommend that you avoid using them. Many test publishers report grade and age equivalents and occasionally you will find a testing expert that favors them (at least at the lower grade levels). Nevertheless they are subject to misinterpretation and should be avoided when possible. If you are required to use them, we recommend that you also report standard scores and percentile ranks and emphasize these more precise derived scores when explaining test results.

Criterion-Referenced Interpretations

As noted previously, with criterion-referenced interpretations the examinee's performance is not compared to that of other people, but to a specified level
of performance (i.e., a criterion). Criterion-referenced
interpretations emphasize what the examinees know
or what they can do, not their standing relative to other
test takers, but their standing relative to an absolute
standard or criterion. Although some authors appear
to view criterion-referenced score interpretations as a

> *Criterion-referenced
> interpretations emphasize
> what the examinee knows or
> what he or she can do, not the
> person's standing relative to
> other test takers.*

relatively new approach dating back to only the 1960s or 1970s, criterion-referenced interpretations actually predate norm-referenced interpretations. For example, educators were scoring their
students' papers and tests using "percentage correct," a criterion-referenced interpretation, long
before test developers started developing norm-referenced scores. Nevertheless, since the 1960s
there has been renewed interest in and refinement of criterion-referenced score interpretations.
A number of different labels has been applied to this type of score interpretation in the last 40
years, including *content-referenced, domain-referenced,* and *objective-referenced.* In this text
we will be using the term *criterion-referenced* because it is probably the broadest and most common label.

Probably the most common example of a criterion-referenced score is percentage correct.
For example, when a teacher reports that a student correctly answered 85% of the problems
on a classroom test assessing the student's ability to multiply double digits, this is a criterion-
referenced interpretation. Although there is a variety of criterion-referenced scoring systems, they
all involve an absolute evaluation of examinees' performances as opposed to a relative evaluation. That is, instead of comparing their performances to the performances of others (a relative
interpretation), a criterion-referenced interpretation attempts to describe what they know or are
capable of doing—the absolute level of performance.

In addition to percentage correct, another type
of criterion-referenced interpretation is referred to as
mastery testing. Mastery testing involves determining whether the examinee has achieved a specific level
of mastery of the knowledge or skills domain and is
usually reported in an all-or-none score such as a pass/
fail designation (AERA et al., 1999). Most of us have
had experience with mastery testing in obtaining a
driver's license. The written exam required to obtain
a driver's license is designed to determine whether
the applicant has acquired the basic knowledge necessary to operate a motor vehicle successfully and safely

> **Mastery testing** *involves
> determining whether the
> examinee has achieved a
> specific level of mastery of the
> knowledge and skills domain
> and is usually reported in an
> all-or-none score such as a
> pass/fail designation.*

(e.g., state motoring laws and standards). A cut score had been previously established, and all
scores equal to or above this score are reported as "pass" whereas scores below it are reported as
"fail." If the cut score requires correctly answering 85% of the items, all examinees with scores
of 84% or below fail and all with 85% and above pass. There is no practical distinction in such
a decision between an examinee answering 85% of the items correctly and one who answered

100% correctly. They both pass! For many educators, mastery testing is viewed as the preferred way of assessing mastery or proficiency of basic educational skills. For example, a teacher can develop a test to assess students' mastery of multiplication of fractions or addition with decimals. Likewise, a teacher can develop a test to assess students' mastery of spelling words on a third-grade reading list. In both of these situations, the teacher may set the cut score for designating mastery at 85% and all students achieving a score of 85% or higher will be considered to have mastered the relevant knowledge or skills domain.

Another common criterion-referenced interpretative approach is referred to as "standards-based interpretations." Whereas mastery testing typically results in an all-or-none interpretation (i.e., the student either passes or fails), standards-based interpretations usually involve three to five performance categories. For example, the results of an achievement test might be reported as basic, proficient, or advanced. An old variant of this approach is the assignment of letter grades to reflect performance on classroom achievement tests. For example, many teachers assign letter grades based on the percentage of items correct on a test, which is another type of criterion-referenced interpretation. For example, *A* grades might be assigned for percentage correct scores between 90 and 100%, *B*s for scores between 80 and 89%, *C*s for scores between 70 and 79%, *D*s for scores between 60 and 69%, and *F*s for scores below 60%. Note that with this system a student with a score of 95% receives an A regardless of how other students scored. If all of the students in the class correctly answered 90% or more of the items correctly, they would all receive *A* grades on the test.

> *The most important consideration with criterion-referenced interpretations is how clearly the knowledge or skill domain is specified or defined.*

As noted previously, with norm-referenced interpretations the most important consideration is the relevance of the group that the examinee's performance is compared to. However, with criterion-referenced interpretations, there is no comparison group and the most important consideration is how clearly the knowledge or skill domain being assessed is specified or defined (e.g., Popham, 2000). For criterion-referenced interpretations to provide useful information about what a student knows or what skills he or she possesses, it is important that the knowledge or skill domain assessed by the test be clearly defined. To facilitate this, it is common for tests specifically designed to produce criterion-referenced interpretations to assess more limited or narrowly focused content domains than those designed to produce norm-referenced interpretations. For example, a test designed to produce norm-referenced interpretations might be developed to assess broad achievement in mathematics (e.g., ranging from simple number recognition to advanced algebraic computations). In contrast, a math test designed to produce criterion-referenced interpretations might be developed to assess the students' ability to add fractions. In this situation, the criterion-referenced domain is much more focused, which allows for more meaningful criterion-based interpretations. For example, if a student successfully completed 95% of the fractional addition problems, you would have a good idea of his or her math skills in this limited, but clearly defined area. In contrast, if a student scored at the 50th percentile on the norm referenced broad mathematics achievement test, you would know that his or her performance was average for the student's age. However, you would not be able to make definitive statements about the specific types of math problems the student is able to perform. Although criterion-referenced interpretations are most applicable to narrowly defined domains, they are often applied to broader, less clearly defined domains. For example, most tests used for licensing professionals such as physicians, lawyers, teachers, or psychologists involve criterion-referenced interpretations.

Norm-Referenced, Criterion-Referenced, or Both?

Early in this chapter we noted that it is not technically accurate to refer to norm-referenced tests or criterion-referenced tests. It is the interpretation of performance on a test that is either norm-referenced or criterion-referenced. As a result, it is possible for a test to produce both norm-referenced and criterion-referenced interpretations. That being said, for several reasons it is usually optimal for tests to be designed to produce either norm-referenced or criterion-referenced scores. Norm-referenced interpretations can be applied to a larger variety of tests than criterion-referenced interpretations. We have made the distinction between maximum performance tests (e.g., aptitude and achievement) and typical response tests (e.g., interest, attitudes, and behavior). Norm-referenced interpretations can be applied to both categories, but criterion-referenced interpretations are typically applied only to maximum performance tests. That is, because criterion-referenced score interpretations reflect an examinee's knowledge or skills in a specific domain, it is not logical to apply them to measures of personality. Even in the broad category of maximum performance tests, norm-referenced interpretations tend to have broader applications. Consistent with their focus on well-defined knowledge and skills domains, criterion-referenced interpretations are most often applied to educational achievement tests or other tests designed to assess mastery of a clearly defined set of skills and abilities. Constructs such as aptitude and intelligence are typically broader and lend themselves best to norm-referenced interpretations. Even in the context of achievement testing we have alluded to the fact that tests designed for norm-referenced interpretations often cover broader knowledge and skill domains than those designed for criterion-referenced interpretations.

> *It is not technically accurate to refer to norm-referenced or criterion-referenced tests. It is the interpretation of performance on a test that is either criterion-referenced or norm-referenced.*

In addition to the breadth or focus of the knowledge or skills domain being assessed, test developers consider other factors when developing tests intended primarily for either norm-referenced or criterion-referenced interpretations. For example, because tests designed for criterion-referenced interpretations typically have a narrow focus, they are able to devote a relatively large number of items to measuring each objective or skill being measured. In contrast, because tests designed for norm-referenced interpretations typically have a broader focus they may devote only a few items to measuring each objective or skill. When developing tests intended for norm-referenced interpretations, test developers will typically select items of average difficulty and eliminate extremely difficult or easy items (this will be explained in detail in Chapter 6). When developing tests intended for criterion-referenced interpretations, test developers match the difficulty of the items to the difficulty of the knowledge or skills domain being assessed.

> *Tests can be developed that provide both norm-referenced and criterion-referenced interpretations.*

TABLE 3-4 Characteristics of Norm-Referenced and Criterion-Referenced Scores	
Norm-Referenced Scores	**Criterion-Referenced Scores**
Compare performance to a specific reference group—a relative interpretation.	Compare performance to a specific level of performance—an absolute interpretation.
Useful interpretations require a relevant reference group.	Useful interpretations require a carefully defined knowledge or skills domain.
Usually assess a fairly broad range of knowledge or skills.	Usually assess a limited or narrow domain of knowledge or skills.
Typically have only a limited number of items to measure each objective or skill.	Typically have several items to measure each test objective or skill.
Items are typically selected that are of medium difficulty and maximize variance; very difficult and very easy items typically are deleted.	Items are selected that provide good coverage of content domain; the difficulty of the items matches the difficulty of content domain.
Example: Percentile rank—a percentile rank of 80 indicates that the examinee scored better than 80% of the subjects in the reference group.	Example: Percentage correct—a percentage correct score of 80 indicates that the examinee successfully answered 80% of the test items.

Although our discussion to this point has emphasized differences between norm-referenced and criterion-referenced interpretations, they are not mutually exclusive. Tests can be developed that provide both norm-referenced and criterion-referenced interpretations. Both interpretive approaches have positive characteristics and provide useful information (see Table 3–4). Whereas norm-referenced interpretations provide important information about how an examinee performed relative to a specified reference group, criterion-referenced interpretations provide important information about how well an examinee has mastered a specified knowledge or skills domain. It is possible, and sometimes desirable, for a test to produce both norm-referenced and criterion-referenced scores. For example, it would be possible to interpret a student's test performance as "by correctly answering 75% of the multiplication problems, the student scored better than 60% of the students in the class." Although the development of a test to provide both norm-referenced and criterion-referenced scores may require some compromises, the increased interpretive versatility may justify these compromises (e.g., Linn & Gronlund, 2000). As a result, some test publishers are beginning to produce more tests that provide both interpretive formats. Nevertheless, most tests are designed for either norm-referenced or criterion-referenced interpretations. Although the majority of published standardized tests are designed to produce norm-referenced interpretations, tests producing criterion-referenced interpretations play an extremely important role in educational and other settings.

SCORES BASED ON ITEM RESPONSE THEORY

To this point we have focused our discussion on norm-referenced and criterion-referenced score interpretations. In recent years theoretical and technical advances have ushered in new types of scores that are based on **item response theory (IRT)**. IRT is a modern test theory that has greatly impacted test development, and we will discuss it in more detail in Chapter 7. For now we can define IRT as a theory or model of mental measurement that holds that the responses to items on a test are accounted for by latent traits. A latent trait is some ability or characteristic that is inferred to exist based on theories of behavior as well as evidence of its existence, but a latent trait cannot be assessed directly. Intelligence is an example of a latent trait. It is assumed that each examinee possesses a certain amount of any given latent trait and that its estimation is not dependent on any specific set of items or any

> *In recent years theoretical and technical advances have ushered in new types of scores that are based on* **item response theory (IRT).**

assessment procedure. Central to IRT is a mathematical model that describes how examinees at different levels of ability (or whatever latent trait is being assessed) will respond to individual test items. IRT is fundamental to the development and application of computer adaptive testing (CAT). What is most important to us at this point (i.e., a chapter on the interpretation of test scores) is that IRT allows the calculation of scores that do not fit the common norm-referenced/criterion-referenced classification scheme.

To illustrate the basics of the IRT model, consider this simple example. Envision a scale reflecting vocabulary skills (i.e., ability to specify the meaning of words correctly). On the left side of the scale are words that most people can define. As we progress up the scale the words get increasingly more difficult. The words on the far right side of the scale are difficult and few people, only those with strong vocabulary skills, can define them. This is illustrated in the following figure:

cat	table	greater	venture	posit	esoteric

In this example, most examinees can define "cat" whereas very few can define "esoteric." In this illustration we only use six words reflecting six items; however, in the development of an actual test, many word items would be included (e.g., 100 or more).

In the IRT model this scale can also be considered a scale reflecting the ability level of examinees. The specific ability level of an examinee is defined as the level on this scale where the examinee can get half of the items correct. In IRT terminology, an examinee's ability level is designated by the Greek letter theta (Θ). Consider Johnny who is 7 years old and in the second grade. He easily defines "cat" and "table," and although he correctly defines "greater," he misses half of the other items at the same difficulty level as "greater." Now consider Sally who is a junior in college. Her vocabulary skills are understandably better

> *Scores based on the IRT model are similar to the raw scores on tests developed using classical test theory, but they have a distinct advantage in that they are equal-interval-level scores and have stable standard deviations across age groups.*

developed than Johnny and her ability level is at approximately the level of the word "posit." These ability levels of these two examinees are identified in the following figure.

		Johnny		Sally	
cat	table	greater	venture	posit	esoteric

The scores assigned to reflect an individual's ability level in an IRT model are similar to the raw scores on tests developed using traditional models (i.e., classical test theory). For example, they can be transformed into either norm- or criterion-referenced scores. However, they have a distinct advantage in that, unlike traditional raw scores, they are equal-interval-level scores (i.e., having equal intervals between values) and stable standard deviations across age groups. These IRT scores go by different names, including *W*-scores, growth scores, and Change Sensitive Scores (CSS). W-scores are used on the Woodcock-Johnson III (Woodcock, McGrew, & Mather, 2001b) and are set so a score of 500 reflects cognitive performance at the beginning fifth-grade ability level. *W*-scores have proven to be particularly useful in measuring changes in cognitive abilities. For example, they can help measure gains in achievement due to learning or declines in cognitive abilities due to dementia. In terms of measuring gains, if over time an examinee's *W*-score increases by 10 units (e.g., from 500 to 510), he or she can now complete tasks with 75% probability of success that the person originally could complete with only a 50% probability of success. Conversely, if an examinee's *W*-score decreases by 10 *W* units (e.g., 500 to 490) he or she can now complete tasks with only 25% probability of success that originally could complete with 50% probability of success (Woodcock, 1978, 1999). These IRT-based scores are not available for many published tests, but they will likely become more widely available in the future. They are often referred to generically as Rasch or Rasch-type scores, after the originator of the mathematical models.

SO WHAT SCORES SHOULD WE USE: NORM-REFERENCED, CRITERION-REFERENCED, OR RASCH-BASED SCORES?

> *Different types of test scores answer different questions.*

So, what scores should we use? Just as different reference groups or standardization samples provide us with different kinds of information, allowing us to answer different questions, different types of test scores answer different questions. Prior to being able to answer the question of which scores we should we use, we need to know what it is we want the test score to tell us.

- Raw scores tell us the number of points accumulated by a person on a measure and can tell us his or her relative rank among test takers (assuming we know everyone's raw score). Raw scores typically provide us only with ordinal scale measurement.
- Traditional norm-referenced standard scores address the general question of how this person's performance compares to the performance of some specified reference group and typically reflects interval scale measurement.
- Criterion-referenced scores tell us whether or not or to what extent a person's performance has approached a desired level of proficiency.
- Rasch or IRT-based scores are on an equal-interval scale that reflects position on some underlying or latent trait. These scores are particularly useful in evaluating the degree of change in scores over time and in comparing scores across tests of a common latent trait.

To illustrate how the use of different types of test scores might address different questions, consider the issue of whether or not a student's performance in reading has changed following the introduction of specialized teaching methods after it was discovered that the student was having great difficulty acquiring reading skills. In such a circumstance, a student, John, would be administered a reading test prior to initiating an intervention or specialized reading methods to obtain a baseline level of performance. After some period of specialized instruction, John would be tested a second time to determine whether or not his skills in reading had changed. If the test used provided one of the four types of scores noted earlier, what would each of these scores tell us about John's change in reading skill?

- **Common standard scores** that are norm-referenced by age group would answer the following question: "How has John's reading performance changed relative to the average rate of change of other children the same age?"
- **Rasch-type scores** would answer the question, "How has John's reading performance changed relative to the starting point of his specialized instruction?" **Raw scores** would answer this question as well, but are not on an equal-interval scale. This makes it difficult to estimate by how much John's reading performance has really changed. The advantage of a Rasch-type score in this circumstance is that the distance between each score point is the same throughout the entire range of scores.
- **Criterion-referenced scores** answer a different question. Criterion referenced scores address the question, "Has John's performance in reading reached a predetermined level of proficiency or a set goal for his instructional progress?"

All of these questions may be important, but they are in fact quite different and different types of scores are required to answer each of these questions. To understand the difference in the types of information provided, consider if John were running a race instead of learning to read.

- Norm-referenced standard scores would reflect John's position in the race relative to all other runners at any given time.
- Rasch scores would indicate accurately his distance from the starting point, but would not allow us to assess his progress relative to other runners without also knowing their Rasch score. Raw scores would indicate distance from the starting point as well, but unlike measurement in feet or meters in a race, when used with psychological or educational variables, would not indicate the distance accurately at each point of progress.
- A criterion-referenced score would let us know when John had passed specific points on the racetrack or had reached the finish line.

So here we see that each type of score provides us with a different type of information. Which score we should use is dependent on the type of information we desire.

For purposes of evaluating change, in some circumstances standard scores that are age corrected are the most appropriate but in other circumstances, criterion-referenced scores or even Rasch scores may be more appropriate. In an educational environment where we are looking to assess improvement in academic achievement levels of an individual student, the question of acquisition of academic skills relative to an age-appropriate peer group would be the most appropriate question to address in nearly all instances. That is, it is important to know if a student is making progress or keeping pace relative to other students the same age and not relative only to the starting point. If we considered only progress relative to a starting point and looked only at changes in raw scores or some other form of growth score such as reflected in a Rasch scale, we could certainly determine if a student was making progress. However, the student may be progressing at a rate that is less than that of classmates, and as a result is falling further and further behind. By using age-corrected standard scores, we see easily whether the student is progressing at a lesser rate, the same pace, or more quickly than other students of the same age.

In a therapeutic environment, we have very different concerns. A person who is in psychotherapy being treated for depressive symptoms may be making progress; however, we would not want to discontinue therapy until a specific criterion point had been reached. In such cases, we would be more interested in the absolute level of symptomatology present or absolute level of distress experienced by the patient as opposed to his or her relative level of change compared to some peer group.

QUALITATIVE DESCRIPTIONS OF TEST SCORES

Qualitative descriptions of test scores help professionals communicate results in written reports and other formats.

Test developers commonly provide qualitative descriptions of the scores produced by their tests. These qualitative descriptors help professionals communicate results in written reports and other formats. For example, the Stanford-Binet Intelligence Scales, Fifth Edition (SB5; Roid, 2003) provides the following qualitative descriptions:

IQ	Classification
145 and above	Very Gifted or Highly Advanced
130–144	Gifted or Very Advanced
120–129	Superior
110–119	High Average
90–109	Average
80–89	Low Average
70–79	Borderline Impaired or Delayed
55–69	Mildly Impaired or Delayed
40–54	Moderately Impaired or Delayed

These qualitative descriptors help professionals communicate information about an examinee's performance in an accurate and consistent manner. That is, professionals using the SB5 should consistently use these descriptors when describing test performance.

A similar approach is often used with typical response assessments. For example, the Behavior Assessment System for Children (BASC; Reynolds & Kamphaus, 1998) provides the following descriptions of the clinical scales such as the depression or anxiety scales:

T-Score Range	Classification
70 and above	Clinically Significant
60–69	At-Risk
41–59	Average
31–40	Low
30 and below	Very Low

REPORTING INFORMATION ON NORMATIVE SAMPLES AND TEST SCORES

The *Standards for Educational and Psychological Testing* (AERA et al., 1999) devotes an entire chapter to the discussion of test norms and scores. In terms of normative data, the *Standards* specify that "It is important that norms be based on technically sound, representative, scientific samples of sufficient size" (p. 51). The *Standards* stipulate that test developers should report specific information about the normative sample and how the data were collected. They also require that test developers provide information on the meaning and interpretations of test scores and their limitations. (In this and subsequent chapters we often will devise illustrations based on tests developed by one of the authors of this text [CRR]. This is done because of our expertise with these instruments and our ability to access technical information about the tests as well as other information that may be difficult to obtain.)

To illustrate how information on normative data and test scores is reported in test manuals, we will use examples from the Reynolds Intellectual Assessment Scales (RIAS; Reynolds & Kamphaus, 2003). The RIAS is an individually administered intelligence test for clients 3 to 94 years. The RIAS contains a two-subtest Verbal Intelligence Index (VIX) and a two-subtest Nonverbal Intelligence Index (NIX). The two verbal subtests are *Guess What (GWH)* and *Verbal Reasoning (VRZ)*. The two nonverbal subtests are *Odd-Item Out (OIO)* and *What's Missing (WHM)*. All four subtests are combined to form the *Composite Intelligence Index (CIX)*. It takes approximately 20 to 25 minutes to administer the four intelligence scale subtests. The RIAS also includes a conormed, supplemental measure of memory that is composed of two memory subtests that yield a *Composite Memory Index (CMX)*. The two memory subtests are *Verbal Memory (VRM)* and *Nonverbal Memory (NVM)*. The administration of the memory subtests requires approximately 10 to 15 minutes.

The RIAS was standardized on a national sample of 2,438 individuals that is representative of the U.S. population. Tables 3–5 and 3–6 compare the demographic characteristics of the

TABLE 3-5	Comparison of U.S. Population and RIAS Standardization Sample: Age and Gender				
	U.S. Population		**RIAS Standardization Sample**		
Age (years)	**Male**	**Female**	**n**	**Male**	**Female**
3–8	51.0	49.0	703	48.1	51.9
9–12	51.3	48.7	371	52.0	48.0
13–19	51.2	48.8	415	52.0	48.0
20–34	49.4	50.6	319	49.5	50.5
35–54	49.2	50.8	333	53.5	46.5
55–74	46.7	53.3	163	46.0	54.0
75–94	39.7	60.3	134	34.3	65.7
Total	48.9	51.1	2,438	49.4	50.6

Note. U.S. population data are from the *Current Population Survey*, March 2001 [Data File]. Washington, DC: U.S. Bureau of the Census.

Source: Reynolds, C. R., & Kamphaus, R. W. (2003). Reynolds Intellectual Assessment Scales. Lutz, FL: Psychological Assessment Resources. Reprinted with permission of PAR.

TABLE 3-6 Comparison of U.S. Population and RIAS Standardization Sample: Age, Ethnicity, and Educational Attainment

Education/Ethnicity	U.S. Population By Age Group (Years)							RIAS Standardization Sample by Age Group (Years)[a]						
	3–8	9–12	13–19	20–34	35–54	55–74	75–94	3–8	9–12	13–19	20–34	35–54	55–74	75–94
≤ 11 years														
White	4.7	4.7	7.4	4.7	4.8	13.0	25.2	3.3	4.9	7.2	5.3	8.7	13.5	27.6
African American	1.8	1.8	2.5	1.9	1.7	3.4	4.7	0.7	0.0	2.4	6.3	5.7	1.2	2.2
Hispanic American	4.7	4.7	5.2	5.6	4.1	4.0	3.3	3.9	3.5	4.3	2.5	1.2	0.6	0.7
Other	0.5	0.5	0.7	0.4	0.5	1.0	1.2	0.4	0.3	0.0	0.0	0.0	0.0	0.7
12 years/HS[b]														
White	21.8	21.8	21.1	19.0	23.7	29.6	31.7	21.7	24.5	23.4	19.8	25.8	32.5	30.6
African American	4.8	4.8	4.6	5.1	4.6	3.0	1.8	12.8	5.1	7.7	4.4	3.9	1.8	0.0
Hispanic American	3.5	3.5	3.5	4.7	2.7	1.8	0.9	12.7	3.5	2.9	2.2	2.1	2.5	0.7
Other	1.2	1.2	1.2	1.1	1.2	1.0	0.7	0.9	0.5	1.0	0.6	0.0	0.6	0.0
13–15 years														
White	22.3	22.3	21.6	23.6	21.3	18.3	15.9	15.4	18.1	27.1	20.1	20.1	20.9	19.4
African American	4.0	4.0	3.8	4.6	3.6	1.8	0.6	2.4	4.9	3.6	3.5	4.5	2.5	0.7
Hispanic American	2.5	2.5	2.5	3.5	1.9	0.9	0.3	2.4	4.3	1.2	3.1	2.7	0.6	0.0
Other	1.4	1.4	1.4	1.9	1.0	0.6	0.3	1.1	0.8	1.0	0.6	0.3	0.0	0.0
≥ 16 years														
White	21.4	21.4	19.7	18.2	23.6	18.5	12.0	18.4	25.1	15.0	20.8	18.6	22.7	16.4
African American	2.0	2.0	1.8	2.0	2.0	1.3	0.5	1.7	2.4	1.4	4.4	1.5	0.6	0.0
Hispanic American	1.3	1.3	1.2	1.3	1.2	0.6	0.3	1.6	2.2	1.4	4.4	3.9	0.0	0.7
Other	2.2	2.2	2.0	2.4	2.0	1.3	0.6	0.6	0.0	0.2	1.9	0.9	0.0	0.0

Note. U.S. population data are from the *Current Population Survey,* March 2001 [Data File]. Washington, DC: U.S. Bureau of the Census. Education is number of years completed; for individuals ages 3 to 16 years, education is based on parent's education.

[a]N = 2,438. [b]HS = High school diploma, GED, or equivalent.

Source: Reynolds, C. R., & Kamphaus, R. W. (2003). Reynolds Intellectual Assessment Scales. Lutz, FL: Psychological Assessment Resources. Reprinted with permission of PAR.

TABLE 3-7	*T*-Score Conversions for Subtest Raw Scores						
Raw Score	GWH	OIO	VRZ	WHM	VRM	NVM	Raw Score
0	9	9	9	9	19	9	0
1	9	9	9	9	20	9	1
2	9	9	9	9	22	9	2
3	9	9	9	9	23	9	3
4	9	10	9	9	24	9	4
5	9	11	10	9	25	9	5
6	9	11	12	9	26	9	6
7	9	12	14	9	27	9	7
8	9	13	15	9	28	9	8
9	9	14	17	9	30	9	9
10	9	14	19	9	31	9	10
11	9	15	21	9	32	9	11
12	9	16	23	9	33	9	12
13	9	16	25	9	34	9	13
14	9	17	27	9	35	9	14
15	9	18	29	9	36	9	15
16	9	18	31	10	38	9	16
17	9	19	33	11	39	9	17
18	9	20	35	12	40	9	18
19	9	20	37	13	41	9	19
20	9	21	39	14	42	9	20
21	9	22	41	15	43	9	21
22	9	22	43	17	44	9	22
23	9	23	45	18	46	9	23
24	12	24	47	19	47	9	24
25	15	24	49	20	48	9	25
26	17	25	51	21	49	9	26
27	19	26	53	22	50	9	27
28	21	26	54	23	51	9	28
29	23	27	56	24	52	9	29
30	25	28	58	26	54	9	30
31	28	28	60	27	55	9	31
32	30	29	62	28	56	9	32
33	32	30	64	29	57	9	33

(Continued on page 100)

TABLE 3-7	*T*-Score Conversions for Subtest Raw Scores (*Continued*)						
Raw Score	GWH	OIO	VRZ	WHM	VRM	NVM	Raw Score
34	34	30	66	30	58	9	34
35	36	31	68	31	59	9	35
36	38	32	70	32	60	9	36
37	40	32	72	33	62	9	37
38	43	33	74	34	63	13	38
39	45	34	76	36	64	14	39
40	47	34	78	37	65	15	40
41	49	35	80	38	66	16	41
42	51	36	82	39	67	17	42
43	53	36	84	40	68	18	43
44	56	37	86	41	69	18	44
45	58	38	88	42	71	19	45
46	60	38	90	43	72	20	46
47	62	39	91	44	72	21	47
48	64	40	91	46	73	22	48
49	66	40		47	75	23	49
50	68	41		48	76	24	50
51	71	42		49	77	25	51
52	73	43		50		26	52
53	75	43		51		27	53
54	77	44		52		28	54
55	79	45		53		28	55
56	81	45		55		29	56
57	83	46		56		30	57
58	86	47		57		31	58
59	88	47		58		32	59
60	90	48		59		33	60
61	91	49		60		34	61
62	91	49		61		35	62
63		50		62		36	63
64		51		63		37	64
65		51		65		38	65
66		52		66		39	66
67		53		67		39	67

(Continued)

Raw Score	GWH	OIO	VRZ	WHM	VRM	NVM	Raw Score
68		53		68		40	68
69		54		69		41	69
70		55		70		42	70
71		55		71		43	71
72		56		72		44	72
73		57		74		45	73
74		57		75		46	74
75		58		76		47	75
76		59		77		48	76
77		59		78		49	77
78		60		79		49	78
79		61		80		50	79
80		61		81		51	80
81		62				52	81
82		63				53	82
83		63				54	83
84		64				55	84
85		65				56	85
86		65				58	86
87		66				60	87
88		67				62	88
89		67				64	89
90		68				66	90
91		69				68	91
92		69				70	92
93		70					93
94		71					94
95		71					95
96		72					96
97		73					97
98		74					98
99		74					99
100		75					100
101		76					101
102		76					102

Source: From Reynolds, C. R., & Kamphaus, R. W. (2003). Reynolds Intellectual Assessment Scales. Lutz, FL: Psychological Assessment Resources. Reprinted with permission of PAR.

TABLE 3-8   Standard Score Conversions for the RIAS Verbal Intelligence Index

Sum of Subtest T Scores	VIX	%ile Rank	Confidence Interval[a] 90%	95%	T Score	z Score	NCE	Stanine
87–88	92	30	87–98	86–99	45	−0.53	39	4
89	93	32	88–99	87–100	45	−0.47	40	4
90	94	34	89–100	88–101	46	−0.40	42	4
91	95	37	90–101	89–102	47	−0.33	43	4
92	96	39	91–102	89–103	47	−0.27	44	4
93–94	97	42	91–103	90–104	48	−0.20	46	5
95–96	98	45	92–104	91–105	49	−0.13	47	5
97–98	99	47	93–105	92–106	49	−0.07	49	5

Source: Reynolds, C. R., & Kamphaus, R. W. (2003). Reynolds Intellectual Assessment Scales. Lutz, FL: Psychological Assessment Resources. Reprinted with permission of PAR.

standardization sample to that of the U.S. population. These data illustrate that the RIAS standardization sample is representative of the general population.

The RIAS professional manual (Reynolds & Kamphaus, 2003) provides a description of how the age-adjusted subtest *T*-scores were derived. This includes a fairly technical description of sample weighting and continuous norming procedures that were used in developing the normalized subtest *T*-scores. There are also 50 tables in an appendix that allow one to convert raw scores on the subtests to *T*-scores. Table 3–7 reproduces the conversion table for examinees aged 11 years 8 months to 11 years 11 months. In this table, a raw score of 48 on *Guess What (GWH)* translates to a *T*-score of 64. Accordingly, a raw score of 48 on *Odd-Item Out (OIO)* translates to a *T*-score of 40. Using these tables, the examiner is able to convert raw scores to *T*-scores for all of the RIAS subtests.

Once the subtest *T*-scores are calculated, the examiner is able to calculate the index scores. To do this, the age-adjusted *T*-scores comprising the index scores are summed. For example, the *Guess What* and *Verbal Reasoning T*-scores are summed to allow the calculation of the Verbal Intelligence Index (VIX). Once these summed scores are available, the examiner can convert them to index scores using tables provided in the manual. These index scores have a mean of 100 and a standard deviation of 15. Table 3–8 reproduces a portion of the table used for converting summed *T*-scores for the Verbal Intelligence Index (VIX). An examination of Table 3–8 illustrates the variety of supplemental scores available for the RIAS index scores. These include *T*-scores, z-scores, normal curve equivalents (NCEs), and stanines.

The RIAS Record Form is designed to facilitate the accurate calculation of all scores. Figure 3–2 is an example of a completed first page of the RIAS Record Form. The RIAS Record Form also contains graphs that allow the examiner to plot the subtest and index scores. Examples of these graphs are illustrated in Figure 3–3.

RIAS™ Record Form

Cecil R. Reynolds, PhD, and Randy W. Kamphaus, PhD

Name _Scoring Example_ Gender _F_

Ethinicity _White_ Grade/highest level of education _16_

ID# _02401_ Examiner _Dr. Green_

Reason for referral _Post-surgical evaluation_ Referral source _Dr. Maguire_

	Year	Month	Day
	01	14	45
Date Tested	02	03	18
Date of Birth	78	09	24
Age	23	05	21

RIAS Subtest Scores/Index Summary

Age-Adjusted T Scores (refer to Appendix A, Table _A42_)

	Raw Scores	Verbal	Nonverbal		Memory
Guess What (GWH)	54	59			
Odd-Item Out (OIO)	73		52		
Verbal Reasoning (VRZ)	37	57			
What's Missing (WHM)	63		53		
Verbal Memory (VRM)	46				59
Nonverbal Memory (NVM)	83				49

Sum of T Scores: 116 + 105 = 221 108

RIAS Indexes (refer to Appendix B)

VIX	NIX	CIX	CMX
114	105	110	108

Confidence Interval _90_ %

107 – 119	99 – 110	105 – 114	102 – 113

Percentile Rank

82	63	75	70

Verbal Intelligence Index	Nonverbal Intelligence Index	Composite Intelligence Index	Composite Memory Index

Additional Information (optional)

Primary language spoken at home _English_ Parental educational attainment (if applicable) _N/A_

Name of school (if applicable) _N/A_ Occupation (if applicable) _salesperson_

Vision/hearing/language/motor problems (specify) _N/A_

History of learning problems _N/A_

History of medical/neurological problems _Brain tumor resection 1 month ago._

Notes _____

FIGURE 3-2 Example of RIAS Record Form.

Source: Reynolds, C. R., & Kamphaus, R. W. (2003). Reynolds Intellectual Assessment Scales. Lutz, FL: Psychological Assessment Resources. Reprinted with permission of PAR.

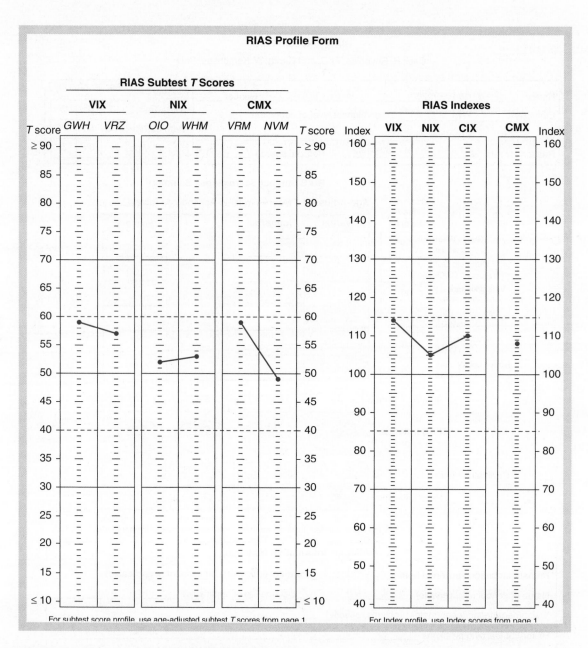

FIGURE 3-3 Example of Completed RIAS Profile Graphs.

Source: Reynolds, C. R., & Kamphaus, R. W. (2003). Reynolds Intellectual Assessment Scales. Lutz, FL: Psychological Assessment Resources. Reprinted with permission of PAR.

Summary

In this chapter we provided an overview of different types of test scores and their meanings. We started by noting that raw scores, although easy to calculate, usually provide little useful information about an examinee's performance on a test. As a result, we usually transform raw scores into derived scores. These derived scores can be classified broadly as either norm-referenced or criterion-referenced. Norm-referenced score interpretations compare an examinee's performance on a test to the performance of other people, typically those in the standardization sample. When making norm-referenced interpretations, it is important to evaluate the adequacy of the standardization sample. This involves determining if the standardization is representative of the examinees the test will be used with; if the sample is current; and if the sample is of adequate size to produce stable statistics.

When making norm-referenced interpretations it is useful to have a basic understanding of the normal distribution (also referred to as the bell-shaped curve). The normal distribution is a distribution that characterizes many naturally occurring variables and has several characteristics that psychometricians find very useful. The most useful of these characteristics is that predictable proportions of scores occur at specific points in the distribution. For example, if you know that an individual's score is 1 standard deviation above the mean on a normally distributed variable, you know that the individual's score exceeds approximately 84% of the scores in the standardization sample. This predictable distribution of scores facilitates the interpretation and reporting of test scores.

Standard scores are norm-referenced derived scores that have a predetermined mean and standard deviation. A variety of standard scores are commonly used today, including:

- z-scores: mean of 0 and standard deviation of 1.
- T-scores: mean of 50 and standard deviation of 10.
- IQs: mean of 100 and standard deviation of 15.
- CEEB scores (SAT/GRE): mean of 500 and standard deviation of 100.

By combining an understanding of the normal distribution with the information provided by standard scores, you can easily interpret an examinee's performance relative to the specified reference group. For example, an examinee with a T-score of 60 scored 1 standard deviation above the mean. You know that approximately 84% of the scores in a normal distribution are below 1 standard deviation above the mean. Therefore, the examinee's score exceeded approximately 84% of the scores in the reference group.

When scores are not normally distributed (i.e., do not take the form of a normal distribution), test publishers often use "normalized" standard scores. These normalized scores often look just like regular standard scores, but they are computed in different manner. Nevertheless, they are interpreted in a similar manner. For example, if a test publisher reports normalized T-scores, they will have a mean of 50 and standard deviation of 10 just like regular T-scores. There are some unique normalized standard scores, including:

- Stanine scores:mean of 5 and standard deviation of 2.
- Wechsler subtest scaled scores:mean of 10 standard deviation of 3.
- Normal curve equivalent (NCE):mean of 50 and standard deviation of 21.06.

Another common type of norm-referenced score is percentile rank. This popular format is one of the most easily understood norm-referenced derived scores. Like all norm-referenced scores, the percentile rank reflects an examinee's performance relative to a specific reference group. However, instead of using a scale with a specific mean and standard deviation, the percentile rank simply specifies the percentage of individuals scoring below a given point in a distribution. For example, a percentile rank of 80 indicates that 80% of the individuals in the reference group scored below this score. Percentile ranks have the advantage of being easily explained to and understood by individuals without formal training in psychometrics.

The final norm-referenced derived scores we discussed were grade and age equivalents. For numerous reasons, we recommend that you avoid using these scores. If you are required to report them, also report standard scores and percentile ranks and emphasize these when interpreting the results.

In contrast to norm-referenced scores, criterion-referenced scores compare an examinee's performance to a specified level of performance referred to as a criterion. Probably the most common criterion-referenced score is the percentage correct score routinely reported on classroom achievement tests. For example, if you report that a student correctly answered 80% of the items on a spelling test, this is a criterion-referenced interpretation. Another type of criterion-referenced interpretation is mastery testing. On a mastery test you determine whether examinees have achieved a specified level of mastery on the knowledge or skill domain. Here, performance is typically reported as either "pass" or "fail." If examinees score above the cut score they pass; if they score below the cut score they fail. Another criterion-referenced interpretation is referred to as standards-based interpretations. Instead of reporting performance as simply pass/ fail, standard-based interpretations typically involve three to five performance categories.

With criterion-referenced interpretations, a prominent consideration is how clearly the knowledge or domain is defined. For useful criterion-referenced interpretations, the knowledge or skill domain being assessed must be clearly defined. To facilitate this, criterion-referenced interpretations are typically applied to tests that measure focused or narrow domains. For example, a math test designed to produce criterion-referenced scores might be limited to the addition of fractions. This way, if a student correctly answers 95% of the fraction problems, you will have useful information regarding the student's proficiency with this specific type of math problems. You are not able to make inferences about a student's proficiency in other areas of math, but you will know this specific type of math problem was mastered. If the math test contained a wide variety of math problems (as is common with norm-referenced tests), it would be more difficult to specify exactly in which areas a student is proficient.

We noted that the terms norm-referenced and criterion-referenced refer to the interpretation of test performance, not the test itself. Although it is often optimal to develop a test to produce either norm-referenced or criterion-referenced scores, it is possible and sometimes desirable for a test to produce both norm-referenced and criterion-referenced scores. This may require some compromises when developing the test, but the increased flexibility may justify these compromises. Nevertheless, most tests are designed for either norm-referenced or criterion-referenced interpretations, and most published standardized tests produce norm-referenced interpretations. That being said, tests that produce criterion-referenced interpretations have many important applications, particularly in educational settings.

We next provided a brief description of scores based on item response theory (IRT). IRT is a modern test theory that holds that the responses to items on a test are accounted for by latent traits. The scores in this model are similar to traditional raw scores in that they can be transformed into either norm or criterion-referenced scores. However, they have an advantage in that they are interval level scores and have stable standard deviations across age groups. This makes them particularly useful in measuring changes in cognitive abilities. These IRT-based scores are not currently available for many published tests, but they will likely become more widely available in the future.

We provided some guidance on determining which type of score interpretation to use. We noted that different types of test scores provide information that allows us to answer different questions. In summary:

- Raw scores tell us the number of points accumulated by a person on a measure and can tell us his or her relative rank among test takers (assuming we know everyone's raw score).
- Traditional norm-referenced standard scores address the general question of how this person's performance compares to the performance of some specified reference group and typically reflects interval scale measurement.
- Criterion-referenced scores tell us whether or not or to what extent a person's performance has approached a desired level of proficiency.
- Rasch or IRT-based scores are on an equal-interval scale that reflects position on some underlying or latent trait. These scores are particularly useful in evaluating the degree of change in scores over time and in comparing scores across tests of a common latent trait.

We closed the chapter by illustrating the way test developers report information on normative samples and test scores using examples from the Reynolds Intellectual Assessment Scales (RIAS; Reynolds & Kamphaus, 2003).

Key Terms and Concepts

Criterion-referenced score
    interpretations, 73
Grade equivalents, 87
Item response theory (IRT), 93
Linear transformation, 79

Mastery testing, 89
Normalized standard scores, 83
Norm-referenced score
    interpretations, 72
Percentile rank, 86

Raw score, 72
Standard scores, 78
z-scores, 80

Recommended Readings

American Educational Research Association, American Psychological Association, & National Council on Measurement in Education. (1999). *Standards for educational and psychological testing*. Washington, DC: AERA. For the technically minded, Chapter 4, Scales, Norms, and Score Comparability, is must reading!

Lyman, H. B. (1998). *Test scores and what they mean*. Boston: Allyn & Bacon. This text provides a comprehensive and very readable discussion of test scores. An excellent resource.

Internet Site of Interest

http://www.teachersandfamilies.com/open/parent/scores1.cfm
Understanding Test Scores: A Primer for Parents is a user-friendly discussion of tests that is accurate and readable. A good resource for parents.

Practice Items

1. Transform the following raw scores to the specified standard score formats. The raw score distribution has a mean of 70 and standard deviation of 10.

a. Raw score = 85	z-score =	T-score =
b. Raw score = 60	z-score =	T-score =
c. Raw score = 55	z-score =	T-score =
d. Raw score = 95	z-score =	T-score =
e. Raw score = 75	z-score =	T-score =

2. Convert the following z-scores to T-scores and CEEB scores.

a. z-score = 1.5	T-score =	CEEB score =
b. z-score = −1.5	T-score =	CEEB score =
c. z-score = 2.5	T-score =	CEEB score =
d. z-score = −2.0	T-score =	CEEB score =
e. z-score = −1.70	T-score =	CEEB score =

Answers can be found in Appendix C.

4

Reliability

It is the user who must take responsibility for determining whether or not scores are sufficiently trustworthy to justify anticipated uses and interpretations.—
AERA et al., 1999, p. 31

Chapter Outline

Classical Test Theory and Measurement Error
Sources of Measurement Error
Reliability Coefficients
The Standard Error of Measurement

Modern Test Theories
Reporting Reliability Information
Reliability: Practical Strategies for Educators
Summary

Learning Objectives

After reading and studying this chapter, students should be able to:

1. Define and explain the importance of reliability in psychological assessment.
2. Define and explain the concept of measurement error.
3. Explain classical test theory and its importance to psychological assessment.
4. Describe the major sources of measurement error and give examples.
5. Identify the major methods for estimating reliability and describe how these analyses are performed.
6. Identify the sources of measurement error that are reflected in different reliability estimates.

7. Describe steps that can be taken to improve reliability.
8. Define the standard error of measurement (SEM) and explain its importance.
9. Explain how SEM is calculated and describe its relation to reliability.
10. Explain how confidence intervals are calculated and used in psychological assessment.
11. Explain how reliability is addressed in generalizability and item response theory.
12. Read and interpret information on the reliability of test scores presented in a test manual.

109

> *In simplest terms, in the context of measurement, reliability refers to consistency or stability of assessment results.*

Most dictionaries define *reliability* in terms of dependability, trustworthiness, or having a high degree of confidence in something. Reliability in the context of psychological measurement is concerned to some extent with these same factors, but is extended to such concepts as stability and consistency. In simplest terms, in the context of measurement, **reliability** refers to the consistency, accuracy, or stability of assessment results. Although it is common for people to refer to the "reliability of a test," in the *Standards for Educational and Psychological Testing* (AERA et al., 1999) reliability is considered to be a characteristic of scores or assessment results, not tests themselves. Consider the following example: A teacher administers a 25-item math test in the morning to assess the students' skill in multiplying two-digit numbers.

- If the test had been administered in the afternoon rather than the morning, would Susie's score on the test have been the same?
- Because there are literally hundreds of two-digit multiplication problems, if the teacher had asked a different group of 25 two-digit multiplication problems, would Susie have received the same score?
- What about the ambulance that went by, its siren wailing loudly, causing Johnny to look up and watch for a few seconds? Did this affect his score, and did it affect Susie's who kept working quietly?
- Kareem wasn't feeling well that morning but came to school because he felt the test was so important. Would his score have been better if he had waited to take the test when he was feeling better?
- Would the students have received the same scores if another teacher had graded the test?

All of these questions involve issues of reliability of the scores obtained on the test. They all ask if the test produces stable and consistent scores.

> *Some degree of* **measurement error** *is inherent in all measurement.*

As you can see from these examples, numerous factors can affect reliability. The time the test is administered, the specific set of questions included on the test, distractions due to external (e.g., ambulances) or internal (e.g., illness) events, and the person grading the test are just a few of these factors. In this chapter you will learn to take many of the sources of unreliability into account when selecting or developing assessments and evaluating scores. You will also learn to estimate the degree of reliability in test scores with a method that best fits your particular situation. First, however, we will introduce the concept of measurement error as it is essential to developing a thorough understanding of reliability.

CLASSICAL TEST THEORY AND MEASUREMENT ERROR

Some degree of error is inherent in all measurement. Although **measurement error** has been studied largely in the context of psychological and educational tests, measurement error is clearly not unique to psychological and educational tests. In fact, as Nunnally and Bernstein (1994) pointed out, measurement in other scientific disciplines has as much, if not more, error than that in psychology and education. They gave the example of physiological blood pressure measurement, which is considerably less reliable than scores yielded by many psychological tests. Even in situations in which we generally believe measurement is exact, some error is present. If we asked a dozen people to time a 440-yard race using the same brand of stopwatch, it is extremely unlikely that they would all report precisely the same time. If we had a dozen people and a measuring tape graduated in millimeters, and required each person to measure independently the length of a 100-foot strip of land, it is unlikely all of them would report the same answer to the nearest millimeter. In the physical sciences the introduction of more technologically sophisticated measurement devices has reduced, but not eliminated, measurement error.

Over the last 100 years several theories or models have been developed to help us understand measurement issues, and the most influential is *classical test theory* (CTT), which is also referred to as *true score theory*. Charles Spearman (1907, 1913) laid the groundwork for classical test theory in the early 1900s. Other individuals such as Thurstone (1931), Guilford (1936), Thorndike (1949), Gulliksen (1950), Magnusson (1967), and Lord and Novick (1968) also made significant contributions to the development and statement of CTT. According to this theory, every score on a mental test is composed of two components: the true score (i.e., the score that would be obtained if there were no errors) and the error score. This can be represented in a very simple equation:

$$X_i = T + E$$

Here we use X_i to represent the observed or obtained score (X) of an individual (i). X_i is the score the examinee received on the test. The symbol T is used to represent an individual's true score and reflects the test taker's true skills, abilities, knowledge, attitudes, or whatever the test measures if it could be measured perfectly, with no error. Finally, E represents measurement error.

An individual has only one true score. However, he or she may receive different observed scores on different administrations of a test due to different amounts of measurement error. Consider these examples. On a 100-item multiple-choice test Tim actually knows the answer to 80 items (i.e., his true score) and makes lucky guesses on 5 and gets them correct (i.e., errors of measurement). His observed score is 85. Here $X_i = 85$, $T = 80$, and $E = 5$ (i.e., $85 = 80 + 5$). In this situation measurement error resulted in an increase in his observed score. This is not always the case and measurement errors can also reduce an individual's observed score. For example, if Tim knew the answer to 80 items (i.e., true score) but incorrectly marked the answer sheet on 5 items, his observed scores would now be 75. Here $X_i = 75$, $T = 80$, and $E = -5$ (i.e., $75 = 80 - 5$). In actual practice there are a multitude of factors that can introduce error into a test score, some raising the score and some lowering the score. These errors of measurement have a cumulative or additive effect. For example, if Tim knew the answer to 80 items, correctly guessed the answer on 3, and incorrectly marked the answer sheet on 2 items, his observed scores would be 81. The error score component is now 1 (i.e., $3 - 2$). Here $X_i = 81$, $T = 80$, and $E = 1$ (i.e., $81 = 80 + 1$).

As noted, CTT is concerned with measurement error that is defined as the difference between an individual's obtained and true score. CTT focuses our attention on *random* measurement error. Random measurement error is the result of chance factors that can either increase or decrease an individual's observed score. These random events vary from person to person, from test to test, and from administration to administration. There are also systematic sources of measurement error. *Systematic measurement error* involves systematic or consistent differences in test performance between groups of individuals that are the result of factors unrelated to the construct being measured. Systematic measurement error results in stable or consistent errors of measurement (i.e., the same amount of error every time). CTT is concerned only with random measurement error and does not consider systematic measurement error. Systematic measurement error does not result in inconsistent or unstable test scores and therefore is not considered in reliability analyses. However, we will touch on systematic measurement error in later sections of the text, particularly when addressing test bias, because systematic error is usually associated with a detectable source and biases scores in a consistent direction.

Now that you have a grasp on the basics of CTT, we will delve a little deeper and consider some general principles or assumptions of the theory. These include:

- The mean of error scores in a population is zero. Because random measurement error is random (e.g., sometimes increasing obtained scores, sometimes decreasing the obtained scores), it balances out over a large number of test administrations. Therefore, over a very large number of test administrations random measurement error will balance out and the mean will equal zero.
- The correlation between true score and error score is zero. True score is without error, so it does not have any systematic relationship with error. In other words, there is no relationship between an individual's level on a construct and the amount of measurement error impacting his or her observed score on any given administration of a test.
- The correlation between error scores on different measurements is zero. In other words, the amount of error in an individual's obtained score from one administration of a test is not related to the amount of error on any subsequent independent administrations of the test (or another test).

> *Measurement error limits the extent to which test results can be generalized and reduces the confidence we have in test results (AERA et al., 1999).*

Comprehension of the basic principles of CTT is essential for understanding reliability. CTT highlights the prevalence and characteristics of random measurement error. Measurement error reduces the usefulness of measurement, our ability to generalize test results, and the confidence we have in these results (AERA et al., 1999). Practically speaking, when we administer a test we are interested in knowing the test taker's true score. However, due to the presence of measurement error we can never know with absolute confidence the true score, so we usually refer to obtained scores or estimated true scores. CTT is also important because it presents a mathematical model that allows us to estimate the reliability of test scores. These estimates of reliability inform us about the amount of measurement error associated with test scores and how much confidence we should have in them. With information about the reliability of measurement, we can also establish intervals around an obtained score and calculate the probability that the true score will fall within the specified interval.

Before we proceed, we want to emphasize that our brief introduction to CTT is just that: brief and only an introduction. A thorough discussion of CTT requires presentation of the formal mathematical proofs that underlie the model. Although we will elaborate more on CTT in this chapter, we will not delve into these formal proofs. For the interested reader, more detailed descriptions are provided by Crocker and Algina (1986) and Osterlind (2006). Lord and Novick (1968) provide a detailed discussion of CTT that remains current and is well suited for readers with a more advanced background in mathematics.

SOURCES OF MEASUREMENT ERROR

Because measurement error is so pervasive, it is beneficial to be knowledgeable both about its characteristics and the methods that are available for estimating its magnitude. Generally, whenever you hear a discussion of reliability or read about the reliability of test scores, it is the score's relative freedom from measurement errors that is being discussed. Reliable assessment results are relatively free from measurement error whereas less reliable results are influenced to a larger degree by measurement error. A number of factors may introduce error into test scores and even though all cannot be assigned to distinct categories, it may be helpful to group these sources in some manner and to discuss their relative contributions. The types of errors that are our greatest concern are errors due to content sampling and time sampling.

Content Sampling Error

Tests rarely, if ever, include every possible question or evaluate every possible relevant behavior. Let's revisit the example we introduced at the beginning of this chapter. A teacher administers a math test designed to assess students' skill in multiplying two-digit numbers. We noted that there are literally

> *Content sampling is typically considered the largest source of error in test scores.*

hundreds of two-digit multiplication problems. Obviously it would be impractical (and unnecessary) for the teacher to develop and administer a test that includes all possible items. Instead, a universe or domain of test items is defined based on the content of the material to be covered. From this domain, a sample of test questions is taken. In this example, the teacher decided to select 25 items to measure students' ability. These 25 items are simply a sample of the item domain and, as with any sampling procedure, may or may not be representative of the domain from which they are drawn. The error that results from differences between the sample of items (i.e., the test) and the domain of items (i.e., all the possible items) is referred to as content sampling error. Content sampling error is typically considered the largest source of error in test scores and therefore is the source that concerns us most. Fortunately, content sampling error is also the easiest and most accurately estimated source of measurement error.

The amount of measurement error due to content sampling is determined by how well we sample the total domain of items. If the items on a test are a good sample of the domain, the amount of measurement error due to content sampling will be relatively small. If the items on a test are a poor sample of the domain, the amount of measurement error due to content sampling will be relatively large. Measurement error resulting from content sampling is estimated by analyzing the degree of similarity among the items making up the test. In other words, we analyze the test items to determine how well they correlate with one another and with the examinee's standing on the construct being measured. We will explore a variety of methods for estimating measurement errors due to content sampling later in this chapter.

Time Sampling Error

> *Measurement error due to time sampling reflects random fluctuations in performance from one situation to another and limits our ability to generalize test scores across different situations.*

Measurement error can also be introduced by one's choice of a particular time to administer the test. If Jose did not have breakfast and the math test was just before lunch, he might be distracted or hurried and not perform as well as if he took the test after lunch. But Michael, who ate too much at lunch and was up late last night, was sleepy in the afternoon and might not perform as well on an afternoon test as he would have on the morning test. If during the morning testing session a neighboring class was making enough noise to be disruptive, the class might have performed better in the afternoon when the neighboring class was relatively quiet. These are all examples of situations in which random changes in the test taker (e.g., fatigue, illness, anxiety) or the testing environment (e.g., distractions, temperature) impact performance on the test. This type of measurement error is referred to as time sampling error and reflects random fluctuations in performance from one situation or time to another and limits our ability to generalize test results across different situations. Some assessment experts refer to this type of error as temporal instability. As you might expect, testing experts have developed methods of estimating error due to time sampling.

Other Sources of Error

Although errors due to content sampling and time sampling typically account for the major proportion of random error in testing, administrative and scoring errors that do not affect all test takers equally will also contribute to the random error observed in scores. Clerical errors committed while adding up a student's score or an administrative error on an individually administered test are common examples. When the scoring of a test relies heavily on the subjective judgment of the person grading the test or involves subtle discriminations, it is important to consider differences in graders, usually referred to as inter-rater (interscorer) differences. That is, would the test taker receive the same score if different individuals graded the test? For example, on an essay test would two different graders assign the same scores? These are just a few examples of sources of error that do not fit neatly into the broad categories of content or time sampling errors.

RELIABILITY COEFFICIENTS

You will note that we refer to reliability as being *estimated*. This is because the absolute or precise reliability of assessment results cannot be known. Just as we always have some error in test scores, we also have some error in our attempts to measure reliability. However, the methods of estimating reliability we will discuss are conservative and considered to be lower bound estimates of the true reliability of test scores. In other words, the actual reliability of test scores is at least as high, and possibly higher, than the estimated reliability (Reynolds, 1999).

Earlier in this chapter we introduced CTT, which holds that test scores are composed of two components, the true score and the error score. We represented this with the equation:

$$X_i = T + E$$

As you remember, X_i represents an individual's obtained score, T represents the true score, and E represents random measurement error. This equation can be extended to incorporate the concept of variance. The extension indicates that the variance of test scores is the sum of the true score variance plus the error variance, and is represented in the following equation:

$$\sigma^2_X = \sigma^2_T + \sigma^2_E$$

Here, σ^2_X represents the variance of the total test, σ^2_T represents true score variance, and σ^2_E represents the variance due to measurement error. True score variance reflects differences in test takers due to real differences in skills, abilities, knowledge, attitudes, and so on, whereas the total score variance is made up of true score variance plus variance due to all the sources of random error we have previously described.

> *Reliability can be defined as the proportion of test score variance due to true score differences.*

The general symbol for the reliability of assessment results is r_{xx} and is referred to as the reliability coefficient. We estimate the reliability of a test score as the ratio of true score variance to total score variance. Mathematically, reliability is written:

$$r_{XX} = \sigma^2_T / \sigma^2_X$$

This equation defines the reliability of test scores as the proportion of test score variance due to true score differences. The reliability coefficient is considered to be the summary mathematical representation of this ratio or proportion. Another index of reliability that is useful in the context of measurement theory is the reliability index, and it is briefly discussed in Special Interest Topic 4.1.

SPECIAL INTEREST TOPIC 4.1

The Reliability Index

As noted in this chapter, reliability coefficients are designated with the symbol r_{XX} and are mathematically defined as the ratio of true score variance to observed score variance. Stated another way, reliability coefficients are interpreted as the proportion of observed score variance that is the result of variance in true scores. Although we primarily focus our attention in this chapter on the interpretation of reliability coefficients, there is an equally important correlation that is integral to CTT. That is the *reliability index*. The reliability index is an index that reflects the correlation between true and observed scores. For example, if the reliability index is equal to 1.0, then all true scores (T) and observed scores (X) are equal and there is no measurement error.

Because true scores are not directly observable, the reliability index is a theoretical concept and cannot be calculated directly. However, we do know the mathematical relationship between the reliability coefficient and the reliability index. That is, the reliability index is the square root of the reliability coefficient. For example, if the reliability coefficient is 0.81, the reliability index is 0.90. In this example, the reliability coefficient of 0.81 indicates that 81% of the observed score variance is due to true score variance. The reliability index of 0.90 reflects the correlation between observed and true scores.

Reliability coefficients can be classified into three broad categories (AERA et al., 1999). These include (1) coefficients derived from the administration of the same test on different occasions (i.e., test-retest reliability), (2) coefficients based on the administration of parallel forms of a test (i.e., alternate-form reliability), and (3) coefficients derived from a single administration of a test (internal consistency coefficients). A fourth type, inter-rater reliability, is indicated when scoring involves a significant degree of subjective judgment. The major methods of estimating reliability are summarized in Table 4–1. Each of these approaches produces a reliability coefficient (r_{xx}) that can be interpreted in terms of the proportion or percentage of test score variance attributable to true variance. For example, a reliability coefficient of 0.90 indicates that 90% of the variance in test scores is attributable to true variance. The remaining 10% reflects error variance. We will now consider each of these methods of estimating reliability.

TABLE 4–1	Major Types of Reliability			
Type of Reliability Estimate	**Common Symbol**	**Number of Test Forms**	**Number of Testing Sessions**	**Summary**
Test-retest	r_{12}	One form	Two sessions	Administer the same test to the same group at two different sessions.
Alternate forms				
Simultaneous administration	r_{ab}	Two forms	One session	Administer two forms of the test to the same group in the same session.
Delayed administration	r_{ab}	Two forms	Two sessions	Administer two forms of the test to the same group at two different sessions.
Split-half	r_{oe}	One form	One session	Administer the test to a group one time. Split the test into two equivalent halves.
Coefficient alpha or KR-20	r_{xx}	One form	One session	Administer the test to a group one time. Apply appropriate procedures.
Inter-rater	r	One form	One session	Administer the test to a group one time. Two or more raters score the test independently.

Test-Retest Reliability

Probably the most obvious way to estimate the reliability of a test score is to administer the same test to the same group of individuals on two different occasions. With this approach the reliability coefficient is obtained by simply calculating the correlation between the scores on the two administrations. For example, we could administer our 25-item math test one week after the initial administration and then correlate the scores obtained on the two administrations. This estimate of reliability is referred to as **test-retest reliability** and is primarily sensitive to measurement error due to time sampling. It is an index of the stability of test scores over time, and some authors refer to coefficients obtained with this approach as stability coefficients. Because many tests are intended to measure fairly stable characteristics, we expect tests of these constructs to produce stable scores. Test-retest reliability reflects the degree to which test scores can be generalized across different situations or over time.

> **Test-retest reliability** *is primarily sensitive to measurement error due to time sampling and is an index of the stability of scores over time.*

One important consideration when calculating and evaluating test-retest reliability is the length of the interval between the two test administrations. If the test-retest interval is very short (e.g., hours or days), the reliability estimate may be artificially inflated by memory and practice effects from the first administration. If the test interval is longer, the estimate of reliability may be lowered not only by the instability of the scores but also by actual changes in the test takers during the extended period. In practice, there is no single "best" time interval, but the optimal interval is determined by the way the test results are to be used. For example, intelligence is a construct or characteristic that is thought to be fairly stable, so it would be reasonable to expect stability in intelligence scores over weeks or months. In contrast, an individual's mood (e.g., depressed, elated, nervous) is more subject to transient fluctuations and stability across weeks or months would not be expected. In the latter case, a test-retest study may be telling you more about the stability of the trait, state, or construct being assessed than about the stability of test scores per se. This distinction too often is overlooked in discussions of test score reliability.

In addition to the construct being measured, the way the test is to be used is an important consideration in determining what is an appropriate test-retest interval. Because the SAT is used to predict performance in college, it is sensible to expect stability over relatively long periods of time. In other situations, long-term stability is much less of an issue. For example, the long-term stability of a classroom achievement test (such as our math test) is not a major concern because it is expected that the students will be enhancing existing skills and acquiring new ones due to class instruction and studying. In summary, when evaluating the stability of test scores, one should consider the length of the test-retest interval in the context of the characteristics being measured and how the scores are to be used.

The test-retest approach does have significant limitations, the most prominent being carryover effects from the first to second testing. Practice and memory effects result in different amounts of improvement in retest scores for different test takers.

> *The test-retest approach does have significant limitations, the most prominent being carryover effects from the first to second testing.*

These carryover effects prevent the two administrations from being independent, and as a result the reliability coefficients may be artificially inflated. In other instances, repetition of the test may change either the nature of the test or the test taker in some subtle way (Ghiselli, Campbell, & Zedeck, 1981). As a result, only tests that are not appreciably influenced by these carryover effects are suitable for this method of estimating reliability.

Alternate-Form Reliability

Alternate-form reliability *based on simultaneous administration is primarily sensitive to measurement error due to content sampling.*

Another approach to estimating reliability involves the development of two equivalent or parallel forms of the test. The development of these alternate forms requires a detailed test plan and considerable effort since the tests must be truly parallel in terms of content, difficulty, and other relevant characteristics. The two forms of the test are then administered to the same group of individuals and the correlation is calculated between the scores on the two assessments. In our example of the 25-item math test, the teacher could develop a parallel test containing 25 different problems involving the multiplication of double digits (i.e., from the same item domain). To be parallel the items would need to be presented in the same format and be of the same level of difficulty. Two fairly common procedures are used to establish **alternate-form reliability**. One is alternate-form reliability based on simultaneous administrations and is

Alternate-form reliability *based on delayed administration is sensitive to measurement error due to content sampling and time sampling.*

obtained when the two forms of the test are administered on the same occasion (i.e., back-to-back). The other, alternate-form with delayed administration, is obtained when the two forms of the test are administered on two different occasions. Alternate-form reliability based on simultaneous administration is primarily sensitive to measurement error related to content sampling. Alternate-form reliability with delayed administration is sensitive to measurement error due to both content sampling and time sampling.

Alternate-form reliability has the advantage of reducing the carryover effects that are a prominent concern with test-retest reliability. However, although practice and memory effects may be reduced using the alternate-form approach, typically they are not fully eliminated. Simply exposing examinees to the common format required for parallel tests often results in some carryover effects even if the content of the two tests is different. For example, an examinee given a test measuring nonverbal reasoning abilities may develop strategies during the administration of the first form that alter her approach to the second form, even if the specific content of the items is different. Another limitation of the alternate-form approach to estimating reliability is that relatively few tests, standardized or teacher-made, have alternate forms. As we suggested, the development of alternate forms that are actually equivalent is a time-consuming process, and many test developers do not pursue this option. Nevertheless, at times it is desirable to have more than one form of a test, and when multiple forms exist, alternate-form reliability is an important consideration.

Internal Consistency Reliability

Internal consistency reliability estimates primarily reflect errors related to content sampling. These estimates are based on the relationship between items within a test and are derived from a single administration of the test.

SPLIT-HALF RELIABILITY. Estimating **split-half reliability** involves administering a test and then dividing the test into two equivalent halves that are scored independently. The results on one half of the test are then correlated with results on the other half of the test by calculating the Pearson product-moment correlation. Obviously, there are many ways a test can be divided in half. For example, one might

> *Split-half reliability* can *be calculated from one administration of a test and primarily reflects error due to content sampling.*

correlate scores on the first half of the test with scores on the second half. This is usually not a good idea because the items on some tests get more difficult as the test progresses, resulting in halves that are not actually equivalent. Other factors such as practice effects, fatigue, or declining attention that increases as the test progresses can also make the first and second half of the test not equivalent. A more acceptable approach would be to assign test items randomly to one half or the other. However, the most common approach is to use an odd–even split. Here all "odd"-numbered items go into one half and all "even"-numbered items go into the other half. A correlation is then calculated between scores on the odd-numbered and even-numbered items.

Before we can use this correlation coefficient as an estimate of reliability, there is one more task to perform. Because we are actually correlating two halves of the test, the reliability coefficient does not take into account the reliability of the test scores when the two halves are combined. In essence, this initial coefficient reflects the reliability of only a shortened, half-test. As a general rule, longer tests produce scores that are more reliable than shorter tests. If we have twice as many test items, then we are able to sample the domain of test questions more accurately. The better we sample the domain the lower the error due to content sampling and the higher the reliability of our test scores. To "put the two halves of the test back together" with regard to a reliability estimate, we use a correction formula commonly referred to as the Spearman-Brown formula. To estimate the reliability of scores on the full test, the Spearman-Brown formula is generally applied as:

$$\text{Reliability of Scores on Full Test} = \frac{2 \times \text{Reliability of Half-Test Scores}}{1 + \text{Reliability of Half-Test Scores}}$$

Here is an example. Suppose the correlation between odd and even halves of your midterm in this course was 0.74, the calculation using the Spearman-Brown formula would go as follows:

$$\text{Reliability of Full-Test Score} = \frac{2 \times 0.74}{1 + 0.74}$$

$$\text{Reliability of Full-Test Score} = \frac{1.48}{1.74} = 0.85$$

The reliability coefficient of 0.85 estimates the reliability of the full test score when the odd–even halves correlated at 0.74. This demonstrates that the uncorrected split-half

TABLE 4–2	Half-Test Coefficients and Corresponding Full-Test Coefficients Corrected with the Spearman-Brown Formula	
Half-Test Correlation	**Spearman-Brown Reliability**	
0.50	0.67	
0.55	0.71	
0.60	0.75	
0.65	0.79	
0.70	0.82	
0.75	0.86	
0.80	0.89	
0.85	0.92	
0.90	0.95	
0.95	0.97	

reliability coefficient presents an underestimate of the reliability of the full test score. Table 4–2 provides examples of half-test coefficients and the corresponding full-test coefficients that were corrected with the Spearman-Brown formula. By looking at the first row in this table you will see that a half-test correlation of 0.50 corresponds to a corrected full-test coefficient of 0.67.

Although the odd–even approach is the most common way to divide a test and will generally produce equivalent halves, certain situations deserve special attention. For example, if you have a test with a relatively small number of items (e.g., <8), it may be desirable to divide the test into equivalent halves based on a careful review of item characteristics such as content, format, and difficulty. Another situation that deserves special attention involves groups of items that deal with an integrated problem (this is referred to as a testlet). For example, if multiple questions refer to a specific diagram or reading passage, that whole set of questions should be included in the same half of the test. Splitting integrated problems can artificially inflate the reliability estimate (e.g., Sireci, Thissen, & Wainer, 1991).

An advantage of the split-half approach to reliability is that it can be calculated from a single administration of a test. However, because only one testing session is involved, this approach primarily reflects only errors due to content sampling.

COEFFICIENT ALPHA AND KUDER-RICHARDSON RELIABILITY. Other approaches to estimating reliability from a single administration of a test are based on formulas developed by Kuder and Richardson (1937) and Cronbach (1951). Instead of comparing responses on two halves of the test as in split-half reliability, this approach examined the consistency of responding to all the individual items on the test. Reliability estimates produced with these formulas can be thought of as the average of all possible split-half coefficients and are properly corrected for the length of the whole test. Like split-half reliability, these estimates are sensitive to measurement error introduced by content sampling. Additionally, they are also sensitive to the heterogeneity of the test content. When we refer to content heterogeneity, we are concerned with the degree to which the test items measure related characteristics. For example, our 25-item math test involving multiplying two-digit numbers would probably be more homogeneous than a test designed to measure both multiplication and division. An even more heterogeneous test would be one that involves multiplication and reading comprehension, two fairly dissimilar content domains.

Whereas Kuder and Richardson's formulas and coefficient alpha both reflect item heterogeneity and errors due to content sampling, there is an important difference in terms of their application. In their original article Kuder and Richardson (1937) presented numerous formulas for estimating reliability. The most commonly used formula is known as the **Kuder-Richardson formula 20 (KR-20)**. KR-20 is applicable when test items are scored dichotomously, that is, simply right or wrong, scored 0 or 1. **Coefficient alpha** (Cronbach, 1951) is a more general form of KR-20 that also deals with test items that produce scores with multiple values (e.g., 0, 1, or 2). Because coefficient alpha is more broadly applicable, it has become the preferred statistic for estimating internal consistency (Keith & Reynolds, 1990). Tables 4–3 and 4–4 illustrate the calculation of KR-20 and coefficient alpha, respectively.

> **Coefficient alpha *and* Kuder-Richardson reliability *are sensitive to error introduced by content sampling, but also reflect the heterogeneity of test content.***

Inter-Rater Reliability

If the scoring of a test relies on subjective judgment, it is important to evaluate the degree of agreement when different individuals score the test. This is referred to as inter-scorer or **inter-rater reliability**. Estimating inter-rater reliability is a fairly straightforward process. The test is administered one time and two individuals independently score each test. A correlation is then calculated between the scores obtained by the two scorers. This estimate of reliability primarily reflects differences due to the individuals scoring the test and largely ignores error due to content or time sampling. In addition to the correlational approach, inter-rater agreement can also

> *If the scoring of an assessment relies on subjective judgement, it is important to evaluate the degree of agreement when different individuals score the test. This is referred to as* **inter-rater reliability.**

be evaluated by calculating the percentage of times that two individuals assign the same scores to the performances of students. This approach is typically referred to as *inter-rater agreement* or *percentage agreement* and its calculation is illustrated in Table 4–5. Many authors prefer *Cohen's kappa* over the standard percentage of agreement when analyzing categorical data. Kappa is a more robust measure of agreement as it takes into consideration the degree of agreement expected by chance (Hays, 1994). A weighted kappa coefficient is also available that is appropriate for ordinal-level data and takes into consideration how disparate the ratings are. For comparative purposes, kappa and weighted kappa are also reported in Table 4–5. Kappa is also used in any instance where the agreement in classification is of interest. Circumstances where this might occur can include whether a test is administered at two different points in time and used to classify people into diagnostic groups (or other groups, such those to hire and those to reject). In this case, each person would be classified or assigned to a group using the obtained test scores from each occasion and the degree of agreement across times compared via kappa. One could also use two different tests on the same group of people at the same point

TABLE 4–3	Calculating KR-20

KR-20 is sensitive to measurement error due to content sampling and is also a measure of item heterogeneity. KR-20 is applicable when test items are scored dichotomously, that is, simply right or wrong, scored 0 or 1. The formula for calculating KR-20 is:

$$KR\text{-}20 = \frac{k}{k-1}\left(\frac{SD^2 - \sum p_i \times q_i}{SD^2}\right)$$

where:

k = number of items

SD^2 = variance of total test scores

p_i = proportion of correct responses on item

q_i = proportion of incorrect responses on item

Consider these data for a five-item test that was administered to six students. Each item could receive a score of either 1 or 0.

	Item 1	Item 2	Item 3	Item 4	Item 5	Total Score
Student 1	1	0	1	1	1	4
Student 2	1	1	1	1	1	5
Student 3	1	0	1	0	0	2
Student 4	0	0	0	1	0	1
Student 5	1	1	1	1	1	5
Student 6	1	1	0	1	1	4
p_i	0.8333	0.5	0.6667	0.8333	0.6667	$SD^2 = 2.25$
q_i	0.1667	0.5	0.3333	0.1667	0.3333	
$p_i \times q_i$	0.1389	0.25	0.2222	0.1389	0.2222	

Note: When calculating SD^2, n was used in the denominator.

$\sum p_i \times q_i = 0.1389 + 0.25 + 0.2222 + 0.1389 + 0.2222$

$\sum p_i \times q_i = 0.972$

$$KR\text{-}20 = \frac{5}{4}\left(\frac{2.25 - 0.972}{2.25}\right)$$

$$= 1.25\left(\frac{1.278}{2.25}\right)$$

$$= 1.25(0.568)$$

$$= 0.71$$

in time, and classify them separately using each set of test scores, and then compute the cross-test agreement in classification.

On some tests, inter-rater reliability is of little concern. For example, on a test with multiple-choice or true–false items, grading is fairly straightforward and a conscientious grader should produce reliable and accurate scores. In the case of our 25-item math test, a careful grader should be able to determine whether the students' answers are accurate and assign a score consistent with that of another careful grader. However, for some tests inter-rater reliability is a major concern.

TABLE 4–4 Calculating Coefficient Alpha

Coefficient alpha is sensitive to measurement error due to content sampling and is also a measure of item heterogeneity. It can be applied to tests with items that are scored dichotomously or that have multiple values. The formula for calculating coefficient alpha is:

$$\text{Coefficient Alpha} = \left(\frac{k}{k-1}\right)\left(1 - \frac{\sum SD_i^2}{SD^2}\right)$$

where:

k = number of items

SD_i^2 = variance of individual items

SD^2 = variance of total test scores

Consider these data for a five-item test that was administered to six students. Each item could receive a score ranging from 1 to 5.

	Item 1	Item 2	Item 3	Item 4	Item 5	Total Score
Student 1	4	3	4	5	5	21
Student 2	3	3	2	3	3	14
Student 3	2	3	2	2	1	10
Student 4	4	4	5	3	4	20
Student 5	2	3	4	2	3	14
Student 6	2	2	2	1	3	10
SD_i^2	0.8056	0.3333	1.4722	1.5556	1.4722	$SD^2 = 18.81$

Note: When calculating SD_i^2 and SD^2, n was used in the denominator.

$$\text{Coefficient Alpha} = \frac{5}{4}\left(1 - \frac{0.8056 + 0.3333 + 1.4722 + 1.5556 + 1.4722}{18.81}\right)$$

$$= 1.25\left(1 - \frac{5.63889}{18.81}\right)$$

$$= 1.25(1 - 0.29978)$$

$$= 1.25(0.70)$$

$$= 0.875$$

TABLE 4–5 Calculating Inter-Rater Agreement

The scoring of many psychological and educational assessments requires subjective judgment. For example, in academic settings students might engage in debates, compose poems, or perform pieces of music as part of their course requirements. The evaluation of these types of tasks is typically based on scoring rubrics that specify what aspects of the student's performance should be considered when providing a score or grade. Subjective scoring is not limited to educational assessments but is also common on psychological tests. For example, many intelligence and achievement tests include subtests that require subjective scoring. The Comprehension, Vocabulary, and Similarities subtests on the Wechsler Intelligence Scale for Children—Fourth Edition, for instance, all involve some degree of subjective scoring. When scoring involves the subjective judgment, inter-rater reliability is an important concern. As noted in the text, one approach to estimating inter-rater reliability is to calculate the correlation between the scores that are assigned by two judges. Another approach is to calculate the percentage of agreement between the judges' scores.

Consider an example where two judges rated poems composed by 25 students. The poems were scored from 1 to 5 based on criteria specified in a rubric, with 1 being the lowest performance and 5 being the highest. The results are illustrated in the following table:

(Continued on page 124)

TABLE 4–5	Calculating Inter-Rater Agreement (*Continued*)				
Ratings of Rater 2	**Ratings of Rater 1**				
	1	**2**	**3**	**4**	**5**
5	0	0	1	2	**4**
4	0	0	2	**3**	2
3	0	2	**3**	1	0
2	1	**1**	1	0	0
1	**1**	1	0	0	0

Once the data are recorded you can calculate inter-rater agreement with the following formula:

$$\text{Inter-Rater Agreement} = \frac{\text{Number of Cases Assigned the Same Scores}}{\text{Total Number of Cases}} \times 100$$

In our example the calculation would be:

$$\text{Inter-Rater Agreement} = \frac{12}{25} \times 100$$

$$\text{Inter-Rater Agreement} = 48\%$$

This degree of inter-rater agreement might appear low to you, but this would actually be respectable for a classroom test. In fact the Pearson correlation between these judges' ratings is 0.80 (better than many, if not most, constructed-response assessments).

Instead of requiring the judges to assign the exact same score for agreement, some authors suggest the less rigorous criterion of scores being within one point of each other (e.g., Linn & Gronlund, 2000). If this criterion were applied to these data, the modified agreement percent would be 96% because there was only one score where the judges were not within one point of each other (Rater 1 assigned a 3 and Rater 2, a 5).

As we noted, some authors prefer Cohen's kappa when calculating inter-rater reliability because it takes into consideration chance agreement and is therefore a more robust measure of inter-rater agreement. Using the data previously given, Cohen's kappa is 0.327 (interpreted as reflecting fair agreement) and the weighted kappa is 0.594. If one compares kappa to simple inter-rater agreement (i.e., 0.327 vs. 0.48), it is apparent that kappa is a more rigorous approach when exact agreement is required. Similarly, if one compares the weighted kappa to the modified percent agreement (i.e., 0.594 vs. 0.96), the same pattern appears.

Classroom essay tests are a classic example. It is common for students to feel that a different teacher might have assigned a different score to their essay. It can be argued that the teacher's personal biases, preferences, or mood influenced the score, not only the content and quality of the student's essay. Even on our 25-item math test, if the teacher required that the students "show their work" and this influenced the students' grades, subjective judgment might be involved and inter-rater reliability could be a concern.

Reliability Estimates Are Not Independent

We noted earlier that coefficient alpha is the average of all split-half test score correlations corrected for test length. This means that it is also the average of the correlations of every test item with every other item on the test. We point this out because as a corollary, it is true that anything that reduces the average inter-item correlation also reduces the value of alpha. Thus, although we think of alpha and related reliability coefficients as estimates of the internal consistency reliability (i.e., homogeneity of item domain sampling) of a test score, they are in reality much broader values, making alpha (as the best of its breed) the preferred reliability estimate.

In an attempt to determine the total amount of error in a test score, some researchers will sum the error due to domain sampling as estimated by alpha and the inter-rater error, for example. These estimates are not independent, however, as inter-rater error lowers the average-inter-item correlation and is thus accounted for in alpha due to its method of calculation. Alpha also sets limits on test-retest correlations. The theoretical maximum test-retest coefficient is the square root of alpha. Whereas in practice it is possible to obtain a higher value due to chance factors (i.e., the chance occurrence of a correlation between error terms that are actually not correlated!), the true value of a test-retest correlation cannot exceed the square root of alpha.

> *Any source of error that would reduce the average inter-item correlation is reflected by coefficient alpha.*

Not only is it unnecessary to sum estimates of error in an effort to determine the total amount of error present is a test score, it can be misleading. Any potential source of error that would reduce the average inter-item correlation (e.g., administration errors, scoring errors, differing levels of effort by some examinees on hard items, etc.) is already accounted for by alpha.

Reliability of Composite Scores

Psychological and educational measurement often yields multiple scores that can be combined to form a composite. For example, the assignment of grades in educational settings is often based on a composite of several tests and other assessments administered over a grading period or semester. Many standardized psychological instruments contain several measures that are combined to form an overall **composite score**. For example, the Wechsler Adult Intelligence Scale—Third Edition (Wechsler, 1997) is composed of 11 subtests that are used in the calculation of the Full Scale Intelligence Quotient (FSIQ). Both of these situations involve composite scores that are obtained by combining the scores on several different tests or subtests. The advantage of composite scores is that the reliability of composite scores is generally greater than that of the individual scores that contribute to the composite. More precisely, the reliability of a composite is the result of the number of scores in the composite, the reliability of the individual scores, and the correlation between those scores. The more scores in the composite, the higher the correlation between those scores, and the higher the individual reliabilities the higher the composite reliability. As we noted, tests are simply samples of the test domain, and combining multiple measures is analogous to increasing the number of observations or the sample size. Table 4–6 illustrates the computation of the reliability of a linear combination.

> *Reliability of composite scores is generally greater than the measures that contribute to the composite.*

Reliability of Difference Scores

There are a number of situations where researchers and clinicians want to consider the difference between two scores. Here the variable of interest is a difference score that is calculated as:

$$D = X - Y$$

TABLE 4–6 Calculating the Reliability of a Linear Combination

Nunnally (1978) illustrated a method of calculating the reliability of a linear combination that is often used in psychometric studies. The standard score formula is:

$$r_{yy} = 1 - \frac{k - \Sigma r_{ii}}{\sigma^2_y}$$

where:

r_{yy} = Reliability of the linear combination

k = Number of scores in the linear combination

Σr_{ii} = Sum of the reliabilities of the scores

σ^2_y = Variance of the linear combination

The only quantity in the formula that requires some extra work is σ^2_y. This may be calculated with data derived from the correlation matrix of the measures to be combined in the composite. Consider an example where we have three measures (A, B, and C) we wish to combine into a linear composite. The correlation matrix could be:

Measures	A	B	C
A	1.0	0.70	0.60
B	0.70	1.0	0.80
C	0.60	0.80	1.0

In this example, the correlation between measures A and B is 0.70, between A and C is 0.60, and between B and C is 0.80. One can calculate σ^2_y by summing the values in this matrix. In this example $\sigma^2_y = 7.2$

For this example, we will assume the reliability of the all three measures is 0.80. Therefore, $\Sigma r_{ii} = 2.40$ (i.e., 0.80 + 0.80 + 0.80 = 2.40).

There are three measures, so $k = 3$.

$$r_{yy} = 1 - \frac{3 - 2.4}{7.2}$$

$$= 1 - \frac{0.6}{7.2}$$

$$= 1 - 0.0833$$

$$= 0.92$$

This illustrates how three measures that produce scores with acceptable reliability (i.e., 0.80) and moderate to strong intercorrelations (i.e., between 0.60 and 0.80) can be combined to form a composite with excellent reliability.

where X is the score on one test and Y is the score on the other test. For example, one approach to diagnosing learning disabilities involves calculating difference scores by subtracting an examinee's score on an achievement test (e.g., reading comprehension) from the IQ. The assumption is that if the discrepancy is negative and sufficiently large (e.g., 2 or more SDs), the examinee is not demonstrating academic achievement commensurate with aptitude. If further assessment rules out a number of explanations such as inadequate educational opportunities or

Reliability of difference scores is typically considerably lower than the reliabilities of the individual scores.

sensory impairment (e.g., visual or auditory problems), the discrepancy might reflect an inherent learning disability (this approach to diagnosing learning disabilities has many detractors, and that debate will be discussed in Chapter 9). Another common situation where difference scores are used is when a psychologist wants to consider gains (or losses) in test performance over time. For example, a researcher might want to determine if a specific treatment results in improved performance on a certain task. This is often accomplished by administering pre- and post-intervention tests.

In these situations the variable of interest is a difference score. When dealing with difference scores it is important to remember that the reliability of difference scores is typically considerably lower than the reliabilities of the individual scores. As a general rule, the reliability of difference scores is higher when the original measures have high reliabilities and low correlations with each other. For example, consider an IQ with a reliability of 0.90, an achievement test with a reliability of 0.80, and a correlation between the two of 0.50. The reliability of the difference score would equal 0.70. Although the reliabilities of the initial two measures were reasonable, the reliability of the resulting difference score is marginal at best. If the correlation between the IQ and achievement tests were 0.60 instead of 0.50, the reliability of the difference scores would fall to 0.63.

In summary, one should be cautious when interpreting difference scores. The reliability of difference scores is typically considerably lower than the reliabilities of the individual scores. To exacerbate the problem, difference scores are often calculated using scores that have fairly strong correlations with each other (e.g., IQ and achievement scores; pre- and posttest scores). Table 4–7 provides an illustration of the computation of difference scores.

TABLE 4–7	Calculating the Reliability of Difference Scores

The standard score formula for calculating the reliability of a difference scores is:

$$r_{DD} = \frac{0.5(r_{AA} + r_{BB}) - r_{AB}}{1 - r_{AB}}$$

where

r_{DD} = reliability of the difference score

r_{AA} = reliability of Test A

r_{BB} = reliability of Test B

r_{AB} = correlation between the two tests

Consider the case where the reliability of Test A = 0.80, the reliability of Test B = 0.80, and the correlation between the two tests is 0.60.

$$r_{DD} = \frac{0.5(0.80 + 0.80) - 0.60}{1 - 0.60} = \frac{0.80 - 0.60}{0.40} = \frac{0.20}{0.40} = 0.50$$

If the correlation between the two tests were 0.30, the reliability of the difference score would be considerably higher, as illustrated here:

$$r_{DD} = \frac{0.5(0.80 + 0.80) - 0.30}{1 - 0.30} = \frac{0.80 - 0.30}{0.70} = \frac{0.50}{0.70} = 0.71$$

This illustrates how the reliability of difference scores is influenced by the strength of the correlation between the two tests.

Selecting a Reliability Coefficient

Table 4–8 summarizes the major sources of measurement error reflected in different reliability coefficients. As we have suggested in our discussion of each approach to estimating reliability, different conditions call for different estimates of reliability. One should consider factors such as the nature of the construct and how the scores will be used when selecting an estimate of reliability. If a test is designed to be given more than one time to the same individuals, test-retest and alternate-form reliability with delayed administration are

> *One should consider factors such as the nature of the construct being measured and how the scores will be used when selecting an estimate of reliability.*

appropriate because they are sensitive to measurement errors resulting from time sampling. Accordingly, if a test is used to predict an individual's performance on a criterion in the future, it is also important to use a reliability estimate that reflects errors due to time sampling.

When a test is designed to be administered only one time, an estimate of internal consistency is appropriate. As we noted, split-half reliability estimates error variance resulting from content sampling whereas coefficient alpha and KR-20 estimate error variance due to content sampling and content heterogeneity. Because KR-20 and coefficient alpha are sensitive to content heterogeneity, they are applicable when the test measures a homogeneous domain of knowledge or a unitary characteristic. For example, our 25-item test measuring the ability to multiply double digits reflects a homogeneous domain, and coefficient alpha would provide a good estimate of reliability. However, if we have a 50-item test, 25 measuring multiplication with double digits and 25 measuring division, the domain is more heterogeneous, and coefficient alpha and KR-20 would probably underestimate reliability. In the latter situation, in which we have a test with heterogeneous content (where the heterogeneity is intended and not a mistake), the split-half method is preferred. Because the goal of the split-half approach is to compare two equivalent halves, it would be possible to ensure that each half has equal numbers of both multiplication and division problems.

We have been focusing on tests of achievement when providing examples, but the same principles apply to other types of tests. For example, a test that measures depressed mood may

TABLE 4–8 Major Sources of Error Variance Associated with Types of Reliability	
Type of Reliability	**Major Source of Error Variance**
Test-retest reliability	Time sampling
Alternate-form reliability	
Simultaneous administration	Content sampling
Delayed administration	Time sampling and content sampling
Split-half reliability	Content sampling
Coefficient alpha and KR-20	Content sampling and item heterogeneity
Inter-rater reliability	Differences due to raters/scorers

assess a fairly homogeneous domain, making the use of coefficient alpha or KR-20 appropriate. However, if the test measures depression, anxiety, anger, and impulsiveness, the content becomes more heterogeneous and the split-half estimate would be indicated. In this situation, the split-half approach would allow the construction of two equivalent halves with equal numbers of items reflecting the different traits or characteristics under investigation.

Naturally, if different forms of a test are available, it would be important to estimate alternate-form reliability of the score. If a test involves subjective judgment by the person scoring the test, inter-rater reliability is important. Many contemporary test manuals report multiple estimates of reliability, and we will illustrate this in a later section of this chapter.

Evaluating Reliability Coefficients

Another important question that arises when considering reliability coefficients is "How large do reliability coefficients need to be?" Remember, we said reliability coefficients can be interpreted in terms of the proportion of test score variance attributable to true variance. Ideally we would like our reliability coefficients to equal 1.0 because this would indicate that 100% of the test score variance is due to true differences among individuals on the variable assessed. However, due to measurement error, perfectly reliable measurement does not exist. There is not a single, simple answer to our question about what is an acceptable level of reliability. What constitutes an acceptable reliability coefficient depends on several factors, including the construct being measured, the amount of time available for testing, the way the scores will be used, and the method of estimating reliability. We will now briefly address each of these factors.

> *What constitutes an acceptable reliability coefficient depends on several factors, including the construct being measured, the amount of time available for testing, the way the scores will be used, and the method of estimating reliability.*

CONSTRUCT. Some constructs are more difficult to measure than others simply because the item domain is more difficult to sample adequately. As a general rule, personality variables are more difficult to measure than cognitive abilities. As a result, what might be an acceptable level of reliability for a measure of "dependency" might be regarded as unacceptable for a measure of intelligence. In evaluating the acceptability of a reliability coefficient, one should consider the nature of the variable under investigation and how difficult it is to measure. By carefully reviewing and comparing the reliability estimates of different instruments available for measuring a construct, one can determine which is the most reliable measure of the construct.

TIME AVAILABLE FOR TESTING. If the amount of time available for testing is limited, only a limited number of items can be administered and the sampling of the test domain is open to greater error. This could occur in a research project in which the school principal allows you to conduct a study in his or her school but allows only 20 minutes to measure all the variables in your study. As another example, consider a districtwide screening for reading problems wherein the budget allows only 15 minutes of testing per student. In contrast, a psychologist may have 2 hours to administer a standardized intelligence test. It would be unreasonable to expect the same level of reliability from these significantly different measurement processes. However, comparing the reliability coefficients associated with instruments that can be administered within the parameters of the testing situation can help one select the best instrument for the situation.

TEST SCORE USE. The way the test scores will be used is another major consideration when evaluating the adequacy of reliability coefficients. Diagnostic tests that form the basis for major decisions about individuals should be held to a higher standard than tests used with group research or for screening large numbers of individuals. For example, an individually administered test of intelligence that is used in the diagnosis of mental retardation would be expected to produce scores with a very high level of reliability. In this context, performance on the intelligence test provides critical information used to determine whether the individual meets the diagnostic criteria. In contrast, a brief test used to screen all students in a school district for reading problems would be held to less rigorous standards. In this situation, the instrument is used simply for screening purposes and no diagnosis is to be rendered and no decisions are being made that cannot easily be reversed—only a decision about the need for a more thorough evaluation. It helps to remember that although high reliability is desirable with all assessments, standards of acceptability vary according to the way test scores will be used. High-stakes decisions demand highly reliable information!

METHOD OF ESTIMATING RELIABILITY. The size of reliability coefficients is also related to the method selected to estimate reliability. Some methods tend to produce higher estimates than other methods. As a result, it is important to take into consideration the method used to produce correlation coefficients when evaluating and comparing the reliability of different tests. For example, KR-20 and coefficient alpha typically produce reliability estimates that are smaller than ones obtained using the split-half method. As indicated in Table 4–8, alternate-form reliability with delayed administration takes into account more major sources of error than other methods do and generally produces lower reliability coefficients. In summary, some methods of estimating reliability are more rigorous and tend to produce smaller coefficients, and this variability should be considered when evaluating reliability coefficients.

GENERAL GUIDELINES. Although it is apparent that many factors deserve consideration when evaluating reliability coefficients, we will provide some general guidelines that can provide some guidance.

- If test results are being used to make important decisions that are likely to impact individuals significantly and are not easily reversed, it is reasonable to expect reliability coefficients of 0.90 or even 0.95. This level of reliability is regularly obtained with individually administered tests of intelligence. For example, the reliability of the Full Scale IQ from the Stanford-Binet Intelligence Scales—Fifth Edition (SB5; Roid, 2003), an individually administered intelligence test, is 0.98 at some ages.
- Reliability estimates of 0.80 or more are considered acceptable in many testing situations and are commonly reported for group and individually administered achievement and personality tests. For example, the California Achievement Test/5 (CAT/5; CTB/Macmillan/

> *If a test is being used to make important decisions that are likely to impact individuals significantly and are not easily reversed, it is reasonable to expect reliability coefficients of 0.90 or even 0.95.*

McGraw-Hill, 1993), a set of group-administered achievement tests frequently used in public schools, has reliability coefficients for most of its scores that exceed 0.80.

- For teacher-made classroom tests and tests used for screening, reliability estimates of at least 0.70 for scores are expected. Classroom tests frequently are combined to form linear composites that determine a final grade, and the reliability of these composite scores is expected to be greater than the reliabilities of the individual scores. Marginal coefficients in the 0.70s might also be acceptable when more thorough assessment procedures are available to address concerns about individual cases (e.g., when a psychologist is screening a large number of individuals in a community sample).

Some writers suggest that reliability coefficients as low as 0.60 are acceptable for group research, performance assessments, and projective measures, but we are reluctant to endorse the use of any assessment that produces scores with reliability estimates below 0.70. As you recall, a reliability coefficient of 0.60 indicates that 40% of the observed variance can be attributed to random error. How much confidence can you place in assessment results when you know that 40% of the variance is attributed to random error?

How to Improve Reliability

A natural question at this point is "What can we do to improve the reliability of our assessment results or test scores?" In essence we are asking what steps can be taken to maximize true score variance and minimize error variance. Probably the most obvious approach is simply to increase the number of items on a test. In the context of an individual test, if we increase the number of items while maintaining the same quality as the original items, we will increase the reliability of the test scores obtained. This concept was introduced when we discussed split-half reliability and presented the Spearman-Brown formula. In fact, a variation of the Spearman-Brown formula can be used to predict the effects on reliability of scores achieved by adding items:

$$r = \frac{n \times r_{xx}}{1 + (n - 1)r_{xx}}$$

where r = estimated reliability of test scores with new items

n = factor by which the test length is increased

r_{xx} = reliability of the original test scores

For example, consider the example of our 25-item math test. If the reliability of the test score were 0.80 and we wanted to estimate the increase in reliability we would achieve by increasing the test to 30 items (a factor of 1.2), the formula would be:

$$r = \frac{1.2 \times 0.80}{1 + [(1.2 - 1)0.80]}$$

$$r = \frac{0.96}{1.16}$$

$$r = 0.83$$

TABLE 4–9	Reliability Expected When Increasing the Number of Items			
Current Reliability	**The Reliability Expected When the Number of Items is Increased By:**			
	× 1.25	**× 1.50**	**× 2.0**	**× 2.5**
0.50	0.56	0.60	0.67	0.71
0.55	0.60	0.65	0.71	0.75
0.60	0.65	0.69	0.75	0.79
0.65	0.70	0.74	0.79	0.82
0.70	0.74	0.78	0.82	0.85
0.75	0.79	0.82	0.86	0.88
0.80	0.83	0.86	0.89	0.91
0.85	0.88	0.89	0.92	0.93
0.90	0.92	0.93	0.95	0.96

Table 4–9 provides other examples illustrating the effects of increasing the length of our hypothetical test on reliability. By looking in the first row of this table you see that increasing the number of items on a test with a reliability of 0.50 by a factor of 1.25 results in a predicted reliability of 0.56. Increasing the number of items by a factor of 2.0 (i.e., doubling the length of the test) increases the reliability of our test score to 0.67.

In some situations various factors will limit the number of items we can include in a test. For example, teachers generally develop tests that can be administered in a specific time interval, usually the time allocated for a class period. In these situations, one can enhance reliability by using multiple measurements that are combined for an average or composite score. As noted earlier, combining multiple tests in a linear composite will increase the reliability of measurement over that of the component tests. In summary, anything we do to get a more adequate sampling of the content domain will increase the reliability of our measurement.

In a later chapter we will discuss a set of procedures collectively referred to as "item analyses." These procedures help us select, develop, and retain test items with good measurement characteristics. Although it is premature to discuss these procedures in detail, it should be noted that selecting or developing good items is an important step in developing a good test. Selecting and developing good items will enhance the measurement characteristics of the assessments you use.

Another way to reduce the effects of measurement error is what Ghiselli et al. (1981) referred to as "good housekeeping procedures." By this they mean test developers should provide precise and clearly stated procedures regarding the administration and scoring of tests. Examples include providing explicit instructions for standardized administration, developing high-quality rubrics to facilitate reliable scoring, and requiring extensive training before individuals can administer, grade, or interpret a test.

> *Possibly the most obvious way to improve the reliability of measurement is simply to increase the number of items on a test. If we increase the number of items while maintaining the same quality as the original items, we will increase the reliability of the test.*

Special Problems in Estimating Reliability

RELIABILITY OF SPEED TESTS A speed test generally contains items that are relatively easy but has
a time limit that prevents any examinees from correctly answering all questions. As a result, the examinee's score on a speed test primarily reflects the
speed of his or her performance. When estimating
the reliability of the results of speed tests, estimates
derived from a single administration of a test are not

> *When estimating the reliability
> of the results of speed tests,
> estimates derived from a single
> administration of a test are not
> appropriate.*

appropriate. Therefore, with speed tests, test-retest or alternate-form reliability is appropriate, but
split-half, coefficient alpha, and KR-20 should be avoided.

RELIABILITY AS A FUNCTION OF SCORE LEVEL. Though it is desirable, tests do not always
measure with the same degree of precision throughout the full range of scores. If a group of
individuals is tested for whom the test is either too easy or too difficult, we are likely to have additional error introduced into the scores. At the extremes of the distribution, where scores reflect
mostly all correct or all wrong responses, little accurate measurement has occurred. It would be
inaccurate to infer that a child who missed every question on an intelligence test has "no" intelligence. Rather, the test did not adequately assess the low-level skills necessary to measure the
child's intelligence. This is referred to as the test having an insufficient "floor." At the other end,
it would be inaccurate to report that a child who answers all of the questions on an intelligence
test correctly has an "infinite level of intelligence." The test is simply too easy to provide an
adequate measurement, a situation referred to as a test having an insufficient "ceiling." In both
cases we need a more appropriate test. Generally, aptitude and achievement tests are designed
for use with individuals of certain age, ability, or grade/educational levels. When a test is used
with individuals who fall either at the extremes or outside this range, the scores might not be as
accurate as the reliability estimates suggest. In these situations, further study of the test's reliability is indicated.

RANGE RESTRICTION. The values we obtain when calculating reliability coefficients are dependent on characteristics of the sample or group of individuals on which the analyses are
based. One characteristic of the sample that significantly impacts the coefficients is the degree
of variability in performance (i.e., variance). More precisely, reliability coefficients based on
samples with large variances (referred to as heterogeneous samples) will generally produce
higher estimates of reliability than those based on samples with small variances (referred to as
homogeneous samples). When reliability coefficients are based on a sample with a restricted
range of scores, the coefficients may actually underestimate the reliability of measurement. For
example, if you base a reliability analysis on students in a gifted and talented class in which
practically all of the scores reflect exemplary performance (e.g., >90% correct), you will receive lower estimates of reliability than if the analyses are based on a class with a broader and
more nearly normal distribution of scores. To be accurate, reliability estimates should be calculated using samples that are representative of the population to whom examinees are intended
to be compared or referenced.

> *The reliability estimates discussed in this chapter are usually not applicable to mastery tests. Because mastery tests emphasize classification, a recommended approach is to use an index that reflects the consistency of classification.*

MASTERY TESTING. Criterion-referenced scores are used to make interpretations relative to a specific level of performance. Mastery testing is an example of a criterion-referenced score where an examinee's performance is evaluated in terms of achieving a cut score associated with a predetermined level of mastery instead of the relative degree of achievement (i.e., relative to the achievement of others). The emphasis in this testing situation is on classification. Examinees either score at or above the cut score and are classified as having mastered the skill or domain, or they score below the cut score and are classified as having not mastered the skill or domain. Mastery testing often results in limited variability among test takers, and as we just described, limited variability in performance results in small reliability coefficients. As a result, the reliability estimates discussed in this chapter are typically inadequate for assessing the reliability of mastery tests. Given the emphasis on classification, a recommended approach is to use an index that reflects the consistency of classification (AERA et al., 1999). Special Interest Topic 4.2 illustrates a useful procedure for evaluating the consistency of classification when using mastery tests.

CORRECTION FOR ATTENUATION. Statisticians and psychometricians may apply a *correction for attenuation* to correct for the unreliability of scores being correlated. For example, in a study of the relationship between visual and auditory memory, the researcher is typically interested in only the psychological constructs of visual and auditory memory and would like to eliminate measurement error. This can be achieved mathematically using a correction for attenuation. As another example, consider a test-retest reliability study. Here, both the original "test scores" and the "retest scores" contain some measurement error (e.g., due to content sampling). The test developer might decide to apply a correction for attenuation to correct for the unreliability in the original test and retest scores and focus the test-retest analysis on the stability of scores over time. These are reasonable practices as long as the researchers highlight this in their discussion of the results. It is also recommended that both corrected and uncorrected coefficients be reported. Table 4–10 illustrates the calculation of the correction for attenuation.

THE STANDARD ERROR OF MEASUREMENT

> *Reliability coefficients are useful when comparing the reliability of the scores produced by different tests, but when the focus is on interpreting the test scores of individuals, the standard error of measurement is a more practical statistic.*

Reliability coefficients are interpreted in terms of the proportion of observed variance attributable to true variance and are a useful way of comparing the reliability of scores produced by different assessment procedures. Other things being equal, you will want to select the test that produces scores with the best reliability. However, once a test has been selected and the focus is on interpreting scores, the **standard error of measurement (SEM)** is a more practical statistic. The SEM is the standard deviation of the

SPECIAL INTEREST TOPIC 4.2

Consistency of Classification with Mastery Tests

As noted in the text, the size of reliability coefficients is substantially impacted by the variance of the test scores. Limited test score variance results in lower reliability coefficients. Because mastery tests often do not produce test scores with much variability, the methods of estimating reliability described in this chapter will often underestimate the reliability of these tests. To address this, reliability analyses of mastery tests typically focus on the consistency of classification. That is, because the objective of mastery tests is to determine if a student has mastered the skill or knowledge domain, the question of reliability can be framed as one of how consistent mastery–nonmastery classifications are. For example, if two parallel or equivalent mastery tests covering the same skill or content domain consistently produce the same classifications (i.e., mastery vs. nonmastery), we would have evidence of consistency of classification. If two parallel mastery tests produced divergent classifications we would have cause for concern. In this case the test results are not consistent or reliable.

The procedure for examining the consistency of classification on parallel mastery tests is fairly straightforward. Simply administer both tests to a group of students and complete a table like the one that follows. For example, consider two mathematics mastery tests designed to assess students' ability to multiply fractions. The cut score is set at 80%, so all students scoring 80% or higher are classified as having mastered the skill whereas those scoring less than 80% are classified as not having mastered the skill. In the following example, data are provided for 50 students:

	Form B: Nonmastery (score, 80%)	Form B: Mastery (score of 80% or better)
Form A: Mastery (score of 80% or better)	4	32
Form A: Nonmastery (score <80%)	11	3

Students classified as achieving mastery on both tests are denoted in the upper right-hand cell whereas students classified as not having mastered the skill are denoted in the lower left-hand cell. There were four students who were classified as having mastered the skills on Form A but not on Form B (denoted in the upper left-hand cell). There were three students who were classified as having mastered the skills on Form B but not on Form A (denoted in the lower right-hand cell). The next step is to calculate the percentage of consistency. This is accomplished with the following formula:

$$\text{Percent Consistency} = \frac{\text{Mastery on Both Forms} + \text{Nonmastery on Both Forms}}{\text{Total Number of Students}} \times 100$$

$$\text{Percent Consistency} = \frac{32 + 11}{50} \times 100$$

$$\text{Percent Consistency} = 0.86 \times 100$$

$$\text{Percent Consistency} = 86\%$$

This approach is limited to situations in which you have parallel mastery tests. Another limitation is that there are no clear standards regarding what constitutes "acceptable" consistency of classification. Consistent with the evaluation of all reliability information, the evaluation of classification consistency should take into consideration the consequences of any decisions that are based on the test results (e.g., Gronlund, 2003). If the test results are used to make high-stakes decisions (e.g., awarding a diploma), a very high level of consistency is required. If the test is used only for low-stake decisions (e.g., failure results in further instruction and retesting), a lower level of consistency may be acceptable.

There are more robust approaches to examine consistency of classifications. For example, one could calculate Cohen's kappa, which takes into account the degree of agreement expected by chance.

TABLE 4–10	Applying a Correction for Attenuation

The general formula for a correction for attenuation is:

$$C - r_{xy} = \frac{(r_{xy})}{[(\sqrt{r_{xx}})(\sqrt{r_{yy}})]}$$

where

$C - r_{xy}$ = corrected correlation

r_{xy} = uncorrected correlation

r_{xx} = reliability of X scores

r_{yy} = reliability of Y scores

Consider this example. A researcher is examining the correlation between reading comprehension and word recognition. He or she decides to report both corrected and uncorrected test-retest reliability coefficients. The uncorrected correlation between the reading comprehension and word recognition scores is 0.75. The reliability of the reading comprehension scores is 0.90 and word recognition scores is 0.81.

$$C - r_{xy} = \frac{(0.75)}{[(\sqrt{0.90})(\sqrt{0.81})]}$$

$$C - r_{xy} = \frac{(0.75)}{[0.95 \times 0.90]}$$

$$C - r_{xy} = \frac{0.75}{0.855}$$

$$C - r_{xy} = 0.88$$

Therefore, the uncorrected coefficient is 0.75 and the corrected coefficient is 0.88. This corrected coefficient can be interpreted as the correlation between true scores on the tests of reading comprehension and word recognition.

distribution of scores that would be obtained by one person if he or she were tested on an infinite number of parallel forms of a test comprised of items randomly sampled from the same content domain. That definition is jam packed with information, so allow us to elaborate. If we created an infinite number of parallel forms of a test and had the same person take them with no carryover effects, the presence of measurement error would prevent the person from earning the same score every time. Although each test might represent the content domain equally well, the test taker would perform better on some tests and worse on others simply due to random error (e.g., chance or luck in knowing the answers to items selected for one version of a test but not another). By taking the scores obtained on all of these tests, a distribution of scores would result. The mean of this distribution is the individual's true score (T) and the SEM is the standard deviation of this distribution of error scores. Obviously, we are never actually able to follow these procedures and must estimate the SEM using information that is available to us.

Evaluating the Standard Error of Measurement

The SEM is a function of the reliability (r_{xx}) of test scores and standard deviation (SD) of the test scores. When calculating the SEM, the reliability coefficient takes into consideration measurement errors present in test scores, and the SD reflects the variance of the scores in the distribution. The SEM is estimated using the following formula:

$$SEM = SD\sqrt{1 - r_{xx}}$$

where SD = the standard deviation of the obtained scores, and

r_{xx} = the reliability of the test scores

Let's work through two quick examples. First, let's assume a test with a standard deviation of 10 and reliability of 0.90.

$$\text{Example 1: SEM} = 10\sqrt{1 - 0.90}$$
$$SRM = 10\sqrt{0.10}$$
$$SEM = 3.2$$

Now let's assume a test with a standard deviation of 10 and reliability of 0.80. The SD is the same as in the previous example, but the reliability is lower.

$$\text{Example 2: SEM} = 10\sqrt{1 - 0.80}$$
$$SRM = 10\sqrt{0.20}$$
$$SEM = 4.5$$

Notice that as the reliability of the test decreases, the SEM increases. Because the reliability coefficient reflects the proportion of observed score variance due to true score variance and the SEM is an estimate of the amount of error in test scores, this inverse relationship is what one would expect. The greater the reliability of test scores, the smaller the SEM and the more confidence we have in the precision of test scores. The lower the reliability of a test, the larger the SEM and the less confidence we have in the precision of test scores. Table 4–11 shows the SEM as a function of SD and reliability. Examining the first row in the table shows that on a test with a standard deviation of 30 and a reliability coefficient of 0.95 the SEM is 6.7. In comparison, if the reliability of the test is 0.90 the SEM is 9.5; if the reliability of the test is 0.85 the SEM is 11.6 and so forth. The SEM has been traditionally used in calculating intervals or bands around observed scores in which the true score is expected to fall. We will now turn to this application of the SEM.

> *The greater the reliability of a test score, the smaller the SEM and the more confidence we have in the precision of test scores.*

Calculating Confidence Intervals

A **confidence interval** reflects a range of scores that will contain the individual's true score with a prescribed probability (AERA et al., 1999). We typically use the SEM to calculate confidence intervals. When introducing the SEM, we said it provides information

> *A confidence interval reflects a range of scores that will contain the individual's true score with a prescribed probability (AERA et al., 1999).*

TABLE 4–11	Standard Errors of Measurement for Different Levels of Reliability and Standard Deviations					
Standard Deviation	Reliability Coefficients					
	0.95	0.90	0.85	0.80	0.75	0.70
30	6.7	9.5	11.6	13.4	15.0	16.4
28	6.3	8.9	10.8	12.5	14.0	15.3
26	5.8	8,2	10.1	11.6	13.0	14.2
24	5.4	7.6	9.3	10.7	12.0	13.1
22	4.9	7.0	8.5	9.8	11.0	12.0
20	4.5	6.3	7.7	8.9	10.0	11.0
18	4.0	5.7	7.0	8.0	9.0	9.9
16	3.6	5.1	6.2	7.2	8.0	8.8
14	3.1	4.4	5.4	6.3	7.0	7.7
12	2.7	3.8	4.6	5.4	6.0	6.6
10	2.2	3.2	3.9	4.5	5.0	5.5
8	1.8	2.5	3.1	3.6	4.0	4.4
6	1.3	1.9	2.3	2.7	3.0	3.3
4	0.9	1.3	1.5	1.8	2.0	2.2
2	0.4	0.6	0.8	0.9	1.0	1.1

about the distribution of observed scores around true scores. More precisely, we defined the SEM as the standard deviation of the distribution of error scores. Like any standard deviation, the SEM can be interpreted in terms of frequencies represented in a normal distribution. In the previous chapter we showed that approximately 68% of the scores in a normal distribution are located between 1 SD below the mean and 1 SD above the mean. As a result, approximately 68% of the time an individual's observed score would be expected to be within ±1 SEM of the true score. For example, if an individual had a true score of 70 on a test with a SEM of 3, then we would expect him or her to obtain scores between 67 and 73 two thirds of the time (as long as there are no changes in performance as a function of taking the test). To obtain a 95% confidence interval we simply determine the number of standard deviations encompassing 95% of the scores in a distribution. By referring to a table representing areas under the normal curve (see Appendix A) you can determine that 95% of the scores in a normal distribution fall within ±1.96 SDs of the mean. Given a true score of 70 and SEM of 3, the 95% confidence interval would be 70 ±3(1.96) or 70 ± 5.88. Therefore, in this situation an individual's observed score would be expected to be between 64.12 and 75.88, 95% of the time.

You might have noticed a potential problem with this approach to calculating confidence intervals. So far we have described how the SEM allows us to form confidence intervals around the examinee's true score. The problem is that we don't know an examinee's true score, only the observed score. Although it is possible for us to estimate true scores (see Special Interest Topic 4.3), it is common practice to use the SEM to establish confidence intervals around obtained scores (see Gulliksen, 1950). These

SPECIAL INTEREST TOPIC 4.3

Asymmetrical Confidence Intervals

It is common practice for test developers and publishers to report confidence intervals using the procedure described in this chapter. However, to correct for true score regression to the mean, several researchers (e.g., Dudek, 1979; Glutting, McDermott, & Stanley, 1987) have suggested an approach that establishes confidence intervals based on estimated true scores and the standard error of estimation (SE_E). Using this approach, the estimated true score is obtained with the following formula:

$$\text{Estimated True Score} = \text{Mean} + r_{xx}(X - \text{Mean})$$

where the Mean is the mean on the standard scores, X is the observed score, and r_{xx} is the reliability coefficient. The standard error of estimation is obtained using the following formula:

$$SE_E = SD\sqrt{1 - r_{xx}}\,(r_{xx})$$

where the SD of the standard scores r_{xx} is the reliability coefficient.

This approach results in confidence intervals that are asymmetrical around the observed score. For example, an observed score of 120 might have a 95% confidence interval of 113–123. Note that this range extends 7 points below the observed scores (i.e., 120) and only 3 points above it. The more common approach described in this chapter results in symmetrical confidence intervals. For example, an observed score of 120 might have a 95% confidence interval of 115–125 (i.e., observed score ±5 points).

The approach based on estimated true scores and the standard error of estimation has appeal from a technical perspective, and in recent years some test developers have adopted it (e.g., Reynolds & Kamphaus, 2003; Wechsler, 1997).

confidence intervals are calculated in the same manner as just described, but the interpretation is slightly different. In this context the confidence interval is used to define the range of scores that will contain the individual's true score. For example, if an individual obtains a score of 70 on a test with a SEM of 3.0, we would expect his or her true score to be between 67 and 73, 68% of the time (obtained score ±1 SEM). Accordingly, we would expect his or her true score to be between 64.12 and 75.88, 95% of the time (obtained score ±1.96 SEM). In practice, the score delineating confidence intervals are rounded to the nearest whole number since most tests do not yield fractional scores. For example, "64.14 to 75.88" is rounded to "64 to 76."

A major advantage of the SEM and the use of confidence intervals is that they remind us that measurement error is present in all scores and that we should interpret scores cautiously.

It may help to make note of the relationship between the reliability of a test score, the SEM, and confidence intervals. We stated that as the reliability of scores increase the SEM decreases. The same relationship exists between test score reliability and confidence intervals. As the reliability of test scores increases (denoting less measurement error) the confidence intervals become smaller (denoting more precision in measurement).

A major advantage of the SEM and the use of confidence intervals is that they remind us that measurement error is present in all scores and that we should interpret scores cautiously. A single numerical score is often interpreted as if it is precise and involves no error. For example, if you report that Susie has a Full Scale IQ of 113, her parents might interpret this as implying that Susie's IQ is exactly 113. If you are using a high-quality IQ test such as the Reynolds Intellectual Assessment Scales or the Stanford-Binet Fifth Edition, the obtained IQ is very likely a good estimate of her true IQ. However, even with the best assessment instruments the obtained scores contain some degree of error, and the SEM and confidence intervals help us illustrate this. This information can be reported in different ways in written reports. For example, Kaufman and Lichtenberger (1999) recommend the following format:

> Johnny obtained a Full Scale IQ of 113 (between 108 and 118 with 95% confidence).

Kamphaus (2001) recommends a slightly different format that is illustrated below:

> Susie obtained a Full Scale IQ in the High Average range, with a 95% probability that her true IQ falls between 108 and 118.

Regardless of the exact format used, the inclusion of confidence intervals highlights the fact that test scores contain some degree of measurement error and should be interpreted with caution. Most professional test publishers either report scores as bands within which the examinee's true score is likely to fall or provide information on calculating these confidence intervals.

MODERN TEST THEORIES

We have focused on classical test theory in this chapter due to its prominent role in the development of tests and the estimation and reporting of reliability information. There are two newer test theories that were developed in the latter part of the 20th century. These are generalizability theory and item response theory. These deserve mention at this point in our discussion of reliability because they both complement and extend CTT in terms of reliability information.

Generalizability Theory

Lee Cronbach and colleagues (e.g., Cronbach, Rajaratnam, & Gleser, 1963) developed an extension of classical test theory (CTT) known as *generalizability theory* in the 1960s and 1970s. CTT provides only an undifferentiated error component, but in real-life situations more than one source of measurement error is reflected in any reliability coefficient. For example, in this chapter we noted that internal consistency estimates of reliability primarily reflect errors due to domain sampling. Although this is true, errors due to faulty administration, errors in scoring, and errors associated with time sampling may all act to lower the average inter-item correlation, which reduces the internal consistency reliability of test scores. Likewise, test-retest coefficients are confounded by internal consistency errors. Under CTT it is not possible to determine how much error is contributed by the different sources of error. The main advantage of generalizability theory is that it gives researchers the opportunity to design studies that reveal how much variance is associated with various sources of error.

Generalizability theory typically uses analysis of variance (ANOVA) to estimate reliability coefficients and partition the error variance components. The methods and designs for partitioning variance components in ANOVA are beyond the scope of this text, but the general procedure is to use a statistical analysis program such as Statistical Package for the Social Sciences (SPSS) or Statistical Analysis System (SAS). These statistical programs have analysis options that will estimate the variance components (i.e., the variances associated with each source of variation specified by the analyst). A numerical value for each source is obtained, and generalizability coefficients can be calculated using rules that have been developed over the past few decades. Some psychometricians advocate simply examining the magnitude of the variances. An example of this was provided by Cronbach (1990) where he described how a researcher interested in generalizing the results of a typing test across different test passages (i.e., the selection the students are required to type) and different testing occasions (i.e., what day the test is administered). For this study, 25 students were given five different typing passages on five consecutive days (i.e., a different passage on each day). Using a two-way ANOVA design, the results indicated that the variance associated with the use of different passages on different days was small (i.e., 0.28) relative to the observed score variance (i.e., 12.4). These results indicate that the selection of a specific typing passage or a specific day to administer the test had relatively little impact on the score the students received. In other words, in this situation it is reasonable to generalize across test passages and testing occasions. The author noted that this is a common finding when using professionally developed alternate test forms that are technically comparable. Alternate test forms developed by the typical classroom teacher might not reach as high a level of technical equivalence and the results might be different (i.e., more variance associated with the use of different test forms).

> *The main advantage of generalizability theory is that it gives researchers the opportunity to design studies that reveal how much variance is associated with various sources of error.*

Most test manuals report information on the reliability of test scores based on classical test theory. However, generalizability theory provides a flexible and often more informative approach to reliability analysis. Given enough information about reliability, one can partition the error variance into its components as demonstrated in Figure 4–1 when each component is calculated independent of the others. It should be noted that generalizability theory is an extension of CTT and the theories are not incompatible. Cronbach, who was instrumental in developing generalizability theory, was also instrumental in developing CTT decades earlier.

FIGURE 4–1 Partitioning the Variance to Reflect Sources of Variance

Item Response Theory

Another modern test theory is *item response theory (IRT)*. We will discuss IRT in more detail in Chapter 7. For now we can define it as a theory or model of mental measurement that posits that the responses to items on a test are accounted for by latent traits. It is assumed that each examinee possesses a certain amount of any given latent trait and that its estimation is not dependent on any particular set of items or any assessment procedure. Central to IRT is a mathematical

In IRT, information on the reliability of scores is typically reported as a test information function (TIF) that illustrates the reliability of measurement at different points along the distribution.

cal model that describes how examinees at different levels of ability will respond to individual test items. IRT is fundamental to the development and application of computer adaptive testing. What is most important to us at this point is that in IRT information on the reliability of measurement takes a different form than either CTT or generalizability theory.

In IRT information on the reliability of scores is typically reported as a test information function (TIF). A TIF illustrates the reliability of measurement at different points along the distribution. This implies that the reliability of measurement is not constant across the distribution, and this is the case (as mentioned earlier in this chapter). A test (or an item) may provide more reliable measurement for examinees at one level of ability, and less reliable measurement for those at another level. TIFs can also be converted into an analog of the standard error of measurement for specific points in the distribution. Figure 4–2 shows a TIF (solid line) with its analogous standard error of measurement (dotted line) curve. The graph shows both curves, each with a scale on different sides of the graph (i.e., TIF values on the left; standard error values on the right). This graph indicates that the most reliable information, as represented by higher TIF

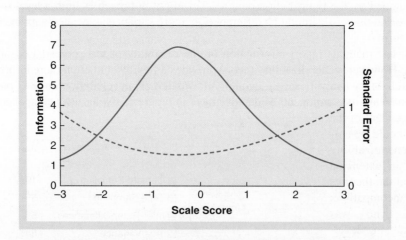

FIGURE 4–2 Test Information Function (TIF) and Standard Errors

Source: Osterlind, Steven J., *Modern Measurement: Theory, Principles, and Applications of Mental Appraisal*, 1st ©2006. Printed and electronically reproduced by permission of Pearson Education, Inc., Upper Saddle River, New Jersey.

values and lower error values, is available around the middle of the distribution. At both the high and low ends of the distribution, there is more measurement error. Although CTT provides only one estimate of reliability, as shown here IRT can provide information about reliability at different points along the distribution. This is an advantage of IRT. However, its mathematical complexity has been a drawback to its widespread application as well as its failure to improve on CTT models except in specialized testing models.

REPORTING RELIABILITY INFORMATION

The *Standards for Educational and Psychological Testing* (AERA et al., 1999) devoted an entire chapter to the discussion of reliability and errors of measurement. This emphasized the importance of information on reliability to all professionals developing and/or using tests. For test developers, the *Standards* (1999) specified that "developers and distributors of tests have primary responsibility for obtaining and reporting evidence of reliability and test infor-mation functions" (p. 30). Standard 2.1 stipulates that for all scores that are to be interpreted, relevant reliability coefficients and standard errors of measurement should be reported. For psychologists (and all other users of tests), the *Standards* noted, "It is the user who must take responsibility for determining whether or not scores are sufficiently trustworthy to justify anticipated uses and interpretations" (p. 31). In other words, psychologists should carefully consider the reliability of test scores when selecting tests to administer and when interpreting test results.

Psychological researchers often use tests, questionnaires, and other assessments in con-ducting their research. It is important for these researchers to provide adequate information about the psychometric properties of the scores reported in their research. Wilkinson and the Task Force on Statistical Inference (an APA task force; 1999) emphasized that all authors of research articles should provide information on the reliability of the measures they use in their research (e.g., reliability coefficients). They emphasized that to interpret meaningfully the size of the ob-served effects it is necessary to have information on the reliability of assessment scores. Whereas information on the psychometric properties of professionally developed published tests is avail-able typically in the professional manual or in research literature, this may not be the case with instruments developed by researchers to measure constructs in their research. It is important to remember that the quality of all research is intricately tied to the quality of the measurement instruments used.

How Test Manuals Report Reliability Information: The Reynolds Intellectual Assessment Scales (RIAS)

To illustrate how reliability information is reported in test manuals, we will use examples from the Reynolds Intellectual Assessment Scales (RIAS; Reynolds & Kamphaus, 2003). The RIAS is an individually administered intelligence test for clients 3 years to 94 years of age. The RIAS contains a two-subtest Verbal Intelligence Index (VIX) and a two-subtest Nonverbal Intelligence Index (NIX). The two verbal subtests are Guess What (GWH) and Verbal Reasoning (VRZ). The two nonverbal subtests are Odd-Item Out (OIO) and What's Missing (WHM). All four subtests are combined to form the Composite Intelligence Index (CIX). It takes approximately 20 to 25 minutes to administer the four intelligence scale subtests. The RIAS also includes a conormed, supplemental measure of memory that is composed of two memory subtests that yield a Composite Memory Index (CMX). The two memory subtests are Verbal Memory (VRM) and Nonverbal Memory (NVM). The administration of the memory subtests requires approximately 10 to 15 minutes. The RIAS was standardized on a national sample of 2,438 individuals that is representative of the U.S. population.

Chapter 5 of the test manual is titled Test Score Reliability. To examine measurement error associated with content sampling, Reynolds and Kamphaus (2003) presented coefficient alphas for all subtests and indexes. The coefficient alphas for the subtest scores are shown in Table 4–12. In the table, coefficient alphas are reported for different age groups, with median values presented in the bottom row. A review of Table 4–12 shows that the RIAS subtest score alpha coefficients were 0.84 or greater for all age groups. The median coefficients for all subtests were 0.90 or greater. Although the reliability estimates for the subtest scores are clearly adequate for clinical use, the authors recommended the interpretation of index scores when making clinical decisions. The reliability estimates for the RIAS indexes are presented in Table 4–13. A review

TABLE 4–12	Coefficient Alpha for RIAS Subtests					
	Subtest					
Age (Years)	Guess What (*GWH*)	Verbal Reasoning (*VRZ*)	Odd-Item Out (*OIO*)	What's Missing (*WHM*)	Verbal Memory (*VRM*)	Nonverbal Memory (*NVM*)
3	.89	.84	.93	.84	.93	.93
4	.92	.87	.91	.89	.94	.93
5	.95	.86	.90	.85	.95	.94
6	.93	.86	.94	.92	.89	.96
7	.93	.89	.95	.94	.93	.96
8	.92	.88	.94	.92	.90	.95
9	.92	.90	.95	.93	.92	.96
10	.91	.88	.94	.93	.92	.96
11–12	.89	.90	.94	.93	.90	.95
13–14	.90	.92	.94	.93	.91	.96
15–16	.91	.92	.95	.92	.93	.95
17–19	.92	.92	.94	.90	.94	.90
20–34	.92	.94	.95	.93	.94	.95
35–54	.95	.94	.95	.93	.94	.96
55–74	.91	.93	.95	.91	.93	.95
75–94	.94	.93	.95	.92	.94	.96
Median	.92	.90	.94	.92	.93	.95

Source: From Reynolds, C. R., & Kamphaus, R. W. (2003). Reynolds Intellectual Assessment Scales. Lutz, FL: *Psychological Assessment Resources.* Reprinted with permission of PAR.

TABLE 4–13	Coefficient Alpha for Indexes			
	Index			
Age (Years)	**VIX**	**NIX**	**CIX**	**CMX**
3	.91	.92	.94	.94
4	.94	.93	.95	.95
5	.94	.92	.96	.95
6	.94	.94	.96	.94
7	.94	.95	.97	.95
8	.94	.94	.96	.93
9	.94	.95	.97	.95
10	.93	.95	.95	.95
11–12	.94	.95	.96	.93
13–14	.95	.95	.97	.95
15–16	.95	.95	.97	.95
17–19	.95	.94	.96	.93
20–34	.96	.96	.97	.96
35–54	.97	.96	.98	.97
55–74	.95	.95	.97	.95
75–94	.96	.96	.98	.97
Median	.94	.95	.96	.95

Note. VIX = Verbal Intelligence Index; NIX = Nonverbal Intelligence Index; CIX = Composite Intelligence Index: CMX = Composite Memory Index.

Source: From Reynolds, C. R., & Kamphaus, R. W. (2003). Reynolds Intellectual Assessment Scales. Lutz, FL: *Psychological Assessment Resources.* Reprinted with permission of PAR.

of these data shows that the RIAS index alpha coefficients for all age groups equal or exceed 0.91, with the median coefficients all 0.94 or greater. These results indicate that the RIAS subtest scores and indexes provide reliable measurement. There is some variability across age groups, but with lower reliability estimates generally limited to the younger age groups, they all meet or exceed recommended standards for the recommended clinical applications.

The data just described demonstrate that the RIAS subtests and indexes are reliable in the general population. The authors took an additional step by examining the internal consistency reliability of the RIAS scores in major subgroups within the general population. Specifically, they examined the coefficient alphas of the subtests and indexes across gender and ethnic groups. These data are not reproduced here, but the results indicate consistently high coefficient alphas across ethnicity and gender.

In the next section of the chapter the authors provided information on the standard error of measurement (SEM). The standard errors of measurement for the RIAS indexes are presented in Table 4–14. Standard errors of measurement are again reported for different age groups, with

TABLE 4–14	Standard Errors of Measurement of the RIAS Indexes by Age Group			
	Index			
Age (Years)	**VIX**	**NIX**	**CIX**	**CMX**
3	4.50	4.24	3.67	3.67
4	3.67	3.97	3.35	3.35
5	3.67	4.24	3.00	3.35
6	3.67	3.67	3.00	3.67
7	3.67	3.35	2.60	3.35
8	3.67	3.67	3.00	3.97
9	3.67	3.35	2.60	3.35
10	3.97	3.35	3.35	3.35
11–12	3.67	3.35	3.00	3.97
13–14	3.35	3.35	2.60	3.35
15–16	3.35	3.35	2.60	3.35
17–19	3.35	3.67	3.00	3.97
20–34	3.00	3.00	2.60	3.00
35–54	2.60	3.00	2.12	2.60
55–74	3.35	3.35	2.60	3.35
75–94	3.00	3.00	2.12	2.60
Median	3.67	3.35	2.80	3.35

Note. VIX = Verbal Intelligence Index; NIX = Nonverbal Intelligence Index; CIX = Composite Intelligence Index; CMX = Composite Memory Index.

Source: From Reynolds, C. R., & Kamphaus, R. W. (2003). Reynolds Intellectual Assessment Scales. Lutz, FL: *Psychological Assessment Resources.* Reprinted with permission of PAR.

median values presented in the bottom row. Examination of the data indicates that the standard errors of measurement for the specific age groups range from 2.12 to 4.5. The median standard errors of measurement ranged from 3.67 to 2.80. In summary, again these data indicate highly reliable measurement.

Appendix B of the professional manual accompanying the RIAS provides 90% and 95% confidence intervals for the RIAS indexes. Instead of basing these confidence intervals on the standard errors of measurement, the confidence intervals were calculated with the estimated true score in place of the observed score and the standard error of estimate in place of the standard error of measurement. This procedure (as described in Special Interest Topic 4.3) results in asymmetrical confidence intervals. A brief example of selected confidence intervals for the Composite Intelligence Index (CIX) from the RIAS manual is provided in Table 4–15 (in the actual appendix confidence intervals are provided for every score between 40 and 160). Based on these

TABLE 4–15	Examples of RIAS Confidence Intervals	
Composite Intelligence Index (CIX)	**Confidence Interval**	
	90%	**95%**
70	66–76	66–77
80	76–86	75–86
90	86–95	85–96
100	95–105	94–106
110	105–114	104–115
120	114–124	114–125
130	124–134	123–134

data, for an examinee with a CIX of 120, the examiner could expect with 90% confidence that the examinee's true score is between 114 and 124, and with 95% that it is between 114 and 125.

The authors of the RIAS next examined measurement error associated with temporal instability by reporting test-retest reliability coefficients (in this manual referred to as stability coefficients). Test-retest coefficients were reported for 86 examinees. The median test-retest interval was 21 days. The results are presented in Table 4–16. The coefficients for the subtests range from 0.70 (i.e., Visual Memory) to 0.82 (i.e., Guess What). The coefficients for the indexes range from 0.79 (i.e., CMX) to 0.86 (i.e., VIX). Table 4–16 also contains coefficients that were corrected for attenuation (i.e., $C\text{-}r_{tt}$). The corrected coefficients "correct" for unreliability in the test and retest scores (this procedure was discussed in Special Interest Topic 4.4). As expected, the corrected coefficients are somewhat larger than the uncorrected coefficients. The authors also reported test-retest coefficients for four different age groups (3–4 years, 5–8 years, 9–12 years, and 13–82 years). The test-retest stability coefficients across age groups are consistent with the results from the total sample. Together, these results support the short-term stability of RIAS scores.

In closing, the authors examined the amount of error due to examiner differences. To this end, two professionals independently scored a random sample of 35 test protocols, and the subtest raw scores were correlated. The inter-rater reliability coefficients were Guess What, 0.99; Verbal Reasoning, 1.00; Odd-Item Out, 1.00; What's Missing, 1.00; Verbal memory, 0.95; and Nonverbal memory, 1.00. These strong coefficients support the high reliability of RIAS results when scored by qualified examiners.

This example using the RIAS illustrates the type of information that test manuals typically provide about the reliability of the test. You can expect some differences in the presentation of information, but the important feature is that test authors and publishers should provide adequate information for psychologists to make informed decisions about the reliability of the scores produced by a test.

RELIABILITY: PRACTICAL STRATEGIES FOR EDUCATORS

We are often asked by teachers how they can estimate reliability of their classroom test scores. First, for teachers using multiple-choice or other tests that can be scored by a computer scoring program, the score printout will typically report some reliability estimate (e.g., coefficient alpha

TABLE 4–16	Stability Coefficients of Scores for the RIAS Subtests and Indexes					
	First testing		**Second testing**			
Subtest/index	**M**	**SD**	**M**	**SD**	r_{tt}	$C\text{-}r_{tt}{}^a$
Guess What	49.07	10.31	50.28	10.25	.82	.89
Verbal Reasoning	49.18	11.64	52.03	11.88	.78	.87
Odd-Item Out	50.44	10.09	52.38	9.46	.72	.77
What's Missing	50.09	11.89	53.13	14.00	.81	.88
Verbal Memory	50.42	10.52	52.03	9.16	.70	.76
Nonverbal Memory	51.50	9.88	53.96	9.83	.80	.84
VIX	101.10	16.02	105.04	15.27	.86	.91
NIX	100.79	15.18	102.38	15.44	.81	.86
CIX	101.70	14.73	104.35	16.14	.84	.86
CMX	100.67	11.86	103.60	12.53	.79	.83

Note. $N = 86$. VIX = Verbal Intelligence Index; NIX = Nonverbal Intelligence Index; CIX = Composite Intelligence Index; CMX = Composite Memory Index. r_{tt} = test-retest reliability; $C\text{-}r_{tt}$ = corrected test-retest reliability. Median test-retest interval is 21 days (range = 9 to 39 days).

[a]Correlations were corrected for attenuation using the formula: $(r_{xy})/[(\sqrt{r_{xy}})(\sqrt{r_{yy}})]$.

Source: From Reynolds, C. R., & Kamphaus, R. W. (2003). Reynolds Intellectual Assessment Scales. Lutz, FL: *Psychological Assessment Resources.* Reprinted with permission of PAR.

or KR-20). If a teacher doesn't have access to computer scoring, but the items on a test are of approximately equal difficulty and scored dichotomously (i.e., correct–incorrect), one can use an internal consistency reliability estimate known as the Kuder-Richardson formula 21 (KR-21). This formula is actually an estimate of the KR-20 discussed earlier and is usually adequate for classroom tests. To calculate KR-21 you need to know only the mean, variance, and number of items on the test. The formula is:

$$KR\text{--}21 = 1 - \frac{X(n - X)}{n\sigma^2}$$

where X = mean

σ^2 = variance

n = number of items

Consider the following set of 20 scores: 50, 48, 47, 46, 42, 42, 41, 40, 40, 38, 37, 36, 36, 35, 34, 32, 32, 31, 30, 28. Here the $X = 38.25$, $\sigma^2 = 39.8$, and $n = 50$. Therefore,

$$KR\text{--}21 = 1 - \frac{38.25(50 - 38.25)}{50(39.8)}$$

$$= 1 - \frac{449.4375}{1990}$$

$$= 1 - 0.23 = 0.77$$

SPECIAL INTEREST TOPIC 4.4

A Quick Way to Estimate Reliability for Classroom Exams

Saupe (1961) provided a quick method for teachers to calculate reliability for a classroom exam in the era prior to easy access to calculators or computers. It is appropriate for a test in which each item is given equal weight and each item is scored either right or wrong. First, the standard deviation of the exam must be estimated from a simple approximation:

SD = [sum of top 1/6th of scores − sum of bottom 1/6th of scores]/[total # of scores −1]/2

Then reliability can be estimated from:

Reliability = 1 − [0.19 × number of items]/ SD^2

Thus, for example in a class with 24 student test scores, the top 6th of the scores are 98, 92, 87, and 86, while the bottom 6th of the scores are 48, 72, 74, and 75. With 25 test items, the calculations are:

$$SD = [98 + 92 + 87 + 86 − 48 + 72 + 74 + 75]/[23/2]$$

$$= [363 − 269]/11.5$$

$$= 94/11.5 = 8.17$$

So, reliability = 1 − [0.19 × 25]/8.17^2

$$= 1 − 07$$

$$= 0.93$$

Source: Saupe, J. L. (1961). Some useful estimates of the Kuder-Richardson formula number 20 reliability coefficient. *Educational and Psychological Measurement, 2,* 63–72.

As you see, this is a fairly simple procedure. If one has access to a computer with a spreadsheet program or a calculator with mean and variance functions, you can estimate the reliability of classroom test scores easily in a matter of minutes with this formula.

Special Interest Topic 4.4 presents a shortcut approach for calculating Kuder-Richardson Formula 21 (KR-21). If one wants to avoid even these limited computations, we have prepared Table 4–17, which allows you to estimate the KR-21 reliability for dichotomously scored classroom

TABLE 4–17	KR-21 Reliability Estimates for Tests with a Mean of 80%		
	Standard Deviation of Test		
Number of Items (n)	**0.10(n)**	**0.15(n)**	**0.20(n)**
10	—	0.29	0.60
20	0.20	0.64	0.80
30	0.47	0.76	0.87
40	0.60	0.82	0.90
50	0.68	0.86	0.92
75	0.79	0.91	0.95
100	0.84	0.93	0.96

tests if you know the standard deviation and number of items (this table was modeled after tables originally presented by Deiderich, 1973). Table 4–17 is appropriate for tests with a mean of approximately 80% correct (we are using a mean of 80% correct because it is fairly representative of many classroom tests). To illustrate its application, consider the following example. If your test has 50 items and an SD of 8, select the Number of Items row for 50 items and the Standard Deviation of Test column for $0.15n$ [because $0.15(50) = 7.5$, which is close to your actual SD of 8]. The number at the intersection is 0.86, which is very respectable reliability for a classroom test (or a professionally developed test for that matter).

If you examine Table 4–17 you will likely detect a few fairly obvious trends. First, the more items on the test, the higher the estimated reliability coefficients. We alluded to the beneficial impact of increasing test length previously in this chapter, and the increase in reliability is due to enhanced sampling of the content domain. Second, tests with larger standard deviations (i.e., variance) produce more reliable results. For example, a 30-item test with an SD of 3 [i.e., $0.10(n)$] results in an estimated reliability of 0.47, whereas one with an SD of 4.5 [i.e., $0.15(n)$] results in an estimated reliability of 0.76. This reflects the tendency we described earlier that restricted score variance results in smaller reliability coefficients. We should note that although we include a column for standard deviations of $0.20(n)$, standard deviations this large are rare with classroom tests (Deiderich, 1973). In fact, from our experience it is more common for classroom tests to have standard deviations closer to $0.10(n)$. Before leaving our discussion of KR-21 and its application to classroom tests, we do want to caution you that KR-21 is only an approximation of KR-20 or coefficient alpha. KR-21 assumes the test items are of equal difficulty and it is usually slightly lower than KR-20 or coefficient alpha (Hopkins, 1998). Nevertheless, if the assumptions are not grossly violated it is probably a reasonably good estimate of reliability for many classroom applications.

Our discussion of shortcut reliability estimates to this point has been limited to tests that are dichotomously scored. Obviously, many of the assessments teachers use are not dichotomously scored and this makes the situation a little more complicated. If your items are not scored dichotomously, you can calculate coefficient alpha with relative ease using a commonly available spreadsheet such as Microsoft Excel. With a little effort you should be able to use a spreadsheet to perform the computations illustrated previously in Tables 4–3 and 4–4.

Summary

Reliability refers to consistency in test scores. If a test or other assessment procedure produces consistent measurements, its scores are reliable. Why is reliability so important? As we have emphasized, assessments are useful because they provide information that helps scientists and professionals make better decisions. However, the reliability (and validity) of that information is of paramount importance. For us to make good decisions, we need reliable information. By estimating the reliability of our assessment results we get an indication of how much confidence we can place in them. If we have highly reliable and valid information, it is probable that we can use that information to make better decisions. If the results are unreliable, they are of little value to us.

Over the last century several measurement theories have been developed that help us understand measurement error and related issues. The oldest and most widely applied theory is classical test theory (CTT). We discussed CTT in some detail because it provided the foundation for most contemporary approaches to estimating reliability. We also briefly introduced generalizability theory and item response theory, two modern test theories that have expanded our understanding of reliability and measurement error.

Errors of measurement undermine the reliability of measurement and therefore reduce the utility of the measurement. Although there are multiple sources of measurement error, the major sources are content sampling and time sampling errors. Content sampling errors are the result of less than perfect sampling of the content domain. The more representative tests are of the content domain, the less content sampling errors threaten the reliability of the test scores. Time sampling errors are the result of random changes in the examinee or environment over time. Experts in testing and measurement have developed methods of estimating errors due to these and other sources. The major approaches to estimating reliability include:

- Test-retest reliability involves the administration of the same test to a group of individuals on two different occasions. The correlation between the two sets of scores is the test-retest reliability coefficient and primarily reflects errors due to time sampling.
- Alternate-form reliability involves the administration of parallel forms of a test to a group of individuals. The correlation between the scores on the two forms is the reliability coefficient. If the two forms are administered at the same time, the reliability coefficient primarily reflects content sampling error. If the two forms of the test are administered at different times, the reliability coefficient primarily reflects both content and time sampling errors.
- Internal-consistency reliability estimates are derived from a single administration of a test. Split-half reliability involves dividing the test into two equivalent halves and calculating the correlation between the two halves. Instead of comparing performance on two halves of the test, coefficient alpha and the Kuder-Richardson approaches examine the consistency of responding among all of the individual items of the test. Split-half reliability primarily reflects errors due to content sampling whereas coefficient alpha and the Kuder-Richardson approaches reflect both item heterogeneity and errors due to content sampling.
- Inter-rater reliability is estimated by administering the test once but having the responses scored by different examiners. By comparing the scores assigned by different examiners, one can determine the influence of different raters or scorers. Inter-rater reliability is important to examine when scoring involves considerable subjective judgment.

We also discussed a number of issues that are important for understanding and interpreting reliability estimates. We provided some guidelines for selecting the type of reliability estimate that is most appropriate for specific assessment procedures, some guidelines for evaluating reliability coefficients, and some suggestions on improving the reliability of measurement.

Reliability coefficients are useful when comparing the reliability of different tests, but the standard error of measurement (SEM) is more useful when interpreting scores.

The SEM is an index of the amount of error in test scores and is used in calculating confidence intervals within which we expect the true score to fall. An advantage of the SEM and the use of confidence intervals is that they remind us that measurement error is present in all scores and that we should use caution when interpreting scores. In closing this chapter, we provided an example of how test manuals should provide information on reliability and measurement error using the Reynolds Intellectual Assessment Scales (RIAS). We also provided some practical strategies for estimating the reliability of classroom tests.

Key Terms and Concepts

Alternate-form reliability, 118
Coefficient alpha, 121
Composite score, 125
Confidence interval, 137
Inter-rater reliability, 121

Kuder-Richardson formula 20
   (KR-20), 121
Measurement error, 110
Reliability, 110
Split-half reliability, 119

Standard error of measurement
   (SEM), 134
Test-retest reliability, 117

Recommended Readings

American Educational Research Association, American Psychological Association, & National Council on Measurement in Education. (1999). *Standards for educational and psychological testing.* Washington, DC: AERA. Chapter 5, Reliability and Errors of Measurement, is a great resource!

Feldt, L. S., & Brennan, R. L. (1989). Reliability. In R. L. Linn (Ed.), *Educational measurement* (3rd ed., pp. 105–146). Upper Saddle River, NJ: Merrill/Prentice Hall. A little technical at times, but a great resource for students wanting to learn more about reliability.

Ghiselli, E. E., Campbell, J. P., & Zedeck, S. (1981). *Measurement theory for the behavioral sciences.* San Francisco: Freeman. Chapters 8 and 9 provide outstanding discussions of reliability. A classic!

Nunnally, J. C., & Bernstein, I. H. (1994). *Psychometric theory* (3rd edition). New York: McGraw-Hill. Chapter 6, The Theory of Measurement Error, and Chapter 7, The Assessment of Reliability, are outstanding chapters. Another classic!

Subkoviak, M. J. (1984). Estimating the reliability of mastery–nonmastery classifications. In R. A. Berk (Ed.), *A guide to criterion-referenced test construction* (pp. 267–291). Baltimore: Johns Hopkins University Press. An excellent discussion of techniques for estimating the consistency of classification with mastery tests.

Practice Items

1. Consider these data for a five-item test that was administered to six students. Each item could receive a score of either 1 or 0. Calculate KR-20 using the following formula:

$$\text{KR-20} = \frac{k}{k-1}\left(\frac{\text{SD}^2 - \sum p_i \times q_i}{\text{SD}^2}\right)$$

where

k = number of items
SD^2 = variance of total test scores
p_i = proportion of correct responses on item
q_i = proportion of incorrect responses on item

	Item 1	Item 2	Item 3	Item 4	Item 5	Total Score
Student 1	0	1	1	0	1	
Student 2	1	1	1	1	1	
Student 3	1	0	1	0	0	
Student 4	0	0	0	1	0	
Student 5	1	1	1	1	1	
Student 6	1	1	0	1	0	
p_i						SD^2
q_i						
$p_i \times q_i$						

Note: When calculating SD^2, use n in the denominator.

2. Consider these data for a five-item test that was administered to six students. Each item could receive a score ranging from 1 to 5. Calculate coefficient alpha using the following formula:

$$\text{Coefficient Alpha} = \left(\frac{k}{k-1}\right)\left(1 - \frac{\sum SD_i^2}{SD^2}\right)$$

where:

k = number of items
SD_i^2 = variance of individual items
SD^2 = variance of total test scores

	Item 1	Item 2	Item 3	Item 4	Item 5	Total Score
Student 1	4	5	4	5	5	
Student 2	3	3	2	3	2	
Student 3	2	3	1	2	1	
Student 4	4	4	5	5	4	
Student 5	2	3	2	2	3	
Student 6	1	2	2	1	3	
SD_i^2					$SD^2 =$	

Note: When calculating SD_i^2 and SD^2, use n in the denominator.

Answers can be found in Appendix C.

Chapter Five

Validity

Validity refers to the degree to which evidence and theory support the interpretations of test scores entailed by proposed uses of the test. Validity is, therefore, the most fundamental consideration in developing and evaluating tests.

AERA ET AL., 1999, P. 9

Chapter Outline

Learning Objectives

After reading and studying this chapter, students should be able to:

1. Define validity and explain its importance in the context of psychological assessment.
2. Describe the major threats to validity.
3. Explain the relationship between reliability and validity.
4. Trace the development of the contemporary conceptualization of validity.
5. Describe the five categories of validity evidence specified in the 1999 *Standards*.
6. For each category of validity evidence, give an example to illustrate the type of information provided.
7. Explain how validity coefficients are interpreted.
8. Define the standard error of estimate and explain its interpretation.
9. Describe the steps in factor analysis and how factor analytic results can contribute evidence of validity.
10. Explain how validity evidence is integrated to develop a sound validity argument.
11. Review validity evidence presented in a test manual and evaluate the usefulness of the test scores for specific purposes.

In the previous chapter we introduced you to the concept of the reliability (i.e., the accuracy and consistency of measurement). Now we turn our attention to validity, another fundamental psychometric property. Messick (1989) defined validity as "an integrated evaluative judgment of the degree to which empirical evidence and theoretical rationales support the adequacy and appropriateness of inferences and actions based on test scores or other modes of assessment" (p.13). Similarly, the *Standards for Educational and Psychological Testing* (AERA et al., 1999) defined validity as "the degree to which evidence and theory support the interpretations of test scores entailed by proposed uses of the tests" (p. 9). Reynolds (1998) defined validity similarly, arguing that **validity** refers to the appropriateness and accuracy of the interpretation of performance on a test, such performance usually expressed as a test score. Validity is illustrated in the following series of questions: If test scores are interpreted as reflecting intelligence, do they actually reflect intellectual ability? If test scores are interpreted as reflecting depressed mood, do they actually reflect a client's level of depression? If test scores are used (i.e., interpreted) to predict success in college, can they accurately predict who will succeed in college? Naturally the validity of the interpretations of test scores is directly tied to the usefulness of the interpretations. Valid interpretations help us make better decisions; invalid interpretations do not!

> **Validity *refers to the appropriateness or accuracy of the interpretation of test scores.***

There is a consensus in the profession of psychometrics that older concepts of validity as referring to a test are abandoned in favor of an approach that emphasizes that validity refers to the appropriateness or accuracy of the interpretations of *test scores*. In other words, it is not technically correct to refer to the validity of a test. Validity is a characteristic of the interpretations given to test scores. As a result, it is not technically correct to ask the question "Is the Wechsler Intelligence Scale for Children—Fourth Edition (WISC-IV) a valid test?" It is preferable to ask the question "Is the interpretation of performance on the WISC-IV as reflecting intelligence valid?" Validity must always have a context and that context is interpretation. What does performance on this test mean? The answer to this question is the interpretation given to performance, and it is this interpretation that possesses the construct of validity, not the test itself.

Additionally, when test scores are interpreted in multiple ways, each interpretation needs to be validated. For example, an achievement test can be used to evaluate a student's performance in academic classes, to assign the student to an appropriate instructional program, to diagnose a learning disability, or to predict success in college. Each of these uses involves different interpretations and the validity of each interpretation needs to be evaluated (AERA et al., 1999).

> **When test scores are interpreted in multiple ways, each interpretation needs to be evaluated.**

To establish or determine validity is a major responsibility of the test authors, test publishers, researchers, and even test users. A test manual presents essentially a summary of evidence for espoused interpretations of test scores, as the evidence is known at the time the manual is prepared. However, validation is a process, one that involves an ongoing, dynamic effort to accumulate evidence for a sound scientific basis for proposed test score interpretations (AERA et al., 1999; Reynolds, 1998). Validation, then, is not static but a constantly moving target. Validation continues in the scientific literature, and test users should not be constrained

---

SPECIAL INTEREST TOPIC 5.1:

Are Psychological Tests as Accurate as Medical Tests?

Many, if not most, people assume that tests used by medical professionals are more reliable and valid than those used by psychologists. That is, medical tests such as magnetic resonance imaging (MRI), X-rays, Pap smears, and electrocardiograms provide more reliable and accurate results than common psychological tests such as intelligence, neuropsychological, and personality tests. However, Meyer et al. (2001) reviewed research that examined the validity of a large number of medical and psychological tests and concluded that psychological tests often provide results that equal or exceed the validity of medical tests. For example, the Pap smear test that is used to detect cervical abnormalities produces an effect size of 0.36 whereas the average ability of scores from the Minnesota Multiphasic Personality Inventory—Second Edition to detect depressive or psychotic disorders has an effect size of 0.37 (larger effect sizes indicate superior validity). Even when you examine the validity of medical and psychological tests to detect the same disorder, psychological tests can provide superior results. For example, the effect size of MRI results in detecting dementia is 0.57 whereas the effect size for neuropsychological tests in detecting dementia is 0.68. This paper reported effect sizes for over 140 medical and psychological tests. So the answer to the question is "Yes, psychological tests can provide information that is as valid as common medical tests."

---

by the necessary limitations imposed on information in a test manual and should follow the accumulated literature of the ongoing process of validation. This premise is also supported in the *Standards* (AERA et al., 1999), which noted that "validation is the joint responsibility of the test developer and test user" (p. 11).

This chapter is one of the longest you will face in this text. However, validity is the most important of all psychometric characteristics and is misconstrued surprisingly often by practicing professional psychologists. Because we have introduced you to the central issue of validity, you might be interested in knowing how psychological tests compare to medical tests in terms of validity. You might be surprised by the answer to this question! Special Interest Topic 5.1 provides a brief overview of a research article that examines this issue.

THREATS TO VALIDITY

Messick (1994) and others have identified the two major threats to validity as construct underrepresentation and construct-irrelevant variance. To translate this into everyday language, validity is threatened when a test measures either less (construct underrepresentation) or more (construct-irrelevant variance) than the construct it is supposed to measure (AERA et al., 1999). Construct underrepresentation occurs when a test does not measure important aspects of the specified construct (later, in Chapter 6, we will explain in detail how to avoid this problem if you are developing a test). Consider a test designed to be a comprehensive measure of the mathematics skills covered in a third-grade curriculum and to convey information regarding mastery of each skill. If the test contained only division problems, it would not be an adequate representation of the broad array of math skills typically covered in a third-grade curriculum

> *Validity is threatened when a test measures either less or more than the construct it is designed to measure.*

(although a score on such a test may predict performance on a more comprehensive measure). Division is an important aspect of the math curriculum, but not the only important aspect. To address this problem, the content of the test would need to be expanded to reflect all of the skills typically taught in a third-grade math curriculum.

Construct-irrelevant variance is present when the test measures characteristics, content, or skills that are unrelated to the test construct. For example, if our third-grade math test has extensive and complex written instructions, it is possible that in addition to math skills, reading comprehension skills are being measured. If the test is intended to measure only math skills, the inclusion of reading comprehension would reflect construct-irrelevant variance. To address this problem, one might design the test to minimize written instructions and to ensure the reading level is low. As you might imagine, most tests leave out some aspects that some users might view as important and include aspects that some users view as irrelevant (AERA et al., 1999).

In addition to characteristics of the test itself, factors external to the test can impact the validity of the interpretation of results. Linn and Gronlund (2000) identified numerous factors external to the test that can influence validity. They highlighted the following factors:

- *Examinee characteristics.* Any personal factors that alter or restrict the examinees' responses in the testing situation can undermine validity. For example, if an examinee experiences high levels of test anxiety this may impact his or her performance on a maximum performance test. Low motivation might also impact the validity of interpretations based on maximum performance tests. The same principle applies to typical response tests. For example, instead of responding in a truthful manner when completing a personality test, a client might attempt to present himself or herself in either a more pathological (i.e., fake-bad) or a less pathological (i.e., fake-good) manner. All of these can undermine validity.
- *Test administration and scoring procedures.* Deviations from standard administrative and scoring procedures can undermine validity. In terms of administration, failure to provide the appropriate instructions or follow strict time limits can lower validity. To accommodate the special needs of individuals with disabilities, there are occasions when it is appropriate to modify standard administrative procedures. However, even in these situations it is required that examiners provide evidence that the validity of score interpretations is not compromised (Lee, Reynolds, & Willson, 2003). In terms of scoring, unreliable or biased scoring can lower validity .
- *Instruction and coaching.* In addition to the content of the test influencing validity, prior instruction and/or coaching can also impact validity. For example, consider a test of critical thinking skills. If the examinees were coached and given solutions to the particular problems included on a test, validity would be compromised. Recall that a test presents a sample of the domain of potential questions related to a specific construct, so if someone takes this sample of questions and teaches the examinees how to respond, the test is no longer useful in determining where the examinee stands on the construct represented by the item sample. This is a potential problem when educators "teach the test" and when attorneys sometimes obtain copies of tests and coach their clients in particular ways to answer so as to present themselves in a way favorable to their legal case.

Additionally, the validity of norm-referenced interpretations of performance on a test is influenced by the appropriateness of the reference group or standardization sample (AERA et al., 1999). As these examples illustrate, a multitude of factors can influence the validity of assessment-based

> *Validity is not an all-or-none concept, but exists on a continuum.*

interpretations. Due to the cumulative influence of these factors, validity is not an all-or-none concept. Rather, it exists on a continuum, and we usually refer to degrees of validity or to the relative validity of the interpretation(s) given to a particular score.

RELIABILITY AND VALIDITY

In the preceding chapter we addressed the issue of the reliability of measurement. *Reliability* refers to the stability, or consistency, and accuracy of test scores and reflects the amount of random measurement error present. Reliability is a necessary but insufficient condition for validity. A test that does not produce reliable scores cannot produce valid interpretations. However, no matter how reliable measurement is, it is not a guarantee of validity. From our discussion of reli-

> *Reliability is a necessary but insufficient condition for validity.*

ability you will remember that obtained score variance is composed of two components: true score variance and error variance. Only true score variance is reliable, and only true score variance can be related systematically to any construct the test is designed to measure. If reliability is equal to zero, then the true score vari-

ance component must also be equal to zero, leaving our obtained score to be composed only of error—that is, random variations in responses. Thus, without reliability there can be no validity.

Reliability also places limits on the magnitude of validity coefficients when a test score is correlated with variables external to the test itself (e.g., if we compute the correlation between an IQ and achievement in reading). In such research, the internal consistency reliability coefficient imposes a theoretical limit on the true value of the correlation that is equal to the square root of the reliability coefficient (i.e., maximum correlation $= \sqrt{r_{xx}}$).

Although low reliability limits validity, high reliability does not ensure validity. It is entirely possible that a test can produce reliable scores but inferences based on the test scores can be completely invalid. Consider the following rather silly example involving head circumference. If we use some care we can measure the circumferences of our clients' heads in a reliable and consistent manner. In other words, the measurement is reliable. However, if we considered head circumference to be an index of intelligence, our inferences would not be valid. The measurement of head circumference is still reliable, but when interpreted as a measure of intelligence it would result in invalid inferences.

A more relevant example can be seen in the various intelligence scales that produce highly reliable verbal and nonverbal scales. There is also a rather substantial body of research demonstrating these scores are interpreted appropriately as reflecting types of intelligence. However, some psychologists have drawn the inference that score differences between the verbal and nonverbal scales indicate some fundamental information about personality and even forms of psychopathology. For example, one author argued that a person who scores higher on the verbal scale relative to the nonverbal scale by 15 points or more is highly likely to have an obsessive-compulsive personality disorder! There is no evidence or research to support such an interpretation, and, in fact, a large percentage of the population of the United States score higher on the verbal scales relative to the nonverbal scales (about 12.5% in fact on the scale in question here). Thus, although the scores are themselves highly reliable and some interpretations are highly valid (the scales measure intellectual ability), other interpretations wholly lack validity despite the presence of high reliability.

"TYPES OF VALIDITY" VERSUS "TYPES OF VALIDITY EVIDENCE"

We have already introduced you to the influential *Standards for Educational and Psychological Testing* (AERA et al., 1999). This is actually the latest in a series of documents providing guidelines for the development and use of tests. At this point we are going to trace the evolution of the concept of validity briefly by highlighting how it has been defined and described in this series of documents. In the early versions (i.e., APA, 1954, 1966; APA, AERA, & NCME, 1974, 1985) validity was divided into three distinct types. As described by Messick (1989), these are:

> *Validity is a unitary concept.*

- Content validity involves how adequately the test samples the content area of the identified construct. In other words, is the content of the test relevant and representative of the content domain? We speak of it being representative because every possible question that could be asked cannot as a practical matter be asked, so questions are chosen to sample or represent the full domain of questions. Content validity is typically based on professional judgments about the appropriateness of the test content.
- Criterion-related validity involves examining the relationships between the test and external variables that are thought to be direct measures of the construct. Studies of criterion-related validity empirically examine the relationships between test scores and criterion scores using correlation or regression analyses.
- Construct validity involves an integration of evidence that relates to the meaning or interpretation of test scores. This evidence can be collected using a wide variety of research strategies and designs.

This classification terminology has been widely accepted by researchers, authors, teachers, and students and is often referred to as the traditional nomenclature (AERA et al., 1999). However, in the late 1970s and 1980s, measurement professionals began moving toward a conceptualization of validity as a unitary concept. That is, whereas we previously had talked about different types of validity (i.e., content, criterion-related, and construct validity), these "types" really only represent different ways of collecting evidence to support the validity of interpretations of performance on a test, which we commonly express as a test score. To emphasize the view of validity as a unitary concept and get away from the perception of distinct types of validity, the 1985 *Standards for Educational and Psychological Testing* (APA et al., 1985) referred to "types of validity evidence" in place of "types of validity." Instead of content validity, criterion-related validity, and construct validity, the 1985 *Standards* referred to content-related evidence of validity, criterion-related evidence of validity, and construct-related evidence of validity.

This brings us to the current *Standards* (AERA et al., 1999). According to the 1999 *Standards*:

> Validity is a unitary concept. It is the degree to which all of the accumulated evidence supports the intended interpretation of test scores for the proposed purposes. (p. 11)

The 1999 document is conceptually similar to the 1985 document (i.e., "types of validity evidence" versus "types of validity"), but the terminology has expanded and changed somewhat. The change in terminology is not simply cosmetic, but is substantive and intended to promote a new way of conceptualizing validity, a view that has been growing in the profession for over two decades. The 1999 *Standards* identified the following five categories of evidence that are related to the validity of test score interpretations:

- *Evidence based on test content* includes evidence derived from an analysis of the test content, which includes the type of questions or tasks included in the test and administration and scoring guidelines.
- *Evidence based on relations to other variables* includes evidence based on an examination of the relationships between test performance and external variables or criteria.
- *Evidence based on internal structure* includes evidence regarding relationships among test items and components.
- *Evidence based on response processes* includes evidence derived from an analysis of the processes engaged in by the examinee or examiner.
- *Evidence based on consequences of testing* includes evidence based on an examination of the intended and unintended consequences of testing.

> *Sources of validity evidence differ in their importance according to factors such as the construct being measured, the intended use of the test scores, and the population being assessed.*

These sources of evidence differ in their importance or relevance according to factors such as the construct being measured, the intended use of the test scores, and the population being assessed. Those using tests should carefully weight the evidence of validity and make judgments about how appropriate a test is for each application and setting. Table 5–1 provides a brief summary of the different classification schemes that have been promulgated over the past four decades in the *Standards*.

At this point you might be asking, "Why are the authors wasting my time with a discussion of the history of technical jargon?" There are at least two important reasons. First, it is likely that in your readings and studies you will come across references to various "types of validity." Many older test and measurement textbooks refer to content, criterion, and construct validity, and some newer texts still use that or a similar nomenclature. We hope that when you come across different terminology you will not be confused, but instead will understand its meaning and

TABLE 5–1	Tracing Historical Trends in the Concept of Validity	
1974 *Standards* (Validity as Three Types)	**1985** *Standards* (Validity as Three Interrelated Types)	**1999** *Standards* (Validity as Unitary Construct)
Content validity	Content-related validity	Validity evidence based on test content
Criterion validity	Criterion-related validity	Validity evidence based on relations to other variables
Construct validity	Construct-related validity	Validity evidence based on response processes
		Validity evidence based on internal structure
		Validity evidence based on consequences of testing

origin. Second, the *Standards* are widely accepted and serve as professional guidelines for the development and evaluation of tests. For legal and ethical reasons test developers and publishers generally want to adhere to these guidelines. Several of the major journals in the field of tests and measurements (e. g., *Educational and Psychological Measurement* and *Psychological Assessment*) require all published manuscripts to conform to the language recommendations of the *Standards*. As a result, we expect all test publishers will adopt the new nomenclature in the next few years as some have already. Currently test manuals and other test-related documents are adopting this new nomenclature (e.g., Reynolds, 2002). However, older tests typically have supporting literature that uses the older terminology, and you need to understand its origin and meaning. When reviewing test manuals and assessing the psychometric properties of a test, you need to be aware of the older as well as the newer terminology.

SOURCES OF VALIDITY EVIDENCE

Evidence Based on Test Content

The *Standards* (AERA et al., 1999) noted that valuable validity evidence can be gained by examining the relationship between the content of the test and the construct or domain the test is designed to measure. In this context, test content includes the "themes, wording, and format of the items, tasks, or questions on a test, as well as the guidelines … regarding administration and scoring" (p. 11). Oth-

> *Valuable validity evidence can be gained by examining the relationship between the content of the test and the construct it is designed to measure.*

er writers provide similar descriptions. For example, Reynolds (1998b) notes that validity evidence based on test content focuses on how well the test items sample the behaviors or subject matter the test is designed to measure. In a similar vein, Anastasi and Urbina (1997) stated that validity evidence based on test content involves the examination of the content of the test to determine whether it provides a representative sample of the domain being measured. Popham (2000) succinctly framed it as "Does the test cover the content it's supposed to cover?" (p. 96). In the past, this type of validity evidence was primarily subsumed under the label "content validity."

Test developers routinely begin considering the appropriateness of the content of the test at the earliest stages of development. Identifying what we want to measure is the first order of business, because we cannot measure anything very well that we have not first clearly defined. Therefore, the process of developing a test should begin with a clear delineation of the construct or content domain to be measured. Once the construct or content domain has been clearly defined, the next step is to develop a table of specifications. This table of specifications is essentially a blueprint that guides the development of the test. It delineates the topics and objectives to be covered and the relative importance of each topic and objective. Finally, working from this table of specifications the test developers write the actual test items. Professional test developers often bring in external consultants who are considered experts in the content area(s) covered by the test. For example, if the goal is to develop an achievement test covering American history, the test developers will likely recruit experienced teachers of

> *Item relevance and content coverage are two important factors to be considered when evaluating the correspondence between the test content and its construct.*

American history for assistance developing a table of specifications and writing test items. If the goal is to develop a typical response scale to assess the presence of symptoms associated with a psychological disorder (e.g., depression, anxiety), the test developers will typically recruit expert consultants to help review the clinical and research literature and develop items designed to assess the theoretical construct being measured. If care is taken with these procedures, the foundation is established for a correspondence between the content of the test and the construct it is designed to measure. Test developers may include a detailed description of their procedures for writing items as validity evidence, including the number, qualifications, and credentials of their expert consultants.

After the test is written, it is common for test developers to continue collecting validity evidence based on content. This typically involves having expert judges systematically review the test and evaluate the correspondence between the test content and its construct or domain. These experts can be the same ones who helped during the early phase of test construction or a new, independent group of experts. During this phase, the experts typically address two major issues, item relevance and content coverage. To assess **item relevance** the experts examine each individual test item and determine whether it reflects essential content in the specified domain. To assess **content coverage** the experts look at the overall test and rate the degree to which the items cover the specified domain. To understand the difference between these two issues, consider these examples. For a test intended to assess obsessive-compulsive symptoms, a question about the presence and frequency of ritualistic hand-washing would clearly be deemed a relevant item whereas a question about calculating algebraic equations would be judged to be irrelevant. This distinction deals with the relevance of the items to the construct or content domain. In contrast, if you examined the total test and determined that all of the questions dealt with the ritualistic behaviors and no other obsessive-compulsive symptoms were covered, you would conclude that the test had poor content coverage. That is, because obsessions and compulsions include many important symptoms in addition to ritualistic behaviors that are not covered in the test, the test does not reflect a comprehensive and representative sample of the specified construct or content domain. The concepts of item relevance and content coverage are illustrated in Figures 5–1 and 5–2.

As you can see, the collection of content-based validity evidence is typically qualitative in nature. However, although test publishers might rely on traditional qualitative approaches (e.g., the judgment of expert judges to help develop the tests and subsequently to evaluate the completed test), they can take steps to report their results in a more quantitative manner. For example, they can report the number and qualifications of the experts, the number

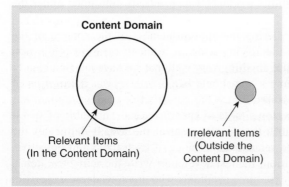

FIGURE 5-1 Illustration of Item Relevance.

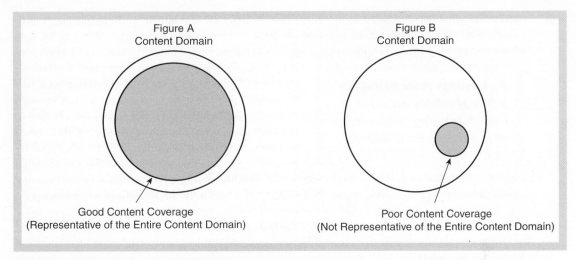

FIGURE 5-2 Illustration of Content Coverage.

of chances the experts had to review and comment on the assessment, and their degree of agreement on content-related issues. Taking these efforts a step further, Lawshe (1975) developed a quantitative index that reflects the degree of agreement among the experts making content-related judgments. Newer approaches are being developed that use a fairly sophisticated technique known as multidimensional scaling analysis (Sireci, 1998).

> *Content-based validity evidence is often the preferred approach for establishing the validity of achievement tests and tests used in the selection and classification of employees.*

As we suggested previously, different types of validity evidence are most relevant, appropriate, or important for different types of tests. For example, content-based validity evidence is often seen as the preferred approach for establishing the validity of academic achievement tests. This applies to both teacher-made classroom tests and professionally developed achievement tests. Another situation in which content-based evidence is of primary importance is with tests used in the selection and classification of employees. For example, employment tests may be designed to sample the knowledge and skills necessary to succeed at a job. In this context, content-based evidence can be used to demonstrate consistency between the content of the test and the requirements of the job. The key factor that makes content-based validity evidence of paramount importance with both achievement tests and employment tests is that they are designed to provide a representative sample of the knowledge, behavior, or skill domain being measured. In contrast, content-based evidence of validity is usually less important, though certainly not unimportant, for personality and aptitude tests (Anastasi & Urbina, 1997).

FACE VALIDITY. Before leaving our discussion of content-based validity evidence, we need to highlight the distinction between it and face validity. **Face validity** is an older term that you may yet encounter. It is technically not a form of validity at all, but instead refers to a test "appearing" to measure what it is designed to measure. That is, does the test appear valid to untrained individuals who take, administer, or examine the test? Face validity really has nothing to do with what a test actually measures, just what it appears to measure. For example, does a test of person-

> **Face validity** *is not technically a form of validity, but refers to a test "appearing" to measure what it is designed to measure.*

ality look like the general public expects a personality test to look? Does a test of intelligence look like the general public expects an intelligence test to look? Naturally, the face validity of a test is closely tied to the content of a test. In terms of face validity, when untrained individuals inspect a test they are typically looking to see whether the items on the test are what they expect. Whereas content-based evidence of validity is acquired through a systematic and technical analysis of the test content, face validity involves only the superficial appearance of a test. A test can appear "face valid" to the general public, but not hold up under the systematic scrutiny involved in a technical analysis of the test content.

This is not to suggest that face validity is an undesirable or even irrelevant characteristic. A test that has good face validity is likely to be better received by the general public. If a test appears to measure what it is designed to measure, examinees are more likely to be cooperative and invested in the testing process, and the public is more likely to view the results as meaningful (Anastasi & Urbina, 1997). Research suggests that on maximum performance tests, good face validity can increase examinee motivation, which in turn can increase test performance (Chan, Schmitt, DeShon, Clause, & Delbridge, 1997). If a test has poor face validity, those using the test may have a flippant or negative attitude toward the test and as a result put little effort into completing it. If this happens, the actual validity of the test can suffer. The general public is not likely to view a test with poor face validity as meaningful, even if there is technical support for the validity of the test. There are times, however, when face validity is undesirable. These occur primarily in forensic settings in which detection of malingering may be emphasized. Malingering is a situation in which an examinee intentionally feigns symptoms of a mental or physical disorder in order to gain some external incentive (e.g., receiving a financial reward, avoiding punishment). In these situations face validity is not desirable because it may help the examinee fake pathological responses. In fact, false forms of face validity are useful in detecting malingered responses (see Chapter 18 for an explanation).

Evidence Based on Relations to Other Variables

Important validity evidence also can be secured by examining the relationships between test scores and other variables (AERA et al., 1999). In describing this type of validity evidence, the *Standards* recognized several related but fairly distinct applications. One involves the examination of test-criterion evidence, one convergent and discriminant evidence, and one based on group differences. For clarity, we will address these applications separately.

TEST-CRITERION EVIDENCE. Many tests are designed to predict performance on some variable that is typically referred to as a criterion. The *Standards* (AERA et al., 1999) defined a criterion as "a measure of some attribute or outcome that is of primary interest" (p. 14). The criterion can be academic performance as reflected by the grade point average (GPA), job performance as measured by a supervisor's ratings, or anything else that is of importance to the user of the test.

Historically, this type of validity evidence has been re-ferred to as "predictive validity," "criterion validity," or "criterion-related validity." There are two differ-ent types of validity studies typically used to collect **test-criterion evidence: predictive studies** and **concurrent studies**. In a predictive study the test is administered, there is an intervening time interval, and then the criterion is measured. In a concurrent study the test is administered and the criterion is measured at about the same time.

> *There are two different types of validity studies typically used to collect* **test-criterion** *evidence:* **predictive studies** *and* **concurrent studies***.*

To illustrate these two approaches we will consider the Scholastic Assessment Test (SAT). The SAT is designed to predict how well high school students will perform in college. To complete a predictive study, one might administer the SAT to high school students, wait until the students have completed their freshman year of college, and then examine the relationship between the predictor (i.e., SAT scores) and the criterion (i.e., first-year-student GPA). Researchers often use a correlation coefficient to examine the relationship between a predictor and a criterion, and in this context the correlation coefficient is referred to as a validity coefficient. To complete a concurrent study of the relationship between the SAT and college performance, the researcher might administer the SAT to a group of students completing their first year and then simply correlate their SAT scores with their GPAs. In predictive studies there is a time interval between the predictor test and the criterion; in a concurrent study there is no time interval. Figure 5–3 illustrates the temporal relationship between administering the test and measuring the criterion in predictive and concurrent studies.

A natural question is "Which type of study, predictive or concurrent, is best?" As you might expect (or fear), there is not a simple answer to that question. Very often in education and other settings we are interested in making predictions about future performance. Consider our example of the SAT; the question is which students will do well in college and which will not. Inherent in this question is the passage of time. You want to administer a test before students

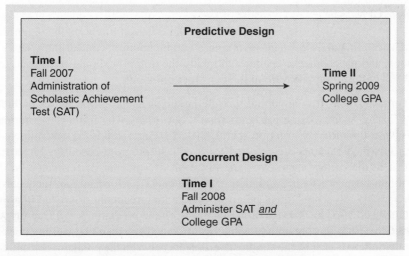

FIGURE 5-3 Illustration of Predictive and Concurrent Studies.

graduate from high school that will help predict the likelihood of their success in college. In situations such as this, predictive studies maintain the temporal relationship and other potentially important characteristics of the real-life situation (AERA et al., 1999).

Because a concurrent study does not retain the temporal relationship or other characteristics of the real-life situation, a predictive study is preferable when prediction is the ultimate goal of assessment. However, predictive studies take considerable time to complete and can be extremely expensive. As a result, although predictive studies might be preferable from a technical perspective, for practical reasons test developers and researchers might adopt a concurrent strategy to save time and/or money. In some situations this is less than optimal and you should be cautious when evaluating the results. However, in certain situations concurrent studies are the preferred approach. Concurrent studies clearly are appropriate when the goal of the test is to determine current status of the examinee as opposed to predicting future outcome (Anastasi & Urbina, 1997). For example, a concurrent approach to validation would be indicated for a test designed to diagnose the presence of psychopathology in elementary school students. Here we are most concerned that the test gives us an accurate assessment of the child's conditions at the time of testing, not at some time in the future. The question is not "Who will develop the disorder?" but "Who has the disorder?" In these situations, the test being validated is often a replacement for a more time-consuming or expensive procedure. For example, a relatively brief screening test might be evaluated to determine whether it can serve as an adequate replacement for a more extensive psychological assessment process. However, if we were interested in selecting students at high risk of developing a disorder in the future, say, for participation in a prevention program, a prediction study would be in order. We would need to address how well or accurately our test predicts who will develop the disorder in question.

Selecting a Criterion. In both predictive and concurrent studies, it is important that the criterion itself be reliable and valid. As noted earlier, reliability is a prerequisite for validity. If a measure is not reliable, whether it is a predictor test or a criterion measure, it cannot be valid. At the same time, reliability does not ensure validity. Therefore, we need to select criterion measures that are also valid. In our example of using the SAT to predict first-year-student GPA, we consider our criterion, GPA, to be a valid measure of success in college. In a concurrent study examining the ability of a test to diagnose psychopathology, the criterion might be the diagnosis provided by an extensive clinical assessment involving a combination of clinical interviews, behavioral observations, and psychometric testing. Optimally the criterion should be viewed as the "gold standard," the best existing measure of the construct of interest.

Criterion Contamination. It is important that the predictor and criterion scores be independently obtained. That is, scores on the predictor should not in any way influence criterion scores. If predictor scores do influence criterion scores, the criterion is said to be contaminated. Consider a situation in which students are selected for a college program based on performance on an aptitude test. If the college instructors are aware of the students' performance on the aptitude test, this might influence their evaluation of the students' performance in their class. Students with high aptitude test scores might be given preferential treatment or graded in a more lenient manner. In this situation knowledge of performance on the predictor is influencing performance on the criterion. Criterion contamination has occurred and any resulting validity coefficients will be artificially inflated. That is, the validity coefficients between the predictor test and the criterion will be larger than they would be had the criterion not been contaminated. The coefficients will suggest the validity is greater than it actually is. To avoid this undesirable situation, test developers must ensure that no individual who evaluates criterion performance has knowledge of the examinees' predictor scores.

Interpreting Validity Coefficients. Predictive and concurrent validity studies examine the relationship between a test and a criterion and the results are often reported in terms of a validity coefficient. At this point it is reasonable to ask, "How large should validity coefficients be?" For example, should we expect validity coefficients greater than 0.80? Although there is no simple answer to this question, validity coefficients should be large enough to indicate that information from the test will help predict how individuals will perform on the criterion measure (e.g., Cronbach & Gleser, 1965). Returning to our example of the SAT, the question is whether the relationship between the SAT and the first-year-student GPA is sufficiently strong so that information about SAT performance helps predict who will succeed in college. If a test provides information that helps predict criterion performance better than any other existing predictor, the test may be useful even if its validity coefficients are relatively small. As a result, testing experts avoid specifying a minimum coefficient size that is acceptable for validity coefficients.

> *If a test provides information that helps predict criterion performance better than any other existing predictor, the test may be useful even if the validity coefficients are relatively small.*

In this context it is useful to also recall the arguments of McCall and Treat (1999):

"The aim of clinical assessment is to gather data that allow us to reduce uncertainty regarding the probabilities of events" (p. 215). Test scores "have information value or are illuminating to the degree they allow us to predict or control events with greater accuracy or with less error than we could have done without them" (p. 217).

Prediction can be an outcome such as accurately receiving a clinical diagnosis, graduating from college, or completing fighter pilot training without crashing! If a test allows us to reduce the uncertainty surrounding the probability of any such event, it is useful.

We cannot overemphasize the importance in the context of assessment, measurement, and prediction (i.e., reducing the error in our estimation of the probability of some event) in deciding whether a validity coefficient is of a sufficiently large magnitude for useful application in that setting. In the prediction of classroom achievement, we tend to look for tests that have coefficients in the mid to high 0.50s and above before we consider them useful. However, much smaller coefficients can have enormous impacts on our ability to improve certain outcomes. For example, Hunter, Schmidt, and Rauschenberger (1984) have demonstrated the far-reaching implications on productivity of workers and subsequently the gross domestic product of the United States (reaching into the 100s of billions of dollars) if employers used employment tests to place workers in the best jobs, even if the employment tests had validity coefficients in only the 0.20s to 0.30s.

Although we cannot set a minimum size for acceptable validity coefficients, certain techniques are available that can help us evaluate the usefulness of test scores for prediction purposes. In Chapter 2 we introduced linear regression, a mathematical procedure that allows you to predict values on one variable given information on another variable. In the context of validity analysis,

> *The* standard error of estimate *is used to describe the amount of prediction error due to the imperfect validity of interpretation of a test score.*

linear regression allows you to predict criterion performance based on predictor test scores. When using linear regression, a statistic called the **standard error of estimate** is used to describe the amount of prediction error due to the imperfect validity of the test. The standard error of estimate is the standard deviation of prediction errors around the predicted score. The formula for the standard error of estimate is quite similar to that for the SEM introduced in the last chapter. We will not go into detail about the use of the S_E, but it allows one to calculate confidence intervals around a client's predicted score that reflect a range of scores that will include his or her actual score with a prescribed probability. It is common for test publishers to provide tables that allow users to calculate 90 and 95% confidence intervals. Psychologists are encouraged to report these confidence intervals as they highlight the fact that our predictions are not perfect and should be interpreted with appropriate caution.

> **Decision-theory models** *help the test user determine how much information a predictor test can contribute when making classification decisions.*

DECISION-THEORY MODELS. When tests are used for making decisions such as in student or personnel selection, factors other than the correlation between the test and criterion are important to consider. For example, factors such as the proportion of applicants needed to fill positions (i.e., selection ratio) and the proportion of applicants who can be successful on the criterion (i.e., base rate) can impact the usefulness of test scores. As an example of how the selection ratio can influence selection decisions, consider an extreme situation in which you have more positions to fill than you have applicants. Here you do not have the luxury of being selective and have to accept all the applicants. In this unfortunate situation no test is useful, no matter how strong a relationship there is between it and the criterion. However, if you have only a few positions to fill and many applicants, even a test with a moderate correlation with the criterion may be useful. As an example of how the base rate can impact selection decisions, consider a situation in which practically every applicant can be successful (i.e., a very easy task). Because almost any applicant selected will be successful, no test is likely to be useful regardless of how strong a relationship there is between it and the criterion. However, if you have a difficult task and few applicants can be successful, even a test with a moderate correlation with the criterion may be useful. To take into consideration these factors, decision-theory models of utility have been developed (Messick, 1989). In brief, **decision-theory models** help the test user determine how much information a predictor test can contribute when making classification decisions. We will not go into detail about decision theory at this point, but we will discuss the use of tests in personnel selection in some detail in Chapter 12. Other good discussions of decision-theory and selection methods for those with interests in this area can be found in Hunter et al. (1984) and Schmidt and Hunter (1998).

Sensitivity and Specificity. Whenever a test score (or even a clinician's opinion or conclusions) is used to classify individuals or some characteristic of an individual into groups, the sensitivity and specificity of the classification method is important. This is best illustrated in the cases of diagnosis or in making hiring decisions. The *sensitivity* of a measure to a diagnostic condition is essentially the ability of the test at a predetermined cut score to detect the presence of the disorder. The *specificity* of a measure is the ability of the test at a predetermined cut score to determine the absence of the disorder. Sensitivity and specificity may sound like mirror images of each other, but they are not. It may be very easy to tell when someone does not have a disorder—but very difficult to tell when they do! Attention deficit hyperactivity disorder (ADHD) is a prime

> *Whenever a test score is used to classify individuals or some characteristic of an individual into groups, the sensitivity and specificity of the classification method is important.*

example, and a controversial diagnosis. ADHD has many so-called mimic disorders—disorders that have similar symptom patterns but a different underlying cause. So it is easy to determine that a child or adolescent does not have the disorder if he or she is absent impulsive, overactive, and inattentive behaviors; determining that the person has the disorder in the presence of these symptoms is far more difficult.

For example, if we give a child a comprehensive measure of behavior to determine if he or she has ADHD, the manual for the scale might give a cut score of $T \geq 70$ on certain subscales as indicative of a high probability of the presence of ADHD—thus it is used to predict the presence of the disorder. Because neither test scores nor clinicians are always right, we should be interested in the relative accuracy of such predictions—which is not apparent from a correlation coefficient. Rather, a type of contingency table such as shown in Table 5–2 is used to analyze the sensitivity and specificity of classifications. Often, recommended cut scores for declaring a classification (e.g., ADHD–not ADHD, hire–do not hire) are investigated using just such tables. Cut scores are then varied and the effects of different scores on the sensitivity and specificity values are determined. Typically as cut scores are used that have increased sensitivity, specificity goes down and vice versa. The trick is to find the appropriate balance in terms of the errors we will make—false positive errors (e.g., diagnosing ADHD when it is not present) and false negative errors (e.g., failing to diagnose ADHD when it is present).

TABLE 5–2	Calculating Sensitivity and Specificity		
Test Results	**Actual Outcome**		**Row Totals**
	Positive	**Negative**	
Positive	**True Positives (Cell A)**	**False Positives (Cell B)**	A + B = Number of Predicted Positive Cases
Negative	**False Negatives (Cell C)**	**True Negatives (Cell D)**	C + D = Number of Predicted Negative Cases
Column Totals =	A + C = Number of Cases with Positive Outcome	B + D = Number of cases with Negative Outcome	

Sensitivity: the ability of the instrument to detect a disorder when it is present. Calculated as **A**/(**A** + **C**)

Specificity: is the ability of an instrument to detect the absence of a disorder when it is (i.e., detect normality). Calculated as **D**/(**B** + **D**)

Positive Predictive Values (PPV): represents the proportion of positive cases that will be detected accurately. Calculated as **A**/(**A** + **B**)

Negative Predictive Values (NPV): represents the proportion of "normal" cases that will be detected accurately. Calculated as **D**/(**C** + **D**)

Given that we will always make mistakes in diagnosis or other judgments about people, which is better—a higher false positive or higher false negative error rate? There is no one-size-fits-all response to this question. In making a determination of which type of error is better to make, we must ask ourselves about the consequences of each type of error for the person involved. Screening measures are designed to detect a high probability of a condition in an economical and efficient manner. If the results of the screening measure suggest the presence of the condition, more extensive and expensive testing or evaluation can be conducted. Screening measures should always emphasize sensitivity over specificity. For example, if we are screening for a deadly cancer, we would want our screener to have extremely high sensitivity so that virtually all who have the disease would be detected and receive early treatment—the cost of false negative errors would be too high. On the other hand, when failing to detect a disorder may have minimal consequences, we may look for better rates of specificity. Table 5–2 demonstrates how sensitivity and specificity values are calculated.

To help us interpret these values better, we also look at positive predictive value (PPV) and negative predictive values (NPV). PPV represents the proportion of positive cases that will be detected accurately, and NPV represents the proportion of "normal" cases that will be detected accurately. As we have noted, this type of analysis can be applied to any set of classifications where the categories to be predicted are mutually exclusive.

Validity Generalization. An important consideration in the interpretation of predictive and concurrent studies is the degree to which they can be generalized to new situations, that is, to circumstances similar to but not the same as those under which the validity studies were conducted. When a test is used for prediction in new settings, research has shown that validity coefficients can vary considerably. For example, a validation study may be conducted using a national sample, but different results may be obtained when the study is repeated using a restricted sample such as a local school district. Originally these results were interpreted as suggesting that test users were not able to rely on existing validation studies and needed to conduct their own local validation studies. However, subsequent research using a new statistical procedure known as meta-analysis indicated that much of the variability previously observed in validity coefficients was actually due to statistical artifacts (e.g., sampling error). When these statistical artifacts were taken into consideration the remaining variability was often negligible, suggesting that validity coefficients can be generalized more than previously thought (AERA et al., 1999). Currently, in many situations local validation studies are not seen as necessary. For example, if there is abundant meta-analytic research that produces consistent results, local validity studies will likely not add much useful information. However, if there is little existing research or the results are inconsistent, then local validity studies may be particularly useful (AERA et al., 1999).

CONVERGENT AND DISCRIMINANT EVIDENCE. Convergent and discriminant evidence of validity have traditionally been incorporated under the category of construct validity. Convergent evidence of validity is obtained when you correlate a test with existing tests that measure the same or similar constructs. For example, if you are developing a new intelligence test you might elect to correlate scores on your new test with scores on the Wechsler Intelligence Scale for Children—Fourth Edition (WISC-IV; Wechsler, 2003). Because the WISC-IV is a well-respected test of intelligence with considerable validity evidence, a strong correlation between the WISC-IV and your new intelligence test would provide evidence that your test is actually measuring the construct of intelligence. Discriminant evidence of validity is obtained when you correlate a test with existing tests that measure dissimilar constructs. For example, if you were validating a test designed to measure anxiety, you might correlate your anxiety scores with a measure of sensation seeking. Because anxious individuals do not typically engage in sensation-seeking behaviors, you would expect a negative correlation between the measures. If your analyses produce the expected negative correlations, this would support your hypothesis.

There is a related, relatively sophisticated validation technique referred to as the **multitrait-multimethod matrix** that combines convergent and divergent strategies (Campbell & Fiske, 1959). This approach requires that you examine two or more traits using two or more measurement methods. The researcher then examines the resulting correlation matrix, comparing the actual relationships with a priori (i.e., preexisting) predictions about the relationships. Table 5–3 presents a hypothetical multitrait-multimethod matrix with depression, hyperactivity, and socialization as the traits, and self-report, parent report, and teacher report as the methods. The reliability coefficients are designated by r_{xx} and are along the principal diagonal (referred to as monotrait-monomethod correlations). The validity coefficients are designated by r_{xy} and are along three shorter diagonals. The validity coefficients are the correlations of scores of the same trait measured by

> *There is a relatively sophisticated validation technique referred to as the* **multitrait-multimethod matrix** *that combines convergent and divergent strategies.*

different methods (i.e., referred to as monotrait-heteromethod correlations). In the matrix **HM** indicates heterotrait-monomethod correlations that reflect relationships between different traits measured by the same method. *HH* indicates heterotrait-heteromethod correlations that reflect relationships between different traits measured by different methods. Campbell and Fiske noted

TABLE 5–3	A Multitrait-Multimethod Matrix								
		Self-Report			Parent Rating			Teacher Rating		
		D	H	S	D	H	S	D	H	S
Self- Report Scale	Depression	r_{xx}								
	Hyperactivity	**HM**	r_{xx}							
	Socialization	**HM**	**HM**	r_{xx}						
Parent Rating Form	Depression	r_{xy}	*HH*	*HH*	r_{xx}					
	Hyperactivity	*HH*	r_{xy}	*HH*	**HM**	r_{xx}				
	Socialization	*HH*	*HH*	r_{xy}	**HM**	**HM**	r_{xx}			
Teacher Rating Form	Depression	r_{xy}	*HH*	*HH*	r_{xy}	*HH*	*HH*	r_{xx}		
	Hyperactivity	*HH*	r_{xy}	*HH*	*HH*	r_{xy}	*HH*	**HM**	r_{xx}	
	Socialization	*HH*	*HH*	r_{xy}	*HH*	*HH*	r_{xy}	**HM**	**HM**	r_{xx}

Note: D, H, and S refers to depression, hyperactivity, and socialization, respectively. Monotrait-monomethod values are reliability coefficients (r_{xx}) and monotrait-heteromethod values are validity coefficients (r_{xy}). HM indicates heterotrait-monomethod correlations and *HH* indicates heterotrait-heteromethod correlations.

that validity coefficients should obviously be greater than correlations between different traits measured by different measures (designated *HH* correlations in Table 5–3), and also greater than different traits measured by the same method (designated **HM** correlations in Table 5–3). In addition to revealing information about convergent and discriminant relationships, this technique provides information about the influence of common method variance. When two measures show an unexpected correlation due to similarity in their method of measurement, we refer to this as method variance. Thus, the multitrait-multimethod matrix allows one to determine what the test correlates with, what it does not correlate with, and how the method of measurement influences these relationships. This approach has considerable technical and theoretical appeal, yet difficulty with implementation and interpretation has somewhat limited its application to date.

CONTRASTED GROUPS STUDIES. Validity evidence can also be garnered by examining different groups, which are expected, based on theory, to differ on the construct the test is designed to measure. This is referred to as a contrasted group study. For example, if you are attempting to validate a new measure of intelligence, you might form two groups, individuals with mental retardation and normal control participants. In this type of study, the diagnoses or group assignment would have been made using assessment procedures that do not involve the test under consideration. Each group would then be administered the new test, and its validity as a measure of intelligence would be supported if the predefined groups differed in performance in the predicted manner. Although the preceding example is rather simplistic, it illustrates a general approach that has numerous applications. For example, many constructs in psychology and education have a developmental component. That is, you expect younger participants to perform differently than older participants. Tests designed to measure these constructs can be examined to determine whether they demonstrate the expected developmental changes by looking at the performance of groups reflecting different ages and/or education. In the past, this type of validity evidence typically has been classified as construct validity.

Evidence Based on Internal Structure

By examining the internal structure of a test (or battery of tests) one can determine whether the relationships between test items (or, in the case of test batteries, component tests) are consistent with the construct the test is designed to measure (AERA et al., 1999). For example, one test might be designed to measure a construct that is hypothesized to involve a single dimension, whereas another test might measure a construct thought to involve multiple dimensions.

> *By examining the internal structure of the test, we can determine if its actual structure is consistent with the hypothesized structure of the construct it measures.*

By examining the internal structure of the test, we can determine whether its actual structure is consistent with the hypothesized structure of the construct it measures. Factor analysis is a sophisticated statistical procedure used to determine the number of conceptually distinct factors or dimensions underlying a test or battery of tests. Because factor analysis is a prominent approach to collecting validity evidence based on internal structure, we will briefly discuss it.

FACTOR ANALYSIS: A GENTLE INTRODUCTION. As noted, factor analysis plays a prominent role in test validation. The *Standards* (AERA et al., 1999) defined factor analysis as:

> Any of several statistical methods describing the interrelationships of a set of variables by statistically deriving new variables, called factors, that are fewer in number than the original set of variables. (p. 175)

Reynolds and Kamphaus (2003) provided a slightly more theoretical definition, noting that factor analysis is a statistical approach that allows one to evaluate the presence and structure of any latent constructs existing among a set of variables. These definitions are in agreement, because in factor analysis terminology a factor is a hypothetical variable reflecting a latent construct—the factor underlies and is at least partly responsible for the way examinees respond to questions on the variables that make up the factor. The mathematical process of factor analysis scrutinizes the intercorrelation matrix of a set of variables to see if patterns of relationships emerge that are useful in explaining any patterns of test scores that may occur. The "set of variables" mentioned in these explanations can be either the individual items of a test or the subtest scores of a test battery. For example, a hypothetical personality test with 200 individual items might be analyzed with the results indicating that five factors, or dimensions, exist among the items. Chapter 10 on personality assessment describes the five-factor model that holds that five major factors or dimensions underlie the construct of personality. These factors include:

- *Neuroticism*: Individuals who score high on this factor tend to experience high levels of negative affects (e.g., sadness, anxiety, and anger) and are particularly sensitive to stress. In contrast, individuals who score low tend to be emotionally stable and less reactive to stress.
- *Extraversion*: Individuals with high scores on this factor tend to be sociable, active, and prefer large-group activities whereas those with low scores tend to be reserved, appreciate solitude, and are independent.
- *Openness to experience*: Individuals with high scores tend to be curious and appreciate novel experiences whereas those with low scores prefer familiar and conventional behavior.
- *Agreeableness*: Individuals with high scores tend to be compassionate and altruistic whereas those with low scores tend to be disagreeable, egocentric, and antagonistic.
- *Conscientiousness*: Individuals with high scores tend to be self-controlled, organized, and dependable whereas those with low scores tend to be less disciplined and unreliable.

If the author of our hypothetical personality test had developed the personality test based on the five-factor model, the results of this factor analysis could be used to support the validity of the test. The test author could also develop five-factor scores that summarize the examinees' responses on the test.

Factor analysis can also be applied to the subtest scores of a test battery. This is often pursued with intelligence and other maximum performance test batteries (e.g., neuropsychological batteries). For example, the Wechsler Intelligence Scale for Children—Fourth Edition (WISC-IV; Wechsler, 2003) is a battery that contains 15 subtests. Based on factor analytic studies, the subtests of the WISC-IV were found to measure four major dimensions and the test produces the following factor-based scores:

- *Verbal Comprehension Index*: Reflects verbal reasoning, verbal conceptualization, and knowledge of facts.

- *Perceptual Reasoning Index*: Reflects perceptual and nonverbal reasoning, spatial processing, and visual-spatial-motor integration.
- *Working Memory Index*: Reflects working memory capacity and includes attention, concentration, and mental control.
- *Processing Speed Index*: Reflects ability to process nonverbal material quickly when adequate levels of attention are present as well as visual-motor coordination.

The WISC-IV and other intelligence tests will be discussed in more detail in Chapter 9.

Factor Analysis: The Process. Factor analysis begins with a table of intercorrelations among the variables (individual items or subtests) that is referred to as a correlation matrix. Table 5–4 illustrates a correlation matrix showing the correlations between two subtests measuring memory (i.e., story memory and word list memory) and two subtests measuring visual-spatial abilities (visual analysis and visual-spatial design). A review of these correlations reveals that the two memory subtests showed moderate correlations with each other (i.e., $r = 0.52$), but small correlations with the visual-spatial subtests (ranging from 0.14 to 0.18). Likewise, the two visual-spatial subtests showed moderate correlations with each other (i.e., $r = 0.64$), but small correlations with the memory subtests (ranging from 0.14 to 0.18).

Several different factor analytic methods have been developed (often referred to as factor extraction techniques), and each has it own supporters and detractors. For example, principal component analysis (PCA) begins with the assumption that the variables have perfect reliability and places a value of 1.0 in the diagonal of the correlation matrix. With PCA all of the variance is analyzed, including shared variance (i.e., variance shared with other variables), unique variance (i.e., variance unique to individual variables), and error variance (i.e., variance due to measurement error). In contrast, principal factor analysis (PFA) does not assume the variables have perfect reliability and begins by placing the squared multiple correlation of all the other variables with the variable being considered (R^2) in the diagonal of the correlation matrix. With PFA, only shared variance is analyzed, with unique and error variance excluded. There are

> *Several different factor analytic methods have been developed and each has it own supporters and detractors.*

a number of other factor analytic methods available, but when the underlying factor structure is robust, it will typically emerge regardless of which extraction method is used—although the relative strength of the factors will vary across methods.

After selecting a factoring technique and applying it to the data, one must determine how many factors to retain. On one hand, the more factors retained the more variance that is explained

TABLE 5–4	Correlation Matrix			
	Story Memory	**Word List Memory**	**Visual Analysis**	**Visual-Spatial Design**
Story memory	1.00	0.52	0.15	0.18
Word list memory	0.52	1.00	0.14	0.16
Visual analysis	0.15	0.14	1.00	0.64
Visual-spatial design	0.18	0.16	0.64	1.00

by the factor solution. On the other hand, retaining too many factors can result in a complex solution that does not facilitate interpretation. Selecting the number of factors to retain is not as straightforward a process as one might imagine, but researchers have a number of guidelines to help them. One common approach, referred to as the Kaiser-Guttman criteria, is to examine eigenvalues and retain values greater than 1.0. Eigenvalues reflect variance when each variable being analyzed contributes a variance value of 1.0. Retaining factors with eigenvalues greater than 1.0 ensures that each factor that is retained accounts for more variance than any single variable being analyzed. Another approach to determine how many factors to retain is the scree test (Cattell, 1966). Here factors are plotted on the horizontal axis and eigenvalues are plotted on the vertical axis. The researcher then examines the graph and looks for an "elbow," a point where previous factors explain substantially more variance than those past the point. Figure 5–4 presents a hypothetical scree plot. Examination of this plot suggests the presence of an elbow at the fifth factor. If you draw a line through the first five points you get a reasonably good fit. However, another line with a different slope would need to be drawn to fit the remaining points. Another important consideration is the interpretability of the factor solution. That is, does the factor solution make sense from a psychological perspective? Put another way, do the variables loading on a factor share a common theme or meaning? For example, on an intelligence test all the variables loading on a single factor might be measuring verbal processing skills. On a personality test, all the variables loading on a factor might reflect a propensity to experience negative affect. A factor solution that is not interpretable has little or no practical value and will likely provide scant evidence of validity.

All factor extraction methods produce a factor matrix that reflects the correlations between the variables and the factors (i.e., latent constructs). Table 5–5 presents a hypothetical factor matrix. In this example there are two subtests that measure memory-related abilities (i.e., story memory and word list memory) and two subtests that measure visual processing abilities

FIGURE 5-4 Scree Plot.

TABLE 5-5	Factor Matrix	
Variables	**Factor 1**	**Factor 2**
Story memory	0.77	−0.49
Word list memory	0.74	−0.52
Visual analysis	0.62	0.61
Visual-spatial design	0.61	0.62

> *To enhance interpretability (i.e., understanding the meaning of the factors), most researchers geometrically rotate the axes of the factors.*

(i.e., visual analysis and visual-spatial design). This initial factor matrix is difficult to interpret. All the subtests have moderate-to-high loadings on Factor 1. On Factor 2, the first two variables have negative loadings and the second two factors have loadings that approximate their loadings on Factor 1. To enhance interpretability (i.e., understanding the meaning of the factors), most researchers geometrically rotate the axes of the factors. The goals of these rotations are typically to eliminate any large negative loadings and to yield a solution where each variable has high loadings on only one factor and small loadings on all other factors (referred to as "simple structure"). If these goals are achieved, the rotated factor pattern should be easier to interpret.

Table 5–6 presents a rotated factor pattern for the same subtests presented in Table 5–5. This rotated factor pattern is more interpretable, revealing that the two variables involving memory load on Factor 1, and the two variables involving visual processing load on Factor 2. Researchers have a number of options when selecting a rotation method. Some rotation methods produce orthogonal factors—the term orthogonal means the factors are not correlated. The most popular orthogonal rotation method is the Varimax technique. Other rotation techniques allow oblique factors—the term oblique as used here means the factors can be correlated. Most researchers select orthogonal rotations, because they are simpler to interpret, but oblique rotations may be appropriate when the factors are correlated in real-world applications (e.g., ability test batteries).

Confirmatory Factor Analysis. Our discussion of factor analysis to this point has focused on exploratory factor analysis. As described, exploratory factor analysis examines or "explores" a data set in order to detect the presence and structure of latent constructs existing among a set of variables. Confirmatory factor analysis is an alternative set of procedures that is gaining popularity among researchers. With confirmatory factor analysis the researcher specifies a hypothetical

TABLE 5-6	Rotated Factor Matrix	
Variables	**Factor 1**	**Factor 2**
Story memory	0.90	0.06
Word list memory	0.90	0.11
Visual analysis	0.08	0.87
Visual-spatial design	0.09	0.87

factor structure and then examines the data to see if there is a reasonable fit between the actual and the hypothesized structure of the data set. There are a number of statistics available (referred to as model-fit statistics) that statistically test the fit or match between the actual and hypothesized factor structure. As Cronbach (1990) observed, a positive finding in confirmatory factor analysis does not necessarily indicate that the hypothesized structure is optimal, only that the

> *A positive finding in confirmatory factor analysis does not necessarily indicate that the hypothesized structure is optimal, only that the data do not clearly contradict it.*

data do not clearly contradict it. In summary, test publishers and researchers use factor analysis either to confirm or to refute the proposition that the internal structure of the tests is consistent with that of the construct being measured. Later in this chapter we will describe the results of both exploratory and confirmatory factor analytic studies of the Reynolds Intellectual Assessment Scales (RIAS; Reynolds & Kamphaus, 2003).

Factor analysis is not the only approach researchers use to examine the internal structure of a test. Any technique that allows researchers to examine the relationships between test components can be used in this context. For example, if the items on a test are assumed to reflect a continuum from very easy to very difficult, empirical evidence of a pattern of increasing difficulty can be used as validity evidence. If a test is thought to measure a one-dimensional construct, a measure of item homogeneity might be useful (AERA et al., 1999). The essential feature of this type of validity evidence is that researchers empirically examine the internal structure of the test and compare it to the structure of the construct of interest. This type of validity evidence traditionally has been incorporated under the category of construct validity and is most relevant with tests measuring theoretical constructs such as intelligence or personality.

Evidence Based on Response Processes

Validity evidence based on the response processes invoked by a test involves an analysis of the fit between the performance and actions the examinees actually engage in and the construct being assessed. Although this type of validity evidence has not received as much attention as the approaches previously discussed, it has considerable potential and in terms of the traditional nomenclature it would likely be classified under construct validity. For example, consider a test designed to measure mathematical reasoning ability. In this situation it would be important to investigate the examinees' response processes to verify that they are actually engaging in analysis and reasoning as opposed to applying rote mathematical algorithms (AERA et al., 1999). There are numerous ways of collecting this type of validity evidence, including interviewing examinees about their response processes and strategies, recording behavioral indicators such as response times and eye movements, or even analyzing the types of errors committed (AERA et al., 1999; Messick, 1989).

The *Standards* (AERA et al., 1999) noted that studies of response processes are not restricted to individuals taking the test, but may also examine the assessment professionals who administer or grade the tests. When testing personnel records or evaluating the performance of examinees, it is important to make sure that their processes or actions are in line with the construct being measured. For example, many tests provide specific criteria or rubrics that are intended to guide the scoring process. The Wechsler Individual Achievement Test—Second Edition (WIAT-II;

The Psychological Corporation, 2002) has a section to assess written expression that requires the examinee to write an essay. To facilitate grading, the authors include an analytic scoring rubric that has four evaluative categories: mechanics (e.g., spelling, punctuation), organization (e.g., structure, sequencing, use of introductory/concluding sentences, etc.), theme development (use of supporting statements, evidence), and vocabulary (e.g., specific and varied words, unusual expressions). In validating this assessment it would be helpful to evaluate the behaviors of individuals scoring the test to verify that the criteria are being carefully applied and that irrelevant factors are not influencing the scoring process.

Evidence Based on Consequences of Testing

Recently, researchers have started examining the consequences of test use, both intended and unintended, as an aspect of validity. In many situations the use of tests is based largely on the assumption that their use will result in some specific benefit (AERA et al., 1999; also see McFall & Treat, 1999). For example, if a test is used to identify qualified applicants for employment, it is assumed that the use of the test will result in better hiring decisions (e.g., lower training costs, lower turnover). If a test is used to help select students for admission to a college program, it is assumed that the use of the test will result in better admissions decisions (e.g., greater student success and higher retention). This line of validity evidence simply asks the question, "Are these benefits being achieved?" This type of validity evidence, often referred to as consequential validity evidence, is most applicable to tests designed for selection and promotion.

> *Researchers have started examining the consequences of test use, both intended and unintended, as an aspect of validity.*

Some authors have advocated a broader conception of validity, one that incorporates social issues and values. For example, Messick (1989) in his influential chapter suggested that the conception of validity should be expanded so that it "formally brings consideration of value implications and social consequences into the validity framework" (p. 20). Other testing experts have criticized this position. For example, Popham (2000) suggested that incorporating social consequences into the definition of validity would detract from the clarity of the concept. Popham argued that validity is clearly defined as the "accuracy of score-based inferences" (p. 111) and that the inclusion of social and value issues unnecessarily complicates the concept. The *Standards* (AERA et al., 1999) appeared to avoid this broader conceptualization of validity. The *Standards* distinguished between consequential evidence that is directly tied to the concept of validity and evidence that is related to social policy. This is an important but potentially difficult distinction to make. Consider a situation in which research suggests that the use of a test results in different job selection rates for different groups. If the test measures only the skills and abilities related to job performance, evidence of differential selection rates does not detract from the validity of the test. This information might be useful in guiding social and policy decisions, but it is not technically an aspect of validity. If, however, the test measures factors unrelated to job performance, the evidence is relevant to validity. In this case, it may suggest a problem with the validity of the test such as the inclusion of construct-irrelevant factors.

Another component to this process is to consider the consequences of not using tests. Even though the consequences of testing may produce some adverse effects, these must be contrasted with the positive and negative effects of alternatives to using psychological tests. If more subjective approaches to decision making are employed, for example, the likelihood of cultural, ethnic, and gender biases in the decision-making process will likely increase. This typically raises many controversies, and many professionals in the field attempt to avoid these issues, especially at the level of training students. We disagree. We believe this issue is of great importance and address concerns related to cultural bias in testing later in this book, devoting an entire chapter to these issues.

INTEGRATING EVIDENCE OF VALIDITY

The *Standards* (AERA et al., 1999) stated that "Validation can be viewed as developing a scientifically sound validity argument to support the intended interpretation of test scores and their relevance to the proposed use" (p. 9). The development of this **validity argument** typically involves the integration of numerous lines of evidence into a coherent commentary. As we have noted, different types of validity evidence are most applicable to different types of tests. Here is a brief review of some of the prominent applications of different types of validity evidence.

> *The development of a* **validity argument** *typically involves the integration of numerous lines of evidence into a coherent commentary.*

- Evidence based on test content is most often reported with academic achievement tests and tests used in the selection of employees.
- Evidence based on relations to other variables can be either test-criterion validity evidence, which is most applicable when tests are used to predict performance on an external criterion, or convergent and discriminant evidence of validity, which can be useful with a wide variety of tests, including intelligence tests, achievement tests, personality tests, and so on.
- Evidence based on internal structure can be useful with a wide variety of tests, but has traditionally been applied with tests measuring theoretical constructs such as personality or intelligence.
- Evidence based on response processes can be useful with practically any test that requires examinees to engage in any cognitive or behavioral activity.
- Evidence based on consequences of testing is most applicable to tests designed for selection and promotion, but can be useful with a wide range of tests.

You might have noticed that most types of validity evidence have applications to a broad variety of tests, and this is the way it should be. The integration of multiple lines of research or types of evidence results in a more compelling validity argument. It is also important to remember that every interpretation or intended use of a test must be validated. As we noted earlier, if a test is used for different applications, each use or application must be validated. In these situations it is imperative that different types of validity evidence be provided. Table 5–7 provides a summary of the major applications of different types of validity evidence.

Although we have emphasized a number of distinct approaches to collecting evidence to support the validity of score interpretations, validity evidence is actually broader than the strategies described in this chapter. The *Standards* (AERA et al., 1999) stated:

TABLE 5-7	Sources of Validity Evidence	
Source	**Example**	**Major Applications**
Evidence based on test content	Analysis of item relevance and content coverage	Achievement tests and tests used in the selection of employees
Evidence based on relations to other variables	Test criterion; convergent and discriminant evidence; contrasted groups studies	Wide variety of tests
Evidence based on internal structure	Factor analysis, analysis of test homogeneity	Wide variety of tests, but particularly useful with tests of constructs such as personality or intelligence
Evidence based on response processes	Analysis of the processes engaged in by the examinee or examiner	Any test that requires examinees to engage in a cognitive or behavioral activity
Evidence based on consequences of testing structure	Analysis of the intended and unintended consequences of testing	Most applicable to tests designed for selection and promotion, but useful on a wide range of tests

Ultimately, the validity of an intended interpretation of test scores relies on all the evidence relevant to the technical quality of a testing system. This includes evidence of careful test construction; adequate score reliability; appropriate test administration and scoring, accurate score scaling; equating, and standard setting; and careful attention to fairness for all examinees. (p. 17)

In other words, when considering the validity of score interpretations, one should consider in totality the evidence of the technical quality of the test. Obviously the five sources of validity evidence described in this chapter are central to building a validity argument, but other information should be carefully considered. Does the test produce reliable scores, is the standardization sample representative and of sufficient size, is there adequate standardization of both administration and scoring? In sum, is the test a well-developed and technically sound instrument? In Chapter 6 we will add to this discussion and provide practical guidance to ensuring the validity of test score interpretations. This is a process that begins when you first begin thinking about developing a test.

Finally, the development of a validity argument is an ongoing process; it considers existing research and incorporates new scientific findings. Whereas test developers are obligated to provide initial evidence of the validity of the score interpretations they are proposing, research from independent researchers subsequent to the release of the test is also essential. A number of excellent professional journals (e.g., *Psychological Assessment, Psychometrika*) routinely publish empirical research articles covering the psychometric properties of different tests. Additionally, those using tests are expected to weigh the validity evidence and make their own judgments about the appropriateness of the test in their own situations and settings. This places the clinical practitioners using psychological tests in the final, most responsible role in the validation process.

HOW TEST MANUALS REPORT VALIDITY EVIDENCE: THE REYNOLDS INTELLECTUAL ASSESSMENT SCALES (RIAS)

To illustrate how validity evidence is reported in test manuals, we will use examples from the Reynolds Intellectual Assessment Scales (RIAS; Reynolds & Kamphaus, 2003). The RIAS is an individually administered intelligence test for clients 3 years to 94 years of age. The RIAS contains a two-subtest Verbal Intelligence Index (VIX) and a two-subtest Nonverbal Intelligence Index (NIX). The two verbal subtests are Guess What (GWH) and Verbal Reasoning (VRZ). The two nonverbal subtests are Odd-Item Out (OIO) and What's Missing (WHM). All four subtests are combined to form the Composite Intelligence Index (CIX). It takes approximately 20 to 25 minutes to administer the four intelligence scale subtests. The RIAS also includes a conormed, supplemental measure of memory that is composed of two memory subtests that yield a Composite Memory Index (CMX). The two memory subtests are Verbal Memory (VRM) and Nonverbal Memory (NVM). The administration of the memory subtests requires approximately 10 to 15 minutes. The RIAS was standardized on a national sample of 2,438 individuals that is representative of the U.S. population.

Chapter 6 of the test manual is titled Validity of Test Score Interpretations. The authors reported validity evidence using the nomenclature presented in the *Standards* (AERA et al., 1999). They started by describing Carroll's (1993) three-stratum theory of intelligence (this theory will be discussed in detail in Chapter 9) and noted that the RIAS focuses on the assessment of stratum-three and stratum-two abilities from Carroll's theory. The authors then described how the different subtests and index scores of the RIAS match the three-stratum theory of intelligence, and hypothesized validity evidence that would support this relationship.

In terms of validity evidence based on test content, they examined the stimuli, items, and format of the individual RIAS subtests. The authors noted that although the individual items are new, the general formats of the subtests have a long history of use in cognitive assessment and have been thoroughly studied. They supported these statements in a subtest-by-subtest manner providing citations of research supporting the validity of these tasks in intellectual assessment.

The item-review and item-selection process that was used in developing the RIAS was also described. Early in the development process a panel of minority psychologists experienced in assessment reviewed all items to determine if they were appropriate as measures of the relevant constructs and were applicable across the U.S. cultures. A second panel with psychologists with diverse training (e.g., school, clinical, neuropsychology) also reviewed the items. Items questioned by either panel were either eliminated or revised. Final items were selected based on traditional item statistics such as item difficulty, item discrimination, and item consistency (these will be discussed in detail in Chapter 7). Item analyses were also conducted across age, gender, and ethnic groupings to ensure they were appropriate. In summary, the authors held that a review of test content supported the validity of the RIAS. The test formats are longstanding and have been well researched and the individual items passed multiple levels of expert and statistical review and analysis.

Validity evidence based on the internal structure is the next topic described in the test manual. First, the internal consistencies of the index scores are examined. It is noted that Cronbach's coefficient alphas for all index scores exceeded 0.90. In addition to this suggesting strong reliability, these strong coefficients reflect high internal consistency among the subtests comprising the indexes. The results of exploratory and confirmatory factor analysis are described

TABLE 5-8	RIAS Intelligence Subtest Loadings for Individuals 19–54 Years	
Subtests	**Factor 1**	**Factor 2**
Guess What	0.74	0.48
Verbal Reasoning	0.73	0.45
Odd-Item Out	0.42	0.62
What's Missing	0.36	0.60

next. The results of principal factor analyses with Varimax rotations are reported for four subtests (i.e., the four intelligence subtests) and six subtests (i.e., the four intelligence subtests and the two memory subtests). Although an examination of scree plots suggested that two and three factors solutions were both viable, a two-factor solution was selected because it made the most psychological and psychometric sense. The two factors identified reflect verbal and nonverbal abilities. All of the verbal subtests loaded on the rotated Factor 1 and all of the nonverbal subtests loaded on Factor 2. This pattern emerged when the analysis was limited to the four intelligence subtests and also when the memory subtests were included. Table 5–8 presents the intelligence subtest loadings for individuals in the 19–54 age group. To assess the stability of the two-factor solution across different groups, the authors examined the factor structure across age groups, gender, and ethnicity. They presented tables with the factor loadings for these groups, and presented statistics that test the comparability of factor solutions across groups. These analyses demonstrate that the two-factor solution is stable across these groups.

A series of confirmatory factor analyses was also conducted. In these analyses several models were examined including a one-factor solution, a two-factor solution (reflecting verbal and nonverbal factors), and a three-factor solution (reflecting verbal, nonverbal, and memory factors). The results support the one-factor and two-factor solutions, which supports the validity of the Composite Intelligence Index (CIX), Verbal Intelligence Index (VIX), and Nonverbal Intelligence Index (NIX). The authors suggested that further research is needed to assess the validity of the Composite Memory Index (CMX) in clinical populations.

The authors next turned their attention to validity evidence based on relations to other variables. This included an examination of developmental trends. The authors noted that intellectual ability grows rapidly in young children, starts to plateau in adolescence with some continued growth, and finally declines in the elderly. Correlations and plots of smoothed polynomial curves were presented that document the predicted relationship between performance on RIAS raw scores and age. Correlations between RIAS scores and performance and the Wechsler intelligence scales and academic achievement were also presented. These correlations revealed the expected relationships between the RIAS scores and other measures of intelligence and achievement. The analyses also indicated that RIAS scores were not strongly impacted by motor coordination and motor speed. The authors also examined performance on the RIAS in a number of clinical groups (e.g., adults with mild mental retardation, children with learning disabilities). All the clinical groups demonstrated deviations from the population mean as expected, again supporting the validity of the RIAS score interpretations.

In closing, the authors considered validity evidence based on the consequences of testing. In this context they noted that although this category of validity evidence is most applicable to tests designed for selection purposes, evidence that the RIAS can provide an accurate estimate of intelligence and memory across gender and ethnic groups supports the diagnostic utility of this instrument. The authors also noted that the development of a validity argument should incorporate not only the validity evidence presented in a test manual's chapter on validity, but also the totality of information provided on the development, standardization, scaling, reliability, and so on related to the test.

Summary

In this chapter we introduced the concept of validity. In the context of psychological tests and measurement, validity refers to the degree to which theoretical and empirical evidence supports the meaning and interpretation of test scores. In essence the validity question is "Are the intended interpretations of test scores appropriate and accurate?" Numerous factors can limit the validity of interpretations. The two major internal threats to validity are construct underrepresentation (i.e., the test is not a comprehensive measure of the construct it is supposed to measure) and construct-irrelevant variance (i.e., the test measures content or skills unrelated to the construct). Other factors that may reduce validity include instructional and coaching procedures, test administration/scoring procedures, and client characteristics. There is also a close relationship between validity and reliability. For a test to be valid it must be reliable, but at the same time reliability does not ensure validity. Put another way, reliability is a necessary but insufficient condition for validity.

As a psychometric concept, validity has evolved and changed over the last half century. Until the 1970s validity was generally divided into three distinct types: content validity, criterion-related validity, and construct validity. This terminology was widely accepted and is still often referred to as the traditional nomenclature. However, in the 1970s and 1980s measurement professionals started conceptualizing validity as a unitary construct. That is, although there are different ways of collecting validity evidence, there are not distinct types of validity. To get away from the perception of distinct types of validity, today we refer to different types of validity evidence. The most current typology includes the following five categories:

- Evidence based on test content. Evidence derived from a detailed analysis of the test content includes the type of questions or tasks included in the test and guidelines for administration and scoring. Collecting content-based validity evidence is often based on the evaluation of expert judges about the correspondence between the test's content and its construct. The key issues addressed by these expert judges are whether the test items assess relevant content (i.e., item relevance) and the degree to which the construct is assessed in a comprehensive manner (i.e., content coverage).
- Evidence based on relations to other variables. Evidence based on an examination of the relationships between test performance and external variables or criteria can actually be divided into two subcategories of validity evidence: test-criterion evidence and convergent and discriminant evidence. Test-criterion evidence is typically of interest when a test is designed to predict performance on a criterion such as job performance or success in college. Two types of studies are often used to collect test-criterion evidence: predictive and concurrent studies. They differ in the timing of test administration and criterion measurement. In a

predictive study the test is administered and there is an interval of time before the criterion is measured. In concurrent studies the test is administered and the criterion is measured at approximately the same time. The collection of convergent and discriminant evidence involves examining the relationship between a test and other tests that measure similar constructs (convergent evidence) or dissimilar constructs (discriminant evidence). If the test scores demonstrate the expected relationships with these existing measures, this can be used as evidence of validity.

- Evidence based on internal structure. Evidence examining the relationships among test items and components, or the internal structure of the test, can help determine whether the structure of the test is consistent with the hypothesized structure of the construct it measures.
- Evidence based on response processes. Evidence analyzing the processes engaged in by the examinee or examiner can help determine if test goals are being achieved. For example, if the test is designed to measure mathematical reasoning, it is helpful to verify that the examinees are actually engaging in mathematical reasoning and analysis as opposed to performing rote calculations.
- Evidence based on consequences of testing. Evidence examining the intended and unintended consequences of testing is based on the common belief that some benefit will result from the use of tests. Therefore, it is reasonable to confirm that these benefits are being achieved. This type of validity evidence has gained considerable attention in recent years and there is continuing debate regarding the scope of this evidence. Some authors feel that social consequences and values should be incorporated into the conceptualization of validity, whereas others feel such a broadening would detract from the clarity of the concept.

Different lines of validity evidence are integrated into a cohesive validity argument that supports the use of the test for different applications. The development of this validity argument is a dynamic process that integrates existing research and incorporates new scientific findings. Validation is the shared responsibility of the test authors, test publishers, researchers, and even test users. Test authors and publishers are expected to provide preliminary evidence of the validity of proposed interpretations of test scores, whereas researchers often pursue independent validity studies. Ultimately, those using tests are expected to weigh the validity evidence and make their own judgments about the appropriateness of the test in their own situations and settings, placing the practitioners or consumers of psychological tests in the final, most responsible role in this process.

Key Terms and Concepts

Concurrent studies, 165

Content coverage, 162

Decision-theory models, 168

Face validity, 163

Item relevance, 162

Multitrait-multimethod matrix, 171

Predictive studies, 165

Standard error of estimate, 168

Test-criterion evidence, 165

Validity, 155

Validity argument, 179

Recommended Readings

American Educational Research Association, American Psychological Association, & National Council on Measurement in Education. (1999). *Standards for educational and psychological testing.* Washington, DC: AERA. Chapter 1 is a must read for those wanting to gain a thorough understanding of validity.

Cronbach, L. J., & Gleser, G. C. (1965). *Psychological tests and personnel decisions* (2nd ed.). Champaign: University of Illinois Press. A classic, particularly with regard to validity evidence based on relations to external variables.

Gorsuch, R. L. (1983). *Factor analysis* (2nd ed.). Hillsdale, NJ: Erlbaum. A classic for those really interested in understanding factor analysis.

Hunter, J. E., Schmidt, F. L., & Rauschenberger, J. (1984). Methodological, statistical, and ethical issues in the study of bias in psychological tests. In C. R. Reynolds & R. T. Brown (Eds.), *Perspectives on bias in mental testing* (pp. 41–100). New York: Plenum Press.

Lee, D., Reynolds, C. R., & Willson, V. L. (2003). Standardized test administration: Why bother? *Journal of Forensic Neuropsychology, 3*, 55–81.

McFall, R. M., & Treat, T. T. (1999). Quantifying the information value of clinical assessments with signal detection theory. *Annual Review of Psychology, 50,* 215–241.

Messick, S. (1989). Validity. In R. L. Linn (Ed.), *Educational measurement* (3rd ed., pp. 13–103). Upper Saddle River, NJ: Merrill/Prentice Hall. A little technical at times, but very influential.

Schmidt, F. L., & Hunter, J. E. (1998). The validity and utility of selection methods in personnel psychology: Practical and theoretical implications of 85 years of research findings. *Psychological Bulletin, 124,* 262–274. A must read on personnel selection!

Sireci, S. G. (1998). Gathering and analyzing content validity data. *Educational Assessment, 5,* 299–321. This article provides a good review of approaches to collecting validity evidence based on test content, including some of the newer quantitative approaches.

Tabachnick, B. G., & Fidel, L. S. (1996). *Using multivariate statistics* (3rd ed.). New York: HarperCollins. A great chapter on factor analysis that is less technical than Gorsuch (1993).

Chapter Six

Item Development

Everyone thinks it is easy to develop good test items, until they try!

Learning Objectives

After reading and studying this chapter, students should be able to:

1. Distinguish between objective and subjective items.
2. Distinguish between selected-response and constructed-response items.
3. Specify the strengths and limitations of selected-response and constructed-response items and the specific item formats.
4. Understand, describe, and apply general guidelines for developing items.
5. Demonstrate entry-level skills in developing multiple-choice items.
6. Demonstrate entry-level skills in developing true–false items.
7. Demonstrate entry-level skills in developing matching items.
8. Demonstrate entry-level skills in developing essay items.
9. Demonstrate entry-level skills in developing short-answer items.
10. Demonstrate entry-level skills in developing typical response items.

In this chapter we will review many of the different item formats available to test authors and provide some basic guidelines for developing items. We will devote more time to the development of items for maximum performance tests, but we will also address the development of items for typical response tests. We will start with a brief survey of the most popular item formats before proceeding to a discussion of guidelines for developing items.

ITEM FORMATS

Different authors use different classification systems or schemes when categorizing test items. Historically a popular approach has been to classify test items as either "objective" or "subjective." This distinction usually referred to how the items were scored (i.e., either in an objective or subjective manner). If experts

> *One popular approach has been to classify test items as either objective or subjective.*

in the area would demonstrate a high level of agreement on whether the item has been answered correctly or in the keyed direction, the item is considered to be **objective**; where much disagreement might exist, the item is classified as **subjective**. The relative objectivity and subjectivity of items anchor two ends of a continuum, and there is often no bright shining line for declaring an item as totally objective or subjective. However, in the context of maximum performance tests, there should be no disagreement among individuals grading multiple-choice items. The items should be easily scored "correct" or "incorrect" according to the scoring criteria. The same goes for true–false and matching items. They can all be scored in an objective manner and are classified as objective: Everyone agrees on which answers are keyed as correct and incorrect. This rationale also applies to objective items on typical response tests. For example, true–false items are also used on typical response tests and these can be scored in an objective manner.

In contrast, essay items are considered subjective because grading them involves subjective judgments on the part of the individuals grading the test. It is not too surprising that two graders might assign different grades to the same essay item. Another example could be an examinee's responses on an oral examination. Here there also might be considerable subjectivity in scoring and two individuals might score the responses differently. Our own personal experiences in administering the oral section of state board licensing examinations for psychologists—where oral examiners are trained, provided a manual, and allowed to observe experienced examiners, and need only score the examinee's answers as pass–fail—indicate such exams to be highly subjective, with a surprising amount of disagreement among examiners. Primarily for this reason, many credentialing bodies are doing away with oral exams in favor of objective examination procedures for such critical decisions. As a result, essay and other test items involving more subjective scoring are classified as subjective. In the context of typical response tests there are also item formats that require subjective judgment. For example, projective personality tests are typical response tests that require the respondent to respond to ambiguous stimuli. The Rorschach inkblot test is an example of a projective personality test where the test taker is shown an inkblot and asked "What might this be?" One person might envision a boat, another sees a swan, another sees a dragon. The scoring of this type of test typically involves considerable subjective judgment.

Although the objective–subjective distinction is generally useful there are some limitations. For example, are short-answer items objective or subjective? Many authors refer

> *A more direct approach is to classify items as either* selected-response *or* constructed-response items, *and this is the one adopted in this textbook.*

to them as objective items, but scoring short-answer items often involves considerable subjectivity. A more direct approach is to classify items as either selected-response or constructed-response items. With this approach, if an item requires an examinee to select a response from available alternatives, it is classified as a **selected-response item**. Multiple-choice, true–false, and matching items are all selected-response items. If an item requires examinees to create or construct a response it is classified as a **constructed-response item**. Constructed-response items include *fill-in-the-blank, short-answer,* and *essay items,* and would also include typical *oral examination procedures* as well as *interviews.* In a broader sense, constructed-response assessments also include *performance assessments, portfolios,* and even *projective techniques.* The selected-response–constructed-response classification system is the one we will use in this textbook.

As we indicated, on selected-response items, the examinee selects the appropriate response from options that are provided. On a true–false item the examinee simply selects true or false to answer the item. On multiple-choice items he or she selects the best response from a list of alternatives. On matching items the examinee matches premises (typically listed on the left) with the appropriate responses (typically listed on the right). The key factor is that all selected-response items provide the answer; the examinee simply selects the appropriate one. There are considerable differences among these selected-response item formats, but we can make some general statements about their strengths and limitations. Strengths include:

- Examinees generally can respond to a relatively large number of selected-response items in a limited amount of time. This means you can include more items in your test. Because tests are essentially samples of the content domain, and large samples are better than small samples, the inclusion of a large number of items tends to enhance the measurement characteristics of the test.
- Selected-response items can be scored in an efficient, objective, and reliable manner. A computer can often score selected-response items. As a result, scoring takes less time and there are fewer grading errors. This can produce tests with desirable measurement characteristics.

> *Examinees generally can respond to a relatively large number of selected-response items in a limited amount of time and items can be scored in an efficient, objective, and reliable manner.*

- Selected-response items are flexible and can be used to assess a wide range of constructs with greatly varying levels of complexity.
- Selected-response items decrease the influence of certain construct-irrelevant factors that can impact test scores (e.g., the influence of writing ability on a test measuring scientific knowledge).

Naturally, there are limitations associated with the use of selected-response items. These include:

- Selected-response items are challenging to write. Relative to constructed-response items, they typically take more effort and time to write. This is not to say that writing constructed-response

---

SPECIAL INTEREST TOPIC 6.1

Do Multiple-Choice Items Penalize Creative Examinees?

Critics of multiple-choice and other selected-response items have long asserted that these items measure only superficial knowledge and conventional thinking and actually penalize examinees who are creative, deep-thinkers. In a recent study, Powers and Kaufman (2002) examined the relationship between performance on the Graduate Record Examination (GRE) General Test and selected personality traits, including creativity, quickness, and depth. In summary, their analyses revealed that there was no evidence that "deeper-thinking" examinees were penalized by the multiple-choice format. The correlation between GRE scores and depth were as follows: Analytical = 0.06, Quantitative = 0.08, and Verbal = 0.15. The results in terms of creativity were more positive. The correlation between GRE scores and creativity were as follows: Analytical = 0.24, Quantitative = 0.26, and Verbal = 0.29 (all p <.001). Similar results were obtained with regard to quickness. The correlation between GRE scores and quickness were as follows: Analytical = 0.21, Quantitative = 0.15, and Verbal = 0.26 (all p <.001).

   In summary, there is no evidence that individuals who are creative, deep-thinkers, and mentally quick are penalized by multiple-choice items. In fact, the research reveals modest positive correlations between the GRE scores and these personality traits. To be fair, there was one rather surprising finding, a slightly negative correlation between GRE scores and conscientious (e.g., careful, avoids mistakes, completes work on time). The only hypothesis the authors proposed was that "conscientious" does not benefit examinees particularly well on timed tests such as the GRE that place a premium on quick performance.

---

items is an easy task—just that the development of effective selected-response items is usually more difficult and time-consuming.

- There are some constructs that cannot be measured using selected-response items. For example, if you want to measure an individual's ability to play the flute or write a poem, you need to have them actually create the response by performing. Special Interest Topic 6.1 summarizes research that examines unsubstantiated claims that selected-response items penalize creative examinees.

- Selected-response items are subject to blind guessing and random responding. Because the examinee is required only to "select" a response, he or she can do this randomly.

As we stated, constructed-response items include short-answer items, essays, performance assessments, and portfolios. Most people are familiar with short-answer items and essays. Short-answer items require the examinee to supply a word, phrase, or number in response to a direct question. Short-answer items may also take the form of an incomplete sentence that the examinee completes (i.e., fill-in-the-blank). Essay items pose a question or problem for the examinee to respond to in a written format. Essay items can typically be classified as either restricted-response or extended-response. As the name suggests, restricted-response essays are highly structured and place restrictions on the nature and scope of the examinee's responses. In contrast, extended-response essays are less structured and provide more freedom to examinees in how they respond. We have mentioned performance assessments previously in this text, but you may not be very familiar with them. Performance assessments require examinees to complete a process or produce a product in a context that closely resembles real-life situations. An example is an airline pilot being required to demonstrate aviation skills in a flight simulator that mimics the flying characteristics on a specific airplane. Portfolio assessments, a form of performance assessment, involve the systematic collection of examinee work products over a specified period of time according to a specific set of guidelines (AERA et al., 1999). Artists, architects, writers, and others have long used portfolios to represent their work. In the context of typical response tests, projective personality tests require respondents to construct a unique response to ambiguous stimuli, not to select a response from a list of alternatives. Constructed-response assessments have their own associated strengths and weaknesses. Their strengths include:

- Compared to selected-response items, some constructed-response assessments (e.g., short-answer and essays) may be easier to write or develop. Not easy, but *easier*!
- Constructed-response items are well suited for assessing higher order cognitive abilities and complex task performance, and some tasks simply require a constructed-response format (e.g., composing a letter, demonstrating problem-solving skills). As a result they expand the range of constructs that can be assessed.
- Constructed-response items eliminate blind guessing. Because the examinee has to actually "construct" or create a response, random guessing is nearly eliminated.

> *Constructed-response items are well suited for assessing higher order cognitive abilities and complex task performance.*

Constructed-response item weaknesses include:

- Constructed-response items take more time for examinees to complete. You cannot include as many constructed-response items or tasks on a test as you can selected-response items. As a result, you are not able to sample the content domain as thoroughly.
- Constructed-response items are more difficult to score in a reliable manner. In addition to scoring being more difficult and time-consuming compared to selected-response items, scoring is more subjective and less reliable.
- Whereas constructed-response items practically eliminate blind guessing, they are vulnerable to "feigning." For example, examinees who do not actually know the correct response might feign a response that superficially resembles a correct response (in Texas we have another name for this act that our publisher will not allow us to use here!).
- Constructed-response items are vulnerable to the influence of extraneous or construct-irrelevant factors that can impact test scores (e.g., the influence of writing ability on a test measuring scientific knowledge).

As you see, selected-response and constructed-response assessments have specific strengths and weaknesses, and these strengths and weaknesses deserve careful consideration when selecting an assessment format. However, typically the key factor in selecting an assessment or item format involves identifying the format that most directly measures the construct. That is, you want to select the item format or task that will be the purest, most direct measure of the construct of interest. For example, if you want to assess an examinee's writing abilities, an essay is the natural choice. If you want to assess an examinee's ability to engage in oral debate, a performance assessment would be the logical choice. However, if you wanted to predict the person's ability to develop such a skill with proper training, a selected-response measure of logical and deductive reasoning might work very well. Although the nature of some constructs or objectives dictates

TABLE 6–1	Strengths and Weaknesses of Selected-Response Items

Strengths of Selected-Response Items

1. You can typically include a relatively large number of selected-response items in your test. This facilitates adequate sampling of the content domain.
2. They can be scored in an efficient, objective, and reliable manner.
3. They are flexible and can be used to assess a wide range of abilities.
4. They can reduce the influence of certain construct-irrelevant factors.

Weaknesses of Selected-Response Items

1. They are relatively difficult to write.
2. They are not able to assess all abilities (e.g., writing ability).
3. They are subject to random guessing.

the use of constructed-response items (e.g., writing skills), some can be measured equally well using either selected-response or constructed-response items. If after careful consideration you determine that both formats are appropriate, we generally recommend the use of selected-response items as they allow broader sampling of the content domain and more objective/reliable scoring procedures. Both of these factors enhance the measurement characteristics of your test. Tables 6–1 and 6–2 summarize the strengths and weaknesses of selected-response and constructed-response items.

Selected-response and constructed-response assessments have specific strengths and weaknesses that should be considered when selecting an item format. However, typically the key factor in selecting an assessment or item format involves identifying the format that most directly measures the construct you want to measure.

TABLE 6–2	Strengths and Weaknesses of Constructed-Response Items

Strengths of Constructed-Response Items

1. Compared to selected-response items, they are often easier to write.
2. They are well suited for assessing higher order cognitive abilities and complex task performance.
3. They eliminate random guessing.

Weaknesses of Constructed-Response Items

1. Because they typically require more time than selected-response items for the examinees to complete, you cannot include as many items in a test. As a result, you are not as able to sample the content domain as thoroughly.
2. They are more difficult to score in a reliable manner.
3. They are vulnerable to feigning.
4. They are vulnerable to the influence of construct-irrelevant factors.

GENERAL ITEM WRITING GUIDELINES

> *The overriding goal is to develop items that measure the specified construct and contribute to psychometrically sound tests.*

In the remainder of this chapter we will provide guidelines for developing different types of items. We recommend you apply these guidelines in a flexible manner. *The overriding goal is to develop items that measure the specified construct and contribute to psychometrically sound tests.* Many of these suggestions are tied to specific item types. For example, we will first discuss the broad topic of maximum performance tests. In that section we will cover the development of both selected-response and constructed-response items. We will then turn our attention to the development of typical response tests. Here we will focus on the development of selected-response items. However, before providing guidelines for developing specific item types, we will provide some general guidelines that are applicable to almost all items. These general guidelines are listed as follows.

Provide Clear Directions

It is common for inexperienced test developers to assume that test takers understand how to respond to different item formats. This may not be the case! When developing a test always include thorough directions that clearly specify how the examinee should respond to each item format. Just to be safe, assume that the examinees have never seen a test like it before and provide directions in sufficient detail to ensure they know what is expected of them.

Present the Question, Problem, or Task in as Clear and Straightforward a Manner as Possible

When writing items, keep it as simple as possible! Unless you are assessing reading ability, aim for a low reading level. You do not want an examinee to answer an item incorrectly due to ambiguous wording, complex syntax, or unnecessarily difficult vocabulary. This does not mean to avoid scientific or technical terms necessary to state the problem, but simply to avoid the unnecessary use of complex incidental words.

In addition, generally avoid using items that contain *no*, *none*, and *not*. The use of negative statements can make the statement more ambiguous, which is not desirable. Do not make vocabulary a part of the question or problem *unintentionally*. Along these same lines, whenever possible you should avoid complex, compound sentence constructions unless their understanding and comprehension is actually being assessed. Otherwise, you will almost certainly introduce construct-irrelevant variance as some people will simply be confused by the wording or have difficulty attending to such constructions when knowledge or understanding of a distinct concept is being assessed. They will then answer incorrectly for reasons irrelevant to the construct being measured.

Develop Items and Tasks That Can Be Scored in a Decisive Manner

Ask yourself if the items have clear answers on which virtually every expert would agree. In terms of essays and performance assessments, the question may be if experts would agree about the quality of performance on the task. The scoring process can be challenging even when your items have clearly "correct" answers. When there is ambiguity regarding what represents a definitive answer or response, scoring can become much more difficult.

Avoid Inadvertent Cues to the Answers

A cue is something in the stem that provides a clue to the answer that is not based on knowledge. It is easy for unintended cues to correct responses to become embedded in a test. For example, information in one item may provide information that reveals the answer to another item. It is also possible for an item to contain a clue to its own answer. Consider the following examples.

EXAMPLE 1A Poor Item—Stem Contains a Cue to the Correct Answer

1. Which type of validity study examines the ability of test scores to predict a criterion that is measured in the future?

    A. interval study
    B. content study
    C. factorial study
    D. predictive study <

EXAMPLE 1B Better Item—Cues Avoided

2. Which type of validity study involves a substantial time interval between when the test is administered and when the criterion is measured?

    A. interval study
    B. content study
    C. factorial study
    D. predictive study <

EXAMPLE 2A Poor Item—Stem Contains a Definitive Clue to the Correct Answer *(this is an actual item taken from a classroom test administered by a physical education, not math, teacher)*

1. How many quarters are there in a football game ? _____

EXAMPLE 2B Better Item—Cues Avoided

2. How many time periods of play are there in a football game? _____

In Example 1, in the first item, the use of *predict* in the stem and *predictive* in the correct alternative provides a cue to the correct answer. This is corrected in the second example. In Example 2, the vocabulary gives away the answer—*quarters* refers to 4, and indeed 4 is the correct answer.

Arrange the Items in a Systematic Manner

You should arrange the items in your assessment in a manner that promotes the optimal performance of your examinees. If your test contains multiple item formats, the items should be arranged in sections according to the type of item. That is, place all the multiple-choice items together, all the short-answer items together, and so on. This is recommended because it allows the examinees to maintain the same mental set throughout the section. It has the added benefit of making it easier for you to score the items. After arranging the items by format, in the case of a maximum performance measure you should arrange the items in each section according to their level of difficulty. That is, start with the easy items and move progressively to the more difficult items. This arrangement tends to reduce anxiety, enhance motivation, and allows examinees to progress quickly through the easier items and devote the remaining time to the more difficult items.

Ensure That Individual Items Are Contained on One Page

For selected-response items, ensure that they are contained on one page. For example, for multiple-choice, true–false, and matching items, do not divide them so that part of the item is on one page, and it is completed on another. This can contribute to examinees making errors as they switch back and forth between pages, errors that are irrelevant to the construct you are measuring.

Tailor the Items to the Target Population

Carefully consider the type of clients your test will be used with and tailor the items accordingly. For example, young children and elderly people do not respond well to tasks with manipulatives and these should be avoided unless assessment of dexterity is actually the purpose of the item.

Minimize the Impact of Construct-Irrelevant Factors

Look for and minimize cognitive, motor, and other factors that are necessary to answer items correctly, but irrelevant to the construct being measured. For example, the inclusion of extensive and complex written instructions on a test intended to measure math skills will likely result in the test measuring not only math skills, but also reading comprehension. In Chapter 5 we identified construct-irrelevant variance as one of the major threats to validity of test score interpretation.

Avoid Using the Exact Phrasing From Study Materials

When preparing achievement tests, avoid using the exact wording used in the textbook or other study materials. Exact phrasing may be appropriate if rote memorization is what you desire, but it is of limited value in terms of encouraging concept formation and the ability to generalize.

Avoid Using Biased or Offensive Language

Carefully review your items for potentially biased or otherwise offensive language. We also encourage you to ask a diverse group of colleagues to review your test items. Although reviewers are no better than chance at nominating or detecting culturally biased items, the language or symbols contained in a test item may be inadvertently offensive to some cultural and religious groups, and if you are not a member of the group, you may well be unaware of the issue with the item content. Commercial test publishers routinely ask members of both genders as well as ethnic and other cultural groups, including different religious denominations, to review test item content for offensiveness.

Use a Print Format That Is Clear and Easy to Read

Use a font size and spacing that is clear and appropriate for the examinees. For example, with tests designed for use with very young or with elderly clients a larger font size may be appropriate. Carefully examine the test in its final form to ensure that it is easy to follow and does not hinder performance.

Determine How Many Items to Include

There is no simple answer to the question of how many items to include in a test. The optimal number of items to include in an assessment is determined by factors such as the time available, age of the examinees, the types of items, the breadth of the material or topics being assessed (i.e., scope of the test), and the type of test. Let's consider several of these factors separately:

- *Time available.* Obviously it is important to consider the amount of time available for assessment when determining how many items to include in a test. For example, if you are developing a classroom test to be administered in a standard 1-hour period you must plan accordingly. If you are developing a brief screening instrument designed to screen a large number of subjects for depression, it is important to limit the number of items so the test can be administered in a brief time period (e.g., 15 minutes).
- *Age of examinees.* For young examinees it is probably best to limit tests to no more than about 30 minutes in order to maximize effort, concentration, and motivation. The same might apply for elderly clients. For adolescents and most adults you can increase this period considerably, but it is probably desirable to limit most assessments to 2–4 hours in order to maximize performance. Naturally these are just flexible guidelines. For example, when administering comprehensive achievement, aptitude, or personality assessments, more time may be necessary to assess the constructs adequately. Also, tests that are administered individually by a trained examiner—skilled at developing and maintaining rapport; evaluating effort, attention, and fatigue; and recognizing when breaks are appropriate—may be considerably longer if necessary.
- *Types of items.* Obviously, examinees can complete more true–false or multiple-choice items than they can essay items in a given period of time. As we have already alluded to, the inclusion of more "time-efficient" items will enhance the sampling of the content domain and produce more reliable scores.
- *Type and purpose of the test.* Maximum performance tests can typically be categorized as either *speed* or *power* tests. Pure speed tests generally contain items that are relatively easy but have strict time limits that prevent examinees from successfully completing all the items. On pure power tests, the speed of performance is not an issue. Everyone is given

TABLE 6–3 General Item Development Guidelines
1. Provide clear directions.
2. Present the question, problem, or task in as clear and straightforward a manner as possible.
3. Develop items and tasks that can be scored in a decisive manner.
4. Avoid inadvertent cues to the answers.
5. Arrange the items in a systematic manner.
6. Ensure that individual items are contained on one page.
7. Tailor the items to the target population.
8. Minimize the impact of construct-irrelevant factors.
9. Avoid using the exact phrasing from study materials.
10. Avoid using biased or offensive language.
11. Use a print format that is clear and easy to read.
12. Determine how many items to include in an assessment.

enough time to attempt all the items, but the items are ordered according to difficulty, with some items being so difficult that almost no examinees are expected to answer them all. The distinction between speed and power tests is one of degree rather than being absolute. Most often a test is not a *pure* speed test or a *pure* power test, but incorporates some combination of the two approaches. The decision to use a speed test, a power test, or some combination of the two will influence the number and type of items you include on your test.

- *Scope of the test.* In addition to the power versus speed test distinction, the scope of the test will influence how many items you include in an assessment. For a weekly classroom exam designed to assess progress in a relatively narrow range of skills and knowledge, a brief test will likely be sufficient. However, for a 6-week or semester assessment covering a broader range of skills and knowledge, a more comprehensive (i.e., longer) assessment is typically indicated.

When estimating the time needed to complete the test you should also take into consideration any test-related activities such as handing out the test, giving directions, and collecting the tests. Most professional test developers design power tests that approximately 95% of their samples will complete in the allotted time. This is probably a good rule-of-thumb for most maximum performance tests. If fewer than 95% of examinees reach the final item before a time limit expires, the test is considered speeded, and not a true power test. The purpose of the test (i.e., what you are attempting to measure) should always be considered in determining whether you need time limits and if so, how stringent they should be. Many tests have no time limits at all. Table 6–3 provides a summary of these general guidelines for developing test items.

MAXIMUM PERFORMANCE TESTS

In the next sections we provide guidelines for writing items for maximum performance tests. In this section we will focus primarily on the development of items for achievement tests that are designed to measure educational or learning objectives. However, many of these guidelines will apply to aptitude tests that use these types of items. We will first address selected-response items, then constructed-response items. In subsequent sections we will provide suggestions for developing guidelines for typical performance tests.

Multiple-Choice Items

Multiple-choice items are by far the most popular of the selected-response items. They have gained this degree of popularity because they can be used in a variety of content areas and can assess both simple and complex objectives. Multiple-choice items take the general form of a question or incomplete statement with a set of possible answers, one of which is correct. The part of the item that is either a question or an incomplete statement is referred to as the stem. The possible answers are referred to as alternatives. The correct alternative is simply called the answer and the incorrect alternatives are referred to as distracters (i.e., they serve to "distract" examinees who don't actually know the correct response).

> **Multiple-choice items** *are the most popular of the selected-response items largely because they can be used in a variety of content areas and can assess both simple and complex objectives.*

Multiple-choice items can be written so the stem is in the form of a direct question or an incomplete sentence. Most writers prefer the direct-question format because they feel it presents the problem in the clearest manner. The advantage of the incomplete-statement format is that it may present the problem in a more concise manner. If the question is formatted as an incomplete statement, it is suggested that the omission occur near the end of the stem. Our recommendation is to use the direct-question format unless the problem can be stated more concisely using the incomplete-sentence format without any loss of clarity.

Another distinction in made between multiple-choice items that have what is known as the correct-answer versus the best-answer format. The correct-answer format is appropriate when there is only one correct answer (e.g., what is the square root of 100?). However multiple-choice items can also be written to handle situations where there is more than one correct answer and the objective is to identify the "best-answer." Consider the following example of a best-answer item.

EXAMPLE 3 Best-Answer Format

1. Which variable is generally thought to be the most important influence on the resale value of a house?

    A. initial cost per square foot
    B. the builder's reputation
    C. contemporariness of the design
    D. location <

In Example 3, all the variables listed are important to consider when considering resale value of a house, but as almost any realtor will tell you, location is the most important. Most test developers prefer the best-answer format for two reasons. First, in some situations it is difficult to write an answer that everyone will agree is correct. The best-answer format allows you to frame it as an answer that most experts will agree with. Second, the best-answer format often requires the examinee to make more subtle distinctions among the alternatives, which results in more demanding items that measure more complex educational objectives. Following are more suggestions for developing multiple-choice items.

USE A FORMAT THAT MAKES THE ITEM AS CLEAR AS POSSIBLE. Although there is not a universally accepted format for multiple-choice items, here are a few recommendations regarding the physical layout that can enhance clarity.

- The item stem should be numbered for easy identification, whereas the alternatives are indented and identified with letters.
- There is no need to capitalize the beginning of alternatives unless they begin with a proper name.
- Keep the alternatives in a vertical list instead of placing them side by side as it is easier for examinees to scan a vertical list quickly.

THE ITEM STEM SHOULD CONTAIN ALL THE INFORMATION NECESSARY TO UNDERSTAND THE PROBLEM OR QUESTION. When writing multiple-choice items, the problem or question should be fully developed in the item stem. Poorly developed multiple-choice items often contain an inadequate stem that leaves the test taker unclear about the central problem or question. One way to determine if the stem is adequate is to read the stem without examining the alternatives. If the stem is adequate, a knowledgeable individual should be able to answer the question with relative ease without needing to read the alternatives.

PROVIDE BETWEEN THREE AND FIVE ALTERNATIVES. There is no "correct" number of alternatives to provide, but it is recommended that you use between three and five alternatives. Four is the most common number of alternatives, but some test developers suggest using five alternatives because using more alternatives reduces the chance of correctly guessing the answer when you know nothing at all about which answer is correct. For example, the chance of correctly guessing the answer with three alternatives is 1 in 3 (i.e., 33%); with four alternatives, 1 in 4 (i.e., 25%); and with five alternatives, 1 in 5 (i.e., 20%). The use of five alternatives is probably the upper limit because many computer scoring programs accommodate only five alternatives and due to the difficulty in developing plausible distracters (the addition of distracters that are clearly wrong and not selected by any examinees does not reduce the chance of correctly guessing the answer). In some situations three alternatives may be sufficient. It takes examinees less time to read and answer items with three alternatives instead of four (or five) and it is easier to write two good distracters than three (or four). There is even research that suggests that multiple-choice items with three alternatives can be as effective as items with four or five alternatives (e.g., Costin, 1970; Grier, 1975; Sidick, Barrett, & Doverspike, 1994).

KEEP THE ALTERNATIVES BRIEF AND ARRANGE THEM IN AN ORDER THAT PROMOTES EFFICIENT SCANNING. As we noted, the item stem should contain as much of the content as possible and should not contain irrelevant material. A correlate of this is that the alternatives should be as brief as possible. This brevity makes it easier for examinees to scan the alternatives looking for the correct answer. When applicable, alternatives should be arranged in a logical order that promotes efficient scanning. For example, numbers should be placed in ascending order, dates ordered in temporal sequence, and nouns and names alphabetized. When there is no logical order for the distracters, they should be arranged randomly to avoid a pattern where one lettered distracter is more likely to be correct over the course of the test items (e. g., many people believe that option C is the most frequent correct answer among four-choice multiple-choice items).

IN MOST SITUATIONS YOU SHOULD AVOID NEGATIVELY STATED STEMS. As a general rule we recommend that you avoid using negatively stated stems. By this we mean you should limit the use of terms such as *except*, *least*, *never*, or *not*. Examinees might overlook these terms and miss the question even when they have mastered the learning objective measured by the item. Unless your intention is to measure the examinee's ability to read the items carefully and attend to details, this is not a desired outcome and the correct interpretation of the test's results is undermined. In most situations this can be avoided simply by rephrasing the stem. Occasionally it may be necessary or desirable to state stems in the negative. For example, in some situations it is important for examinees to know what not to do (e.g., what should you *not* do if you smell gas?) or identify an alternative that differs in some way from the other alternatives. In these situations you should highlight the negative terms by capitalizing, underlining, or printing them in bold type.

Double negatives should be avoided always (a word we generally detest in testing circles!). Although logicians know that a double negative indicates a positive case, examinees should not have to ferret out this logic problem!

MAKE SURE ONLY ONE ALTERNATIVE IS CORRECT OR CLEARLY REPRESENTS THE BEST ANSWER. Carefully review your alternatives to ensure there is only one correct or best answer. It is common for professors to be confronted by upset students who feel they can defend one of the distracters as a correct answer. Although it is not possible to avoid this situation completely, you can minimize it by carefully evaluating the distracters. We recommend setting aside the test for a period of time and returning to it for proofing after a break. Occasionally it might be appropriate to include more than one correct alternative in a multiple-choice item and require the examinees to identify all of the correct alternatives. In these situations it is usually best to format the question as a series of true–false items, an arrangement referred to as a cluster-type or multiple true–false item. This format is illustrated in the following example.

EXAMPLE 4 Multiple True–False Item

1. Which of the following states have a coastline on the Gulf of Mexico? Circle the T if the state has a Gulf coastline or the F if the state does not have a Gulf coastline.

Alabama	**T**	F
Florida	**T**	F
Tennessee	T	**F**
Texas	**T**	F

ALL ALTERNATIVES SHOULD BE GRAMMATICALLY CORRECT RELATIVE TO THE STEM. Another set of cues that may help the uninformed examinee select the correct answer is based on grammatical rules. These grammatical cues are usually the result of inadequate proofreading and can be corrected once they are detected. Examine the following examples.

EXAMPLE 5 Poor Item—Grammatical Cue Present

1. Which individuals are credited with making the first successful flights in a heavier-than-air aircraft that was both powered and controlled?

   A. Octave Chanute
   B. Otto Lilienthal
   C. Samuel Langley
   D. Wilbur and Orville Wright <

EXAMPLE 6 Better Item—Grammatical Cue Avoided

2. Which individuals are credited with making the first successful flights in a heavier-than-air aircraft that was both powered and controlled?

   A. Octave Chanute and Sir George Cayley
   B. Otto Lilienthal and Francis Herbert Wenham
   C. Samuel Langley and Alphonse Penaud
   D. Wilbur and Orville Wright <

In the first example the phrase "individuals are" in the stem indicates a plural answer. However, only the fourth alternative (i.e., D) meets this requirement. This is corrected in the second example by ensuring that each alternative reflects a plural answer. Another common error is inattention to the articles *a* and *an* in the stem. Review the following examples.

EXAMPLE 7 Poor Item—Grammatical Cue Present

1. A coherent and unifying explanation for a class of phenomena is a_____

   A. analysis.
   B. experiment.
   C. observation.
   D. theory. <

EXAMPLE 8 Better Item—Grammatical Cue Avoided

2. A coherent and unifying explanation for a class of phenomena is a(n) _____

   A. experiment.
   B. hypothesis.
   C. observation.
   D. theory. <

In Example 7, the use of the article *a* indicates an answer beginning with a consonant instead of a vowel. An observant examinee relying on cues will detect this and select the fourth alternative (i.e., D) because it is the only one that is grammatically correct. This is corrected in Example 8 by using *a(n)* to accommodate alternatives beginning with either consonants or vowels.

ALL DISTRACTERS SHOULD APPEAR PLAUSIBLE. Distracters should be designed to distract unknowledgeable examinees from the correct answer. Therefore, all distracters should appear plausible and should be based on common errors. After you have administered the test once, analyze the distracters and determine which ones are effective and which are not. Replace or revise the ineffective distracters. There is little point in including a distracter that can be easily eliminated by uninformed examinees. Such distracters simply waste time and space.

USE ALTERNATIVE POSITIONS IN A RANDOM MANNER FOR THE CORRECT ANSWER. This guideline suggests that the correct answer should appear in each of the alternative positions approximately the same number of times. When there are four alternatives (e.g., A, B, C, and D), there is a tendency for test developers to overuse the middle alternatives (i.e., B and C). Alert examinees are likely to detect this pattern and use this information to answer questions of which they are unsure. For example, we have had examinees indicate that when faced with a question they can't answer based on knowledge they simple select B or C. An easy way to reach this goal is to attempt random assignment when possible and once the test is complete count the number of times the correct answer appears in each position. If any positions are over- or underrepresented, simply make adjustments to correct the imbalance.

MINIMIZE THE USE OF *NONE OF THE ABOVE* AND AVOID USING *ALL OF THE ABOVE.* There is some disagreement among test development experts regarding the use of *none of the above* and *all of the above* as alternatives. The alternative *none of the above* is criticized because it automatically forces the item into a correct-answer format. Although there are times when *none of the above* is appropriate as an alternative, it should be used sparingly. Testing experts are more unified in their criticism of *all of the above* as an alternative. There are two primary concerns. First, an examinee may read alternative A, see that it is correct and mark it without ever reading alternatives B, C, and D. In this situation the response is incorrect because the examinee did not read all of the alternatives, not necessarily because he or she did not know the correct answer. Second, examinees may know only that two of the alternatives are correct and therefore conclude that *all of the above* is correct. In this situation the response is correct but is based on incomplete knowledge. Our recommendation is to use *none of the above* sparingly and avoid using *all of the above*.

LIMIT THE USE OF *ALWAYS* AND *NEVER* IN THE ALTERNATIVES. The use of *always* and *never* should generally be avoided because it is only in mathematics that their use is typically justified. Savvy examinees know this and will use this information to rule out distracters.

Multiple-choice items are the most popular selected-response format. They have numerous strengths including versatility, objective and reliable scoring, and efficient sampling of the

TABLE 6–4 Checklist for the Development of Multiple-Choice Items	
1. Are the items clear and easy to read?	_____
2. Does the item stem clearly state the problem or question?	_____
3. Are there between three and five alternatives?	_____
4. Are the alternatives brief and arranged in an order that promotes efficient scanning?	_____
5. Have you avoided negatively stated stems?	_____
6. Is there only one alternative that is correct or represents the best answer?	_____
7. Are all alternatives grammatically correct relative to the stem?	_____
8. Do all distracters appear plausible?	_____
9. Did you use alternative positions in a random manner for the correct answer?	_____
10. Did you minimize the use of "none of the above" and avoid using "all of the above"?	_____
11. Did you limit the use of "always" and "never" in the alternatives?	_____

content domain. The only substantive weaknesses are that multiple-choice items are not effective for measuring all learning objectives (e.g., organization and presentation of material, writing ability, and performance tasks) and they are not easy to develop. Testing experts generally support the use of multiple-choice items as they can contribute to the development of reliable and valid assessments. Table 6–4 provides a checklist for developing multiple-choice items. Special Interest Topic 6.2 summarizes research that has empirically examined the question "Is it in your best interest to change your answer on a multiple-choice test?"

SPECIAL INTEREST TOPIC 6.2

What Research Says About Changing Your Answer

Have you ever heard that it is usually not in your best interest to change your answer on a multiple-choice test? Many examinees *and* educators believe that you are best served by sticking with your first impression. That is, don't change your answer. Surprisingly, this is not consistent with the research! Pike (1979) reviewed the literature and came up with these conclusions:

◆ Examinees change their answers on only approximately 4% of the questions.

◆ When they do change their answers, more often than not it is in their best interest. Typically there are approximately two favorable changes (i.e., *incorrect* to *correct*) for every unfavorable one (i.e., *correct* to *incorrect*).

◆ These positive effects tend to decrease on more difficult items.

◆ High-scoring examinees are more likely to profit from changing their answers than low-scoring examinees.

This does not mean that you should encourage your examinees to change their answers on a whim. However, if an examinee feels a change is indicated based on careful thought and consideration, he or she should feel comfortable doing so. Research suggests that examinees are probably doing the right thing to enhance their score.

True–False Items

The next selected-response format we will discuss is the true–false format. True–false items are very popular, second only to the multiple-choice format. We will use the term true–false items to actually refer to a broader class of items. Sometimes this category is referred to as binary items, two-option items, or alternate-choice items. The common factor is that all these items involve a statement or question that the examinee marks as true or false, agree or disagree, correct or incorrect, yes or no, fact or opinion, and so on. Because the most common form is true–false, we will use this term generically to refer to all two-option or binomial items. Below are our guidelines for developing true–false items.

AVOID INCLUDING MORE THAN ONE IDEA IN THE STATEMENT. True–false items should address only one central idea or point. Consider the following examples.

EXAMPLE 9 Poor Item—Statement Contains More than One Idea

1.   T   F   The study of biology helps us understand living organisms and predict the weather.

EXAMPLE 10 Better Item—Statement Contains Only One Idea

2.   **T**   F   The study of biology helps us understand living organisms.

Example 9 contains two ideas, one that is correct and one that is false—therefore it is partially true and partially false. This can cause confusion as to how examinees should respond. Example 10 addresses only one idea and is less likely to be misleading. Even if both ideas are correct, the specificity of the item content is suspect and the test results become more difficult to interpret correctly. For example, if the examinee missed the item, was it because he or she did not know the first idea, the second idea, or neither of them?

AVOID SPECIFIC DETERMINERS AND QUALIFIERS THAT MIGHT SERVE AS CUES TO THE ANSWER. Specific determiners such as *never*, *always*, *none*, and *all* occur more frequently in false statements and serve as cues to uninformed examinees that the statement is too broad to be true. Accordingly, moderately worded statements including *usually*, *sometimes*, and *frequently* are more likely to be true and these qualifiers also serve as cues to uninformed examinees. Although it would be difficult to avoid using qualifiers in all true–false items, they can be used equally in true and false statements so their value as cues is diminished.

ENSURE THAT TRUE AND FALSE STATEMENTS ARE OF APPROXIMATELY THE SAME LENGTH. There is a tendency among item writers to write *true* statements (most likely to ensure their exactness) that are longer than *false* statements. To prevent statement length from serving as an unintentional cue, visually inspect your statements and ensure that there is no conspicuous difference between the length of true and false statements.

INCLUDE AN APPROPRIATELY EQUAL NUMBER OF TRUE AND FALSE STATEMENTS. Some examinees are more likely to select *true* when they are unsure of the correct response (i.e., acquiescence set) and there are also examinees who have adopted a response set where they mark *false* when unsure of the answer. To prevent examinees from artificially inflating their scores with either of these response sets you should include an approximately equal number of *true* and *false* items. Some earlier writers recommended that in a true–false format, 60% of the items be written so that *true* is the correct response. This was promulgated as a means of promoting learning because a majority of the statements the examinee would read would be accurate. This helps in very limited circumstances, does not apply to typical performance tests (a common application of the binary format—some using yes–no instead of true–false), and is outweighed by the issue of response sets and guessing strategies. Balance is better.

True–false items are a popular selected-response format for maximum performance tests. Although true–false items can be scored in an objective and reliable manner and examinees can answer many items in a short period of time, they have numerous weaknesses. For example, they are often limited to the assessment of fairly simple learning objectives and are vulnerable to guessing. Whereas true–false items have a place in maximum performance tests, before using them we recommend that you weigh their strengths and weaknesses and ensure that they are the most appropriate item format for assessing the specific learning objectives. Table 6–5 provides a brief checklist for developing true–false items. Many of these will also apply to yes–no formats that are often used with younger individuals as these ideas are a little easier to understand.

Matching Items

The final selected-response format we will discuss is matching items.

Matching items usually contain two columns of words or phrases. One column contains words or phrases for which the examinee seeks a match. This column is traditionally placed on the left and the phrases are referred to as *premises*. The second column contains words that are available for selection. The items in this column are referred to as *responses*. The premises are numbered and the responses are identified with letters. Directions are provided that indicate the basis for matching the items in the two lists. Following is an example of a matching item.

TABLE 6–5 Checklist for the Development of True–False Items	
1. Does each statement include only one idea?	_____
2. Have you avoided using specific determiners and qualifiers that can serve as cues to the answer?	_____
3. Are true and false statements of approximately the same length?	_____
4. Are there an approximately equal number of true and false statements?	_____

EXAMPLE 11   Matching Items

Directions: Column A lists major functions of the brain. Column B lists different brain structures. Indicate which structure primarily serves which function by placing the appropriate letter in the blank space to the left of the function. Each brain structure listed in Column B can be used once, more than once, or not at all.

Column A	Column B
__b__ **1.** Helps initiate and control rapid movement of the arms and legs.	**a.** basal ganglia
__g__ **2.** Serves as a relay station connecting different parts of the brain.	**b.** cerebellum
__e__ **3.** Involved in the regulation of basic drives and emotions.	**c.** corpus callosum
__a__ **4.** Helps control slow, deliberate movements of the arms and legs.	**d.** hypothalamus
__c__ **5.** Connects the two hemispheres.	**e.** limbic system
__d__ **6.** Controls the release of certain hormones important in controlling the internal environment of the body.	**f.** medulla
	g. thalamus

This item demonstrates an imperfect match because there are more responses than premises. Additionally, the instructions also indicate that each response may be used once, more than once, or not at all. These procedures help prevent examinees from matching items simply by elimination. Following are some additional suggestions for developing matching items.

LIMIT MATCHING ITEMS TO HOMOGENEOUS MATERIAL. Possibly the most important guideline to remember when writing matching items is to keep the lists as homogeneous as possible. By this we mean you should base the lists on a common theme. For example, in Example 11 all of the premises specified functions served by brain structures and all of the responses were brain structures. Other examples of homogeneous lists could be the achievements matched with famous individuals, historical events matched with dates, definitions matched with words, and so on. What should be avoided is including heterogeneous material in your lists.

IN THE DIRECTIONS, INDICATE THE BASIS FOR MATCHING PREMISES AND RESPONSES. Clearly state in the directions the basis for matching responses to premises. If you have difficulty specifying the basis for matching all the items in your lists, it is likely that your lists are too heterogeneous.

INCLUDE MORE RESPONSES THAN PREMISES. By including more responses than premises you reduce the chance that an uninformed examinee can narrow down options and successfully match items by guessing.

INDICATE THAT RESPONSES MAY BE USED ONCE, MORE THAN ONCE, OR NOT AT ALL. By adding this statement to your directions and writing responses that are occasionally used more than once or not at all, you also reduce the impact of guessing.

TABLE 6–6	Checklist for the Development of Matching Items	
1. Is the material homogeneous and appropriate for the matching format?		_____
2. Do the directions indicate the basis for matching premises and responses?		_____
3. Are there more responses than premises?		_____
4. Do the directions indicate that responses may be used once, more than once, or not at all?		_____
5. Are the lists relatively short to facilitate scanning (e.g., less than 10)?		_____
6. Are the responses brief and arranged in a logical order?		_____

KEEP THE LIST FAIRLY BRIEF. For several reasons, it is desirable to keep the list of items fairly brief. It is easier for the person writing the test to ensure that the lists are homogeneous when the lists are brief. For the examinee taking the test it is easier to read and respond to a shorter list of items without the introduction of confounding factors such as short-term memory and attention skills. Although there is not universal agreement regarding the number of items to include in a matching list, a maximum of 10 appears reasonable with lists between 5 and 8 items generally recommended.

ENSURE THAT THE RESPONSES ARE BRIEF AND ARRANGE THEM IN A LOGICAL ORDER. Examinees should be able to read the longer premises and then scan the briefer responses in an efficient manner. To facilitate this process, keep the responses as brief as possible and arrange them in a logical order when appropriate (e.g., alphabetical, numerically).

Matching items can be scored in an objective and reliable manner, can be completed in a fairly efficient manner, and are relatively easy to develop. Their major limitations include a rather limited scope and the possibility of promoting rote memorization of material by your examinees. Nevertheless, when carefully developed, matching items can effectively assess some constructs. Table 6–6 provides a checklist for developing matching items.

Essay Items

> *An **essay item** is a test item that poses a question or problem for the examinee to respond to in an open-ended written format.*

The first constructed-response format we will address are essay items. An **essay item** is a test item that poses a question or problem for the examinee to respond to in an open-ended written format. Being a constructed-response item, the examinees must respond by constructing a response, not by selecting among alternatives. Even though essay items vary in the degree of structure they impose on the examinee's response, they generally provide considerable freedom to the examinee in composing a response. Good essay items challenge the examinee to organize, analyze, integrate, and synthesize information. At their best, essay items elicit novel and creative cognitive processes. At their worst they present an ambiguous task that is difficult, if not impossible, to score in a reliable manner.

Essay items are often classified as either *restricted-response* or *extended-response*. Restricted-response items are highly structured and clearly specify the form and scope of examinees' responses.

Restricted-response items typically require examinees to list, define, describe, or give reasons. Extended-response items provide more latitude and flexibility in how examinees can respond to the item. There is little or no limit on the form and scope of the response. When limitations are provided they are usually held to a minimum (e.g., page and time limits). Extended-response items provide less structure, and this promotes greater creativity, integration, and organization of material.

As you might expect, restricted-response and extended-response essay items have their own strengths and limitations. Restricted-response essay items can be answered in a timely fashion and are easier to score in a reliable manner than extended-response items. However, by their very nature there are some objectives that simply cannot be measured in a restricted format (e.g., ability to write an essay explaining the reasons for the Civil War). In contrast, extended-response items give examinees more latitude in responding. However, they are more difficult to score in a reliable manner and, because they take considerable time to complete (as does scoring), you typically have to limit your test to relatively few items, which results in limited sampling of the content domain. Following are our guidelines for developing essay items.

CLEARLY SPECIFY THE ASSESSMENT TASK. The most important criterion for a good essay item is that it clearly specifies the assessment task. The assessment task is simply what you want the examinee to do. We recommend that you provide enough information in your essay item that there is no doubt about what you expect. If you want the examinee to list reasons, specify that you want a list. If you want them to make an evaluative judgment, clearly state it. If you want a restricted response, specify that. If you want an extended response, make that clear. We are not suggesting that your essay item stems be unnecessarily lengthy; in fact, we recommend that they be as brief as possible—that is, as brief as possible and still clearly specify the assessment task.

USE MORE RESTRICTED-RESPONSE ITEMS IN PLACE OF A SMALLER NUMBER OF EXTENDED-RESPONSE ITEMS. Restricted-response items have measurement characteristics that may make them preferable over extended-response items. First, they are easier to score in a reliable manner. They are not as easy to score in a reliable manner as selected-response items, but they are easier than extended-response essays. Second, because examinees can respond to a larger number of items in a given amount of time, they can provide superior sampling of content domain. Some objectives simply require the use of extended-response items; however, when you have a choice we recommend using multiple restricted-response items.

DEVELOP AND USE A SCORING RUBRIC. The major limitation of essay items is they are notoriously difficult to score in a reliable manner, without a carefully designed scoring rubric. To facilitate the scoring of essays, it is important to develop and consistently use a scoring rubric, which is a written guide that helps you score a constructed response. For restricted-response essay items the criteria for scoring can often be specified by writing a sample answer or simply listing the major elements. However, for extended-response items more complex rubrics are often required. For extended-response items, due to the freedom given to the examinee, it may not be possible to write a sample answer that takes into consideration all possible "good" responses. As a result the exact form and content of the response cannot be anticipated and a simple model response cannot be delineated.

Scoring rubrics are often classified as either analytic or holistic. *Analytic scoring rubrics* identify different aspects or dimensions of the response and the grader scores each dimension separately. For example, an analytic scoring rubric might distinguish between response content, writing style, and grammar/mechanics. With this scoring rubric the grader scores each response in terms of these three categories. An advantage of analytic scoring rubrics is that they provide specific feedback to examinees regarding the adequacy of their response in different areas. The major drawback of analytic rubrics is that their use can be fairly time-consuming, particularly when the rubric specifies many dimensions to be graded individually. With a *holistic rubric,* the grader assigns a single score based on the overall quality of the examinee's response. Holistic rubrics are often less detailed than analytic rubrics. They are easier to develop and scoring usually proceeds faster. Their primary disadvantage is that they do not provide specific feedback to examinees about the strengths and weaknesses of their response. We will not go into detail about the development and application of scoring rubrics, but we do strongly encourage those of you interested in developing and using essay items to read textbooks that address this important topic in greater detail (e.g., Reynolds, Livingston, & Willson, 2009).

LIMIT THE USE OF ESSAY ITEMS TO OBJECTIVES THAT CANNOT BE MEASURED USING SELECTED-RESPONSE ITEMS. Essays are extremely popular among many teachers and have their strengths; nevertheless, they do have significant limitations (primarily unreliable scoring and reduced content sampling, as well as the time required to do high-quality scoring). As a result we recommend that you restrict the use of essay items to the measurement of objectives that cannot be measured adequately using selected-response items. For example, if you want to assess the examinee's ability to organize and present material in a written format, an essay item would be a natural choice.

Essay items vary in terms of the limits they place on examinee responses, yet most essay items give examinees considerable freedom in developing their responses. The most prominent weaknesses of essay items involve difficulty scoring in a reliable manner and limited content sampling. Both of these issues can result in reduced reliability and validity. On the positive side, essay items are well suited for measuring many complex objectives and are relatively easy to write. We provided numerous suggestions for writing and scoring essay items, but encouraged test developers to limit the use of essay items to the measurement of objectives that are not easily assessed using selected-response items. Table 6–7 provides a checklist for developing essay items.

Short-Answer Items

Short-answer items are items that require the examinee to supply a word, phrase, number, or symbol in response to a direct question. Short-answer items can also be written as incomplete sentences instead of direct questions (this format is sometimes referred to as a *completion item*).

TABLE 6–7	Checklist for the Development of Essay Items	
1. Have you clearly specified the assessment task?		_____
2. Have you used more restricted-response items in place of a smaller number of extended-response items?		_____
3. Have you developed a scoring rubric?		_____
4. Have you limited the use of essay items to objectives that cannot be measured using selected-response items?		_____

Relative to essay items, short-answer items place stricter limits on the nature and length of the response. Practically speaking, short-answer items can be viewed as a type of restricted-response essay items. As we noted, restricted-response essay items provide more structure and limit the form and scope of examinee's response relative to an extended-response essay item. Short-answer items take this a step further, providing even more structure and limits on the examinee's response. Following are specific suggestions for writing short-answer items.

STRUCTURE THE ITEM SO THAT THE RESPONSE IS AS SHORT AS POSSIBLE. As the name implies, you should write short-answer items so that they require a short answer. This makes scoring easier, less time-consuming, and more reliable.

MAKE SURE THERE IS ONLY *ONE* CORRECT RESPONSE. In addition to brevity, it is important that there only be one correct response. This is more difficult than you might imagine. When writing a short-answer item, ask yourself if the examinee can interpret it in more than one way. Consider this example:

> John Adams was born in _____.

The correct response could be "Massachusetts." Or it could be "Braintree" (now Quincy) or even the "United States of America." It could also be "1735" or even "the 18th century." All of these would be correct! This highlights the need for specificity when writing short-answer items. A much better item would be:

> John Adams was born in what state?_____

AS A GENERAL RULE, THE DIRECT-QUESTION FORMAT IS PREFERABLE TO THE INCOMPLETE-SENTENCE FORMAT. There is usually less chance of examinee confusion when the item is presented in the direct-question format. This is particularly true when writing tests for young examinees, but even older examinees may find direct questions more understandable than incomplete sentences. Most experts recommend using only the incomplete-sentence format when it results in a briefer item without any loss in clarity.

WHEN USING THE INCOMPLETE-SENTENCE FORMAT IT IS BEST TO HAVE ONLY ONE BLANK SPACE, GENERALLY NEAR THE END OF THE SENTENCE. As we noted, unless incomplete-sentence items are carefully written, they may be confusing or unclear to examinees. Generally the more blank spaces an item contains, the less clear the task becomes. Therefore, we recommend that you usually limit each incomplete sentence to one blank space. We also recommend that the blank space be located near the end of the sentence. This arrangement tends to provide more clarity than if the blank appears early in the sentence.

MAKE SURE THE BLANKS PROVIDE ADEQUATE SPACE FOR EXAMINEE RESPONSE. You should ensure that each blank provides adequate space for the examinee to write a response. In order for space length not to serve as a possible cue to the answer, you should determine how much space is necessary for providing the longest response in a series of short-answer items, and use that length for all other items.

TABLE 6–8 Checklist for the Development of Short-Answer Items	
1. Does the item require a short response?	_____
2. Is there only one correct response?	_____
3. Did you use an incomplete sentence only when there was no loss of clarity relative to a direct question?	_____
4. Do incomplete sentences contain only one blank space?	_____
5. Are blanks in incomplete sentences near the end of the sentence?	_____
6. Do the blanks provide adequate space for the answers?	_____
7. For questions requiring quantitative answers, have you indicated the degree of precision expected?	_____
8. Have you created a scoring rubric for each item?	_____

FOR QUESTIONS REQUIRING QUANTITATIVE ANSWERS, INDICATE THE DEGREE OF PRECISION EXPECTED. For example, if you want your answer stated in inches, specify that. If you want all fractions reduced to their lowest terms or all numerical answers rounded to the second decimal point, specify these expectations.

CREATE A SCORING RUBRIC AND CONSISTENTLY APPLY IT. As with essay items, it is important to create and consistently use a scoring rubric when scoring short-answer items. When creating this rubric, take into consideration any answers beside the preferred or "best" response that will give full or partial credit.

Short-answer items, like essay items, require the examinee to provide a written response. However, instead of having a large degree of freedom in drafting the response, on short-answer items the examinee is usually required to limit his or her response to a single word, a brief phrase, or a symbol/number. Similar to essay items, short-answer items are somewhat difficult to score in a reliable manner. On the positive side, short-answer items are well suited for measuring certain learning objectives (e.g., math computations) and are relatively easy to write. As with essay items, short-answer items have distinct strengths, but should be used in a judicious manner. Table 6–8 provides a checklist for developing short-answer items.

TYPICAL RESPONSE ITEMS

> *We believe the assessment of feelings, thoughts, self-talk, and other covert behaviors is best accomplished by self-report.*

Now that we have covered many of the common item formats used in maximum performance tests, we will turn to the items commonly used in typical response tests such as personality and attitude scales. We will first describe the different item formats commonly used with these tests and then provide some general guidelines for developing items. We believe the assessment of feelings, thoughts, self-talk, and other covert behaviors is best accomplished by self-report, and this will be the focus of our discussion. However, like maximum performance tests, there are a number of item formats available when using self-report measures.

Typical Response Item Formats

The first format we will discuss is the true–false format. True–false items are common in both maximum performance and typical response tests. The MMPI-2 is a typical response test that uses the true–false format. Other common forms of binomial items use yes–no and agree–disagree as alternatives. Following are examples of true–false items that might be used to assess depressive symptoms.

EXAMPLE 12   True-False Items

Directions: Read the following statements and circle *true* if you agree with the statement and *false* if you do not agree with the statement. There are no right or wrong answers. Please do your best to answer every item.

I feel sad.	True	False
I think about harming myself.	True	False
I sleep well at night.	True	False

These items focus primarily on the individual's current experiences. Is your client currently feeling sad, thinking about harming himself or herself, and sleeping well at night?

Another common item format used on self-reports is rating scales. The term rating scale is defined differently by different researchers and authors. Some authors use rating scales only when the individual completing the scale is rating another individual. An example would be students rating their professors on instructional effectiveness and course quality. In this text we take a broader definition of rating scales, one that includes the rating of self or others. A major distinction between true–false items and ratings is the number of options. That is, true–false items allow only two choices whereas rating scales typically have four or five alternatives. Another difference is that rating scales of thoughts, feelings, and moods, as well as behaviors typically denote frequency (e.g., *never, sometimes, often, almost always*), whereas true–false and yes–no items force the respondent to make a more definitive or absolute judgment call. True–false items can of course be introduced with stems to mimic such frequencies (e.g., I always have good manners; Often, my hands feel sweaty) but more items are typically required with such a series of binomial response items in order to obtain reliable scores. Review the following rating scale items and compare them to the previous true–false items.

EXAMPLE 13   Rating Scale Items

Directions: Read the following sentences and circle the response that is most descriptive for you. There are no right or wrong answers. Please do your best to answer every item.

I feel sad.	Never	Sometimes	Often	Almost always
I think about harming myself.	Never	Sometimes	Often	Almost always
I sleep well at night.	Never	Sometimes	Often	Almost always

As you see, these items ask that the respondent indicate the frequency of the thoughts, feelings, or behaviors. Another rating scale format is illustrated next that is more specific in soliciting information about frequencies.

EXAMPLE 14   Frequency Rating Scale Items

Directions: Read the following sentences and circle the response that is most descriptive for you. There are no right or wrong answers. Please do your best to answer every item.

I feel sad.	Daily	Weekly	Monthly	Once a year or less	Never
I think about harming myself.	Daily	Weekly	Monthly	Once a year or less	Never
I sleep well at night.	Daily	Weekly	Monthly	Once a year or less	Never

---

There are several factors to consider when deciding between the true–false format and rating scales with frequency ratings. As a general rule, frequency ratings have advantages over true–false items. First, frequency ratings provide more information per item than true–false items and can increase the range of scores, produce more reliable scores, and/or reduce overall scale length. Second, frequency ratings can enhance measurement at the extremes because options such as n*ever* and *almost always* are inherently extreme ratings. Finally, frequency ratings are better suited to the content of some items than true–false and make responding simpler. These advantages argue for the use of rating scales over true–false items, but true–false items are appropriate for use on some scales. In fact, Reynolds and Kamphaus (2004) found that self-report scales using a combination of true–false items and rating scales with four options produced the higher alpha reliabilities than scales containing only one format (see Special Interest Topic 6.3 for more on this topic).

As we noted, rating scales are often used to solicit ratings from individuals who are familiar with the person you are assessing. This is very common when completing assessments of children and adolescents. For example, the Behavior Assessment System for Children—Second Edition (Reynolds & Kamphaus, 2004) includes two rating scales for assessing children and adolescents, one completed by parents and one completed by teachers. The primary difference between these rating scales and those used on self-reports is the focus. Self-report rating scales are routinely applied to a wide range of feelings, thoughts, and behaviors. Self-report scales, being completed by the client, are able to assess the client's subjective experiences. On the other hand, rating scales completed by a third party typically focus on overt behaviors because those are what they have the opportunity to observe. Because of this some authors use the term behavior rating scales to describe these instruments. Like self-report items, these items have been shown to provide reliable and valid information when used appropriately. Following are examples of items that might be used on a behavior rating scale that is designed to be completed by parents regarding their child.

SPECIAL INTEREST TOPIC 6.3

Mixing Item Formats

It has been common practice for personality scales to contain only one item type. For example, the Minnesota Multiphasic Personality Inventory—Second Edition (MMPI-2), like its predecessor the MMPI, contains all true–false items. Similarly, the Self-Report of Personality, a component of the Behavior Assessment System for Children (BASC) contained all true–false items. Although this practice was based more on tradition than empirical research, it was assumed that respondents might have difficulty switching between item formats and this might result in reduced reliability and validity.

When developing the Behavior Assessment System for Children—Second Edition (BASC-2; Reynolds & Kamphaus, 2004), the authors considered ways of increasing the range and reliability of scores on the SRP. They noted that some items could be viewed best as reflecting a continuum and not the dichotomy implied by true–false response options. As a result they evaluated the utility of a response format based on frequency: *never, sometimes, often, almost always*, or N/S/O/A (note that some researchers refer to such multiple point response scales on self-report instruments as a "fuzzy response scale" or a "fuzzy metric"). To do this they created and evaluated two parallel forms of the SRP that differed in terms of response format: true–false versus N/S/O/A. In some cases this also involved minor modifications to the wordings of items. For example, the true–false item "I often have nightmares" was changed to "I have nightmares" for the N/S/O/A format. The study evaluated the formats with regard to test-retest reliability, internal-consistency reliability, and the size of the individual standardized item loadings in a form of factor analysis, contrasting the items under each response condition.

The authors examined coefficient alpha for different combinations including all true–false, all N/S/O/A, and a mixture of the two. For the mixture condition, the format was the one that seemed most appropriate based on both content and psychometric grounds. The results revealed that scales containing a mixture of formats consistently had higher coefficient alphas than scales containing only one format. Also, examinees found it easier to respond to certain types of questions in a binomial, absolute sense (true–false) while finding it easier to respond to other items using a more detailed scale, allowing the expression of a gradient of the behavior in question. Additionally, the inclusion of the N/S/O/A items increased the range of scores, therefore reducing potential floor and ceiling effects. Despite these authors' wealth of experience with test development, this result was unexpected—it had been anticipated that the four-choice response option would be superior in nearly every case. These results demonstrate that at times it is useful to look beyond "traditional" practices and empirically evaluate novel approaches to test development, and that it is important to listen to the data and not assume what will work best.

It should be noted that the final tests do keep all of the true–false items and N/S/O/A items together or segregated from one another. For example, on the adolescent SRP form (ages 12–21) the first 69 items are true–false whereas items 70–176 are N/S/O/A. This way respondents do not have to switch between response formats more than once, which could be confusing.

EXAMPLE 15   Behavior Rating Scale Items

Directions: Following are some phrases that describe how children may act. Read the phrases and circle the response that is most descriptive of your child. Please do your best to answer every item.

Appears sad.	Never	Sometimes	Often	Almost always
Harms self.	Never	Sometimes	Often	Almost always
Sleeps well at night.	Never	Sometimes	Often	Almost always

The use of these behavior rating scales has proven very useful in the assessment of children and adolescents. For example, school psychologists routinely collect behavior ratings from both parents and several teachers when completing psychological assessments. This provides useful information because it allows clinicians to identify behavioral problems that are observed by different raters in different settings, and identify settings where the behaviors are less problematic. We will discuss the use of these scales more in Chapter 11.

The assessment of attitudes, as opposed to feelings, thoughts, self-talk, and behaviors, often uses **Likert items** (Likert, 1932). Likert items are similar to rating scales, but instead of focusing on frequency, the focus is on degree of agreement. That is, does the respondent agree or disagree with a statement? These scales are also referred to as *summative rating scales*. Following are examples of Likert items to assess attitudes toward politicians.

EXAMPLE 16

Directions: Read the following sentences and circle the response that best describes your position or belief. The responses are: Strongly Agree = SA, Agree = A, Neutral = N, Disagree = D, and Strongly Disagree = SD.

Politicians can be trusted.	SA	A	N	D	SD
Politicians lose sight of those they serve.	SA	A	N	D	SD
I would like to enter politics.	SA	A	N	D	SD

> **Likert items** *have become the most popular item format for assessing attitudes.*

Likert items have become the most popular item format for assessing attitudes. In the past other formats were very popular, namely Thurstone and Guttman scales. These have lost some popularity in recent years, primarily because Likert items are easier to develop and tend to produce more reliable results. Nevertheless, you will likely come across examples of Thurstone and Guttman scales, and we briefly discuss these in Special Interest Topic 6.4.

Many of the general guidelines we presented at the beginning of the chapter apply to the development of items for typical response tests. Following are brief guidelines for developing items for self-report measures.

Typical Response Item Guidelines

FOCUS ON THOUGHTS, FEELINGS, AND BEHAVIORS—NOT FACTS. With typical-response tests you are trying to assess the examinee's experiences—his or her typical thoughts, feelings, and behaviors. As a result, you should avoid statements based on factual information and can be scored as "correct" or "incorrect."

LIMIT STATEMENTS TO A SINGLE THOUGHT, FEELING, OR BEHAVIOR. Each statement should focus on just one thought, feeling, behavior, or attitude. Don't make the mistake of combining more than one construct, as illustrated in the example on page 217.

SPECIAL INTEREST TOPIC 6.4

Guttman Scales and Thurstone Scales

You have read about scales of measurement in this text and perhaps elsewhere and their importance to the use and interpretation of test scores as well as their importance for defining appropriate level for the mathematical analysis of numbers. It was Louis Guttman in 1944 who really explained in a most approachable way that all forms of measurement belong to one of four types of scales: categorical, ordinal, interval, and ratio. However, many actually attribute these scales of measurement to Stevens (1951), who referred to them as nominal, ordinal, interval, and ratio. The mathematical foundations of these scales have since been examined in detail in a variety of sources, and for the mathematically inclined we recommend some older presentations such as that by Hays (1973, pp. 81–91), but if these are not accessible, the Pedhazur and Schmelkin (1991) discussions are also strong.

Guttman is better known for his ideas about developing a deterministic (absolute) scale that carries his name (i.e., Guttman scales) in this same 1944 paper. Guttman scaling is also sometimes known as *cumulative scaling*. The purpose of Guttman scaling is to establish a one-dimensional continuum for a concept you wish to measure. Items having binary (e.g., yes–no) answers form a Guttman scale if they can be ranked in some order so that, for a rational respondent, the response pattern can be captured by a single index on that ordered scale. On a Guttman scale, items are arranged in a perfect hierarchical order so that an individual who agrees with a particular item on a survey or attitudinal dimension also agrees with items of lower rank, or statements that are in some way subordinate to the last statement one answers in the affirmative. In aptitude or achievement testing, a Guttman scale would exist when all persons tested answered every question correctly until missing one, and then failed to answer any additional questions correctly. The strength of a Guttman scale, indeed, its purpose, is to enable us to predict item responses perfectly knowing only the total score for the respondent. For example, if we asked a person to solve arithmetic problems, and the test had 100 items, if the examinee earned a score of 51, we would know immediately the person answered items 1–51 correctly and missed items 52–100. There are many obvious advantages of such a scale, one being the great reduction in testing time—as soon as a person misses or responds differently to just 1 item, we can cease testing!

Guttman scales are very appealing from an intuitive perspective, and you may wonder why all tests are not constructed in this manner—indeed, one rarely (if ever) sees a test with a true Guttman scale. First, Guttman scales are highly impractical; and second, when they are developed, they are rather simplistic in the information they provide. Oddly enough, to develop a Guttman scale, one ends up having only ordinal data—that is, Guttman scales rank-order people by their responses, but give us little information about the distance they are apart in the distribution of the underlying trait or construct we seek to assess. In some areas such as math, Guttman scales are easy to derive and are also a good illustration of the simplicity of the information. Consider the following five-item test, which is extremely likely to produce a Guttman scale:

1. How much is $2 + 2$?
2. How much is $20 - 10$?
3. How much is 10×55?
4. Solve for x: $x - 3 + 7 = 15$
5. Solve for x: $(x + 3)(x + 3) = 16$

A person who answers item 5 correctly will almost certainly have answered items 1–4 correctly, and a person who answers item 4 but misses item 5, will almost certainly have answered items 1–3 correctly, and so on. However, to develop such a scale, we sacrifice a great deal of precision in assessing real skill in mathematics. For example, there may be great differences in the skills of students who only answer 4 items correctly compared to those who can answer all 5 items. For most purposes of psychological assessment, the Guttman scale, however appealing intuitively, is illogical and does not fit our need for information. Guttman scales that are not highly simplistic are more difficult to develop

(Continued on page 216)

SPECIAL INTEREST TOPIC 6.4 *(Continued)*

than typical scales and aspire only to ordinal level data, whereas most scales give us at least interval scale data.

Another approach to developing a cumulative scale was developed by Thurstone (e.g., 1928). Unlike Guttman scales that can be used with maximum performance or typical response tests, Thurstone scales are limited to typical response assessments, usually attitude scales. In developing a Thurstone scale one begins by writing a large number of statements that reflect the full range of attitudes from very negative to very positive with reference to a specific topic or issue. It is important for these items to reflect the full range of attitudes, including neutral statements. These statements are then reviewed by judges who assign a scale value to each statement along a continuum ranging from extremely favorable to extremely unfavorable. When doing this the judges often use a scale with 11 equal-width intervals. For example, the most negative statements are assigned values of 1 whereas the most favorable statements are assigned values of 11. With this scale neutral statements would be then assigned values of 6.

To illustrate this, consider the development of a scale to measure attitudes about the use of cell phones while driving. Following are three items that might be assigned different scale values by the judges.

Item	Scale Value
It should be illegal to drive while using a cell phone—period!	1 (very negative)
I don't have a strong opinion about the use of cell phones while driving.	6 (neutral)
I believe we should be able to use our cell phones at any time and any place we desire.	11 (very positive)

Once the judges have rated all of the statements, their ratings are reviewed with the goal of selecting a final set of statements that will be included on the scale. There are two primary criteria considered in selecting items to retain on the final scale. First, it is important to select items that are evenly distributed across the whole continuum ranging from very positive to very negative. In other words, you want items that have ratings ranging from 1 to 11, with all 11 values represented. Second, it is desirable to select items that the judges rated in a consistent manner. If an item received inconsistent ratings (i.e., some positive ratings, some negative ratings), this suggests that the item may be ambiguous and it is dropped from further consideration. There are statistics that can be calculated to help determine which items received the most consistent ratings.

The result is a final scale where examinees indicate their attitudes by endorsing items using a binary format, typically indicating that they *agree* or *disagree* with the statements. The total score an examinee receives is the median of the scale values of the items they endorsed. If we use our example of an 11-point scale, with 1 indicating the most unfavorable statements and 11 indicating the most favorable statements, an individual with a low total score (i.e., the median value of the items they endorsed) would be expressing an unfavorable attitude toward the issue or topic. An examinee with a favorable attitude would be expected to receive a high total score, whereas someone receiving a total score of 6 would have expressed a neutral response pattern. Although Thurstone scales were popular for many years (and still have their advocates), they are used less commonly today. This decrease in popularity is partly due to the rather complex process used in developing Thurstone scales and research showing that other item formats (e.g., Likert scales) can produce more reliable scores with the same number of items (Friedenberg, 1995).

For more information on this topic, we recommend the following references:

Guttman, L. (1944). A basis for scaling qualitative data. *American Sociological Review, 9,*139–150

Hays, W. (1973). *Statistics for the social sciences.* New York: Holt, Rinehart & Winston.

Pedhazur, E., & Schmelkin, L. (1991). *Measurement, design, and analysis.* Hillsdale, NJ: Erlbaum.

Stevens, S. S. (1951). Mathematics, measurement, and psychophysics. In S. S. Stevens (Ed.), *Handbook of experimental psychology* (pp. 1–49). New York: Wiley.

Thurstone, L. L. (1928). Attitudes can be measured. *American Journal of Sociology, 33,* 529–554.

EXAMPLE 17   Poor Item—Statement Contains More than One Thought, Feeling, or Behavior

I feel sad and angry.	True	False

This can be corrected by replacing the item with two separate items.

EXAMPLE 18   Better Items—Each Statement Contains Only One Thought, Feeling, or Behavior

I feel sad.	True	False
I feel angry.	True	False

AVOID STATEMENTS THAT EVERYONE WILL ENDORSE IN A SPECIFIC MANNER. To increase variance and enhance reliability, you should strive to write items that measure individual differences. If everyone or almost everyone responds to an item in the same way, it is not contributing to the measurement of the identified constructs.

INCLUDE ITEMS THAT ARE WORDED IN BOTH POSITIVE/FAVORABLE AND NEGATIVE/ UNFAVORABLE DIRECTIONS. As a general rule, use a combination of items that are worded in "positive" and "negative" directions. This may encourage examinees to avoid a response style where they are simply marking one response option on all items. This is most applicable on true– false items and Likert scales and less applicable to rating scales where you are trying to assess the frequency of problematic thoughts, feelings, and behaviors.

USE AN APPROPRIATE NUMBER OF OPTIONS. For rating scales, either four or five response options seem to be optimal in developing reliability without unduly lengthening the time required by the person completing the ratings. Rating scales with more than four or five options rarely improve reliability or validity of test score interpretation and take longer for examinees to complete. For Likert items, the maximum number of options appears to be seven steps, with little increase in reliability after that.

WEIGH THE BENEFITS OF USING AN ODD OR EVEN NUMBER OF OPTIONS. On Likert items, it is generally recommended that you use an odd number of choices with the middle choice being *neutral* or *undecided*. This is not universally accepted as some authors support the use of an even number of choices with no neutral option. This is based on the fact that some respondents tend to overuse the neutral choice if it is available, which can result in reduced variance and reliability. The downside of eliminating the neutral choice is that some respondents might become frustrated and simply not complete items when they don't have a strong opinion. Missing data can be a significant problem in these cases. Our recommendation is to use an odd number of options with a neutral option. With frequency rating scales this is less important because there is not a need for a neutral option.

TABLE 6–9	Checklist for the Development of Typical Response Items	
1. Do the items focus on thoughts, feelings, and behaviors—not facts?		_____
2. Is each item limited to a single thought, feeling, or behavior?		_____
3. Did you avoid statements that everyone will endorse in a specific manner?		_____
4. Did you include items that are worded in both positive/favorable and negative/unfavorable directions?		_____
5. Did you use an appropriate number of options?		_____
6. Did you weigh the benefits of using an odd or even number of options?		_____
7. For rating scales and Likert items, did you clearly label the options?		_____
8. Did you minimize the use of specific determiners?		_____
9. For young children, did you consider structuring the scale as an interview?		_____

FOR RATING SCALES AND LIKERT ITEMS, CLEARLY LABEL THE OPTIONS. For example, don't just use a format such as:

Strongly Agree   1   2   3   4   5   6   7   Strongly Disagree

This format might leave the respondent wondering about the difference between a 2 and a 3.

MINIMIZE THE USE OF SPECIFIC DETERMINERS. The use of specific determiners such as *never*, *always*, *none*, and *all* should be used cautiously as they can complicate the response process.

WITH YOUNG CHILDREN YOU MAY WANT TO STRUCTURE THE SCALE AS AN INTERVIEW. For young children, you may consider using an interview format where the items are read to the child. This may help reduce construct irrelevant variance being introduced by eliminating the impact of reading skills.

Table 6–9 provides a checklist for the development of items for typical response tests.

Summary

At the beginning of this chapter we noted that all test items can be classified as either selected-response or constructed-response items. We started by focusing on maximum performance test items. Selected-response items include multiple-choice, true–false, and matching items whereas constructed-response items include short-answer and essay items. We briefly discussed the specific item types, highlighting both their strengths and weaknesses. These are summarized as follows:

- Multiple-choice items are the most popular selected-response format for maximum performance tests. They have numerous strengths including versatility, objective and reliable scoring, and efficient sampling of the content domain. The only weaknesses are that multiple-choice items are not effective for measuring all objectives and they are not easy to develop. Testing experts generally support the use of multiple-choice items as they can contribute to the development of reliable and valid assessments.

- True–false items are another popular selected-response format. Although true–false items can be scored in an objective and reliable manner and examinees can answer many items in a short period of time, they have numerous weaknesses. For example, they are limited to the assessment of fairly simple objectives and are very vulnerable to guessing. Whereas true–false items have a place in maximum performance assessment, before using them we recommend that you weight their strengths and weaknesses and ensure that they are the most appropriate item format for assessing the specific learning objectives.
- Matching items can be scored in an objective and reliable manner, can be completed in a fairly efficient manner, and are relatively easy to develop. Their major limitations include a rather limited scope and the possibility of promoting rote memorization of material by your examinees. Nevertheless, when carefully developed, matching items can effectively assess many lower-level learning objectives.
- Essay items pose a question or problem that the examinee responds to in a written format. Although essay items vary in terms of the limits they place on responses, most essay items give examinees considerable freedom in developing their responses. The most prominent weaknesses of essay items include difficulty scoring them in a reliable manner and limited content sampling. Both of these issues can result in reduced reliability and validity. On the positive side, essay items are well suited for measuring many complex objectives and are relatively easy to write.
- Short-answer items, like essay items, require examinees to respond by providing a written response. However, instead of having considerable freedom in drafting their responses, examinees are usually required to limit their responses to a single word, a brief phrase, or a symbol/number. Similar to essay items, short-answer items are somewhat difficult to score in a reliable manner. On the positive side, short-answer items are well suited for measuring certain learning objectives (e.g., math computations) and are relatively easy to write.

At this point we turned our attention to items for typical response tests. We initially focused on the assessment of feelings, thoughts, self-talk, and other covert behaviors using self-report items. These are briefly described as follows:

- True–false items and other binomial items (e.g., yes–no, agree–disagree) are commonly used on typical response tests. These items generally focus on the examinee's current experiences. For example, is your client currently feeling sad, thinking about harming himself or herself, and sleeping well at night?
- Rating scales can be designed both for self-report measures and for the rating of other individuals (typically referred to as behavior rating scales). Although true–false items allow only two choices, rating scales typically have four or five alternatives. Rating scales also typically denote frequency (e.g., *never, sometimes, often, almost always*); true–false and yes–no items ask the respondent to make a more definitive or absolute judgment call.

As a general rule, rating scales have advantages over true–false items because (*a*) they provide more information per item than true–false items and can increase the range of scores, (*b*) they can enhance measurement at the extremes because options such as *never* and *almost always* are inherently extreme ratings, and (*c*) they are better suited to the content of some items than true–false and make responding simpler. Nevertheless, true–false items are appropriate, and even show better measurement properties for the content of some items.

In closing, we addressed the assessment of attitudes. Likert items are similar to rating scales, but instead of focusing on frequency they focus on the degree of agreement. That is, does the respondent agree or disagree with a statement? These scales are also referred to as summative rating scales. In the past cumulative rating scales such as Guttman and Thurstone scales were popular, but Likert scales have proven to be easier to develop and to have equivalent if not superior psychometric properties, and as a result have become the most popular.

It should be noted that this chapter presents fairly brief coverage of a very complicated and technical topic. For those of you interested in more information, we encourage you to read the more comprehensive coverage of this topic in *Measurement and Assessment in Education* (Reynolds et al., 2009).

Key Terms and Concepts

Constructed-response items, 188
Essay items, 206
Likert items, 214
Multiple-choice items, 197

Objective items, 187
Selected-response items, 188
Subjective items, 187

Recommended Readings

Aiken, L. R. (1982). Writing multiple-choice items to measure higher order educational objectives. *Educational & Psychological Measurement, 42,* 803–806. A respected author presents suggestions for writing multiple-choice items that assess higher order learning objectives.

Ebel, R. L. (1970). *The case for true–false items. School Review, 78,* 373–389. Although many assessment experts are opposed to the use of true–false items for the reasons cited in the text, Ebel comes to their defense in this article.

Edwards, A. (1957). *Techniques of attitude scale construction.* New York: Appleton. A classic text on developing attitude scales.

Reynolds, C. R., Livingston, R. B., & Willson, V. (2009). *Measurement and Assessment in Education.* Boston: Allyn & Bacon.

7

Item Analysis
Methods for Fitting the Right
Items to the Right Test

The better the items, the better the test.

Learning Objectives

After reading and studying this chapter, students should be able to:

1. Discuss the relationship between the reliability and validity of test scores and the quality of the items on a test.
2. Describe the importance of the item difficulty index and demonstrate its calculation and interpretation.
3. Describe the importance of the item discrimination index and demonstrate its calculation and interpretation.
4. Describe the relationship between item difficulty and discrimination.
5. Describe how item-total correlations can be used to examine item discrimination.

6. Describe the importance of the distracter analysis and demonstrate its calculation and interpretation.
7. Describe how the selection of distracters influences item difficulty and discrimination.
8. Show how item analysis statistics can be used to improve test items.
9. Describe qualitative approaches to improving test items.
10. Describe the major concepts related to and interpret item characteristic curves.
11. Explain the major aspects of item response theory.
12. Identify major contemporary applications of item response theory.

221

A number of quantitative procedures are useful in assessing the quality and measurement characteristics of the individual items that make up tests. These procedures are collectively referred to as item analysis statistics or procedures. Unlike reliability and validity analyses that evaluate the measurement characteristics of a test as a whole, item analysis procedures examine individual items separately, not the overall test. Item analysis statistics are useful in helping test developers decide which items to keep on a test, which items to modify, and which items to eliminate.

> *The reliability and validity of test scores are dependent on the quality of the items on the test. If you can improve the quality of the individual items, you will improve the overall quality of your test.*

The reliability of test scores and the validity of the interpretation of test scores are dependent on the quality of the items on the test. If you can improve the quality of the individual items, you will improve the overall quality of your test. When discussing reliability we noted that one of the easiest ways to increase the reliability of test scores is to increase the number of items that go into making up the test score. This statement is generally true and is based on the assumption that when you lengthen a test you add items of the same quality as the existing items. If you use item analysis to delete poor items and improve other items, it is actually possible to end up with a test that is shorter than the original test and that also produces scores that are more reliable and result in more valid interpretations.

Although quantitative procedures for evaluating the quality of test items will be the focus of the chapter, there are some qualitative procedures that may prove useful when evaluating the quality of test items. These qualitative procedures typically involve an evaluation of validity evidence based on the content of the test and an examination of individual items to ensure that they are technically accurate and clearly stated. Whereas these qualitative procedures have not received as much attention as their quantitative counterparts, it is often beneficial to use a combination of quantitative and qualitative procedures. In this chapter we will also introduce item characteristic curves in the context of item response theory, a modern test theory that complements and extends classical test theory in a number of test development applications.

We will begin our discussion by describing the major quantitative item analysis procedures. First, however, it should be noted that different types of items and different types of tests require different types of item analysis procedures. Items that are scored dichotomously (i.e., either right or wrong) are handled differently than items that are scored on a continuum (e.g., an essay that can receive scores ranging from 0 to 10). Tests that are designed to maximize the variability of scores (e.g., norm-referenced) are handled differently than mastery tests (i.e., scored pass or fail). As we discuss the different item analysis procedures we will specify what types of procedures are most appropriate for what types of items and tests.

ITEM DIFFICULTY INDEX (OR ITEM DIFFICULTY LEVEL)

> *Item difficulty is defined as the percentage or proportion of test takers who correctly answer the item.*

When evaluating items on maximum performance or ability tests, an important consideration is the difficulty level of the items. **Item difficulty** is defined as the percentage or proportion of test takers who correctly answer the item. The item difficulty level or index is abbreviated as *p* and calculated with the following formula:

$$p = \frac{\text{Number of Examinees Correctly Answering the Item}}{\text{Number of Examinees}}$$

For example, in a class of 30 students, if 20 students get the answer correct and 10 are incorrect, the item difficulty index is 0.66. The calculations are illustrated as follows:

$$p = \frac{20}{30} = 0.66$$

In the same class, if 10 students get the answer correct and 20 are incorrect, the item difficulty index is 0.33. The item difficulty index can range from 0.0 to 1.0 with easier items having larger decimal values and difficult items having lower decimal values. An item that is answered correctly by all students receives an item difficulty of 1.00 whereas an item that is answered incorrectly by all students receives an item difficulty of 0.00. Items with p values of either 1.0 or 0.00 provide no information about individual differences and are of no value from a measurement perspective. Some test developers will include one or two items with p values of 1.0 at the beginning of a test to instill a sense of confidence in test takers. This is a defensible practice from a motivational perspective, but from a technical perspective these items do not contribute to the measurement characteristics of the test. Another factor that should be considered about the inclusion of very easy or very difficult items is the issue of time efficiency. The time examinees spend answering ineffective items is largely wasted and could be better spent on items that enhance the measurement characteristics of the test.

*For maximizing variability among test takers, the **optimal item difficulty level is 0.50**, indicating that 50% of the test takers answered the item correctly and 50% answered the item incorrectly.*

For maximizing variability and reliability, the optimal item difficulty level is 0.50, indicating that 50% of the test takers answered the item correctly and 50% answered the item incorrectly. Based on this statement, you might conclude that it is desirable for all test items to have a difficulty level of 0.50, but this is not necessarily true for several reasons. One reason is that items on a test are often correlated with each other. When items on a test are correlated the measurement process may be confounded if all the items have p values of 0.50. As a result, it is often desirable to select some items that have p values below 0.50 and some with values greater than 0.50, but with a mean of 0.50. Aiken (2000) recommended that there should be approximately a 0.20 range of these p values around the optimal value. For example, a test developer might select items with difficulty levels ranging from 0.40 to 0.60, with a mean of 0.50.

Another reason that 0.50 is not the optimal difficulty level for every testing situation involves the influence of guessing. On constructed-response items (e.g., essay and short-answer items) where guessing is not a major concern, 0.50 is typically considered the optimal difficulty level. However, with selected-response items (e.g., multiple-choice and true–false items) where test takers might answer the item correctly simply by guessing, the optimal difficulty level varies. To take into consideration the effects of guessing, the optimal item difficulty level

Whereas a mean p of 0.50 is optimal for maximizing variability and reliability, different levels are desirable in many different testing applications.

TABLE 7–1	Optimal p Values for Items with Varying Numbers of Choices
Number of Choices	**Optimal Mean p Value**
2 (e.g., true–false)	0.85
3	0.77
4	0.74
5	0.69
Constructed response (e.g., essay)	0.50

Source: Based on Lord (1952).

is set higher than for constructed-response items. For example, for multiple-choice items with four options the average p should be approximately 0.74 (Lord, 1952). That is, the test developer might select items with difficulty levels ranging from 0.64 to 0.84 with a mean of approximately 0.74. Table 7–1 provides information on the optimal mean p value for selected-response items with varying numbers of alternatives or choices.

Special Assessment Situations and Item Difficulty

Our discussion of item difficulty so far is most applicable to norm-referenced tests. For criterion-referenced tests, particularly mastery tests, item difficulty is evaluated differently. On mastery tests the test taker typically either passes or fails and there is the expectation that most test takers will eventually be successful. As a result, on mastery tests it is common for items to have average p values as high as 0.90. Other tests that are designed for special assessment purposes may vary in terms of what represents desirable item difficulty levels. For example, if a test were developed to help employers select the upper 25% of job applicants, it would be desirable to have items with p values that average around 0.25. If it is desirable for a test to be able to distinguish between the highest-performing examinees (e.g., in testing gifted and talented students), it may also be desirable to include at least some very difficult items. In summary, whereas a mean p of 0.50 is optimal for maximizing variability among test takers, different difficulty levels are desirable in many testing applications (see Special Interest Topic 7.1 for another example).

It should be noted that p values are sample dependent. That is, it is possible for one to achieve different item p values from different samples. For example, it is expected that item difficulty values will differ according to grade level. A specific item would likely be more difficult for a test administered to third-grade students compared to fourth-grade students.

Percent Endorsement

As we noted, the item difficulty index is applicable to only maximum performance tests where items are scored correct–incorrect—either right or wrong. However, there is a conceptually similar index referred to as the percent endorsement statistic that can be calculated for typical response tests (Friedenberg, 1995). In brief, the percent endorsement statistic indicates the percentage of examinees that responded to an item in a given manner. For example, a possible item on a depression scale might be:

1. I often feel sad.	True	False

SPECIAL INTEREST TOPIC 7.1

Item Difficulty Indexes and Power Tests

As a rule of thumb and for psychometric reasons explained in this chapter, we have noted that item difficulty indexes of 0.50 are desirable in most circumstances on standardized tests. However, it is also common to include some very easy items so all or most examinees get some questions correct as well as some very hard items, so the test has enough ceiling. With a power test, such an IQ test, that covers a wide age range and whose underlying construct is developmental, item selection becomes much more complex. Items that work very well at some ages may be far too easy, too hard, or just developmentally inappropriate at other ages. If a test covers the age range of say 3 years up to 20 years, and the items all had a difficulty level of 0.5, you could be left with a situation where the 3-, 4-, 5-, and even 6-year-olds typically pass no items and perhaps the oldest individuals nearly always get every item correct. This would lead to very low reliability estimates at the upper and lower ages and just poor measurement of the constructs generally, except near the middle of the intended age range. For such power tests covering a wide age span, item statistics such as the difficulty index and the discrimination index are examined at each age level and plotted across all age levels. In this way, items can be chosen that are effective in measuring the relevant construct at different ages. When the item difficulty indexes for such a test are examined across the entire age range, some will approach 0 and some will approach 1.00. However, within the age levels (e.g., for 6-year-olds) there will be many items that are close to 0.50. This affords better discrimination and gives each examinee a range of items on which they can express their ability on the underlying trait.

A percent endorsement analysis might reveal that 15% of the respondents endorsed the item *true*. As with item difficulty, the endorsement rate is dependent on the sample. Using this example, one might find that 15% of the respondents in a community sample endorsed the *true*, but that a much higher percentage from a clinical sample composed of individuals with psychological disorders endorsed the item in a positive manner (e.g., 80%).

> *The percent endorsement statistic indicates the percentage of examinees who responded to an item in a given manner.*

Later in this chapter we will provide some examples of how test developers use information about item difficulty and other item analysis statistics to select items to retain, revise, or delete from future administrations of the test. First, we will discuss another popular item analysis procedure—the item discrimination index.

ITEM DISCRIMINATION

Item discrimination refers to how well an item can discriminate or differentiate among test takers who differ on the construct being measured by the test. For example, if a test is designed to measure reading comprehension, item discrimination reflects an item's ability to distinguish between individuals with good reading comprehension skills and those with poor

> *Item discrimination refers to how well an item can accurately discriminate between test takers who differ on the construct being measured.*

> *One popular method of calculating an index of item discrimination is based on the difference in performance between those who score well on the overall test and those who score poorly.*

reading skills. Unlike item difficulty level where there is agreement on how to calculate the statistic, more than 50 different indexes of item discrimination have been developed over the years (Anastasi & Urbina, 1997). Luckily most of these indexes produce similar results (Engelhart, 1965; Oosterhof, 1976). We will focus our discussion on two of the most popular indexes of item discrimination: the discrimination index and item-total correlations.

Discrimination Index

One popular method of calculating an index of item discrimination is based on the difference in performance between two groups. Although there are different ways of selecting the two groups, they are typically defined in terms of total test performance. One common approach is to select the top and bottom 27% of test takers in terms of their overall performance on the test, and exclude the middle 46% (Kelley, 1939). Some assessment experts have suggested using the top and bottom 25%, some the top and bottom 33%, and some the top and bottom halves. In practice, all of these are probably acceptable, but our recommendation is to use the traditional top and bottom 27%. The difficulty of the item is computed for each group separately, and these are labeled p_T and p_B (*T* for top, *B* for bottom). The difference between p_T and p_B is the discrimination index, designated as *D*, and is calculated with the following formula (e.g., Johnson, 1951):

$$D = p_T - p_B$$

where *D* = discrimination index

  p_T = proportion of examinees in the top group getting the item correct

  p_B = proportion of examinees in the bottom group getting the item correct

To illustrate the logic behind this index, consider an achievement test designed to measure academic achievement in some specified area. If the item is discriminating between examinees who know the material and those who do not, then examinees who are more knowledgeable (i.e., those in the "top" group) should get the item correct more often than examinees who are less knowledgeable (i.e., those in the "bottom" group). For example, if $p_T = 0.80$ (indicating 80% of the examinees in the top group answered the item correctly) and $p_B = 0.30$ (indicating 30% of the examinees in the bottom group answered the item correctly), then

$$D = 0.80 - 0.30 = 0.50$$

Hopkins (1998) provided guidelines for evaluating items in terms of their *D* values (see Table 7–2). According to these guidelines, *D* values of 0.40 and above are considered excellent, between 0.30 and 0.39 are good, between 0.11 and 0.29 are fair, and between 0.00 and 0.10 are poor. Items with negative *D* values are likely miskeyed or there are other serious problems. Other testing assessment experts have provided different guidelines, some more rigorous and some more lenient.

TABLE 7–2	Guidelines for Evaluating *D* Values
Difficulty	
0.40 and larger	Excellent
0.30–0.39	Good
0.11–0.29	Fair
0.00–0.10	Poor
Negative values	Miskeyed or other major flaw

Source: Based on Hopkins (1998).

As a general rule, we suggest that items with D values over 0.30 are acceptable (the larger the better), and items with D values below 0.30 should be carefully reviewed, and possibly revised or deleted. However, this is only a general rule and there are exceptions. For example, most indexes of item discrimination, including the item discrimination index (D), are biased in favor of items with intermediate difficulty levels. That is, the maximum D value of an item is related to its p value (see Table 7–3). Items that all examinees either pass or fail (i.e., p values of either 0.00 or 1.0) cannot provide any information about individual differences and their D values will always be zero. If half of the examinees correctly answered an item and half failed (i.e., p value of 0.50) then it is possible for the item's D value to be 1.0. This does not mean that all items with p values of 0.50 will have D values of 1.0; just that the item can conceivably have a D value of 1.0. As a result of this relationship between p and D, items that

> As a general rule, we recommend that items with **D** values over 0.30 are acceptable, and items with **D** values below 0.30 should be carefully reviewed, and possibly revised or deleted.

TABLE 7–3	Maximum *D* Values at Different Difficulty Levels
Item Difficulty Index (*p*)	**Maximum *D* Value**
1.0	0
0.90	0.20
0.80	0.40
0.70	0.60
0.60	0.70
0.50	1.0
0.40	0.70
0.30	0.60
0.20	0.40
0.10	0.20
0.00	0

have excellent discrimination power (i.e., D values of 0.40 and above) will necessarily have p values between 0.20 and 0.80. In testing situations where it is desirable to have either very easy or very difficult items, D values can be expected to be lower than those normally desired. Additionally, items that measure abilities or objectives that are not emphasized throughout the test may have poor discrimination due to their unique focus. In this situation, if the item measures an important ability or learning objective and is free of technical defects it should be retained (e.g., Linn & Gronlund, 2000).

In summary, whereas low D values often indicate problems, the guidelines provided in Table 7–2 should be applied in a flexible, considered manner. Our discussion of the calculation of item difficulty and discrimination indexes has used examples with items that are dichotomously scored (i.e., correct–incorrect, 1 or 0). Special Interest Topic 7.2 provides a discussion of the application of these statistics with constructed-response items that are not scored in a dichotomous manner.

SPECIAL INTEREST TOPIC 7.2

Item Analysis for Constructed-Response Items

Our discussion and examples of the calculation of the item difficulty index and discrimination index used examples that were dichotomously scored (i.e., scored right or wrong: 0 or 1). Although this procedure works well with selected-response items (e.g., true–false, multiple-choice), you need a slightly different approach with constructed response items that are scored in a more continuous manner (e.g., an essay item that can receive scores between 1 and 5 depending on quality). To calculate the item difficulty index for a continuously scored constructed-response item, you use the following formula (Nitko, 2001):

$$p = \frac{\text{Average Score on the Item}}{\text{Range of Possible Scores}}$$

The range of possible scores is calculated as the maximum possible score on the item minus the minimum possible score on the item. For example, if an item has an average score of 2.7 and is scored on a 1 to 5 scale, the calculation would be:

$$p = \frac{2.7}{5 - 1} = \frac{2.7}{4} = 0.675$$

Therefore, this item has an item difficulty index of 0.675. This value can be interpreted the same as the dichotomously scored items we discussed. To calculate the item discrimination index for continuously scored constructed-response item, you use the following formula:

$$D = \frac{\text{Average Score for the Top Group} - \text{Average Score for the Bottom Group}}{\text{Range of Possible Scores}}$$

For example, if the average score for the top group is 4.3, the average score for the bottom group is 1.7, and the item is scored on a 1 to 5 scale, the calculation would be:

$$D = \frac{4.3 - 1.7}{5 - 1} = \frac{2.6}{4} = 0.65$$

Therefore, this item has an item discrimination index of 0.65. Again, this value can be interpreted the same as the dichotomously scored items we discussed.

Item Discrimination on Mastery Tests

As we noted previously, the item difficulty indexes on mastery tests tend to be higher (indicating easier items) than on tests designed primarily to produce norm-referenced scores. This is because with mastery testing it is usually assumed that most examinees will be successful. As a result, on mastery tests it is common for items to have average p values as high as 0.90. As a result, the standard approach to interpreting item difficulty levels needs to be modified to accommodate this tendency.

The interpretation of indexes of discrimination is also complicated on mastery tests. Because it is common to obtain high p values for both high- and low-scoring examinees, it is normal for traditional item discrimination indexes to underestimate an item's true measurement characteristics. Several different approaches have been suggested for determining **item discrimination on mastery tests** (e.g., Aiken, 2002; Popham, 2000). One common approach involves administering the test to two groups of examinees: one group that has received instruction and one that has not received instruction. The formula is:

> *Several different approaches have been suggested for determining **item discrimination on mastery tests**.*

$$D = p_{\text{instruction}} - p_{\text{no instruction}}$$

where $p_{\text{instruction}}$ = proportion of instructed examinees getting the answer correct

$p_{\text{no instruction}}$ = proportion of examinees without instruction getting the answer correct

This approach is technically adequate, with the primary limitation being potential difficulty obtaining access to an adequate group that has not received instruction or training on the relevant material. If one does have access to an adequate sample, this is a promising approach.

Another popular approach involves administering the test to the same sample twice, once before instruction and once after instruction. The formula is:

$$D = p_{\text{posttest}} - p_{\text{pretest}}$$

where p_{posttest} = proportion of examinees getting the answer correct on posttest

p_{pretest} = proportion of examinees getting the answer correct on pretest

Some drawbacks are associated with this approach. First, it requires that the test developers write the test, administer it as a pretest, wait while instruction is provided, administer it as a posttest, and then calculate the discrimination index. This can be an extended period of time in some situations, and test developers often want feedback in a timely manner. A second limitation is the possibility of carryover effects from the pre- to posttest. For example, examinees might remember items or concepts emphasized on the pretest, and this carryover effect can influence how they respond to instruction, study, and subsequently prepare for the posttest.

Aiken (2000) proposed another approach for calculating discrimination for mastery tests. Instead of using the top and bottom 27% of examinees (or the top and bottom 50%), he recommended using item difficulty values based on the test takers who reached the mastery cut-off score (i.e., mastery group) and those who did not reach mastery (i.e., nonmastery group). The formula is:

$$D = p_{\text{mastery}} - p_{\text{nonmastery}}$$

where p_{mastery} = proportion of mastery examinees getting the answer correct

$p_{\text{nonmastery}}$ = proportion of nonmastery examinees getting the answer correct

The advantage of this approach is that it can be calculated based on the data from one test administration with one sample. A potential problem is that because it is common for the majority of examinees to reach mastery, the p value of the nonmastery group might be based on a small number of examinees. As a result the statistics might not be stable and lead to erroneous conclusions.

Item-Total Correlation Coefficients

> *Another approach to examining item discrimination is to correlate performance on the item with the total test score.*

Another approach to examining item discrimination is to correlate performance on the items (scored as either 0 or 1) with the total test score. This is referred to as an item-total correlation. The total test score is usually the total number of items answered correctly (unadjusted) or the total number of items answered correctly omitting the item being examined (adjusted). Either way, the item-total correlation is usually calculated using the point-biserial correlation. As you remember from our discussion of basic statistics the point-biserial is used when one variable is a dichotomous nominal score and the other variable is measured on an interval or ratio scale. Here the dichotomous variable is the score on a single item (e.g., right or wrong) and the variable measured on an interval scale is the total test score. A large item-total correlation is taken as evidence that an item is measuring the same construct as the overall test measures and that the item discriminates between individuals high on that construct and those low on the construct. An item-total correlation calculated on the adjusted total will be lower than that computed on the unadjusted total and is preferred because the item being examined does not "contaminate" or inflate the correlation. The results of an item-total correlation will be similar to those of an item discrimination index and can be interpreted in a similar manner (Hopkins, 1998).

In the past some test developers preferred the item discrimination index over item correlations because it was easier to calculate. However, as computers and statistical programs have become widely available, the item-total correlation has become easier to compute and is becoming the dominant approach for examining item discrimination. Table 7–4 provides examples of two commercial test scoring and item analysis programs.

Item Discrimination on Typical Response Tests

Item-total correlations can also be used with typical response tests. For example, consider a test designed to measure "sensation-seeking" tendencies using true–false items. Following is an example of an item that might be on such a test:

I would like to go parachuting.	True	False

TABLE 7–4	Two Examples of Test Scoring and Item Analysis Programs

Assessment Systems Corporation

One of the company's products, ITEMAN, scores and analyzes a number of item formats including multiple-choice and true–false items. This product computes common item analysis and test statistics (e.g., mean, variance, standard deviation, KR-20). Its Internet site is http://www.assess.com/Software/sItemTest.htm.

Principia Products

One of this company's products, Remark Office OMR, grades tests and produces statistics and graphs reflecting common item analysis and test statistics. Its Internet site is http://www.principiaproducts.com/office/index.html.

If all *true* responses are scored 1 and indicate a tendency to engage in sensation-seeking behaviors and all *false* responses are scored 0 and indicate a tendency to avoid sensation-seeking behaviors, high scores on the test would indicate that the respondent enjoys high-sensation behaviors. Accordingly, low scores would suggest that the respondent tend to avoid high-sensation behaviors. Calculating item-total correlations would allow the test developer to select items with high correlations—that is, those items that discriminate between respondents that are high and low in sensation-seeking behaviors.

Difficulty and Discrimination on Speed Tests

Based on our discussion up to this point it should be clear that there are situations where the interpretation of indexes of item difficulty and discrimination is complicated. One situation where the interpretation of item analysis results is complicated is with "speed tests." On speed tests, performance depends primarily on the speed of performance. Items on speed tests are often fairly easy and could be completed by most test takers if there were no time limits. However, there are strict time limits and these limits are selected so that

> *On speed tests, measures of item difficulty and discrimination will largely reflect the position of the item in the test rather than the actual difficulty of the item or its discriminative ability.*

no test taker will be able to complete all of the items. The key factor is how many items the test taker is able to complete in the allotted time. On power tests everyone is given sufficient time to attempt all the items, but the items vary in difficulty with some being so difficult that no test takers will answer them all correctly. In many situations tests incorporate a combination of speed and power, so the speed–power distinction is actually one of degree.

On speed tests, measures of item difficulty and discrimination will largely reflect the location of the item in the test rather than the item's actual difficulty level or ability to discriminate. Items appearing late on a speed test will be passed by fewer individuals than items that appear earlier simply because the strict time limits prevent examinees from being able to attempt them. The items appearing later on the test are probably not actually more difficult than the earlier items, but their item difficulty index will suggest that they are more difficult.

Similar complications arise when interpreting indexes of discrimination with speed tests. Because the individuals completing the later items also tend to be the most capable test takers, indexes of discrimination may exaggerate the discriminating ability of these items. Although different procedures have been developed to take into consideration these and related factors, they all have limitations and none have received widespread acceptance (e.g., Aiken, 2000; Anastasi & Urbina, 1997). Our recommendation is that you be aware of these issues and take them into consideration when interpreting the item analyses of highly speeded tests.

Examples of Item Difficulty and Discrimination Indexes

To illustrate the results of common item analyses, we will present a few examples based on items administered in our upper-division undergraduate Test and Measurement class. These three examples illustrate some common patterns.

1. A test that measures what it is designed to measure is_____; a test that produces consistent/stable scores is _____.
   a. reliable; valid
   b. valid; reliable <
   c. marginal; optimal
   d. optimal; marginal

Item difficulty (p):	0.97
Discrimination index:	0.00
Item-total correlation:	0.05

Item 1 is an easy item that almost all students answer correctly. Because it is so easy it does not discriminate between students who know the material and those who do not. We often use this (or a similar item) as the first item in a test to help relax students and ease them into the assessment process.

2. Approximately what percentage of scores falls below an IQ of 130 if the scores are normally distributed?
   a. 16%
   b. 34%
   c. 50%
   d. 84%
   e. 98% <

Item difficulty (p):	0.78
Discrimination index:	0.53
Item-total correlation:	0.59

Item 2 is fairly easy for a five-alternative multiple-choice item (remember that the optimal mean p value for selected-response items with five choices was 0.69), but it does discriminate well.

3. Which of the following is an appropriate estimate of reliability when one is assessing the reliability of a highly speeded test?
   a. Coefficient alpha
   b. Kuder-Richardson (KR-20)
   c. Split-half reliability
   d. Test-retest reliability <
   e. all of the above

Item difficulty (p):	0.44
Discrimination index:	0.82
Item-total correlation:	0.66

Item 3 is a fairly difficult multiple-choice item for one with five alternatives. It shows excellent discrimination and can help identify high-achieving students.

DISTRACTER ANALYSIS

The final quantitative item analysis procedure we will discuss in this chapter involves the analysis of individual distracters. On multiple-choice items, the incorrect alternatives are referred to as distracters because they "distract" examinees who don't actually know the correct response. **Distracter analysis** allows you to examine how many examinees in the top and bottom groups selected each option on a multiple-choice item.

> **Distracter analysis** *allows you to examine how many examinees in the top and bottom groups selected each option on a multiple-choice item.*

The key is to examine each distracter and ask two questions. First, did the distracter distract some examinees? If no examinees selected the distracter it is not doing its job. An effective distracter must be selected by some examinees. If a distracter is so obviously incorrect that no examinees select it, it is ineffective and needs to be revised or replaced. The second question involves discrimination. Effective distracters should attract more examinees in the bottom group than in the top group. When looking at the correct response we expect more examinees in the top group to select it than examinees in the bottom group (i.e., it demonstrates positive discrimination). With distracters we expect the opposite. We expect more examinees in the bottom group to select a distracter than examinees in the top group. That is, distracters should demonstrate *negative* discrimination! Consider the following example:

	Options			
Item 1	**A***	**B**	**C**	**D**
Number in top group	22	3	2	3
Number in bottom group	9	7	8	6

*Correct answer.

For this item, $p = 0.52$ (moderate difficulty) and $D = 0.43$ (excellent discrimination). This item serves as an example of what might be expected with a "good" item. As reflected in the D value, more examinees in the top group than the bottom group selected the correct answer (i.e., option A). By examining the distracters (i.e., options B, C, and D) you see that they were all selected by some examinees, which indicates that they are serving their purpose (i.e., distracting examinees who don't know the correct response). Additionally, all three distracters were selected more by members of the bottom group than the top group. This is the desired outcome! Although we want more high-scoring examinees to select the correct answer than low-scoring examinees (i.e., positive discrimination), we want more low-scoring examinees to select distracters than high-scoring examinees (i.e., negative discrimination). In summary, this is a good item and all of the distracters are performing well.

Now we will consider an example that illustrates some problems. Consider the following example:

	Options			
Item 1	**A***	**B**	**C**	**D**
Number in top group	17	9	0	4
Number in bottom group	13	6	0	11

*Correct answer.

> *The selection of distracters can significantly impact the difficulty of the item and consequently the ability of the item to discriminate.*

For this item, $p = 0.50$ (moderate difficulty) and $D = 0.14$ (fair discrimination but further scrutiny suggested). Based on these values, this item needs closer examination and possibly revision. Examining option B you will notice that more examinees in the top group than in the bottom group selected this distracter. This is not a desirable situation since it indicates that more top-performing examinees selected this distracter than poor-performing examinees. As a result, option B needs to be examined to determine why it is attracting top examinees. It is possible that the wording is ambiguous or that the option is similar in some way to the correct answer, and as a result it is attracting top examinees. Examining option C you note that no one selected this distracter. It attracted no examinees, suggesting that it was obviously not the correct answer, and as a result needs to be replaced. To be effective, a distracter must distract some examinees. Finally, option D performed well. More poor-performing examinees selected this option than top-performing examinees (i.e., 11 vs. 4). It is likely that if the test developer revises options B and C this will be a more effective item.

How Distracters Influence Item Difficulty and Discrimination

Before leaving our discussion of distracters, we want to highlight how the selection of distracters impacts both item difficulty and discrimination. Consider the following item:

1. In what year did Albert Einstein first publish his full general theory of relativity?
   a. 1910
   b. 1912
   c. 1914
   d. 1916
   e. 1918

Unless you are very familiar with Einstein's work, this is probably a fairly difficult question. Now consider this revision:

1. In what year did Albert Einstein first publish his full general theory of relativity?
   a. 1655
   b. 1762
   c. 1832
   d. 1916 <
   e. 2001

This is the same question but with different distracters. The revised item would likely be a much easier item in a typical high school science class. The point is that the selection of distracters can significantly impact the difficulty of the item and consequently the ability of the item to discriminate.

QUALITATIVE ITEM ANALYSIS

In addition to the quantitative item analysis procedures described to this point, test developers can also use **qualitative item analysis** to improve their tests. Along these lines, Popham (2000) provided some useful suggestions. He recommended that after writing the test the developer set aside the test for a few days to gain some distance from it. We can tell you from our own experience this is good advice. Even though you carefully proof a test immediately after writing it,

> *In addition to quantitative item analysis procedures, test developers can also use* **qualitative item analysis** *procedures to improve their tests.*

a review a few days later will often reveal a number of errors. This delayed review often reveals both clerical errors (e.g., spelling or grammar) and less obvious errors that might make an item unclear or inaccurate. After a "cooling off" period we are often amazed that an "obvious" error evaded detection earlier. Somehow the introduction of a period of time provides distance that seems to make errors more easily detected. The time you spend proofing a test is well spent and can help you avoid problems once the test is administered and scored.

Popham (2000) also recommended that you have a colleague review the test. Ideally this should be a colleague familiar with basic psychometric principles and the construct being assessed by the test. In addition to checking for clerical errors, clarity, and accuracy, the reviewer should determine if the test is covering all aspects of the construct that it is designed to cover. This is akin to collecting validity evidence based on the content of the test. Finally, he recommended that you have the examinees provide feedback on the test. For example, after completing the test you might have the examinees complete a brief questionnaire asking if the directions were clear and if any of the questions were confusing.

Ideally a test developer should use both quantitative and qualitative approaches to improve tests. We regularly provide a delayed review of our own tests and use colleagues as reviewers whenever possible. After administering a test and obtaining the quantitative item analyses, we typically question examinees about problematic items, particularly items where the basis of the problem is not obvious. Often a combination of qualitative and quantitative procedures will result in the optimal enhancement of your tests.

Popham (2000) noted that historically quantitative item analysis procedures have been applied primarily to tests using norm-referenced score interpretations and qualitative procedures have been used primarily with tests using criterion-referenced interpretations. This tendency can

> *We recommend the use of both qualitative and quantitative approaches to improve the quality of test items.*

be attributed partly to some of the technical problems we described earlier about using item analysis statistics with mastery tests. Nevertheless, we recommend the use of both qualitative and quantitative approaches with both types of score interpretations. When developing tests, we believe the more information one has, the better!

ITEM CHARACTERISTIC CURVES AND ITEM RESPONSE THEORY

> *Today traditional item analysis procedures such as the item difficulty and discrimination indexes typically complement sophisticated new techniques associated* **with item response theory (IRT).**

The item analysis procedures that we have described so far in this chapter have literally been around for close to a century and are related to classical test theory. Although they are well established and are still useful, they have their limitations and are typically complemented with sophisticated new techniques associated with **item response theory (IRT)**. We have already mentioned IRT several times in this text, specifically when discussing test scores and reliability. In summary, IRT is a theory or model of mental measurement that holds that the responses to items on a test are accounted for by latent traits. A latent trait is an ability or characteristic of an individual that is inferred to exist based on theories of behavior as well as empirical evidence, but a latent trait cannot be assessed directly. Intelligence is an example of a latent trait. It is assumed that each examinee possesses a certain amount of any given latent trait and that its estimation is not dependent on any specific set of items or any assessment procedure. Central to IRT is a rather complex mathematical model that describes how examinees at different levels of ability (or whatever latent trait is being assessed) will respond to individual test items. IRT is also known by other names, including unidimensional scaling, latent trait theory, and item characteristic curve theory. At this point it is helpful to elaborate on IRT and its contribution to contemporary test development and analysis. A description of item characteristic curves is a good place to start our discussion.

Item Characteristic Curves

An **item characteristic curve (ICC)** is a graph with ability reflected on the horizontal axis and the probability of a correct response reflected on the vertical axis. It is important to recognize

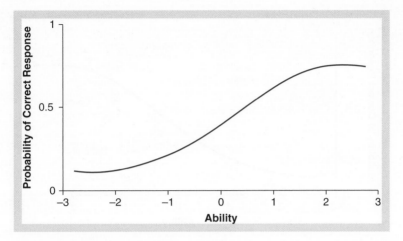

FIGURE 7–1   Typical ICC.

that *each item has its own specific ICC.* These ICCs are plotted from mathematically derived functions and usually involve iterative procedures (Anastasi & Urbina, 1997). Figure 7–1 presents a hypothetical, but typical, ICC for an item with good discrimination. Notice that this ICC takes a "Lazy S" shape and it is an asymptote (i.e., approaches but never intersects with zero or 100%). By examining this graph you see that low levels of ability are associated with a low probability of a correct response. As the ability level increases, the probability of a correct response increases. In other words, test takers with greater ability have a better chance of answering the item correct than those with lower ability. This is what you expect with a good item.

ICCs incorporate information about item measurement characteristics that you are already familiar with: the item's difficulty and discrimination ability. In ICC terminology the point halfway between the lower and upper asymptotes is referred to as the inflection point and represents the difficulty of the item (i.e., the b parameter). That is, it pinpoints the ability level required for a test taker to have a 50% chance of getting the item correct. Discrimination (i.e., the a parameter) is reflected by the slope of the ICC at the inflection point. ICCs with steeper slopes demonstrate better discrimination than those with gentler slopes. Discrimination in this context refers to the ability of the item to differentiate or discriminate one level of ability or one level of the presence of the trait being assessed from another level. Figure 7–2 illustrates how both difficulty and discrimination are represented in an ICC. The vertical dotted line denoting "Difficulty" indicates that it requires a z-score of approximately 0.45 to have a 50% chance of answering the item correctly. The dotted line representing "Discrimination" is at approximately 45 degrees which suggests good discrimination.

> **Item characteristic curves (ICCs)** *incorporate information about item measurement characteristics that you are already familiar with: the item's difficulty and discrimination ability.*

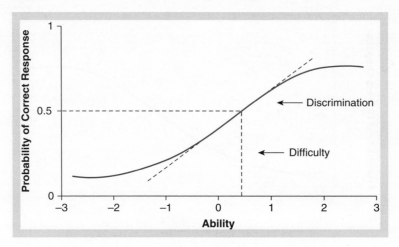

FIGURE 7–2   ICC Illustrating Difficulty and Discrimination.

This is further illustrated in Figures 7–3 and 7–4. Figure 7–3 depicts two items with equal slopes, but Item 2 is shifted to the right of Item 1. This shifting to the right indicates that relative to Item 1, Item 2 requires more ability to answer correctly—that is, it is more difficult. Figure 7–4 depicts two items that are of equal difficulty, but different discrimination. Item 1 has a steeper slope which indicates that it is better at discriminating between test takers low and high in ability compared to Item 2.

IRT Models

There are three major IRT models that differ in assumptions made about items' characteristics. The simplest model (if one can realistically use "simple" in the context of IRT) is referred to as the Rasch model after the Danish mathematician and statistician Georg Rasch who was a pioneer in

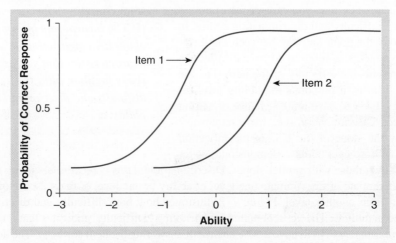

FIGURE 7–3   Two ICCs With the Same Discrimination but Different Difficulties.

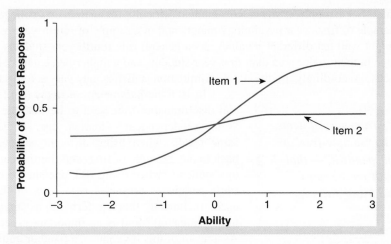

FIGURE 7–4 Two ICCs With the Same Difficulty but Different Discrimination.

the development of IRT. This model is referred to as a one-parameter IRT model because it assumes that items differ in only one parameter—difficulty (i.e., b parameter). That is, all items have equal discrimination (or differences in discrimination are negligible). This implies that all items have ICCs with the same S shape with the same slope; they differ in only the location of their inflection point along the horizontal (i.e., ability) axis.

A more complex IRT model is the two-parameter IRT model that assumes that items differ in both difficulty and discrimination. In this model the ICCs differ not only in their inflection points, but also in their slopes. Although test developers might attempt to develop tests that contain items with the same degree of discrimination, in practice this is difficult, if not impossible, to accomplish. As a result, the two-parameter IRT model better reflects real-life test development applications than the one-parameter IRT model.

As you might have anticipated, the third model is the three-parameter IRT model. In both the one- and two-parameter IRT models the ICCs asymptote toward a probability of zero— assuming essentially a zero percent possibility of answering the items by chance. The three-parameter model assumes that even if the respondent essentially has no "ability," there is still a chance he or she may answer the item correctly simply by chance. Obviously this occurs on selected-response items. For example, a multiple-choice item with four alternatives has a 25% chance of being answered correctly with random guessing. A true–false item has a 50% chance of being answered correctly with random guessing. The three-parameter model essentially adjusts the lower tail of the ICC to take into consideration the probability of answering an item correctly simply by chance (i.e., the c parameter). This model is mathematically very complex and this complexity has prevented it from being widely applied.

Invariance of Item Parameters

The item statistics we discussed earlier in this chapter such as item difficulty (i.e., p) and item discrimination (i.e., D) are based on classical test theory (CTT). These item statistics are dependent on the sample they are derived with. That is, one may obtain different p and D values in different samples. For example, if you calculated item difficulty for an item on a college psychology test in a sample of first- year psychology majors and in a sample of fourth-year psychology majors, you might well get different p values. As a general rule fourth-year students will have more knowledge in their major area than first-year students and a higher percentage will answer the item correctly. Accordingly, traditional discrimination statistics may vary across samples.

> *In IRT the parameters of items are said to be "sample-free" or "sample-independent"— that is, one should get the same results when using different samples.*

In IRT the parameters of items (e.g., difficulty and discrimination) are said to be "sample- free" or "sample-independent"—that is, one should get the same results when using different samples. Going back to our example of first- and fourth-year psychology students, when using IRT one should obtain the same parameter estimates regardless of the sample used. Technically this is referred to as "invariance of item parameters" and is an important aspect of IRT. As a result of this invariance, a fixed or uniform scale of measurement can be developed and used in different groups. Accordingly, examinees can be tested using different sets of items and their scores will be comparable (Anastasi & Urbina, 1997). These properties of IRT make it particularly useful in a number of special test development applications such as computer-based testing and development of equivalent or alternate forms of tests.

Special Applications of IRT

> *IRT has made significant contributions to contemporary test development.*

As we discussed earlier, IRT is a modern psychometric theory that has extended, but not replaced, classical test theory. Following are a few specific applications where IRT has made significant contributions to contemporary test development.

COMPUTER ADAPTIVE TESTING. IRT is fundamental to the development and application of computer adaptive testing (CAT). In CAT the test taker is initially given an item that is of medium difficulty. If the test taker correctly responds to that item, the computer selects and administers a slightly more difficult item. If the examinee misses the initial item, the computer selects a somewhat easier item. As the testing proceeds the computer continues to selects items on the basis on the test taker's performance on previous items. CAT continues until a specified level of precision is reached. Research has shown that CAT can produce the same levels of reliability and validity as conventional paper-and-pencil tests, but requires the administration of fewer test items, which means enhanced efficiency.

DETECTING BIASED ITEMS. IRT has proved particularly useful in identifying biased test items. To this end, ICCs for different groups (e.g., males, females) are generated and statistically compared to determine the degree of differential item function (DIF). Figure 7–5 depicts an item with substantially different ICCs for two different groups. This application of IRT will be discussed in more detail in Chapter 15.

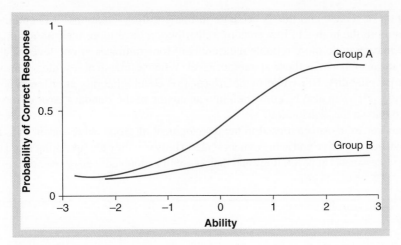

FIGURE 7–5 ICCs for a Biased Item.

SCORES BASED ON ITEM RESPONSE THEORY. As we stated in Chapter 3, in addition to the norm-referenced and criterion-referenced score interpretations, IRT provides an additional approach for interpreting scores. Because we introduced IRT scores in Chapter 3, we will not go into great detail in them at this point. However, a brief review is warranted. In summary, the scores assigned to reflect an examinee's performance in IRT models are similar to raw scores on tests developed using classical test theory. For example, they can be transformed into either norm- or criterion-referenced scores. However, they have an advantage in that unlike traditional raw scores, they are equal-interval level scores (i.e., having equal intervals between values) and have stable standard deviations across age groups. These IRT scores go by different names, including *W*-scores, growth scores, change sensitive scores (CSS), or Rasch scores. The *W*-scores used on the Woodcock-Johnson III (Woodcock, McGrew, & Mather, 2001a) provide a good example of these scores. *W*-scores are set so a score of 500 reflects cognitive performance at the beginning fifth-grade ability level. *W*-scores have proven to be particularly useful in measuring changes in cognitive abilities. For example, they can help measure gains in achievement due to learning or declines in cognitive abilities due to dementia. In terms of measuring gains, if over time an examinee's *W*-score increases by 10 units (e.g., from 500 to 510), he or she can now complete tasks with 75% probability of success that originally could be completed only with a 50% probability of success. Conversely, if an examinee's *W*-score decreases by 10 *W* units (e.g., 500 to 490) he or she can now complete tasks with only 25% probability of success that originally could be completed with 50% probability of success (Woodcock, 1999). Although these IRT-based scores are not currently widely available, they will likely become more available in the future.

RELIABILITY. In Chapter 4 we stated that in IRT models information on the reliability of scores is reported as a test information function (TIF). A TIF illustrates the reliability of measurement at different points along the distribution. This implies that the reliability is not constant across the distribution of scores, and this is accurate in many testing situations. It is common to find that scores at both the high and low ends of a distribution have more measurement error. As a result, a test may provide more reliable measurement for examinees at one level of ability, and less reliable measurement for those at another level. Whereas classical test theory provides only one estimate of reliability, IRT can provide information about reliability at different points along the distribution. TIFs can also be converted into an analog of the standard error of measurement for specific points in the distribution.

IRT models are most often used in the development of group achievement tests and in the various Woodcock cognitive and achievement scales. However, they are becoming more widely applied in other assessments in psychology and their use will undoubtedly grow over the next decades.

Summary

In this chapter we described several procedures that can be used to assess the quality of the individual items making up a test. These include:

- Item difficulty level. The item difficulty level or index is defined as the percentage or proportion of examinees correctly answering the item. The item difficulty index (i.e., p) ranges from 0.0 to 1.0 with easier items having larger decimal values and difficult items having smaller values. For maximizing variability among examinees, the optimal item difficulty level is 0.50, indicating that half of the examinees answered the item correctly and half answered it incorrectly. Although 0.50 is optimal for maximizing variability, there are many situations where other values are preferred. As a general rule, in most testing situations test developers will select items with p values between 0.20 and 0.80.
- Item discrimination. Item discrimination refers to the extent to which an item accurately discriminates between examinees that vary on the test's construct. For example, on an achievement test the question is can the item distinguish between examinees who are high achievers and those who are poor achievers? Whereas a number of different approaches have been developed for assessing item discrimination, we focused our discussion on the popular item discrimination index (i.e., D). We provided guidelines for evaluating item discrimination indexes, and as a general rule items with D values over 0.30 are acceptable, and items with D values below 0.30 should be reviewed. However, this is only a general rule and we discussed a number of situations when smaller D values might be acceptable. Another approach to examining item discrimination is to correlate performance on individual item with the total test score. This is referred to as an item-total correlation. The results of an item-total correlation will be similar to those of an item discrimination index and can be interpreted in a similar manner. In the past some preferred the item discrimination index over item correlations because it was easier to calculate. However, the broad availability of computers has made calculating item-total correlations easy and they are becoming the dominant approach for examining item discrimination.
- Distracter analysis. The final quantitative item analysis procedure we described was distracter analysis. In essence, distracter analysis allows the test developer to evaluate the distracters on multiple-choice items (i.e., incorrect alternatives) and determine if they are functioning properly. This involves two primary questions. First, a properly functioning

distracter should "distract" some examinees. If a distracter is so obviously wrong that no examinees selected it, it is useless and deserves attention. The second question involves discrimination. Effective distracters should attract more examinees in the bottom group than in the top group. Distracter analysis allows you to answer these two questions.

- Qualitative approaches. In addition to quantitative item analysis procedures, test developers can also use qualitative approaches to improve their tests. Popham (2000) suggested that the test developer carefully proof the test after setting it aside for a few days. This break often allows the test author to gain some distance from the test and provide a more thorough review of the test. He also recommended getting a trusted colleague to review the test. Finally, he recommended that the test developer solicit feedback from the examinees regarding the clarity of the directions and the identification of ambiguous items. Test developers are probably best served by using combination of quantitative and qualitative item analysis procedures.

- Item characteristic curves and item response theory. An item characteristic curve (ICC) is a graph with ability reflected on the horizontal axis and the probability of a correct response reflected on the vertical axis. ICCs incorporate information about an item's difficulty and discrimination ability and are a component of item response theory (IRT). IRT is a modern theory of mental measurement that holds that responses to items on a test are accounted for by latent traits. IRT assumes that each examinee possesses a certain amount of any given latent trait and that its estimation is not dependent on any specific set of items or any assessment procedure. IRT has significantly impacted contemporary test development, particularly in the development and application of computer adaptive testing.

Key Terms and Concepts

Distracter analysis, 233
Item characteristic curves, (ICCs) 236
Item difficulty, 222

Item discrimination on mastery tests, 229
Item response theory, 236
Qualitative item analysis, 235

Recommended Readings

Embretson, S., & Reise, S. (2000). *Item response theory for psychologists*. London: Taylor & Francis.

Johnson, A. P. (1951). Notes on a suggested index of item validity: The U-L index. *Journal of Educational Measurement, 42*, 499–504. This is a seminal article on the history of item analysis.

Kelley, T. L. (1939). The selection of upper and lower groups for the validation of test items. *Journal of Educational Psychology, 30*, 17–24. A real classic!

Chapter Eight

Achievement Tests in the Era of High-Stakes Assessment

Depending on your perspective, standardized achievement tests are either a bane or boon to public schools. Many politicians and citizens see them as a way of holding educators accountable and ensuring students are really learning. On the other hand, many educators feel standardized tests are often misused and detract from their primary job of educating students.

Chapter Outline

The Era of High-Stakes Assessments
Group-Administered Achievement Tests
Individual Achievement Tests
Selecting an Achievement Battery

Teacher-Constructed Achievement Tests and
   Student Evaluation
Achievement Tests—Not Only in the Public Schools!
Summary

Learning Objectives

After reading and studying this chapter, students should be able to:

1. Describe the characteristics of standardized tests and explain why standardization is important.
2. Describe the major characteristics of achievement tests.
3. Describe the major uses of standardized achievement tests in schools.

4. Explain what high-stakes testing means and trace the historical development of this phenomenon.
5. Identify the major publishers of group achievement tests and their major tests.
6. Discuss the major issues and controversies surrounding state and high-stakes testing programs.
7. Describe and evaluate common procedures used for preparing students for standardized tests.

8. Describe and evaluate the major individual achievement tests.
9. Describe and explain the major factors that should be considered when selecting standardized achievement tests.
10. Describe and explain major factors that should be considered when developing a classroom achievement test.
11. Describe major factors that should be considered when assigning student grades.
12. Describe some uses of achievement tests outside the school setting.

In this chapter we will focus on standardized achievement tests, primarily as they are used in schools. As noted in Chapter 1, a standardized test is a test that is administered, scored, and interpreted in a standard manner. Most standardized tests are developed by testing professionals or test publishing companies. The goal of standardization is to ensure that testing conditions are as nearly the same as is possible for all individuals taking the test. If this is accomplished, no examinee will have an advantage over

> **Achievement tests** *are designed to assess students' knowledge in a skill or content domain in which they have received instruction.*

another due to variance in administration procedures, and assessment results will be comparable. An **achievement test** is a test to assess an examinee's knowledge or skills in a content domain in which he or she has received instruction (AERA et al., 1999). Naturally the vast majority of teacher-constructed classroom tests qualify as achievement tests, but they are not standardized. In this chapter we will focus on standardized achievement tests, but we will briefly address teacher-constructed achievement tests, and their development and application later in this chapter. In describing standardized achievement tests, Linn and Gronlund (2000) highlighted the following characteristics:

- Standardized achievement tests typically contain high-quality items that were selected on the basis of both quantitative and qualitative item analysis procedures.
- They have precisely stated directions for administration and scoring so that consistent procedures can be followed in different settings.
- Many contemporary standardized achievement tests provide both norm-referenced and criterion-referenced interpretations. The norm-referenced interpretation allows comparison to the performance of other examinees, whereas criterion-referenced interpretation allows comparisons to an established criterion.
- The normative data are based on large, representative samples.
- Equivalent or parallel forms of the test are often available.
- They have professionally developed manuals and support materials that provide extensive information about the test, how to administer, score and interpret it, and its measurement characteristics.

There are many different types of standardized achievement tests. Some achievement tests are designed for group administration whereas some are designed for individual administration. Individually administered achievement tests must be given to only one examinee at a time and require specially trained examiners. Some achievement tests focus on a single-subject area (e.g., reading); others cover a broad range of academic skills and content areas (e.g., reading, language, and mathematics). Some use selection type items exclusively whereas others contain constructed-response and performance assessments. In addition to coming in a variety of formats, standardized achievement tests have a number of different uses or applications. These include:

- One of the most common uses of standardized achievement tests is to track student achievement over time or to compare group achievement across classes, schools, or districts.
- Standardized achievement tests are increasingly being used in high-stakes decision making in the public schools. For example, they may be used to determine which students are promoted or allowed to graduate. They may also be used in evaluating and rating teachers, administrators, schools, and school districts.
- Achievement tests can help identify academic strengths and weaknesses of individual examinees.
- Achievement tests can be used to evaluate the effectiveness of instructional programs or curricula and help educators identify areas of concern.
- Achievement tests are used in employment settings to determine if the job applicant has the requisite knowledge for the job.
- Achievement tests are used in licensing and certification in a broad array of professions including psychology, medicine, electrical engineering, and even driving—the written test for a driver's license is an achievement test covering a prescribed area of content (i.e., the rules of the road and knowledge required to drive safely).
- A final major use of standard achievement tests is the identification of students with special educational requirements. For example, achievement tests might be used in assessing children to determine if they qualify for special education services.

As is apparent from these applications, achievement tests are most commonly used in our public schools. In the next section we trace some of the historical factors that have influenced the contemporary use of achievement tests in today's schools.

THE ERA OF HIGH-STAKES ASSESSMENTS

> *The current trend is toward more, rather than less, standardized testing in public schools.*

The current trend is toward more, rather than less, standardized achievement testing in public schools. This trend is largely attributed to the increasing emphasis on educational accountability and high-stakes testing programs. Popham (2000) noted that even though there have always been critics of public schools, calls for increased accountability became more strident and widespread in the 1970s. During this period news reports began to surface that publicized incidences where high school graduates were unable to demonstrate even the most basic academic skills such as reading and writing. In 1983 the National Commission of Excellence in Education published *A Nation at Risk: The Imperative for Educational Reform*. This important report sounded an alarm proclaiming that the United States was falling behind other nations in terms of educating our children. Parents, who as taxpayers were footing the bill for their children's education, increasingly began to question the quality of the education being provided and demand evidence that schools were actually educating our children. In efforts to assuage taxpayers, legislators started implementing statewide minimum-competency testing programs. These programs were intended to guarantee that graduates of public schools were able to meet minimum academic standards. Many students passed these exams, but a substantial number of students failed and the public schools and teachers were largely blamed for the failures. In this era of increasing accountability, many schools developed more sophisticated assessment programs that used both state-developed tests and commercially produced nationally standardized achievement tests. As the trend continued, it became common for local newspapers to rank schools according to their students' performance on these tests with the implication that a school's ranking reflected the effectiveness or quality of teaching. Special Interest Topic 8.1 provides a brief description of the National Assessment of Educational Progress (NAEP) that has been used for several decades to monitor academic progress across the nation, as well as the results of fourth-grade reading assessments.

SPECIAL INTEREST TOPIC 8.1

The "Nation's Report Card"

The National Assessment of Educational Progress (NAEP), also referred to as the "Nation's Report Card," is the only ongoing nationally administered assessment of academic achievement in the United States. NAEP provides a comprehensive assessment of our students' achievement at critical periods in their academic experience (i.e., Grades 4, 8, and 12). NAEP assesses performance in mathematics, science, reading, writing, world geography, U.S. history, civics, and the arts. New assessments in world history, economics, and foreign language are currently being developed. NAEP has been administered regularly since 1969. It does not provide information on the performance of individual students or schools, but presents aggregated data reflecting achievement in specific academic areas, instructional practices, and academic environments for broad samples of students and specific subgroups. The NAEP has an excellent website that can be accessed at http://nces.ed.gov/nationsreportcard/. Of particular interest to teachers is the NAEP *Questions Tool*. This tool provides access to NAEP questions, student responses, and scoring guides that have been released to the public. This tool can be accessed at http://nces.ed.gov/nationsreportcard/itmrls/. The following table contains fourth-grade reading scores for the states, Department of Defense Education Agency, and the District of Columbia.

NAEP Results: 2007 Fourth-Grade Average Reading Scores

	State	Score			State	Score
1	Massachusetts	235.75		13	Wyoming	225.29
2	New Jersey	230.65		14	Delaware	225.07
3	DoDEA	229.18		15	Minnesota	224.92
4	New Hampshire	229.02		16	Iowa	224.89
5	Vermont	228.25		17	Maryland	224.78
6	Connecticut	227.20		18	Kansas	224.66
7	Virginia	227.14		19	Washington	224.00
8	Montana	226.67		20	New York	223.75
9	Pennsylvania	226.35		21	Colorado	223.73
10	North Dakota	226.33		22	Florida	223.53
11	Ohio	225.67		23	Idaho	223.40
12	Maine	225.54		24	South Dakota	223.40

(Continued on page 248)

SPECIAL INTEREST TOPIC 8.1 (*Continued*)

	State	Score		State	Score
25	Wisconsin	223.32	39	Alabama	216.39
26	Nebraska	222.90	40	Tennessee	215.75
27	Kentucky	222.43	41	West Virginia	215.13
28	Indiana	221.67	42	Oregon	215.02
29	Utah	221.26	43	Alaska	214.48
30	Missouri	220.78	44	South Carolina	213.84
	National Average	**220.52**	45	Hawaii	213.50
31	Michigan	220.12	46	New Mexico	211.63
32	Texas	219.60	47	Nevada	210.82
33	Illinois	219.39	48	Arizona	209.52
34	Georgia	218.89	49	California	208.52
35	Rhode Island	218.76	50	Mississippi	207.81
36	North Carolina	217.93	51	Louisiana	207.41
37	Arkansas	217.03	52	District of Columbia	197.09
38	Oklahoma	216.96			

Note: DoDEA = Department of Defense Education Agency.

Source: Data retrieved from http://nces.ed.gov/nationsreportcard/ on April 16, 2009.

> *The No Child Left Behind Act of 2001 required that each state develop high academic standards and implement annual assessments to monitor the performance of states, districts, and schools.*

Subsequent legislation and reports continued to focus attention on the quality of our educational system and promote increasing levels of accountability, which translated into more testing. In recent years, the No Child Left Behind Act of 2001 required that each state develop high academic standards and implement annual assessments to monitor the performance of states, districts, and schools. It requires that state assessments meet professional standards for reliability and validity, and requires that states achieve academic proficiency for all students within 12 years. As this text goes to print Congress is beginning to debate the reauthorization of NCLB. It is likely that there will be significant changes to the act in the next years, but in our opinion it is likely that standardized achievement tests will continue to see extensive use in our public schools. Special Interest Topic 8.2 succinctly describes NCLB and two other major federal laws that impact assessment practices in the public schools.

SPECIAL INTEREST TOPIC 8.2

Federal Law and Achievement Assessment

There are numerous federal laws that have significantly impacted the assessment of students in public schools. Following are brief descriptions of three major statutes that significantly impact the way students are assessed.

No Child Left Behind (NCLB) Act of 2001

The Elementary and Secondary Education Act of 1965 (ESEA) was one of the first federal laws to focus on education. Although the federal government recognizes that education is primarily the responsibility of the individual states, it holds that the federal government has a responsibility to ensure that an adequate level of educational services is being provided by all states (Jacob & Harthshorne, 2007). The No Child Left Behind Act of 2001 is the most recent reauthorization of the ESEA. Major aspects of this act include:

- ◆ *Increased State Accountability.* The NCLB Act requires that each state develop rigorous academic standards and implement annual assessments to monitor the performance of states, districts, and schools. It requires that these assessments meet professional standards for reliability and validity and that states achieve academic proficiency for all students within 12 years. To ensure that no group of children is neglected, the act requires that states and districts include all students in their assessment programs, including those with disabilities and limited English proficiency. However, the act does allow 3% of all students to be given alternative assessments. Alternative assessments are defined as instruments specifically designed for students with disabilities that preclude their assessment using the standard assessment.

- ◆ *More Parental Choice.* The act allows parents with children in schools that do not demonstrate adequate annual progress toward academic goals to move their children to another, better performing school.

- ◆ *Greater Flexibility for States.* A goal of the NCLB Act is to give states increased flexibility in the use of federal funds in exchange for increased accountability for academic results.

- ◆ *Reading First Initiative.* A goal of the NCLB Act is to ensure that every student can read by the end of third grade. To this end, the Reading First initiative significantly increased federal funding of empirically based reading instruction programs in the early grades.

  Although the NCLB Act received broad support when initiated, it has been the target of increasing criticism in recent years. The act's focus on increased accountability and statewide assessment programs typically receive the greatest criticism. For example, it is common to hear teachers and school administrators complain about "teaching to the test" when discussing the impact of statewide assessment programs.

Individuals with Disabilities Education Improvement Act of 2004 (IDEA 2004)

The Education of All Handicapped Children Act (EAHCA) of 1975 was the original law that required that all children with disabilities be given a free appropriate public education (FAPE). At that time it was estimated that there were more than 8 million children with disabilities. Of these, over half were not receiving an appropriate public education and as many as 1 million were not receiving a public education at all (Jacob & Hartshorne, 2007). The Individuals with Disabilities Education Improvement Act of 2004 (commonly abbreviated as IDEA 2004 or simply IDEA) is the most current reauthorization of the EAHCA. IDEA designates 13 disability categories (e.g., mental retardation, visual or hearing impairment, specific learning disabilities, emotional disturbance) and provides funds to states and school districts that meet the requirements of the law. IDEA provides guidelines for conducting evaluations for students

(Continued on page 250)

SPECIAL INTEREST TOPIC 8.2 (*Continued*)

suspected of having a disability. Students who qualify under IDEA have an individualized educational program (IEP) developed specifically for them that designates the special services and modifications to instruction and assessment that they must receive. Possibly most important for regular education teachers is the move for students with disabilities to receive instruction in the "least restrictive environment," a movement referred to as "mainstreaming." In application, this means that most students with disabilities receive educational services in the regular education classroom. As a result, more regular education teachers are involved in the education of students with disabilities and are required to implement the educational modifications specified in their students' IEPs. These modifications can include modifications in both instructional strategies and assessment practices. For more information on IDEA 2004, go to the following site: http://idea.ed.gov.

Section 504 of the Rehabilitation Act of 1973

This law mandates that any institution that receives federal funds must ensure that individuals with disabilities have equal access to all programs and services provided by the institution. More specifically, schools cannot exclude students with disabilities from any activities or programs based on their disability, and schools must make reasonable accommodations to ensure that students with disabilities have an equal opportunity to benefit from those activities or programs (Jacob & Harthshorne, 2007). Section 504 differs from IDEA in several important ways. First, it defines a handicap or disability very broadly, much broader than IDEA. Therefore, a child may not qualify for services under IDEA, but qualify under Section 504. Second, Section 504 is an antidiscrimination act, not a grant program like IDEA. Although IDEA provides funds for the required services, Section 504 does not. In terms of the assessment of disabilities, Section 504 provides less specific guidance than IDEA. Similar to IDEA, students qualified under Section 504 may receive modifications to their instruction and assessments that are implemented in the classrooms. In recent years there has been a rapid expansion in the number of students receiving accommodations under Section 504.

In the remainder of this chapter we will introduce a number of standardized achievement tests. First we will provide brief descriptions of some major group achievement tests and discuss their applications in schools. We will then briefly describe a number of individual achievement tests that are commonly used in schools and clinical settings. Because teacher-constructed classroom tests play such a prominent role in educational settings, we also briefly cover these instruments. The goal of this chapter is to familiarize you with some of the prominent characteristics of these tests and their contemporary use.

GROUP-ADMINISTERED ACHIEVEMENT TESTS

> *The main attraction of group-administered tests is that they are an efficient way to collect information about students' achievement.*

Achievement tests can be classified as either individual or group tests. Individual tests are administered in a one-to-one testing situation. One testing professional (i.e., the examiner) administers the test to one individual (i.e., the examinee) at a time. In contrast, **group-administered tests** are those that can be administered to more than one examinee at a time. The main attraction of group administration is that it is an efficient way to collect information about students or other examinees. By efficient, we mean a large number of examinees can be assessed with a minimal time commitment from educational professionals. As you might expect, group administered tests are very popular in school settings. For example, most teacher-constructed classroom tests are designed to be administered to the whole class at one time. Accordingly, if a school district wants to test all the students in Grades 3 through 8, it would probably be impossible to administer a lengthy test to each student on a one-to-one basis. There is simply not enough time or enough teachers (or other educational professionals) to accomplish such a task without significantly detracting from the time devoted to instruction. However, when you can have one professional administer a test to 20 to 30 examinees at a time, the task can be accomplished in a reasonably efficient manner.

Although efficiency is the most prominent advantage of group-administered tests, there are at least three other positive attributes of group testing that warrant mentioning. First, because the role of the individual administering the test is limited, group tests will typically involve more uniform testing conditions than individual tests. Second, group tests frequently involve items that can be scored objectively, often even by a computer (e.g., selected-response items). This reduces or eliminates the measurement error introduced by the scoring procedures that are more common in individual tests, many of which require the examiner to judge the adequacy of the response to open-ended questions. Finally, group tests often have very large standardization or normative samples. Normative samples for professionally developed group tests are often in the range of 100,000 to 200,000, whereas professionally developed individually administered tests will usually have normative samples ranging from 1,000 to 8,000 participants (Anastasi & Urbina, 1997).

Naturally, group tests have some limitations. For example, in a group-testing situation the individual administering the test has relatively little personal interaction with the individual examinees. As a result, there is little opportunity for the examiner to develop rapport with the examinees and closely monitor and observe their progress. Accordingly they have limited opportunities to make qualitative behavioral observations about the performance of their examinees and how they approach and respond to the assessment tasks. Another concern involves the types of items typically included on group achievement tests. Some testing experts applaud group tests for often using objectively scored items; others criticize them as these items restrict the type of responses examinees can provide. This parallels the same argument for-and-against selected-response items we discussed in earlier chapters. Another limitation of group tests involves their lack of flexibility. For example, when administering individual tests the examiner is usually able to select and administer only those test items that match to examinee's ability level. With group tests, however, all examinees are typically administered all the items. As a result, examinees might find some items too easy and others too difficult, resulting in boredom and/or frustration and lengthening the actual testing time beyond what is necessary to assess the student's knowledge accurately (Anastasi & Urbina, 1997). It should be noted that publishers of major group achievement tests are taking steps to address these criticisms. For example, to address concerns about the extensive use of selected-response items, an increasing number of standardized achievement tests are being developed that incorporate more constructed-response items and performance tasks. To address concerns about limited flexibility in administration, online and computer-based assessments are becoming increasingly available.

In this section we will be discussing a number of standardized group achievement tests. Many of these tests are developed by large test publishing companies and are commercially available to all qualified buyers (e.g., legitimate educational institutions). In addition to these commercially available tests, many states have started developing their own achievement tests that are specifically tailored to assess the state curriculum. These are often standards-based assessments that are used in high-stakes testing programs. We will start by briefly introducing some of the major commercially available achievement tests.

Commercial Standardized Achievement Tests

Commercially developed group achievement tests are test batteries developed for use in public schools around the nation and are available for purchase by qualified professionals or institutions. The most popular tests are comprehensive batteries designed to assess achievement in multiple academic areas such as reading, language arts, mathematics, science, social studies, and so on. These comprehensive tests are often referred to as survey batteries. As noted, many school districts use standardized achievement tests to track student achievement over time or to compare performance across classes, schools, or districts. These batteries typically contain multiple subtests that assess achievement in specific curricular areas (e.g., reading, language, mathematics, and science). These subtests are organized in a series of test levels that span different grades. For example, a subtest might have four levels with one level covering kindergarten through the 2nd grade, the second level covering Grades 3 and 4, the third level covering Grades 5 and 6, and the fourth level covering Grades 7 and 8 (Nitko, 2001). The most widely used standardized group achievement tests are produced and distributed by three publishers: CTB McGraw-Hill, Pearson Assessment, and Riverside Publishing.

> *The most widely used standardized group achievement tests are produced by CTB McGraw-Hill, Pearson Assessments, and Riverside Publishing.*

CTB MCGRAW-HILL. CTB McGraw-Hill publishes three popular standardized group achievement tests, the California Achievement Tests—Fifth Edition (CAT/5), the TerraNova CTBS, and the TerraNova—The Second Edition (CAT/6).

California Achievement Tests—Fifth Edition (CAT/5). The CAT/5 is designed for use with students from kindergarten through Grade 12 and is described as a traditional achievement battery. The CAT/5 assesses content in Reading, Spelling, Language, Mathematics, Study Skills, Science, and Social Studies. It is available in different formats for different applications (e.g., Complete Battery, Basic Battery, Short Form). The CAT/5 can be paired with the Test of Cognitive Skills—Second Edition (TCS/2), a measure of academic aptitude, to allow comparison of achievement–aptitude abilities.

TerraNova CTBS. This is a revision of Comprehensive Tests of Basic Skills—Fourth Edition. The TerraNova CTBS was designed for use with students from kindergarten through Grade 12 and was published in 1997. It combines selected-response and constructed-response items that allow students to respond in a variety of formats. The TerraNova CTBS assesses content in Reading/Language Arts, Mathematics, Science, and Social Studies. An expanded version adds Word Analysis, Vocabulary, Language Mechanics, Spelling, and Mathematics Computation. The TerraNova CTBS is available in different formats for different applications (e.g., Complete Battery, Complete Battery Plus, Basic Battery). The TerraNova CTBS can be paired with the Test of Cognitive Skills—Second Edition (TCS/2), a measure of academic aptitude, to compare aptitude–achievement abilities.

TerraNova—The Second Edition (CAT/6). The TerraNova—The Second Edition, or CAT/6, is described as a comprehensive modular achievement battery designed for use with students from kindergarten through Grade 12 and contains year 2005 normative data. The CAT/6 assesses content in Reading/Language Arts, Mathematics, Science, and Social Studies. An expanded version adds Word Analysis, Vocabulary, Language Mechanics, Spelling, and Mathematics Computation. It is available in different formats for different applications (e.g., CAT Multiple Assessments, CAT Basic Multiple Assessment, CAT Plus). The CAT/6 can be paired with InView, a measure of cognitive abilities, to compare aptitude–achievement abilities.

PEARSON ASSESSMENTS. Pearson Assessments publishes the Stanford Achievement Test Series—Tenth Edition (Stanford 10) and the Metropolitan Tests of Achievement—Eighth Edition (MAT8).

Stanford Achievement Test Series—Tenth Edition (Stanford 10). Originally published in 1923, the Stanford Achievement Test Series has a long and rich history of use. The Stanford 10 can be used with students from kindergarten through Grade 12 and has year 2007 normative data. It assesses content in Reading, Mathematics, Language, Spelling, Listening, Science, and Social Science. The Stanford 10 is available in a variety of forms, including abbreviated and complete batteries. The Stanford 10 can be administered with the Otis-Lennon School Ability Test—Eighth Edition (OLSAT-8). Also available from Pearson Assessments are the Stanford Diagnostic Mathematics Test—Fourth Edition (SDMT 4) and Stanford Diagnostic Reading Test—Fourth Edition (SDRT 4), which provide detailed information about the specific strengths and weaknesses of students in mathematics and reading.

Metropolitan Tests of Achievement—Eighth Edition (MAT8). The MAT8 can be used with students from kindergarten through Grade 12. It assesses content in Reading, Mathematics, Language, Science, and Social Science. The MAT8 is untimed (but provides guidelines) and can be administered with the Otis-Lennon School Ability Test—Seventh Edition (OLSAT-7).

RIVERSIDE PUBLISHING. Riverside Publishing produces two major achievement tests: the Iowa Tests of Basic Skills (ITBS) and Iowa Tests of Educational Development (ITED).

Iowa Tests of Basic Skills (ITBS). The ITBS is designed for use with students from kindergarten through Grade 8, and as the name suggests is designed to provide a thorough assessment of basic academic skills. The most current ITBS form was published in 2001. The ITBS assesses content in Reading, Language Arts, Mathematics, Science, Social Studies, and Sources of Information. The ITBS is available in different formats for different applications (e.g., Complete Battery, Core Battery, Survey Battery). The ITBS can be paired with the Cognitive Abilities Test (GogAT), Form 6 a measure of general and specific cognitive skills, to allow comparison of aptitude–achievement abilities.

Iowa Tests of Educational Development (ITED). The ITED is designed for use with students from Grades 9 through 12 and was published in 2001. The ITED is designed to measure the long-term goals of secondary education. The ITED assesses content in Vocabulary, Reading Comprehension, Language: Revising Written Materials, Spelling, Mathematics: Concepts and Problem Solving, Computation, Analysis of Science Materials, Analysis of Social Studies Materials, and Sources of Information. The ITED is available as both a complete battery and a core battery.

It can be paired with the Cognitive Abilities Test (CogAT), Form 6 a measure of general and specific cognitive skills, to allow comparison of aptitude–achievement abilities.

SUPPLEMENTAL CONSTRUCTED-RESPONSE AND PERFORMANCE ASSESSMENTS. As we discussed in earlier chapters there are many educators who criticize tests that rely extensively on selected-response items and advocate the use of constructed-response and performance assessments. To address this criticism, many of the survey batteries previously discussed provide open-ended and performance assessments to complement their standard batteries. For example, Riverside Publishing offers the *Performance Assessments for ITBS and ITED*. These are norm-referenced open-ended assessments in Integrated Language Arts, Mathematics, Science, and Social Studies. These free-response assessments give students the opportunity to demonstrate content-specific knowledge and higher order cognitive skills in a more lifelike context. Other publishers have similar products available that supplement their survey batteries.

DIAGNOSTIC ACHIEVEMENT TESTS. The most widely used achievement tests have been the broad survey batteries designed to assess the student's level of achievement in broad academic areas. Although these batteries do a good job in this context, they typically have too few items that measure specific skills and learning objectives to be useful to teachers when making instructional decisions. For example, the test results might suggest that a particular student's performance is low in mathematics, but the results will not pinpoint exactly what the student's strengths and weaknesses are. To address this limitation, many test publishers have developed diagnostic achievement tests. These diagnostic batteries contain a larger number of items linked to each specific learning objective. In this way they can provide more precise information about which academic skills have been achieved and which have not. Examples of group-administered diagnostic achievement tests include the Stanford Diagnostic Reading Test—Fourth Edition (SDRT 4) and Stanford Diagnostic Mathematics Test—Fourth Edition (SDMT 4) both published by Pearson Assessments. Most other publishers have similar diagnostic tests to complement their survey batteries.

Obviously these have been very brief descriptions of these major test batteries. These summaries were based on information current at the time of this writing. However, these tests are continuously being revised to reflect curricular changes and to update normative data. For the most current information interested readers should access the Internet sites for the publishing companies (see Table 8–1) and/or refer to the current edition of the *Mental Measurements Yearbook* or other reference resources. See Special Interest Topic 8.3 for information on these resources.

TABLE 8-1 Major Publishers of Standardized Group Achievement Tests
CTB McGraw-Hill. Website: http:/ctb.com/ California Achievement Tests—Fifth Edition (CAT/5) TerraNova CTBS TerraNova—The Second Edition (CAT/6)
Pearson Assessments. Website: http://pearsonassess.com/ Stanford Achievement Test Series—Tenth Edition (Stanford 10) Metropolitan Tests of Achievement—Eighth Edition (MAT8)
Riverside Publishing. Website: http://www.riverpub.com/ Iowa Tests of Basic Skills (ITBS) Iowa Tests of Educational Development (ITED)

SPECIAL INTEREST TOPIC 8.3

Finding Information on Standardized Tests

When you want to locate information on a standardized test, it is reasonable to begin by examining information provided by the test publishers. This can include their Internet sites, catalogs, test manuals, specimen test sets, score reports, and other supporting documentation. However, you should also seek out resources that provide independent evaluations and reviews of the tests you are researching. The Testing Office of the American Psychological Association Science Directorate (see the website at http://www.apa.org/science/programs/testing/find-tests.aspx) provides the following description of the four most popular resources:

- **Mental Measurements Yearbook (MMY).** *MMY* is published by the Buros Institute for Mental Measurements and lists tests alphabetically by title. Each listing provides basic descriptive information about the test (e.g., author, date of publication) plus information about the availability of technical information and scoring and reporting services. Most listings also include one or more critical reviews.

- **Tests in Print (TIP).** *TIP* is also published by the Buros Institute for Mental Measurements and is a bibliographic encyclopedia of information on practically every published test in psychology and education. Each listing provides basic descriptive information on tests, but does not contain critical reviews or psychometric information. After locating a test that meets your criteria, you can turn to the *MMY* for more detailed information on the test.

- **Test Critiques.** *Test Critiques* is published by Pro-Ed, Inc. and contains a three-part listing for each test that includes an Introduction, Practical Applications/Uses, and Technical Aspects, followed by a critical review of the test.

- **Tests.** *Tests* is also published by Pro-Ed, Inc. and is a bibliographic encyclopedia covering thousands of assessments in psychology and education. It provides basic descriptive information on tests, but does not contain critical reviews or information on reliability, validity, or other technical aspects of the tests. It serves as a companion to *Test Critiques*.

These resources can be located in the reference section of most college and larger public libraries. In addition to these traditional references, Test Reviews Online is a web-based service of the Buros Institute of Mental Measurements (http://www.unl.edu/buros). This service makes test reviews available online to individuals precisely as they appear in the *Mental Measurements Yearbook*. For a relatively small fee (currently $15) users can download information on any of over 2,000 tests.

State-Developed Achievement Tests

As we discussed earlier, standardized achievement tests are increasingly being used in making high-stakes decisions at the state level (e.g., determining which students are promoted or graduate; rating teachers, administrators, schools, and school districts). All states now have statewide testing programs, but different states have adopted different approaches. Some states utilize commercially available achievement batteries such as those described in the previous section (often referred to as off-the-shelf tests). An advantage of these commercial tests is that they provide normative data based on national samples. This allows one to compare a student's performance to that of students across the

> *Standardized achievement tests are increasingly being used in making high-stakes decisions at the state level.*

nation, not only students from one's state or school district. For example, one could find that Johnny's reading performance was at the 70th percentile relative to a national normative group. Using these commercial tests it is also possible to compare state or local groups (e.g., a district, school, or class) to a national sample. For example, one might find that a school district's mean fourth-grade reading score was at the 55th percentile based on national normative data. These comparisons can provide useful information to school administrators, parents, and other stakeholders.

All states have developed educational standards that specify the academic knowledge and skills their students are expected to achieve (see Special Interest Topic 8.4 for information on state standards). One significant limitation of using a commercial off-the-self national test is that it might not closely match the state's curriculum standards. Boser (1999) noted that commercial achievement tests typically are not designed to measure the content standards of specific states, but instead reflect a blend of the content of major textbooks, state standards, and national standards. He described a study commissioned by the California education department that examined a number of commercially available achievement tests to see how they align with the state's math standards. These studies found that the off-the-shelf tests focused primarily on basic math skills and did not adequately assess if students had mastered the state's standards. This comes down to a question of test validity. If you are interested in assessing what is being taught in classrooms across the nation, the commercially available group achievement tests probably give you a good measure. However, if you are more interested in determining if your students are mastering your state's content standards, off-the-shelf achievement tests are less adequate and state developed content-based assessments are preferable.

SPECIAL INTEREST TOPIC 8.4

Standards-Based Assessments

AERA et al. (1999) defines standards-based assessments as tests that are designed to measure clearly defined content and performance standards. In this context, content standards are statements that specify what students are expected to achieve in a given subject matter at a specific grade (e.g., Mathematics, Grade 5). In other words, content standards specify the skills and knowledge we want our students to master. Performance standards specify a level of performance, typically in the form of a cut score or a range of scores that indicates achievement levels. That is, performance standards specify what constitutes acceptable performance. National and state educational standards have been developed and can be easily accessed via the Internet. Following are a few examples of state educational Internet sites that specify the state standards.

- ◆ *California:* Content Standards for California Public Schools, http://www.cde.ca.gov/standards/
- ◆ *Florida:* Sunshine State Standards, http://sunshinestatestandards.net/
- ◆ *New York:* Learning Standards, http://www.emsc.nysed.gov/guides/
- ◆ *Texas:* Texas Essential Knowledge and Skills, http://www.tea.state.tx.us/teks

Education World provides a website that allows you to easily access state and national standards. The site for state standards is http://www.education-world.com/standards/state/index.shtml. The site for national standards is http://www.education-world.com/standards/national/.

To address this limitation, many states have developed their own achievement batteries that are designed to closely match the state's curriculum. In contrast to the commercial tests that typically report normative scores, state developed often emphasize criterion referenced score interpretations. In Texas there is a statewide program that includes the Texas Assessment of Knowledge and Skills (TAKS). The TAKS measures success of students in the state's curriculum in reading (Grades 3 through 9), mathematics (Grades 3 through 11), writing (Grades 4 and 7), English language arts (Grades 10 and 11), science (Grades 5, 10, and 11), and social studies (Grades 8, 10, and 11). There is a Spanish TAKS that is administered in Grades 3 through 6. The decision to promote a student to the next grade may be based on passing the reading and math sections, and successful completion of the TAKS at Grade 11 is required for students to receive a high school diploma. The statewide assessment program contains two additional tests. There is a Reading Proficiency Test in English (RPTE) that is administered to limited English proficient students to assess annual growth in reading proficiency. Finally there is the State-Developed Alternative Assessment (SDAA) that can be used with special education students when it is determined that the standard TAKS is inappropriate. All of these tests are designed to measure the educational objectives specified in the state curriculum, the Texas Essential Knowledge and Skills (TEKS) curriculum (see http://www.tea.state.tx.us).

Some states have developed hybrid assessment strategies to assess student performance and meet accountability requirements. For example, some states use a combination of state developed tests and commercial off-the-shelf tests, using different tests at different grade levels. Another approach, commonly referred to as augmented testing, involves the use of a commercial test that is administered along with test sections that address any misalignment between state standards and the content of the commercial test. Table 8–2 provides information on the assessment strategies used 2007 in state assessment programs. A review of this table reveals that the majority of states (i.e., 45) have state-developed tests that are specifically designed to align with their standards. Only one state (i.e., Iowa) reported exclusively using an off-the-shelf test. It should be noted that any report of state assessment practices is only a snapshot of an ever changing picture. The best way to get information on your state's current assessment practices is to go to the website of the state's board of education and verify the current status.

There is considerable controversy concerning statewide testing programs. Proponents of high-stakes testing programs see them as a way of increasing academic expectations and ensuring that all students are judged according to the same standards. They say these testing programs guarantee that students graduating from public schools have the skills necessary to be successful in life after high school. Critics of these testing programs argue that the tests emphasize rote learning and often neglect critical thinking, problem solving, and communication skills. To exacerbate the problem, critics feel that too much instructional time is spent preparing students for the tests instead of teaching the really important skills teachers would like to focus on. Additionally, they argue that these tests are culturally biased and are not fair to minority students (Doherty, 2002). For additional information on the pros and cons of high-stakes testing programs, see Special Interest Topic 8.5. Special Interest Topic 8.6 provides an overview of a promising and sophisticated approach to high-stakes assessment referred to as *value-added assessment.* This debate is likely to continue for the foreseeable future, but in the meantime these tests will continue to play an important role in public schools.

> *Proponents of high-stakes testing programs believe they increase academic expectations and ensure that all students are judged according to the same standards.*

TABLE 8–2	State Assessment Practices		
	State-Developed Tests (Criterion-Referenced)	**Augmented/ Hybrid Tests**	**Off-the-Shelf Tests (Norm-Referenced)**
Alabama	Yes	No	Yes
Alaska	Yes	No	Yes
Arizona	Yes	Yes	Yes
Arkansas	Yes	No	Yes
California	Yes	No	Yes
Colorado	Yes	No	Yes
Connecticut	Yes	No	No
Delaware	No	Yes	No
District of Columbia	Yes	No	No
Florida	Yes	No	Yes
Georgia	Yes	No	Yes
Hawaii	No	Yes	No
Idaho	Yes	No	No
Illinois	Yes	Yes	No
Indiana	Yes	No	No
Iowa	No	No	Yes
Kansas	Yes	No	No
Kentucky	Yes	No	Yes
Louisiana	Yes	Yes	No
Maine	Yes	No	Yes
Maryland	Yes	Yes	No
Massachusetts	Yes	No	No
Michigan	Yes	No	Yes
Minnesota	Yes	No	No
Mississippi	Yes	No	No
Missouri	No	Yes	No
Montana	Yes	No	Yes
Nebraska	Yes	No	No
Nevada	Yes	No	Yes
New Hampshire	Yes	No	No
New Jersey	Yes	No	No
New Mexico	Yes	No	Yes
New York	Yes	No	No
North Carolina	Yes	No	No
North Dakota	Yes	No	No

(Continued)

	State-Developed Tests (Criterion-Referenced)	Augmented/ Hybrid Tests	Off-the-Shelf Tests (Norm-Referenced)
Ohio	Yes	No	No
Oklahoma	Yes	No	No
Oregon	Yes	No	No
Pennsylvania	Yes	No	No
Rhode Island	Yes	Yes	No
South Carolina	Yes	No	No
South Dakota	No	Yes	Yes
Tennessee	Yes	No	No
Texas	Yes	No	No
Utah	Yes	No	Yes
Vermont	Yes	No	No
Virginia	Yes	No	No
Washington	Yes	No	No
West Virginia	Yes	No	Yes
Wisconsin	No	Yes	No
Wyoming	Yes	No	No
Totals	**45**	**10**	**18**

Note: **State-Developed Tests (Criterion-Referenced):** defined as tests that are custom-made to correspond to state content standards; **Augmented/Hybrid Tests:** defined as tests that incorporate aspects of both commercially developed norm referenced and state developed criterion referenced tests (includes commercial tests augmented or customized to match state standards); **Off-the-Shelf Tests (Norm-Referenced):** defined as commercially developed norm-referenced tests that have not been modified to specifically reflect state standards.

Source: Data provided by Education Week, retrieved from http://www.edcounts.org/createtable/step1.php?clear=1 on August 9, 2007.

SPECIAL INTEREST TOPIC 8.5

American Educational Research Association (AERA) Position Statement on High-Stakes Testing

The American Educational Research Association (AERA) is a leading organization that studies educational issues. The AERA (2000) presented a position statement regarding high-stakes testing programs employed in many states and school districts. Its position is summarized in the following points:

1. Important decisions should not be based on a single test score. Ideally, information from multiple sources should be taken into consideration when making high-stakes decisions. When tests are the basis of important decisions, students should be given multiple opportunities to take the test.

2. When students and teachers are going to be held responsible for new content or standards, they should be given adequate time and resources to prepare themselves before being tested.

(Continued on page 260)

SPECIAL INTEREST TOPIC 8.5 (*Continued*)

3. Each test should be validated for each intended use; for example, if a test is going to be used for determining which students are promoted *and* for ranking schools based on educational effectiveness, both interpretations must be validated.

4. If there is the potential for adverse effects associated with a testing program, efforts should be made to make all involved parties aware of them.

5. There should be alignment between the assessments and the state content standards.

6. When specific cut scores are used to denote achievement levels, the purpose, meaning, and validity of these passing scores should be established.

7. Students who fail a high-stakes test should be given adequate opportunities to overcome any deficiencies.

8. Adequate consideration and accommodations should be given to students with language differences.

9. Adequate consideration and accommodations should be given to students with disabilities.

10. When districts, schools, or classes are to be compared, it is important to clearly specify which students are to be tested and which students are exempt, and ensure that these guidelines are followed.

11. Test scores must be reliable.

12. There should be an ongoing evaluation of both the intended and unintended effects of any high-stakes testing program.

These guidelines may be useful when trying to evaluate the testing programs employed in your state or school. For more information, the full text of this position statement can be accessed at http://www.aera.net/about/policy/stakes.htm.

SPECIAL INTEREST TOPIC 8.6

Value-Added Assessment: A New Approach to Educational Accountability

Victor Willson, PhD

Texas A&M University

The term *value-added* has been used in business and industry to mean the economic value gain that occurs when material is changed through manufacturing or manipulation. In education this has been interpreted as the change in a student's knowledge that occurs as the result of instruction. In many ways, it can be seen as determining the value of instruction in raising knowledge levels (however, the model does not attempt to determine many benefits of schooling that go beyond knowledge acquisition). One of the most complex models of value-added assessment has been developed in Tennessee (Ceperley & Reel, 1997; Sanders, Saxton, & Horn, 1997). This model also has been implemented in a different form in Dallas (Webster & Mendro, 1997). Value-added assessment is a rather complex model, and the basic ideas are presented here in a hypothetical situation.

Consider students who attend Washington School in East Bunslip, New Jersey, in Ms. Jones's third-grade class (all names are made up). These students may be typical or representative of third-grade students, or there may be a substantial proportion of excellent or poor students. Ms. Jones teaches in her style, and the students are given the state achievement test at the end of the year.

(Continued)

For this example, let's assume that statewide testing begins in Grade 3. The results of the state test, student by student, are used to build a model of performance for each student, for Ms. Jones, for Washington School, and for the East Bunslip school district. One year's data are inadequate to do more than simply mark the levels of performance of each focus for achievement: student, teacher, school, and district.

The next year Ms. Jones's previous students have been dispersed to several fourth-grade class-rooms. A few of her students move to different school districts, but most stay in East Bunslip and most stay at Washington School. All of this information will be included in the modeling of performance. Ms. Jones now has a new class of students who enter the value-added assessment system. At the end of this year there are now data on each student who completed fourth grade, although some students may have been lost through attrition (e.g., missed the testing, left the state). The Tennessee model includes a procedure that accounts for all of these "errors." The performance of the fourth-grade students can now be evaluated in terms of their third-grade performance and the effect of their previous teacher, Ms. Jones, and the effect of their current teacher (assuming that teacher also taught last year and there was assessment data for the class taught). In addition, a school-level effect that can be estimated. Thus, the value-added system attempts to explain achievement performance for each level in the school system by using information from each level. This is clearly a very complex undertaking for an entire state's data. As of 1997, Sanders et al. noted that over 4 million data points in the Tennessee system were used to estimate effects for each student, teacher, school, and district.

The actual value-added component is not estimated as a gain, but as the difference in perform-ance from the expected performance based on the student's previous performance, current grade in school effect, sum of current and previous teacher effectiveness, and school effectiveness. When 3 or more years' data become available, longitudinal trend models can be developed to predict the perform-ance in each year for the various sources discussed.

Student achievement is what it is. A student either passes or fails the state test according to criteria the state establishes. What is unique in the value-added model of accountability is that the fo-cus is on teacher, school, and district effectiveness rather than on individual student performance. The system is intended to (1) guide instructional change through inspection of the teacher and grade-level estimates of average performance and (2) evaluate teachers and administrators by examining consist-ency of performance averages across years. The second purpose is certainly controversial and has its detractors. In particular, teacher evaluation based on state assessments has been criticized due to the limited coverage of the state tests. This, it is argued, has resulted in reduced coverage of content, focus on low-level conceptual understanding, and overemphasis on teaching to the test at the expense of content instruction. Nevertheless, there is continued interest in the value-added models and their use will likely increase.

Best Practices in Preparing Students for Standardized Assessment

As you can see from our discussion of standard-ized achievement tests to this point, these tests have widespread applications in public education. As a result, educators are often asked to prepare students for these tests. Much has been written in recent years about the proper procedures or practices for preparing students to take standardized achieve-ment tests. As we noted earlier, high-stakes testing programs are in place in every state and these tests are used to make important decisions such as which

Critics of high-stakes testing programs believe too much instructional time is spent preparing students for the tests instead of teaching the really important skills necessary for success in life.

> *Only* **test preparation practices** *that introduce generic test-taking skills and use multiple instructional techniques can be recommended enthusiastically.*

students graduate or get promoted, which teachers receive raises, and which administrators retain their jobs. As you might imagine, the pressure to ensure that students perform well on these tests has also increased. Legislators put pressure on state education officials to increase student performance, who in turn put pressure on local administrators, who in turn put pressure on teachers. An important question is what **test preparation practices** are legitimate and acceptable, and what practices are unethical or educationally contraindicated? This is a more complicated question than one might first imagine.

A popular phrase currently being used in both the popular media and professional educational literature is **teaching to the test**. The phrase generally implies efforts by teachers to prepare students to perform better on a standardized achievement test. Many writers use teaching to the test in a derogatory manner referencing unethical or inappropriate preparation practices. Other writers use the phrase more broadly to reference any instruction that is designed to enhance performance on a test. As you will see, there is a wide range of test preparation practices that can be applied. Some of these practices are clearly appropriate whereas others are clearly inappropriate. As an extreme example, consider a teacher who shared the exact items from a standardized test that is to be administered to students. This practice is clearly a breach of test security and is tantamount to cheating. It is unethical and educationally indefensible and most responsible educators would not even consider such a practice. In fact, such a breach of test security could be grounds for the dismissal of the educator, revocation of license, and possible legal charges (Kober, 2002).

> **Teaching to the test** *has become a popular concept in both the popular media and professional literature.*

Thankfully such flagrantly abusive practices are relatively rare, but they do occur. However, the appropriateness of some of the more common methods of preparing students for tests is less clear. With one notable exception, which we will describe, it is generally accepted that *any test preparation practice that raises test scores without also increasing mastery of the underlying knowledge and skills is inappropriate*. In other words, if a practice *artificially* increases test performance while failing to increase mastery of the domain of knowledge or skills reflected on the test, the practice is inappropriate. You may recognize this involves the issue of test validity. Standardized achievement tests are meant to assess the academic achievement of students in specific areas. If test preparation practices increase test scores without increasing the level of achievement, the validity of the test is compromised. Consider the following examples of various test preparation procedures.

INSTRUCTION IN GENERIC TEST-TAKING SKILLS. This involves instruction in general test-taking skills such as completing answer sheets, establishing an appropriate pace, narrowing choices on selected-response items, and introducing students to novel item formats (e.g., Kober, 2002). This is the "notable exception" to the general rule we noted previously. Although instruction in general test-taking skills does not increase mastery of the underlying knowledge and skills, it does make students more familiar and comfortable with standardized tests. As a result, their

TABLE 8–3	Important Test-Taking Skills to Teach Students

1. Carefully listen to or read the instructions.
2. Carefully listen to or read the test items.
3. Establish an appropriate pace. Don't rush carelessly through the test, but don't proceed so slowly you will not be able to finish.
4. If you find an item to be extremely difficult, don't spend an inordinate amount of time on it. Skip it and come back if time allows.
5. On selected-response items, make informed guesses by eliminating alternatives that are clearly wrong.
6. Unless there is a penalty for guessing, make an effort to complete every item. It is better to try and guess the correct answer than to simply leave it blank.
7. Ensure that you carefully mark the answer sheet. For example, on computer-scored answer sheets make sure the entire space is darkened and avoid extraneous marks.
8. During the test periodically verify that the item numbers and answer numbers match.
9. If time permits, go back and check your answers.

Source: Based on Linn and Gronlund (2000) and Sarnacki (1979).

scores are more likely to reflect accurately their true academic abilities and not the influence of deficient test-taking skills (e.g., Linn & Gronlund, 2000; Popham, 1999; Stroud & Reynolds, 2006). This practice enhances the validity of the assessment. This type of instruction is also typically fairly brief and, as a result, not detrimental to other educational activities. Therefore, instruction in generic test-taking skills is an appropriate preparation practice (see Table 8–3). Stroud and Reynolds (2006) in fact included a test-taking strategies scale on their School Motivation and Learning Strategies scale so that educators can assess the need to teach these skills to individual students or entire classes.

PREPARATION USING PRACTICE FORMS OF THE TEST. Many states and commercial test publishers release earlier versions of their exams as practice tests. Because these are released as practice tests, their use is not typically considered unethical. However, if these tests become the focus of instruction at the expense of other teaching activities, this practice can be harmful. Research suggests that direct instruction using practice tests may produce short-term increases in test scores without commensurate increases in performance on other measures of the test domain (Kober, 2002). Like instruction in generic test-taking skills, the limited use of practice tests may help familiarize students with the format of the test. However, practice tests should be used in a judicious manner to ensure that they do not become the focus of instruction.

PREPARATION EMPHASIZING TEST-SPECIFIC ITEM FORMATS. Here teachers provide instruction and assignments that prepare students to deal exclusively with the specific item formats that are used on the standardized test. For example, teachers might use classroom tests and homework assignments that resemble actual items on the test (Kober, 2002). If the writing section of a test requires single-paragraph responses, teachers will restrict their writing assignments to a single paragraph. If a test uses only multiple-choice items, the teachers will limit their classroom tests to multiple-choice items. The key feature is that students are given instruction that exposes them to only the material as presented and measured on the test. With this approach students will be limited in their ability to generalize acquired skills and knowledge to novel situations (Popham, 1999). Test scores may increase, but the students' mastery of the underlying domain is limited. As a result, this practice should be avoided.

PREPARATION EMPHASIZING TEST CONTENT. This practice is somewhat similar to the previous practice, but instead of providing extensive exposure to items resembling those on the test, the goal is to emphasize the skills and content most likely to be included on the standardized tests. Kober (2002) stated that this practice often has a "narrowing effect" on instruction. Because many standardized achievement tests emphasize basic skills and knowledge that can be easily measured with selected-response items, this practice may result in teachers neglecting more complex learning objectives such as the analysis and synthesis of information or development of complex problem-solving skills. Test scores may increase, but the students' mastery of the underlying domain is restricted. This practice should be avoided.

PREPARATION USING MULTIPLE INSTRUCTIONAL TECHNIQUES. With this approach students are given instruction that exposes them to the material as conceptualized and measured on the test, but also presents the material in a variety of different formats. Instruction covers all salient knowledge and skills in the curriculum and addresses both basic and higher order learning objectives (Kober, 2002). With this approach, increases in test scores are associated with increases in mastery of the underlying domain of skills and knowledge (Popham, 1999). As a result, this test preparation practice is recommended.

Although this list of test preparation practices is not exhaustive, we have tried to address the most common forms. In summary, only preparation that introduces generic test-taking skills and uses multiple instructional techniques can be recommended enthusiastically. Teaching generic test-taking skills makes students more familiar and comfortable with the assessment process, and as a result enhances the validity of the assessment. Because test-taking skills may vary greatly among students, teaching these skills to all students levels the playing field so to speak, so no one has an undue advantage simply by being a sophisticated test taker. The use of multiple instructional techniques results in enhanced test performance that reflects an increased mastery of the content domain. As a result, with both of these practices the validity of the score interpretation as reflecting domain-specific knowledge is not compromised. Other test preparation practices generally fall short of this goal. For example, practice tests may be useful when they are used cautiously, but they are often overused and become the focus of instruction with detrimental results. Any procedures that emphasize test-specific content or test-specific item formats should be avoided as they may increase test scores without actually enhancing mastery of the underlying test domain. In addition to preparing students to take standardized achievement tests, educators are often expected to help administer these tests. Special Interest Topic 8.7 provides some guidelines for administering standardized group achievement tests.

SPECIAL INTEREST TOPIC 8.7

Administering Standardized Group Achievement Tests

When introducing this chapter we stated that standardized tests are professionally developed and must be administered and scored in a standard manner. For standardized test scores to be meaningful and useful, it is imperative that these standard procedures be followed precisely. These procedures are explicitly specified so that the tests can be administered in a uniform manner in different settings. The administration of individual intelligence (e.g., Wechsler intelligence scales) or achievement tests (Woodcock-Johnson III Tests of Achievement) requires extensive training at the graduate level. For example, every master's or doctorate level psychology and counseling program we are aware of has specific courses that prepare students to administer and interpret intelligence and other individualized tests.

The administration of group tests such as the Iowa Tests of Basic Skills (ITBS) or state-developed achievement tests requires less rigorous training. Teachers and other educational professionals are often responsible for administering group achievement tests to their students and as a result should understand the basics of standardized test administration. Following are a few guidelines to help teachers administer standardized tests to their students that are based on our own experience and a review of the literature (e.g., Kubiszyn & Borich, 2003; Linn & Gronlund, 2000; Popham, 1999, 2000).

- ◆ *Review the test administration manual before the day of the test.* Administering standardized tests is not an overly difficult process, but it is helpful to review the administration instructions carefully before the day of the test. This way you will be familiar with the procedures and there should be no surprises. This review will alert you to any devices (e.g., stopwatch) or supporting material (e.g., scratch paper) you may need during the administration. It is also beneficial to do a mock administration by reading the instructions for the test in private before administering it to the students. The more familiar you are with the administration instructions the better prepared you will be to administer the test. Additionally, you will find the actual testing session to be less stressful.

- ◆ *Encourage the students to do their best.* Standardized achievement tests (and most other standardized tests used in schools) are maximum performance tests and ideally students will put forth their best efforts. This is best achieved by explaining to the students how the test results will be used to their benefit. For example, with achievement tests you might explain to the students that the results can help them and their parents track their academic progress and identify any areas that need special attention. Although it is important to motivate students to do their best, it is equally important to avoid unnecessarily raising their level of anxiety. For example, you would probably not want to focus on the negative consequences of poor performance immediately before administering the test. This presents a type of balancing act; you want to encourage the students to do their best without making them excessively anxious.

- ◆ *Closely follow instructions.* As we noted, the reliability and validity of the test results are dependent on the individual administering the test closely following the administration instructions. First, the instructions to students must be read word-for-word. You should not alter the instructions in any way, paraphrase them, or try to improvise. It is likely that some students will have questions, but you are limited in how you can respond. Most manuals indicate that you can clarify procedural questions (e.g., Where do I sign my name?), but you cannot define words or in any other way provide hints to the answers.

- ◆ *Strictly adhere to time limits.* Bring a stopwatch and practice using it before the day of the test.

- ◆ *Avoid interruptions.* Avoid making announcements or any other types of interruptions during the examination. To help avoid outside interruptions you should post a "Testing in Session—Do Not Disturb" sign on the door.

(Continued on page 266)

SPECIAL INTEREST TOPIC 8.7 (*Continued*)

♦ *Avoid distractions.* Don't check your e-mail or voice-mail or engage in texting during the assessment. It is your professional responsibility to focus on the task at hand—proctoring the examination.

♦ *Be alert to cheating.* Although you don't want to hover over the students to the extent that it makes them unnecessarily nervous, active surveillance is indicated and can help deter cheating. Stay alert and monitor the room from a position that provides a clear view of the entire room. Walk quietly around the room occasionally. If you note anything out of the ordinary, increase your surveillance of those students. Document any unusual events that might deserve further consideration or follow-up.

By following these suggestions you should have a productive and uneventful testing session. Nevertheless, you should be prepared for unanticipated events to occur. Keep the instruction manual close so you can refer to it if needed. It is also helpful to remember that you can rely on your professional educational training to guide you in case of unexpected events.

INDIVIDUAL ACHIEVEMENT TESTS

As we mentioned, standardized achievement tests are also used in the identification, diagnosis, and classification of examinees with special learning needs. Some group-administered achievement tests might be used in identifying children with special needs, but in many situations individually administered achievement tests are used. For example, if a student is having learning difficulties and parents or teachers are concerned about the possibility of a learning disability, the student would likely be given a thorough assessment that would include an individual achievement test. A testing professional, with extensive training in psychometrics and test administration, administers these tests to one student at a time. Because these tests are administered individually they can contain a wider variety of item formats. For example, the questions are often presented in different modalities, with some questions being presented orally and some in written format. Some questions may require oral responses whereas some require written responses. In assessing writing abilities, some of these tests elicit short passages while others require fairly lengthy essays. Relative to the group tests, individual achievement tests typically provide a more thorough assessment of the student's skills. Because they are administered in a one-to-one context the examiner is able to observe the student closely and hopefully gain insight into the source of learning problems. Additionally, these tests are scored individually so they are more likely to incorporate open-ended item formats (e.g., essay items) requiring qualitative scoring procedures. In the following section we will briefly introduce you to some of the most popular individual achievement tests in use today.

> *Relative to the group tests, individual achievement tests typically provide a more thorough assessment of the student's skills.*

Wechsler Individual Achievement Test—Second Edition (WIAT-II)

The WIAT-II (Psychological Corporation, 2002) is a comprehensive individually administered norm-referenced achievement test published by the Psychological Corporation. By comprehensive we mean it covers a broad spectrum of academic skill areas in individuals from 4 to 85 years. It contains the following composites and subtests:

- *Reading Composite:* Composed of the Word Reading subtest (letter knowledge, phonological awareness and decoding skills), Reading Comprehension subtest, (comprehension of short passages, reading rate, and oral reading prosody), and Pseudoword Decoding (phonetic decoding skills).
- *Mathematics Composite:* Composed of the Numerical Operations subtest (number knowledge, ability to solve calculation problems and simple equations) and Math Reasoning subtest (ability to reason mathematically including identifying geometric shapes, solving word problems, interpreting graphs, etc.).
- *Written Language Composite:* Composed of the Spelling subtest (ability to write dictated letters and words) and Written Language subtest (transcription, handwriting, written word fluency, generate and combine sentences, extended writing sample).
- *Oral Language Composite:* Composed of the Listening Comprehension subtest (ability to listen and comprehend verbal information) and Oral Expression subtest (verbal word fluency, repetition, story generation, and providing directions).

The WIAT-II produces a variety of derived scores, including standard scores and percentile ranks. The test has excellent psychometric properties and documentation. Additionally, the WIAT-II has the distinct advantage of being statistically linked to the Wechsler intelligence scales. Linkage with these popular intelligence tests facilitates the aptitude–achievement discrimination analyses often used to diagnose learning disabilities (this will be discussed more in the next chapter on aptitude tests). As this text goes to press, the Wechsler Individual Achievement Test—Third Edition is expected to be released in the near future.

Woodcock-Johnson III Tests of Achievement (WJ III ACH)

The WJ III ACH (Woodcock, McGrew, & Mather, 2001b) is a comprehensive individually administered norm-referenced achievement test distributed by Riverside Publishing. The standard battery contains the following cluster scores and subtests:

- *Broad Reading:* Composed of the Letter-Word Identification subtest (identify letters and pronounce words correctly), Reading Fluency subtest (ability to read simple sentences quickly and decide if the statement is true or false), and the Passage Comprehension subtest (ability to read passages and demonstrate understanding).
- *Oral Language:* Composed of the Story Recall subtest (ability to recall details of stories that are presented on an audio tape) and Understanding Directions subtest (ability to follow directions presented on an audio tape).
- *Broad Math:* A comprehensive measure of math skills composed of the Calculation subtest (ability to perform mathematical computations), the Math Fluency subtest (ability to solve simple math problems quickly), and the Applied Problems subtest (ability to analyze and solve math word problems).
- *Math Calculation Skills:* A math aggregate cluster composed of the Calculation and Math Fluency subtests.
- *Broad Written Language:* A comprehensive measure of writing abilities composed of the Spelling subtest (i.e., ability to spell words presented orally), the Writing Fluency subtest

(ability to formulate and write simple sentences quickly), and the Writing Samples subtest (ability to write passages varying in length, vocabulary, grammatical complexity, and abstractness).

- *Written Expression:* A writing aggregate cluster composed of the Writing Fluency and Writing Samples subtests.

Other special-purpose clusters can be calculated using the 12 subtests in the standard battery. In addition, there are 10 more subtests in an extended battery that allows the calculation of supplemental clusters. The WJ III ACH provides a variety of derived scores and has excellent psychometric properties and documentation. A desirable feature of the WJ III ACH is that it is available in two parallel forms. The availability of different forms is an advantage when testing a student on more than one occasion because the use of different forms can help reduce carryover effects. Additionally, the WJ III ACH and the Woodcock-Johnson III Tests of Cognitive Abilities (WJ III COG; Woodcock, McGrew, & Mather, 2001c) compose a comprehensive diagnostic system, the Woodcock-Johnson III (WJ III; Woodcock, McGrew, & Mather, 2001a). When administered together they facilitate the aptitude–achievement discrimination analyses often used to help diagnose learning disabilities. An additional advantage of the WJ III ACH is that it covers all areas of specified by IDEA 2004 for assessing learning disabilities.

Wide Range Achievement Test 4 (WRAT-4)

The WRAT-4 is a brief achievement test that measures reading, spelling, and arithmetic skills in individuals 5 through 95 years. It contains the following subtests:

- *Word Reading:* Assesses ability to recognize and name letters and pronounce printed words.
- *Reading Comprehension:* Assesses ability to read and comprehend the meaning of sentences.
- *Spelling:* Assesses ability to write letters, names, and words that are presented orally.
- *Arithmetic:* Assesses ability to recognize numbers, count, and perform written computations.

The WRAT-4 can be administered in 30 to 45 minutes and comes in two parallel forms. Relative to the WIAT-II and WJ III ACH, the WRAT-4 measures a restricted range of skills. However, when only a quick estimate of achievement in reading, spelling, and math computation is needed, the WRAT-4 can be a useful instrument.

The individual achievement batteries described to this point measure skills in multiple academic areas. As with the group achievement batteries, there are also individual tests that focus on specific skill domains. In the following section we will briefly describe two tests that are examples of individual achievement tests that focus on specific skill areas.

Gray Oral Reading Test—Fourth Edition (GORT-4)

The GORT-4 is a measure of oral reading skills and is often used in the diagnosis of reading problems. The test contains 14 passages of increasing difficulty that the student reads aloud. The examiner records reading rate and reading errors (e.g., skipping or inserting words, mispronunciation). Additionally, each reading passage contains questions to assess comprehension. There are two parallel forms available.

KeyMath—Revised/NU: A Diagnostic Inventory of Essential Mathematics— Normative Update (KeyMath R/NU)

The KeyMath R/NU, published by American Guidance Services, measures mathematics skills in the following areas: Basic Concepts (numeration, rational numbers, and geometry), Operations (addition, subtraction, multiplication, division, and mental computations), and Applications (measurement, time and money, estimation, interpreting data, and problem solving). The Key-Math R/NU is available in two parallel forms.

SELECTING AN ACHIEVEMENT BATTERY

Numerous factors should be considered when selecting a standardized achievement battery. If you are selecting a test for administration to a large number of students you will more than likely need a group achievement test. Nitko (1990, 2001) provided some suggestions for selecting a group achievement battery. He noted that although most survey batteries assess the common educational objectives that are covered in most curricula, there are some potentially important differences in the content covered. In some instructional areas such as reading and mathematics there is

> *When selecting a standardized achievement test many factors should be considered, including the content covered, its technical properties, and practical issues such as cost and time requirements.*

considerable consistency in the curricula used in different schools. In other areas such as science and social studies there is more variability. As a result, potential users should examine closely any potential battery to determine if its content corresponds with the school, district, or state curriculum. Naturally it is also important to evaluate the technical adequacy of a test. This includes issues such as the adequacy of the standardization sample, the reliability of test scores, and the availability of validity evidence supporting the intended use. This is best accomplished using some of the resources we discussed earlier in this chapter (Special Interest Topic 8.3). Finally, it is also useful to consider practical issues such as cost, testing time required, availability of scoring services, and the quality of support materials such as administration and interpretative guides.

Many of the same factors should be considered when selecting an individual achievement test. You should select a test that adequately assesses the specific content areas you are interested in. For example, whereas a test such as the WRAT-4 might be sufficient for screening purposes, it is not adequate for in-depth diagnostic purposes. If one is testing a student to determine if he or she has a specific learning disability, it would be important to use a battery such as the WJ III ACH that covers all recognized areas of learning disability under IDEA.

TEACHER-CONSTRUCTED ACHIEVEMENT TESTS AND STUDENT EVALUATION

It is probably safe to say that you have literally taken hundreds of classroom achievement tests in your academic career—from kindergarten through college! It is also likely that most of these tests were developed by your teachers. It has been estimated that teachers devote at least one

> *It has been estimated that teachers devote at least one third of their professional time to assessment-related activities.*

third of their professional time to assessment-related activities (Stiggins & Conklin, 1992). Classroom assessments should provide relevant information that both enhances instruction and promotes student learning. They should provide objective feedback about what the students have learned, how well they have learned it, how effective the instruction has been, and what information, concepts, and objectives require more attention. Another important feature is that course grades are often based on the results of these tests. The following quote from Stiggins and Conklin (1992) highlights the important role teacher-made tests play in the overall process of educational assessment.

> As a nation, we spend billions of dollars on educational assessment, including hundreds of millions for international and national assessments, and additional hundreds of millions for statewide testing programs. On top of these, the standardized tests that form the basis of district-wide testing programs represents a billion dollar industry. If we total all of these expensive highly visible, politically important assessments, we still account for less than 1 percent of all the assessments conducted in America's schools. The other 99 percent are conducted by teachers in their classrooms on a moment-to-moment, day-to-day, and week-to-week basis. (back cover)

Given your years of experience taking classroom tests, you have probably noticed that some of these tests were well developed and clearly covered the material presented in class—that is, they had "face validity." You probably also noticed that some were poorly developed and seemed to have little to do with the material covered in class and your readings. In the following section we will highlight some key steps teachers should follow when developing tests and using the results to assign grades.

Specify Educational Objectives

The first step in developing a classroom achievement test should be to specify the educational objectives or goals a teacher has for the students. Although we will not go into detail about developing educational objectives, some general guidelines include (1) write objectives that cover a broad spectrum of knowledge and abilities, (2) identify behaviors that are observable and directly measurable, (3) state any special conditions (e.g., the use of calculators), and (4) when appropriate, specify an outcome criterion. For more information on writing educational objectives, refer to Reynolds et al. (2009).

Develop a Test Blueprint

The next step in developing a classroom test is to write a table of specifications. A table of specifications is essentially a blueprint for the test that helps one organize the educational objectives and make sure that the test content matches what was taught in class. A table of specifications also helps one include items of varying degrees of complexity. We will provide more information on test blueprints in Chapter 18.

Determine How the Scores Will Be Interpreted

Teachers must decide if they will use a norm-referenced or criterion-referenced score interpretation and this decision should be based on how the test results will be used. If one needs to determine a student's standing relative to a specified norm group, a norm-referenced interpretation is indicated. If one needs to determine what the student knows or what tasks he or she can perform, a criterion-referenced interpretation is indicated. With classroom achievement tests we are most interested in the student's level of mastery of the educational objectives and as a result criterion-referenced interpretations are usually most useful.

Select Item Formats

Teachers must also decide which type of items to include in the test. We spent considerable time discussing different item formats and their development in Chapter 6. In that chapter we noted that the overriding goal is to develop items that measure the specified constructs and contribute to psychometrically sound tests. Selected-response items have characteristics that can contribute to psychometrically sound tests (e.g., objective and reliable scoring, good sampling of content domain), but it is often necessary to use constructed-response items to adequately measure a student's knowledge or abilities. For example, if you want to determine if a student can write a poem, you need him or her to actually write a poem. Once item formats have been selected, it is important to follow best practices in actually developing the items.

Assignment of Grades

As we noted, teacher-made classroom tests often serve as the basis for student evaluation and assigning course grades. Grading has a long and rich history and this is briefly described in Special Interest Topic 8.8. As stated in an earlier chapter, evaluation in the schools is often divided into formative and summative evaluation. *Formative evaluation* involves evaluative activities that are aimed at providing feedback to students. In this context, feedback implies the communication of information concerning a student's performance or achievement that is intended to have a corrective effect. *Summative evaluation* involves the determination of the worth, value, or quality of an outcome. In the classroom summative evaluation typically involves the formal evaluation of performance or progress in a course, often in the form of a numerical or letter grade or mark.

> *The assignment of grades has both positive and negative aspects.*

The assignment of grades has both positive and negative aspects. On the positive side, grades can represent a fair system for comparing students that minimizes irrelevant characteristics such as gender or race. Additionally, because most people are familiar with grades and their meaning, grades are an effective and efficient means of providing information about student achievement. On the down side, a grade is only a brief summary of a student's performance and does not convey detailed information about specific strengths and weaknesses. Additionally, whereas most people understand the general meaning of grades, there is variability in what grades actually mean in different classes and schools. For example, some schools are plagued with grade inflation where practically everyone receives good grades (e.g., As and Bs), whereas other schools are much more rigorous in assigning grades. Finally, student competition for grades

---

SPECIAL INTEREST TOPIC 8.8

A Brief History of Grading

Brookhart (2004) provided a discussion of the history of grading in the United States. Following are a few of the key developments she noted in this timeline.

- ◆ *Pre-1800:* Grading procedures were first developed in universities. Brookhart's research suggested that the first categorical grading scale was used at Yale in 1785 and classified students as *Optimi* (i.e., best), *Second Optimi* (i.e., second best), *Inferiores* (i.e., lesser), and *Pejores* (i.e., worse). In 1813 Yale adopted a numerical scale where students were assigned grades between 1 and 4, with decimals used to reflect intermediary levels. Some universities developed scales with more categories (e.g., 20) whereas others tried simple pass–fail grading.

- ◆ *1800s:* The common school movement of the 1800s saw the development of public schools designed to provide instruction to the nation's children. Initially these early schools adopted grading scales similar to those in use at universities. In about 1840, schools started the practice of distributing report cards. Teachers at the time complained that assessment and grading were too burdensome and parents complained that the information was difficult to interpret. These are complaints that are still with us today!

- ◆ *1900s:* Percentage grading was common in secondary schools and universities at the beginning of the 20th century. By 1910, however, educators began to question the reliability and accuracy of using a scale with 100 different categories or scale points. By the 1920s the use of letter grades (A, B, C, D, and F) was becoming the most common practice. During the remainder of the 1900s a number of grading issues came to the forefront. For example, educators became increasingly aware that nonachievement factors (e.g., student attitudes and behaviors and teacher biases) were influencing the assignment of grades and recognized that this was not a desirable situation. Additionally, there was a debate regarding the merits of norm-referenced versus criterion-referenced grading systems. Finally, there were efforts to expand the purpose of grades so they not only documented the students' level of academic achievement, but also enhanced the learning of students. As you might expect, these are all issues that educators continue to struggle with to this day.

In some aspects we have come a long way in refining the ways we evaluate the performance of our students. At the same time, we are still struggling with many of the same issues we struggled with 100 years ago.

---

may become more important than actual achievement and students may have difficulty separating their personal worth from their grades, both undesirable situations. Nevertheless, grades are viewed as an essential component of our educational process and efforts should be made to assign them in an accurate and responsible manner. To this end we have the following suggestions:

- ● *Base Grades on Academic Achievement.* We recommend that grades be assigned *solely* on the basis of academic achievement. Some teachers will penalize students for missing class or inappropriate behavior by lowering their grades. Although factors such as class behavior and attitude are certainly important, if they are combined with achievement when assigning grades they blur the meaning of grades.

- ● *Choose a Frame of Reference.* Once a teacher has decided what to base student grades on (hopefully academic achievement), he or she must decide what frame of reference to use. When assigning grades, it is common to use either a relative or absolute approach. These approaches are comparable to the norm-referenced (i.e., relative) and criterion-referenced (i.e., absolute) score interpretations we have discussed throughout this text. In a relative or norm-referenced approach, grades are assigned by comparing each student's performance to that of other students in the class. For example, the top 10% of the students might receive As, the next 20% might receive Bs, and so on. In an absolute or criterion-referenced approach, grades are assigned by comparing each student's performance to a specified level of performance. One of the most common criterion-referenced grading systems is the traditional percentage-based system. Here students with cumulative grades between 90 and 100% would receive As, those between 80 and 89% would receive Bs, and so forth. We believe that both relative (i.e., norm-referenced) and absolute (i.e., criterion-referenced) grading approaches can be used successfully. They both have advantages and limitations, but when used conscientiously either approach can be effective. In contrast, some educators have suggested that grades should be based on effort or improvement. For example, if a student with very poor skills at the beginning of instruction achieves a moderate level of achievement, he or she should receive a better grade than a high-achieving student who demonstrated a smaller gain, but a higher overall level of achievement. Another variation is to base grades on achievement relative to ability or aptitude. Here a student with average intelligence who scores above average on tests of achievement is considered an overachiever and receives good grades. Accordingly, an underachiever is a student whose achievement is considered low in relation to their level of intelligence, and these students would receive lower grades (regardless of the absolute level of achievement). There are a number of technical and practical problems with these approaches and they should be avoided (see Reynolds et al., 2009 for more information).

- **Report Student Progress.** A number of different approaches have been proposed, but *letter grades* (i.e., A, B, C, D, and F) are the most popular method of reporting student progress and are used in the majority of schools and universities today. Although there might be some variation in the meaning attached to them, letter grades are typically interpreted as follows:

$$A = \text{Excellent/superior achievement}$$

$$B = \text{Above-average achievement}$$

$$C = \text{Average achievement}$$

$$D = \text{Below-average or marginal achievement}$$

$$F = \text{Failing/poor performance}$$

Students and parents generally understand letter grades, and the evaluative judgment represented by letter grades is probably more widely accepted than any other system available.

- **Keep Grades Confidential.** Students and parents should be informed of their grades in a timely manner and this information should be conveyed in a confidential and protected manner. Grades or test scores should not be posted or otherwise displayed in any way that reveals a student's individual performance. A federal law, the Family Educational Rights and Privacy Act (FERPA; also known as Public Law 93-380 or the Buckley Amendment) governs the maintenance and release of educational records, including grades, test scores, and related evaluative material.

This has been a very brief review of some important issues related to the development of classroom achievement tests and their use in assigning grades. There are a number of texts that cover these topics in more detail (e.g., Reynolds et al., 2009), and if you aspire to become a teacher or professor, we encourage you to study this topic further.

ACHIEVEMENT TESTS—NOT ONLY IN THE PUBLIC SCHOOLS!

Our discussion of achievement assessment to this point has focused on their application in public schools. Although it is true that achievement tests are widely used in schools, that is not their only application. For example, most of you have taken a test to obtain a driver's license. This is an example of an achievement test being used outside public schools. They are also used in personnel selection (i.e., discussed in Chapter 12) and in allowing students to gain college credit by examination (e.g., College-Level Examination Program; CLEP testing). Another major application of achievement assessment is in licensing and certification of a multitude of professions (e.g., psychologists, physicians, lawyers, plumbers, and electricians). Police officers and firefighters often take achievement tests for promotions to certain levels of authority or rank in their jobs. In the following sections we will briefly discuss two achievement tests that are used for professional licensing.

> *It is true that achievement tests are widely used in schools, but that is not their only application.*

Examination for Professional Practice in Psychology (EPPP)

Licensing of professionals is a state right and each state has boards that are responsible for testing and licensing professionals in their state. The EPPP is administered by the Association of State and Provincial Psychology Boards and is used by individual state licensing boards to license psychologists. The EPPP contains 225 items, 200 of which are actual test items and 25 pilot test items. The content areas of the test are outlined as follows:

- *Biological Basis of Behavior (11%):* Knowledge of the biological and neural basis of behavior and psychopharmacology.
- *Cognitive & Affective Basis of Behavior (13%):* Knowledge of theories and empirical research on learning, memory, motivation, affect, emotion, and executive function.
- *Social & Cultural Basis of Behavior (12%):* Knowledge of group processes, theories of personality, and diversity issues.
- *Growth & Lifespan Development (13%):* Knowledge of normal and abnormal development and factors that impact developmental outcomes.
- *Assessment & Diagnosis (14%):* Knowledge of psychometrics, assessment instruments, and diagnostic/classification systems.
- *Treatment, Intervention, & Prevention (15%):* Knowledge of a broad range of treatment and intervention models for addressing concerns in a diverse clientele.

- *Research Methods & Statistics (7%):* Knowledge of research methods and statistical procedures.
- *Ethical, Legal, & Professional Issues (15%):* Knowledge of major ethical codes, standards of practice, and legal issues related to psychological services and mental health issues.

Performance on the EPPP is reported in scaled scores that are conversions of raw scores. The recommended passing scaled score for independent practice is 500 (which reflects approximately 70% correct responses) and for supervised practice is 450 (approximately 65% correct responses). These cut scores are simply recommendations, and each state's licensing board typically establishes its own standards. More information about the EPPP can be found at http://www.asppb.org.

United States Medical Licensing Examination (USMLE)

The USMLE is a three-stage examination for licensing physicians for practice in the United States. It is administered by the Federation of State Medical Boards (FSMB) and the National Board of Medical Examiners (NBME). It involves the following three steps:

Step 1. This computer-based multiple-choice assessment is designed to determine if the applicant is knowledgeable about the essential scientific facts and concepts that are fundamental to the practice of medicine. In addition to assessing basic scientific knowledge this assessment is designed to determine if the applicant understands the scientific principles needed to be a lifelong learner and maintain competence throughout his or her professional career.

Step 2. This step contains two assessments: Step 2 Clinical Knowledge (CK) and Clinical Skills (CS). Step 2 CK is a computer-based multiple-choice test designed to determine if the applicant can apply medical knowledge and skills in a clinical setting under supervision. The goal of this assessment is to determine if the applicant can practice medicine in a safe and competent manner. Step 2 CS is a test of clinical skills that uses standardized patients to assess an applicant's clinical, cognitive, and communication skills. This assessment is administered only at five testing centers in the United States.

Step 3. This computer-based multiple-choice assessment is designed to determine if the applicant can apply medical knowledge and skills in an unsupervised setting. This step includes multiple-choice items and computer-based case simulations. The computer-based simulations present clinical vignettes and allows the applicant to select appropriate tests and interventions—and there are literally thousands of tests and interventions he or she can select from. This is the final assessment and is intended to ensure that applicants are prepared for the independent practice of medicine. More information on the USMLE is available at http://www.usmle.org.

We have reviewed only two of the many tests used by state boards for licensing professionals. Many such tests exist—for licensing lawyers, realtors, engineers, teachers, nurses, counselors, and so on. Table 8–4 provides a brief list of some of the many uses of achievement tests outside our public schools.

TABLE 8-4	Sample of Achievement Test Applications Outside Public Schools
Application	**Examples**
Personnel selection and promotion	Wonderlic Personnel Test
	Wide Range Achievement Test
	Tests specific to the job (e.g., clerical knowledge, knowledge of policy and procedures, knowledge of law applicable to one job, etc.)
College credit by examination	College-Level Examination Program (CLEP)
	ACT Proficiency Examination Program (PEP)
Professional licenses	Examination in the Professional Practice of Psychology (EPPP)
	United States Medical Licensing Examination (USMLE)
	The Praxis Series: Teacher Licensure and Certification
Nonprofessional licenses	Driver's licenses of all types including chauffeur's licenses

Summary

In this chapter we discussed achievement tests and their applications. The bulk of the chapter focused on standardized achievement tests, which are designed to be administered, scored, and interpreted in a standard manner. The goal of standardization is to ensure that testing conditions are the same for all individuals taking the test. If this is accomplished, no examinee will have an advantage over another, and test results will be comparable. These tests have different applications in the schools, including:

- Tracking student achievement over time
- Using high-stakes decision making (e.g., promotion decisions, teacher evaluations)
- Identifying individual strengths and weaknesses
- Evaluating the effectiveness of educational programs
- Identifying students with special learning needs

Of these uses, high-stakes testing programs are probably the most controversial. These programs use standardized achievement tests to make important decisions such as determining which students will be promoted and evaluating educational professionals and schools. Proponents of high-stakes testing programs see them as a way of improving public education and ensuring that students are all judged according to the same standards. Critics of high-stakes testing programs argue that they encourage teachers to focus on low-level academic skills at the expense of higher level skills such as problem solving and critical thinking.

We next described several of the most popular commercial group achievement tests. The chapter included a discussion of the current trend toward increased high-stakes assessments in the public schools and how this is being implemented by states using a combination of commercial and state-developed assessments. We introduced a potentially useful approach for assessing and monitoring student achievement that is referred to as value-added assessment.

We also provided some guidelines to help teachers prepare their students for these tests. We noted that any test preparation procedure that raises test scores without also increasing the mastery of the underlying knowledge and skills is inappropriate. After evaluating different test preparation practices we concluded that preparation that introduces generic test-taking skills and uses multiple instructional techniques can be recommended. These practices should result in improved performance on standardized tests that reflects increased mastery of the underlying content domains. Preparation practices that emphasize the use of practice tests or focus on test-specific content or test-specific item formats should be avoided because they may increase test scores, but not increase mastery of the underlying test domain.

We next briefly described some popular individual achievement tests that are used in schools. These individually administered tests are used by professionals with specialized training in assessment for a variety of purposes, including assessment of learning disabilities under the Individuals with Disabilities Education Act (IDEA). We also provided suggestions regarding the selection of achievement tests for different applications. We also briefly reviewed some of the applications of achievement tests outside of schools, such as their use in licensing professionals.

In closing, we discussed teacher-constructed classroom achievement tests and their use in assigning grades. We noted that these tests are administered in great numbers and have significant impact on students. When developing classroom tests, we emphasized the need to clearly specify student learning objectives, develop and follow a test blueprint, select a score interpretation approach based on how the results will be used, and include items that measure the specified constructs and contribute to the reliability and validity of test results. In terms of grade assignment, we recommended that grades be based solely on academic achievement and not contaminated with factors such as behavior or attitude. We stated that both relative (i.e., norm-referenced) and absolute (i.e., criterion-referenced) grading approaches can be used successfully, but recommended that teachers avoid basing grades on effort, improvement, or achievement relative to aptitude. We noted that letter grades are the most popular method of reporting student progress and that they are typically well understood by both students and parents. In closing we noted that it is important to keep grades confidential and that this is mandated by the Family Educational Rights and Privacy Act (FERPA).

Key Terms and Concepts

Achievement tests, 245
Group-administered tests, 250

Teaching to the test, 262
Test preparation practices, 262

Recommended Readings

Reynolds, C.R., Livingston, R.B., & Willson, V.L. (2009). *Measurement and Assessment in Education.* Boston: Allyn & Bacon.

Chapter Nine

Assessment of Intelligence

Conventional intelligence tests and even the entire concept of intelligence testing are perennially the focus of considerable controversy and strong emotion.

—REYNOLDS AND KAUFMAN, 1990

Learning Objectives

After reading and studying this chapter, students should be able to:

1. Compare and contrast the constructs of achievement and aptitude/intelligence.
2. Explain how achievement and aptitude can be conceptualized as different aspects of a continuum and provide examples to illustrate this continuum.
3. Discuss the major milestones in the history of intelligence assessment.
4. Describe the major uses of aptitude and intelligence tests.
5. Describe and evaluate the major individually administered intelligence tests.
6. Understand the central concepts of neuropsychological testing.
7. Understand the central concepts of memory testing.
8. Describe and evaluate the major individually administered memory tests.
9. Understand a report of an intellectual assessment.
10. Identify the major college admission tests and describe their use.

In Chapter 1, when describing maximum performance tests we noted that they are often classified as either achievement tests or aptitude tests. (In some professional sources the term *aptitude* is being replaced with *ability*. For historical purposes we will use *aptitude* to designate this type of test in this chapter, but we do want to alert readers to this variability in terminology.) We defined achievement tests as those designed to assess students' knowledge or skills in a content domain in which they have received instruction (AERA et al., 1999). In contrast, **aptitude tests** are designed to measure the cognitive skills, abilities, and knowledge that individuals have accumulated as the result of their overall life experiences. In some instances, such as with measures of general intelligence, aptitude measures are much broader than achievement measures, but some aptitude measures can be very narrow and focus on something as distinctive as visual attention or psychomotor speed. Whereas achievement tests are tied to a specific program of instruction, aptitude tests reflect the cumulative impact of life experiences as a whole in concert with an individual's underlying or latent ability to use information. Aptitude measures are more likely to focus on cognitive processes as opposed to content of knowledge domains as well. Some interpret the use of the term *aptitude* to denote the maximum level at which a person can perform now and in the future—we do not ascribe to immutability as an attribute of any aptitude assessed by any psychological test. Rather, aptitude scores as used here reflect how well a person performed on a task at that point in time, which we understand will predict future levels of performance, but far from perfectly. A person's aptitude score and the aptitude underlying performance may both change over time.

> **Aptitude tests** *are designed to measure the cognitive skills, abilities, and knowledge that individuals have accumulated as the result of their overall life experiences.*

These introductory comments might lead you to believe there is a clear and universally accepted distinction between achievement and aptitude tests. However, in practice this is not the case and the distinction is actually a matter of degree. Many, if not most, testing experts conceptualize both achievement and aptitude tests as tests of developed cognitive abilities that can be ordered along a continuum in terms of how closely linked the assessed abilities are to specific learning experiences. This continuum is illustrated in Figure 9–1. At one end of the continuum you have teacher-constructed classroom tests that are tied directly to the instruction provided in a specific classroom or course. For example, a classroom mathematics test should assess specifically the learning objectives covered in the class during a specific instructional period. This is an example of a test that is linked clearly and directly to specific academic experiences (i.e., the result of curriculum and instruction). Next along the continuum are the survey achievement batteries that measure a fairly broad range of knowledge, skills, and abilities. Although there should be alignment between the learning objectives measured by these tests and the academic curriculum, the scope of a survey battery is considerably broader and more comprehensive than that of a teacher-constructed classroom test. The group-administered survey batteries described in Chapter 8 are dependent on direct school experiences, but there is variability in how direct the linkage is. For example, the achievement tests developed by states specifically to assess the state's core curriculum are more directly linked to instruction through the state's specified curriculum than the commercially developed achievement tests that assess a more generic curriculum.

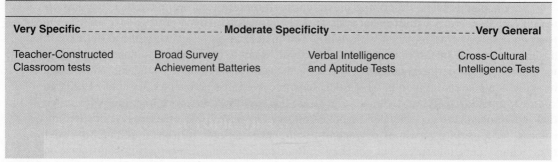

FIGURE 9–1 A Continuum of General Abilities.

Source: Modeled after Anastasi and Urbina (1997); Cronbach (1990); and others.

Next are intelligence and other aptitude tests that emphasize verbal, quantitative, and visual–spatial abilities. Many traditional intelligence tests can be placed in this category, and even though they are not linked to a specific academic curriculum, they do assess many skills that are commonly associated with academic success. The Otis-Lennon School Ability Test (OLSAT); Stanford-Binet Intelligence Scales—Fifth Edition; Tests of Cognitive Skills—Second Edition (TCS/2); Wechsler Intelligence Scale for Children—Fourth Edition (WISC-IV); and Reynolds Intellectual Assessment Scales (RIAS) are all examples of tests that fit in this category (some of these will be discussed later in this chapter). In developing these tests, the authors attempt to measure abilities that are acquired through common, everyday experiences—not only those acquired through formal educational experiences. For example, a quantitative section of one of these tests will typically emphasize mental computations and quantitative reasoning as opposed to the developed mathematics skills traditionally emphasized on achievement tests. Novel problem-solving skills are emphasized on many portions of these tests as well. Modern intelligence tests are not just measures of knowledge or how much you know, but also how well you think and can manipulate information.

Finally, at the most "general" end of the continuum are the nonverbal and cross-cultural intelligence or aptitude tests. These instruments attempt to minimize the influence of language, culture, and educational experiences. They typically emphasize the use of nonverbal performance items and often completely avoid language-based content (e.g., reading, writing, etc.). The Naglieri Nonverbal Ability Test—Multilevel Form (NNAT—Multilevel Form) is an example of a test that belongs in this category. The NNAT—Multilevel Form is a group-administered test of nonverbal reasoning and problem solving that is thought to be relatively independent of educational experiences, language, and cultural background (however, no test is truly culture-free or independent of all of one's life experiences). The NNAT—Multilevel Form (like many nonverbal IQ tests) employs items

> *Both achievement and aptitude tests measure developed abilities and can be arranged along a continuum according to how dependent the abilities are on direct school experiences.*

in which the test taker must find the missing pattern in a series of designs or figures. The matrices in the NNAT—Multilevel Form are arranged in order of difficulty and contain designs and shapes that are not specific to any one culture but appear across most cultures or are novel to nearly all test takers. Promoters of the test suggest that this test may be particularly useful for students with limited English proficiency, minorities, or those with hearing impairments.

In summary, both achievement and aptitude tests measure developed cognitive abilities and can be arranged along a continuum according to how dependent the abilities are on direct school experience. As we progress from the specific to the general end of the continuum, test performance becomes less and less dependent on specific learning experiences. The abilities measured by achievement tests are specifically linked to academic instruction or training. In contrast, the abilities measured by aptitude tests are acquired through a broad range of life experiences, including those at school, home, work, and all other settings.

Although we feel it is important to recognize that the distinction between achievement and aptitude tests is not absolute, we also feel the aptitude–achievement distinction is useful. In schools and other settings (e.g., clinical, employment), aptitude and achievement tests traditionally have been used for different purposes, and these labels help us identify their intended applications. For example, achievement tests typically are used to measure what has been learned or "achieved" at a specific point in time. In contrast, aptitude tests usually are used to predict future performance (e.g., academic or job performance). Even college quarterbacks who are trying out for the National Football League routinely take a specialized aptitude test to gauge their ability to learn complex offensive schemes and to recognize defensive alignments and make adjustments quickly and effectively. Special Interest Topic 9.1 provides a brief discussion differentiating between "predicting performance" and "measuring potential."

Although many sources use the terms *aptitude* and *intelligence* interchangeably, general intelligence tests are not the only type of aptitude test in use today. In addition to intelligence tests, special aptitude tests and multiple aptitude batteries frequently are used in many educational, clinical, and employment settings. Special aptitude tests were developed originally in the context of employment settings to help employers select job applicants based on their aptitudes in specific areas such as mechanical or clerical ability. Subsequently, test developers developed multiple-aptitude batteries to measure a number of distinct abilities.

> *General intelligence tests historically have been the most popular and widely used aptitude tests in school settings.*

General *intelligence tests* historically have been the most popular and widely used aptitude tests in psychology whether in clinical practice, school settings, or even in employment environments. Intelligence tests are the most advanced, psychometrically, of all tests in the armamentarium of psychologists, yet psychology as a discipline as well as the media and lay public seem to have a "love–hate" relationship with intelligence and intelligence testing in particular. It is not uncommon for parents of a child, when reviewing the results of an intellectual assessment of the child with a psychologist, to dismiss the idea of IQ in one breath and inquire as to the results of the child's IQ testing in the next! Intelligence testing research spawns strong emotions. As one example, consider the following. In the 1980s when the APA held its annual convention in Anaheim, California, Arthur Jensen, who became famous following a 1969 article in *Harvard Educational Review* ("How Much Can We Boost IQ and Scholastic Achievement?"), was scheduled to deliver an invited address on his research on intelligence.

SPECIAL INTEREST TOPIC 9.1

Do Intelligence Tests Reveal Your Potential for Learning or Other Achievements?

The short answer is an emphatic "No!"

Intelligence tests are among the very best predictors of performance in school as well as on the job, especially in vocational training programs or nearly anything related to academic achievement. This fact is often misconstrued and interpreted to mean that an intelligence test measures your potential to acquire knowledge and skills.

Intelligence tests do predict very well compared to most other indicators of what you will most likely achieve in these domains. However, the predictions made by an IQ about your future performance are actually the mean levels of performance by others at the same IQ point who have the average level of motivation, spend the same average amount of time studying, have the same average level of study and learning skills and strategies, have the same average level of opportunity to learn or develop these skills, have the same average level of quality of instruction, have the same average level of attentional skills, and so on, as the average of other persons with the exact same IQ.

This means that if any one of these assumptions is untrue for you, you will most likely not perform at the predicted level. In fact, around each predicted level of achievement or performance, there is a normal distribution of actual performance. So, if you study harder than others with the same IQ as you, you will perform at a higher level than predicted by the IQ you obtained—if you have a higher level of motivation than others who have the same IQ as you, you will most likely perform at a higher level over time. On the other hand, if you spend less time studying than the average person with the same IQ as you, you will most likely perform at a lower level than others at this IQ point.

An IQ then is not a determinant or indicator of your potential, it is only a very good predictor of what you are most likely to achieve. You have a great deal of control over the accuracy of this prediction. Work harder, study harder and smarter, and attend better and you will perform at a higher level than most people with your IQ, thus beating the prediction; but do less than others with the same IQ, and you will perform at a lower level. You get to choose on which side of the predicted level of performance you will actually fall.

One of the authors of this text (CRR) had been asked by the APA to introduce Jensen, whose conclusions on racial differences in intelligence based on his research were often seen as controversial by many (and led to the coining of the term *Jensenism*). Several weeks before the convention, CRR was contacted by the Anaheim police and told they had received what they considered a credible threat that if Jensen were to speak, he would be assassinated during his address. Despite this threat, Jensen spoke and CRR did introduce him, but the police patrolled the venue of the invited address that day quite heavily (with canines in attendance as well) and screened the audience as they entered the convention center hall, a hall that was completely filled for Jensen's address. Few topics in psychology can engender such strong and polemic responses (also see Special Interest Topics 9.2 and 9.3 as well as Chapter 15 of this text on cultural bias in testing).

A BRIEF HISTORY OF INTELLIGENCE TESTS

Although practically everyone is familiar with the concept of **intelligence** and uses the term in everyday conversations, it is not easy to develop a definition of intelligence on which everyone agrees. Although practically all psychologists and psychometricians have their own personal

SPECIAL INTEREST TOPIC 9.2

The Controversial IQ: Knowns and Unknowns

A task force established by the American Psychological Association produced a report titled "Intelligence: Knowns and Unknowns" (Neisser et al., 1996). Its authors summarize the state of knowledge about intelligence and conclude by identifying seven critical questions about intelligence that have yet to be answered. These issues are summarized here and remain unconquered.

1. It is widely accepted that there is a substantial genetic contribution to the development of intelligence, but the pathway by which genetic differences are expressed is not known.

2. It is also accepted that environmental factors contribute significantly to the development of intelligence, but no one really knows the mechanism by which they express their influence.

3. The role of nutrition in the development of intelligence is unclear. It is clear that profound early malnutrition is detrimental, but the effects of more subtle nutritional differences in populations that are "adequately fed" are not well understood.

4. Research has revealed significant correlations between information-processing speed and intelligence, but these findings have not resulted in clear theoretical models.

5. The "Flynn Effect" is real! That is, mean IQs are increasing worldwide. No one is really sure what factors are driving these gains. (See Chapter 3 for more on this topic.)

6. Mean IQ differences between races cannot be attributed to obvious test bias or simply to differences in socioeconomic status. There is also no support for genetic explanations. Simply put, no one really knows the basis of these differences.

7. It is widely accepted that standardized intelligence tests do not measure all aspects of intelligence such as creativity, common sense, and interpersonal finesse. However, we do not know very much about these abilities such as how they relate to more traditional aspects of intelligence or how they develop.

In concluding their report, Neisser et al. (1996) noted:

In a field where so many issues are unresolved and so many questions unanswered, the confident tone that has characterized most of the debate on these topics is clearly out of place. The study of intelligence does not need politicized assertions and recriminations; it needs self-restraint, reflection, and a great deal more research. The questions that remain are socially as well as scientifically important. There is no reason to think them unanswerable, but finding the answers will require a shared and sustained effort as well as the commitment of substantial scientific resources. Just such a commitment is what we strongly recommend. (p. 97)

definition of intelligence, most of these definitions will incorporate abilities such as problem solving, abstract reasoning, and the ability to acquire knowledge—how well you can think and problem solve (e.g., Gray, 1999; Reynolds & Kamphaus, 2003). Developing a consensus beyond this point is more difficult (see Special Interest Topic 9.2 and 9.3 for more on the controversial state of intelligence). For our present purpose, instead of pursuing a philosophical discussion of the meaning of intelligence, we will focus only on intelligence as measured by contemporary intelligence tests. These tests typically

> *Most definitions of* **intelligence** *incorporate abilities such as problem solving, abstract reasoning, and the ability to acquire knowledge.*

SPECIAL INTEREST TOPIC 9.3

The Controversial IQ: Schools and IQ Tests

Although IQ tests had their origin in the schools, they have been the source of considerable controversy essentially since their introduction. Opponents of IQ tests often argue IQ tests should be banned from schools altogether whereas proponents can hardly envision the schools without them. Many enduring issues contribute to this controversy, and we will mention only the most prominent ones. These include the following.

Mean IQ Differences among Ethnic Groups

There is considerable research that documents mean IQ differences among various ethnic groups, and this has often been the source of considerable controversy. Although the basis for these differences has not been identified, there is ample evidence the differences cannot be attributed merely to test bias (something we address in more detail in Chapter 15). Nevertheless, because mean group differences in IQ may result in differential educational treatment and placement, there continues to be the *appearance* of test bias, and this *appearance* promulgates the controversy regarding the use of IQ tests in schools (Canter, 1997). For example, because of the perception of test bias the state of California has prohibited the use of a number of popular IQ tests for making placement decisions with certain ethnic minorities. This is not based on the psychometric properties of the IQ tests, but on public perception and legal cases. Other states have examined the same tests and concluded that the tests are not biased and supported their use with minorities.

Can IQ Be Increased?

Given the importance society places on intelligence and a desire to help children excel, it is reasonable to ask how much IQ can be improved. Hereditarians, those who see genetics as playing the primary role in influencing IQ, hold that efforts to improve it are doomed to failure. In contrast, environmentalists, who see environmental influences as primary, see IQ as being highly malleable. So who is right? In summary, the research suggests that IQ can be improved to some degree, but the improvement is rather limited. For example, adoption studies indicate that lasting gains of approximately 10 to 12 IQ points are the most that can be accomplished through even the most pervasive environmental interventions. The results of preschool intervention programs such as Head Start are much less impressive. These programs may result in modest increases in IQ, but even these gains are typically lost in a few years (Kranzler, 1997). The programs do have other benefits to children, however, and should not be judged only on their impact on IQ.

Do We Really Need IQ Tests in Schools?

Although public debate over the use of IQ tests in schools typically has focused on ethnic differences and the malleability of intelligence, professional educators and psychologists also have debated the usefulness of IQ tests in educational settings. Different terms have been applied to this question over the years. For example, Wigdor and Garner (1982) framed it as the *instructional validity* of IQ test results, Hilliard (1989) referred to it as the *pedagogical utility question,* and Gresham and Witt (1997) indicated it was essentially an issue of *treatment validity*. Whatever label you use, the question is "Does the use of IQ tests result in educational benefits for students?" Proponents of IQ tests highlight evidence that intelligence plays a key role in success in many areas of life, including school achievement. As an extension they argue that information garnered from IQ tests allows educators to tailor instruction so that it meets the specific needs of their students. As a result more students are able to succeed academically. Opponents of IQ tests argue that there is little evidence that the use of IQ tests results in any real improvement in the education of students. A contemporary debate involves the use of IQ tests in the identification of students with learning disabilities. Historically the diagnosis of learning disabilities has been based on a discrepancy model in which students' level of achievement is compared to their overall level of

(Continued on page 285)

intelligence. If students' achievement in reading, mathematics, or some other specific achievement area is significantly below that expected based on their IQ, they may be diagnosed as having a learning disability (actually the diagnosis of learning disabilities is more complicated than this, but this explanation is sufficient in this context). Currently some researchers are presenting arguments that IQs need not play a role in the diagnosis of learning disabilities and are calling for dropping the use of a discrepancy model, and the 2004 federal law governing special education eligibility (the Individuals with Disabilities Education Act of 2004) no longer requires such a discrepancy, but does allow its use in diagnosing disabilities.

So what does the future hold for IQ testing in the schools? We believe that when used appropriately IQ tests can make a significant contribution to the education of students. Braden (1997) noted that

> eliminating IQ is different from eliminating intelligence. We can slay the messenger, but the message that children differ in their learning rate, efficiency, and ability to generalize knowledge to new situations (despite similar instruction) remains. (p. 244)

At the same time we recognize that on occasion IQ tests (and other tests) have been used in inappropriate ways that are harmful to students. The key is to be an informed user of assessment results. To this end a professional educator should have a good understanding of the topics covered in this text, including basic psychometric principles and the ethical use of test results.

produce an overall score referred to as an intelligence quotient (IQ), and this is the most common operational definition of intelligence in research on intelligence.

Intelligence tests had their beginning in the schools. In the early 1900s, France initiated a compulsory education program. Recognizing that not all children had the cognitive abilities necessary to benefit from regular education classes, the minister of education wanted to develop special educational programs to meet the particular needs of these children. To accomplish this, he needed a way of identifying children who needed special services. Alfred Binet and his colleague Theodore Simon had been attempting to develop a measure of intelligence for some years, and the French government commissioned them to develop a test that could predict academic performance accurately. The result of their efforts was the first **Binet-Simon Scale**, released in 1905. This test contained problems arranged in the order of their difficulty and assessing a wide range of abilities. The test contained some sensory-perceptual tests, but the emphasis was on verbal items assessing comprehension, reasoning, judgment, and short-term memory. Subsequent revisions of the Binet-Simon Scale were released in 1908 and 1911. These scales gained wide acceptance in France and were soon translated and standardized in the United States, most successfully by Louis Terman at Stanford University. This resulted in the Stanford-Binet Intelligence Scale, which has been revised numerous times (the fifth revision, SB5, remains in use today). Ironically, Terman's version of the Binet-Simon Scale became even more popular in France and other parts of Europe than the Binet-Simon Scale!

The development and success of the Binet-Simon Scale, and subsequently the Stanford-Binet Intelligence Scale, ushered in the era of widespread intelligence testing in the United States. Following Terman's lead, other assessment experts developed and released their own intelligence tests. Some of

> *The development and success of the* **Binet-Simon Scale,** *and subsequently the* **Stanford-Binet,** *ushered in the era of widespread intelligence testing in the United States.*

the tests were designed for individual administration (like the Stanford-Binet Intelligence Test) whereas others were designed for group administration. Some of these tests placed more emphasis on verbal and quantitative abilities whereas others focused more on visual–spatial and abstract problem-solving abilities. As a general rule, research has shown with considerable consistency that contemporary intelligence tests are good predictors of academic success. This is to be expected considering this was the precise purpose for which they were initially developed over 100 years ago. In addition to being good predictors of school performance, research has shown that IQs are fairly stable over time. Nevertheless, these tests have become controversial themselves as a result of the often emotional debate over the meaning of intelligence. To try and avoid this association and possible misinterpretations, many test publishers have adopted more neutral names such as *academic potential, scholastic ability, school ability, mental ability,* and simply *ability* to designate essentially the same construct.

The concept of ability testing received a major boost in the United States in the 1915–1920 period as a result of World War I. The U.S. Army needed a way to assess and classify recruits as suitable for the military or not and to classify them for jobs in the military. The APA and one of its presidents, Robert M. Yerkes, worked to develop a group of experts in the field who devised a series of aptitude test that came to be known as the Army Alpha and Army Beta—one was verbal (Alpha) and one nonverbal (Beta). Through their efforts and those of the Army in screening recruits literally millions of Americans became familiar with the concept of intelligence or ability testing. Subsequently, in the following decade, the College Entrance Examination Board (CEEB) commissioned the development of what is now the Scholastic Assessment Test (SAT), to assist in developing objective criteria for college admissions. Prior to the advent of the SAT, admission to colleges and universities was largely determined by legacy systems and who was willing to recommend you—not by what we consider today to be academic credentials or successes.

Intelligence testing received another boost in the next decade, the 1930s, when David Wechsler developed an intelligence test that included measures of verbal ability and nonverbal (or so-called performance abilities) on the same test. Prior to Wechsler, and the Wechsler-Bellevue I (so named because Wechsler was chief of psychology at the famous Bellevue Hospital in New York—it was common in this era for authors to name tests after where they were employed, hence the Stanford Binet, named after Terman's place of employment, the Hiskey-Nebraska Test of Learning Aptitude, etc.), intelligence tests typically assessed verbal or nonverbal intelligence, not both. Wechsler saw the clinical value in having an assessment of both on the same person with a common standardization sample used to calculate the scores. Wechsler broke ranks with Binet (whose test yielded a score for general intelligence only) and other intelligence test authors on another important front as well. Binet and many other tests computed IQs based on age curves as well as computing IQs using the old formula of 100 × (Mental Age/ Chronological Age), which produces an ordinal scale of measurement at best (it is an odd scale we know because it mixes ratio scales such as chronological age with ordinal measurement (e.g., mental age) and manipulates them in statistically inappropriate ways (see Chapter 2)). Wechsler instead created age-corrected deviation-scaled scores for his tests, which are interval scales of measurement and quite likely rise to the level of equal-interval scaling in most cases. With only a few psychometric improvements in their derivation, these are the same types of scores yielded by nearly every intelligence test in use today.

Wechsler subsequently developed versions of his Wechsler-Bellevue for different age groups, including preschoolers (Wechsler Preschool and Primary Scale of Intelligence [WPPSI]), school-aged children (Wechsler Intelligence Scale for Children [WISC]), and adults (Wechsler Adult Intelligence Scale [WAIS]). These tests have been revised multiple times, most occurring after Wechsler's death in the early 1980s, and are the most frequently used individually administered intelligence tests by school and clinical psychologists today. Until the 1980s, the various Wechsler scales and the Stanford-Binet truly dominated the individual intelligence testing market. However, with the success of Alan and Nadeen Kaufman's Kaufman Assessment Battery for Children (KABC), published in 1983, numerous other competitors emerged over the next 20 years. Although the Wechsler scales remain the most frequently used measure of intelligence (the Stanford-Binet has lost allegiances due to problems and dissatisfaction with several of its revisions over the years), many clinicians also now use other individually administered intelligence tests to meet current demands of practice including such scales as the Universal Nonverbal Intelligence Test (UNIT), Reynolds Intellectual Assessment Scales (RIAS), Cognitive Assessment System (CAS), Woodcock-Johnson Tests of Cognitive Abilities (WJ III COG), and the Differential Ability Scales (DAS).

THE USE OF APTITUDE AND INTELLIGENCE TESTS IN SCHOOL SETTINGS

As you can see from the previous discussion, aptitude and intelligence tests have a long history of use in the schools settings. Their widespread use continues to this day, with major applications including:

- Providing alternative measures of cognitive abilities that reflect information not captured by standard achievement tests or school grades
- Helping educators tailor instruction to meet a student's unique pattern of cognitive strengths and weaknesses
- Assessing how well students are prepared to profit from school experiences
- Identifying clients who are underachieving and may need further assessment to rule out learning disabilities or other cognitive disorders, including mental retardation, as well as disability determination
- Identifying students for gifted and talented programs
- Providing a baseline against which other client characteristics may be compared
- Helping guide students and parents with educational and vocational planning

Although we have identified the most common uses of aptitude/intelligence tests in the public schools, the list clearly is not exhaustive. Today's educators need to be familiar with these tests and their interpretations. Even classroom teachers are involved to varying degrees with these applications. For example, teachers are frequently called on to administer and interpret many of the group aptitude tests for their own students. School psychologists and other professionals with specific training in administering and interpreting clinical and diagnostic tests typically administer and interpret the individual intelligence and aptitude tests. Even though they are not directly involved in administering individual intelligence tests, it is important for teachers to be familiar with these individual tests. Teachers frequently need to read and understand psychological reports describing student performances on these tests. Additionally, teachers are often on committees that plan and develop educational programs for students with disabilities based on information derived from the tests.

Aptitude–Achievement Discrepancies

> *One common assessment practice employed in schools and in clinical settings in determining a specific learning disability is referred to as* **aptitude–achievement discrepancy** *analysis.*

One common assessment practice employed in schools and in clinical settings since the mid-1970s is referred to as **aptitude–achievement discrepancy** analysis. This involves comparing a client's performance on an aptitude test with his or her performance on an achievement test. The basic rationale behind this practice is that normally clients' achievement scores should be commensurate with their aptitude scores. In other words, their performance on an aptitude test serves as a type of baseline from which to compare their performance on an achievement test with the expectation that they will be similar. In the majority of cases this is what you will discover when you compare aptitude and achievement scores. This is not to suggest that the scores will be identical, but that they will be similar, or that there will not be a statistically significant discrepancy. If clients' achievement scores are significantly higher than their aptitude scores, they are considered academic overachievers. This may be attributed to a number of factors such as strong motivation and/or an enriched learning environment. This may not necessarily be a reason for concern, but may suggest that whereas they perform well with the specific skills that are emphasized in school, they have more difficulty solving novel problems and generalizing their skills to new situations. These clients may benefit from instructional activities that emphasize transfer of learning, generalization, and creativity (Riverside Publishing, 2002).

If clients' achievement scores are significantly lower than their aptitude scores, they may be considered academic underachievers, which may be cause for concern. Academic underachievement may be the result of a number of factors. The client may not be motivated to perform well in school or may have had inadequate opportunities to learn. This could include limited exposure to instruction or an impoverished home environment. It could also reflect cultural or language differences that impact academic achievement. Naturally a number of medical factors could also be involved such as impaired hearing or vision, or chronic illnesses that cause children to have high rates of absenteeism or that affect them in other ways (e.g., creating fatigue, causing attentional problems, or degrading new learning skills). Additionally a number of psychological disorders or factors could be implicated. For example, children with attention deficit hyperactivity disorder (ADHD) experience attentional problems that may interfere with achievement. Emotional disorders such as depression or anxiety can be detrimental to academic performance. Finally, learning disabilities are often characterized by significant discrepancies between aptitude and achievement. In fact, many contemporary definitions of learning disabilities incorporate a significant discrepancy between aptitude and achievement as a diagnostic criterion for the disorder. Although reliance on aptitude–achievement discrepancies to diagnose learning disabilities is currently the focus of considerable debate (e.g., Fletcher et al., 2002; Reynolds & Shaywitz, 2009), many psychologists continue to use it as an essential element in the diagnosis of learning disabilities. The Individuals with Disabilities Education Act of 2004 mandates that an aptitude–achievement discrepancy can no longer be required for diagnosis of a learning disability in public school settings, but other state, local, federal, and private agencies continue to require such a discrepancy as does the *Diagnostic and Statistical Manual of Mental Disorders* (4th ed., text revision; *DSM–IV–TR*) of the American Psychiatric Association. The CEEB also considers such factors in deciding whether to grant accommodations to students taking the SAT and related college entrance exams.

In practice there are a number of methods for determining whether there is a significant discrepancy between aptitude and achievement scores. Reynolds (1985, 1990) chaired a federal task force that developed criteria for conducting aptitude–achievement discrepancy analyses. These included the requirement that correlation and regression analyses, which are used in predicting achievement levels and establishing statistical significance, must be based on representative samples. To help meet this requirement, many of the popular aptitude/intelligence tests are either conormed (i.e., their normative data were based on the exact same sample of children), or linked (i.e., there is some overlap in the standardization sample so that a proportion of the sample received both tests) with a standardized achievement test, or specific studies are conducted to establish the mathematical relationship between an IQ and an achievement measure (e.g., Reynolds & Kamphaus, 2007). This is a desirable situation and whenever possible one should use conormed or linked aptitude–achievement tests when performing aptitude–achievement analyses. When aptitude–achievement discrepancy analyses are conducted using tests that are not conormed or linked, or when studies to establish the relationship between the measures are poorly constructed, the results should be interpreted with caution (Psychological Corporation, 2002; Reynolds, 1985).

Some of the popular individual intelligence tests have been conormed with a standardized achievement test to facilitate the calculation of aptitude–achievement comparisons. These comparisons typically involve the identification of a statistically significant discrepancy between ability and achievement. Although approaches differ, the simple-difference method and predicted-achievement method are most commonly used (Psychological Corporation, 2002; Reynolds, 1985). In the brief descriptions of major aptitude/intelligence tests that follow, we will indicate which instruments have been conormed or linked to achievement tests and which tests they have been paired with.

> *Although it is common for educators and clinicians to make aptitude–achievement comparisons, many testing experts criticize the practice.*

Before proceeding, we should note that although it is common for educators and clinicians to make ability–achievement comparisons, many testing experts criticize this practice. Critics of this approach argue that ability–achievement discrepancies usually can be attributed simply to measurement error, differences in the content covered, and variations in student attitude and motivation on the different tests (Anastasi & Urbina, 1997; Linn & Gronlund, 2000). Reynolds (1985) provided methods to overcome the psychometric problems, but noncognitive factors are more difficult to control. Also, as we noted, there is considerable debate about relying on ability–achievement discrepancies to diagnose learning disabilities. Our position can probably be best described as middle of the road. Analysis of ability–achievement discrepancies may help identify children who are experiencing some academic problems, but they should be interpreted cautiously. That is, interpret such discrepancies in the context of other information you have about the client (e.g., observations, school grades, classroom behavior), and if there is reason for concern, pursue additional assessment.

A New Assessment Strategy for Specific Learning Disabilities—Response to Intervention (RTI)

There has been growing criticism of reliance on aptitude–achievement discrepancies for diagnosing learning disabilities. If the profession is going to move away from the use of aptitude–achievement discrepancies, the natural question is "What is the best way to identify students with learning disabilities?" The approach that has garnered the most attention and enthusiasm in recent years is referred to as response to intervention (RTI). RTI has been defined and applied in a number of different ways, but Fuchs, Mock, Morgan, and Young (2003) provided a broad but succinct definition, when they described it as follows:

1. Students are provided with "generally effective" instruction by their classroom teacher.
2. Their progress is monitored.
3. Those who do not respond get something else, or something more, from a teacher or someone else.
4. Again, their progress is monitored.
5. Those who still do not respond either qualify for special education or for special education evaluation. (p. 159)

Additionally, Fuchs et al. (2003) outlined the perceived benefits of RTI relative to the aptitude–achievement discrepancy approach. For example, RTI is purported to provide help to struggling students sooner. That is, RTI will help identify students with learning disabilities in a timely manner, not waiting for them to fail before providing assistance. Additionally, proponents hold that RTI effectively distinguishes between students with actual disabilities and students who simply have not received adequate instruction. With RTI different instructional strategies of increasing intensity are implemented as part of the process. It is also believed by some that RTI will result in a reduced number of students receiving special education services and an accompanying reduction in costs.

Although RTI appears to hold promise in the identification of students with learning disabilities (LD), a number of concerns remain. The RTI process has been defined and applied in different ways, by different professionals, in different settings (e.g., Christ, Burns, & Ysseldyke, 2005; Fuchs et al., 2003). For example, some professionals envision RTI as part of a behavioral problem-solving model whereas others feel it should involve the consistent application of empirically validated protocols for students with specific learning problems. Even when there is agreement on the basic strategy (e.g., a problem-solving model), differences exist in the number of levels (or tiers) involved, who provides the interventions, and if RTI is a precursor to a formal assessment or if the RTI process replaces a formal assessment in identifying students with disabilities (Fuchs et al., 2003). Some argue in favor of RTI as a stand-alone method of disability determination, but many (e.g., Reynolds & Shaywitz, 2009) see it as substantially flawed as a means of diagnosis. However, even among those who propose using it for diagnosis, there is little agreement and many problems exist from a testing and measurement standpoint in determining just how to assess whether a student has responded (the R in RTI) to an intervention (see Reynolds, 2008, 2009, and Reynolds & Shaywitz, 2009, for detailed discussions). This is a crucial point because different methods of determining whether a response has occurred will identify different children as having disabilities! These inconsistencies present a substantial problem because they make it difficult to establish empirically the utility of the RTI process. Currently, the RTI model has been evaluated primarily in the context of reading disabilities with children in the early grades, and this research is generally promising. However, much less research is available supporting the application of RTI with other learning disorders and with older children (Feifer & Della Toffalo, 2007; Reynolds, 2005 Reynolds & Shaywitz, 2009). In summary, there is much to be learned!

> *A more moderate and measured approach that incorporates the best of RTI and psychometric assessment practices seems most reasonable at this time.*

At this point, we view RTI as a useful process that can help identify struggling students and ensure that they receive early attention and more intensive instructional interventions. We also feel that students who do not respond to more intensive instruction should receive a formal psychological assessment that includes, among other techniques, standardized cognitive tests (i.e., aptitude, achievement, and possibly neuropsychological tests). We do not agree with those who support RTI as a stand-alone process for identifying students with LD. This position excludes the use of standardized tests and essentially ignores 100 years of empirical research supporting the use of psychometric procedures in identifying and treating psychological and learning problems. A more moderate and measured approach that incorporates the best of RTI and psychometric assessment practices seems most reasonable at this time. If future research demonstrates that RTI can be used independently to identify and develop interventions for students with learning disabilities, we will reevaluate our position.

Diagnosing Mental Retardation/Intellectual Disabilities

The diagnosis of mental retardation is made in many settings, but the most common is in the public schools or a public school setting. There are three primary reasons for this. The first is that the category Mild Mental Retardation, associated with IQs ranging from 55 to 70, accounts for the majority of cases of mental retardation. Second, mild mental retardation may not be evident until a child begins the formal schooling process and experiences broad failures to learn at a pace near that of agemates. This broad pattern of academic failure prompts a referral to the school psychologist or related staff for a comprehensive evaluation. More severe forms of mental retardation, termed moderate, severe, and profound, and associated with IQs below 55, are more likely to be evidenced prior to formal schooling and most cases are diagnosed before age 5 or 6 years. Third, mental retardation is considered broadly under the category of developmental disabilities and one of the key (indeed mandatory) criteria for a diagnosis of mental retardation is that characteristics and evidence of the disorder must have been present prior to the age of 18, when most individuals are attending school.

The diagnosis of mental retardation thus has three major prongs requiring (1) performance on an individually administered test of intelligence (with consideration for the standard error of measurement of the test score) 2 or more standards deviations below the population mean; (2) significant deficits in adaptive behavior (meaning behavior such as self-help skills, activities of daily living, ability to communicate with others, and ability to function in a social system); and (3) evidence that these deficiencies in function occurred during the developmental period (i.e., before the age of 18). Thus, even though intelligence is not the only consideration in a diagnosis of mental retardation, such a diagnosis should not be made in the absence of a comprehensive assessment of intelligence.

> *IQs two or more standard deviations below the mean on an individually administered test of intelligence is a necessary but insufficient condition for a diagnosis of mental retardation.*

When an individual first evidences the intellectual and behavioral characteristics of mental retardation after the age of 18, alternative diagnoses are given that are typically reflective of the cause of the onset of these symptoms (which may be permanent, degenerative, or transitory). Such characteristics may be caused by a dementia such as Alzheimer's disease, by a brain injury, illegal drug use or other prolonged substance abuse, or as an iatrogenic response to treatment of certain medical conditions.

It is also notable that as of this writing, the diagnostic terminology for mental retardation is being reconsidered. Whereas the outcome is several years away, it has been proposed that the term *mental retardation* be removed from diagnostic nomenclature in favor of *intellectual disability* as the new lexicon.

THE USE OF APTITUDE AND INTELLIGENCE TESTS IN CLINICAL SETTINGS

Psychologists involved in various health care settings including private clinical practice use intelligence tests for many purposes, both with children and adults. Clinical child and pediatric psychologists may use intelligence tests for all the reasons discussed previously to be useful in schools in addition to other reasons. Clinical neuropsychologists who specialize in pediatrics will do likewise. In addition to common school applications, intelligence tests might be used in such clinical settings to evaluate a patient's suitability for certain types of psychological interventions, to monitor recovery following a brain injury, to assess the appropriateness of different levels of care when intellectual decline is seen to exist, and to determine disability status for government programs. Some specific examples where intelligence tests may be used include the following: to assess the intelligence of a soldier exposed to a nearby explosion that caused no apparent external injury but caused a concussive injury to the brain serious enough to cause the soldier to be unable to work in a competitive setting in civilian life; to assess the undesirable side effects of treatments for medical conditions (e.g., leukemia treatments and other forms of chemotherapy) that may lessen intellectual function; to assess damage to intellectual skills caused by prolonged surgery under general anesthesia requiring a heart–lung machine or long-term treatment on moderate to high doses of corticosteroids; to assist in determining whether a juvenile offender is suitable to be tried as an adult; and to make recommendations regarding appropriate vocational training programs for adults with other disabilities. Intelligence tests can even be used to monitor dietary compliance in children with certain metabolic disorders such as phenylketonuria, where the failure to maintain a strict diet (in this instance, free of all phenylalanine) causes a drop in intelligence that can be measured via repeat administrations of intelligence tests! This long list represents but a few of the many purposes for which intelligence tests may be applied in clinical settings. Intelligence tests also are used in personnel selection (which is addressed in Chapter 12) and in a variety of other settings where selection or sorting as a function of intellectual level may be an issue of importance.

MAJOR APTITUDE/INTELLIGENCE TESTS

Group Aptitude/Intelligence Tests

As with the standardized achievement tests discussed in a previous chapter, it is common for schools routinely to administer standardized aptitude/intelligence tests to a large number of students. Also as with standardized achievement tests, the most commonly used aptitude tests are group administered, largely due to the efficiency of these tests. In contrast to individually administered intelligence tests, teachers and other school personnel are often called on to help administer and interpret the results of these tests. Other large institutions such as prisons and juvenile facilities also use group intelligence or aptitude measures on a large scale, for screening and classification purposes, and these are often conducted by intake counselors or related staff. The guidelines presented in the previous chapter for administering and interpreting standardized tests apply equally well to both achievement and aptitude tests. However, even group aptitude/intelligence measures need to be interpreted by appropriately trained professionals. Currently, the most widely used group aptitude/intelligence tests in school and clinical settings are produced and distributed by three publishers: CTB McGraw-Hill, Pearson Assessments, and Riverside Publishing.

TESTS OF COGNITIVE SKILLS—SECOND EDITION (TCS/2). The Tests of Cognitive Skills— Second Edition (TCS/2), published by CTB McGraw-Hill, is designed for use with children in Grades 2 through 12. It measures verbal, nonverbal, and memory abilities that are thought to be important for academic success. It includes the following subtests: Sequences (ability to comprehend rules implied in a series of numbers, figures, or letters), Analogies (ability to recognize literal and symbolic relationships), Verbal Reasoning (deductive reasoning, analyzing categories, and recognizing patterns and relationships), and Memory (ability to remember pictures or nonsense words). Although the TCS/2 does not assess quantitative abilities like many other aptitude tests, its assessment of memory abilities is unique. When administered with TerraNova—The Second Edition, CAT/5, or CTBS/4, anticipated achievement scores can be calculated.

PRIMARY TEST OF COGNITIVE SKILLS (PTCS). The Primary Test of Cognitive Skills (PTCS), published by CTB McGraw-Hill, is designed for use with students in kindergarten through first grade (ages 5.1 to 7.6 years). It has four subtests (Verbal, Spatial, Memory, and Concepts) that require no reading or number knowledge. The PTCS produces an overall Cognitive Skills Index (CSI), and when administered with TerraNova—The Second Edition, anticipated achievement scores can be calculated.

INVIEW. InView, published by CTB McGraw-Hill, is designed for use with students in Grades 2 through 12. It is actually the newest version of the Tests of Cognitive Skills and assesses cognitive abilities in verbal reasoning, nonverbal reasoning, and quantitative reasoning. InView contains five subtests: Verbal Reasoning—Words (deductive reasoning, analyzing categories, and recognizing patterns and relationships), Verbal Reasoning—Context (ability to identify important concepts and draw logical conclusions), Sequences (ability to comprehend rules implied in a series of numbers, figures, or letters), Analogies (ability to recognize literal and symbolic relationships), and Quantitative Reasoning (ability to reason with numbers). When administered with TerraNova—The Second Edition, anticipated achievement scores can be calculated.

OTIS-LENNON SCHOOL ABILITY TEST—EIGHTH EDITION (OLSAT-8). The Otis-Lennon School Ability Test—Eighth Edition (OLSAT-8) published by Pearson Assessments, is designed for use with students from kindergarten through Grade 12. The OLSAT-8 is designed to measure verbal processes and nonverbal processes that are related to success in school. This includes tasks such as detecting similarities and differences, defining words, following directions, recalling words/numbers, classifying, sequencing, completing analogies, and solving mathematics problems. The OLSAT-8 produces Total, Verbal, and Nonverbal School Ability Indexes (SAIs). The publishers note that although the total score is the best predictor of success in school, academic success is dependent on both verbal and nonverbal abilities, and the Verbal and Nonverbal SAIs can provide potentially important information. When administered with the Stanford Achievement Test Series—Tenth Edition (Stanford 10), one can obtain aptitude–achievement comparisons (Achievement/Ability Comparisons, or AACs).

COGNITIVE ABILITIES TEST (COGAT), FORM 6. The Cognitive Abilities Test (CogAT), distributed by Riverside Publishing, is designed for use with students from kindergarten through Grade 12. It provides information about the development of verbal, quantitative, and nonverbal reasoning abilities that are related to school success. Students in kindergarten through Grade 2 are given the following subtests: Oral Vocabulary, Verbal Reasoning, Relational Concepts, Quantitative Concepts, Figure Classification, and Matrices. Students in Grades 3 through 12 undergo the following subtests: Verbal Classification, Sentence Completion, Verbal Analogies, Quantitative Relations, Number Series, Equation Building, Figure Classification, Figure Analogies, and Figure Analysis. Verbal, quantitative, and nonverbal *battery scores* are provided along with an overall composite score. The publishers encourage educators to focus on an analysis of the profile of the three battery scores rather than the overall composite score. They feel this approach provides the most useful information to teachers regarding how they can tailor instruction to meet the specific needs of students (see Special Interest Topic 9.4 for examples). When given with the Iowa Tests of Basic Skills or Iowa Tests of Educational Development, the CogAT provides predicted achievement scores to help identify students whose level of achievement is significantly higher or lower than expected. Table 9–1 illustrates the organization of the major group aptitude/intelligence tests.

PERSONNEL AND VOCATIONAL ASSESSMENT. In the personnel and vocational arena, you are likely to encounter the use of the Miller Analogies Test (MAT), an entirely verbal measure that relies heavily on vocabulary development in addition to reasoning skills, and the Wonderlic Personnel Test, which is really an IQ measure from our perspective. The Wonderlic samples a broad range of reasoning and knowledge capacities in a short period of time—it is one of the few speeded measures of intelligence available and has rigid time limits set such that few make it to the last item on the test. In large institutional settings where individuals with below-average intelligence levels are more common, such as in the prison system, the use of group nonverbal intelligence tests is more common, such as the Beta-III Test, a current incarnation of what was once known as the Army Beta, a nonverbal measure of intelligence devised to screen recruits in WWI.

> College admission tests *were specifically designed to predict academic performance in college.*

SPECIAL INTEREST TOPIC 9.4

Ability Profiles on the CogAT

The Cognitive Abilities Test (CogAT) is an aptitude test that measures the level and pattern of a student's cognitive abilities. When interpreting the CogAT, Riverside Publishing (2002) encourages teachers to focus on the student's performance profile on the three CogAT batteries: Verbal Reasoning, Quantitative Reasoning, and Nonverbal Reasoning. To facilitate interpretation of scores, the profiles are classified as A, B, C, or E profiles. These are described next:

- ◆ **A Profiles:** Students with A profiles perform at approximately the same level on verbal, quantitative, and nonverbal reasoning tasks. That is, they don't have any relative strengths or weaknesses. Approximately one third of students receive this profile designation.

- ◆ **B Profiles:** Students with B profiles have one battery score that significantly above or below the other two scores. That is, they have either a relative strength or a relative weakness on one subtest. B profiles are designated with symbols to specify the student's relative strength or weakness. For example, B (Q+) indicates that a student has a relative strength on the Quantitative Reasoning battery, whereas a B (V−) indicates that a student has a relative weakness on the Verbal Reasoning battery. Approximately 40% of students have this type of profile.

- ◆ **C Profiles:** Students with C profiles have *both* a relative strength and a relative weakness. Here the *C* stands for contrast. For example, C (V+N−) indicates that a student has a relative strength in Verbal Reasoning and a relative weakness in Nonverbal Reasoning. Approximately 14% of the students demonstrate this profile type.

- ◆ **E Profiles:** Some students with B or C demonstrate strengths and/or weaknesses that are so extreme they deserve special attention. With the CogAT, score differences of 24 points or more (on a scale with a mean of 100 and SD of 16) are designated as E profiles (*E* stands for extreme). For example, E (Q−) indicates that a student has an extreme or severe weakness in Quantitative Reasoning. Approximately 14% of students have this type of profile.

- ◆ **Level of Performance:** In addition to the pattern of performance, it is also important to consider the level of performance. To reflect the level of performance, the letter code is preceded by a number indicating their middle stanine score. For example, if a student received stanines of 4, 5, and 6 on the Verbal, Quantitative, and Nonverbal Reasoning batteries their middle stanine is 5. In classifying stanine scores, they classify Stanine 1 as Very Low, Stanines 2–3 as Below Average, Stanines 4–6 as Average, Stanines 7–8 as Above Average, and Stanine 9 as Very High.

As an example of a complete profile, the profile 8A would indicate a student with relative evenly developed Verbal, Quantitative, and Nonverbal Reasoning abilities with their general level of performance in the Above Average Range.

Riverside Publishing (2002) delineates a number of general principles for tailoring instruction to meet the needs of students (e.g., build on strengths as well as more specific suggestions for working with students with different patterns and levels of performance). *CogAT, Form 6: A Short Guide for Teachers* (Riverside Publishing, 2002) is an easy-to-read and very useful resource. It is available online at http://www.riverpub.com/products/cogAt/pdf/cogATshort.pdf.

COLLEGE ADMISSION TESTS. A final type of aptitude test includes those used to make admission decisions at colleges and universities. **College admission tests** were specifically designed to predict academic performance in college, and although they are less clearly linked to a specific educational curriculum than most standard achievement tests, they do focus on abilities and skills that are highly academic in nature. Higher education admission decisions are typically based on

TABLE 9–1	Organization of Major Group Aptitude/Intelligence Tests	
Aptitude Test	**Subtests**	**Composite Scores**
Tests of Cognitive Skills—Second Edition (TCS/2)	Sequences Analogies Verbal Reasoning Memory	Verbal ability Nonverbal ability Memory ability
Primary Tests of Cognitive Skills (PTCS)	Verbal Spatial Memory Concepts	Cognitive Skills Index (CSI)
InView	Verbal Reasoning—Words Verbal Reasoning—Context Sequences Analogies Quantitative Reasoning	Verbal reasoning Nonverbal reasoning Quantitative reasoning
Otis-Lennon School Ability Test—Eighth Edition (OLSAT-8)	Verbal Comprehension Verbal Reasoning Pictorial Reasoning Figural Reasoning Quantitative Reasoning	Verbal School Ability Index Nonverbal School Ability Index Total School Ability Index
Cognitive Abilities Test (CogAT), Form 6 (Levels K, 1, and 2)	Oral Vocabulary Verbal Reasoning Relational Concepts Quantitative Concepts Figure Classification Matrices	Verbal battery score Quantitative score Nonverbal score Overall composite score
Cognitive Abilities Test (CogAT), Form 6 (Levels A–H: Grades 3–12)	Verbal Classification Sentence Completion Verbal Analogies Quantitative Relations Number Series Equation Building Figure Classification Figure Analogies Figure Analysis	Verbal battery score Quantitative score Nonverbal score Overall composite score

a number of factors including high school GPA, letters of recommendation, personal interviews, written statements, and extracurricular activities, but in many situations scores on standardized admission tests are a prominent factor. The two most widely used admission assessment tests are the Scholastic Assessment Test (SAT) and the American College Test (ACT). Prior to the advent of these tests, admissions decisions were highly subjective and strongly influenced by family background and status, so another purpose for the development of these instruments was to make the selection process increasingly objective.

Scholastic Assessment Test. The College Entrance Examination Board (CEEB), commonly referred to as the College Board, was originally formed to provide colleges and universities with a valid measure of students' academic abilities. Its efforts resulted in the development of the first Scholastic Aptitude Test in 1926. The test has undergone numerous revisions and in 1994 the title was changed to Scholastic Assessment Test (SAT). The newest version of the SAT was administered for the first time in the fall of 2005 and includes the following three sections: Critical Reading, Mathematics, and Writing. Although the Critical Reading and Mathematics sections assess new content relative to previous exams, the most prominent change is the introduction of the Writing section. This section contains both multiple-choice questions concerning grammar and a written essay. The SAT is typically taken in a student's senior year. The College Board also produces the Preliminary SAT (PSAT), which is designed to provide practice for the SAT. The PSAT helps students identify their academic strengths and weaknesses so they can better prepare for the SAT. The PSAT is typically taken during a student's junior year. Several programs (e.g., the Duke Talent Search) also use these measures with younger students to locate highly capable students for participation early in advanced programs. More information about the SAT can be assessed at the College Board's website: http://www.collegeboard.com.

American College Test. The American College Testing Program (ACT) was initiated in 1959 and is the major competitor of the SAT. The American College Test (ACT) is designed to assess the academic development of high school students and predict their ability to complete college work. The test covers four skill areas—English, Mathematics, Reading, and Science Reasoning—and includes 215 multiple-choice questions. When describing the ACT, the producers emphasize that it is not an aptitude or IQ test, but an achievement test that reflects the typical high school curriculum in English, mathematics, and science. To assist in developing appropriate content, the ACT reviews and assesses the curriculum trends in the public schools of the United States every other year. In addition to the four subtests, the ACT also incorporates an interest inventory that provides information that may be useful for educational and career planning. Beginning in the 2004–2005 academic year, the ACT included an optional 30-minute writing test that assesses an actual sample of students' writing. More information about the ACT can be assessed at the ACT's website: http://www.act.org.

Individual Aptitude/Intelligence Tests

As with achievement tests, both group and individual intelligence tests are commonly used by psychologists in different areas of practice. The measures discussed in the following text are the most commonly used individually administered tests of intelligence in various settings. We caution our readers, however, that because intelligence tests are constantly being revised and updated, the following tests may not be the latest published versions. We present below information on the most recent versions of these tests at the time of preparation of this manuscript, but those who may use such tests need to be vigilant for revisions!

WECHSLER INTELLIGENCE SCALE FOR CHILDREN—FOURTH EDITION (WISC-IV). The Wechsler Intelligence Scale for Children—Fourth Edition (WISC-IV) is the fourth edition of the most popular individual test of intellectual ability for children. Empirical surveys of school psychologists and

> *Surveys of psychologists and other assessment personnel have consistently shown that the Wechsler scales are the most popular individual intelligence tests used in clinical and school settings with children and adults.*

other assessment personnel have consistently shown that the Wechsler scales are the most popular individual intelligence test used in clinical and school settings with children (e.g., Livingston, Eglsaer, Dickson, & Harvey-Livingston, 2003). The first version, known simply as the WISC, was published in 1949, and the first revision was not until 1974. Wechsler scales now are revised approximately every 10 to 12 years. The WISC-IV, which takes approximately 2 to 3 hours to administer and score, must be administered by professionals with extensive graduate-level training and supervised experience in psychological assessment. It is normed for use with children aged 6 through 16 years. For younger and older individuals, different versions of the Wechsler scales must be used. Here are brief descriptions of the subtests of the WISC-IV (Wechsler, 2003):

- *Arithmetic.* The client is presented a set of arithmetic problems to solve mentally (i.e., no pencil and paper) and answer orally. This subtest involves numerical reasoning ability, mental manipulation, concentration, and auditory memory.
- *Block Design.* The client reproduces a series of geometric patterns using red-and-white blocks. This subtest measures the ability to analyze and synthesize abstract visual stimuli, nonverbal concept formation, and perceptual organization.
- *Cancellation.* The client scans sequences of visual stimuli and marks target forms. This subtest involves processing speed, visual attention, and vigilance.
- *Coding.* The client matches and copies symbols that are associated with either objects (i.e., Coding A) or numbers (Coding B). This subtest is a measure of processing speed, short-term visual memory, mental flexibility, attention, and motivation.
- *Comprehension.* The client responds to questions presented orally involving everyday problems or social situations. This subtest is a measure of verbal comprehension and reasoning as well as the ability to apply practical information.
- *Digit Span.* The client is presented sequences of numbers orally to repeat verbatim (i.e., Digits Forward) or in reverse order (i.e., Digits Backwards). This subtest involves short-term auditory memory, attention, and on Digits Backwards, mental manipulation.
- *Information.* The client responds to questions that are presented orally involving a broad range of knowledge (e.g., science, history, geography). This subtest measures the student's general fund of knowledge.
- *Letter-Number Sequencing.* The client reads a list of letters and numbers and then recalls the letters in alphabetical order and the numbers in numerical order. This subtest involves short-term memory, sequencing, mental manipulation, and attention.
- *Matrix Reasoning.* The client examines an incomplete matrix and then selects the item that correctly completes the matrix. This subtest is a measure of fluid intelligence and is considered a largely language-free and culture-fair measure of intelligence.
- *Picture Completion.* The client is presented a set of pictures and must identify what important part is missing. This subtest measures visual scanning and organization as well as attention to essential details.

- *Picture Concepts.* The client examines rows of objects and then selects objects that go to-gether based on an underlying concept. This subtest involves nonverbal abstract reasoning and categorization.
- *Similarities.* Two words are presented orally to the client, who must identify how they are similar. This subtest measures verbal comprehension, reasoning, and concept formation.
- *Symbol Search.* The client scans groups of symbols and indicates whether a target symbol is present. This subtest is a measure of processing speed, visual scanning, and concentration.
- *Vocabulary.* The client is presented a series of words orally to define. This subtest is pri-marily a measure of word knowledge and verbal conceptualization.
- *Word Reasoning.* The client must identify the underlying or common concept implied by a series of clues. This subtest involves verbal comprehension, abstraction, and reasoning.

Information, Word Reasoning, Picture Completion, Arithmetic, and Cancellation are sup-plemental subtests whereas the other subtests are core subtests. The administration of supple-mental subtests is not mandatory, but they may be used to "substitute" for a core subtest if the core subtest is seen as being inappropriate for a particular student (e.g., due to physical limita-tion). A supplemental subtest may also be used if a core subtest is "spoiled" or invalidated for some reason (e.g., its administration is interrupted).

The WISC-IV produces four index scores, brief descriptions of which follow (Wechsler, 2003):

- *Verbal Comprehension Index (VCI).* The VCI is a composite of Similarities, Vocabulary, and Comprehension. Information and Word Reasoning are supplemental VCI subtests. The VCI reflects verbal reasoning, verbal conceptualization, and knowledge of facts.
- *Perceptual Reasoning Index (PRI).* The PRI is a composite of Block Design, Picture Concepts, and Matrix Reasoning. Picture Completion is a supplemental PRI subtest. The PRI reflects perceptual and nonverbal reasoning, spatial processing abilities, and visual–spatial–motor integration.
- *Working Memory Index (WMI).* The WMI is a composite of Digit Span and Letter–Number Sequencing. Arithmetic is a supplemental WMI subtest. The WMI reflects the student's working memory capacity that includes attention, concentration, and mental control.
- *Processing Speed Index (PSI).* The PSI is a composite of Coding and Symbol Search. Cancellation is a supplemental PSI subtest. The PSI reflects the student's ability to quickly process nonverbal material as well as attention and visual–motor coordination.

This four-index framework is based on factor analytic and clinical research (Wechsler, 2003). Similar index scores have a rich history of clinical use and have been found to provide reliable information about the student's abilities in specific areas (Kaufman, 1994; Kaufman & Lichtenberger, 1999; Wechsler, 2003). Whereas previous Wechsler scales have produced a Verbal IQ, Performance IQ, and Full Scale IQ, the WISC-IV reports only a Full Scale IQ (FSIQ), which reflects the student's general level of intelligence. The organization of the WISC-IV is depicted in Table 9–2. To facilitate the calculation of aptitude–achievement discrepancies, the WISC-IV is statistically linked to the Wechsler Individual Achievement Test—Second Edition (WIAT-II), which was described in Chapter 8.

The WISC-IV and its predecessors are designed for use with children between the ages of 6 and 16. For early childhood assessment the Wechsler Preschool and Primary Scale of Intelligence—Third

TABLE 9–2	Organization of the Wechsler Intelligence Scale for Children—Fourth Edition (WISC-IV)		
Subtests	**Index Scores**	**IQs**	
Information Vocabulary Similarities Comprehension Word Reasoning	Verbal Comprehension		
Block Design Picture Completion Matrix Reasoning Picture Concepts	Perceptual Reasoning		
Coding Symbol Search Cancellation	Processing Speed	Full Scale IQ	
Digit Span Arithmetic Letter–Number Reasoning	Working Memory		

Edition (WPPSI-III, which is now in revision) is available and is appropriate for children between 2 years 6 months and 7 years 3 months. The Wechsler Adult Intelligence Scale—Fourth Edition (WAIS-IV) is appropriate for individuals between the ages of 16 and 89 years. The WAIS-IV was published in 2008 and is structured almost identically to the WISC-IV.

STANFORD-BINET INTELLIGENCE SCALES, FIFTH EDITION (SB5).   As we noted, the Stanford-Binet Intelligence Test was the first intelligence test to gain widespread acceptance in the United States. Whereas the Wechsler scales have become the most popular and widely used intelligence tests in schools, the Stanford-Binet scales have maintained a strong following. The most recent edition of these scales is the **Stanford-Binet Intelligence Scale—Fifth Edition (SB5)**, released in 2003. The SB5 is designed for use with individuals from 2 to 85 years of age. It contains 10 subtests, which are combined to produce five factor indexes (i.e., Fluid Reasoning, Knowledge, Quantitative Reasoning, Visual–Spatial Processing, and Working Memory), two domain scores (i.e., Verbal IQ and Nonverbal IQ), and a Full Scale IQ reflecting overall intellectual ability. The organization of the SB5 is depicted in Table 9–3 (Riverside, 2003). A potentially appealing aspect of the SB5 is the availability of an Extended IQ scale that allows the calculation of FSIQs higher than 160. This can be useful in the assessment of extremely gifted individuals. At the time of this writing, SB5 is also under revision. The revision will be published by Pro-Ed, Inc.

> *An appealing aspect of the Stanford-Binet Intelligence Scales—Fifth Edition is the availability of an Expanded IQ scale that allows the calculations of IQs higher than 160.*

TABLE 9–3	Organization of the Stanford-Binet Intelligence Scales—Fifth Edition (SB5)	
Subtests	**Factor Scores**	**IQs**
Verbal Fluid Reasoning Nonverbal Fluid Reasoning	Fluid Reasoning (FR)	Verbal IQ (composite of 5 verbal subtests)
Verbal Knowledge Nonverbal Knowledge	Knowledge (KN)	
Verbal Quantitative Reasoning Nonverbal Quantitative Reasoning	Quantitative Reasoning (QR)	Nonverbal IQ (composite of 5 nonverbal subtests)
Verbal Visual–Spatial Processing Nonverbal Visual–Spatial Processing	Visual–Spatial Processing (VS)	
Verbal Working Memory Nonverbal Working Memory	Working Memory (WM)	Full Scale IQ (composite of all 10 subtests)

WOODCOCK-JOHNSON III TESTS OF COGNITIVE ABILITIES (WJ III COG). The **Woodcock-Johnson III Tests of Cognitive Abilities (WJ III COG)** has gained a loyal following and has some unique qualities that warrant mentioning. The battery is designed for use with individuals 2 to 90 years of age. The WJ III Tests of Cognitive Abilities is based on the Cattell-Horn-Carroll (CHC) theory of cognitive abilities, which incorporates Cattell's and Horn's *Gf-Gc* theory and Carroll's three-stratum theory. Special Interest Topic 9.5 presents a brief description of the CHC theory of intelligence. The CHC theory provides a comprehensive model for assessing a broad range of cognitive abilities, and many clinicians like the WJ III because it allows coverage of this broad range of abilities. The organization of the WJ III Tests of Cognitive Abilities is depicted in Table 9–4 (Riverside, 2003). The WJ III Tests of Cognitive Abilities is conormed with the WJ III Tests of Achievement described in Chapter 8.

> *The* WJ III Tests of Cognitive Abilities *is based on the Cattell-Horn-Carroll (CHC) theory of cognitive abilities, which incorporates Cattell's and Horn's Gf-Gc theory and Carroll's three-stratum theory.*

SPECIAL INTEREST TOPIC 9.5

The Cattell-Horn-Carroll (CHC) Theory of Intelligence and Its Impact on Contemporary Intelligence Test Batteries

Kevin S. McGrew
Woodcock-Muñoz Foundation University of Minnesota

Each mind has its own method.
—Emerson, 1841

Since the beginning of our existence, humans have searched for order in their world. Part of this search has focused on observed individual differences between and among different individuals and groups. This search has been propelled by the only universal proven law of human behavior—the law of individual differences. People differ on many characteristics and are more different than they are alike.

1. ***Psychometric theories of intelligence.*** The concept of *intelligence*, which has long attracted the interests of scholars and laypersons alike, has been the result of people observing that "individuals differ from one another in their ability to understand complex ideas, to adapt

(Continued on page 302)

SPECIAL INTEREST TOPIC 9.5 (*Continued*)

effectively to the environment, to learn from experience, to engage in various forms of reasoning, to overcome obstacles by taking thought" (Neisser et al., 1996, p. 77). "Though rarely appreciated outside academe, the breakthrough in objectively gauging the nature and range of mental abilities is a pivotal development in the behavioral sciences" (Lamb, 1994, p. 386). The objective measurement of mental abilities is referred to as the *psychometric* approach to intelligence. To date, of the different approaches to conceptualizing intelligence, the psychometric approach has been the most influential, has generated the most systematic research and, more importantly, has facilitated the development of the reliable, valid, and practical intelligence test batteries (Neisser et al., 1996).

2. **CHC theory has narrowed the intelligence theory testing gap.** Since the recognition of CHC theory as the first consensus-based, comprehensive, empirically validated working taxonomy (or table) of human cognitive elements (McGrew, 1997, 2005) in the early 1990s, it "has formed the foundation for most contemporary IQ tests" (Kaufman, 2009, p. 91). CHC theory has served, either explicitly or implicitly, as the main test blueprint for most all contemporary, comprehensive, individually administered intelligence test batteries (Differential Abilities Scales—Second Edition, DAS-II; Stanford—Binet Intelligence Scale—Fifth Edition, SB5; Kaufman Assessment Battery for Children—Second Edition, KABC-II; Woodcock-Johnson Battery—Third Edition, WJ III). CHC influence can also be seen in recent revisions of the Wechsler intelligence battery trilogy (WPPSI-III; WISC-IV; WAIS-IV; Kaufman, 2009) and has been acknowledged as a design influence for entirely new batteries (e.g., the Reynolds Intellectual Assessment Scales, RIAS; Reynolds & Kamphaus, 2003).

3. **Broad strokes of CHC theory.** The birth of psychometric efforts to measure, describe, and catalog human intelligence is typically associated with Spearman (1904). The psychometric study of human intelligence has since been lengthy and extensive and, recently converged on a generally accepted psychometric-based consensus taxonomy of human cognitive abilities namely, the *Cattell-Horn-Carroll (CHC)* theory of cognitive abilities (see McGrew, 2005, 2009). CHC theory is a hierarchical model of intelligence that combines the Cattell-Horn *Gf-Gc* (Horn, 1989) and Carroll (1993) tri-stratum models of cognitive abilities (see McGrew, 2005, 2009; also see Kaufman, 2009). CHC theory is a three-stratum model that includes over 70 narrow abilities at stratum I, 9 broad abilities at stratum II, and an overall *g* (general intelligence) ability at the apex of the hierarchy (stratum III).[1] The model is the results of decades of psychometric research by many intelligence scholars, primarily via factor analytic (structural evidence) research. Support for the CHC structure is also based on neurocognitive, heritability (genetic), developmental, and prediction of differential outcomes evidence (Horn & Noll, 1997). This model is depicted below.

4. **Broad CHC ability domains.** Nine broad (stratum II) CHC ability domains are generally accepted as the hallmark feature of CHC theory, of which typically five to seven broad abilities are represented by tests in contemporary intelligence batteries.[2] Brief definitions of the nine primary broad CHC abilities follow:[3]

   a. *Fluid reasoning* (*Gf*): The use of deliberate and controlled mental operations to solve novel problems that cannot be performed automatically. Inductive and deductive reasoning and logic are generally considered the hallmark indicators of *Gf*. *Gf* has been linked to the ability to handle greater degrees of cognitive complexity which is typically defined as more efficiency in processing a wider and diverse array of elementary cognitive processes (in active working memory) during cognitive performance.

---

[1]John Horn (no *g*) and John Carroll (*g* exists) were in sharp disagreement regarding the validity of the construct of *g*. Horn felt it was a statistical artifact of the positive manifold of correlation matrices whereas Carroll believed it did represent some form of essential mental energy. This author had the privilege to participate in small private meetings (during the development of the WJ III and SB5 intelligence test batteries) with both Horn and Carroll and can attest to many "spirited" exchanges regarding the "*g* or not to *g*" disagreement between these two giants in the field of human intelligence.

[2]Other broad domains that are relatively new to the CHC model, or which have not been deemed relevant to practical intelligence batteries, include decision and reaction speed (*Gt*), general (domain-specific) knowledge (*Gkn*), tactile abilities (*Gh*), kinesthetic abilities (*Gk*), olfactory abilities (*Go*), psychomotor abilities (*Gp*), and psychomotor speed (*Gps*). See McGrew (2009).

[3]Space does not allow for a list (with definitions) of the 70+ narrow abilities that are subsumed under the broad CHC domains. See McGrew (2005) for the names and definitions of the various narrow CHC abilities.

(Continued)

b. *Comprehension-knowledge* (*Gc*): A person's breadth and depth of acquired knowledge of the language, information and concepts of a culture, and/or the application of this knowledge. *Gc* is primarily a store of verbal or language-based declarative (knowing *what*) and procedural (knowing *how*) knowledge acquired through the investment of other abilities during formal and informal educational and general life experiences.

c. *Short-term memory* (*Gsm*): The ability to apprehend and maintain awareness of a limited number of elements of information in the immediate situation (events that occurred in the last minute or so). A limited resource-capacity system that loses information quickly through the decay of memory traces, unless an individual activates other cognitive resources to maintain the information in immediate awareness.

d. *Visual–spatial processing* (*Gv*): The ability to generate, store, retrieve, and transform visual images and sensations in the "mind's eye." *Gv* abilities are typically measured by tasks (viz., figural or geometric stimuli) that require the perception and transformation of visual shapes, forms, or images or tasks that require maintaining spatial orientation with regard to objects that may change or move through space.

e. *Auditory processing* (*Ga*): Abilities that depend on sound as input and on the functioning of hearing. A key characteristic of *Ga* is the extent an individual can cognitively control (i.e., handle the competition between signal and noise) the perception of auditory information. The *Ga* domain circumscribes a wide range of abilities involved in the interpretation and organization of sounds, such as discriminating patterns in sounds and musical structure (often under background noise and/or distorting conditions) and the ability to analyze, manipulate, comprehend and synthesize sound elements, groups of sounds, or sound patterns.

f. *Long-term storage and retrieval* (*Glr*): The ability to store and consolidate new information in long-term memory and later fluently retrieve the stored information (e.g., concepts, ideas, items, names) through association. Memory consolidation and retrieval can be measured in terms of information stored for minutes, hours, weeks, or longer. Some *Glr* narrow abilities have been prominent in creativity research (e.g., production, ideational fluency, or associative fluency).

g. *Cognitive processing speed* (*Gs*): The ability to automatically and fluently perform relatively easy or overlearned elementary cognitive tasks, especially when high mental efficiency (i.e., attention and focused concentration) is required over a sustained period of time. Typically measured by timed tasks.

h. *Reading and writing* (*Grw*): The breadth and depth of a person's acquired store of declarative and procedural reading and writing skills and knowledge. *Grw* includes both basic skills (e.g., reading and spelling of single words) and the ability to read and write complex connected discourse (e.g., reading comprehension and the ability to write a story).

i. *Quantitative knowledge* (*Gq*): The breadth and depth of a person's acquired store of declarative and procedural quantitative or numerical knowledge. *Gq* is largely acquired through the investment of other abilities primarily during formal educational experiences. *Gq* represents an individual's store of acquired mathematical knowledge, not reasoning with this knowledge.

5. ***Concluding comments and caveats.*** The connection between intelligence theorists and applied test developers has resulted in a small revolution in the field of applied intelligence testing. Most all comprehensive intelligence batteries implicitly or explicitly acknowledge the role of the CHC framework during test design. Yet, CHC theory should not be viewed as static. One should not succumb to the "hardening of the CHC categories" (McGrew, 2005, 2007) as new factor analytic research has already suggested possible modifications and revisions in the model. More importantly, a number of contemporary researchers are examining causal or dynamic CHC models (i.e., causal relations between CHC broad abilities), models that place the CHC structure within the framework of information processing theories, and research that seeks to understand the relations between CHC abilities and neurocognitive constructs and functioning. The CHC human ability taxonomy, although relatively new on the psychometric scene, should be considered just one major landmark accomplishment on the road to mapping the complete terrain of human cognitive performance. CHC has provided researchers and intelligence testing practitioners with a common nomenclature around

(Continued on page 304)

SPECIAL INTEREST TOPIC 9.5 (*Continued*)

which to frame and investigate research questions and issues. At this time the CHC taxonomy should be considered the first accurate starting point from which scholars of human intelligence can finally ground their research with an eye on refining, extending, and/or fundamentally revising the CHC framework to eventually better describe and explain human cognitive performance.

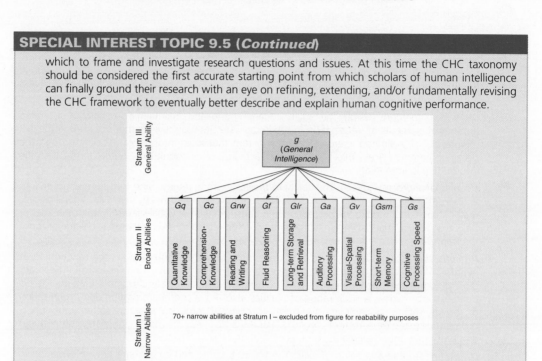

TABLE 9–4	Organization of the Woodcock-Johnson III Tests of Cognitive Abilities (WJ III COG)	
Subtests	**Factor Scores**	**IQs**
Verbal Comprehension General Information	Comprehension/Knowledge (*Gc*)	
Visual–Auditory Learning Retrieval Fluency Visual–Auditory Learning: Delayed	Long-Term Retrieval (*Glr*)	
Spatial Relations Picture Recognition Planning (*Gv/Gf*)	Visual–Spatial Thinking (*Gv*)	
Sound Blending Auditory Attention Incomplete Words	Auditory Processing (*Ga*)	General Intellectual Ability (GIA)
Concept Formation Analysis–Synthesis Planning (*Gv/Gf*)	Fluid Reasoning (*Gf*)	
Visual Matching Decision Speed Rapid Picture Naming Pair Cancellation	Processing Speed (*Gs*)	
Numbers Reversed Memory for Words Auditory Working Memory	Short-Term Memory (*Gsm*)	

REYNOLDS INTELLECTUAL ASSESSMENT SCALES (RIAS). The **Reynolds Intellectual Assessment Scales (RIAS)** by Reynolds and Kamphaus (2003) is a relative newcomer to the clinician's collection of intelligence tests rapidly growing in popularity in schools and in clinical settings. It is designed for use with individuals between 3 and 94 years of age and incorporates a conormed supplemental memory scale. One particularly desirable aspect of the RIAS is the ability to obtain a reliable, valid measure of intellectual ability that incorporates both verbal and nonverbal abilities in a relatively brief period (i.e., 20 to 25

> *One particularly desirable aspect of the Reynolds Intellectual Assessment Scales (RIAS) is the ability to obtain a reliable, valid measure of intellectual ability that incorporates both verbal and nonverbal abilities in a relatively brief period (20 to 25 minutes).*

minutes). Most other tests that assess verbal and nonverbal cognitive abilities require considerably more time. The supplemental memory tests require about 10 minutes for administration, so a clinician can assess both memory and intelligence in approximately 35 minutes. The organization of the RIAS is depicted in Table 9–5.

TABLE 9–5 Organization of the Reynolds Intellectual Assessment Scales (RIAS)		
Subtests	**Factor Scores**	**IQs**
Verbal Reasoning	Verbal Intelligence Index (VIX)	
Guess What		
Odd-Item Out	Nonverbal Intelligence Index (NIX)	Composite Intelligence Index (CIX)
What's Missing		
Verbal Memory	Composite Memory Index (CMX)	
Nonverbal Memory		

SELECTING APTITUDE/INTELLIGENCE TESTS

A natural question at this point is "Which of these tests should I use?" There are numerous factors to consider when selecting an aptitude or intelligence test. An initial consideration involves the decision to use a group or individual test. As is the case with standardized achievement tests, group aptitude tests are used almost exclusively for mass testing applications because of their efficiency. Even a relatively brief individual intelligence test typically requires

> *When selecting an intelligence or aptitude test, it is important to consider factors such as how the information will be used and how much time is available for testing.*

approximately 20 to 30 minutes per person to administer. Additionally, assessment professionals with special training in test administration are needed to administer these individual tests. A limited amount of time to devote to testing and a limited number of assessment personnel combine to make it impractical to administer individual tests to a large numbers of individuals, especially when screening procedures can be applied to cull individuals for more expensive, comprehensive assessment procedures. However, some situations demand the use of an individual intelligence test. This is often the case when disability determination is an issue or more complex diagnostic questions are to be addressed.

The first question to ask in deciding what measure to use is "What information do I really need about this person's level of intellectual function?" Tests should be chosen to provide information that answers important questions. When selecting an intelligence or aptitude test, it is also important to consider how the information will be used. Are you primarily interested in predicting performance in school or a vocational training program, or do you need a test that provides multiple scores reflecting different sets of cognitive abilities? As a general rule intelligence tests have been shown to be good at predicting academic success. Therefore, if you are simply interested in predicting school success practically any of these tests will meet your needs. If you want to identify the cognitive strengths and weaknesses of your students, you should look at the type of scores provided by the different test batteries and select one that meets your needs from either a theoretical or practical perspective. For example, a clinician who has embraced the Cattell-Horn-Carroll (CHC) theory of cognitive abilities would be well served using the RIAS, SB5, or the Woodcock-Johnson III Tests of Cognitive Abilities because they are based to different degrees on that model of cognitive abilities. The key is to select a test that provides the specific type of information you need for your application. Look at the type of factor and intelligence scores the test produces, and select a test that provides meaningful and practical information for your application.

If you are interested in making aptitude–achievement comparisons, ideally you should select an aptitude test that is conormed with an achievement test that also meets your specific needs. All of the major group aptitude tests we discussed are conormed or linked to a major group achievement test. When selecting a combination aptitude–achievement battery, you should examine both the achievement test and the aptitude test to determine which set best meets your specific assessment needs. In reference to the individual intelligence tests we discussed, only the WISC-IV and WJ III Tests of Cognitive Abilities have been conormed with or linked to an individual achievement test battery. Although it is optimal to use conormed instruments when aptitude–achievement comparisons are important, in actual practice many clinicians rely on aptitude and achievement tests that are not conormed or linked. In this situation, it is important that the norms for both tests be based on samples that are as nearly identical as possible. For example, both tests should be normed on samples with similar characteristics (e.g., age, race, geographic region) and obtained at approximately the same time (Reynolds, 1990).

Another important question involves the population you will use the test with. For example, if you will be working with children with speech, language, or hearing impairments or diverse cultural/language backgrounds, you may want to select a test that emphasizes nonverbal abilities and minimizes cultural influences. Finally, as when selecting any test, you want to examine the psychometric properties of the test. You should select a test that produces reliable scores and has been validated for your specific purposes. All of the aptitude/intelligence tests we have discussed have good psychometric properties, but it is the test user's responsibility to ensure that the selected test has been validated for the intended purposes.

UNDERSTANDING THE REPORT OF AN INTELLECTUAL ASSESSMENT

Special Interest Topic 9–6 presents an unedited computer-generated report of the intellectual assessment of a 64-year-old female referred for a psychological evaluation. Typically, you will not encounter an unedited computer-generated report. Such reports are, however, used by a school, clinical, and other psychologists as the foundation for their own individualized reporting on students. We thought it would be instructive for you to have the opportunity to read such a report in its raw state.

The report begins with a review of all the data gathered as a result of the administration and scoring of the intelligence test. You will see a number of terms employed that you have already learned throughout this text. You will see, for example, that confidence intervals based on the standard errors of measurement are applied to the various intelligence indexes and that not only standard scores but also percentile ranks are provided to assist in the interpretation. The report continues by providing brief background information on why Becky was being evaluated accompanied by several behavioral observations considered important by the person administering the test.

The next section of the report provides some caveats regarding proper administration and use of the results of the intellectual assessment. This section will clue the reader in to the assumptions that underlie the interpretation of the results that follow later in the report. A computer-generated report cannot take into account as yet the behavior of the examinee or any other extraneous factors that may necessitate altering standard interpretations of test performance as well as the professional examiner is capable of doing.

The next section of the report provides a narrative summary of Becky's scores on this intellectual assessment and provides norm-referenced interpretations. *Norm-referenced interpretations* are those that compare Becky's performance to other individuals of the same chronological age and who belong to the population sampled for development of the norms for this particular test. You will also see references within this section to the practical application of a confidence interval as well as estimates of true scores, all terms with which you have become acquainted earlier in this text.

Once the more global indexes of intellectual function have been reviewed, the report provides information on more specific intellectual tasks Becky completed. This is followed by a section where the pattern of Becky's intellectual development is discussed by the use of normreferenced discrepancy interpretations. Essentially, this section presents an actuarial analysis of the differences among Becky's scores across the different subdomains of intelligence evaluated during this assessment. Such an analysis logically leads to recommendations for understanding Becky's particular pattern of intellectual development and ways that it may be relevant to altering interventions. The next major section of the report deals precisely with feedback and recommendations. Here the reader is provided with a general understanding of the implications of these findings for Becky's behavioral concerns and alternative interventions are recommended. These are based on various studies of the implications of intelligence test results for examinee's behavior over many decades. In particular, the actuarial analyses of discrepancies in Becky's various areas of intellectual development have led to recommendations for some additional assessment as well as changes in interventions.

The purpose of all of the commentary in this report is ultimately to achieve an understanding of Becky's development and how it may be related to furthering her behavioral functioning.

The sample report focuses on recommendations for long-term care facilities. Other specialized reports can be generated separately for specialized clinical settings that make quite different recommendations and even provide provisional diagnoses that should be considered by the professional psychologist administering and interpreting the intellectual assessment. The reader should be aware that it is rare for a report to be based only on an intellectual assessment, and we doubt you will ever see such a report based on a singular instrument.

Typically, reports of the assessment of a client conducted by a diagnostic professional will include not only a thorough assessment of intellectual functions, such as reported in Special In-

(Continued on page 318)

SPECIAL INTEREST TOPIC 9.6

Example of a Computerized Report of an Intellectual Assessment of an Adult

RIAS™ Interpretive Report

Cecil R. Reynolds, PhD and Randy W. Kamphaus, PhD

Name: Becky R. Gibson	Gender: Female				
Ethnicity: Caucasian/White	Grade/Education: 12 years			Year	Month	Day
ID#:	Examiner: (not specified)	Date Tested	2009	4	7
Reason for referral: (not specified)	Referral source: (not specified)	Date of Birth	1944	9	1
		Age	64	7	6

RIAS Subtest Scores/Index Summary

Age-Adjusted *T* Scores

	Raw Scores	Verbal	Nonverbal		Memory
Guess What (GWH)	47	49			
Odd-Item Out (OIO)	33		28		
Verbal Reasoning (VRZ)	31	47			
What's Missing (WHM)	32		2		
Verbal Memory (VRM)	37				60
Nonverbal Memory (NVM)	30				16
Sum of *T* Scores		96 +	51 =	147	76

(Continued)

RIAS Indexes	VIX	NIX	CIX	CMX
	98	59	79	80

	VIX	NIX	CIX	CMX
Confidence Interval 95%	91–105	55–67	74–85	75–87
Confidence Interval 90%	92–104	56–66	75–85	76–86
Percentile Rank	45	0.31	8	9
	Verbal Intelligence Index	Nonverbal Intelligence Index	Composite Intelligence Index	Composite Memory Index

RIAS Total Battery Scores	TVB	TNB	TTB
	104	52	76

	TVB	TNB	TTB
Confidence Interval 95%	98–109	48–60	72–82
Confidence Interval 90%	99–109	49–59	73–81
Percentile Rank	61	0.07	5
	Total Verbal Battery Score	Total Nonverbal Battery Score	Total Test Battery Score

Background Information

Becky R. Gibson is a 64-year-old female. Becky has completed 12 years of education and is currently not attending school.

Caveat and Descriptive Text

The test scores, descriptions of performance, and other interpretive information provided in this computer report are predicated on the following assumptions. First, it is assumed that the various subtests were administered and scored correctly in adherence with the general and specific administration and scoring guidelines provided in Chapter 2 of the RIAS/RIST Professional Manual (Reynolds & Kamphaus, 2003). Second, it also is assumed that the examinee was determined to be appropriately eligible for testing by the examiner according to the guidelines for testing eligibility provided in Chapter 2 of the RIAS Professional Manual and that the examiner was appropriately qualified to administer and score the RIAS/RIST.

This report is intended for revelation, transmission to, and use by individuals appropriately qualified and credentialed to interpret the RIAS/RIST under the laws and regulations of their local jurisdiction and meeting the guidelines for use of the RIAS/RIST as stated in the RIAS Professional Manual (Reynolds & Kamphaus, 2003) (see Chapter 2).

(Continue on page 310)

SPECIAL INTEREST TOPIC 9.6 (*Continued*)

Becky was administered the Reynolds Intellectual Assessment Scales (RIAS). The RIAS is an individually administered measure of intellectual functioning normed for individuals between the ages of 3 and 94 years. The RIAS contains several individual tests of intellectual problem solving and reasoning ability that are combined to form a Verbal Intelligence Index (VIX) and a Nonverbal Intelligence Index (NIX). The subtests that compose the VIX assess verbal reasoning ability along with the ability to access and apply prior learning in solving language-related tasks. Although labeled the Verbal Intelligence Index, the VIX also is a reasonable approximation of crystallized intelligence. The NIX comprises subtests that assess nonverbal reasoning and spatial ability. Although labeled the Nonverbal Intelligence Index, the NIX also provides a reasonable approximation of fluid intelligence. These two indexes of intellectual functioning are then combined to form an overall Composite Intelligence Index (CIX). By combining the VIX and the NIX to form the CIX, a stronger, more reliable assessment of general intelligence (*g*) is obtained. The CIX measures the two most important aspects of general intelligence according to recent theories and research findings: reasoning or fluid abilities and verbal or crystallized abilities. Each of these indexes is expressed as an age-corrected standard score that is scaled to a mean of 100 and a standard deviation of 15. These scores are normally distributed and can be converted to a variety of other metrics if desired.

The RIAS also contains subtests designed to assess verbal memory and nonverbal memory. Depending on the age of the individual being evaluated, the verbal memory subtest consists of a series of sentences, age-appropriate stories, or both, read aloud to the examinee. The examinee is then asked to recall these sentences or stories as precisely as possible. The nonverbal memory subtest consists of the presentation of pictures of various objects or abstract designs for a period of 5 seconds. The examinee is then shown a page containing six similar objects or figures and must discern which object or figure was previously shown. The scores from the verbal memory and nonverbal memory subtests are combined to form a Composite Memory Index (CMX), which provides a strong, reliable assessment of working memory and also may provide indications as to whether or not a more detailed assessment of memory functions may be required. In addition, the high reliability of the verbal and nonverbal memory subtests allows them to be compared directly to each other.

For reasons described in the RIAS/RIST Professional Manual (Reynolds & Kamphaus, 2003), it is recommended that the RIAS subtests be assigned to the indexes described above (e.g., VIX, NIX, CIX, and CMX). For those who do not wish to consider the memory scales as a separate entity and prefer to divide the subtests strictly according to verbal and nonverbal domains, the RIAS subtests can be combined to form a Total Verbal Battery (TVB) score and a Total Nonverbal Battery (TNB) score. The subtests that compose the Total Verbal Battery score assess verbal reasoning ability, verbal memory, and the ability to access and apply prior learning in solving language-related tasks. Although labeled the Total Verbal Battery score, the TVB also is a reasonable approximation of measures of crystallized intelligence. The TNB comprises subtests that assess nonverbal reasoning, spatial ability, and nonverbal memory. Although labeled the Total Nonverbal Battery score, the TNB also provides a reasonable approximation of fluid intelligence. These two indexes of intellectual functioning are then combined to form an overall Total Test Battery (TTB) score. By combining the TVB and the TNB to form the TTB, a stronger, more reliable assessment of general intelligence (*g*) is obtained. The TTB measures the two most important aspects of general intelligence according to recent theories and research findings: reasoning, or fluid, abilities and verbal, or crystallized, abilities. Each of these scores is expressed as an age-corrected standard score that is scaled to a mean of 100 and a standard deviation of 15. These scores are normally distributed and can be converted to a variety of other metrics if desired.

Composite Norm-Referenced Interpretations

On testing with the RIAS, Becky earned a Composite Intelligence Index or CIX of 79. On the RIAS, this level of performance falls within the range of scores designated as moderately below average and exceeds the performance of 8% of individuals at Becky's age. The chances are 90 out of 100 that Becky's true CIX falls within the range of scores from 75 to 85.

Becky earned a Verbal Intelligence Index (VIX) of 98, which falls within the average range of verbal intelligence skills and exceeds the performance of 45% of individuals Becky's age. The chances are 90 out of 100 that Becky's true VIX falls within the range of scores from 92 to 104.

(Continued)

Becky earned a Nonverbal Intelligence Index (NIX) of 59, which falls within the significantly below average range of nonverbal intelligence skills and exceeds the performance of less than one percent of individuals Becky's age. The chances are 90 out of 100 that Becky's true NIX falls within the range of scores from 56 to 66.

Becky earned a Composite Memory Index (CMX) of 80, which falls within the below average range of working memory skills. This exceeds the performance of 9% of individuals Becky's age. The chances are 90 out of 100 that Becky's true CMX falls within the range of scores from 76 to 86.

On testing with the RIAS, Becky earned a Total Test Battery or TTB score of 76. This level of performance on the RIAS falls within the range of scores designated as moderately below average and exceeds the performance of 5% of individuals at Becky's age. The chances are 90 out of 100 that Becky's true TTB falls within the range of scores from 73 to 81.

Becky's Total Verbal Battery (TVB) score of 104 falls within the range of scores designated as average and exceeds the performance of 61% of individuals her age. The chances are 90 out of 100 that Becky's true TVB falls within the range of scores from 99 to 109.

Becky's Total Nonverbal Battery (TNB) score of 52 falls within the range of scores designated as significantly below average and exceeds the performance of less than one percent of individuals her age. The chances are 90 out of 100 that Becky's true TNB falls within the range of scores from 49 to 59.

Subtest Norm-Referenced Interpretations

The Guess What subtest measures vocabulary knowledge in combination with reasoning skills that are predicated on language development and acquired knowledge. On testing with the RIAS, Becky earned a T score of 49 on Guess What.

Odd-Item Out measures analytical reasoning abilities within the nonverbal domain. On testing with the RIAS, Becky earned a T score of 28 on Odd-Item Out.

Verbal Reasoning measures analytical reasoning abilities within the verbal domain. English vocabulary knowledge is also required. On testing with the RIAS, Becky earned a T score of 47 on Verbal Reasoning.

What's Missing measures spatial and visualization abilities. On testing with the RIAS, Becky earned a T score of 23 on What's Missing.

Verbal Memory measures the ability to encode, briefly store, and recall information in the verbal domain. English vocabulary knowledge also is required. On testing with the RIAS, Becky earned a T score of 60 on Verbal Memory.

Nonverbal Memory measures the ability to encode, briefly store, and recall information in the nonverbal and spatial domains. On testing with the RIAS, Becky earned a T score of 16 on Nonverbal Memory.

RIAS Discrepancy Score Summary Table

Discrepancy Score	Score Difference	Statistically Significant?	Prevalence in Standardization Sample
VIX > NIX	39	yes	<1%
CIX < CMX	1	no	93.80%
VRM > NVM	44	yes	<1%
TVB > TNB	52	yes	<1%

Note: VIX = Verbal Intelligence Index; NIX = Nonverbal Intelligence Index; CIX = Composite Intelligence Index; CMX = Composite Memory Index; VRM = Verbal Memory Subtest; NVM = Nonverbal Memory Subtest; TVB = Total Verbal Battery Index; TNB = Total Nonverbal Battery Index.

(Continued on page 312)

SPECIAL INTEREST TOPIC 9.6 (*Continued*)

Discrepancy Norm-Referenced Interpretations

Although the CIX is a good estimate of Becky's general intelligence, a statistically significant discrepancy exists between her VIX of 98 and her NIX of 59, demonstrating better developed verbal or crystallized abilities. The magnitude of the difference observed between these two scores is potentially important and should be considered when drawing conclusions about Becky's current status. A difference of this size is relatively uncommon, occurring in less than one percent of cases in the general population. In such cases, interpretation of the CIX or general intelligence score may be of less value than viewing Becky's verbal and nonverbal abilities separately.

Becky's overall level of performance on the CMX is consistent with her level of performance on the CIX, indicating that her working memory skills are developed in a manner consistent with her overall, general intellectual ability.

Within the subtests making up the CMX, Becky's performance in the verbal memory domain significantly exceeded her level of performance within the nonverbal memory domain. This difference is reliable and indicates that Becky functions at a significantly higher level when asked to recall or engage in working memory tasks that are easily adapted to verbal linguistic strategies, as opposed to tasks relying on visual–spatial cues and other nonverbal memory features. This discrepancy between verbal and nonverbal memory may take on special diagnostic significance because the magnitude of the difference observed here is relatively uncommon, occurring in less than 1 percent of the population at Becky's age.

Although the TTB is a good estimate of Becky's general intelligence, a significant discrepancy exists between her TVB score of 104 and her TNB score of 52, demonstrating better developed verbal or crystallized intellectual abilities. The magnitude of the difference observed between these two scores is potentially important and should be considered when drawing conclusions about Becky's current status. A difference of this size is relatively uncommon, occurring in less than one percent of cases in the general population. In such cases, interpretation of the TTB or general intelligence score may be of less value than viewing Becky's verbal and nonverbal abilities separately.

If interested in comparing the TTB and CIX scores or the TTB and CMX scores, it is better to compare the CIX and CMX directly. As noted in the RIAS/RIST Professional Manual (Reynolds & Kamphaus, 2003), the TTB is simply a reflection of the sum of the *T* scores of the subtests that compose the CIX and CMX. Thus, it is more appropriate to make a direct comparison of the CMX and CIX because any apparent discrepancy between the TTB and the CIX or the TTB and the CMX will in fact be a reflection of discrepancies between the CIX and the CMX, so this value is best examined directly. To compare the CMX or CIX to the TTB may exaggerate some differences inappropriately.

General Interpretive Caveats

Examiners should be familiar with the cultural and linguistic background of Becky (which may radically alter the suggestions contained herein) and be certain to consider these factors before arriving at a final decision regarding any diagnosis, classification, or related decision and before making any form of recommendations.

Assisted Living and Long-Term-Care Facility Feedback and Recommendations
Composite Score Feedback and Recommendations

Becky's CIX score of 79 and TTB score of 76 indicate moderate deficits in overall development of general intelligence relative to others at Becky's age. Individuals earning general intelligence scores in this range frequently experience at least moderate difficulty acquiring information through traditional educational methods, whether in the classroom, a vocational training program, or in another setting.

The TTB measures the same general construct as the CIX with the exception that six tests are included rather than four. Evidence in the RIAS/RIST Professional Manual (Reynolds & Kamphaus, 2003) documents the equivalence of these two scores based on evidence that a first factor solution is defensible at all age levels of the RIAS whether four or six subtests are used. There also is evidence from a variety of intelligence tests to suggest the "indifference of the indicator" (Kamphaus, in press). In other words, general intelligence may be assessed using a variety of cognitive tests providing further

(Continued)

evidence that for most individuals the TTB and CIX will be interchangeable. There will be exceptions to this well-documented scientific finding, in the case of severe brain injury, for example, where significant memory impairment may be present, but these cases will be exceptions rather than the rule.

Individuals with general intelligence scores in this range will experience difficulty following complex instructions and also may experience difficulty understanding and explaining their needs for care as well as other desires. They often require specialized cognitive and behavioral care plans including memory supports to ensure recall of and compliance with necessary routines such as self-care, as well as counseling and redirection when ill-informed or impulsive decisions are made. These individuals should be monitored for the presence or emergence of mental health disorders because of greater risk associated with lower general intelligence scores. A full mental health evaluation may be warranted if symptoms appear. However, in all instances, greater patience will be required on the part of caregivers in the caregiving process with Becky than might be necessary with others at the same age.

Becky's NIX score of 59 and TNB score of 52 indicate severe deficits in overall development of visual–spatial ability relative to others at Becky's age. Individuals at this score level on the TNB nearly always have accompanying nonverbal memory difficulties that can easily be moderate to severe in nature. Special attention to Becky's NVM score is necessary, as well as considerations for any extant nonverbal memory problems and their accompanying level of severity in making specific recommendations.

Visual–spatial skills are less highly correlated with general intelligence than verbal abilities and, therefore, deficits in this area may not cause as much functional impairment in settings where verbal skills are emphasized, such as training and educational programs. Nevertheless, visual–spatial impairment may cause problems in specialized settings and during tasks such as map reading, following flow charts, the visualization of directions given orally, puzzle solving requiring visualization, and the interpretation of symbols and relationships among them (e.g., in mathematics). Interpersonal impairment may occur in some cases where visual–spatial limitations cause an individual to miss visual cues (e.g., facial expressions).

Individuals at this age who are residing in assisted living or long-term care facilities and have visual–spatial information processing functions that are impaired at a level significantly below that of other seniors at the same age will experience a number of additional difficulties that require intervention. Difficulties with visual–spatial functions pose special problems that generally have a greater impact on day-to-day functions because visual–spatial knowledge is crucial for daily functioning (e.g., finding one's way around the house or facility; finding materials, possessions, and implements that are needed to enhance functioning). These individuals may have problems in conducting routine affairs of daily life and may have difficulty finding their belongings, room, or other locations, particularly when new learning is required. Even individuals in this age range with mild deficits, but especially those with more moderate to severe deficits relative to agemates, will experience difficulty in managing routine affairs (e.g., remembering faces). Regular assistance in the management of possessions is necessary for individuals within this age range who experience impaired visual–spatial functions relative to agemates, like Becky.

For individuals in assisted living or other long-term care facilities, special precautions are necessary in the presence of difficulties with visual–spatial functioning. When presenting visual–spatial information to Becky, verbal cues for future recall should be provided and a discussion of strategies for recall of visual–spatial information would be helpful. The use of multiple modalities is typically recommended to increase recall, such as routinely pairing visual–spatial stimuli with verbal stimuli in order to enhance recall. The use of lists, oral language and written language directions, and verbal reminders may be especially helpful. Translation of visual–spatial material into verbal material is recommended. For example, substituting or adding verbal directions to directions given via a map, graph, or picture (i.e., visually) is advised. Frequent verbal directions and reminders are recommended in most circumstances where recall needs to be enhanced. Family members or other caregivers also should be taught to use such techniques with Becky. Verbal reminders of activities and directions may be helpful if they are brief. For individuals who show only mild impairment relative to agemates (i.e., scores between 80 and 89), the use of verbal directions may be adequate.

(Continued on page 314)

SPECIAL INTEREST TOPIC 9.6 (*Continued*)

Becky's CMX of 80 falls within the low average range and indicates mild difficulties with recall of verbal and visual–spatial information relative to others Becky's age. This may cause mild problems and some consternation in the acquisition of new learning or academic or training material, but is unlikely to disturb most functions of day-to-day living.

Individuals at this age who are residing in assisted living or long-term care facilities and who have memory functions that are impaired at a level significantly below that of other seniors at the same age will experience a number of additional difficulties that require intervention. These individuals may have problems in conducting routine affairs of daily life and may have difficulty tracking the current year, month, and day, for example, in addition to being forgetful regarding even routinely scheduled activities. Even individuals in this age range with mild memory deficits, but especially those with more moderate to severe deficits relative to agemates, will experience difficulty in managing routine affairs such as the payment of bills and the recollection of due dates. Regular assistance in managing financial affairs is virtually always necessary for individuals within this age range who experience impaired memory function relative to agemates, as did Becky. If taking medication that is time sensitive, such individuals may forget to take their medication at the appointed time, forget whether they have taken their medication, and experience general confusion over which medications to take at which time. In assisted living and long-term care facilities, it is best for medication to be handled by appropriate staff and not left with the resident. If this cannot occur, and medication must be left with the resident, then medication should be sorted into a daily pill minder that is clearly marked with the day and time at which these medications are to be taken.

Often, the use of a large-print dry-erase wall calendar is helpful in maintaining schedules and assisting the individual in understanding not only their daily routine but any special activities that are scheduled for particular days such as doctor visits, visits with relatives, birthdays, anniversaries, and other important events. These calendars can be marked for a month in advance in most cases and hung in a highly visible position in Becky's room. To facilitate tracking of day and time, someone in the facility should be responsible for placing an *X* over each passing day when checking on this person at the time of the morning visit. Additionally, the use of radio frequency controlled clocks, commonly referred to as "atomic clocks," that automatically adjust the time, day of the week, and complete date are useful and have become relatively inexpensive in recent years. These clocks may be located next to the erasable calendar for ease of reference.

If Becky has a valid driver's license and continues to operate a motor vehicle, a formal driving evaluation also is recommended. Individuals at this age, even with mild levels of memory impairment relative to agemates, may experience difficulty with driving because of the common attentional deficits that accompany such memory problems as well as difficulty recalling specific directions and the ease of becoming lost. When these factors are coupled with routine decreases in reaction time that occur with age, motor vehicle operation requires special attention and clear discussion with family members. Although clearly some of these individuals continue to be able to operate a motor vehicle safely for an extended period of time, many do not, and a formal driving evaluation is urged as a safety precaution for the individual as well as the public.

For individuals like Becky, who show only mild impairment relative to agemates, the use of such common cognitive strategies as a daily calendar or small notebook may be useful as well as practice with rehearsal strategies. Research also has documented beneficial effects from routine, low-impact exercise such as walking including the use of a treadmill in the improvement of memory function in some elderly individuals, particularly those who are sedentary. Exercise has additional overall health benefits and whenever possible should be considered as a recommendation for improvement of lifestyle for seniors.

Becky's NVM score of 16 suggests that she will experience severe difficulties in the learning and recall of visual–spatial material, including maps, figures, graphs, drawings, locations, the arrangement of items on a written work, signs, faces, and directions that require visualization. These difficulties will likely occur even when Becky is presented material in a meaningful or experiential context, which should be performed because the use of concrete objects often aids recall.

(Continued)

The general recommendations provided for a CMX score of less than 90 or a VRM score of less than 43 are also applicable when NVM is less than 43. Because of Becky's visual–spatial deficits, however, the pairing of verbal material with visual–spatial information becomes particularly important when following these recommendations.

Individuals at this age who are residing in assisted living or long-term care facilities and who have visual–spatial memory functions that are impaired at a level significantly below that of other seniors at the same age will experience a number of additional difficulties that require intervention. Difficulties with visual–spatial memory functions pose special problems that generally have a greater impact on day-to-day functions because visual–spatial knowledge is crucial for daily functioning (e.g., finding one's way around the house or facility; finding materials, possessions, and implements that are needed to enhance functioning). These individuals may have problems in conducting routine affairs of daily life and may have difficulty finding their belongings, room, or other location, particularly if new learning is required. Even individuals in this age range with mild memory deficits, but especially those with more moderate to severe deficits relative to agemates, will experience difficulty in managing routine affairs such as remembering faces. Routine assistance in the management of possessions is necessary for individuals within this age range who experience impaired visual–spatial memory functions relative to agemates, as does Becky.

For individuals in assisted living or other long-term care facilities, special precautions are necessary because of difficulties with visual–spatial memory. When visual–spatial information is presented to Becky, verbal cues for future recall should be provided along with a discussion of strategies for the recall of visual–spatial information are helpful. The use of multiple modalities is typically recommended to increase recall, such as routinely pairing visual–spatial stimuli with verbal stimuli in order to enhance recall. The use of lists, oral language and written language directions, and verbal reminders may be especially helpful. Translation of visual–spatial material into verbal material is recommended (e.g., substituting or adding verbal instructions to directions given via a map, graph, or picture). Frequent verbal directions and reminders are recommended in most circumstances where recall needs to be enhanced. Family members or other caregivers also should be taught to use such techniques with Becky. A tape recording of instructions regarding an individual's daily activities, and the belongings or implements needed for each activity, may be helpful. Verbal reminders of activities and directions may be helpful if they are brief.

Discrepancy Feedback and Recommendations

The magnitude of discrepancy between Becky's VIX score of 98 and NIX score of 59 as well as the magnitude of the discrepancy between her TVB score of 104 and TNB score of 52 are relatively unusual within the normal population. This is especially true in referral populations where it is much more common for NIX or TNB to exceed VIX or TVB. In general, this pattern represents substantially disparate skills in the general domains of verbal and nonverbal reasoning with clear superiority evident in the verbal domain.

Residents with this pattern will experience great difficulty with spatial relationships and following demonstrations. Careful verbal explanation of what is expected of the resident along with a clear step-by-step guide to any actions the resident is expected to perform will be useful. Written directions to places that the resident frequents should be made available in large print and in an easily accessible location in the resident's room. Depending on the resident's overall level of intellectual function and degree of spatial confusion, Becky may become easily confused when outside familiar environments and should be verbally coached on where she is going, what to expect when she arrives, and any sequence of events that is not part of the daily routine. Careful verbal explanations of any medical procedures, changes in medication, and in the daily routine should be provided and the Becky should be allowed to explain these back to the caregiver to be sure they are understood. If reading ability is intact, the use of a written daily log or daily diary of events also can be useful to aid recall as well as to review and familiarize herself with her daily routine.

The magnitude of discrepancy between Becky's VRM score of 60 and NVM score of 16 is relatively unusual within the normative population, suggesting that memory for verbal material is greater

(Continued on page 316)

SPECIAL INTEREST TOPIC 9.6 (*Continued*)

than that for visual–spatial information. This profile indicates that adaptation could be improved by helping Becky develop compensatory skills to mitigate the impact of visual–spatial memory problems.

For individuals in assisted living or other long-term care facilities, special precautions are necessary in the presence of difficulties with visual–spatial memory. When presenting visual–spatial information to Becky, verbal cues for future recall should be provided along with a discussion of strategies for recall of visual–spatial information. The use of multiple modalities is typically recommended to increase recall, such as routinely pairing visual–spatial stimuli with verbal stimuli in order to enhance recall. The use of lists, oral language and written language directions, and verbal reminders may be especially helpful. Translation of visual–spatial material into verbal material is recommended (e.g., substituting or adding verbal directions to directions given via a map, graph, or picture). Frequent verbal directions and reminders are recommended in most circumstances where recall needs to be enhanced. Family members or other caregivers also should be taught to use such techniques with Becky.

A recording of directions for an individual's daily activities, along with the belongings or implements needed for each activity, may be helpful. Verbal reminders of activities and directions may be helpful if they are brief.

Recommendations for Additional Testing

In cases where the CMX falls below 90, additional follow-up assessment with a more comprehensive memory battery often provides additional clues and insights into appropriate instructional practices as well as rehabilitative exercises that may be most useful. Follow-up evaluation with a comprehensive memory battery should be given even stronger consideration when the CMX is below 90 and also falls at a level that is significantly below the CIX. Comprehensive memory batteries are recommended for such assessments because of the high degree of variability in performance produced by even small changes in memory tasks. The two most comprehensive batteries available are the Test of Memory and Learning—Second Edition (TOMAL-2; Reynolds & Voress, 2007) and the Wide Range Assessment of Memory and Learning—Second Edition (WRAML-2; Sheslow & Adams; 2003). Becky's VIX score of 98 and her TVB score of 104 are significantly higher than her NIX score of 59 score and her TNB score of 52. As such, follow-up evaluation may be warranted. Evaluations that consider disturbances in spatial functions and other right hemisphere related tasks may prove helpful. Evaluation of visual perceptual skills with measures such as the Developmental Test of Visual Perception-Adolescent and Adult (for ages 11 through 75 years; DTVP-A; Reynolds, Pearson, & Voress, 2002) may be particularly useful. This scale allows for evaluation of motor-reduced as well as motor-enhanced visual perceptual functions and spatial abilities. Other tests of specific nonverbal cognitive functions that might be considered include the age appropriate version of the Tactual Performance Test (Reitan & Wolfson; 1993), the Koppitz-2 Developmental Bender Scoring System for the Bender Gestalt Test (Reynolds, 2006), subtests of the Neuropsychological Assessment Battery (NAB; Stern & White; 2003), and other related tests of visual organization and nonverbal skills with which you are familiar and skilled. In addition, behavioral assessments are recommended when this pattern occurs in a referral population because this pattern has been associated with the presence of nonverbal learning disability and is more common in cases of Asperger's syndrome (i.e., not diagnostic in itself, but only suggestive of the need for additional evaluation if behavioral issues are present). Given Becky's age it is doubtful these will be fruitful areas to explore but should nevertheless be considered.

Becky's VRM score of 60 is significantly higher than her NVM score of 16. As such, follow-up evaluation may be warranted. Additional testing with the WRAML-2 (Sheslow & Adams, 2003), TOMAL-2 (Reynolds & Voress, 2007), or similar measure is suggested to determine if Becky's memory difficulties are modality-specific in that it is localized to either verbal or visual–spatial information, or if the impairment exists in short-term acquisition or long-term retrieval of previously learned material. A thorough history, supplemented by questions about qualitative aspects of memory, should be used as well. It also may be helpful to inquire about the individual's perception of memory problems and have her describe the onset, duration, and environmental contexts that are affected.

(Continued)

RIAS Extended Score Summary Table

Score	GWH	OIO	VRZ	WHM	VRM	NVM	VIX	NIX	CIX	CMX	TVB	TNB	TTB
Raw score	47	33	31	32	37	30							
T score (Mean = 50, SD = 10)	49	28	47	23	60	16	49	23	36	37	53	18	34
z-score (Mean = 0, SD = 1)	−0.10	−2.20	−0.30	−2.70	1.00	−3.40	−0.13	−2.73	−1.40	−1.33	0.27	−3.20	−1.60
Subtest scaled score (Mean = 10, SD = 3)	10	3	9	2	13	1							
Sum of subtest T scores							96	51	147	76	156	67	223
Index score (Mean = 100, SD = 15)							98	59	79	80	104	52	76
Percentile rank							45	0.31	8	9	61	0.07	5
95% confidence interval							91–105	55–67	74–85	75–87	98–109	48–60	72–82
90% confidence interval							92–104	56–66	75–85	76–86	99–109	49–59	73–81
NCE (Mean = 50, SD = 21.06)							47	1	21	22	56	1	16
Stanine (Mean = 5, SD = 2)							5	1	2	2	6	1	2

Source: From Reynolds, C. R., & Kamphaus, R. W. (2003). Reynolds Intellectual Assessment Scales. Lutz, FL: Psychological Assessment Resources. Reprinted with permission of PAR.

(Continued from page 307)

terest Topic 9.6, but also will include evaluations of mental status, personality, and behavior that may affect functioning, and specialized areas of cognitive abilities such as auditory perceptual skills, visual perceptual skills, visual motor integration, attention, concentration, and memory skills, among other important aspects of the development, that are dictated by the nature of the referral and information gathered during the ongoing assessment process.

Summary

In this chapter we discussed the use of standardized intelligence and aptitude tests in many settings. We started by noting that aptitude/intelligence tests are designed to assess the cognitive skills, abilities, and knowledge that are acquired as the result of broad, cumulative life experiences. We compared aptitude/intelligence tests with achievement tests that are designed to assess skills and knowledge in areas in which specific instruction has been provided. We noted that this distinction is not absolute, but rather one of degree. Both aptitude and achievement tests measure developed cognitive abilities. The distinction lies with the degree to which the cognitive abilities are dependent on or linked to formal learning experiences. Achievement tests should measure abilities that are developed as the direct result of formal instruction and training whereas aptitude tests should measure abilities acquired from all life experiences, not only formal schooling. In addition to this distinction, achievement tests are usually used to measure what has been learned or achieved at a fixed point in time, whereas aptitude tests are often used to predict future performance. Although the distinction between aptitude and achievement tests is not as clear as one might expect, the two types of tests do differ in their focus and are used for different purposes.

The most popular type of aptitude tests used by psychologists today is the general intelligence test. Intelligence tests actually had their origin in the public schools approximately 100 years ago when Alfred Binet and Theodore Simon developed the Binet-Simon Scale to identify children who needed special educational services to be successful in French schools. The test was well received in France and was subsequently translated and standardized in the United States to produce the Stanford-Binet Intelligence Test. Subsequently other test developers developed their own intelligence tests and the age of intelligence testing had arrived. Some of these tests were designed for group administration and others for individual administration. Some of these tests focused primarily on verbal and quantitative abilities whereas others placed more emphasis on visual–spatial and abstract problem-solving skills. Some of these tests even avoided verbal content altogether. Research suggests that, true to their initial purpose, intelligence tests are fairly good predictors of academic success. Nevertheless, the concept of intelligence has taken on different meanings for different people, and the use of general intelligence tests has been the focus of controversy and emotional debate for many years. This debate is likely to continue for the foreseeable future. In an attempt to avoid negative connotations and misinterpretations, many test publishers have switched to more neutral titles such as *school ability* or simply *ability* to designate the same basic construct.

Contemporary intelligence tests have numerous applications in today's practice of psychology. These include providing a broader measure of cognitive abilities than traditional achievement tests, helping teachers tailor instruction to meet students' unique patterns of cognitive strengths and weaknesses; determining whether students are prepared for educational experiences; identifying students who are underachieving and may have learning or other cognitive disabilities; identifying students for gifted and talented programs; helping students and parents make educational and career decisions; monitoring a variety of changes in mental functions in medical disorders, Alzheimer's disease, and other dementias; and many other clinical applications. For example, intelligence tests play a key role in the diagnosis of mental retardation, with performance 2 or more standard deviations below the mean on an individually administered test of intelligence being a necessary but insufficient condition for such a diagnosis.

One common practice when interpreting intelligence tests is referred to as aptitude–achievement discrepancy analysis and is often used when a learning disability is expected. This simply involves comparing a student's performance on an aptitude test with performance on an achievement test. The expectation is that achievement will be commensurate with aptitude. Students with achievement scores significantly greater than ability scores may be considered academic overachievers whereas those with achievement scores significantly below ability scores may be considered underachievers. There are a number of possible causes for academic underachievement ranging from poor student motivation to specific learning disabilities. We noted that there are different methods for determining whether a significant discrepancy between ability and achievement scores exists and that standards have been developed for performing these analyses. To meet these standards, many of the popular aptitude and achievement tests have been conormed or statistically linked to permit comparisons. We cautioned that although ability–achievement discrepancy analysis is a common practice, not all assessment experts support the practice. As we have emphasized throughout this text, test results should be interpreted in addition to other sources of information when making important decisions. This suggestion applies when making ability–achievement comparisons.

An alternative to the use of ability–achievement discrepancies for diagnosing learning disabilities is referred to as response to intervention (RTI). Currently, RTI appears to be a useful process that can help identify struggling students and ensure that they receive early attention and intervention. However, current research does not support the use of RTI as a stand-alone process for identifying students with LD. We believe the best approach for identifying students with LD is one that incorporates the best of RTI and psychometric assessment practices (e.g., intelligence tests).

In the next sections we examined a number of the popular group and individual intelligence tests. This included a brief review of college admissions testing where we noted their original purpose was to enhance the objectivity of college admissions procedures. In closing we provided some guidelines for selecting intelligence and provided an extended example of a report of an intellectual assessment.

Key Terms And Concepts

Aptitude tests, 279
Aptitude–achievement
    discrepancy, 288
Binet-Simon Scale, 285
College admission tests, 295
Intelligence, 282

Reynolds Intellectual Assessment Scales, (RIAS), 305
Stanford-Binet Intelligence Scale—Fifth Edition (SB5), 300

The Woodcock-Johnson III Tests of Cognitive Ability (WJ III COG), 301

Recommended Readings

Cronbach, L. J. (1975). Five decades of public controversy over mental testing. *American Psychologist, 36,* 1–14. An interesting and readable chronicle of the controversy surrounding mental testing during much of the twentieth century.

Fletcher-Janzen, E., & Reynolds, C. R. (Eds.). (2009). *Neuroscientific and clinical perspectives on the RTI initiative in learning disabilities diagnosis and intervention.* New York: Wiley. This text provides a review of the use of RTI in the identification of learning disabilities.

Kamphaus, R. W. (2001). *Clinical assessment of child and adolescent intelligence.* Boston: Allyn & Bacon. This text provides an excellent discussion of the assessment of intelligence and related issues.

Chapter Ten

Assessment
of Personality

*Once studied solely by introspection, assessment of personality is now
an objective science.*

Learning Objectives

After reading and studying this chapter, students should be able to:

1. Compare and contrast maximum performance tests and typical response tests.
2. Define and give examples of response sets.
3. Explain how test validity scales can be used to guard against response sets and give examples.
4. Explain factors that make the assessment of personality more challenging in terms of reliability and validity.
5. Distinguish between objective and projective personality tests and give examples of each.
6. Describe the major approaches to developing objective personality scales and give an example of each.

7. Describe the major features of the MMPI-2, its prominent applications, and its psychometric properties.
8. Describe the five-factor model of personality.
9. Describe special considerations related to the assessment of personality in children and adolescents and give examples of scales used with this population.
10. Define and give an example of a narrow-band personality scale.
11. Explain the central hypothesis of projective techniques and give examples of popular projective techniques.
12. Discuss the debate over the use of projective techniques.

321

In Chapter 1, when describing the different types of tests, we noted that tests typically can be classified as measures of either maximum performance or typical response. Maximum performance tests are often referred to as ability tests. On these tests, items are usually scored as either correct or incorrect, and examinees are encouraged to demonstrate the best performance possible. Achievement and aptitude tests are common examples of maximum performance tests. In contrast, typical response tests attempt to measure the typical behavior and characteristics of examinees. Typical response tests typically assess constructs such as personality, behavior, attitudes, or interests (Cronbach, 1990). In this chapter we will focus on the assessment of personality, but in other chapters we will address other instruments such as behavior (Chapter 11) and career interests (Chapter 12). Gray (1999) defined personality as "the relatively consistent patterns of thought, feeling, and behavior that characterize each person as a unique individual" (p. G12). This definition probably captures most people's concept of personality. In conventional assessment terminology, personality is defined in a similar manner, incorporating a host of emotional, motivational, interpersonal, and attitudinal characteristics (Anastasi & Urbina, 1997; Cronbach, 1990). Many of the tests we will address will be broad measures of personality. However, in this chapter we will also introduce some tests that measure narrow constructs such as depression or anxiety. It is common for both broad and narrow measures of personality to be referred to as inventories, but other terms are also used (e.g., *questionnaire, scale*).

ASSESSING PERSONALITY

> *Even though we might not consciously be aware of it, we all engage in the assessment of personality on a regular basis.*

Even though we might not consciously be aware of it, we all engage in the assessment of personality on a regular basis. When you note that "Johnny has a good personality," "Tammy is trustworthy," or "Tamiqua is extroverted," you are making a judgment about personality. We use these informal evaluations to determine whom we want to associate with and whom we want to avoid, among many other ways. The development of the first formal instrument for assessing personality typically is traced to the efforts of Robert Woodworth. In 1918, he developed the Woodworth Personal Data Sheet which was designed to help collect personal information about military recruits. Much as the development of the Binet scales ushered in the era of intelligence testing, the introduction of the Woodworth Personal Data Sheet, developed during World War I, ushered in the era of personality assessment. Subsequent instruments for assessing personality took on a variety of forms, but they all had the same basic purpose of helping us understand the personal characteristics of ourselves and others. Special Interest Topic 10.1 provides a brief description of an early informal test of personality.

Psychologists use personality inventories in different settings to answer different questions. Any attempt to list all of these applications would inevitably be incomplete, but we will highlight some major uses here:

- Psychologists and other mental health professionals use personality inventories to facilitate diagnosis and help plan treatment. It is often apparent from clinical interviews and observations that a client is experiencing some form of psychopathology, but identifying the specific disorder(s) can often be quite challenging. A review of the

SPECIAL INTEREST TOPIC 10.1

The Handsome and the Deformed Leg

Sir Francis Galton (1884) related a tale attributed to Benjamin Franklin about a crude test of personality. Franklin describes two basic types of people, those who are optimistic and focus on the positive and those who are pessimistic and focus on the negative. Franklin reported that one of his philosophical friends desired a test to help him identify and avoid people who were pessimistic, offensive, and prone to acrimony.

> In order to discover a pessimist at first sight, he cast about for an instrument. He of course possessed a thermometer to test heat, and a barometer to tell the air-pressure, but he had no instrument to test the characteristic of which we are speaking. After much pondering he hit upon a happy idea. He chanced to have one remarkably handsome leg, and one that by some accident was crooked and deformed, and these he used for the purpose. If a stranger regarded his ugly leg more than his handsome one he doubted him. If he spoke of it and took no notice of the handsome leg, the philosopher determined to avoid his further acquaintance. Franklin sums up by saying, that every one has not this two-legged instrument, but every one with a little attention may observe the signs of a carping and fault-finding disposition. (pp. 9–10)

Source: This tale was originally reported by Sir Francis Galton (1884). Galton's paper was reproduced in Goodstein & Lanyon (1971).

DSM–IV–TR reveals that many disorders present with overlapping symptoms, and identifying the correct disorder and ruling out competing diagnosis is referred to as *differential diagnosis*. Personality inventories can help with this process. Repeated assessments are also used in clinical practice to monitor the client's progress. This applies to the efficacy of both psychopharmacological and psychological interventions. That is, repeated assessments can reveal what is working to help the client and what is not.

- Psychologists frequently use personality inventories to enhance their client's self-understanding and self-actualization. Although some personality measures are designed to facilitate clinical diagnosis (as described previously), some are designed to assess normal personality functioning and enhance the individual's functioning in a number of spheres (e.g., personal, social, and marital adjustment). Special Interest Topic 10.2 describes therapeutic assessment, a novel approach that uses assessment as the centerpiece of a clinical intervention.

- Psychologists routinely use measures of personality to identify children with emotional and behavioral disorders that interfere with the ability to learn in schools. Some of these children may receive special education services under the Individuals with Disabilities Education Act (IDEA). For example, psychologists in the schools use personality tests to assist in determining eligibility for special education programs under the designation of emotionally disturbed and to assist in arriving at the appropriate intervention for the emotional issues present.

- Psychologists use a variety of personality measures to help determine which job applicants will become successful employees. Likewise they use personality measures to help current employees better understand themselves and their colleagues, thus enhancing the workplace environment.

- Psychologists use measures of personality to answer questions relevant to legal proceedings such as competency to stand trial or future dangerousness.
- Psychologists in academic and research settings use personality tests to measure a multitude of constructs in a wide range of psychological research.

SPECIAL INTEREST TOPIC 10.2

Therapeutic Assessment

Hale Martin, PhD

University of Denver

Can psychological assessment change someone's life? Some psychologists believe it can, and have research to back it up. Stephen E. Finn at the Center for Therapeutic Assessment in Austin, Texas, has led the way in developing and empirically grounding an approach to assessment that research suggests works as a brief therapy. Time-honored psychological tests can yield insights about people's persistent problems and difficulties. Finn and others contend that if these insights are offered back to clients in a supportive, sensitive, and clinically astute way, it will have a positive impact on clients' lives. This argument is a far cry from previous concerns that hearing testing results could damage people. The accumulating evidence is on the side of Finn and others who are working to develop strategies for using testing to help clients overcome problems, grow emotionally, and improve relationships.

Collaboration is a central aspect of the semistructured approach developed by Dr. Finn, which he calls *therapeutic assessment*. Finn built on the seminal work of Dr. Constance Fischer at Duquesne University who first advanced the value of collaborative assessments in the 1970s. Her sensible approach began the movement of assessment from esoteric—and often unhelpful—understanding to practical, helpful interventions that had a positive impact on the client. Fischer focuses on the practical. For example, for an assessment of a food server with organizational problems, Fischer might begin by visiting the coffee shop where the server worked to watch how she functioned in that setting. Then, when they met in the office, Fischer might ask her to copy a set of geometric figures on paper (the Bender Gestalt Test) and talk about the disorganization that appeared in those drawings. Fischer might then ask if the woman could think of a better way to approach the drawings, have her try out that way and assess the success of that strategy. If it worked, Fischer would talk with the woman about how to export that new approach back to the coffee shop. If it did not work, Fischer would guide the woman to a solution that might work, then try out that solution. This approach can be more helpful than a feedback session and traditional report written to the referring professional focusing on a diagnosis, such as ADHD.

In therapeutic assessment, collaboration between assessor and client begins from the start with clients identifying what questions they need answered to better deal with their current struggles in life. Typically, clients ask such questions as "Why do I have so much trouble keeping relationships?", "Where does all my anger come from?", or "Am I depressed?" The assessor then directs the assessment in search of those answers and helps the client understand the assessment findings in useful ways. Finn believes that psychological assessment can produce longstanding change if it helps clients improve the accuracy and quality of their "story" about themselves and the world. This can't be done recklessly because our stories about ourselves and the world are central props that we all use to feel safe in the world. However, by using clients' motivation, which is often high when they come in for assessment, and their active involvement in examining and revising their story, a new story can emerge that better explains the clients' behaviors and the world around them. This new story coauthored by the client can produce changes that last long after an assessment is completed.

Helping the client feel safe and emotionally supported is essential. The empathy that the assessor can develop through the tests and the resulting relationship between assessor and client provide a

(Continued)

powerful basis for decreasing shame and increasing self-esteem. Research has demonstrated that increases in self-esteem, elusive in even some long courses of therapy, can be realized quickly as a result of the therapeutic assessment process. With increases in self-compassion, clients are able to make meaningful changes in their lives.

Furthermore, therapeutic assessment applies our growing understanding that experience, not just intellectual insight, is important for change to occur. One of the last steps in a therapeutic assessment, called the assessment intervention session, creates an *in vivo* experience related to the main struggles clients face and works to help clients have a different experience with their problems. For example, an assessor might use a picture story technique like the Thematic Apperception Test to put a client face–to-face with her issues. When working with a client who the testing suggests avoids emotions, the assessor might select cards that pull for strong emotions. By noting the client's characteristic responses and eliciting the client's curiosity about them, the assessor guides the client to greater self-insight.

It doesn't stop there. Recognizing the importance of felt experience, the assessor devises ways for the client to handle the challenging situation in a new way that offers hope of new solutions to old problems. The assessor and client explore the resistances, fears, and obstacles as well as the excitement and hope the new experience offers. This experiential learning is carefully built from the insights derived from the empirical testing results. It can be a pivotal experience for the client and paves the way to deeper and more meaningful discussion of testing results. Therapeutic assessment can have a powerful impact on assessors as well, as they closely attune to the lives of others and learn how others change their life trajectories.

An example comes from Finn's book *In Our Clients' Shoes,* in which he reports a therapeutic assessment with David, a 28-year-old man whose therapy was floundering. David had been in treatment for several years with a therapist named Elizabeth, focusing on being more successful at work and in relationships. As a child David had been diagnosed with attention deficit disorder (ADD), which he believed explained his lack of attention, poor memory, disorganization, and perhaps the meandering course of therapy. However, Elizabeth had come to wonder whether bipolar or dissociative disorder might better explain the problems. David readily agreed to the assessment and the journey to new understanding began.

Through a careful initial interview, Dr. Finn helped David frame his own questions for the assessment:

1. Do I really have ADD, and if not, why do I have trouble concentrating and remembering things?
2. Why can't I break up with girlfriends when they're treating me badly? What in me is too weak to do this?
3. Why is it so hard for me to be alone?

Subsequent testing sessions were designed to collaboratively answer these questions, the results of which were shared along the way. The results revealed an unrecognized, severe, chronic depression that David had coped with since childhood by attempting to screen out distressing emotions that threatened to push him into an abyss. David reported a childhood with divorced parents who were absorbed in their own problems and clearly were unable to meet his emotional needs. He was left to cope with the world as best as he could.

The assessment intervention session alternated stimulating strong feelings through telling stories to highly emotional pictures and measuring David's ability to remember numbers. This tactic clearly demonstrated that when his emotions were high, David's memory suffered—which illustrated *in vivo* an important answer: His struggle to manage difficult emotions impaired his attention and memory. Furthermore it became apparent that David was easily overwhelmed and disorganized by emotions, especially anger. Additionally, his early relationship experiences led him to expect his emotional needs would not be met, while at the same time he held on to whatever hope of being nurtured he found. Finally in this session, through telling stories to the carefully selected pictures, David had a breakthrough emotional experience and was able to feel how overwhelmed and lonely he had been as a child. Dr. Finn handled this feared vulnerability gently, which helped David assimilate it.

(Continued on page 326)

In the final session with David and Elizabeth, David himself explained "how 'old feelings' were causing his 'brain to melt down.'" Dr. Finn added that those old feelings also made it difficult for David to be alone and kept him in bad relationships. Dr. Finn stressed the importance of having people in our lives, beginning with parents, who can keep us from being too overwhelmed and help us become increasingly competent in managing emotions. He outlined a way that David could grow in this regard. Through the assessment process, the answers to the initial questions had become clear. David's struggles were not rooted in ADHD, bipolar, or dissociative disorder but rather in the limitations of his early adaptation to difficult emotions.

The impact of the assessment was substantial. Six years later as Dr. Finn wrote about the case, Elizabeth reported that David had worked in treatment for 5 years and that his emotional facility had grown. He had married a loving woman a year previously, and they were expecting their first child, which if a female, he would name Elizabeth. He had received the help that he needed to get his life unstuck. Elizabeth also had grown from the experience, recognizing her own need to reach out for help when she felt overwhelmed.

The therapeutic assessment approach can be applied to a range of assessments. Most research to this point has been with individuals, but Finn has used variations of therapeutic assessment with couples and to help families change the inaccuracies in the stories they have about their children. A couple's assessment strives to help both members understand themselves better but also to see their contribution to problems the couple has. The couple is videotaped to highlight problematic patterns in their interactions, and this often has a powerful effect in changing those interactions. A child–family assessment involves the parents throughout the assessment process with the child. Research that Finn and Dr. Deborah Tharinger are spearheading at the University of Texas at Austin shows powerful outcomes that result from addressing the all-important system in which the child grows up. The child–family assessor also gives the child a new perspective by writing and presenting an age-appropriate fable or story that captures the child's dilemma and offers alternatives. Others are working to adapt the therapeutic assessment approach to neuropsychological assessment and even as an alternative to some forensic assessments.

How far can therapeutic assessment go in changing the way assessors work with their clients? Could this therapeutic approach have utility for managed care, which is constantly looking for short-term, effective, interventions? The future will tell, but with the accumulating supporting research and the increasing prominence of therapeutic assessment in the psychology community, the answers are on the way.

Personality is a complex, multidimensional construct. As such, it cannot be summarized in one omnibus score, and personality tests typically attempt to measure multiple dimensions or aspects of personality. This is accomplished through the use of multiple scale or factor scores. The scales on a personality test vary greatly from test to test depending on the purpose of the instrument. For example, personality tests that are designed to be used in clinical settings to facilitate the diagnosis of mental disorders often contain scales reflecting constructs such as depression, anxiety, psychosis, and aggressiveness. Personality tests that are designed to be used in a general population will typically have reflecting dimensions such as introversion–extroversion, agreeableness, and dependability. As you will see there are different approaches to developing these scales. However, before we describe them we will introduce the concept of response sets, an important topic when considering the use of personality tests.

Response sets and dissimulation *are test responses that misrepresent a person's true characteristics.*

Response Sets and Dissimulation

Response sets and dissimulation are test responses that misrepresent a person's true characteristics. When a person unconsciously responds in either a negative or positive manner he or she is evidencing a response set; when the person purposefully misrepresents himself or herself it is dissimulation. In both cases the respondent's true characteristics are distorted or misrepresented. For example, an individual completing an employment-screening test might attempt to present an overly positive image by answering all of the questions in the most socially appropriate manner possible, even if the responses do not accurately represent the person. On the other hand, an individual who is hoping to win a large settlement in a court case might exaggerate the mental distress he or she is experiencing as the result of a traumatic event. In both of these situations the individual completing the test or scale consciously or unconsciously responded in a manner that distorted reality.

Response sets and dissimulation can be present when completing maximum performance tests. For example, an individual with a pending court case claiming neurological damage resulting from an accident might "fake bad" on an intelligence test in an effort to substantiate the presence of brain damage and enhance his or her legal case. However, they are an even bigger problem on typical performance tests. Because many of the constructs measured by typical performance tests (e.g., personality, behavior, attitudes, and beliefs) have dimensions that may be seen as either socially "desirable" or "undesirable," the tendency to employ a response set is heightened. When response sets or dissimulation are present, the validity of the test results may be compromised because they introduce construct-irrelevant error to test scores (e.g., AERA et al., 1999). That is, the test results do not accurately reflect the construct the test was designed to measure. To combat this, many typical performance tests incorporate some type of validity scale designed to detect the presence of response sets and dissimulation. **Validity scales** take different forms, but the general principle is that they are designed to detect individuals who are not responding in an accurate manner.

> **Validity scales** *take different forms, but the general principle is that they are designed to detect individuals who are not responding in an accurate manner.*

To illustrate some different types of validity scales we will briefly review the validity scales included in the Behavior Assessment System for Children—Self-Report of Personality (SRP; Reynolds & Kamphaus, 2004). The SRP includes three validity scales, an F index, L index, and V index. The F index is composed of items that are "infrequently" endorsed in a specific manner in a normal population. For example, very few children or adolescents indicate that they are "not a good friend" or that they "often cheat on tests." This type of validity scale is often referred to as an *infrequency index*. If an examinee endorses enough of these items in the keyed direction, his or her F index will be elevated. High scores on the F index can be the result of numerous factors, ranging from reading difficulties to an intentional desire to "fake bad" to look more disturbed or pathological. The second SRP validity scale is the L index, which also contains items that are rarely endorsed in a specific manner in a normal population. The distinction is that items on this scale are intended to identify individuals with a "social desirability" response set (i.e., examinees who are trying to "fake good"). For example, few adolescents who are responding honestly will indicate that "their life is perfect" or that "their teachers are always

> *The development and use of personality assessments are plagued with challenges above and beyond those present in other areas of psychological assessment.*

right." High scores on the L index may suggest that the SRP clinical scales underestimate any existing emotional or behavioral problems. The final validity scale is the V index, which is composed of nonsensical items that may be endorsed due to carelessness, reading difficulty, or simply a refusal to cooperate. An example of an item that might be included in the V index is "Batman is my best friend." Special Interest Topic 10.3 provides an example of a fake good response set and how the use of the SRP Lie scale helps identify this response set.

SPECIAL INTEREST TOPIC 10.3

An Example of a "Fake Good" Response Set

Self-report inventories, despite the efforts of test developers, always remain susceptible to response sets. The following case is an authentic example. In this case the Behavior Assessment System for Children—Self-Report of Personality (SRP) was used.

Maury was admitted to the inpatient psychiatric unit of a general hospital with the diagnoses of impulse control disorder and major depression. She is repeating the seventh grade this school year because she failed to attend school regularly last year. When skipping school, she spent time roaming the local shopping mall or engaging in other relatively unstructured activities. She was suspended from school for lying, cheating, and arguing with teachers. She failed all of her classes in both semesters of the past school year.

Maury's responses to the diagnostic interview suggested that she was trying to portray herself in a favorable light and not convey the severity of her problems. When asked about hobbies, for example, she said that she liked to read. When questioned further, however, she could not name a book that she had read.

Maury's father reported that he has been arrested many times. Similarly, Maury and her sisters have been arrested for shoplifting. Maury's father expressed concern about her education. He said that Maury was recently placed in an alternative education program designed for youth offenders.

Maury's SRP results show evidence of a social desirability or fake good response set. All of her clinical scale scores were lower than the normative T-score mean of 50 and all of her adaptive scale scores were above the normative mean of 50. In other words, the SRP results suggest that Maury is optimally adjusted, which is in stark contrast to the background information obtained.

Maury's response set, however, was identified by the Lie scale of the SRP, where she obtained a score of 9, which is on the border of the caution and extreme caution ranges. The following table shows her full complement of SRP scores.

Clinical Scales		Adaptive Scales	
Scale	*T*-Score	Scale	*T*-Score
Attitude to School	41	Relations with Parents	53
Attitude to Teachers	39	Interpersonal Relations	57
Sensation Seeking	41	Self-Esteem	54
Atypicality	38	Self-Reliance	52
Locus of Control	38		
Somatization	39		
Social Stress	38		
Anxiety	34		
Depression	43		
Sense of Inadequacy	41		

Source: Clinical Assessment of Child and Adolescent Personality and Behavior (2nd ed., Box 6.1, p. 99), by R. W. Kamphaus and P. J. Frick, 2002, Boston: Allyn & Bacon. Copyright 2002 by Pearson Education. Reprinted with permission.

Factors Affecting Reliability and Validity

Anastasi and Urbina (1997) noted that the development and use of personality assessments are plagued with challenges above and beyond those present in other areas of psychological assessment. For example, as just discussed response sets are often present in personality assessment and may compromise the validity of the results. Whereas responses biases may influence performance on maximum performance tests, they are far more problematic on personality assessments. Additionally, the constructs measured by personality tests may be less stable than the constructs measured by maximum performance tests. In this context it is useful to distinguish between psychological traits and states. A trait is a stable internal characteristic that is manifested as a tendency for an individual to behave in a particular manner. For example, introversion–extraversion is often considered a trait that is fairly stable over time. Cronbach (1990) stated that 6-year test-retest reliability coefficients of approximately 0.80 have been reported for broad personality traits and that these correlations can exceed 0.90 when correcting for short-term fluctuations. In contrast, psychological states are transient emotional states that fluctuate over time. Test-retest reliability coefficients will naturally be lower when measuring state-related constructs compared to constructs reflecting broad traits, and as Cronbach noted, these transient emotional states may influence attempts to measure more stable constructs.

We also have to be careful when talking about or considering the test-retest reliability of all measures, but especially personality test scores. For some reason, the field continues to confuse the accuracy of measurement at one point in time with the stability of the underlying attribute. Often, when measuring unstable variables, psychologists will refer to the test-retest reliability of the score as poor or as having poor accuracy when in fact the test has measured the variable quite well on both occasions. If you had a piece of wood and measured it under extremely dry conditions and it was 100 millimeters long, and you then soaked it in water overnight and measured it the next day and it was 103 millimeters long—would you say your ruler was unreliable? Probably not: The length of the board has actually changed and the measuring device measured it with a very high degree of accuracy both times.

Special Interest Topic 10.4 presents a discussion of the "Forer Effect." The discovery of this effect significantly influenced the way validity evidence for personality tests was collected.

OBJECTIVE PERSONALITY TESTS: AN OVERVIEW

A search of the *Mental Measurements Yearbook* results in the identification of over 600 tests listed in the category on personality tests. Obviously we will not be discussing all of these tests, but we will introduce a few major contemporary personality measures in this chapter. We will describe two broad categories of personality measures: objective self-report measures and projective techniques. Objective self-report measures are those where respondents endorse selected-response items to reflect their characteristic ways of behaving, feeling, thinking, and so on. Projective techniques are steeped in psychodynamic theory traditionally and involve the presentation of unstructured or ambiguous stimuli that allows an almost infinite range of responses from the respondent. For example, the clinician shows the examinee an inkblot and asks: "What might this be?" With projective measures the stimuli are thought to serve as a blank screen on which the examinee "projects" his or her thoughts, desires, fears, needs, and conflicts.

SPECIAL INTEREST TOPIC 10.4

The Forer Effect—or, You and Your Aunt Fanny!

Read the following paragraph carefully and then stop and immediately ask yourself this question: *How accurately does this describe me and my personality in general?* Answer the question to yourself before reading on.

> You have a need for other people to like and admire you, and yet you tend to be critical of yourself. While you have some personality weaknesses you are generally able to compensate for them. You have considerable unused capacity that you have not turned to your advantage. Disciplined and self-controlled on the outside, you tend to be worrisome and insecure on the inside. At times you have serious doubts as to whether you have made the right decision or done the right thing. You prefer a certain amount of change and variety and become dissatisfied when hemmed in by restrictions and limitations. You also pride yourself as an independent thinker and do not accept others' statements without satisfactory proof. But you have found it unwise to be too frank in revealing yourself to others. At times you are extroverted, affable, and sociable, while at other times you are introverted, wary, and reserved. Some of your aspirations tend to be rather unrealistic.

Our bet is that this statement describes you reasonably well—how did we know that? Are we just impossibly psychic?

In the early days of personality assessment, one approach to the validation of the interpretation of personality test scores that was quite popular was to have people take the test and then have aa psychologist familiar with the test write a description of the examinee's personality structure. This description would be given to the examinee, along with the interpretation given by the psychologist based on the examinee's own scores. Each examinee would then complete a rating scale, indicating to what extent he or she agreed with the description, and its overall level of accuracy as applied to the individual examinee. Not surprisingly, this approach to validating the interpretations of personality test scores usually turned out well for the test and its interpretation.

However, the level of agreement was dependent on a variety of factors beyond the actual personality test profile. Clinicians tend to want to include things they know about people in general in such interpretations and one can easily devise descriptions that most people will agree are consistent with how they view themselves.

In 1949, Bertram Forer conducted a study in which he had a group of college students took a personality test. A short time later, he provided each with an interpretation of the results and description of their personality. Students were then asked to read the description privately and complete a rating scale indicating how well the interpretations matched their own views of their personality characteristics. Unbeknownst to the students, they were not given individualized interpretations but a common interpretation—they all got the same statement. It was in fact the interpretation that you read above. As a group, the students rated the personality description and interpretation given to them as being highly consistent with their view of themselves. Since the publication of Forer's study, the use of such validation procedures has diminished greatly, as it should. However, occasionally one finds just such an approach or a variation on this method used where clinicians interview examinees and then are asked to rate the agreement between an interpretation based on a personality test and their own view of the examinee from the interview. Such approaches remain subject to the Forer Effect. Interpretations such as the one given in the Forer study are also referred to often as "Aunt Fanny" personality descriptions because they seem to fit everyone—and their Aunt Fanny!

These same basic principles that go into creating Aunt Fanny descriptions are often used in the writing of horoscopes as well as the results of nonstandardized personality surveys often published in the lay press in books as well as popular magazines. These are reasonably easy to create. You might even consider writing one yourself and having four or five of your friends each read it independently and ask how well they think it describes them. They may be amazed at your insights.

We will first focus on objective self-report measures of personality. Two of the most popular item types with objective self-report measures are true–false items and self-rating scales (e.g., *never, sometimes, often, almost always*). Some personality instruments have also used forced-choice item formats. An example of a forced-choice item is one that presents two phrases that are of equal acceptability in terms of social desirability. For example, "I enjoy reading novels" and "I enjoy watching sports." The respondent must select the one that best describes him or her. In the past it was believed that forced-choice items might help reduce response biases, but research has shown that these items were not very effective in reducing response biases and also introduced other technical problems (e.g., Anastasi & Urbina, 1997). As a result, forced-choice items are not very common in contemporary typical response tests (but you will still occasionally see tests that use these items).

We will organize our discussion around the major approaches to scale development— that is, the way test developers select and group the items on their personality tests. The major methods we will discuss are content–rational, empirical keying, factor analytic, and theoretical. Although we discuss these procedures separately, in actual practice it is common for test authors to combine them when developing tests. For example, an author might initially develop items based on content themes, but retain items and develop scales based on factor analytic procedures.

Content–Rational Approach

The earliest approach to developing objective personality scales is to develop items based on their apparent relevance to the construct being measured. This is typically referred to as the content–rational approach to scale development. For example, in developing items to measure depression you might include items addressing feelings of sadness, hopelessness, isolation, and inferiority. The inclusion of these items is based on your understanding of the construct you want to measure (i.e., depression) rather than an empirical analysis of the items. The Woodworth Personal Data Sheet, which we noted was the first formal instrument for assessing personality, was developed primarily using a content-based approach. Whereas there are some more contemporary personality measures that have used this approach (e.g., Symptom Checklist–90— Revised; Derogatis, 1994), this approach has largely fallen out of favor as a stand-alone approach to scale development. One major limitation of this approach is that the scales are transparent to the extent that examinees can easily manipulate the results to present themselves in a specific way (e.g., Anastasi & Urbina, 1997). For example, if one wants to appear depressed, endorsing items reflecting feelings of sadness, hopelessness, isolation, and inferiority will result in a "high" depression score. Likewise, avoiding the endorsement of such items will result in a "low" depression score. Another limitation of relying solely on a content–rational approach is that the assumption that an item measures a specific construct is not always correct. We might believe that individuals with major depression will endorse the item "I feel inferior" in a positive direction more than those without the diagnosis, but this might not be the case! What an item actually measures is an empirical question that can only be answered through careful statistical analysis (e.g., Friedenberg, 1995). Most test authors on some occasions have been surprised to discover that one of their favored items based on subjective content analysis failed to hold up under empirical scrutiny.

> *The earliest approach to developing objective personality scales was to develop items based on their apparent relevance to the construct being measured.*

Although contemporary test developers rarely rely exclusively on a content–rational approach to scale development, it is common to start with this approach when writing items for personality tests. Once items have been written based on their content, empirical studies can reveal which items are actually measuring the constructs of interest.

Empirical Criterion Keying

> *The* Minnesota Multiphasic Personality Inventory (MMPI) *is a prime example of a test developed using the empirical criterion keying approach.*

Empirical criterion keying is a process in which a large pool of items is administered to two groups, one typically a clinical group composed of individuals with a specific diagnosis and the other a control or normal group representative of the general population. The items are then statistically examined with the goal of identifying and retaining items that discriminate between the two groups. With this approach it is not necessary that the items have logical appeal or content relevance. For example, if the item "I like classical music" discriminates well between depressed and nondepressed individuals it might be retained even though its content does not appear to be relevant to depression. (Don't worry—this is just an example and enjoying classical music is not indicative of depression!)

The **Minnesota Multiphasic Personality Inventory (MMPI)** is a prime example of a test developed using the empirical criterion keying approach. The original MMPI was published in the early 1940s (Hathaway & McKinley, 1940, 1943) to aid in the diagnosis of psychiatric disorders. By the 1960s the MMPI was the most widely used and thoroughly researched personality test and was used not only in clinical settings to facilitate diagnosis, but also in nonclinical settings to assess examinees in employment, military, medical, forensic, and other settings. By the 1980s there was increased criticism of the MMPI, with detractors noting that advances in personality theory, our understanding of psychopathology, and psychometrics all called for a revision of the original MMPI (Anastasi & Urbina, 1997). The revision, the Minnesota Multiphasic Personality Inventory—Second Edition, was published in 1989 (MMPI-2; Butcher et al.). To allow continuity with its predecessor, the MMPI-2 retained the overall structure of the original MMPI. However, it did incorporate changes intended to modernize and improve the instrument including the development of contemporary norms using a national standardization sample and removal or revision of outdated and objectionable items.

The MMPI-2 (like the original MMPI) contains 10 Clinical Scales that are summarized in Table 10–1 (based on information provided by Graham, 1993; Hathaway & McKinley, 1989). Eight of these scales were originally developed using empirical criterion keying; the Masculinity-Femininity and Social Introversion scales were added after the publication of the original MMPI and were developed using content-based procedures (Graham, 1993). In clinical practice most psychologists utilize a configural approach to interpreting MMPI-2 scores. That is, instead of examining single scales in isolation, they examine scores as a profile or in relation to each other. The most popular approach is to examine the highest two scores in a client's profile. With this approach the highest two clinical scales produce a 2-point code. For example, consider a profile with the highest score being scale 4 (Psychopathic Deviate) followed by scale 9 (Hypomania). This would be coded as a 4–9 2-point code. Considerable research has been completed regarding the behavioral correlates of MMPI-2 code types and this information is condensed in a number of interpretive clinical guides. For example, consider these excerpted descriptive comments regarding a 4–9 (or 9–4) code type. Figure 10–1 depicts a completed MMPI-2 profile with a 4–9 code type. According to Graham (1993):

> The most salient characteristic of 49/94 individuals is a marked disregard for social standards and values. They frequently get into trouble with the authorities because of antisocial behavior. They have poorly developed conscience, easy morals, and fluctuating ethical values. Alcoholism, fighting, marital problems, sexual acting out, and a wide array of delinquent acts are among the difficulties in which they may be involved. (p. 95)

In addition to the original 10 clinical scales a number of additional scales are available. In fact, close to 60 additional scales are listed in the MMPI-2 manual (Hathaway & McKinley, 1989). Some of these supplementary scales have received considerable research and clinical attention. For example, the MacAndrew Alcoholism Scale—Revised (MAC-R) is a 49-item scale that research indicates may be sensitive in detecting substance abuse problems. Another example is the Negative Treatment Indicators scale. Elevated scores on

TABLE 10–1	MMPI-2 Clinical Scales			
#	Name	Symbol	Items	High Scores
1	Hypochondriasis	Hs	32	High scores are associated with somatic complaints and excessive concern about health issues.
2	Depression	D	57	High scores are associated with depressive symptoms such as pessimism, hopelessness, and discouragement.
3	Hysteria	Hy	60	High scores are associated with the development of physical symptoms in response to stress and to avoid responsibility.
4	Psychopathic Deviate	Pd	50	High scores are associated with difficulty incorporating societal standards and values.
5	Masculinity-Femininity	Mf	56	High scores are associated with tendency to reject stereotypical gender roles.
6	Paranoia	Pa	40	High scores are associated with behaviors ranging from general oversensitivity to paranoid delusions.
7	Psychasthenia	Pt	48	High scores are associated with anxiety, agitation, and discomfort.
8	Schizophrenia	Sc	78	High scores may be associated with psychotic symptoms, confusion, or disorientation.
9	Hypomania	Ma	46	High scores are associated with high energy levels, narcissism, and possibly mania.
0	Social Introversion	Si	69	High scores are associated with social introversion.

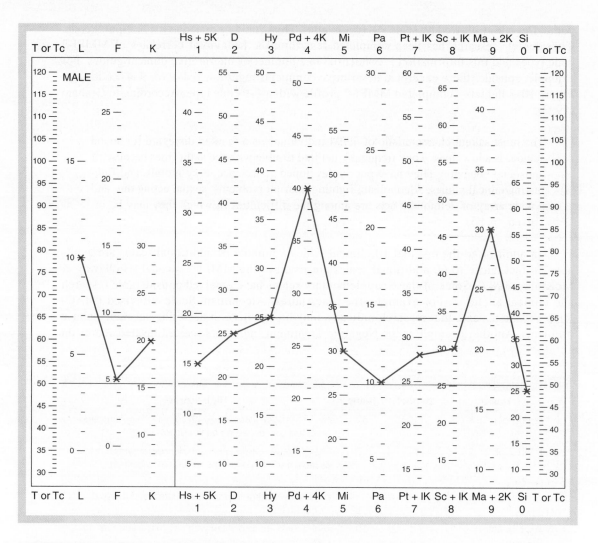

FIGURE 10–1   MMPI-2 Profile With a 4–9 Code Type.
Source: Excerpted from the MMPI®-2 (Minnesota Multiphasic Personality Inventory®-2) Manual for Administration, Scoring, and Interpretation, Revised Edition. Copyright © 2001 by the Regents of the University of Minnesota. Used by permission of the University of Minnesota Press. All rights reserved. "MMPI" and "Minnesota Multiphasic Personality Inventory" are trademarks owned by the Regents of the University of Minnesota.

> *One of the most impressive features of the MMPI and its revision is the development and application of validity scales.*

this scale may reflect client attitudes that interfere with psychological treatment such as resistance to change or the belief that change is simply not possible (Butcher et al., 1989).

One of the most impressive features of the MMPI and its revision is the development and application of validity scales. These scales are designed to detect response sets (e.g., faking good or bad), resistance, carelessness, random responding, or errors due to misunderstanding or poor reading ability. The original MMPI included four validity scales that are listed in Table 10–2. The MMPI-2 includes three new validity scales, the Back F scale (FB), Variable Response Inconsistency scale (VRIN), and the True Response Inconsistency scale (TRIN). These will not be described here, but interested readers can find more information in a number of resources (e.g., Graham, 1993). Interpretation strategies for the validity scales varies from the simple to the complex. One simple strategy is to consider any protocol with an excessive number of omitted items as invalid. However, authors disagree about what constitutes an excessive number, with some suggesting a "Cannot Say (?)" score greater than 10 as the cutoff, and others setting the cutoff as high as 30. Likewise, some clinicians will discount any protocol with a validity scale score greater than 65 whereas others utilize a more complex configural approach that considers the pattern formed by the validity scales as a whole (Graham, 1993).

In addition to the MMPI-2 there is also the Minnesota Multiphasic Personality Inventory—Adolescents (MMPI-A). This instrument is designed for adolescents between the ages of 14 and 18 and contains the basic clinical and validity scales from the original MMPI and an assortment of supplementary and content-based scales.

The reliability of the MMPI-2 can generally be described as adequate. For example, 1-week test-retest data for the basic validity and clinical scales ranged from 0.67 to 0.92 in a sample of 82 males and 0.58 to 0.91 in a sample of females (Butcher et al., 1989). Granted this is not impressive compared to the reliability of many intelligence and other cognitive tests, but it is in line with scores produced by many personality measures. Another aspect of reliability is often overlooked when evaluating the MMPI-2. Because many MMPI-2 interpretive strategies emphasize configural analysis, it is also important to evaluate the stability of profile configurations. Graham (2000) noted that many clinicians assume that if individual scales have adequate reliability, profiles or configurations using multiple scores will also be reliable. However, the evidence supporting this belief is meager at best. The most common approach to examining the stability of MMPI-2 profile configurations has been to examine code type congruence. That is, what percentage of subjects obtain the same MMPI-2 code type on two separate administrations of the test? Graham (2000) reviewed the research on the stability of 1-, 2-, and 3-point codes for the MMPI and MMPI-2 and noted that approximately one quarter to one half will have the same 2-point code types on two

TABLE 10–2	Original MMPI-2 Validity Scales	
Name	**Symbol**	**High Scores**
Cannot Say	?	Number of items not answered for any of a number of reasons such as defiance, confusion, depression, poor reading, and suspiciousness.
Lie scale	L	High scores indicate a tendency to present oneself in a favorable way. Although it may indicate deliberate attempt to fake good, it might simply reflect a strong moral and virtuous self-image. Very low scores may reflect an attempt to "fake bad."
Infrequency scale	F	High scores may indicate random responding, faking bad, or a cry for help.

administrations and only about one quarter will have the same 3-point code type. These results are found in fairly short test-retest intervals (e.g., 1–2 weeks). This does not mean that these configural approaches to interpretation should be abandoned, but it does mean the interpretive strategies should be used with an appropriate degree of caution (something that can be said for all interpretive approaches).

In terms of validity evidence, it is safe to say that a very large amount of validity evidence accumulated over 50 years of research with the original MMPI. Because the MMPI-2 retained the overall structure of the original MMPI, much of the existing validity evidence can also be used to support the MMPI-2. The downside of retaining the original structure is that the MMPI-2 inherited many problems from its predecessor. These problems include:

- The MMPI was developed in the 1930s and was based on a taxonomy of psychopathology that is clearly outdated in the 21st century (e.g., consider the use of the term *psychasthenia*). Instead of using this outdated terminology, many clinicians simply refer to the scales using the scale number (e.g., the Psychasthenia scale is simply referred to as scale 7).
- The "normal" group used in the original empirical analysis was comprised of people visiting a hospital in Minnesota. This presents obvious problems as the group is clearly not representative of the national population. To exacerbate the problem, most were visiting patients at the hospital and were likely experiencing some degree of distress as the result of the illness of a relative or friend when they completed the instrument (e.g., Thorndike, 2005).
- Reliance on what has been described as "flawed" application of empirical criterion keying resulted in numerous psychometric problems (e.g., Anastasi & Urbina, 1997). For example, there is a high degree of overlap in items across the clinical scales and this results in high-scale intercorrelations.

To address these problems a new version MMPI referred to as the MMPI-2-Restructured Format (MMPI-2-RF) has been released recently. In Special Interest Topic 10.5 one of the authors of the MMPI-2-RF describes the development of this promising new instrument.

SPECIAL INTEREST TOPIC 10.5

An MMPI Test for the 21st Century: The MMPI-2-RF

Yossef S. Ben-Porath

Kent State University

The original MMPI was developed in the late 1930s by psychologist Starke Hathaway and psychiatrist Charnley McKinley. These authors did not view the MMPI as the final word on personality assessment. Commenting on the state of the MMPI some 20 years after its completion, Hathaway (1960) observed: "That the MMPI will be a steppingstone to a higher level of validity, I still sincerely hope. . . . In the meantime I see it as a steppingstone that permits useful communication at its own level even though the stone is rather wobbly."

(Continued)

Returning to this topic on the 30th anniversary of its publication, Hathaway (1972) commented:

If another twelve years were to go by without our having gone on to a better instrument or better procedure for the practical needs, I fear that the MMPI, like some other tests, might have changed from a hopeful innovation to an aged obstacle. Do not misunderstand me. I am not agreeing with a few critics who have already called for the funeral and written the epitaph. They have not yet identified what is better. We cannot lay down even a stone-age axe if we have no better one to hew with. (p. xiv)

As reflected in these quotes, Hathaway perceived some significant limitations in the original MMPI, but doubted whether the science of personality assessment had, 30 years later, yielded a more solid foundation upon which a better instrument could be built. Although his reference to stone-age technology was undoubtedly an exaggeration designed for effect, judged by contemporary standards the original MMPI clinical scales cannot be viewed as state of the art. They targeted a now partially outdated nosological system, and the methodology used in their development, empirical keying, is no longer preferentially employed by contemporary test constructors.

In the early 1980s, a team of psychologists assembled by the test publisher, the University of Minnesota Press, began a project to update the MMPI. Their effort yielded the MMPI-2. Consistent with Hathaway's view that the field of assessment psychology had yet to produce a better framework upon which to construct measures of psychopathology, the test's original clinical scales were essentially left unchanged in the revision. The primary change offered by the MMPI-2 was a much-needed update of the test's norms. However, shortly after it was completed, a member of the team that restandardized the test, Professor Auke Tellegen, of the University of Minnesota, embarked on a project that initially yielded revised versions of the original MMPI clinical scales and eventually produced the MMPI-2-RF.

Two primary shortcomings of the original MMPI clinical scales motivated Tellegen's efforts: their heterogeneous and overinclusive content, and its result—the considerable overlap and higher than clinically and theoretically expected correlations between the scales. These problems and the methods used to address them are described in full by Tellegen, Ben-Porath, McNulty, Arbisi, Graham, and Kaemmer (2003). Briefly, correlations between the clinical scales exceed (in some cases appreciably) the covariation of the phenomena they assess. This problem significantly limits the discriminant validity of scores on these scales. Their heterogeneous content, including some items thought initially to provide subtle measures of the constructs they assess but recognized later as largely invalid measure of these constructs, places substantial limits on both the convergent and discriminant validities of the clinical scale scores.

Over the years, MMPI researchers and users developed a number of effective, albeit cumbersome ways to overcome these challenges (e.g., interpretation of patterns of scores on the scales [code types], and various subscales and supplementary scales designed to guide and clarify further their interpretation). Tellegen sought to address these difficulties directly and parsimoniously by developing a set of Restructured Clinical (RC) scales, each designed to measure a major distinctive core component of an original clinical scale. In developing the RC scales, Tellegen employed modern test-construction techniques. This meant conducting hundreds of factor analyses, any one of which would have literally taken Hathaway and McKinley several months to complete using the technology at their disposal at the time the MMPI was developed.

Development of the RC scales proceeded in four steps. First, an MMPI-2 dimension called Demoralization was identified through a series of item factor analyses. This broad, affectively colored latent variable is represented in varying degrees in each of the clinical scales. Next, item factor analyses of each of the scales identified for each a major distinctive and clinically meaningful non-Demoralization core component, defined by a selected subset of the items of that scale. To achieve this aim, the clinical scale items were augmented in each of these analyses with a set of the earlier identified Demoralization items. This addition ensured in each analysis the appearance of separate Demoralization and core dimensions, and thus the ability to distinguish the latter from the former. In the next step, any core item identified in the prior step found to be too highly correlated with the core set of items for another scale was deleted. Thus, at the end of this third step Tellegen had identified a subset of each of the original clinical scale items (Called "seed scales") designed to be maximally distinctive from Demoralization and

(Continued on page 338)

SPECIAL INTEREST TOPIC 10.5 (*Continued*)

from the other core components. In the final step, Tellegen expanded the RC scales by identifying in the entire pool of items the ones sufficiently correlated with a given seed scale and minimally correlated with the others.

In the monograph introducing the RC scales (Tellegen et al., 2003), we reported findings from a series of empirical analyses designed to compare their psychometric properties with those of the original clinical scales. In several large samples we found that scores on the appreciably shorter RC scales showed comparable and in some cases substantially improved reliability, substantially reduced correlations with Demoralziation, and lower intercorrelations. Based on correlations with a variety of extra-test criteria, we concluded that in comparison with the clinical scales, scores on the RC scales showed evidence of comparable or largely improved convergent validities and substantially improved discriminant validities.

In the closing pages of the monograph we commented that the methodology used to develop the RC scales could be applied further and perhaps yield a set of new scales that captures all of the core constructs represented by the MMPI-2 item pool in a more transparent and effective manner. That was our goal in using the RC scales as a starting point for construction of the MMPI-2-RF. Our first step toward that goal involved constructing a set of 23 Specific Problems (SP) scales and 2 Interest scales designed to assess clinical scale components not targeted by the RC scales, facets of the RC scales worthy of separate assessment, and elements of the remarkably rich MMPI-2 item pool that were not (directly) captured by the clinical or RC scales. In addition, guided by factor analyses of the RC scales, we developed a set of Higher-Order (H-O) scales, designed to provide broad-band measures of problems associated with mood and affect, disordered thinking, and undercontrolled behavior. Filling out the MMPI-2-RF, our colleagues Alan Harkness and John McNulty, of the University of Tulsa, developed revised versions the Personality-Psychopathology Five (PSY-5) scales, measures of a five-dimensional model of personality disorder symptoms they had previously introduced (Harkness & McNulty, 1994). In addition, Tellegen and I constructed a set of 8 validity scales (7 of which are revised versions of MMPI-2 validity scales).

The 50 scales of the MMPI-2-RF are composed of 338 of the 567 items of the MMPI-2. Norms for these scales are based on the MMPI-2 normative data. Its two manuals detail the construction of the MMPI-2-RF scales and their psychometric properties (Tellegen & Ben-Porath, 2008), and provide guidance on the administration, scoring, and interpretation of the test (Ben-Porath & Tellegen, 2008).

Our goal for the MMPI-2-RF was to construct a modern assessment device linked to current concepts and models of personality and psychopathology, by applying contemporary scale construction techniques to the highly diverse item pool assembled by Hathaway and McKinley for the original MMPI, and augmented by Butcher et al. (1989) for the MMPI-2. This effort reflects our view that 70 years after Hathaway and McKinley embarked on its development, conditions had ripened for the first comprehensive effort to revise the instrument and introduce an MMPI test for the 21st century. An example of a detailed computer-generated MMPI-2-RF interpretive report is presented in Appendix B.

Factor Analysis

> **Factor analysis *also plays a prominent role in the development of personality and other tests.***

We initially discussed factor analysis in Chapter 5 as it plays a prominent role in test validation. It also plays a prominent role in the development of personality and other tests. To refresh your memory Reynolds and Kamphaus (2003) described **factor analysis** as a statistical approach that allows one to evaluate the presence and structure of latent constructs existing among a set of variables. Factor analysis has a long and important role in identifying the structure of personality with models including from as few as three to several dozen factors (see Goldberg,

1993, for a readable summary). Raymond Cattell is typically credited with being a leader in the use of factor analysis to understand the structure of the normal personality. He published the original 16 Personality Factor Questionnaire (16 PF) in 1949 and the most recent fifth edition was released in 1993. As the name suggests the 16 PF is based on a 16-factor model of personality. The 16 primary factors are Warmth, Reasoning, Emotional Stability, Dominance, Liveliness, Rule-Consciousness, Social Boldness, Sensitivity, Vigilance, Abstractedness, Privateness, Apprehensiveness, Openness-to-Change, Self-Reliance, Perfectionism, and Tension. The 16 PF adopts a hierarchical model that contains second-order factors obtained by factor analyzing the 16 primary factors. These five global factors are Extraversion, Anxiety, Tough-Mindedness, Independence, and Self-Control. The 16 PF—Fifth Edition is more psychometrically sound than earlier editions; however, problems remain. Possibly the most problematic issue is that the 16 primary factors are not statistically independent. Accordingly other researchers have not been able to reproduce the 16-factor structure when examining Cattell's data (e.g., Anastasi & Urbina, 1997). Nevertheless, the 16 PF has a fairly strong following and is a popular measure of normal personality functioning, particularly in counseling, school, and industrial–organizational settings.

In recent years a **five-factor model (FFM) of personality** has received widespread (but not universal) acceptance. This model holds that five major factors or dimensions underlie the construct of personality. Some have suggested that Cattell was actually the founder of the contemporary FFM citing the five global factors in the 16 PF as evidence. However, Cattell

> *The* **five-factor model of personality** *has received widespread acceptance.*

never accepted this recognition or embraced the five-factor model (he maintained that there were more than five factors underlying personality). It appears that Fiske's (1949) research attempting to reproduce Cattell's 16 factors actually resulted in a five-factor solution, and he is usually credited as the first in identifying the five factors contained in the FFM. Ironically, Fisk never followed up on his findings and left the development of the FFM to others (Goldberg, 1993). The five factors included in the contemporary five-factor model are as follows:

- *Neuroticism:* Individuals who score high on this factor tend to experience high levels of negative affects (e.g., depression, anxiety, and anger). In contrast, individuals who score low tend to be emotionally stable.
- *Extraversion:* Individuals with high scores on this factor tend to be gregarious, active, and enjoy group activities, whereas those with low scores tend to be more reserved and enjoy solitary activities.
- *Openness to Experience:* Individuals with high scores tend to be curious and value adventure and novel experiences whereas those with low scores prefer familiar and conventional behavior.
- *Agreeableness:* Individuals with high scores tend to be courteous, tolerant, and compassionate whereas those with low scores tend to be disagreeable, egocentric, and antagonistic.
- *Conscientiousness:* Individuals with high scores tend to be self-disciplined, responsible, and dependable whereas those with low scores tend to be unreliable and display less self-control.

The test that most exemplifies the five-factor model is the NEO Personality Inventory—Revised (NEO PI-R) by Costa and McCrae (1992). The NEO PI-R is a 240-item inventory based largely on the results of factor analytic studies. It produces five domain scores reflecting Neuroti-

TABLE 10–3 Domain and Facet Scales for the NEO PI-R	
Domain	**Facet Scales**
Neuroticism	Anxiety
	Angry Hostility
	Depression
	Self-Consciousness
	Impulsivity
	Vulnerability
Extraversion	Warmth
	Gregariousness
	Assertiveness
	Activity
	Excitement-Seeking
	Positive Emotions
Openness	Fantasy
	Aesthetics
	Feelings
	Actions
	Ideas
	Values
Agreeableness	Trust
	Straightforwardness
	Altruism
	Compliance
	Modesty
	Tender-Mindedness
Conscientiousness	Competence
	Order
	Dutifulness
	Achievement Striving
	Self-Discipline
	Deliberation

cism, Extraversion, Openness, Agreeableness, and Conscientious. Each of the five domain scores have six subordinate facet scores that are listed in Table 10–3. There are two forms available, one for self-report and one for completion by an observer (i.e., a third party such as a spouse or friend). The NEO PI-R contains 3 items that are intended to serve as a validity check (e.g., Did you respond in an honest/accurate manner?), but it has no formal validity scales.

The NEO PI-R scale scores have good reliability and there is reasonable evidence of the validity of the score interpretations. The primary limitation of the NEO PI-R involves its somewhat limited range of applications. The NEO PI-R clearly has a role in basic research on personality, but it has not proven particularly effective in predicting performance or facilitating decision making in clinical settings (e.g., Thorndike, 2005). As a result it is a good measure of normal personality development, but it has not proved to be especially useful in clinical or other applied settings.

Theoretical Approach

A number of objective personality scales have been developed based on a specific theory of personality, or theoretical approach. For example, the **Myers-Briggs Type Indicator (MBTI)** by Myers and McCaulley (1985) was based on the theory of psychological types proposed by C. G. Jung postulating the existence of dichotomies reflecting psychological dispositions or personal preferences. The dichotomies measured by the MBTI are described here:

> *A number of objective personality scales have been developed based on a specific theory of personality.*

- *Introversion (I)–Extraversion (E):* Introversion reflects an individual's preference to focus on the inner world of thoughts and ideas, whereas Extraversion reflects a preference to focus on the external world of people and objects.
- *Sensing (S)–Intuition (N):* Sensing suggests a preference to focus on what can be perceived by the five senses whereas Intuition indicates a preference for focusing on complex relationships and patterns.
- *Thinking (T)–Feeling (F):* Thinking reflects a preference for basing decisions on a logical analysis of the facts whereas Feeling reflects a preference for basing decisions on personal values and situational features.
- *Judging (J)–Perceiving (P):* In dealing with the external world, Judging indicates a preference for structure and decisiveness whereas Perceiving reflects a preference for flexibility and adaptability.

The first three dichotomies were postulated by Jung; the Judging–Perceiving dichotomy was later added by Isabel Briggs Myers and Katherine Briggs when developing the MBTI.

The scores on these four dimensions are used to assign people to 1 of 16 personality types that are designated by letters reflecting the individual's preference. For example, the code type ISTJ indicates a person with preferences reflecting Introversion, Sensing, Thinking, and Judging. The test manual (Myers, McCaulley, Quenk, & Hammer, 1998) provides interpretive guides describing characteristics of each personality code type. For example, the ISTJ type is described as quiet, serious, and dependable. They are practical, realistic, and responsible. Their lives are organized and they value traditions and loyalty.

> *The* Myers-Briggs Type Indicator *and the* Millon Clinical Multiaxial Inventory—III *are examples of theoretically based contemporary objective personality tests.*

The MBTI is one of the most widely used psychological tests today. As might be expected it has both supporters and distracters. Many psychologists and professional counselors find the instrument useful in their clinical practice. In contrast, many psychometricians have criticized the MBTI with regard to its psychometric properties. An often-cited criticism is that it is possible for examinees to be assigned the same four-letter code type while differing greatly in their actual response patterns. For example, two people classified as an ISTJ may vary greatly in the strength of their preferences. One examinee may demonstrate strong preferences on one or more dimensions (e.g., extremely introverted) and the other might demonstrate only moderate or weak preferences (e.g., mild preference for introversion). The MBTI actually does provide scores reflecting the strength of the preferences, but overreliance on categorical code types without considering the strength of the preferences is probably a common interpretive error. The stability of the MBTI code types has also been criticized. For example, the MBTI manual reports that after 4 weeks 65% of the examinees obtain the same four-letter code type whereas 35% change (most on only one dichotomy). This is often cited as a significant weakness of the MBTI. However, when compared to the stability of MMPI-2 2-point code types (i.e., 25 to 50% will obtain the same code type), this criticism appears somewhat overstated.

Another example of a theoretically based personality inventory is the **Millon Clinical Multiaxial Inventory—Third Edition (MCMI-III)** by Millon, Millon, and Davis (1994). This inventory is based on Theodore Millon's theory of personality (Millon & Davis, 1996) and like the MMPI-2, was designed to facilitate the assessment and diagnosis of clients with psychological disorders. Many clinicians find the MCMI-III particularly useful in the assessment of individuals with personality disorders. It is a self-report measure containing 175 statements that are marked as true or false. The inventory's scales include 14 Clinical Personality Patterns scales, 3 Severe Personality Pathology scales, 7 Clinical Syndrome scales, and 3 Severe Clinical Syndrome scales. The personality and clinical syndrome scales parallel *DSM–IV–TR* diagnostic categories and are grouped into two levels of severity. There are also four correction scales, three modifying indexes that can be used to modify clinical scale scores to take into consideration the client's response style, and a Validity scale to help detect potentially invalid protocols. These scales are listed in Table 10–4.

The MCMI-III scores have adequate reliability and validity evidence. One innovative feature of the test is the use of base rate scores. Instead of using the normalized standard scores like most other personality measures, these scores are based on actuarial base rate information. As a result, they take into account the base or prevalence rate of different disorders in different settings, which can enhance the diagnostic accuracy of the scales. A limitation of the MCMI-III is that it, like the MMPI-2, has high intercorrelations between the scale scores, and this complicates the instrument's use for differential diagnosis (e.g., Thorndike, 2005).

Before ending our discussion of the MCMI-III we must note that although we use this as an example of a personality measure developed from a theoretical perspective, like many contemporary personality scales it also has incorporated empirical–statistical methods. The author's website (http://www.millon.net) notes that item and scale development involved the following three steps:

- **Theoretical–Substantive.** In this stage items were developed based on Millon's theory of personality and to align with *DSM–IV* criteria.
- **Internal–Structural.** In this stage the internal consistency of the scales was examined. Items that did not behave as expected were modified or removed.
- **External–Criterion.** In this final stage the items were examined to determine if they facilitated discrimination between diagnostic groups. In these analyses the authors examined the ability of the items to discriminate between clinical groups (e.g., depression vs. anxiety)

TABLE 10–4	MCMI-III Scales
Category	**Diagnostic Scales**
Clinical Personality Patterns scales	Schizoid Avoidant Depressive Dependent Histrionic Narcissistic Antisocial Sadistic Compulsive Negativistic Masochistic
Severe Personality Pathology scales	Schizotypal Borderline Paranoid
Clinical Syndrome scales	Anxiety Somataform Bipolar Manic Dysthymia Alcohol Dependency Drug Dependence Post-Traumatic Stress
Severe Clinical Syndrome scales	Thought Disorder Major Depression Delusional Disorder
Modifying scales	Disclosure Desirability Debasement
Validity scale	

rather than simply between clinical groups and a control or normal group. This was done to enhance the ability of the test to not only identify those with psychopathology, but also to help the clinical differentiate between different psychological disorders (i.e., differential diagnosis).

The test authors indicated that items had to clear each developmental stage successfully to proceed to the following stage. As you see, this is essentially an amalgamation of what we described as the content–rational and empirical criterion keying (with internal consistency analysis used to enhance the psychometric properties of the scales). This is characteristic of the modern trend in the development of personality measures. That is, most contemporary personality measures use multiple approaches to scale development.

ASSESSMENT OF PERSONALITY IN CHILDREN AND ADOLESCENTS

> *In the context of child and adolescent assessment, the term personality is used cautiously.*

In the context of child and adolescent assessment, the term *personality* is used cautiously. Measures of personality in children demonstrate that the personality characteristics of children show less stability than comparable characteristics in adults. This is not particularly surprising given the rapid developmental changes characteristic of children and adolescents. As a result, when using the term *personality* in the context of child and adolescent assessment, it is best to interpret it cautiously and understand that it does not necessarily reflect a fixed construct, but one that is subject to development and change. Although the use of objective personality measures has a long and rich history with adults, their use with children is a relatively new development because it was long believed that children did not have the personal insights necessary to understand and accurately report their subjective experiences. To further complicate the situation, skeptics noted that young children typically do not have the reading skills necessary to complete written self-report tests (e.g., Kamphaus & Frick, 2002). However, numerous self-report measures have been developed and used successfully with children and adolescents. Although insufficient reading skills do make these instruments impractical with very young children, these new self-report measures are being used with older children (e.g., >7 years) and adolescents with considerable success. Objective measures have proven to be particularly useful in the assessment of internalizing disorders such as depression and anxiety that have symptoms that are not always readily apparent to observers. The development and use of self-report measures with children are still at a relatively early stage, but several instruments are gaining widespread acceptance. We will now briefly describe one of the most popular child and adolescent self-report personality measures.

Behavior Assessment System for Children—Self-Report of Personality (SRP)

The Behavior Assessment System for Children—Self-Report of Personality (SRP) (Reynolds & Kamphaus, 2004) is a component of the Behavior Assessment System for Children (BASC-2) and research suggests it is the most popular self-report measure among school psychologists (Livingston et al., 2003). There are three forms of the SRP, one for children 8 to 11 years and one for adolescents 12 to 18 years. A third version, the SRP-I (for interview), is standardized as an interview version for ages 6 and 7 years. The SRP has an estimated third-grade reading level, and if there is concern about the student's ability to read and comprehend the material, the instructions and items can be presented using audio. The SRP contains brief descriptive statements that children or adolescents mark as *true* or *false* to some questions, or *never, sometimes, often,* or *almost always* to other questions, as it applies to them. Reynolds and Kamphaus (2004) describe the subscales as follows:

- *Anxiety:* feelings of anxiety, worry, and fears and a tendency to be overwhelmed by stress and problems
- *Attention Problems:* being easily distracted and unable to concentrate
- *Attitude to School:* feelings of alienation and dissatisfaction with school

- *Attitude to Teachers:* feelings of resentment and dissatisfaction with teachers
- *Atypicality:* unusual perceptions, behaviors, and thoughts that are often associated with severe forms of psychopathology
- *Depression:* feelings of rejection, unhappiness, and sadness
- *Hyperactivity:* being overly active, impulsive, and rushing through work
- *Interpersonal Relations:* positive social relationships
- *Locus of Control:* perception that events in one's life are externally controlled
- *Relations with Parents:* positive attitude toward parents and feeling of being important in the family
- *Self-Esteem:* positive self-esteem characterized by self-respect and acceptance
- *Self-Reliance:* self-confidence and ability to solve problems
- *Sensation Seeking:* tendency to take risks and seek excitement
- *Sense of Inadequacy:* feeling unsuccessful in school and unable to achieve goals
- *Social Stress:* stress and tension related to social relationships
- *Somatization:* tendency to experience and complain about physical discomforts and problems

The SRP produces five composite scores. The most global composite is the Emotional Symptoms Index (ESI) composed of the Anxiety, Depression, Interpersonal Relations, Self-Esteem, Sense of Inadequacy, and Social Stress scales. The ESI is an index of global psychopathology, and high scores usually indicate serious emotional problems. The four lower order composite scales are:

- *Inattention/Hyperactivity:* This scale combines the Attention Problems and the Hyperactivity scales to form a composite reflecting difficulties with the self-regulation of behavior and ability to attend and concentrate in many different settings.
- *Internalizing Problems:* This is a combination of the Anxiety, Atypicality, Locus of Control, Social Stress, and Somatization scales. This scale reflects the magnitude of internalizing problems, and clinically significant scores (i.e., *T*-scores >70) suggest significant problems.
- *School Problems:* This is composed of the Attitude to School, Attitude to Teachers, and Sensation Seeking scales. High scores on this scale suggest a general pattern of dissatisfaction with schools and teachers. Clinically significant scores suggest pervasive school problems, and adolescents with high scores might be at risk for dropping out.
- *Personal Adjustment:* This is composed of the Interpersonal Relationships, Relations with Parents, Self-Esteem, and Self-Reliance scales. High scores are associated with positive adjustment whereas low scores suggest deficits in interpersonal relationships and identity formation.

High scores on the SRP clinical composites and scales reflect abnormality or pathology. The authors provided the following classifications: *T*-score >70 is Clinically Significant; 60–69 is At-Risk; 41–59 is Average; 31–40 is Low; and <30 is Very Low. Scores on the adaptive composite and scales are interpreted differently, with high scores reflecting adaptive or positive behaviors. The authors provided the following classifications to facilitate diagnosis: *T*-score >70 is Very High; 60–69 is High; 41–59 is Average; 31–40 is At-Risk; and <30 is Clinically Significant. An example of a completed SRP profile is depicted in Figure 10–2.

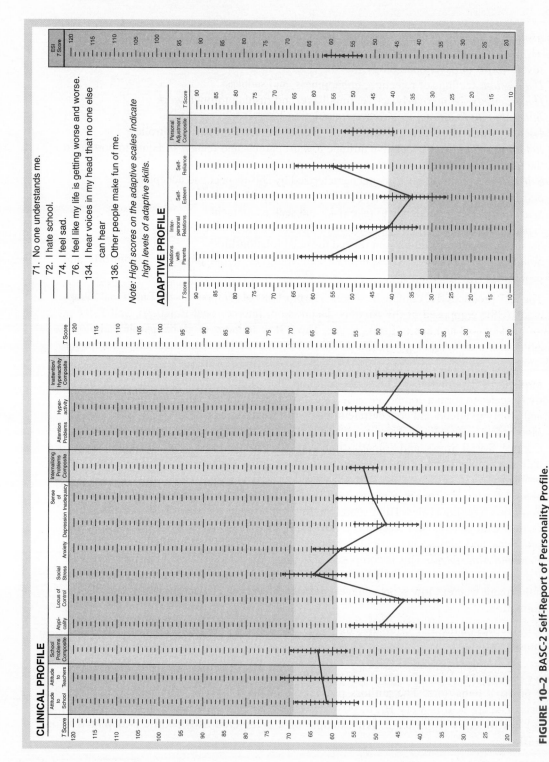

FIGURE 10–2 BASC-2 Self-Report of Personality Profile.

Source: *Behavior Assessment System for Children,* Second Edition *(BASC-2).* Copyright © 2004 NCS Pearson, Inc. Reproduced with permission. All rights reserved. "BASC" is a trademark, in the US and/or other countries, of Pearson Education, Inc. or its affiliates(s).

Single-Domain Self-Report Measures

In addition to broad measures of personality and behavior, there are also brief, more focused scales designed to measure narrow aspects of personality or to focus on a single clinical syndrome.

The personality inventories we have reviewed to this point have been omnibus or broad-band scales. That is, they are designed to measure personality broadly and to cover many aspects of personality and behavior. There are also a number of briefer, more focused scales that are designed to measure narrow aspects of personality or to focus on a single clinical syndrome (often referred to as syndrome-specific). It is common practice in psychological assessment to start with a broad-band instrument like the MMPI-2 or BASC-2 to get a comprehensive view of your client. This helps the clinician identify problematic areas and narrow the focus of subsequent assessment. For example, the results of the MMPI-2 might suggest a potential depressive or anxiety disorder, and the clinician can then follow up with syndrome-specific anxiety and depression scales to develop a more refined understanding of presenting problem. Even within one disorder there is typically considerable variation in symptom presentation. For example, one person with major depression may have symptoms including depressed mood, weight gain, insomnia, fatigue, and suicidal ideations whereas another person with the same diagnosis may present with anhedonia (loss of pleasure from activities that once brought pleasure), loss of appetite, psychomotor agitation, and difficulty concentrating. Although they are both depressed, they have distinctive patterns of symptoms and would likely benefit from different interventions. A targeted assessment using a combination of broad and narrow personality measures and can help identify each client's unique pattern of symptoms which can then help the psychologist tailor treatment to best meet the needs of each client.

An example of a single-domain (or syndrome-specific) self-report measure is the Beck Depression Inventory—Second Edition (BDI-II) by Beck, Steer, and Brown (1996). As the name suggests, the BDI is designed to assess the depression in individuals between 13 and 80 years and is aligned with the diagnostic criteria for major depression in the *DSM–IV–TR*. The BDI contains 21 items reflecting depressive symptoms. Each item includes four statements of increasing severity that describe a specific depressive symptom (0 indicates the symptom is not present, 3 indicates the symptom is severe). The BDI produces a total score that is interpreted with the use of specific cut scores that delineate ranges reflecting the severity of depressive symptoms. The BDI score has good reliability, including good test-retest reliability with a 1-week interval (i.e., $r_{xx} = .93$). Different versions of the BDI have been in use for over 30 years and it continues to be one of the widely used self-report measures of depression.

An example of a single-domain self-report measure used with children is the Children's Depression Inventory (CDI; Kovacs, 1991). The CDI is a 27-item self-report inventory designed for use with children between 7 and 17 years (it parallels the BDI in format). The CDI presents a total score as well as five-factor scores: Negative Mood, Interpersonal Problems, Ineffectiveness, Anhedonia, and Negative Self-Esteem. The CDI is easily administered and scored, is time efficient and inexpensive, and has a fairly extensive research database. As with other single-domain measures, the BDI and CDI do not provide coverage of a broad range of psychological disorders or personality characteristics, but they do give a fairly in-depth assessment of depressive symptoms in their targeted populations.

PROJECTIVE PERSONALITY TESTS: AN OVERVIEW

> *Projective techniques involve the presentation of unstructured or ambiguous materials that allows an almost infinite range of responses from the examinee.*

Projective techniques involve the presentation of unstructured or ambiguous materials that allows an almost infinite range of responses from the examinee. For example, the clinician shows the examinee an inkblot and asks: "What might this be?" The central hypothesis of projective techniques is that examinees will interpret the ambiguous material in a manner that reveals important and often unconscious aspects of their psychological functioning or personality. In other words, the ambiguous material serves as a blank screen on which the examinees "project" their most intimate thoughts, desires, fears, needs, and conflicts (Anastasi & Urbina, 1997; Finch & Belter, 1993). Although extremely popular in clinical settings, the use of projective techniques in the assessment of personality has a controversial history. In fact, Chandler (1990) noted that projective techniques have been the focus of controversy practically since they were initially introduced. Proponents claim that they are the richest source of clinical information available and are necessary to gain a thorough understanding of the individual. They suggest that self-report personality measures reflect only what the examinee wants to reveal. Whereas self-report measures are susceptible to response sets, projective techniques are thought to be relatively free of response sets because the examinee has little idea of what type of responses are expected or are socially appropriate.

Critics of the use of projective techniques note that these procedures typically do not meet even minimum psychometric standards (e.g., having appropriate evidence to support the reliability of their scores and validity of score interpretations), and as a result, their use cannot be justified from an ethical or technical perspective. To justify their use advocates often argue that they don't use projective techniques in a psychometric or diagnostic manner, but simply use them to supplement their objective instruments and gain insight that may be treated as clinical hypotheses. The critics argue that even if projective techniques are used simply to supplement a psychometrically sound battery of objective measures, their questionable reliability and validity will still detract from the technical soundness of the overall assessment process (Kamphaus & Frick, 2002). Psychodynamic theory (which is a theory of Freudian origin), which forms the foundation of the projective hypothesis, also is controversial and not nearly as popular as in the early days of the 20th century.

The debate over the use of projective techniques has been going on for decades. Although there is evidence of diminished use of projective techniques in the assessment, these techniques are still popular and used in clinical and educational settings (Livingston et al., 2003). This debate is apt to continue, but it is highly likely that projective techniques will continue to play a prominent role in psychological assessments for the foreseeable future. Next, we will briefly describe a few of the major projective techniques.

Projective Drawings

Some of the most popular projective techniques in contemporary use, especially with children and adolescents, involve the interpretation of projective drawings. This popularity is usually attributed to two factors. First, young children with limited verbal abilities are hampered in their ability to respond to clinical interviews, objective self-report measures, and even most other projective techniques. However, these young children can produce drawings because this activity is largely nonverbal. Second, because children are usually familiar with and enjoy drawing, this technique provides a nonthreatening "child-friendly" approach to assessment (Finch & Belter, 1993; Kamphaus & Frick, 2002). There are several different projective drawing techniques in use today.

DRAW-A-PERSON (DAP) TEST. The Draw-A-Person (DAP) Test is the most widely used projective drawing technique. The client is given a blank sheet of paper and a pencil and asked to draw a whole person. Although different scoring systems have been developed for the DAP, no system has received universal approval. The figure in the drawing is often interpreted as a representation of the "self." That is, the figure reflects how examinees feel about themselves and how they feel as they interact with their environment (Handler, 1985).

HOUSE-TREE-PERSON (H-T-P). With the House-Tree-Person (H-T-P), the examinee is given paper and a pencil and asked to draw a house, a tree, and a person of each gender, all on separate sheets. The clinician then typically asks a standard set of questions for each picture. After these drawings are completed, the examinee is then given a set of crayons and the process is repeated. The House is typically interpreted as reflecting feelings associated with home life and family relationships. The Tree and Person are thought to reflect aspects of the self, with the Tree representing deep unconscious feelings about the self and the Person reflecting a closer-to-conscious view of self (Hammer, 1985).

KINETIC FAMILY DRAWING (KFD). With the Kinetic Family Drawing (KFD), examinees are given paper and pencil and asked to draw a picture of everyone in their family, including themselves, doing something (hence the term *kinetic*). After completing the drawing the examinees are asked to identify each figure and describe what each one is doing. The KFD is thought to provide information regarding the examinee's view of their family and their interactions (Finch & Belter, 1993).

Despite their popularity and appeal to clinicians, little empirical data support the use of projective drawings as a means of predicting behavior or classifying examinees by diagnostic type (e.g., depressed, anxious, etc.). These techniques may provide a nonthreatening way to initiate the assessment process and an opportunity to develop rapport, but otherwise they should be used with considerable caution and an understanding of their technical limitations (Finch & Belter, 1993; Kamphaus & Frick, 2002).

Sentence Completion Tests

Sentence completion tests are another popular projective approach. These tests typically present incomplete-sentence stems that are completed by the examinee. The sentence completion forms either can be given to the examinee to complete independently or can be read aloud and the responses recorded. Examples of possible incomplete sentence stems include "I really enjoy _____" and "My greatest fear is _____." Numerous sentence completion forms are available, and as with the projective drawings, there are different ways of interpreting the results. Because incomplete-sentence stems provide more structure than most projective tasks (e.g., drawings or inkblots), some have argued that they are not actually "projective" in nature, but are more or less a type of structured interview. As a result, some prefer the term semiprojective to characterize these tests. Regardless of the classification, relatively little empirical evidence documents the psychometric properties of these tests (Kamphaus & Frick, 2002). Nevertheless, they remain popular, are nonthreatening to examinees, and in the hands of skilled clinicians may enhance rapport and provide an opportunity to enhance their understanding of their clients.

Apperception Tests

Another type of projective technique is an apperception test. With this technique the examinee is given a picture and asked to make up a story about it. Figure 10–3 depicts a picture similar to those in some apperception tests. These techniques are also sometimes referred to as thematic, pictorial, or storytelling techniques. The Thematic Apperception Test (TAT; Murray, 1943) is the most widely used apperception test and has a long history of clinical use. It is comprised of 19 black and white cards (pictures and drawings) and 1 blank card (for the blank card the examinee is asked to imagine a picture, describe it, and then tell a story about it). The examinee is typically presented 10 cards and the stories are analyzed in a qualitative manner intended to identify personal factors such as needs for achievement, affiliation, and so on. Like most other projective techniques, limited empirical evidence supports the use of the TAT.

A more recently developed apperception test is the Roberts Apperception Test for Children, which is now titled the Roberts-2 (Roberts & Gruber, 2005). It is designed for children and adolescents 6 to 18 years and includes a standardized scoring system and normative data. The standardized scoring approach results in increased reliability relative to other apperception tests; however, there are still concerns about the technical adequacy of this instrument in terms of contemporary psychometric standards (e.g., Valleley, 2009). Nevertheless, the Roberts-2 is a step in the right direction in terms of enhancing the psychometric qualities of projective techniques.

FIGURE 10–3 Picture Similar to Those Used in the TAT.

Source: Gregory, Psychological testing: History principles & applications, Fig. 13.5 p. 505, © 2000 Allyn & Bacon, Inc. Reproduced by permission of Pearson Education, Inc.

Inkblot Techniques

The final projective approach we will discuss is the inkblot technique. With this technique the examinee is presented an ambiguous inkblot and asked to interpret it in some manner, typically by asking: "What might this be?" Figure 10–4 presents an example of an inkblot similar to those used on inkblot tests. Of all the inkblot techniques, the Rorschach is the most widely used. Hermann Rorschach developed the Rorschach inkblots in the 1920s (Rorschach, 1921) and died soon after publishing the test. In his absence a number of different researchers developed distinctive systems for administering, scoring, and interpreting the instrument. By the 1960s there were five major Rorschach systems in use and this division resulted in a piecemeal approach to establishing the psychometric properties of the technique (Anastasi & Urbina, 1997). John E. Exner Jr. undertook the task of developing a comprehensive system that integrated the most empirically supported features of the existing systems. The Exner Comprehensive System (Exner, 1974, 1991, 1993; Exner & Weiner, 1995) provides a complex standardized scoring system that produces approximately 90 possible scores. Relative to other Rorschach interpretive systems, the Exner system produces more reliable measurement and has adequate normative data. However, validity evidence is somewhat limited (Kamphaus & Frick, 2002). For example, Anastasi and Urbina (1997) found that meta-analytic research suggests that convergent validity evidence for the Rorschach is comparable to that of the MMPI, but in terms of facilitating diagnosis and predicting behavior, the results are not as impressive. Nevertheless, Exner's efforts to produce a more psychometrically sound approach to administering, scoring, and interpreting the Rorschach is clearly a step in the right direction.

> *In light of the paucity of empirical evidence supporting the utility of projective techniques, we recommend that they be used cautiously.*

In summary, in spite of relatively little empirical evidence supporting their utility, projective techniques continue to be popular among psychologists and other clinicians. Our

FIGURE 10–4 Inkblots Similar to Those Used in the Rorschach.

recommendation is to use these instruments cautiously. They should not be used for making important clinical and diagnostic decisions, but they may have merit in introducing the examinee to the assessment process, establishing rapport, and developing hypotheses that can be pursued with more technically adequate assessment techniques.

Summary

In this chapter we focused on the assessment of personality. Personality is generally defined as relatively stable patterns of thinking, feeling, and behaving, and in assessment terminology this is expanded to incorporate a host of emotional, motivational, interpersonal, and attitudinal characteristics. We described a number of ways psychologists use personality measure, including:

- Psychologists and other mental health professionals use personality inventories to facilitate diagnosis and help plan treatment.
- Psychologists frequently use personality inventories to enhance their client's self-understanding and self-actualization.
- Psychologists use measures of personality to identify children with emotional and behavioral disorders that interfere with the ability to learn in schools.
- Psychologists use a variety of personality measures to help determine which job applicants will become successful employees.
- Psychologists use measures of personality to answer questions relevant to legal proceedings such as competency to stand trial or future dangerousness.
- Psychologists in academic and research settings use personality tests to measure a multitude of constructs in a wide range of psychological research.

We next introduced the concept of response biases and discussed how they can impact personality assessment. Response biases or response sets are test responses that misrepresent an examinee's true characteristics. For example, they may answer questions in a way that makes them appear more socially appropriate, even if their responses are not truthful or accurate. When response sets are present, the validity of the test results may be compromised because they introduce construct-irrelevant error to test scores. To combat this, many personality tests incorporate validity scales designed to detect the presence of response sets.

Most of the chapter was devoted to describing two broad categories of personality measures: objective self-report measures and projective techniques. Objective self-report measures are those where respondents endorse selected-response items to reflect their characteristic ways of behaving, feeling, thinking, and so on. Projective techniques involve the presentation of unstructured or ambiguous stimuli that allows an almost infinite range of responses from the respondent. We initially focused on objective self-report measures and used the major approaches employed in developing the scales to structure the presentation. These included:

- Content–rational approach. In the content–rational approach items are selected based on their apparent relevance to the construct being measured. The Woodworth Personal Data Sheet is a notable example of a personality measure developed primarily using a content-based approach. Although contemporary test developers rarely rely exclusively on a content–rational approach to scale development, it is common to start with this approach when writing items for personality tests.

- Empirical criterion keying. Empirical criterion keying is a process in which a large pool of items is administered to two groups, one typically a clinical group composed of individuals with a specific diagnosis and the other a control or normal group representative of the general population. The items are then statistically examined with the goal of identifying and retaining items that discriminate between the two groups. The Minnesota Multiphasic Personality Inventory (MMPI) is a prime example of a test developed using the empirical criterion keying approach. The MMPI was revised in 1989 (MMPI-2) and retained much of the overall structure of the original MMPI. This allowed continuity between the two inventories, but it also meant the MMPI-2 inherited many of the limitations of its predecessor. To address these problems a new version MMPI referred to as the MMPI-2 Restructured Format (MMPI-2-RF) has been developed.
- Factor analysis. Factor analysis has played a prominent role in identifying the structure of personality with models ranging from three to several dozen factors. Raymond Cattell has been a leader in the use of factor analysis to understand the structure of the normal personality. He published the original 16 Personality Factor Questionnaire (16 PF) in 1949 and the most recent edition was released in 1993. As the name suggests, the 16 PF is based on a 16-factor model of personality. In recent years a five-factor model (FFM) of personality has received widespread acceptance. The test that most exemplifies the five-factor model is the NEO Personality Inventory—Revised.
- Theoretical approach. A number of tests have been designed largely based on a specific theory of personality. We described two examples of personality tests based on theories of personality. The Myers-Briggs Type Indicator (MBTI) is based on the theory of psychological types proposed by C. G. Jung and is a broad measure of normal personality development. The Millon Clinical Multiaxial Inventory—Third Edition (MCMI-III) is based on Theodore Millon's theory of personality and was designed to facilitate the assessment and diagnosis of clients with psychological disorders.

The contemporary trend in developing personality assessments is to employ multiple strategies in developing items and scales (and this was actually evident in many of the inventories we described). For example, a test author might initially develop items based on their apparent relevance to the construct being measured, and then use multiple statistical techniques to select items and refine the scales.

In child and adolescent assessment, the term *personality* is used cautiously due to the rapid developmental changes characteristic of children and adolescents. When using the term *personality* in the context of child and adolescent assessment it does not necessarily reflect a fixed construct, but one that is subject to development and change. The Behavior Assessment System for Children—Self-Report of Personality (SRP) was described as an example of an objective personality measure used with children and adolescents.

Projective techniques involve the presentation of an ambiguous task that places little structure or limitation on the examinee's response. A classic example is the presentation of an inkblot followed by the question: "What might this be?" In addition to inkblot tests, projective techniques include projective drawings, sentence completion tests, and apperception (or storytelling) tests. The hypothesis behind the use of projective techniques is that the examinees will respond to the ambiguous stimuli in a manner that reveals basic, often unconscious aspects of their personality. There is considerable controversy over the use of projective techniques. Proponents of their use claim projective techniques represent the richest source of information about the subjective experience of the examinee. Supporters also hold that behavior rating scales and self-report measures are vulnerable to the distorting effects of response sets, whereas projective techniques are relatively free from these effects because it is not obvious what type of response is expected or socially appropriate. In contrast, critics claim that most projective techniques do not meet even minimal psychometric standards and their use cannot be ethically or technically justified. Whereas the use of these projective techniques is vigorously debated in the professional literature, they continue to be among the most popular approaches to assessing personality. Our position is that although projective techniques should not be used as the basis for making important educational, clinical, or diagnostic decisions, they may have merit in developing rapport with clients and in generating hypotheses that can be pursued using technically superior assessment techniques.

Key Terms and Concepts

Factor analysis, 336
Five-factor model (FFM) of personality, 339
Millon Clinical Multiaxial Inventory—Third Edition (MCMI-III), 342

Minnesota Multiphasic Personality Inventory (MMPI), 332
Myers-Briggs Type Indicator (MBTI), 341

Response sets and dissimulation, 327
Validity scales, 327

Recommended Readings

Dawes, R. M., Faust, D., & Meehl, P. E. (1989). Clinical versus actuarial judgment. *Science, 243,* pp. 1668–1674. An interesting article that compares clinical versus actuarial approaches to decision making (e.g., diagnosis, treatment planning),with the actuarial approach coming out on top!

Graham, J. R. (2005). MMPI-2: Assessing personality and psychopathology (4th ed.). New York: Oxford. An excellent guide to using the MMPI-2.

Green, R. L. (2011). The MMPI-2/MMPI-2-RF: An interpretive manual (3rd ed.). Boston: Allyn & Bacon. Another excellent guide to using the MMPI-2.

Chapter Eleven

Behavioral Assessment

The study of behavior is the raison d'être of psychology as a science and objective assessment of behavior a necessity.

Learning Objectives

After reading and studying this chapter, students should be able to:

1. Define and describe behavioral assessment and explain how it is similar to as well as different from other forms of assessment, especially personality testing.
2. Explain how response sets can impact behavioral assessments.
3. Describe how behavioral assessments are used in public schools to assess emotional and behavioral disorders.
4. Explain the difference between behavioral interviewing and traditional clinical interviews.
5. Explain how validity scales can be used to guard against response sets and give examples.

6. Compare and contrast categorical and dimensional diagnostic models.
7. Compare and contrast omnibus and single-domain (syndrome-specific) rating scales. Explain how each can facilitate diagnosis and treatment planning and give examples.
8. Describe the strengths and limitations of behavior rating scales.
9. Describe and evaluate the major behavior rating scales.
10. Describe the history and use of direct observations.
11. Describe continuous performance tests and their application.
12. Describe psychophysiological assessments, their use, and their current status.

The study of behavior is the raison d'être of psychology as a science and objective assessment of behavior a necessity.

Behavioral assessment has a storied history in psychology and has evolved from a simple counting of behavioral occurrences to more sophisticated rating scales and observational schemes. Although professional psychologists traditionally have focused primarily on assessment of cognitive abilities and personality characteristics, the drive for less inferential measures of behavior as well as a movement toward establishing diagnoses based on observable behavior has led to a renewal of interest and use of behavioral assessment methods. Additionally, federal laws mandate that schools provide special education and related services to students with emotional disorders. Before these services can be provided, the schools must be able to identify children with these disorders. The process of identifying these children often involves a psychological evaluation completed by a school psychologist or other clinician wherein behaviors consistent with the federal definition of emotional disturbance must be documented clearly. This has also led to the derivation of increasingly sophisticated measures of actual behavior.

> **Behavioral assessment**
> *emphasizes what a person does.*
> *Most methods of personality*
> *assessment emphasize what*
> *a person has (e.g., attributes,*
> *character, or other latent traits*
> *such as anxiety).*

In Chapter 1, when describing the different types of tests, we noted that tests typically can be classified as measures of either maximum performance or typical response. Maximum performance tests are often referred to as ability tests. On these tests, items are usually scored as either correct or incorrect, and examinees are encouraged to demonstrate the best performance possible. Achievement and aptitude tests are common examples of maximum performance tests. In contrast, typical response tests attempt to measure the typical behavior and characteristics of examinees.

Typical response tests typically assess constructs such as personality, behavior, attitudes, or interests (Cronbach, 1990). **Behavioral assessment** as most commonly conducted is a measure of typical responding (i.e., what a person does on a regular basis) as are personality scales. Behavioral assessments can be constructed that measure maximum levels of performance, but such measures are better conceptualized as aptitude, ability, or achievement measures.

Behavioral assessment also differs from traditional personality assessment in several ways. Behavioral assessment emphasizes what a person does and in this context emphasizes observable behavior as opposed to covert thoughts and feelings. Behavioral assessment attempts then to define how a person behaves overtly on a day-to-day basis using observable expression and acts as the primary means of evaluating behavior. Most methods of personality assessment emphasize what a person has (e.g., his or her character, attributes, or reported feelings and thoughts). How we say we think and feel is not always congruent with what we do. Behavioral assessment is generally seen as more objective than personality assessment as well because most behavioral assessment scales do not ask for interpretations of behavior, only observations of the presence and frequency of a specified behavior. Thus, many see behavioral assessment as having a lower level of inference for its interpretations than traditional personality assessment, where the level of inference between scores and predictions of behavior can be quite high.

Early conceptualizations of behavioral assessment dealt only with overtly observable behavior. Typically, behavioral assessment in its formative years (from the 1930s into the late 1970s) relied on observation and counting of specific behaviors of concern. For example, in the

1960s and early 1970s many school psychologists were issued behavior counters (often referred to as clickers because of the clicking sound they made each time a behavior was "counted") along with other standardized test materials. Behavior was also seen as being highly contextually or setting specific—this perception is still characteristic of behavioral assessment, but is viewed with less rigidity today. For example, there are clear tendencies for children to behave similarly in the presence of their father and their mother, but it is not unusual for some clear differences to emerge in how a child behaves with each parent. The same is true across classrooms with different teachers—a child will have a tendency to respond in similar ways in all classrooms, but there will be clear differences depending on the teacher present and the teacher's approach to classroom management, and the teacher's personality and experience in working with children. As the field of behavioral assessment has matured, practitioners of behavioral assessment have come to recognize the importance of chronic characteristics such as anxiety and depression, locus of control, impulsivity, and other latent traits that do generalize across many settings to a significant extent, though far from perfectly. However, in assessing these traits, behavioral assessment scales ask about observable behaviors that are related to anxiety or depression as opposed to asking about thoughts and feelings. Examples might be, "Says, I have no friends," and "Says, no one likes to be with me," on a behavioral assessment scale, whereas on a self-report personality scale, an item asking about a similar construct might be worded, "I feel lonely much of the time."

> *Early conceptualizations of behavioral assessment relied on observation and counting of specific behaviors of concern in highly specific settings.*

Many traditional scales of personality assessment (though certainly not all) have come to be used in conjunction with behavioral assessment. However, these scales, such as the BASC-2 Self-Report of Personality (Reynolds & Kamphaus, 2004) discussed in the preceding chapter, do rely less on high-inference items and constructs and instead focus on more behavioral questions (e.g., "My parents blame me for things I do not do" as opposed to an item stem such as "People are out to get me"). This distinction may seem subtle, but behavioral assessment professionals argue in favor of the use of terms and items that describe actual behavior as opposed to states.

Thus the lines between behavioral assessment and some forms of traditional personality assessment do blur at points. The key difference in our minds is the level of inference involved in the interpretations of the test scores obtained under these two approaches. They are also quite complementary—it is important to know both how people typically behave *and* how they think and feel about themselves and others. Behavioral assessment also is not a specific or entirely unique set of measuring devices, but rather more of a paradigm, a way of thinking about and obtaining assessment information. Even responses to projective tests, which most psychologists would view as the antithesis of behavioral assessment, can be reconceptualized and interpreted as behavioral in nature (e.g., see the very interesting chapter by Teglasi, 1998) by altering the method of interpretation, moving toward low-inference interpretations of responses as samples of actual behavior. It is common practice now for clinicians to use a multimethod, multimodal approach to behavioral assessment. Practitioners will collect data or assessment information via behavioral interviewing, direct observation, and impressionistic behavior rating scales, as well as self-report "personality scales" designed to reduce the level of inference involved in their interpretation.

ASSESSING BEHAVIOR

Just as we noted about personality in the preceding chapter, whereas we might not consciously be aware of it, we all engage in the assessment and interpretation of behavior on a regular basis. When you note that "Tommy is a difficult child" or "Tamiqua is extroverted" you are making an assessment (albeit a crude and general one) and then forming a judgment about their behavior. We use these informal evaluations to determine with whom we want to associate and who we want to avoid, among many other ways. Clinicians use behavioral assessment to produce far more objective determinations about the behavior of individuals. By using standardized behavioral assessment methods such as behavior rating scales, practitioners can also determine the degree to which behaviors cluster together to reflect broader behavioral dimensions. For example, most behavior rating scales produce scores that reflect dimensions such as distractibility, aggression, hyperactivity, depression, or anxiety. In addition to telling us if clients behave in particular ways, behavior rating scales also indicate how common or rare these behaviors are in the general population. In other words, is the strength of the exhibited tendency to behave in particular ways strong enough or severe enough to warrant clinical interventions, or are these tendencies of a level similar to other people? With clients referred for an evaluation, this information is helpful in helping the clinician determine if there are real behavioral problems requiring psychological interventions or if the behavior is within normal limits. At times one determines the problem is one of a caregiver or teacher who simply has a very low tolerance level for what is a common, normal set of behaviors, and thus a different intervention is required—with a different target! Additionally, through repeated behavioral assessments, which are quite efficient and also have no so-called practice effect, one can monitor treatment effects regularly and accurately when behavioral change is the goal of intervention.

RESPONSE SETS

Response sets also occur in behavioral assessments.

We discussed response sets in more detail in the preceding chapter and will refer to them again in Chapter 18. However, response sets occur in behavioral assessments as well. As you recall, response biases or response sets are test responses that misrepresent a person's true characteristics. For example, an individual completing an employment-screening assessment that asks about behaviors on the job might attempt to present an overly positive image by answering all of the questions in the most socially appropriate manner possible, even if these responses do not accurately represent the person. On the other hand, a teacher who is hoping to have a disruptive student transferred from his or her class might be inclined to exaggerate the student's misbehavior when completing a behavior rating scale to hasten that student's removal. A parent may be completing a rating scale of his or her child's behavior and not want to be seen as a poorly skilled parent and so may deny common behavior problems that are present with the child being rated. In each of these situations the individual completing the test or scale responded in a manner that systematically distorted reality. This is often referred to as dissimulation that is, making another person (or yourself) appear dissimilar from how he or she really is or behaves. When response sets are present, the validity of the test results may be compromised because they introduce construct-irrelevant error to test scores (e.g., AERA et al., 1999). That is, the test results do not accurately reflect the construct the test was designed to measure. To combat this, many behavioral assessment scales incorporate several types of validity scales designed to detect the presence of response sets. Validity scales take different forms, but the general principle is that they are designed to detect individuals who are not responding in an accurate manner. Special Interest Topic 11–1 provides an example of a fake bad response set that might appear on a behavior rating scale completed by parents about their child. Why would parents want the

SPECIAL INTEREST TOPIC 11–1

An Example of a "Fake Bad" Response Set on a Parent Behavior Rating Scale

Typical response measures, despite the efforts of test developers, always remain susceptible to response sets. The following case is an authentic example. In this case the Behavior Assessment System for Children—Second Edition (BASC-2) was used.

Susan was brought to a private psychologist's office on referral from the State Department of Rehabilitation Services. Her mother is applying for disability benefits for Susan and says Susan has Bipolar Disorder. She is 14 years old and repeating the seventh grade this school year because she failed to attend school regularly last year. When skipping school, she spent time roaming the local shopping mall or engaging in other relatively unstructured activities. She failed all of her classes in both semesters of the past school year. Her mother says this is because she is totally out of control behaviorally and "has Bipolar Disorder." Susan's father expressed concern about her education, especially her lack of interest and unwillingness to do homework, but did not describe the hyperirritability and depressive attributes that are common with PBD.

Susan's responses to the diagnostic interview suggested that she was not interested in school and wanted to spend time with friends and engaged in social activities. She complained about having trouble keeping up in school as well, noting that reading was especially difficult for her. She acknowledged some attentional problems that she attributed to lack of interest in academic work, but did not note any other behavioral issues commonly associated with Pediatric Bipolar Disorder

Susan's Parent Rating Scale—Adolescent version (PRS-A) completed by the mother indicates evidence of a "fake bad" response set. All of her clinical scale scores were above the normative *T*-score mean of 50 and all of her adaptive scale scores were below the normative mean of 50. In other words, the PRS-A results suggest that Susan is severely maladjusted in all behavioral domains, which, although possible, is not likely.

The mother's response set was identified by the Infrequency or F scale, where she obtained a score of 16, and is in the Extreme Caution range, indicating a high probability that the overall ratings provide a far more negative picture of the child's behavior than is actually the case. The following table shows her full complement of PRS-A scores based on the mother's ratings.

Clinical Scales		Adaptive Scales	
Scale	*T*-Score	Scale	*T*-Score
Aggression	81	Activities of Daily Living	44
Anxiety	73	Adaptability	35
Attention Problems	70	Functional Communication	28
Atypicality	66	Leadership	39
Conduct problems	65	Social Skills	49
Depression	91		
Hyperactivity	67		
Somatization	85		
Withdrawal	59		

behavior ratings on their child to represent behavior that is worse than what actually is occurring? There are many reasons, but the two most common are a plea for immediate help with the child, so overwrought ratings are provided to get the clinician's attention to the desperate plight of the parents, and the second is to obtain a diagnosis for which services or disability payments might be received. We will talk more about detecting response sets later in the chapter.

ASSESSMENT OF BEHAVIOR IN THE SCHOOLS

> **Public Law 94–142** *and its most current reauthorization, the* **Individuals with Disabilities Education Improvement Act of 2004 (IDEA 2004),** *mandate that schools provide special education services to students with emotional disorders.*

Public Law 94–142 (IDEA) and its most current reauthorization, the **Individuals with Disabilities Education Improvement Act of 2004 (IDEA 2004)**, mandate that schools provide special education and related services to students with emotional disorders. These laws compel schools to identify students with emotional disorders and, as a result, expand school assessment practices, previously focused primarily on cognitive abilities, to include the evaluation of personality, behavior, and related constructs. We emphasize schools as a setting and children as a group in this chapter because that is the location and the population with whom behavioral assessments are most common, although behavioral assessments are also often used in clinics, private psychology practices, and other settings. A small number of behavioral assessment devices are available for assessment of adults.

The instruments used to assess behavior and personality in the schools can usually be classified as behavior rating scales, self-report measures, or projective techniques. The results of a national survey of school psychologists indicated that 5 of the top 10 instruments were behavior rating scales, 4 were projective techniques, and 1 was a self-report measure (Livingston et al., 2003; see Table 11–1 for a listing of these assessment instruments). These are representative of

Table 11-1 10 Most Popular Tests of Child Personality and Behavior	
Name of Test	**Type of Test**
1. BASC Teacher Rating Scale	Behavior rating scale
2. BASC Parent Rating Scale	Behavior rating scale
3. BASC Self-Report of Personality	Self-report measure
4. Draw-A-Person	Projective technique
5. Conners Rating Scales—Revised	Behavior rating scale
6. Sentence Completion Tests	Projective technique
7. House-Tree-Person	Projective technique
8. Kinetic Family Drawing	Projective technique
9. Teacher Report Form (Achenbach)	Behavior rating scale
10. Child Behavior Checklist (Achenbach)	Behavior rating scale

Note: BASC = Behavior Rating System for Children. The Conners Rating Scales—Revised and Sentence Completion Tests actually were tied. Based on a national sample of school psychologists (Livingston et al., 2003).

the instruments school psychologists use to assess children suspected of having an emotional, behavioral, or other type of disorder. The distribution is quite interesting to observe. The field of psychology has moved strongly, as has medicine and some other fields, to what is often termed *evidence-based practice,* referring to engagement in professional practices that have clear support in the science that underlies the profession. Traditionally, stemming from work from the late 1800s into the 1960s, projective assessment dominated assessment and diagnosis of emotional and behavioral disorders. In Chapter 10 we discussed the polemic, staunch emotional controversy surrounding projective testing. Nowhere is the division of opinion more evident than in these survey results. About half of the most frequently used tests in this assessment area in the schools are behavior rating scales—the most objective of behavior assessments and those with the strongest scientific evidence to support their use—whereas 40% are projective tests, clearly the most subjective of our assessment devices and the class of assessments with the least scientific support!

When behavioral assessments are conducted in schools, psychologists or other behavior specialists will often conduct an observational assessment in a classroom or perhaps even on the playground, counting the frequency of specified behaviors. However, teachers are often called on to provide relevant information on students' behavior. Classroom teachers are often asked to help with the assessment of students in their classrooms—for example, by completing behavior rating scales on students in their class. This practice provides invaluable data to school psychologists and other clinicians because teachers have a unique opportunity to observe children in their classrooms. Teachers can provide information on how the child behaves in different contexts, both academic and social. Those who do behavioral assessments understand the need for information on how children behave in different contexts—school, home, and community being the most important—and are interested in the consistencies as well as inconsistencies in behavior across settings.

> *Those who do behavioral assessments understand the need for information on how children behave in different contexts and are interested in the consistencies as well as inconsistencies in behavior across settings.*

BEHAVIORAL INTERVIEWING

Most assessments begin with a review of the referral information and statement of the referral questions. Next comes a form of interview with the person to be evaluated, or in the case of a child or adolescent, an interview with a parent or caregiver may occur first. The traditional clinical interview usually begins with broad, sweeping questions such as "Why are you here?", "How can I help you?", or perhaps with a child, "Why do you think you were asked to come here?" The clinician brings out the presenting problem in this way and then solicits a detailed history and attempts to understand the current mood states of the interviewee as well as any relevant traits of interest and seeks to understand the psychodynamics of the behaviors or states of concern. Behavioral interviewing has a different emphasis.

> *A behavioral interview tends to focus on the antecedents and consequences of behaviors of concern as well as what attempts at change have been made. An attempt to look at the relevant reinforcement history is made as well.*

When conducting a **behavioral interview**, once the issue to be addressed has been established, the clinician focuses on the antecedents and consequences of behaviors of concern as well as what attempts at change have been made. An attempt to look at the relevant reinforcement history is made as well (i.e., what has sustained the behavior and why has it not responded to efforts to create change). Problem-solving strategies are then introduced that are intended to lead to an intervention. Ramsay, Reynolds, and Kamphaus (2002) described six steps in behavioral interviewing that can be summarized as follows:

1. Identify the presenting problem and define it in behavioral terms.
2. Identify and evaluate environmental contingencies supporting the behaviors.
3. Develop a plan to alter these contingencies and reinforcers to modify the behavior.
4. Implement the plan.
5. Evaluate the outcomes of treatment or intervention. (This often involves having done a behavioral assessment using standardized rating scales for example to establish a baseline rate of behaviors of concern and then reassessing with the same scales later to look for changes from baseline.)
6. Modify the intervention plan if the behavior is not responding and evaluate the outcome of these changes.

The first three steps are the heart of the interview process in a behavioral interview, whereas the follow-up steps are conducted on a continuing basis in a behavioral paradigm. One of the key goals of the behavioral interview, contrasted with a traditional clinical interview, is to minimize the levels of inference used to obtain and interpret information. By stressing behavior as opposed to subjective states, a more definitive plan can be derived, clear goals can be set, and the progress of the individual monitored more clearly.

BEHAVIOR RATING SCALES

A **behavior rating scale** is essentially an inventory that asks a knowledgeable informant to rate an individual on a number of dimensions. When working with children and adolescents the informants are typically parents or teachers. On behavior rating scales designed for adults the informants might be a spouse, adult child, or health care worker. The instructions of the behavior rating scale typically ask an informant to rate a person by indicating whether he or she observes the behavior described:

0 = rarely or never

1 = occasionally

2 = often

3 = almost always

The scale will then present a series of item stems for which the informant rates the individual. For example:

Reacts to minor noises from outside the classroom.	0	1	2	3
Tells lies.	0	1	2	3
Interacts well with peers.	0	1	2	3
Is irritable.	0	1	2	3

As we have noted, behavior rating scales have been used most often with children and adolescents, but there is growing interest in using behavior rating scales with adults. The following discussion will initially focus on some major behavior rating scales used with children and adolescents, but we will also provide an example of a scale used with adults.

Behavior rating scales have a number of positive characteristics (e.g., Kamphaus & Frick, 2002; Piacentini, 1993; Ramsay et al., 2002; Witt, Heffer, & Pfeiffer, 1990). For example, children may have difficulty accurately reporting their own feelings and behaviors due to a number of factors such as limited insight or verbal abilities or, in the context of self-report tests, limited reading ability. However, when using behavior rating scales, information is solicited from the important adults in a child's life. Ideally these adult informants will have had adequate opportunities to observe the child in a variety of settings over an extended period of time. Behavior rating scales also represent a cost-effective and time-efficient method of collecting assessment information. For example, a clinician may be able to collect information from both parents and one or more teachers with a minimal investment of time or money. Most popular child behavior rating scales have separate inventories for parents and teachers. This allows the clinician to collect information from multiple informants who observe the child from different perspectives and in various settings. Behavior rating scales can also help clinicians assess the presence of rare behaviors. Although any responsible clinician will interview the client and other people close to the client, it is still possible to miss important indicators of behavioral problems. The use of well-designed behavior rating scales may help detect the presence of rare behaviors, such as fire setting and animal cruelty that might be missed in a clinical interview.

> **Behavior rating scales** *have been used most often with children and adolescents, but there is growing interest in using them with adults.*

There are some limitations associated with the use of behavior rating scales. Even though the use of adult informants to rate children provides some degree of objectivity, as we noted these scales are still subject to response sets that may distort the true characteristics of the child. For example, as a "cry for help" a teacher may exaggerate the degree of a student's problematic behavior in hopes of hastening a referral for special education services or even in the hope the child will be removed form the classroom to a different placement. Accordingly, parents might not be willing or able to acknowledge their child has significant emotional or behavioral problems and tend to underrate the degree and nature of problem behaviors. Although behavior rating scales are particularly useful in diagnosing "externalizing" problems such as aggression and hyperactivity, which are easily observed by adults, they may be less helpful when assessing "internalizing" problems such as depression and anxiety, which are not as apparent to observers.

Ratings of behavior on such omnibus behavior rating scales are **impressionistic** (i.e., based on the impressions of the person completing the scale) to a large extent. Test authors do not ask or expect the person completing the rating to count behaviors and typically items that ask for a specific count are avoided (e.g., one would rarely see an item such as "Gets out of seat without permission or at an inappropriate time 1 time per day"). Rather, behavior rating scales ask "Gets out of seat without permission or at an inappropriate time" with a range of responses such as *rarely, sometimes, often, almost always.* Not everyone will interpret such terms as rarely, sometimes, often, and so on in the same way and this does introduce some error into the ratings. However, the research on carefully developed behavior rating scales generally demonstrates their

> *Behavior rating scale scores, despite their impressionistic basis, predict diagnoses accurately, predict future behavior and learning problems, help detect changes in behavior, and can even predict what types of interventions are most likely to work to change a behavior.*

scores to be very reliable and also shows them to differentiate better among various groups of diagnostic conditions in the emotional and behavioral domain than any other single form of assessment available to us. Behavior rating scale scores, despite their impressionistic basis, predict diagnosis accurately, predict future behavior and learning problems, help us detect changes in behavior, and can even predict what types of interventions are most likely to work to change a behavior (e.g., see Vannest, Reynolds, & Kamphaus, 2009).

It is no surprise, then, that over the past two decades behavior rating scales have gained popularity and become increasingly important in the psychological assessment of children and adolescents (Livingston et al., 2003). It is common for a clinician to have both parents and teachers complete behavior rating scales for one child. This is desirable because parents and teachers have the opportunity to observe the child in different settings and can contribute unique yet complementary information to the assessment process. The consistencies as well as inconsistencies of a child's behavior in different settings and with different adults are also quite informative. Next, we will briefly review some of the most popular scales.

Behavior Assessment System for Children—Second Edition—
Teacher Rating Scale and Parent Rating Scale (TRS and PRS)

The Behavior Assessment System for Children (BASC) is an integrated set of instruments that includes a Teacher Rating Scale (TRS), a Parent Rating Scale (PRS), self-report scales, a classroom observation system, a scale that assesses the parent–child relationship (the Parenting Relationship Questionnaire), and a structured developmental history (Reynolds & Kamphaus, 1992). Although the BASC is a relatively new set of instruments, a 2003 national survey of school psychologists indicates that the TRS and PRS are the most frequently used behavior rating scales in the public schools today (Livingston et al., 2003). Information obtained from the publisher estimates the BASC was used with more than 1 million children in the United States alone in 2003. By 2006, following the release of the second edition of the BASC, known as the BASC-2, this estimate had grown to 2 million children per year. The TRS and PRS are appropriate for children from 2 to 21 years. Both the TRS and PRS provide item stems describing a behavior to which the informant responds *never, sometimes, often,* or *almost always.* The TRS is designed to provide a thorough examination of school-related behavior whereas the PRS is aimed at the home and community environment (Ramsay et al., 2002). In 2004, Reynolds and Kamphaus released the **Behavior Assessment System for Children—Second Edition (BASC-2)**, with updated scales and normative samples. Table 11–2 depicts the 5 composite scales, 16 primary scales, and 7 content scales for all the preschool, child, and adolescent versions of both instruments. Reynolds and Kamphaus (2004) described the individual primary subscales of the TRS and PRS as follows:

- *Adaptability:* ability to adapt to changes in one's environment
- *Activities of Daily Living:* skills associated with performing everyday tasks
- *Aggression:* acting in a verbally or physically hostile manner that threatens others

- *Anxiety:* being nervous or fearful about actual or imagined problems or situations
- *Attention Problems:* inclination to be easily distracted or have difficulty concentrating
- *Atypicality:* reflects behavior that is immature, bizarre, or suggestive of psychotic processes (e.g., hallucinations)
- *Conduct Problems:* inclination to display antisocial behavior (e.g., cruelty, destructive)
- *Depression:* reflects feelings of sadness and unhappiness
- *Functional Communication:* expression of ideas and communication in any way others can understand
- *Hyperactivity:* inclination to be overactive and impulsive
- *Leadership:* reflects ability to achieve academic and social goals, particularly the ability to work with others
- *Learning Problems:* reflects the presence of academic difficulties (only on the TRS)
- *Social Skills:* reflects the ability to interact well with peers and adults in a variety of settings
- *Somatization:* reflects the tendency to complain about minor physical problems
- *Study Skills:* reflects skills that are associated with academic success, for example, study habits, organization skills (only on the TRS)
- *Withdrawal:* the inclination to avoid social contact

New to the BASC-2 are the content scales, so-called because their interpretation is driven more by item content than actuarial or predictive methods. These scales are intended for use by advanced-level clinicians to help clarify the meaning of the primary scales and as an additional aid to diagnosis.

In addition to these individual scales, the TRS and PRS provide several different composite scores. The composite scores for the BASC and the subsequent BASC-2 were derived from a series of exploratory and confirmatory factor analyses, supplemented by a technique called structural equation modeling and are thus empirically derived composite scores. Table 11–2 summarizes the structure and organization of scores produced by the BASC-2.

The authors recommend that interpretation follow a "top-down" approach, by which the clinician starts at the most global level and progresses to more specific levels (e.g., Reynolds & Kamphaus, 2004). The most global measure is the Behavioral Symptoms Index (BSI), which is a composite of the Aggression, Attention Problems, Anxiety, Atypicality, Depression, and Somatization scales. The BSI reflects the overall level of behavioral problems and provides the clinician with a reliable but nonspecific index of pathology. For more specific information about the nature of the problem behavior, the clinician proceeds to the four lower order composite scores:

> *The authors of the* **Behavior Assessment System for Children—Second Edition (BASC-2)** *recommend that interpretation follow a "top-down" approach, by which the clinician starts at the most global level and progresses to more specific levels.*

- *Internalizing Problems.* This is a composite of the Anxiety, Depression, and Somatization scales. Some authors refer to internalizing problems as "overcontrolled" behavior. Students with internalizing problems experience subjective or internal discomfort or distress, but they do not typically display severe acting-out or disruptive behaviors (e.g., aggression, impulsiveness). As a result, these children may go unnoticed by teachers and school-based clinicians. There are some notable exceptions. Children with depression, especially boys,

Table 11–2 Composites, Primary Scales, and Content Scales in the TRS and PRS

	Teacher Rating Scales			Parent Rating Scales		
	P 2–5	C 6–11	A 12–21	P 2–5	C 6–11	A 12–21
COMPOSITE						
Adaptive Skills	•	•	•	•	•	•
Behavioral Symptoms Index	•	•	•	•	•	•
Externalizing Problems	•	•	•	•	•	•
Internalizing Problems	•	•	•	•	•	•
School Problems		•	•			
PRIMARY SCALE						
Adaptability	•	•	•	•	•	•
Activities of Daily Living				•	•	•
Aggression	•	•	•	•	•	•
Anxiety	•	•	•	•	•	•
Attention Problems	•	•	•	•	•	•
Atypicality	•	•	•	•	•	•
Conduct Problems		•	•		•	•
Depression	•	•	•	•	•	•
Functional Communication	•	•	•	•	•	•
Hyperactivity	•	•	•	•	•	•
Leadership		•	•		•	•
Learning Problems		•	•			
Social Skills		•	•	•	•	•
Somatization	•	•	•	•	•	•
Study Skills		•	•			
Withdrawal	•	•	•	•	•	•
CONTENT SCALE						
Anger Control	•	•	•	•	•	•
Bullying	•	•	•	•	•	•
Developmental Social Disorders	•	•	•	•	•	•
Emotional Self-Control	•	•	•	•	•	•
Executive Functioning	•	•	•	•	•	•
Negative Emotionality	•	•	•	•	•	•
Resiliency	•	•	•	•	•	•
NUMBER OF ITEMS	100	139	139	134	160	150

Note: Shaded cells represent new scales added to the BASC-2. P = preschool version; C = child version; A = adolescent version.

Source: Behavior Assessment System for Children, Second Edition (BASC-2). Copyright © 2004 NCS Pearson, Inc. Reproduced with permission. All rights reserved. "BASC" is a trademark, in the US and/or other countries, of Pearson Education, Inc. or its affiliates.

are often irritable and have attentional difficulties, and can be misdiagnosed as having attention deficit hyperactivity disorder (ADHD) if one looks only at these symptoms and does not obtain a full picture of the child's behavior.

- *Externalizing Problems.* This is a composite of the Aggression, Conduct Problems, and Hyperactivity scales. Relative to the behaviors and symptoms associated with internalizing problems, the behaviors associated with externalizing problems are clearly apparent to observers. Children with high scores on this composite are typically disruptive to both peers and adults, and usually will be noticed by teachers and other adults.
- *School Problems.* This composite consists of the Attention Problems and Learning Problems scales. High scores on this scale suggest academic motivation, attention, and learning difficulties that are likely to hamper academic progress. This composite is available only for the BASC-TRS.
- *Adaptive Skills.* This is a composite of Activities of Daily Living, Adaptability, Leadership, Social Skills, and Study Skills scales. It reflects a combination of social, academic, and other positive skills (Reynolds & Kamphaus, 2004).

The third level of analysis involves examining the 16 clinical (e.g., Hyperactivity, Depression) and adaptive scales (e.g., Leadership, Social Skills). Finally, clinicians will often examine the individual items. Although individual items are often unreliable, when interpreted cautiously they may provide clinically important information. This is particularly true of what is often referred to as "critical items." Critical items, when coded in a certain way, suggest possible danger to self or others or reflect an unusual behavior that may be innocuous, but also may not, and requires questioning by the clinician for clarification. For example, if a parent or teacher reports that a child often "threatens to harm self or others," the clinician would want to determine whether these statements indicate imminent danger to the child or others.

When interpreting the Clinical Composites and Scale scores, high scores reflect abnormality or pathology. The authors provide the following classifications: *T*-score ≥70 is Clinically Significant; 60–69 is At-Risk; 41–59 is Average; 31–40 is Low; and ≤30 is Very Low. Scores on the adaptive composite and scales are interpreted differently, with high scores reflecting adaptive or positive behaviors. The authors provided the following classifications: *T*-score ≥70 is Very High; 60–69 is High; 41–59 is Average; 31–40 is At-Risk; and ≤30 is Clinically Significant. Computer software is available to facilitate scoring and interpretation, and the use of this software is recommended because hand scoring can be challenging for new users. An example of a completed TRS profile is depicted in Figure 11–1.

The TRS and PRS have several unique features that promote their use. First, they contain a validity scale that helps the clinician detect the presence of response sets. As noted previously, validity scales are specially developed and incorporated in the test for the purpose of detecting response sets. Both the parent and teacher scales contain a fake bad (F) index that is elevated when an informant excessively rates maladaptive items as *almost always* and adaptive items as *never*. If this index is elevated, the clinician should consider the possibility that a negative response set has skewed the results. Another unique feature of these scales is that they assess both negative and adaptive behaviors. Before the advent of the BASC, behavior rating scales were often criticized for focusing only on negative behaviors and pathology. Both the TRS and PRS address this criticism by assessing a broad spectrum of behaviors, both positive and negative. The identification of positive characteristics can facilitate treatment by helping identify strengths to build on. Still

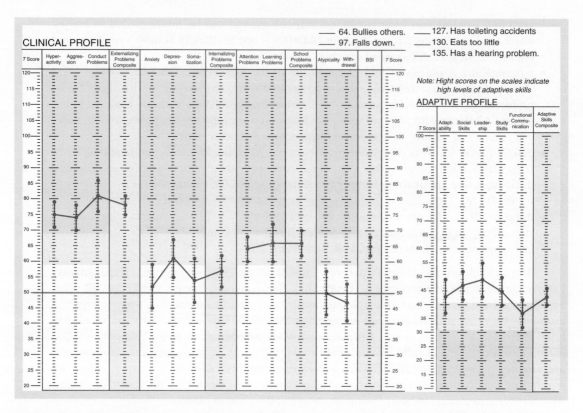

FIGURE 11–1 An example of a completed TRS profile

Source: Behavior Assessment System for Children, Second Edition (BASC-2). Copyright © 2004 NCS Pearson, Inc. Reproduced with permission. All rights reserved. "BASC" is a trademark, in the US and/or other countries, of Pearson Education, Inc. or its affiliates.

another unique feature is that the TRS and PRS provide three norm-referenced comparisons that can be selected depending on the clinical focus. The child's ratings can be compared to a general national sample, a gender-specific national sample, or a national clinical sample composed of children who have a clinical diagnosis and are receiving treatment. In summary, the BASC-2 PRS and BASC-2 TRS are psychometrically sound instruments that have gained considerable support in recent years.

Currently there is an interesting discussion under way regarding the relative merits of categorical diagnostic systems (such as that employed in the *DSM–IV–TR*) versus dimensional models of diagnosis. Special Interest Topic 11–2 presents a brief introduction to this topic.

Achenbach System of Empirically Bvased Assessment— Child Behavior Checklist (CBCL) and Teacher Report Form (TRF)

The Child Behavior Checklist (CBCL) and the Teacher Report Form (TRF) (Achenbach, 1991a, 1991b) are two components of the Achenbach System of Empirically Based Assessment (ASEBA) that also includes a self-report scale and a direct observation system. There are two forms of the

SPECIAL INTEREST TOPIC 11–2

Categorical Versus Dimensional Diagnosis

There are many approaches to grouping individuals as well as objects. Whenever we engage in diagnosis, we are engaged in grouping via the assignment of a label or designation to a person as having or not having a disorder or disease—and, having a disorder or not having a disorder typically are mutually exclusive decisions. In the traditional medical approach to diagnosis, categorical systems and methods are used. Typically, categorical approaches to diagnosis of mental and developmental disorders rely heavily on observation and interview methods designed to detect the presence of particular symptoms or behaviors, both overt and covert. The degree or severity of the symptom is rarely considered except that it must interfere in some way with normal functioning in some aspect of one's life (i.e., it must have a negative impact on the patient). A symptom is either present or absent. A dichotomous decision is then reached on a diagnosis based on a declaration of presence or absence of a set of symptoms known to cluster into a pattern designated as a disorder or syndrome.

In dimensional approaches to diagnosis, the clinician recognizes that many traits and states exists that contribute to a diagnosis and that all of these exist at all times to some greater or lesser extent (i.e., they are present on a continuum). Psychologists, the primary practitioners of dimensional diagnosis, then measure each of the relevant constructs using psychological tests of various types. The relative relationship of each of the constructs to one another and their overall levels are used to derive a diagnosis or classification. Typically, a mathematical algorithm is used such as discriminant analysis, cluster analysis, latent profile analysis, configural frequency analysis, logistic regression, or some other multivariate classification approach in order to arrive at a correct diagnosis or classification. More often than not, psychologists will refer to a diagnosis made using such a dimensional and actuarial approach as a classification as opposed to traditional diagnosis to assist in making the distinction in the methods applied.

Dimensional approaches can at times blur the lines between "normality" and "psychopathology;" however, this is not necessarily a negative outcome. Dimensional approaches can allow individuals who may not meet a strict symptom count to receive services when the combination of behavioral and emotional issues they are experiencing results in clear impairment but a count of symptoms might deny a diagnosis. There is also considerable evidence to show that mathematical or actuarial models of diagnosis and classification tend to be more accurate and objective overall than are traditional methods. The math algorithms are not swayed by subjective impression—however, some see this as a criticism as well, arguing that diagnosis is as much or more an art than a science and that good clinicians should be swayed by subjective information. For this reason, dimensional classification and diagnosis has been very slow to catch on and is particularly resisted by the medical community, although the current trend toward the practice of evidence-based medicine that has moved into many professional health care fields has invited greater acceptance of dimensional approaches to diagnosis and classification.

The use of dimensional models continues to grow more so in psychology than elsewhere, but we see growth in other areas of health care as well. The issues are complex, but the data are compelling. If you want to know more about these approaches, we suggest the following two sources:

Grove, W., & Meehl, P. (1996). Comparative efficiency of the informal (subjective, impressionistic) and formal 9 (mechanical, algorithmic) prediction procedures: The clinical-statistical controversy. *Psychology, Public Policy, and Law. 2*, 293–323.

Kamphaus, R., & Campbell, J. (Eds.). (2006). *Psychodiagnostic assessment of children: Dimensional and categorical approaches.* New York: Wiley.

CBCL, one for children 2 to 3 years and one for children 4 to 18 years. The TRF is appropriate for children from 5 to 18 years. The CBCL and TRF have long played an important role in the assessment of children and adolescents and continue to be among the most frequently used psychological tests in schools today. The scales contain two basic sections. The first section collects information about the child's activities and competencies in areas such as recreation (e.g., hobbies and sports), social functioning (e.g., clubs and organizations), and schooling (e.g., grades). The second section assesses problem behaviors and contains item stems describing problem behaviors. On these items the informant records a response of *not true, somewhat true/sometimes true,* or *very true/often true.* The clinical subscales of the CBCL and TRF are as follows:

- *Withdrawn:* reflects withdrawn behavior, shyness, and a preference to be alone
- *Somatic Complaints:* a tendency to report numerous physical complaints (e.g., headaches, fatigue)
- *Anxious/Depressed:* reflects a combination of depressive (e.g., lonely, crying, unhappy) and anxious (nervous, fearful, worried) symptoms
- *Social Problems:* reflects peer problems and feelings of rejection
- *Thought Problems:* evidence of obsessions/compulsions, hallucinations, or other "strange" behaviors
- *Attention Problems:* reflects difficulty concentrating, attention problems, and hyperactivity
- *Delinquent Behavior:* evidence of behaviors such as stealing, lying, vandalism, and arson
- *Aggressive Behavior:* reflects destructive, aggressive, and disruptive behaviors

The CBCL and TRF provide three composite scores:

- *Total Problems:* overall level of behavioral problems
- *Externalizing:* a combination of the Delinquent Behavior and Aggressive Behavior scales
- *Internalizing:* a combination of the Withdrawn, Somatic Complaints, and Anxious/Depressed scales

Computer-scoring software is available for the CBCL and TRF and is recommended because hand scoring is a fairly laborious and time-consuming process. The CBCL and TRF have numerous strengths that continue to make them popular among school psychologists and other clinicians. They are relatively easy to use, are time efficient (when using the computer-scoring program), and have a rich history of clinical and research applications (Kamphaus & Frick, 2002).

> **Omnibus rating scales** *measure a wide range of symptoms and behaviors that are associated with different emotional and behavioral disorders.*

The BASC-2 TRS and PRS, the CBCL and TRF, and similar rating scales are typically referred to as **omnibus rating scales**. This indicates that they measure a wide range of symptoms and behaviors that are associated with different emotional and behavioral disorders. Ideally an omnibus rating scale should be sensitive to symptoms of both internalizing (e.g., anxiety, depression) and externalizing (e.g., ADHD, Oppositional Defiant Disorder) disorders to ensure that the clinician is not missing important indicators of psychopathology. This is particularly important when assessing children and adolescents because there is a high degree of comorbidity with this population. *Comorbidity* refers to the presence of two or more disorders occurring simultaneously in the same individual. For example, a child might meet the criteria for both an externalizing disorder (e.g., conduct disorder) and an internalizing disorder (e.g., depressive disorder). However, if a clinician did not adequately screen for internalizing symptoms, the more obvious externalizing symptoms might mask the internalizing symptoms and result in an inaccurate or incomplete diagnosis. Inaccurate diagnosis typically leads to inadequate treatment.

Single-Domain Rating Scales

Although omnibus rating scales play a central role in the assessment of psychopathology, there are also a number of **single-domain** (or syndrome-specific) **rating scales**. These rating scales resemble the omnibus scales in format, but they focus on a single disorder (e.g., ADHD) or behavioral dimension (e.g., social skills). Although they are narrow in scope, they often provide a more thorough assessment of the specific domain they are designed to assess than the omni-

> **Single-domain** *(syndrome-specific)* **rating scales** *often provide a more thorough assessment of the specific domain they are designed to assess than the omnibus scales.*

bus scales. As a result, they can be useful in supplementing more comprehensive assessment techniques (e.g., Kamphaus & Frick, 2002). Single-domain scales include measures limited to ADHD, depression, or obsessive-compulsive disorder, for example. Following are some brief descriptions of some contemporary syndrome-specific behavior rating scales.

CHILDHOOD AUTISM RATING SCALE. The CARS (Schopler, Reichler, & Renner, 1988) is a 15-item scale that is designed to help identify autism in children over 2 years of age. The individual items are summed to form a total score that is used to rate a child on a continuum from nonautistic, to mild-to-moderate autism, to severe autism. The CARS can be completed by a professional such as a psychologist, pediatrician, or teacher based on observations performed in a variety of settings (e.g., classrooms, clinics). In the manual the authors report results of psychometric studies that suggest adequate reliability and validity, and a training video is available that shows how to use and score the instrument.

BASC MONITOR FOR ADHD (KAMPHAUS & REYNOLDS, 1998). The BASC Monitor (Kamphaus & Reynolds, 1998) contains two 45-item ratings scales, one for teachers and one for parents. It is designed for use with children and adolescents 4 to 18 years with ADHD. This instrument is designed to facilitate the treatment of ADHD by assessing the primary symptoms of the disorder in a repeated assessment format. This allows the treatment team to monitor the effectiveness of the treatment program and make adjustments when indicated (e.g., changes in the medication regimen). Both the parent and teacher rating forms produce four scales: Attention Problems, Hyperactivity, Internalizing Problems, and Adaptive Skills. The authors report results of multiple psychometric studies that indicate good reliability and validity. There is also BASC Monitor software that helps the clinician collect and track the results of repeated assessments and any changes in pharmacological and behavioral interventions.

PEDIATRIC BEHAVIOR RATING SCALE. The PBRS (Marshall & Wilkinson, 2008) contains two ratings scales, one for teachers (95 items) and one for parents (102 items). This instrument is for children and adolescents between 3 and 18 years and is intended to help identify early onset bipolar disorder and help distinguish it from other disorders with similar presentations. Both forms produce nine scales: Atypical, Irritability, Grandiosity, Hyperactivity/Impulsivity, Aggression, Inattention, Affect, Social Interactions, and a Total Bipolar Index. The authors report results of preliminary psychometric studies that indicate adequate reliability and validity.

> *Omnibus scales such as the BASC-2 and the CBCL should always be used over single-domain scales for initial diagnosis.*

These are just a few examples of the many single-domain or syndrome-specific behavior rating scales. Many of these scales are available for a number of psychological disorders and behavioral dimensions. They are particularly helpful in the assessment of externalizing disorders such as ADHD and conduct disorder in children and adolescents. Note that they are intended to supplement the omnibus scales such as the BASC-2 and the CBCL, which should always be used over single-domain scales for initial screening and assessment.

ADAPTIVE BEHAVIOR RATING SCALES. A special type of syndrome-specific scale is one designed to assess adaptive behavior. The American Association on Intellectual and Developmental Disabilities, an influential organization that advocates for the rights of individuals with disabilities, describes adaptive behavior as a collection of skills in three broad areas:

- *Conceptual skills:* includes literacy, quantitative skills such as telling time and using money, and the ability for self-direction
- *Practical skills:* includes activities of daily living (e.g., getting dressed, adequate hygiene), health care, using transportation, preparing meals, and house cleaning
- *Social skills:* includes general interpersonal and social skills and the ability to follow rules and obey laws

The measurement of adaptive behaviors is particularly important in the assessment of individuals with developmental and intellectual disabilities. For example, when diagnosing Mental Retardation it is necessary to document deficits in adaptive skills in addition to deficits in intellectual abilities. The assessment of adaptive behaviors can also facilitate treatment planning for individuals with a wide range of disabilities.

The Vineland Adaptive Behavior Scales—Second Edition (Vineland-II) is an example of a scale designed to assess adaptive behavior. There are a number of forms available for the Vineland II. These are:

- **Survey Interview Form:** This form is administered to a parent or other caregiver as a semistructured interview. That is, the survey provides a set of questions that the clinician presents to the respondent. It includes open-ended questions that may allow the clinician to gather more in-depth information than that acquired using standard behavior rating scales. There is also an Expanded Interview Form that provides a more detail assessment than the standard Survey Interview Form and is recommended for low-functioning and young clients.
- **Parent/Caregiver Rating Form:** This behavior rating scale covers essentially the same behaviors as the Survey Interview Form but uses an objective rating scale format. This format is recommended when time limitations prevent

> *The measurement of adaptive behaviors is particularly important in the assessment of individuals with developmental and intellectual disabilities.*

using the more comprehensive interview form and for periodic monitoring of client progress during treatment.

• **Teacher Rating Form:** This behavioral questionnaire is designed to be completed by a teacher who has experience with a child in a school or preschool setting. Its assesses the same behavioral domains as those measured by the Survey Interview Form and Parent/ Caregiver Rating Forms, but focuses on behaviors likely to be observed in a classroom or structured daycare setting.

Adult Behavior Rating Scales

We have thus far emphasized behavior rating scales that are used with children and adolescents. Behavior rating scales at these ages are far more common in clinical and school practice than in the adult age range. Nevertheless, there are adult behavior rating scales and we expect that their use will grow in the future. The Clinical Assessment Scales for the Elderly (CASE) by Reynolds and Bigler (2001) is an example of such a scale. It is an omnibus behavior rating scale for persons aged 55 through 90 years designed to be completed by a knowledgeable caregiver such as a spouse or adult child, or a health care worker who has nearly daily contact with the examinee. The CASE also has a separate self-report scale for cognitively intact seniors to complete, but here we will focus on the behavior rating scale.

The various clinical scales of the CASE focus on diagnosis and evaluation of the presence primarily of Axis I or clinical disorders in this age group. The complete self-report scales and the behavior rating scale of the CASE contain 13 scales each, 10 clinical scales and 3 validity scales. Table 11–3 lists and describes the scales of the CASE. As you can see, there is much overlap with rating scales designed for children and adolescents, in terms of the constructs being assessed, but some key differences as well. For example, the CASE contains a Fear of Aging scale that is often useful in evaluating the source of anxieties as well as depressive symptoms in this age group. A Cognitive Competency screening scale is included to alert clinicians to when a more careful or thorough evaluation of intelligence and related neuropsychological skills might be advised. A Substance Abuse scale is also included to alert clinicians to issues in this domain as well—abuse of common substances and prescription medications are included on this scale because they are far more common in this population than many clinicians perceive and are thus often overlooked. You might wonder why most behavior rating scales for adolescents do not include a substance abuse scale. Although this information is certainly valuable and no one denies that substance abuse is a problem in the 13-to-18-year-old group, most behavior rating scales do not include this for several practical reasons. Most adolescents abuse psychoactive substances in a secretive fashion and so raters are most likely unaware of the issues, and even if aware or suspicious, have no opportunity to observe the use, and if these scales come up within the normal range or indicate "no problem," clinicians may be overconfident they have effectively ruled this out. More importantly, however, most of these scales are commonly used in the public schools, which often have prohibitions against psychologists asking students about substance abuse issues. The 10 clinical scales were designed to assist in the process of differential diagnosis of the primary Axis I clinical disorders that occur in the population over 55 years of age. Scales such as study skills, conduct problems, and hyperactivity are of limited value, if any, in this age group so they were not included.

Table 11-3	Clinical Assessment Scales for the Elderly—Clinical Scales and Descriptions
Clinical Scales	**Description**
Anxiety (ANX)	Items assess a generalized sense of apprehension and fears that tend toward being irrational and nonspecific, including observable and subjective symptoms and worry states.
Cognitive Competence (COG)	Items assess impaired thought processes commonly associated with higher cognitive deficits in such areas as attention, memory, reason, and logical thought.
Depression (DEP)	Items assess indications of depressed mood, general dysthymia, sadness, fatigue, melancholy, and some cognitive symptoms associated with major depressive episodes.
Fear of Aging (FOA)	Items assess a sense of apprehension about aging and overconcern with the natural processes of aging and its effects on oneself and one's family.
Mania (MAN)	Items assess characteristics of manic states including pressured speech, grandiose thought, agitation, distractibility, flight of ideas, and related phenomena.
Obsessive-Compulsive (OCD)	Items assess nonproductive; ruminative thought patterns; excessive, targeted worry; and related phenomena.
Paranoia (PAR)	Items assess the presence of ideas of reference, nonbizarre delusions, suspicions of others' motives, a preoccupation with doubts about others, and related ideas.
Psychoticism (PSY)	Items assess disorders of thought, bizarre delusions, confusion, negative symptoms, and associated problems.
Somatization (SOM)	Items assess hypersensitivity to health concerns and physical symptoms not fully explained by medical problems or excessive numbers of physical complaints.
Substance Abuse (SUB)	Items assess overuse of mood-altering substances of a variety of forms, including common consumer products such as coffee/caffeine, alcohol, and illicit substances, and the tendency toward dependency on such substances.
Infrequency (F)	Items assess a tendency to overreport symptoms across a broad range of disorders not commonly endorsed in concert and potentially reflecting acute stress, frank psychosis, malingering, or a very negative response set.
Lie (L)	Items assess the tendency to deny common problems or difficulties, to respond in a socially desirable manner, or an attempt to present oneself in an overly positive light.
Validity (V)	Items on this scale reflect highly unrealistic responses typically endorsed at high levels only by a failure to read and comprehend the items, a failure to take the test seriously, or by random responding.

Source: From Reynolds, C. R., & Bigler, E. D. (2001). *Clinical Assessment Scales for the Elderly.* Odessa, FL: Psychological Assessment Resources. Reprinted with permission of PAR.

Three validity scales are provided with the full-length scales: a Lie (L) or social desirability scale, an Infrequency (F) scale, and a Validity (V) scale composed of nonsensical items designed to detect random or insincere marking. Screening versions of the CASE are also available and are significantly shortened versions of the same scales noted in Table 11–3, including two of the three validity scales. The Infrequency (F) scale does not appear on the CASE screening scales. Otherwise, the clinical and validity scales are common across the four versions of the CASE, although individual items that make up the scales vary somewhat from scale to scale. The full-length CASE rating scales are typically completed in 30 minutes or less, and may be used in a clinician's office, nursing home, and rehabilitation setting as well as in a general or gerontological medical practice. The CASE screening versions are half or less of the length of the full scales and require proportionately less time. The four forms of the CASE (the self-report, the rating form, and the corresponding short versions of each) are designed to be used independently or in combination.

DIRECT OBSERVATION

Direct observation and recording of behavior counts is the oldest method of behavioral assessment and is still widely used. As Ramsay et al. (2002) noted, some believe this approach to be the true hallmark of what constitutes a behavioral assessment. In direct observation, an observer travels to some natural environment

> **Direct observation** *of behavior is the oldest form of behavioral assessment and remains useful.*

of the individual (a school, a nursing home, etc.) and observes the subject, typically without the person knowing he or she is the target of the observation, although the latter is not always possible or even ethical. In reality it is very difficult to get an accurate sample of typical behavior from a person who knows he or she is being observed—observing the behavior will nearly always change it. This is in some ways analogous to the Heisenberg principle of uncertainty in physics: We can never observe something in its unobserved state (observing something changes it!).

In a direct observation, a set of behaviors are specified, then recorded and counted as they occur. In such an instance it is crucial that the observer-recorder be as impartial and objective as possible and that the behaviors to be recorded are described in clear, crisp terms so there is the least amount of inference possible for the observer. Direct observation adds another dimension to the behavioral assessment—rather than being impressionistic, as are behavior ratings, it provides true ratio scale data that are actual counts of behavior. It also adds another dimension by being a different method of assessment that allows triangulation or checking of results from other methods and allowing the observer to note antecedent events as well as consequences assigned to the observed behaviors.

This form of traditional behavioral assessment can occur with or without a standardized recording scheme. Often, observers will develop a form to aid them in coding and counting behaviors that is specific to the individual circumstance of any one observation period or simply devise one they are comfortable using with all of their observations. However, this can introduce a variety of biases and increase the subjectivity of the observations. It can also enhance the error rates of recording behaviors due to the cognitive demand on the observer. Standardized observation forms are available for many different settings and enhance observer training, objectivity, consistency, and accuracy, but do limit the flexibility of direct observation, which is one of its key strengths. Nevertheless, we view the advantages of using a standardized observational or recording system as outweighing the limitations of such systems.

The most widely used system is the Student Observation System (SOS) which is a component of the BASC-2. The SOS is a standardized, objective observational recording system that allows for the observation of 14 dimensions of behavior (some positive dimensions and some negative dimensions), and is designed to be useful in any structured setting that has educational goals. It is most commonly used in classrooms. The 14 categories of behavior assessed are listed in Table 11–4. Each of these categories or behavioral dimensions is defined specifically and clearly for the observer and research indicates high levels of interobserver agreement

Table 11–4	Behavioral Categories of the BASC-2 Student Observation System (SOS)
Category/Definition	**Specific Behavior Examples**
1. **Response to Teacher/Lesson:** This category describes the student's **appropriate** academic behaviors involving the teacher or class. This category does not include working on school subjects (see Category 3).	Raising hand to ask/answer a question; contributing to class discussion; waiting for help or for an assignment or task
2. **Peer Interaction:** This category assesses positive or appropriate interactions with other students.	Conversing with others in small group or class discussion; lightly touching another student in a friendly or encouraging manner; giving a pat on the back or shaking hands
3. **Work on School Subjects:** This category includes **appropriate** academic behaviors that the student engages in alone, without interacting with others.	Working on a school subject either at the student's own desk or in a learning center
4. **Transition Movement:** This category is for appropriate and nondisruptive behaviors of children while moving from one activity or place to another. Most are out-of-seat behaviors and may be infrequent during a classroom observation period.	Walking to the blackboard; getting a book; sharpening a pencil; lining up; taking a water/bathroom break; performing an errand; following others in line
5. **Inappropriate Movement:** This category is intended for inappropriate motor behaviors that are unrelated to classroom work.	Playing at blackboard inappropriately; being asked to leave the room or being physically removed from the room; hitting others with a classroom-related object (e.g., a musical instrument); refusing to leave a teacher's side to participate in school activities
6. **Inattention:** This category includes inattentive behaviors that are not disruptive.	Scribbling on paper or desks; looking at objects unrelated to classroom activity while not paying attention
7. **Inappropriate Vocalization:** This category includes disruptive vocal behaviors. Only vocal behavior should be checked.	Criticizing another harshly; picking on another student; making disruptive noises such as screaming, belching, moaning, grinding teeth, or "shhh" sounds; refusing to do schoolwork or participate in an activity; talking out of turn, during a quiet time, or without permission
8. **Somatization:** This category includes behaviors regardless of inferred reason (e.g., a student may be sleeping because of medication, boredom, or poor achievement motivation).	Complaining that stomach hurts; complaining that head hurts
9. **Repetitive Motor Movement:** This category includes repetitive behaviors (both disruptive and nondisruptive) that appear to have no external reward. Generally, the behaviors should be of 15-second duration or longer to be checked, and may be more likely to be checked on Part A than on Part B because of their repetitive nature. They may, however, be checked during either part.	Rapping finger(s)/pencil on desk; tapping foot on floor; swinging foot in the air; twirling or spinning a pencil or toy; moving body back and forth or from side to side while sitting; walking back and forth or in a circle in one area; sucking on back of hand; staring fixedly at moving hand; hair-twisting
10. **Aggression:** This category includes harmful behaviors directed at another student, the teacher, or property. The student must attempt to hurt another or destroy property for the behavior to be checked in this category. Aggressive play would not be included here.	Intentionally tearing, ripping, or breaking own or another's work, belongings, or property

Continued

Category/Definition	Specific Behavior Examples
11. **Self-Injurious Behavior:** This category includes severe behaviors that attempt to injure one's self. These behaviors should not be confused with self-stimulatory behaviors. This category is intended to capture behaviors of children with severe disabilities who are being served in special classes in schools and institutions.	Pulling own hair with enough force to pull it out; slapping or punching self with enough force to cause a bruise or laceration; banging head on a wall, floor, or object with enough force to bruise or injure; scratching or poking at own eyes with enough force to cause injury; placing paper, dirt, or grass in mouth and attempting to ingest it
12. **Inappropriate Sexual Behavior:** This category includes behaviors that are explicitly sexual in nature. The student could be seeking sexual gratification. Behaviors that are not flagrant and specifically sexual (such as hitting others) are not included here.	"Petting" self or others, any form of sexual touching—hugging another student quickly as a brief hello or good-bye would not be coded unless it involves sexual touching as well
13. **Bowel/Bladder Problems:** This category includes urination and defecation.	Urinating in his or her pants; having a bowel movement outside the toilet; soiling or smearing in pants
14. **Other:** This category includes behaviors that do not seem to fit in any other categories. It should be used infrequently.	

on the ratings with as few as two *in vivo* training sessions (Reynolds & Kamphaus, 2004). The SOS uses a momentary time sampling (MTS) procedure to ensure that it adequately samples the full range of a child's behavior in the classroom (Reynolds & Kamphaus, 1992). Several characteristics of the SOS exemplify this effort:

- Both adaptive and maladaptive behaviors are observed (see Table 11–4).
- Multiple methods are used including clinician rating, time sampling, and qualitative recording of classroom functional contingencies.
- A generous time interval is allocated for recording the results of each time sampling interval (27 seconds).
- Operational definitions of behaviors and time sampling categories are included in the BASC-2 manual (Reynolds & Kamphaus, 2004).
- Inter-rater reliabilities for the time sampling portion are high, which lends confidence that independent observers are likely to observe the same trends in a child's classroom behavior.

These characteristics of the SOS have contributed to its popularity as a functional behavioral assessment tool. It is crucial, for example, to have adequate operational definitions of behaviors that, in turn, contribute to good inter-rater reliability. Without such reliability clinicians will never know if their observations are unique or potentially influenced by their own biases or idiosyncratic definitions of behavior. MTS is also important in making direct observation practical as well as accurate. The observer watches the target individual for a specified period and looks at the recording sheet, marks the relevant behaviors seen, again does this in a specified period, and then observes the target individual again. The BASC-2 SOS MTS is set to be a total of 15 minutes. With this timeframe an observer can target multiple children in a classroom or efficaciously observe the same target in multiple settings to assess the generalizability of the behavioral occurrences.

Data from the direct observation of behavior is useful in initial diagnosis, treatment planning, and in monitoring changes and treatment effectiveness. It gives the clinician a unique look at the immediate antecedents and consequences of behavior in a relevant context in a way that no other method can document. An electronic version of the BASC-2 SOS, the BASC Portable Observation Program (BASC POP), is available that may be used on a laptop computer.

CONTINUOUS PERFORMANCE TESTS (CPTs)

> **Continuous performance tests** *are a specific type of behavioral test originally designed to measure vigilance, attention, and more generally, executive control.*

Continuous performance tests (CPTs) are a specific type of behavioral test originally designed to measure vigilance, sustained and selective attention, and more generally, executive control. There are many different CPT paradigms that have been devised since the original CPT of Rosvold, Mirsky, Sarason, Bransome, and Beck in 1956, but the basic CPT paradigms have remained similar until just recently. Typically, a CPT requires an examinee to view a computer screen and respond when a specific, but highly simple, stimulus or sequence of stimulating, appears on the screen and to inhibit responding at all other times. For example, in the first CPT, the examinee pressed a lever whenever the letter X appeared on a screen but was to resist pressing the lever whenever any other letter or a number appeared. Gradually, CPTs became more complex and an examinee might be required to respond only when the letter X is preceded by the letter A but inhibit responding whenever the X appears (or any other letter appears) but it has not been immediately preceded by the letter A. CPTs can be made more complex by using sequences that mix color, numbers, letters, and even geometric or nonsense figures. CPTs can also be auditory wherein examinees respond to a target sound but only when preceded by a designated or preparatory sound. The patterns used have always been kept simple in order to minimize the effects of short-term memory and maximize attention and inhibition as key variables being assessed. Although the tasks seem simple enough, and indeed they are intended to be simple so that factors such as general intelligence are minimized, they do require intense levels of concentration and over a period of even 15 or 20 minutes, many people will make mistakes on even such simple tasks.

CPTs have been found highly sensitive over decades of research in detecting disorders of self-regulation in which attention, concentration, and response inhibition systems are impaired. These are often key indicators of disorders such as ADHD, are frequently symptoms appearing following traumatic brain injury and many central nervous system diseases, and attempts have been made to use CPT results as the so-called gold standard for diagnosis of ADHD. However, the disturbances in attention, concentration, and response inhibition apparent on CPT use is not specific to even a small subset of disorders. In fact, not only do individuals with ADHD show abnormal results on CPTs, individuals with bipolar disorder, borderline personality disorder, chronic fatigue syndrome, nearly all forms of dementia, mental retardation, schizophrenia, seizure disorder, and a host of neurodevelopmental disorders that are genetic in origin also demonstrate abnormal CPT results. Nevertheless, CPTs remain widely used and are highly sensitive to symptoms associated with abnormalities of the self-regulatory and executive control systems of the brain.

Based on research indicating that working memory is also associated with the executive control systems of the brain, a recent CPT has been devised to assess the executive system of the brain more broadly and has added working memory assessment to the standard CPT paradigms that also assesses inhibitory control, sustained attention, and vigilance (Isquith, Roth, & Gioia, 2010). Known as the Tasks of Executive Control (TEC), the TEC consists of a set of six different tasks that manipulate working memory load as a component of attention, vigilance, and response inhibition. It yields a wide range of scores associated with each of these tasks, some of which are common to the traditional CPT paradigms and some of which are relatively new. It is too early to determine how well these new approaches to the traditional CPT paradigm, particularly the addition of working memory demands, will fare in the clinical and research communities.

CPTs in general do not correlate highly with behavior rating scale data based on observations of children and adolescents in routine aspects of daily life or when performing academic tasks. It seems clear that CPTs do provide unique forms of performance-based information about the executive control systems of the brain and their continued evolution should provide additional insights into brain function as well as diagnostic issues related to central nervous system problems.

PSYCHOPHYSIOLOGICAL ASSESSMENTS

Psychophysiological assessment is another powerful method of behavioral assessment that typically involves recording physical changes in the body during some specific event. The so-called lie detector or polygraph is perhaps the best-known example. It records a variety of changes in the body of a person while answering yes–no questions, some of which are relevant to what the examiner wants to know and some of which are not. Heart rate, respiration,

> **Psychophysiological assessment** *is another powerful method of behavioral assessment that typically involves recording physical changes in the body during some specific event.*

and the galvanic skin response (the ability of the skin to conduct an electric charge—which changes if you start to sweat even a little bit) are commonly monitored by such devices. There are many examples of psychophysiological assessment including the use of electroencephalographs (EEGs) which monitor brain wave activity, electromyographs which monitor activation of muscle tissue, and one of the most controversial, the penile plethysmograph which monitors blood flow changes in the penis during exposure to different stimuli. The latter device has been used to conduct evaluations of male sex offenders for some years and its proponents claim to be able to diagnose pedophilia and other sexual disorders involving fetishes with high degrees of accuracy—having looked at this literature, we remain skeptical of many of these claims.

All devices in the psychophysiological assessment domain are highly sensitive and require careful calibration along with standardized protocols for their use. However, too many of them do not have adequate standardization or reference samples to make them as useful in clinical diagnosis as they might become. Others, however, such as the EEG, are very common, well-validated applications that are immensely useful in the right hands. We believe this form of assessment holds great promise for the future of psychological assessment.

Summary

Behavioral assessment is not simply a specific set of measuring devices, but more of a paradigm, a way of thinking about and obtaining assessment information. Behavioral assessment differs from traditional personality assessment in that behavioral assessments emphasize what an individual actually does, whereas most personality assessments emphasize characteristics or traits of the individual. Many contemporary clinicians use a multimethod, multimodal approach to assessment. That is, they collect data or assessment information using multiple techniques, including behavioral interviewing, direct observation, and impressionistic behavior rating scales, as well as traditional self-report "personality scales." This approach is designed to reduce the level of inference involved in interpretation.

Although a behavioral approach to assessment is best considered a broad paradigm it does typically involve common techniques. For example, it is common for the clinician to conduct a behavioral interview. In a behavioral interview the clinician focuses on the antecedents and consequences of behaviors of concern as well as what interventions have been used. In contrast with traditional clinical interviews a key goal of the behavioral interview is to minimize the level of inference used to obtain and interpret information. By stressing behavior as opposed to subjective states, a more definitive plan can be derived, clear goals can be set, and the progress of the individual monitored more clearly.

Another popular behavioral approach is the use of behavior rating scales. A behavior rating scale is an objective inventory that asks a knowledgeable informant to rate an individual on a number of dimensions. These ratings of behavior are largely impressionistic in nature (i.e., based on the informant's impression rather than actually counting behaviors), but research has shown they predict diagnosis accurately, predict future behavioral and learning problems, help detect changes in behavior, and can even predict what types of interventions are most likely to work to change a behavior. As a result, behavior rating scales have gained considerable popularity in recent years. Many of the most popular behavior rating scales are referred to as an omnibus rating scales. In this context *omnibus* indicates that they measure a wide range of symptoms and behaviors that are associated with different emotional and behavioral disorders. Ideally an omnibus rating scale should be sensitive to symptoms of both internalizing (e.g., anxiety, depression) and externalizing (e.g., ADHD, Oppositional Defiant Disorder) disorders to ensure that the clinician is not missing important indicators of psychopathology. We provided detailed descriptions of two popular omnibus behavior rating scales: the Behavior Assessment System for Children (BASC) which includes a Teacher Rating Scale (TRS), a Parent Rating Scale (PRS); and the Achenbach System of Empirically Based Assessment (ASEBA) which includes the Child Behavior Checklist (CBCL) and the Teacher Report Form (TRF).

Although omnibus rating scales play a central role in the assessment of psychopathology, there are also a number of single-domain or syndrome-specific rating scales. Single-domain rating scales resemble the omnibus scales in format, but focus on a single disorder or behavioral dimension. Although they are narrow in scope, they often provide a more thorough assessment of the specific domain they are designed to assess than the omnibus scales. As a result, they can be useful in supplementing more comprehensive assessment techniques.

Behavior rating scales have been used most often with children and adolescents, but there are behavior rating scales for adults. As an example we discussed the Clinical Assessment Scales for the Elderly (CASE) which is an omnibus behavior rating scale for individuals aged 55 through 90 years designed to be completed by a knowledgeable caregiver, such as a spouse, adult child, or a health care worker who has frequent contact with the examinee. It is likely that behavior rating scales will be designed and used with adults more frequently in the future.

Direct observation and recording of behavior constitutes one of the oldest approaches to behavioral assessment and is still commonly used. In direct observation, an observer travels to some natural environment of the individual and observes the subject, typically without the person knowing he or she is the target of the observation. Direct observation adds another dimension to the behavioral assessment—rather than being impressionistic, as are behavior ratings, it provides true ratio scale data that are actual counts of behavior. It also adds another dimension by being a different method of assessment that allows triangulation or checking of results from other methods and allowing the observer to note antecedent events as well as consequences assigned to the observed behaviors. As an example of an approach to direct observation, we described the Student Observation System (SOS) which is a component of the BASC-2.

Continuous performance tests (CPTs) are another type of behavioral assessment designed to measure vigilance, sustained and selective attention, and executive control. They have been found to be highly sensitive in detecting disorders of self-regulation in which attention, concentration, and response inhibition systems are impaired. Although often considered essential techniques in the assessment of ADHD, the constructs they measure are also commonly impaired in individuals with a number of other psychological and neuropsychological disorders. Research indicates that CPTs provide performance-based information about executive control systems on the brain and can facilitate both diagnosis and treatment.

The final behavioral approach we discussed was psychophysiological assessment. Psychophysiological assessments typically involve recording physical changes in the body during specific events. The polygraph or so-called lie detector is perhaps the best-known example of psychophysiological assessment. It records a variety of changes in the body of a person while answering yes–no questions, some of which are relevant to what the examiner wants to know and some of which are not. Psychophysiological assessment devices are highly sensitive and require careful calibration along with standardized protocols to produce valid and reliable results. Many of these instruments have inadequate standardization and normative data to make them clinically useful, but this approach holds considerable potential.

Key Terms and Concepts

Behavior Assessment System for Children—Second Edition (BASC-2), 364

Behavior rating scale, 362

Behavioral assessment, 356

Behavioral interview, 361

Continuous performance tests (CPTs), 378

Direct observation, 375

Impressionistic, 363

Individuals with Disabilities Education Improvement Act of 2004 (IDEA 2004), 360

Omnibus rating scales, 370

Psychophysiological assessment, 379

Public Law 94–142 (IDEA), 360

Single-domain rating scales, 371

Recommended Readings

Kamphaus, R. W., & Frick, P. J. (2002). *Clinical assessment of child and adolescent personality and behavior.* Boston: Allyn & Bacon. This text provides comprehensive coverage of the major personality and behavioral assessment techniques used with children and adolescents. It also provides a good discussion of the history and current use of projective techniques.

Reynolds, C. R., & Kamphaus, R. W. (2003). *Handbook of psychological and educational assessment of children: Personality, behavior, and context.* New York: Guilford Press. This is another excellent source providing thorough coverage of the major behavioral and personality assessment techniques used with children. Particularly good for those interested in a more advanced discussion of these instruments and techniques.

Riccio, C., Reynolds, C. R., & Lowe, P. A. (2001), *Clinical applications of continuous performance tests: Measuring attention and impulse of responding in children and adolescents.* New York: Wiley. A good source on CPTs.

Chapter Twelve

Employment and Vocational Testing

ROB ALTMANN
PEARSON ASSESSMENTS

What business does testing have in business? Turns out, a pretty big one ...

Learning Objectives

After reading and studying this chapter, students should be able to:

1. Describe the origins of testing in employment settings.
2. Identify and describe the major types of personnel selection strategies.
3. Summarize the major findings associated with the use of cognitive ability tests in employment settings and how to minimize unintended outcomes.
4. Describe some of the major findings of using personality tests for selecting employees, and summarize the current state of the research.
5. Describe the strengths and weaknesses of each major personnel selection strategy.
6. Provide an example of how meta-analysis is used in employment settings.

7. Define job analysis, identify why it is important in personnel selection, and describe some common techniques for completing a job analysis.
8. Describe some common methods for evaluating job performance.
9. Define some common sources of errors found when rating performance.
10. Identify and define key terms found in the Uniform Guidelines on Employee Selection Procedures.
11. Provide some key points from the Principles for the Validation and Use of Personnel Selection Procedures.
12. Describe some common surveys used in career assessment.

As discussed throughout this book, psychological measurement is used successfully across a variety of applications; thus, it should be no surprise that testing has a rich and successful track record when used in employment and vocational settings. In employment and vocational applications, "tests" are often considered in a broader sense than simply a collection of items with correct and incorrect responses. Although such "tests" do exist in these settings (e.g., cognitive ability tests), a collection of other instruments are often included in this category including surveys, inventories, and questionnaires. These instruments commonly purport to measure abilities, attitudes, knowledge, opinions, interests, or skills that are deemed important to a variety of outcomes, such as successful job performance, productivity, tenure, or absenteeism. When used for personnel selection, tests are also heavily regulated, principally through the Equal Employment Opportunity Commission (EEOC), an agency of the federal government. The regulations require that tests used in this way be demonstrably job related. You can view these regulations at http://www.eeoc.gov.

This chapter reviews a variety of measurement tools commonly used in employment and vocational settings. A brief overview of the history of industrial–organizational (I–O) psychology will be given to provide a context for the origins of personnel selection tests. After a detailed discussion of employee selection tools is presented, a number of related topics are discussed, including applicant reactions to testing, job analysis, evaluation of job performance, and vocational testing.

HISTORICAL VIEW OF INDUSTRIAL–ORGANIZATIONAL (I–O) PSYCHOLOGY

Industrial–organizational (I–O) psychology origins can be traced back to the early 1900s, when psychology was applied to the problems experienced by businesses, particularly with respect to the skills needed to perform a job task successfully (Katzell & Austin, 1992; Landy, 1997). Notable psychologists applying general psychological principles to work settings during this time included Hugo Münsterberg, James McKeen Cattell, Walter Dill Scott, and Walter VanDyke Bingham. The growth of all new things requires a catalyst, and in the case of I–O psychology, growth seemed to be sparked by an economic environment of capitalism and industrialization, as well as the American emphasis on the importance of individual differences (a direct contrast from the European structuralist paradigm). Perhaps the largest contributor to the growth of I–O psychology was World War I. A group of psychologists led by Scott and Bingham helped the United States Army in the selection of officers (Katzell & Austin, 1992; Landy, 1997). The results of this effort helped establish the potential of applied applications of psychology in the business world.

> *Perhaps the largest contributor to the growth of* **industrial–organizational psychology** *was World War I.*

After World War I, several notable organizations were founded, including the Scott Company (1919), the Psychological Corporation (1921), and the Association of Consulting Psychologists (1932), in an effort to advance the applied applications of psychology. Although the Scott Company went out of business a few years after it started, it was largely a victim of its own success; key members of the organization left the company for more attractive offers (Katzell & Austin, 1992). The Psychological Corporation founded by J. McKeen Cattell, included involvement by almost 200 psychologists who either held positions in the company or who owned company stock (Katzell & Austin, 1992). Some of the services it offered have changed, but the Psychological Corporation brand (now called Psych-Corp) still exists today as part of the Pearson publishing group, specifically in Pearson Assessments. The Association of Consulting Psychologists (later the American Association for Applied Psychology and eventually the basis of what is now the Society for Industrial and Organizational Psychology (SIOP), a division of the American Psychological Association) was formed to protect the reputation of I–O psychology from challenges by other professional psychologists who remained resistant to industrial psychology applications and from individuals taking advantage of new-found prosperity without having any psychological training (Benjamin, 1997). Special Interest Topic 12.1 highlights some of the early contributions of female psychologists in the development of I–O psychology.

In addition to these organizations, I–O psychology was involved in several well-known studies that advanced the scientific field of research. One group of studies, commonly known as the Hawthorne studies began in the late 1920s and involved a team of psychologists intent on improving the operating efficiency of a plant owned by the Western Electric Company. These studies are often referenced when highlighting the importance of human variables (e.g., social relationships) on worker performance, and when discussing variables that can confound the results of a study. Although the findings of the Hawthorne studies are often maligned and criticized, they consisted of controlled, scientific field-based research that is consistent with the scientific philosophy that underlies I–O research—a fact often forgotten or omitted from discussion (Katzell & Austin, 1992; Olson, Verley, Santos, & Salas, 2004).

SPECIAL INTEREST TOPIC 12.1

Contributions of Female Psychologists in Early I–O Psychology

In many accounts of the early days of I–O psychology, there is little if any mention of the contributions of female psychologists. However, Koppes (1997) provided a detailed look at their contributions during this period. Specifically, Koppes detailed the lives of four prominent female psychologists. Each of these women was born in late 1800s, and received PhDs in psychology from high-quality institutions (Bryn Mawr College, Columbia University, Brown University, and University of Chicago) during the first quarter of the 20th century. A selective summary of their work is provided next.

Marion A. Bills

Among her many accomplishments, Dr. Bills worked as a research assistant for the Bureau of Personnel Research, where she consulted with businesses on selection, training, and supervision issues. She developed expertise in personnel selection, and studied selection techniques for clerical and sales positions. She conducted predictive validity studies between tests and criteria, including productivity and withdrawal, and was one of the first to note the potential advantages of using a battery of tests, rather than a single test. She also worked for Aetna Life Insurance Company, where she specialized in personnel issues such as wage incentives, job classification, and consultation with top management. She published several of her works in leading scientific journals.

Elsie Oschrin Bregman

Initially hired by R.H. Macy and Company in New York, Dr. Bregman was charged with examining the company's personnel processes. While there, she focused on research examining procedures for

(Continued on page 386)

SPECIAL INTEREST TOPIC 10.2 (*Continued*)

recruitment, selection, training, and management. In an effort to examine the effectiveness of the selection procedures, she computed correlations using the Spearman formula between 13 selection tests and sales ability. Dr. Bregman was later hired by the Psychological Corporation to develop and publish revisions of the Army Alpha General Intelligence Examinations. Eventually, she received royalties for revised versions of these tests that she helped develop for use in private businesses. Because of these royalties, she was considered one of the only individuals to profit from the Psychological Corporation during its early years. In addition, she also published several books with E. L. Thorndike on intelligence and learning, and authored 12 articles in leading scientific journals during the first half of the 20th century.

Lillian Moller Gilbreth

Dr. Gilbreth established an industrial management and engineering consulting business with her husband, and used time and motion studies to determine how worker efficiency could be enhanced and productivity improved. She continued to run the company after her husband's death, and worked with a variety of companies, including Eastman Kodak, Remington Typewriter, U.S. Rubber, and Sears, Roebuck, and Company. Over the course of her career, she published several books and scholarly articles. Her work emphasized ways to reduce employee fatigue and increase job satisfaction, and also emphasized the application of psychological principles to scientific management as a way to compensate for a lack of consideration of human aspects of the job. She also noted the value of observing workers in the workplace, and she described the utility of a questionnaire that today would be referred to as a biodata form. One of her books, *The Psychology of Management*, was considered one of the most influential textbooks on industrial relations.

Mary H. S. Hayes

Dr. Hayes was one of the few women who were directly involved in studies during World War I. She worked as a laboratory technician and civilian expert in the U.S. Army Medical School and Surgeon General's Office, and was associated with a committee that conducted research on personnel problems with the likes of E. L. Thorndike, W. V. Bingham, R. M. Yerkes, E. K. Strong, L. M. Terman, and J. B. Watson. She was one of the original employees of the Scott Company, where she coauthored a book titled *Science and Common Sense in Working with Men*, and helped develop a graphic rating scale method. Dr. Hayes was also employed by the U.S. Department of Labor to conduct a study on the problems of unemployed youth, and later helped make decisions on how to prepare youth for national defense jobs.

World War II led to the further growth of I–O psychology, as hundreds of psychologists were employed by the U.S. armed services or civilian agencies (Katzell & Austin, 1992). Within the armed services a number of tests were designed to place recruits in optimal positions. In addition, a number of other variables common to I–O psychology were studied, including procedures for appraisals, team development, attitude change methods, and equipment design (Katzell & Austin, 1992). Upon completion of the war, educational programs across the country expanded their programs to include the study of I–O psychology, which was met by companies' increased demands for such services. Numerous consulting companies currently exist that provide a number of off-the-shelf or customized selection or talent assessments, as well as a host of other employee or organizational services and trainings. I–O psychology has continued to grow at a fast pace; according to the *Occupational Outlook Handbook* (2008–2009 data, available at http://www.bls.gov/oco/), the need for I–O psychologists is expected to increase 21% from 2006 to 2016, from a total of 1,900 to a projected total of 2,400 psychologists.

PERSONNEL SELECTION APPROACHES

Over the last century a number of employee selection tests have been developed in an effort to hire workers who will be successful on the job. The primary goal of these methods or tests is to save organizations money and effort by helping them hire employees who will be able to perform the required duties of the job and who will be satisfied in the organizations' work environment, thereby reducing the costs associated with poor performance, turnover, or counterproductive work behaviors. The methods most widely used by today's organizations are detailed in the following text.

Cognitive Ability

Cognitive ability tests have a long history in employment settings, dating back to the end of World War I (Schmidt & Hunter, 2004). Their use has been described as one of the most discussed and controversial topics in applied psychology (Murphy, Cronin, & Tam, 2003), even though an extensive body of research shows that cognitive ability scores can predict a variety of job performance variables. Cognitive ability tests measure a variety of mental abilities such as reasoning, verbal and/or math ability, perception, or problem solving. In employment settings, in contrast to clinical settings, items from these tests are most often multiple-choice or short-answer response formats.

According to Wagner (1997), advances in statistical methods such as meta-analysis and the availability of large-scale data sets from military applications brought cognitive ability assessment in employment settings into a new era. The ability to summarize large numbers of studies and the application of cognitive ability tests across a variety of applications and performance criteria helped establish the general predictive ability of cognitive ability tests. These tests were shown to be highly reliable, practical, and easily administered to applicants entering the job market.

Numerous studies document the effectiveness of cognitive ability in predicting job performance. Perhaps the most well-known researchers over the last several decades are John Hunter and Frank Schmidt. A series of meta-analyses and summary research have documented the results of numerous studies incorporating the results of tens of thousands of job applicants. A selection of their findings are included here:

> *Numerous studies document the effectiveness of cognitive ability in predicting job performance.*

- A corrected validity coefficient between cognitive ability and job performance of $r = 0.53$ exists, with higher validity coefficients for professional jobs and lower coefficient for jobs requiring lesser skills (Hunter & Hunter, 1984); thus, cognitive ability is generally a strong predictor of job performance.
- Multiple R values from multiple regression analyses of cognitive ability and one of several other predictors exist at levels in the 0.60s, such as integrity (0.65), work sample tests (0.63), structured interviews (0.63), and conscientiousness (0.60; Schmidt & Hunter, 1998); thus, the ability of cognitive ability test scores to predict job performance can be increased further by including several other variables.
- Cognitive ability test scores predict occupational level attained (in both cross-sectional studies and longitudinal studies) and job performance across a variety of job families; and the relationship between cognitive ability and job performance is mediated by job knowledge (Schmidt & Hunter, 2004).

- When estimating the relative economic value of using cognitive ability tests (in terms of the value of increased productivity resulting from increased job performance), they determined that in 1984, the economic impact resulting from the use of cognitive ability tests for hiring entry-level jobs in the federal government for a single year was over $15 billion.

One of the primary concerns with cognitive ability tests is known performance differences across racial and ethnic groups, with minority groups performing up to 1 standard deviation below white applicants (Hunter & Hunter, 1984; Sackett, Schmitt, Ellingson, & Kabin, 2001); the effects of their use can lead to adverse impact on minority group members (Gottfredson, 1986). Sackett et al. (2001) reviewed a number of strategies that have been tried for reducing the performance differences that are commonly found on cognitive ability tests. Here is a review of these strategies and their findings:

- *Strategy:* Combine cognitive ability tests with other noncognitive predictors that are valid predictors of job performance and that have smaller subgroup differences.

  Findings: Whereas subgroup differences can be reduced when combining multiple predictors, such reductions do not necessitate the elimination of adverse impact. A reduction in adverse impact is a function of many factors, including the validities of each predictor, the relationships between predictors, the size of the subgroup differences for each predictor, the ratio of the number of applicants tested and selected for the job, and the way in which the tests are used (see also Pulakos & Schmitt, 1996; Sackett & Ellingson, 1997).

- *Strategy:* Identify and remove test items that are culturally biased.

  Findings: Studies that have attempted to remove items that are biased toward a certain subgroup (i.e., items that display differential item functioning, or DIF) have shown a negligible impact on differences between the performance of subgroups, although the removal of such items is still recommended.

- *Strategy:* Present test items in a way that reduces the demands of verbal or written skills; for example, using an auditory or visual presentation of items.

  Findings: Studies have shown that such presentation strategies can reduce subgroup differences, but such reductions do not necessitate the elimination of adverse impact. Findings have been inconsistent, and more research is needed to draw more firm conclusions.

- *Strategy:* Manipulate instructional sets in order to increase applicants' motivation to complete preemployment tests.

  Findings: The observed effects on subgroup differences have been small, and have been mainly done in laboratory settings. However, additional research is recommended.

- *Strategy:* Directly measure aspects of the job of interest, using portfolios, accomplishment records, or performance assessments (e.g., work sample tests).

  Findings: Studies have shown some reduction in subgroup differences, although findings have been mixed, and are likely the result of differences in the amount of cognitive load contained in each measure. Results will likely mirror those found in the first strategy discussed.

- *Strategy:* Provide coaching and study and practice materials.

  Findings: Results of studies indicate a negligible impact on reducing subgroup differences. However, applicants generally feel positive about such programs, which might lead to fewer complaints about a test and less litigation.

Overall, cognitive ability tests can cause considerable tension for organizations that choose to use them for employment decisions (Sackett et al., 2001). The tension stems from the potential conflict between maximizing performance (by selecting those who are most likely to succeed on the job based on their performance on preemployment tests) and maximizing diversity. It appears that there is growing consensus by I–O psychologists and researchers that cognitive ability tests are both valid and fair, as evidenced by the extensive meta-analytic studies conducted to date and a survey of SIOP members (Murphy et al., 2003). However, it is also clear that research will continue in areas aimed at reducing the subgroup differences commonly associated with cognitive ability measures.

It appears there is growing consensus by I–O psychologists and researchers that cognitive ability test scores are both valid and fair, as evidenced by the extensive meta-analytic studies conducted to date and survey data from members of the Society for Industrial and Organizational Psychology.

One of the most widely used cognitive ability tests is the Wonderlic Personnel Test. Revised in 2007, the Wonderlic Personnel Test consists of 50 multiple-choice questions covering a wide variety of topics, including math problems, vocabulary words, analogies, problem solving, and other types of problems. Examinees have 12 minutes to complete the test. Whereas used in a variety of different professions, the Wonderlic is perhaps best known for its use when evaluating college football players for their potential to be successful players in the National Football League.

Interviews

Employment interviews are one of the most frequently used approaches to evaluating job candidates (Wilk & Cappelli, 2003). Interviewers typically use an unstructured or structured approach when collecting information from job applicants. Unstructured approaches generally rely on the ability of the interviewer to generate questions that are relevant to the applicant being questioned or the content that is being discussed at a given point in time. The results of such interviews are often subjective, and can be very hard to compare across applicants due to the potential uniqueness of each interview session. Structured approaches, on the other hand, require the development of questions prior to the interview. Applicants who are competing for the same job are presented the same questions, and their responses are typically "scored" using a predetermined scoring key. Campion, Pursell, and Brown (1988) provided a number of suggestions for developing effective structured interviews, which are summarized in Table 12–1.

Employment interviews are one of the most frequently used approaches to evaluating job candidates.

Employment interviews are generally considered to be related to job performance, but the level or extent to which they can predict job performance has been unclear. Hunter and Hunter (1984) indicated that interviews had a mean validity of only $r = 0.14$ for predicting job performance. However, more recent research has indicated stronger relationships with job performance. For example, McDaniel, Whetzel, Schmidt, and Maurer (1994) found higher relationships for both unstructured ($r = 0.33$) and structured ($r = 0.44$) interviews. Similarly, Huffcutt and Arthur (1994) derived a mean validity coefficient between interviews and job performance of $r = 0.37$ that is directly comparable to the Hunter and Hunter (1984) estimate. In addition, Huffcutt and Arthur delineated the amount of structure used during the interview, and found that the mean validity estimate for interviews with the least amount of structure was $r = 0.20$, whereas the mean validity estimate for interviews classified as having the second highest amount of structure was $r = 0.56$ (the mean estimate for interviews with the highest amount of structure was essentially the same, $r = 0.57$). A common explanation given for the differences in predictive validity of unstructured and structured interviews is that the latter method demonstrates higher levels of reliability. Even though such an explanation is intuitive, Schmidt and Zimmerman (2004) presented only limited support for this belief; higher reliabilities were not always associated with higher validity coefficients. Further, they demonstrated that averaging scores from three to four independent unstructured interviews provided the same level of predictive validity as that of a structured interview conducted by a single interviewer, a finding that is somewhat contradictory to Campion et al. (1988). Schmidt and Zimmerman called for additional research in this area before definitive recommendations could be given.

Personality

Perhaps the most spirited line of research in personnel selection over the last two decades has been conducted using personality tests to select job candidates. Morgeson, Campion, Dipboye, Hollenbeck, Murphy, and Schmitt (2007) indicated a ninefold increase in articles published in some of the most popular I–O psychology journals (*Journal of Applied Psychology* and *Personnel Psychology*) and presentations at the SIOP annual conferences from 1990 to 2005. Unfortunately, it is unclear whether the surge in research has led to a consensus among researchers or an advancement of the field.

TABLE 12–1 Steps for Developing Effective Structured Interviews	
Step	**Benefits**
1. Develop questions based on a job analysis to determine characteristics that will lead to job success.	Follows recommendations given in the Uniform Guidelines on Employee Selection Procedures, and its importance in court decisions and potentially reducing bias
2. Ask the same questions of each job candidate.	Consistency across candidates provides a more uniform application of the selection process, and enables a more direct comparison of the results
3. Develop rating scales for scoring answers using examples and illustrations.	Helps make scoring system explicit, which is essential to justifying the validity evidence based on the content of the assessment procedure
4. Use a panel of interviewers.	Reduces the impact of idiosyncratic bias that can result when only a single interviewer is used
5. Be consistent when administering the process to all candidates (e.g., have each interviewer ask the same question[s] across job candidates).	Consistency across candidates provides a more uniform application of the selection process
6. Document the process used to develop the interview questions and scoring procedures.	Can serve as a written summary of the events that took place, and will be helpful for providing to others as needed later down the road (e.g., in the event of a legal challenge)

Personality, as discussed earlier, refers to the unique characteristics that define an individual and are used by the individual when interacting with others. Such characteristics might include traits such as conscientiousness, agreeableness, flexibility, intuition, or aggression. In employment settings, personality is most often assessed by self-report questionnaires or inventories that are generally easy for applicants to complete. It is important to note that within employment settings, use of personality tests requires special consideration with respect to legal issues. Personality tests that are used by mental health professionals to diagnose mental health deficiencies are deemed as medical examinations, and as such are restricted for use only after a job offer has been made (e.g., the Minnesota Multiphasic Personality Inventory–Second Edition [MMPI-2; Butcher et al., 1989]). Personality tests that do not provide information on mental health (i.e., "normal" personality measures) are generally considered appropriate for use prior to the tender of a job offer (provided they do not "invade" a person's privacy by asking a person's innermost thoughts and feelings), and are the basis for much of the research conducted over the past two decades. The remainder of this section focuses on this research.

> *Personality, as discussed in this section, refers to the unique characteristics that define an individual and are used by the individual when interacting with others.*

A seminal and often-cited paper on the use of personality testing in selection contexts is Guion and Gottier (1965), who generally concluded that personality tests were of limited utility for making preemployment decisions about applicants. However, the use of personality tests in employment settings continued over the next several decades, the results of which were summarized in two separate studies in the early 1990s. The first study, Barrick and Mount (1991), examined the relationship between personality traits (as categorized into the Big 5 personality dimensions of Extraversion, Emotional Stability (also referred to as neuroticism), Agreeableness, Conscientiousness, and Openness to Experience) and job performance. Table 12–2 provides a summary of each of these dimensions.

Based on their meta-analytic findings, Barrick and Mount (1991) concluded that Conscientiousness was found to be a consistently valid predictor across a variety of occupational groups and across a variety of criterion types, meaning that persons who tend to be dependable, responsible, organized, and so on tend to be better job performers than those who are not. In addition, they concluded that Extraversion was also a valid predictor across criterion types for two occupations: managers and sales. Openness to Experience was a significant predictor of performance in job training exercises, whereas Emotional Stability and Agreeableness did not appear to be valid predictors of job performance.

Tett, Jackson, and Rothstein (1991) also used meta-analytic techniques to examine the relationship between personality and job performance. Whereas similar to the Barrick and Mount (1991) study, the Tett et al. study also investigated a number of variables that were proposed to moderate the relationship between personality and job performance, and used some slightly different methodological techniques when conducting the analyses. Tett and colleagues found even stronger relationships between personality and job performance (purportedly in part due to a methodological process of using absolute values when averaging validity coefficients within a study). They also found several significant moderating variables, including the type of study (mean validities from confirmatory studies are considerably greater than mean validities from

TABLE 12–2 Big 5 Personality Dimensions	
Personality Dimension	**Common Traits Associated With Each Dimension**
Extraversion	Being sociable, gregarious, assertive, talkative, and active
Emotional Stability	Anxiety, depression, anger, embarrassment, emotionality, worrisome, and insecurity
Agreeableness	Being courteous, flexible, trusting, good-natured, cooperative, forgiving, and tolerant
Conscientiousness	Dependable, careful, thorough, responsible, and organized
Openness to Experience	Being imaginative, cultured, curious, broadminded, and artistically sensitive

exploratory studies), the use of job analysis (personality dimensions that were selected as the result of a job analysis were more strongly related to job performance than personality dimensions that were not selected as the result of a job analysis), and job tenure (personality dimensions were a stronger predictor of performance for employees with longer job tenure than for employees with less job tenure).

Although the 1990s saw a resurgence of personality testing within I–O psychology, the last several years have witnessed a marked split among researchers interpreting the results of these studies. Morgeson et al. (2007) discussed several perceived problems with the research examining personality and personnel selection. These authors, all former editors of leading I–O psychology journals, focused on three key problem areas: low-validity coefficients; the reliance on meta-analyses that may overestimate the true relationship to performance due to the number of statistical corrections being made to both predictor and outcome variables; and the uncertain effects that applicant faking may have on the results of a personality test and the ability of that test to accurately predict job performance.

In response to Morgeson and colleagues (2007), Tett and Christiansen (2007) and Ones, Dilchert, Viswesvaran, and Judge (2007) provided a more positive view on the existing state of preemployment personality testing, arguing for its continued use and expanding lines of research. The true relationship between personality and work outcomes is likely underestimated for a variety of reasons, including an overreliance on exploratory strategies, ignoring personality-oriented job analysis, and ignoring the value of narrow-band personality traits and criterion measures. Table 12–3 presents a summary of these authors' reviews of the current state of personality testing in employment settings, focusing on the interpretation of the existing validity evidence, the impact of faking on the results of personality tests and subsequent validities, and recommendations for future research in this area.

A nonclinical personality inventory commonly used in employment settings is the Hogan Personality Inventory—Revised (HPI-R) (Hogan & Hogan, 1995). Based on the five-factor personality model, it consists of 206 true–false items that are designed to be nonintrusive and noninvasive, and is estimated to take about 15 to 20 minutes to complete. The HPI-R provides scores for each of the following dimensions: Adjustment (degree to which person is steady in the face of pressure), Ambition (degree to which person seems leaderlike and values achievement), Sociability (degree to which person needs or enjoys social interaction), Interpersonal Sensitivity (tact, sensitivity, and perceptiveness), Prudence (self-control and conscientiousness), Inquisitive

	TABLE 12–3	Summary of Contemporary Views Regarding Personality Testing in Job Settings	
Authors	**Test-Criterion Validity Evidence**	**Impact of Faking**	**Recommendations**
Morgeson, Campion, Dipboye, Hollenbeck, Murphy, and Schmitt (2007)	• Levels of validity are disappointingly low, although they might offer some incremental validity over cognitive ability tests (they should not be used as a substitute for cognitive ability tests). • Meta-analyses may be overestimating true relationship due to the number of corrections for statistical artifacts such as range restriction and unreliability of both the predictor and outcome.	• Faking on personality tests should be expected and probably cannot be avoided. • It is currently unclear if faking is problematic when personality tests are used in actual employment settings. • Faking does not distort the criterion-related validity of personality tests. • Attempts to create faking scales and adjusting personality scores will have at best minimal effects on criterion-related validities.	• Establish direct links between personality measures being used and measures of job performance. • Avoid published personality measures in most instances, and construct custom measures that are directly linked to job tasks. • Group items according to scales or similar content (rather than using the item sequence as a way to get more truthful or unguarded responding). • Improve methods for obtaining data by either improving self-report or simply abandoning it.
Tett and Christiansen (2007)	• Meta-analytic data suggests that personality tests validity reaches useful levels under some conditions. • Confirmatory strategies are preferred over exploratory strategies. • The validity of personality is underestimated for many reasons (e.g., variability in estimates is ignored, the value of narrow trait dimensions and criterion measures is ignored, incremental validity when combining scores from multiple-trait measures is ignored).	• Past research on faking is inadequate and uninformative, due to an overreliance on social desirability measures and statistical partialing techniques. • Faking appears to attenuate personality test validity, but enough personality trait variance remains to be useful for predicting job performance.	• Contemporary personality tests have been shown to be psychometrically sound. • Theory-guided predictions between traits and performance are needed. • Greater attention should be given to delineating the conditions under which personality testing is most valid, rather than simply dismissing them.
Ones, Dilchert, Viswesvaran, and Judge (2007)	• Based on the evidence to date, the Big 5 personality variables are predictive of job performance and its facets, leadership, and other work-related criteria. • Personality validity coefficients are at levels similar to that of other selection and assessment techniques.	• Faking does not ruin the validity of personality scores. • Faking studies conducted in lab settings may not be the same phenomenon as faking that might occur in applicant settings.	• Different sets of personality variables are useful in predicting job performance for varying occupational groups. • Customized tests are not necessarily superior to off-the-shelf tests, and there is no reason to believe that homegrown scales would necessarily have superior validity than off-the-shelf tests. • In addition to predicting job performance, personality variables are also useful in understanding and predicting work attitudes (e.g., job satisfaction) and organizational behavior (e.g., motivation, effort).

(degree to which person seems creative and analytical), and Learning Approach (degree to which person enjoys academic activities and values education), along with each of their subdimensions. In addition to scale scores and graphs, the software reports provide a candidate's strengths and shortcomings, identifies characteristics that are relevant for success in most work environments, and identifies the suitability of the candidate for the position.

Integrity

Often considered a form of personality testing, integrity testing typically refers to self-report tests that are designed to identify persons inclined to be dishonest. Developed as an alternative to polygraph tests (which are no longer legal in preemployment situations), self-report integrity testing was met with skepticism (e.g., Guion, 1991). However, attitudes toward integrity testing began to change based on research that established a link between integrity and job performance (Ones, Viswesvaran, & Schmidt, 1993; Schmidt & Hunter, 1998). In Schmidt and Hunter's seminal work on the validity and utility of employee selection procedures, integrity tests were shown to have a corrected validity coefficient of 0.41 with job performance, and were shown to provide the greatest incremental validity in predicting job performance over cognitive ability test scores.

Integrity tests are commonly divided into two groups, overt and personality-oriented (Sackett, Burris, & Callahan, 1989). **Overt integrity tests** typically consist of questions pertaining to general beliefs about or attitudes toward theft, as well as admissions about previous theft or wrongdoing. **Personality-oriented integrity tests** focus primarily on personality traits or areas that may relate to theft, such as conscientiousness (or the lack thereof) and sensation or thrill seeking, among others.

> *In Schmidt and Hunter's seminal work on the validity and utility of employee selection procedures, overt and personality-oriented integrity test scores were shown to have a corrected validity coefficient of 0.41 with job performance, and were shown to provide the greatest incremental validity in predicting job performance over cognitive ability tests.*

Sackett and colleagues have monitored the status of integrity testing in preemployment settings since the late 1970s, providing an interesting and comprehensive analysis of integrity research (Berry, Sackett, & Wiemann, 2007; Sackett, Burris, & Callahan, 1989; Sackett & Decker, 1979; Sackett & Wanek, 1996). Five of the main conclusions from their most recent summary are provided as follows:

1. Integrity seems to reflect in part a complex mix of some of the Big 5 personality dimensions, including conscientiousness, agreeableness, and emotional stability, although a substantial amount of variance in integrity still remains.
2. Whereas integrity was previously thought to be unrelated to cognitive ability (Ones et al., 1993), recent research that has avoided combining positive and negative personality facets together has resulted in stronger correlations with cognitive ability (combining personality facets that had negative and positive correlations with cognitive ability in effect canceled each other out, resulting in a near zero correlation).
3. Criterion-related validation studies continue to show positive (yet modest) correlations between integrity test scores and job performance as well as a number of counterproductive work behaviors.

4. Integrity test scores are subject to change based on coaching or faking, but it remains unclear whether applicants do fake on such tests, and what effect this faking has on the validity of the test scores.

5. When used for the purpose for which they are intended, integrity tests continue to be consistent with EEOC guidelines with respect to legal use in preemployement settings.

Although a number of integrity preemployment tests are commercially available, one of the more well-established tests is the Personnel Selection Inventory (PSI), available from Vangent Human Capital Management (http://www.vangent-hcm.com), which consists of between 60 and 140 items and can be completed in about 30 minutes (depending on the specific PSI version). Similar to other integrity tests, the PSI consists of a series of questions that are rated on a multipoint rating scale (often ranging from 5 to 7 rating scale points) that cover a wide number of work-related domains (see Table 12–4 for a sample of domains covered by the PSI). Oftentimes questions related to the honesty or integrity tests or scales are indirect (e.g., It is OK to bend the rules—*never, seldom, sometimes, often, almost always*) or direct (e.g., During your previous job, please estimate the following value of merchandise you took for personal use: *$0, $5, $15, $25, $100, $500, $1,000, $2,000, or more*). Each of these items is assigned a value, and the values across items are summed to form a total honesty scale score. The last types of questions (i.e., the direct questions) might be surprising to some readers (e.g., you might be asking yourself "Why would someone admit to previously taking anything from a previous worksite?"), but the explanation that is commonly offered by selection professionals relates to the state of mind of the job applicants. When completing tests, job applicants are told to be honest and forthright when providing answers to each item. When reading such questions, oftentimes applicants who have no problem taking company property for their personal use tend to be more willing to admit to at least a small level of theft, believing that it is the norm to engage in such behavior, and fearing that if they do not admit to at least some theft, those administering the tests will think or know that they are lying.

Assessment Centers

An **assessment center** typically refers to a collection of tasks or exercises that are designed to simulate a variety of situations that are experienced in a work environment. Assessment centers are often used in selection and career development/training situations. Small groups of participants or employees participate in a series of tasks over an extended period (usually 1 to 3 days), including activities such as in-basket exercises, simulated interviews, group discussions, fact-finding exercises, and oral-presentation exercises (Byham, 1970). Assessors observe each participant and rate their performance across a variety of dimensions, such as communication, drive, consideration of others, organizing/planning, stress tolerance, and other personality dimensions (Meriac, Hoffman, Woehr, & Fleisher, 2008). Recent guidelines have been established that describe defining characteristics and components of an assessment center, including the use of job analysis to identify critical job-related tasks, classification of candidate behaviors into meaningful dimensions, use of multiple assessment techniques that measure critical behaviors,

> *An* assessment center *typically refers to a collection of tasks or exercises that are designed to simulate a variety of situations that are experienced in a work environment.*

TABLE 12–4	Dimensions From the Personnel Selection Inventory
Dimension	**Description**
Honesty	Assesses how likely a person will be to steal from an employer
Tenure	Assesses how likely a person will be to stay at a job for an extended period of time
Nonviolence	Assesses how likely a person will be to refrain from violence in the workplace
Employee/Customer Relations	Assesses a person's tendency to be courteous and cooperative with customers and coworkers
Customer Service Aptitude	Assesses an applicant's understanding of effective methods of dealing with customers
Sales Aptitude	Assesses an applicant's understanding of effective methods of selling and sales interest
Stress Tolerance	Assesses an applicant's ability to tolerate stress
Risk Avoidance	Assesses an applicant's willingness or desire to engage in high-risk or dangerous behaviors
Safety	Assesses an applicant's attitude toward safety and practicing safe behaviors
Supervision Attitude	Assesses an applicant's attitude toward completing assigned work and appropriately respond to work directives
Work Values	Assesses an applicant's attitude to productive work habits
Responsibility	Assesses an applicant's attitude toward engaging in counterproductive or careless workplace behavior
Candidness	Assesses an applicant's tendency to present himself or herself in a socially desirable manner
Accuracy	Assesses whether the applicant understood and carefully completed the test

use of multiple assessors who are trained in rating participants' performance, and systematic procedures for evaluating participants (International Task Force on Assessment Center Guidelines, 2000).

A sizable amount of research demonstrates the predictive validity of assessment center results. Gaugler, Rosenthal, Thornton, and Bentson (1987), in their meta-analysis of assessment centers, reported a test-criterion validity coefficient for an overall assessment center rating of 0.37, whereas an updated review of similar studies has produced a slightly lower result (0.28; Hermelin, Lievens, & Robertson, 2007). Arthur, Day, McNelly, and Edens (2003), focusing on the predictive validity of individual dimensions assessed in assessment centers rather than an overall composite score, found that individual dimensions of problem solving, influencing others, and organizing and planning met or exceeded the test-criterion validity coefficient of the overall composite found by Gaugler et al., and that individual dimensions could be used to account for significantly more total variance in performance compared to an overall score. This line of research was extended by Meriac and colleagues (2008), who used meta-analytic techniques to examine the relationship between assessment center scores, cognitive ability, and personality, and examined the potential incremental validity of assessment centers. They found that the relationships between assessment center dimensions and cognitive ability and personality were somewhat surprisingly low (uncorrected $r = 0.30$ or less), and that assessment center dimensions are able to predict job performance ratings above and beyond cognitive ability and personality, accounting for an additional 10% of explained variance. Taken together, these studies appear to clearly demonstrate the predictive validity of assessment center ratings, but there is less optimism about the level of construct-related validity evidence across assessment center dimensions. Lance (2008) provides a comprehensive review of the problem, and suggests a paradigm shift from assessing dimensions to focusing on candidate behavior that is more directly tied to roles or tasks performed in various exercises. It is likely that such research will further the contributions provided by assessment centers.

Work Sample Tests

Work sample tests (also called performance-based tests or simulations) have been used to select employees for decades (e.g., see Asher & Sciarrino, 1974). As can be determined from the name, work sample tests require applicants to perform tasks related to the job being applied for; such tasks can be actual work samples (e.g., answering phone calls, operating a drill press) or can be contrived examples of various tasks (e.g., writing a letter to respond to a hypothetical customer's complaints). Work sample tests are thought to provide direct evidence of the applicant's ability to work on a job, are believed to be some of the most effective methods for predicting future job performance (Hunter & Hunter,

> **Work sample tests** *(or performance-based tests or simulations) are thought to provide direct evidence of the applicant's ability to work on a job, are believed to be some of the most effective methods for predicting future job performance (Hunter & Hunter, 1984), and are often considered to have strong face validity.*

1984), and are often considered to have strong face validity. However, their use has not been as widespread as one might expect, for a variety of reasons. Gatewood and Feild (1998) offer three primary limitations of work sample tests: (1) Great care must be taken when constructing work sample tests to ensure a representative sample of tasks are selected; (2) they assume that applicants already have the knowledge, skills, and ability to perform the job behavior; and (3) they are expensive, relative to other selection methods, with respect to both test development and the time it takes to administer and score the tests.

Roth, Bobko, and McFarland (2005) conducted a meta-analysis on work sample tests, reexamining some of the previous work sample research. Although their results demonstrated that work sample tests are generally found to be predictive of job performance, the magnitude of the relationship is somewhat lower than what was previously thought (a corrected mean r of 0.33, compared to 0.54 found in previous studies). In addition, Roth and colleagues have suggested that scores on work sample tests may produce larger than previously thought differences between groups of applicants (Roth, Bobko, McFarland, & Buster, 2008). For example, mean scores between black and white applicants have been shown to differ almost three fourths of a standardized difference between average group scores ($d = .73$), a value that is similar to what is often found on cognitive ability tests and is almost twice as high as had been previously reported. These results should not necessarily rule out the use of work sample tests; rather, as noted by Roth et al., these results will allow decision makers to more accurately compare the adverse impact potential of various selection devices.

Biodata

In psychology, it is often said that the best predictor of future behavior is past behavior. The use of biodata (biographical data) for selecting applicants is steeped in this belief (Farmer, 2006; Guion, 1998). Biodata refer to an applicant's personal experiences and background, and can be collected in many ways, such as structured interviews or self-report questionnaires. Although biodata questions often center on previous educational and work experiences, they can also expand to areas such as hobbies, interests, and attitudes. There is generally overlap between the content found in biodata surveys and personality tests; however, biodata are generally considered to measure broader domains than that of personality tests. Table 12–5 presents a summary developed by Mael (1991) of the attributes of biodata item types that commonly appear on biodata forms.

Biodata surveys have been shown to be predictive of job performance in a variety of studies. Hunter and Hunter (1984) reported a corrected correlation between biodata and job performance of $r = 0.37$. Schmidt and Hunter (1998) reported a corrected correlation of $r = 0.35$, along with a small increase in predictive validity when combined with a measure of cognitive ability. In addition, biodata have been shown to be valid predictors of job performance across a variety of settings and organizations (Rothstein, Schmidt, Erwin, Owens, & Sparks, 1990).

TABLE 12–5	Examples of Attributes Included on Biodata Questionnaires
Attribute	**Description**
Historical	Pertains to past behavior, or general questions on what typical past behavior has been
External	Refers to behaviors that actually have occurred, rather than simply thoughts or attitudes
Objective	Refers to behaviors that can be objectively or factually recalled, considered by some as firsthand knowledge
Discrete Actions	Refers to single events or unique behaviors, rather than a summary or average of behaviors
Verifiable	Refers to a behavior that can be corroborated from an independent source, such as a transcript, written document, or testimony by another person
Controllable	Refers to actions or behaviors that are controlled by the respondent (e.g., how many times have you taken a college entrance exam), rather than events that simply "happened" to the respondent (e.g., what is the greatest number of coworkers you have had on your team)
Equally Accessible	Refers to including only questions that relate to skills and experiences that are equally accessible to all applicants (e.g., opportunity to become a class president might be considered as equal access vs. opportunity to be captain of a volleyball team)
Visibly Job Relevant	Refers to questions demonstrating a face-valid relationship to the job
Noninvasive	Refers to items that do not invade on a person's privacy or items that do not contradict federal, state, or local privacy laws (e.g., a question about religious affiliation would be inconsistent with federal law)

CHOOSING A PERSONNEL SELECTION APPROACH

Advantages and Disadvantages of Different Approaches

A number of factors must be considered when choosing a personnel selection approach; effectiveness, cost, appropriateness to the job, time, and legal considerations are only some of these factors. SIOP (the Society for Industrial and Organizational Psychology), the division of the American Psychological Association that studies human well-being and performance in organizational and work settings, offers an overview of advantages and disadvantages of each approach discussed earlier. This overview is summarized in Table 12–6.

Applicant Reactions

Another factor to consider when choosing a selection method is how applicants will react to the chosen method. Hausknecht, Day, and Thomas (2004) offer five reasons why employee reactions to the selection method are important: (1) Applicants who view the method as invasive may view a company as a less attractive option, which could result in a loss of top candidates; (2) applicants with a negative reaction to the selection method might dissuade other persons from seeking employment within an organization; (3) applicants may be less likely to accept a job offer from

TABLE 12–6 Summary of Advantages and Disadvantages of Personnel Selection Approaches

Method	Advantages	Disadvantages
Cognitive ability tests	• Shown to be valid across a variety of organizational outcomes and job types • Easy to administer, in both paper-and-pencil and computerized formats • Cost-effective • Little training needed for administration • Not subject to attempts to manage impressions or fake responses	• Costly and labor intensive to develop custom versions • Subject to differences among ethnic groups and between sexes
Interviews	• Favorable to applicants (most expect to be interviewed) • Provide opportunity for communication from both the interviewer and applicant • Can serve as a measure of verbal communication (in contrast to tests or surveys) • Typically less likely to result in differences by ethnicity or gender	• Subject to a variety of rating errors and/or biases • Time-consuming, particularly if there are a large number of applicants and available positions • Can be costly to train interviewers • May lead to applicants responding in socially desirable ways
Personality tests	• Shown to be valid across a variety of organizational outcomes • Typically less likely to result in differences by ethnicity or gender • Easy to administer, in both paper-and-pencil and computerized formats	• May be less favorable to applicants, especially if viewed as unrelated to the job or intrusive • May lead to applicants responding in socially desirable ways • May lead to legal challenges if test is used to diagnose a medical condition rather than to assess work-related dimensions

(Continued on page 400)

TABLE 12–6	Summary of Advantages and Disadvantages of Personnel Selection Approaches (*Continued*)	
Method	**Advantages**	**Disadvantages**
Integrity tests	• Shown to be valid across a variety of organizational outcomes • Can reduce business costs by hiring employees who are less likely to engage in counterproductive work behaviors • Suggest to applicants that integrity is important • Typically less likely to result in differences by ethnicity or gender • Easy to administer, in both paper-and-pencil and computerized formats	• May lead to applicants responding in socially desirable ways • May be less favorable to applicants, especially if viewed as unrelated to the job or intrusive
Assessment Centers	• Shown to be valid across a variety of organizational outcomes • Positively viewed by applicants because of job relevance • Can provide useful feedback regarding training needs • Typically less likely to result in differences by ethnicity or gender	• Costly and labor intensive to develop • Longer administration time
Work sample tests	• Typically less likely to result in differences by ethnicity or gender • Positively viewed by applicants because of job relevance • Can provide useful feedback regarding training needs	• Do not assess aptitude to perform complex tasks • Administration can be costly, as well as keeping content up to date • Not conducive to group administration • May be inappropriate for jobs that require only a short period of training to perform the job well
Biodata	• Easy to administer and cost-effective • Shown to be valid across a number of outcomes • Typically less likely to result in differences by ethnicity or gender • Do not required skilled administrators	• Can encourage applicants to present themselves in an overly positive light • Provide little insight into additional areas for development (show only information about one's past) • Customized versions can be expensive

a company that is considered to have unfavorable selection practices; (4) negative reactions can lead to increase filings of legal complaints and court challenges; and (5) negative reactions can lead to a lower likelihood of reapplying to a company or buying a company's products.

In general, research has indicated that individuals do not view various selection methods equally. For example, Hausknecht et al. (2004) reported that interviews and work sample tests were perceived relatively favorably; cognitive ability tests, personality tests, and biodata instruments were perceived moderately favorably; and honesty tests were perceived less favorably. Interestingly, the general patterns of preferences seem to hold up internationally, in places such as the Netherlands, France, Spain, Portugal, and Singapore (Anderson & Witvliet, 2008). It is important to note that many studies reporting on selection method preferences often are conducted using students in university settings, not actual employment scenarios. However, upon graduation college students make up a large percentage of the job applicant pool, so their opinions about selection methods are of concern to organizations seeking employees.

> *In general, research has indicated that individuals do not view various selection methods equally.*

Job Analysis

Before choosing a method to select an employee, one must have a firm understanding of the knowledge, skills, and abilities (often referred to as KSAs) needed to successfully perform a job. The process used to define a job is known as job analysis; Harvey (1991) offered a more formal definition of a job analysis:

> [Job analysis is] the collection of data describing (a) observable (or otherwise verifiable) job behaviors performed by workers, including both what is accomplished as well as what technologies are employed to accomplish the end results and (b) verifiable characteristics of the job environment with which workers interact, including physical, mechanical, social, and informational elements. (p. 74)

> *Before choosing a method to select an employee, one must have a comprehensive understanding of the knowledge, skills, and abilities (often referred to as KSAs) needed to perform a job successfully.*

Harvey (1991) suggested there are three primary characteristics of a job analysis: (1) describe observables, (2) describe work behavior that is independent of personal characteristics or attributes of those that perform a job, and (3) include only observations that are verifiable and replicable. Job analysis is a central and necessary part of a test validation effort, for both intuitive and legal reasons. Although it is beyond the scope of this chapter to describe job analysis methodologies in full, we provide a brief overview of some of the most common ways to gather information about jobs.

INTERVIEW. The interview is one of the most common techniques for collecting information about a particular job (Cascio, 1991). A trained interviewer meets with incumbents and supervisors who are very familiar with the job being studied and records the tasks deemed most important to the job, the KSAs required for the job, the physical activities associated with the job, and the environmental conditions in which the job is performed. Interviews are generally considered to be a relatively inexpensive way to collect information about a job. However, the quality of the data collected can be impacted by the skills of the interviewer and the distortion of information by the interviewee (Cascio, 1991).

DIRECT OBSERVATION. Simply observing workers perform their jobs is another method for collecting information about the job. This method is best used for jobs that include a lot of manual labor and activities that can be completed in a relatively short amount of time—jobs such as an assembly specialist or a retail employee might be good candidates for this approach, whereas jobs such as an electrical engineer or a screenwriter might be poor candidates for this approach. This approach can also be an inexpensive way of collecting job-related information, but the observer must maintain a background presence in order to not interfere with the tasks and work that is being performed.

SUBJECT-MATTER EXPERT PANELS. Employees who are considered experts in their jobs (i.e., subject-matter experts, or SMEs) can be assembled into groups of about 5 to 10 to perform a job analysis. Typically, these persons are led by a trained facilitator who engages the employees in exercises and discussions that includes rating both job tasks and their corresponding KSAs (Gatewood & Feild, 1998). An advantage of this approach is that the SMEs are directly providing much of the information that will be contained in the job analysis, rather than being interpreted by an interviewer or observer. However, this approach can be more costly to implement, and its success can rest on the expertise levels of those forming the panel.

QUESTIONNAIRES. A number of commercially available questionnaires can be used to perform a job analysis (e.g., the Position Analysis Questionnaire and the Work Profiling System). These questionnaires typically consist of many items covering a variety of job tasks. Job incumbents are asked to rate the relevance of each task to their job, and may also be asked to supply importance ratings to each task. Typically, items that are ranked the highest and/or are rated as most important are then used to define the KSAs needed for a job.

EVALUATING JOB PERFORMANCE

Up to this point, we have focused primarily on how employees have been selected for vacant job positions. We have compared these strategies by highlighting how predictive each strategy can be in predicting organizational outcomes, with the most important outcome being job performance. We have taken for granted the concept of job performance, and perhaps have even assumed that job performance is comparable across strategies and various lines of research. However, research on job performance criteria has existed for about as long as personnel selection research, and the corresponding issues and debates are just as complex and challenging. In fact, Austin and Villanova (1992) provided a historical summary of the "criterion problem" that dates back to 1917. In general, the criterion problem refers to the difficulty in conceptualizing and measuring performance criteria that are multidimensional and dependent on specific organizations or situations. Although it is beyond the scope of this chapter to provide a detailed review of the history of the criterion problem (and to increase the likelihood that you might continue to read this chapter), following are some of the most common ways of measuring job performance, along with some of their common pitfalls.

> *In general, the criterion problem refers to the difficulty in conceptualizing and measuring performance criteria that are multidimensional and dependent on specific organizations or situations.*

Once job tasks have been identified and applicants have been selected to fill vacant job positions, managers in organizations need a way to evaluate the performances of their employees. Borman (1991) identified four major types of measures used to assess performance: (1) performance ratings; (2) objective measures (e.g., sales volume, turnover, absenteeism); (3) performance tests or job simulations; and (4) written job knowledge tests. This section focuses on the first measure—performance ratings.

Approaches to Performance Ratings

Four primary sources are used to gather **performance ratings**: supervisor, peer, subordinate, and self. Arguably the most common approach is ratings made by a supervisor. Most of us who have had jobs have been rated at some point by a boss or supervisor. The logic behind supervisor ratings is pretty straightforward. Supervisors are often considered to know the most about an individual's performance at work, and are typically responsible for the success or failure of his or her subordinates. Supervisors often act as the link between an employee and the organization, providing feedback to management concerning the performance levels of their employees, and providing feedback to subordinates on how their actions and behaviors are benefiting or working against an organization's goals. Research has shown that such feedback is important, and is more highly related to performance than information obtained from any other source (Becker & Klimoski, 1989).

> *There are four primary sources used gathering* **performance ratings***: supervisor, peer, subordinate, and self.*

Peer ratings generally refer to performance ratings made by persons who hold a position similar to the position of the person being rated. Perhaps surprisingly, peer performance evaluations have been found to exhibit a number of favorable properties: (1) acceptable reliabilities and above-average predictive validities, (2) stability over time, (3) differentiation between effort and performance, and (4) relatively high accuracy (McEvoy & Buller, 1987). However, a number of concerns about peer appraisal systems have been expressed, including friendship bias, the tendency to inflate ratings for those in the same subgroup as the raters, an overreliance on the use of stereotypes, and the possibility of retaliation in subsequent ratings by those who have been rated low during a previous rating period (DeNisi & Mitchell, 1978). In addition, peer rating programs have generally been perceived negatively by employees (Cederblom & Lounsbury, 1980; Love, 1981), although more favorable results have been obtained when ratings are used for developmental purposes rather than evaluative purposes (McEvoy & Buller, 1987).

Subordinate ratings refer to performance ratings of one's direct supervisor. Subordinate ratings of supervisors are perhaps most commonly used in multisource performance evaluation systems (also called 360-degree feedback programs). In general, there exists a substantial amount of support for the effectiveness of subordinate ratings. For example, they increase the likelihood that relevant information will be included in a performance evaluation (beyond that of supervisor ratings), and they can increase the reliability of ratings because subordinates are often in a better position to rate supervisors on certain performance dimensions, such as delegation, work direction, and communication (Mount, 1984). In addition, there can be a number of other positive benefits of implementing subordinate ratings, including (1) increased formal and informal feedback of supervisor performance, (2) increased management learning (i.e., the learning by those the supervisor reports to), and (3) improvement of supervisor behavior and effectiveness (Morgeson, Mumford, & Campion, 2005).

The final type of performance ratings discussed here are self-ratings, in which individual employees typically rate themselves on a variety of performance dimensions. Rarely are self-ratings of performance gathered in isolation, and oftentimes they use the same rating form used by supervisors in their ratings of performance. Although performance self-ratings are desirable because of their relatively low cost to obtain and their potential value to inform discussions about job performance (e.g., in comparing differences found between supervisor and subordinate ratings), they are often considered to be biased in some fashion, leading to inflated ratings. Cascio (1991) suggested several strategies to improve the effectiveness of self-ratings:

- Ask individuals to rate themselves relative to others rather than in absolute terms (e.g., on the dimension of communication, ask individuals to rate themselves on how well they communicate with others in the organization, rather than asking individuals how good of a communicator they are).
- Provide multiple opportunities for self-appraisal; it is a skill that may well improve with practice.
- Ensure confidentiality of ratings.

Comparison of Rating Approaches

Although significant correlations are found among rating formats, a relatively low amount of the overall variance among scores is shared across formats.

As you might imagine, researchers have been particularly interested in understanding the relationship between these approaches, and the differences they may exhibit when evaluating job performance. Harris and Schaubroeck (1988), in their meta-analysis of self, supervisor, and peer ratings, indicated that using multiple raters leads to a number of advantages, including enhanced ability to observe and measure numerous job facets, greater reliability, fairness, ratee acceptance, and improved defensibility when addressing legal concerns. Results from their study found moderate agreement between self–peer ratings and self–supervisor ratings, but much higher agreement between peer–supervisor ratings. Put another way, although significant correlations were found between rating formats, a relatively low amount of the overall variance between scores was found. In the case of the self–peer and self–supervisor ratings, only about 12% of the variance was shared; for the peer–supervisor ratings, the amount of shared variance was markedly higher, but still only about 38%. Thus, each rating format appears to provide a substantial amount of unique information.

One specific performance criteria area that has received considerable attention is the criteria used when validating selection methods and tools. This area is of key interest to researchers and practitioners alike; both have a keen interest in maximizing the chances of finding a relationship between the variable being studied (e.g., a selection test) and job performance criteria. Using studies of tests that predict a variety of job performance measures (e.g., supervisor ratings, supervisor rankings, production data, and work samples, among others) for clerical positions, Nathan and Alexander (1988) found similar validity coefficients across objective and subjective criteria, regardless of the type of test being used to predict job performance. Hoffman, Nathan, and Holden (1991) came to similar conclusions in a study of mechanical, maintenance, and field service jobs in a gas utility company; both objective and subjective criteria resulted in similar levels of validity. However, Hoffman et al. found that one type of subjective performance ratings—self-appraisals—showed validity levels around zero. They concluded: "While the use of self-appraisal may have merit for other performance appraisal purposes … , its use in test validation research may be problematic" (p. 615). Although these results suggest that both subjective and objective performance result in similar levels of validity, this does not imply they are measuring the same thing. A meta-analysis conducted by Bommer, Johnson, Rich, Podsakoff, and MacKenzie (1995) found a corrected average correlation between these measures of 0.39, suggesting that they are not interchangeable.

Types of Rating Methods

When making performance ratings, the rater often will use a rating system that is either relative or absolute (Cascio, 1991). Relative rating methods involve directly comparing the performance of the ratee to other persons performing similar jobs. For example, five customer service representatives might be evaluated by a rater who simply lists their names on a sheet of paper according to their performance level, with the best performer in the group listed first, and the worst performer in the group listed last. A variation of this approach is one in which paired comparisons are made between all employees within a group. For example, if five employees from a single group were being evaluated, the rater would compare each employee to all other employees and indicate which employee is the better performer. After all employees are compared, the rater sums the number of times each employee was rated the better performer, and employees are then ranked according to the total number of times he or she was ranked superior. A final relative rating method is one that mandates the rater to assign employees a rating based on predetermined percentages (e.g., 20% of employees must receive a "needs improvement" rating, 5% of employees must receive an "outstanding" rating).

Absolute rating methods do not involve making direct comparisons with other employees. Rather, the rater focuses on comparing an individual employee's behavior according to a defined (formally or informally) measure of performance. One such method is a narrative essay, in which the rater describes an employee's strengths, weaknesses, and areas of improvement. Another method is behavioral checklists, in which the rater evaluates the employee based on a series of statements about job-related behaviors. Oftentimes, the rater is asked to rate these behaviors using a Likert-type scale that has a variety of response options (e.g., *never, sometimes, often, almost always*). Such ratings are then summed across behavioral dimensions, providing a total performance score for an employee. A rating format that has received a lot of research attention is the behaviorally anchored rating scale (BARS; Smith & Kendall, 1963). Using the notion of critical incidents, different effectiveness levels of job performance are used to anchor a rating scale. When making a rating, the rater reads through the descriptions of each rating point on the corresponding scale and selects the level of performance that is best reflected by the ratee. Although originally BARS was thought to hold promise for reducing some of the common problems associated with ratings scales (e.g., various forms of error, reliability, and validity), research has shown that BARS is not substantially better than a variety of other rating formats (Borman, 1991; Cascio, 1991).

Sources of Error

In many settings, a substantial amount of effort goes into developing effective measures of job performance. Employee interviews, subject-matter expert reviews, literature reviews, and job

TABLE 12–7	Common Error Types When Evaluating Job Performance
Error Type	**Description**
Leniency	Employee is rated more favorably than is warranted by his or her job performance.
Severity	Employee is rated more negatively or severely than is warranted by his or her job performance.
Central tendency	Raters avoid using the low and high extremes of the rating scale, and simply use the middle values in the scale, resulting in all employees being rated in an "average" range.
Halo	Rater uses a global impression of an employee when rating his or her performance, resulting in either overly positive or negative ratings.

analysis techniques can be used to help human resource professionals create rating forms. However, all ratings will be subject to a variety of sources of error. Some of the most common error types are provided in Table 12–7.

> *These error types are considered to be the result of systematic errors in judgment.*

These error types are considered to be the result of systematic errors in judgment. At times, raters can be too lenient, in which they tend to rate an employee more favorably than the employee's performance would warrant. Other times, a rater may be too harsh or severe, in which the employee is rated at a lower level than what is warranted. Raters can also fall into a pattern in which their ratings are subject to a central tendency bias, in which all employees are rated as "average." And finally, raters can introduce a halo bias, in which a general impression of an employee influence ratings on specific dimensions (Cooper, 1981). Of course, when completing ratings, there are steps that raters can take to minimize the errors introduced into the rating process. For example, many biases can be minimized by trying to reduce ambiguity that might be present in the rating scales themselves, or by using a type of forced distribution in which rates are apportioned according to an approximately normal distribution. Additionally, informing raters about how to use the rating instruments and convincing them of the value and uses of the ratings they provide can also help minimize these biases (Cascio, 1991).

LEGAL ISSUES

Up to this point, this chapter has focused on a number of issues related to selecting employees and measuring how well employees perform on the job. Enormous amounts of time, effort, and energy are devoted to maximizing the efficiency and effectiveness of these methods. However, all of these expenditures can quickly become for naught if human resource professionals ignore laws that affect their hiring, promotion, compensation, and retention practices.

A substantial literature base exists on employment law and personnel selection. Although a number of classic books and articles (e.g., *Fairness in Selecting Employees*, Arvey & Faley, 1992) have been written on the subject, two source documents that anyone working in this field should be familiar with are discussed next.

Uniform Guidelines on Employee Selection Procedures (1978)

The **Uniform Guidelines on Employee Selection Procedures** (1978) presents guidelines describing characteristics of acceptable selection procedures, adopted by a number of federal agencies, including the Equal Employment Opportunity Commission, the Civil Service Commission, the Department of Labor, and the Department of Justice. In addition to hiring procedures, these guidelines apply to any selection procedure that is used as a basis for any employment decision, such as hiring, promotion, retention, or referral. Definitions of some key concepts discussed in the Guidelines are provided in Table 12–8.

> *The* **Uniform Guidelines on Employee Selection Procedures** *(1978) presents guidelines describing characteristics of acceptable selection procedures, adopted by a number of federal agencies, including the Equal Employment Opportunity Commission, the Civil Service Commission, Department of Labor, and the Department of Justice.*

In addition to defining key terms, the Guidelines also provides details on establishing validity evidence for selection procedures, both in terms of the type of studies that can be conducted and parameters for establishing validity when it is not technically feasible to implement a predictive validity study at a given location. The Guidelines also define parameters for documenting selection rate and validation data.

TABLE 12–8	Key Concepts From the Uniform Guidelines on Employee Selection Procedures
Concept	**Definition**
Adverse impact	A substantially different rate of selection that works to the disadvantage of members of a ethnicity, sex, or ethnic group.
Unfairness of a selection measure	A condition in which members of one ethnicity, sex, or ethnic group characteristically obtain lower scores on a selection procedure than members of another group, and the differences are not reflected in measures of job performance.
Four-fifths rule	A selection rate for any ethnicity, sex, or ethnic group that is less than four fifths (or 80%) of the rate for the group with the highest rate will generally be regarded by the federal enforcement agencies as evidence of adverse impact.
Discrimination	The use of any selection procedure that has an adverse impact of members of any ethnicity, sex, or ethnic group will be considered to be discriminatory, unless the procedure has been validated in accordance with these guidelines.

Principles for the Validation and Use of Personnel Selection Procedures— Fourth Edition

In addition to providing an overview of the validation process and describing generally accepted sources of validity evidence, the **Principles for the Validation and Use of Personnel Selection Procedures** *also describes operational considerations in personnel selection and proposes guidelines for documenting the results of validation studies.*

The **Principles for the Validation and Use of Personnel Selection Procedures** (2003) was developed by a task force from the SIOP (Society for Industrial and Organizational Psychology) in an effort to document scientific findings and generally accepted practices for using personnel selection procedures and conducting personnel selection research. In addition to providing an overview of the validation process and describing generally accepted sources of validity evidence, the Principles also describes operational considerations in personnel selection and propose guidelines for documenting the results of validation studies. Table 12–9 provides a selected summary of key points from several of these areas.

Although the Principles is likely to provide an abundance of relevant information to those working in the personnel selection field, it is intended only to provide helpful information; it is not intended to interpret or supplant federal, state, or local laws or regulations. In addition, the Principles is not a "how-to" document that can be used by a novice who wants to go into this field. Individuals with formal training in personnel selection must use their own knowledge to determine which portions of the Principles are most applicable to the situation at hand.

CAREER ASSESSMENT

Although not a personnel selection method, a related field is that of career assessment which is commonly used to provide information about attitudes and interests of a person interested in entering the workforce. Traditionally the use of career assessments has often been through a counselor, but today career assessments are readily found on the Internet and can be taken at one's convenience, without the involvement of a counselor—although such use is better suited for those who simply want to better understand some of their occupational and job-related interests, rather than those who are about to spend a significant amount of time and money pursuing a career path. Following is a summary of several of the more popular career assessments that are in use today.

Strong Interest Inventory—Revised Edition (SII-R)

The Strong Interest Inventory (SII-R) was originally developed by E. K. Strong Jr. in 1927, and recently revised by Donnay, Morris, Schaubhut, and Thompson (2004). It is one of the most well-known career assessment inventories available. Designed for use for high school students through adults, the revised version contains 291 items covering six areas: Occupations, Subject Areas, Activities, Leisure Activities, People, and Your Characteristics. Items are answered using a 5-point rating scale, and take between 30 to 45 minutes to complete.

TABLE 12–9	Key Points From the Principles for the Validation and Use of Personnel Selection Procedures
Key Points	
Sources of validity evidence	• Empirical relationship of predictor scores to external variables.
	• Content-related evidence that documents relationship between predictor and job outcomes.
	• Attributes of the internal structure of a test, with respect to how the items relate to each other and/or to the construct being measured.
	• Attributes related to the processes an individual goes through to perform job task or generate a response.
	• Consequences of personnel decisions, with respect to whether differences found in a predictor are also found in measures of job outcomes.
Key steps in planning a validation effort	• Identify existing validation research that is relevant.
	• Design the study in a way that is consistent with how the predictor will be used.
	• Ensure the adequacy of the methods of analysis used in the study, along with the skills of those performing the analysis.
	• Ensure the study is feasible, given the situation in which the predictor is being used.
Strategies for generalizing existing validity evidence to local situations	• Transportability, in which attributes from a job setting in an existing research study are directly comparable to a local situation.
	• Synthetic validity, in which the relationship between the selection procedure and one or more work domains is clearly delineated and documented.
	• Meta-analysis, in which the results of predictor–criterion relationships in existing research across a large number of settings are summarized and analyzed.
Fairness	• As a social rather than psychometric concept, fairness can be viewed as:
	• Equal group performance on a predictor
	• Equal treatment of all examinees
	• A lack of predictive bias, in which a common regression line can describe the predictor–criterion relationship for all subgroups
Bias	• Any construct-irrelevant source of variance that influences predictor scores.

The Strong Interest Inventory measures four primary categories of scales: General Occupational Themes (covering Holland's RIASEC theory [RIASEC stands for realistic, investigative, artistic, social, enterprising, and conventional]; see Table 12–10), Basic Interest scales (30 clusters of interest related to the occupational themes such as athletics, science, performing arts, and sales), Personal Style scales (including work style, learning environment, leadership style, risk taking, and team orientation), and Occupational scales (122 each for males and females, measuring the extent to which a person's interests are similar to person of the same sex working in 122 diverse occupations).

After completing the survey, a variety of computerized report options are available. In the reports, a person's top interest areas are provided within each RIASEC grouping (e.g., investigative might include medical science, research, and mathematics). Then, a person's top 10 occupational matches (from the 122 occupational scales) are provided, along with ratings for all occupational groups. In addition, a summary of a person's personal style scale ratings are provided, describing a person's preferences across each of the personal style groupings.

As noted in Case and Blackwell (2008), "The Strong's qualitative features ... and its psychometric characteristics continue to distinguish this instrument as a standard of excellence ... and represent another significant step in the continuing evolution of this extremely valuable tool." p. 125.

Career Decision-Making System—Revised (CDM-R)

The Career Decision-Making System—Revised (CDM-R) (Harrington & O'Shea, 2000) is a 96-item (Level 1, used for younger students or less developed readers) or 120- item (Level 2, used with stronger readers) career interest inventory that, like the Strong Interest Inventory, is based on Holland's RIASEC personality type. However, the CDM-R uses slightly different names that are designed to be more occupationally relevant (Realistic is denoted as Crafts, Investigative as Scientific, Artistic as The Arts, Enterprising as Business, and Conventional as Office Operations; Social remained the same). The CDM-R can be hand or computer administered and scored. When completing the inventory, students proceed through the following steps:

1. *Identify career choices.* Using a list of 18 career clusters, each with detailed samples of careers within a cluster, students choose their top 2 career cluster choices.
2. *Identify school subjects.* Using a list of 15 school subject areas, students choose 4 school subjects they like the most.
3. *Identify work values.* Using a list of 14 work values (e.g., creativity, good salary, outdoor work), students choose 4 work values that they feel are most important.
4. *Identify abilities.* Using a list of 14 abilities (e.g., clerical, manual, spatial), students identify their top 4 abilities.
5. *Identify future plans.* Using a list of 10 possible plans for additional training or schooling (e.g., 4-year college degree, military service, 1-year business school), students indicate their current plan for continuing their education.
6. *Identify interests.* Students read a series of activities, and indicate whether they like or dislike an activity (or if they can't make up their mind).

Upon completion of the survey, student responses are scored, and possible matches between their responses and careers are presented. The CDM provides an Internet-based job exploration tool that includes both text-based descriptions about a given job, as well as video clips showing someone performing the job. In addition, the CDM updates its job listings based on the U.S. government's release of the *Occupational Outlook Handbook*, which is released every 2 years (see the Bureau of Labor Statistics website at http://www.bls.gov).

TABLE 12–10	Holland's RIASEC Personality Type Categories
Personality Type	**Characteristics**
Realistic	Practical, to the point, brief
Investigative	Analytical, intellectual
Artistic	Creative, innovative
Social	Nurturing, agreeable
Enterprising	Energetic, persuasive
Conventional	Dependable, careful

Self-Directed Search (SDS)

The Self-Directed Search (SDS) by Holland (1997) is a vocational interest inventory that can be used by vocational counselors or can be self-administered. Also based on Holland's RIASEC model, the SDS provides a description of the congruence between a person's personality type and various occupational codes. Two forms of the SDS are offered, one for those with typical reading skills (Form R), and one for those with limited reading skills or lower educational levels (Form E). Similar to other vocational instruments, the SDS offers a tool designed to link occupations and a person's personality type. Interestingly, a leisure activity finder is also offered (e.g., for retired persons) that is designed to identify leisure activities that are most suitable for a given personality type.

Summary

When used in employment settings, tests are considered more than simply a collection of items with correct and incorrect responses. They refer more broadly to a collection of instruments that measure a variety of factors related to job performance, such as general ability, job-related attitudes, job knowledge, opinions, interests, and specific skills. With origins dating back to World War I, the use of psychological tests for predicting job performance and other work-related outcomes has continued to grow, and has resulted in one of the fastest-growing areas in psychology over the last few decades.

This chapter discussed a number of personnel selection approaches. Cognitive ability tests have a long history of use in employment settings, and have consistently shown to be one of the best predictors of job performance, even though their use can lead to some significant drawbacks and challenges. Interviews, although being one of the most widely used selection strategies, can also be among the most subjective; efforts to develop structured questions and standardized approaches can go a long way in improving their effectiveness. Personality tests have come in and out of vogue over a period of 50 years, and have been one of the most contentious areas in I–O psychology in the last decade. Integrity tests, sometimes considered a close cousin of personality tests, continue to be used when making selection decisions, and have been shown to provide some of the highest levels of incremental validity beyond what can be predicted by cognitive ability tests. Assessment centers, work sample tests, and biodata forms continue to be used for making employment decisions, although to a somewhat lesser degree than the other selection approaches discussed in this chapter.

When using selection tools, we stated that a number of related areas can be important to their success. Using methods that result in favorable reactions by applicants can have a positive outcome for a company. Conducting a thorough job analysis can increase the likelihood of assessing skills and abilities that are truly related to the job.

In addition, we have reviewed some common methods for evaluating and obtaining measures of job performance, an area that directly relates to the evaluation of selection methods, and one that necessitates the same care and consideration. We also reviewed some of the relevant legal considerations for employment settings, and highlighted some of the most important concepts and topics. Finally, we discussed career or vocational assessment, and described some of the most commonly used assessment tools, including the Strong Interest Inventory, the Career Decision-Making System, and the Self-Directed Search.

Key Terms and Concepts

Assessment centers, 395
Employment interviews, 389
Industrial–organizational (I–O) psychology, 384
Overt and personality-oriented integrity tests, 394

Performance ratings, 403
Principles for the Validation and Use of Personnel Selection Procedures, 408
Uniform Guidelines on Employee Selection Procedures, 407

Work sample tests, 397

Recommended Readings

Berry, C. M., Sackett, P. R., & Wiemann, S. (2007). A review of recent developments in integrity test research. *Personnel Psychology, 60,* 271–301.

Campion, M., Pursell, E., & Brown, B. (1988). Structured interviewing: Raising the psychometric properties of the employment interview. *Personnel Psychology, 41,* 25–42.

Hunter, J. E., & Hunter, R. F. (1984). Validity and utility of alternative predictors of job performance. *Psychological Bulletin, 96,* 72–98.

Schmidt, F. L., & Hunter, J. (1998). The validity and utility of selection methods in personnel psychology: Practical and theoretical implications of 85 years of research findings. *Psychological Bulletin, 124*(2), 262–274.

Society for Industrial and Organizational Psychology, Inc. (2003). *Principles for the validation and use of personnel selection procedures.* (3rd ed.). College Park, MD: Author.

Tett, R. P., Jackson, D. N., & Rothstein, M. (1991). Personality measures as predictors of job performance: A meta-analytic review. *Personnel Psychology, 44,* 703–742.

The Uniform Guidelines on Employee Selection Procedures (1978). Federal Register, 43 (166), 38296–38309.

Chapter Thirteen

Neuropsychological Testing

CECIL R. REYNOLDS
TEXAS A&M UNIVERSITY

ANDREW L. SCHMITT
THE UNIVERSITY OF TEXAS AT TYLER

The brain is in charge of all behavior and assessment of its functional integrity is important to understanding behavior, cognition, and emotion.

Chapter Outline

Learning Objectives

After reading and studying this chapter, students should be able to:

1. Explain the basic role of clinical neuropsychological assessment.
2. Identify and describe the two most commonly employed fixed battery approaches to neuropsychological assessment.
3. Describe the Boston Process Approach to neuropsychological assessment.
4. Compare and contrast the relative strengths and weaknesses of the fixed battery and flexible battery approaches.
5. Explain the unique importance of memory assessment.
6. Describe the development and the basic structure of the Test of Memory and Learning.
7. Explain the eight principal components of a neuropsychological evaluation.
8. Describe some of the common brain injuries often prompting a neuropsychological evaluation.
9. Outline the major procedures that are common to most neuropsychological evaluations.
10. Describe the primary elements that influence the selection of tests in a neuropsychological exam.
11. Explain the principal concepts and approaches to deficit measurement.
12. Define premorbid ability and its importance in the measurement of change.

> *Clinical neuropsychology is the application of the knowledge gleaned from the study of brain–behavior relationships to patient care.*

Neuropsychology is the study of brain–behavior relationships. **Clinical neuropsychology** is the application of this knowledge to patient care. Neuropsychological testing is the application of a set of standardized procedures designed to assess and quantify brain function as expressed in overt behavior and leading to additional inferences regarding the covert processes of the brain. Neuropsychological testing may include, for example, assessing the ability of the patient to solve novel problems; to learn new tasks; to execute well-defined simple and complex motor tasks; to deduce relationships using formal logic; to engage in recall, recognition, and related memory tasks; to recognize and/or interpret speech sounds, nonspeech sounds, and visual and tactile stimuli; to pay attention; and to develop and execute plans for behavior, among other specific cognitive functions. Accurate neuropsychological testing requires maximum effort from the patient if valid inferences regarding brain function are to be obtained, more so than any other they are truly maximum performance tests.

Neuropsychological testing remains the premier method of assessing brain–behavior relationships even as neuroimaging methods advance. Although SPECT, PET, fMRI, QEEG, MEG, and other techniques of imaging do tell us if areas of the brain are functioning at normal levels (typically from a metabolic viewpoint), they simply cannot tell us if a patient can still read or add numbers or learn a new job skill or how well the patient may perform at any given cognitive task—they tell us only whether the most common underlying brain structure is functioning properly. Often after viewing a functional neuroimage we can be reasonably certain that particular skills will be impaired, but the specific nature of the impairment and its degree are elusive to even the most advanced neuroimaging technologies. At times, behavior functions will even be normal in the face of abnormal neuroimaging studies, and vice versa, with actual neuropsychological testing and quantification of the results remaining the gold standard.

Neuropsychological assessment examines the relationship between brain functioning and behavior through tests that tap specific domains of functioning—typically much more specific domains than those that are represented on general tests of intelligence, such as attention, memory, forgetting, sensory functions, constructional praxis, and motor skills (Reitan & Wolfson, 1985; Reynolds & Mayfield, 2005), although the use of tests of general intelligence is necessary as a component of the comprehensive neuropsychological examination. Neuropsychologists examine the functioning of the brain based on behavioral expression, and are able to determine whether a brain dysfunction exists or whether atypical patterns of functional neocortical development are present.

> *Neuropsychological tests tend to be more highly specific in what they measure relative to general intelligence measures.*

A neurologist looks at the anatomical construction of the brain as well as the electrochemical systems of the central nervous system (CNS). Working in conjunction with neurologists, neuropsychologists are able to determine the functioning sequelae of CNS dysfunction regardless of etiology. Neurologists use advanced neuroimaging techniques such as those noted. Neuropsychologists focus on behavior and cognition in order to offer educational help and remediation strategies to schools, family members, vocational specialists, and counselors. Clinical neuropsychologists deal with a variety of issues as family members seek to understand the cognitive and psychological needs of children and adults who are coping with neurological deficits, acute or chronic.

Family members frequently want to know what they can do to provide the optimal environment to help their loved one reach the maximum level of functioning and enjoy their lives to the fullest extent possible. They seek to understand the specific deficits and possible compensatory strengths. On the basis of a person's medical, family, and developmental history, as well as the specific behavioral and vocational concerns, a neuropsychological assessment is designed and conducted.

Although this chapter discusses examples of specific neuropsychological tests and batteries of tests, neuropsychology as practiced correctly is not a set of techniques. Rather, it is a way of thinking about behavior, often expressed as test scores; in essence, it is a paradigm for understanding behavior. Because the brain determines and controls our behavior, ultimately all tests are neuropsychological tests; however, most tests carrying this classification (about which there is little agreement for many tests) assess very specific functions, or functions that can be tied to very specific brain systems.

COMPONENTS OF A NEUROPSYCHOLOGICAL EVALUATION

When designing a thorough neuropsychological assessment, just choosing a predesigned battery is typically insufficient. The most common neuropsychological batteries and approaches will need to be supplemented in specific ways, depending on the referral questions posed. The following eight general guidelines should nevertheless be useful and are derived from a variety of sources, including our own practices, the general teachings of Lawrence C. Hartlage, and other specific sources—in particular, Rourke, Bakker, Fisk, and Strang (1983) and Reynolds and Mayfield (2005).

1. *All (or at least a significant majority) of a patient's relevant cognitive skills or higher order information-processing skills should be assessed.* This will often involve an assessment of general intellectual level (*g*) via an IQ test that includes both the verbal and nonverbal domains, such as a Wechsler scale or the Reynolds Intellectual Assessment Scales. Efficiency of mental processing as assessed by strong measures of *g* is essential to provide a baseline for interpreting all other aspects of the assessment process. Assessment of basic academic skills (including reading, writing, spelling, and math) will be necessary, along with tests such as the Test of Memory and Learning—Second Edition (TOMAL-2; Reynolds & Voress, 2007), which also have the advantage of including performance-based measures of attention and concentration. Problems with memory, attention/concentration, and new learning are the most common of all complaints following CNS compromise and frequently are associated with chronic neurodevelopmental disorders (e.g., learning disability, attention deficit hyperactivity disorder [ADHD]) and various forms of brain injury.

   > *Neuropsychological testing should sample the relative efficiency of the right and left hemispheres of the brain.*

2. *Testing should sample the relative efficiency of the right and left hemispheres of the brain.* Asymmetries of performance are of interest on in their own right, but different brain systems are involved in each hemisphere, and these have different implications for treatment. Whereas some neurodevelopmental and genetic disorders produce generalized deficits in cognitive functions, others have greater impact on some brain systems than others. For example, Double Y syndrome (in which male offspring have an XYY instead of XY chromosomal feature)

often produces a pattern with greater relative suppression of left hemisphere and related language skill deficits versus the spatial functions and related skills more influenced by right hemisphere function. Even in a diffuse injury such as anoxia, it is possible to find greater impairment in one portion of an individual's brain than in another. Specific neuropsychological tests such as the Halstead-Reitan Neuropsychological Test Battery (HRNB) are useful here, along with measures of verbal and nonverbal memory processes.

3. *Testing should sample both anterior and posterior regions of cortical function.* The anterior portion of the brain is generative, expressive, and regulatory, whereas the posterior region is principally receptive. Deficits and their nature in these systems will have a great impact on treatment choices. Many common tests, such as tests of receptive (posterior) and expressive (anterior) vocabulary, may be applied here, along with a systematic and thorough sensory perceptual examination and certain specific tests of motor function. In conjunction with point 2, this allows for evaluation of the integrity of the four major quadrants of the neocortex: right anterior, right posterior, left anterior, and left posterior.

4. *Testing should determine the presence of specific deficits.* Any specific functional problems a patient is experiencing must be determined and assessed. In addition to such problems being of importance in the assessment of persons with neurodevelopmental disorders, traumatic brain injury (TBI), stroke, and even some toxins can produce very specific changes in neocortical function that are addressed best by the neuropsychological assessment. As they age, people with neurodevelopmental and genetic disorders are more vulnerable to CNS insult as well, which may have more profound effect on an already compromised CNS and produce additional specific deficits. Similarly, certain transplant patients will display specific patterns of deficits as well. Neuropsychological tests tend to be less *g*-loaded as a group and to have greater specificity of measurement than many common psychological tests. Noting areas of specific deficits is important in both diagnosis and treatment planning.

5. *Testing should determine the acuteness versus the chronicity of any problems or weaknesses found.* The "age" of a problem is important to diagnosis and to treatment planning. When a thorough history is combined with the pattern of test results obtained, it is possible, with reasonable accuracy, to distinguish chronic neurodevelopmental disorders such as dyslexia or ADHD from new, acute problems resulting from trauma, stroke, or disease. Particular care must be taken in developing a thorough, documented history when such a determination is made. Rehabilitation and habilitation approaches take differing routes in the design of intervention and treatment strategies, depending on the acuteness or chronicity of the problems evidenced. As people with neurodevelopmental disorders age, symptoms will wax and wane as well, and distinguishing new from old symptoms is important when treatment recommendations are being made.

> *Neuropsychological testing should locate intact complex functional systems.*

6. *Testing should locate intact complex functional systems.* The brain functions as a series of interdependent, systemic networks often referred to as "complex functional systems." Multiple systems are affected by CNS problems, but some systems are almost always spared except in the most extreme cases. It is imperative in the assessment process to locate strengths and intact systems that can be used to overcome the problems the person is experiencing. Treatment following CNS compromise involves habilitation and rehabilitation, with the understanding that some organic deficits will represent permanently

impaired systems. As the brain consists of complex, interdependent networks of systems that produce behavior, the ability to ascertain intact systems is crucial to enhancing the probability of designing successful treatment. Identification of intact systems also suggests the potential for a positive outcome, as opposed to fostering low expectations and fatalistic tendencies from an identification of brain damage or dysfunction.

7. *Testing should assess affect, personality, and behavior.* Neuropsychologists sometimes ignore their roots in psychology and focus on assessing the neural substrates of a problem. However, CNS compromise will result in deviations from normal developmental pathways for affect, personality, and behavior. Some of these changes will be transient and some will be permanent. Some of the changes will be direct (i.e., the results of CNS compromise at the cellular and systemic levels), and others will be indirect (i.e., reactions to loss or changes in function, or to how others respond to and interact with the individual as a genetic or neurodevelopmental disorder continues to express across age). A thorough history, including times of onset of problem behaviors, can assist in determination of direct versus indirect effects. Such behavioral changes will also require intervention, and intervention will not necessarily be the same if the changes noted are direct versus indirect or if premorbid behavior problems were evident.

8. *Test results should be presented in ways that are useful in a school or work environment, to acute care or intensive rehabilitation facilities, or to physicians (i.e., they should be presented to fit the context of the patient's life).* The majority of individuals with developmental disabilities, brain injury, or neurodevelopmental and genetic disorders will continue into higher education and/or join the adult workforce. They are assisted in such pursuits by various federal laws such as the Individuals with Disabilities Education Act (IDEA), Americans with Disabilities Act (ADA), and Section 504 of the Vocational Rehabilitation Amendment of 1973. It is important to establish the learning and vocational skills of these patients so they may be directed toward proper education, training, and employment and to determine any reasonable accommodations that would be required to make them successful. Neuropsychological test results are often used by vocational rehabilitation specialists to determine appropriate guidance. For those individuals with more serious disorders, for whom postsecondary education and placement ultimately in a competitive work environment are not reasonable expectations, neuropsychological examinations are required typically to document the presence and extent of the disability that has resulted from CNS disorders. Not all CNS disorders result in disability and, especially given the concepts of variable expressivity and modern treatments, disability determination must be made one case at a time, but is crucial to establishing eligibility for such life-changing programs as supplemental security income (SSI) and other government-funded programs (e.g., Medicaid and Medicare) for workers who are permanently disabled.

NEUROPSYCHOLOGICAL ASSESSMENT APPROACHES AND INSTRUMENTS

There are two major conceptual approaches to neuropsychological assessment. In the first approach, a standard battery of tasks designed to identify brain impairment is used (the fixed battery approach). The Halstead-Reitan Neuropsychological Test Battery (HRNB) for Adults (Reitan & Wolfson, 1985) is the most commonly used battery, followed by the Luria-Nebraska Neuropsychological Battery (LNNB; Golden, Purisch, & Hammeke, 1991). The second approach to neuropsychological

> *The major theoretical premise of any neuropsychological battery is the proposition that behavior has an organic basis, and thus performance on behavioral measures can be used to assess brain functioning*

assessment favors the use of a flexible combination of traditional psychological and educational tests. The composition of this battery varies depending upon a number of variables, including history, functional level, and presenting problem. The major theoretical premise of any neuropsychological battery is the proposition that behavior has an organic basis (i.e., the brain controls behavior), and thus performance on behavioral measures can be used to assess brain functioning (Cullum, 1998).

The Halstead-Reitan Neuropsychological Test Battery (HRNB)

The **Halstead-Reitan Neuropsychological Test Battery (HRNB)** was designed to assess the key behavioral correlates of brain function. The HRNB consists of measures in six categories: (1) input; (2) attention, concentration, and memory; (3) verbal abilities; (4) spatial, sequential, and manipulatory abilites; (5) abstraction, reasoning, logical analysis, and concept formation; and (6) output (Reitan & Wolfson, 1993). Right–left differences, dysphasia and related deficits (pathognomonic signs), and cutoff scores associated with absolute levels of performance that differentiate normal from brain-damaged adults for each component of the battery are used to determine scores on the General Neuropsychological Deficit Scale, which is the person's level of performance. Based on normative comparisons, raw scores are weighted as "perfectly normal" (score = 0), "normal" (score = 1), "mildly impaired" (score = 2), or "significantly impaired" (score = 3). Scores for various brain systems and right versus left hemisphere differences also can be derived. Table 13–1 lists the components of the HRNB most appropriate for adults. Versions for children and adolescents are available as well.

As of this writing, there simply is no set of neuropsychological assessment devices with as much clinical history and empirical support as the HRNB. Among clinicians who prefer the strong scientific

Table 13–1	Halstead-Reitan Neuropsychological Test Battery	
Test	**Function or Skills Assessed**	**Hypothesized Localization**
Lateral Dominance Test	Determine dominance	
Aphasia Screening Test	Language and construction	Language items relate to left hemisphere; constructional items relate to right hemisphere
Finger Tapping Test	Motor	Frontal lobe
Grip Strength	Motor	Frontal lobe
Finger Localization Test	Sensory–perceptual	Unilateral errors implicate contralateral parietal lobe; can also occur with bilateral errors
Rhythm Test	Alertness and concentration	Global
Speech Sounds Perception Test	Alertness and concentration	Global; anterior left hemisphere
Category Test	Reasoning	Global
Trail Making Test Parts A and B	Visual–spatial reasoning	Global

(Continued)

Table 13–1	Halstead-Reitan Neuropsychological Test Battery *(Continued)*	
Tactual Performance Test		
Total Time	Motor	Frontal lobe
Memory	Immediate memory	Global
Localization	Immediate memory	Global
Category Test	Reasoning	Global
Sensory–Perceptual Examination		
Tactile Perception Test	Sensory–perceptual	Contralateral parietal lobe
Auditory Perception Test	Sensory–perceptual	Temporal lobe
Visual Perception Test	Sensory–perceptual	Visual pathway; visual fields
Tactile Form Recognition	Sensory–perceptual	Parietal lobe
Fingertip Writing Perception Test	Sensory–perceptual	Peripheral nervous system; Parietal lobe

base of support for a fixed battery approach, the HRNB is the most common choice. However, the HRNB, done correctly, is quite lengthy and can require 8 to 10 hours for administration and scoring, too much for some patients and an examination time infrequently supported by third party payers. The HRNB, although derived initially from Halstead's (1947) biological theory of intelligence, evolved from a more purely actuarial or empirical perspective. Even so, it shortchanges such important functions as memory, assessing only a few aspects of memory

> *As of this writing, there is no set of neuropsychological assessment devices with as much clinical history and empirical support as the* **Halstead-Reitan Neuropsychological Test Battery.**

and doing so briefly. During this time, the theoretical models of Alexander Luria were gaining influence (e.g., Luria, 1966) in Western neuropsychology, all of these factors eventually leading to the development of a second, popular fixed battery based on Luria's model of the working brain.

The Luria-Nebraska Neuropsychological Battery (LNNB) for Adults

The Luria-Nebraska Neuropsychological Battery (LNNB) was developed in the late 1970s and 1980s by Charles Golden and colleagues (see Golden et al., 1991) as a means of standardizing and quantifying the clinical assessment procedures of the famed Russian neuropsychologist, Alexander Luria. The LNNB was designed to diagnose cognitive deficits that are general in their manifestation but also to provide information on the lateralization and localization of any focal CNS deficiencies. Golden et al. (1991) argued that the LNNB detects very specific problems that might go unnoticed in less detailed examinations or interpretations of global scores. The LNNB is administered from the age of 12. There are 12 clinical scales on the LNNB. As Golden (1997; Golden et al., 1991) described, the LNNB lends itself to three levels of interpretation: scale, item, and qualitative. Each of the LNNB scales yields a *T*-score, and the resulting profile has been the subject of significant empirical work. However, the items within these scales vary in modality and other demand characteristics (i.e., are quite heterogeneous compared, for example, to items within subtests of the HRNB), and an analysis of item scores is also used. Finally, Luria was a renowned clinician and approached patients individually. Golden et al. (1991) thus designed the LNNB to allow qualitative analysis as a supplement to the typical Western psychological approach of quantitative analysis of performance on the various scales.

The LNNB has some scales and items where process is the dominant feature, but others where content and learned behavior predominate. Careful review of LNNB performance at all three levels (scale, item, and qualitative) is not just possible but necessary. In a qualitative analysis, the examiner is more concerned with wrong answers than with correct ones and analyzes the nature of the errors committed by the examinee. For example, was the inability to write to dictation caused by a visual–motor problem, a visual–perceptive deficit, a failure of comprehension, or a planning, attention, or execution problem? Only through careful observation and a review of successful tasks can these questions be answered. Examiners must have extensive experience with normal individuals, however, to avoid over-interpretation of such item-level performance and behavioral observations on the LNNB or any other scale for that matter.

The Boston Process Approach (BPA)

Another, newer effort at evaluating process in neuropsychological assessment is known as the **Boston Process Approach (BPA)** and is described in detail in Kaplan (1988, 1990). In contrast to the use of standard batteries, the process approach uses a flexible battery of developmental and psychological tests, which permits the clinician to select tasks appropriate to the specific referral question, functioning levels, and response limitations of the adult. Client variables such as "age, gender, handedness, familial handedness, educational and occupational background, premorbid talents, patient's and family's medical, neurological, and psychiatric history, drug or alcohol abuse, use of medications (past and present), etiology of the CNS dysfunction, and laterality and focus of the lesion" (Kaplan, 1990, p. 72) all provide valuable information in developing the assessment. Furthermore, this process provides an analysis of the person's neuropsychological assets, rather than focusing on a diagnosis or a specific localization of brain impairment, for which the standardized batteries have been noted to be especially useful. The flexible battery approach purportedly translates more directly into educational and vocational interventions, and a major goal of conducting a neuropsychological assessment is to aid in the planning of such interventions. This model also tries to integrate quantitative and qualitative approaches to interpretation and analysis of performance on various cognitive tasks. The BPA alters the format of items on traditional tests such as the various Wechsler scales, and BPA versions of the Wechsler Intelligence Scale for Children–IV and the Wechsler Adult Intelligence Scale–IV are available. Additional, supplementary tests have been devised specifically for the BPA over many years, including the Boston Naming Test, the Boston Diagnostic Aphasia Examination, and the California Verbal Learning Test, along with others. As with other methods of assessment, examiners are advised to use BPA assessments in conjunction with history and interview data and observations of the patient. However, clinicians are also free to pick and choose among a myriad of available neuropsychological measures. Table 13–2 lists a number of neuropsychological instruments that are commonly employed in a flexible battery approach.

> *The strength of the* **Boston Process Approach** *lies in its flexibility, which enables a neuropsychologist to tailor the assessment to the referral problem.*

Table 13–2	Neuropsychological Instruments Commonly Employed in a Flexible Battery

Premorbid Ability

National Adult Reading Test (NART; Nelson & Willison, 1991)

Wechsler Test of Adult Reading (WTAR; Psychological Corporation, 2001)

General Ability

Reynolds Intellectual Assessment Scales (RIAS; Reynolds & Kamphaus, 2003)

Stanford-Binet Intelligence Scale—Fifth Edition (SB5; Roid, 2003)

Wechsler Adult Intelligence Scale—Fourth Edition (WAIS-IV; Wechsler, 2008)

Achievement

Wide Range Achievement Test 4 (WRAT-4; Wilkinson & Robertson, 2006)

Woodcock-Johnson III Tests of Achievement (WJ III ACH; Woodcock, McGrew, & Mather, 2001b)

Executive Functions

Comprehensive Trail Making Test (CTMT; Reynolds, 2002)

Stroop Test (Golden, 1978)

Tower of London (Culbertson & Zillmer, 2001)

Attention

Conner's Continuous Performance Test—Third Edition (CPT-III; Conners, 1992)

Paced Auditory Serial Addition Test (PASAT; Gronwall, 1977)

Trail Making Test (Reitan & Wolfson, 1985)

Memory

California Verbal Learning Test—Second Edition (CVLT-II; Delis, Kramer, Kaplan, & Ober, 2000)

Rey Complex Figure Test and Recognition Trial (RCFT; Meyers & Meyers, 1995)

Test of Memory and Learning—Second Edition (TOMAL-2; Reynolds & Voress, 2007)

Wide Range Assessment of Memory and Learning—Second Edition (WRAML-2, Sheslow & Adams, 2003)

Language Tests

Boston Diagnostic Aphasia Examination—Third Edition (BDAE-3; Goodglass, Kaplan, & Barresi, 2001)

Boston Naming Test—Second Edition (BNT-2; Kaplan, Goodglass, & Weintraub, 2001)

Vocabulary subtest (WAIS-IV; Wechsler, 2008)

Construction

Clock Drawing Test (Goodglass & Kaplan, 1983)

Block Design subtest (WAIS-IV; Wechsler, 2008)

Free Drawing (Bicycle; Piaget, 1930)

Concept Formation and Reasoning

Category Test (Halstead, 1947)

Matrix Reasoning subtest (WAIS-IV; Wechsler, 2008)

Raven's Progressive Matrices (RPM; Raven, 1996)

Similarities subtest (WAIS-IV; Wechsler, 2008)

Motor Function

Finger Tapping Test (FTT; Reitan, 1969)

Grip Strength (Reitan & Wolfson, 1985)

Grooved Pegboard (Klove, 1963)

The strength of the BPA lies in its flexibility, which enables a neuropsychologist to tailor the assessment to the referral problem. There is quite a bit of research on individual aspects of the BPA (e.g., see White & Rose, 1997), but research on the BPA as a whole is lacking—and this is a major weakness of the approach. The modifications made to well-designed, carefully standardized tests such as the Wechsler scales also have unpredictable and at times counterintuitive outcomes in patient examination (e.g., Lee, Reynolds, & Willson, 2003; Slick, Hopp, Strauss, & Fox, 1996). Slick et al. (1996) found that changes made to the BPA version of the Wechsler Adult Intelligence Scale–Revised caused a substantial number of individuals to earn lower scores on the modified items than on the corresponding standardized versions of the items, even though the intent of the modification was in part to make the items easier. This could easily draw a clinician into overinterpretation and overdiagnosis of pathology. Slick et al. (1996) correctly concluded that whenever changes are made to standardized instruments, comprehensive norms are required under the new testing conditions. They also concluded that clinical interpretation of such modified procedures prior to the development and purveyance of the norms is questionable from an ethical standpoint.

The lack of good normative or reference data has been a long-term problem for neuropsychological assessment (e.g., see Reynolds, 2008). This causes a variety of problems related to test interpretation, not the least of which is understanding the relationship of status variables such as gender, ethnicity, and socioeconomic status to test performance. The BPA, because of its principal strengths, also makes inordinate cognitive demands on the examiner. Another major concern about the process approach is the difficulty in establishing validity for the innumerable versions of batteries used, as interpretations may not be uniform or reliable. This issue has been addressed inadequately thus far. Base rates for the number of scores from a BPA approach that fall in the "impaired" range for normal and for clinical samples is also absent from the literature, causing much consternation in determining whether low scores are a common or unusual occurrence. In contrast, base rates for such levels of performance on the HRNB are well established.

The issue of the reliability and validity of conclusions drawn from fixed versus flexible batteries has been a matter of controversy regarding the admittance of testimony based on these approaches in a variety of court cases. Thus far, fixed battery data (e.g., HRNB) have been more readily accepted in court, but flexible battery data and conclusions are also accepted more often than not, but not in all cases. The legal issues surrounding the use of flexible batteries in forensic settings are thus as yet unresolved.

ASSESSMENT OF MEMORY FUNCTIONS

> *Memory complaints seem ubiquitous in nearly all cognitive disorders.*

Memory complaints seem ubiquitous in nearly all cognitive disorders. Nearly every CNS disorder associated with disturbances of higher cognitive functions has memory disturbance in some form noted as a common complaint. In cases of traumatic brain injury (TBI), memory disturbances are the most common of all patient complaints. Three age groups account for a majority of cases of TBI—birth to 5, 15 to 24, and over 75, with males outnumbering females by about 2 to 1. Motor vehicle accidents are the most common cause of TBI; falls and violence are second and third, respectively (Rutland-Brown, Langlois, Thomas, & Xi, 2006). TBI produces the least predictable forms of memory loss with the exception of increased forgetting curves. Persons with learning disabilities of various forms, but especially reading-related learning disabilities, commonly are found to have memory problems, particularly with sequential recall. Memory disturbances are the hallmark of nearly all of the known dementias, such as Alzheimer's disease and Korsakoff's disease (also known as alcoholic amnestic disorder), two of the most common of the dementias, although the form of memory loss varies from one dementia to another. Table 13–3 compares the distinguishing characteristics of the most common forms of dementia. As research becomes more sophisticated, disturbances of memory and learning are being discovered elsewhere as well. In many medical disorders as well as in a variety of neuropsychiatric disturbances, retrieval of information is often compromised along with acquisition of new material.

Memory is almost always one focus of cognitive rehabilitation or retraining with TBI patients of all ages. However, recovery of memory functions post-TBI is less predictable than improvements in more general aspects of intellectual function, likely, at least in part, because of the disturbances of attention and concentration that typically accompany TBI. Problems with memory are some of the most persistent sequelae of TBI. Although some forms of memory tasks (e.g., immediate recall) are suppressed in functional and organic disorders, other memory tasks (e.g., delayed recall or forgetting) provide very good discrimination between psychiatric disorders such as depression and TBI and other CNS insult. Some form of memory assessment is nearly always included in comprehensive evaluations of cognitive functions whether conducted by school, clinical, or neuropsychologists, although neuropsychologists more commonly assess memory skills in greater depth than do other psychologists.

Given the ubiquitous nature of memory in daily affairs, particularly during the school-age years, and the importance of memory in evaluating the functional and the physiological integrity of the brain, it is surprising that comprehensive assessment of memory in children and adolescents is a recent phenomenon. This seems particularly odd given the plethora of such tasks available for adults dating from at least the 1930s.

To some extent, memory assessment with children and adolescents must have been viewed as important since the earliest of modern intelligence tests (e.g., the 1907 Binet) and even the Wechsler scales, in their various children's versions, all included one or two brief assessments of immediate recall. Still, the major texts on child neuropsychology of the 1970s and 1980s (e.g., Bakker, Fisk, & Strang, 1983; Hynd & Obrzut, 1981) do not discuss assessment of memory despite the finding that 80% of a sample of various clinicians who perform testing noted memory as an important aspect of the assessment of cognitive and intellectual functions (Snyderman & Rothman, 1987). By 1995, assessment of memory function in children is discussed in key textbooks (e.g., Reynolds & Fletcher-Janzen, 1997) and its relation to various medical (e.g., Baron, Fennell, & Voeller, 1995) and neuropsychiatric disorders (e.g., Gillberg, 1995) routinely included in major works on child neuropsychology.

Dorothea McCarthy, the noted psycholinguist, was aware of the importance of memory and included a memory index on the then-innovative McCarthy Scales of Children's Abilities (McCarthy, 1972). Koppitz (1977), another pioneer in the assessment of children, noted the need for a more detailed evaluation of children's memory functions and devised the four-subtest Visual–Aural Digit Span Test (VADS; Koppitz, 1977). The VADS quickly became popular with school psychologists, among whom Koppitz was well known because of her work in childhood assessment with the Bender–Gestalt Test (which was updated only recently; Reynolds, 2007) and human figure drawings. The VADS is relatively narrow, assessing only sequential memory for digits but altering modality of input and output. No real attempt at developing a comprehensive

Table 13–3 Symptom Presentations in Subtypes of Dementia

Dementia Type	Alzheimer's Disease	Vascular Dementia	Frontal Lobe Dementia	Lewy Body Dementia	Alcoholic Dementia	Parkinson's Dementia	Huntington's Dementia
Genetic risk	Moderate	Moderate	High	Moderate	Low	Low	Very high
Cortical or subcortical features	Cortical	Both cortical and subcortical	Cortical	Both cortical and subcortical	Both cortical and subcortical	Subcortical	Subcortical
Environmental risk factors	Unknown	Hypertension, hyperlipidemia, smoking, obesity, strokes, diabetes	Unknown	Unknown	Alcohol abuse	Possibly environmental toxins	Little environmental influence
Mean age of onset	60–70 years	60–70 years	50–60 years	60–70 years	60–70 years	40–60 years	30–40 years
Prominent physiological changes	Neurofibrillary plaques and tangles; cholinergic cell depletion; atrophy in hippocampus and temporal lobe	Neuroimaging evidence of multiple strokes diffusely throughout the brain	Temporal and frontal lobe atrophy with reduced blood flow and metabolism	Lewy body deposits; atrophy in cortex, limbic system, and substantia nigra	Cortical atrophy in temporal and frontal lobes and subcortical atrophy	Loss of dopaminergic cells in substantia nigra	Atrophy of caudate nucleus and putamen
Distinguishing neuropsychological features	Prominent memory problems in encoding, storage, and retrieval early in the disease	Low verbal and motoric output; executive function impaired	Social and personality changes precede cognitive changes	Visual hallucinations and delusions; fluctuating cognitive function; visual–spatial deficits	Memory, behavioral, and frontal lobe pathology; visual-spatial deficits	Frontal and prefrontal problems; executive function impairment. Significant motor disturbance	Early memory impairment with similar symptoms to Parkinson's Dementia

assessment of children's memory appears until the introduction of the **Wide Range Assessment of Memory and Learning (WRAML)** for ages 5 through 17 by Sheslow and Adams (1990).

The WRAML was born of the frustration and dissatisfaction of its authors in not having a sound, comprehensive measure of memory functioning in children (Sheslow & Adams, 1990). The WRAML consists of nine subtests divided equally into three scales—Verbal Memory, Visual Memory, and Learning—followed by a brief delayed recall to assess rapidity of decay of memory (i.e., forgetting). The WRAML was a substantial improvement over existing measures of memory for children but still provided a limited sample of memory and learning tasks. To increase the breadth and depth of analysis of memory function from the preschool years through the high school years (ages 5 to 20), Reynolds and Bigler (1994) developed the **Test of Memory and Learning (TOMAL)**. The second edition of the TOMAL, the TOMAL-2 (Reynolds & Voress, 2007), continues to provide professionals with a standardized measure of different memory functions for children and adolescents but was also extended to incorporate assessment of adults. In the adult arena, the various incarnations of the Wechsler Memory Scale (now the WMS-IV), developed by David Wechsler of intelligence test fame, have been available since the 1940s.

> *The WRAML2 (ages 5–90 years), TOMAL-2 (ages 5–59 years), and the WMS-IV (ages 16–90) are the most frequently used memory batteries in individual assessment practice.*

TOMAL-2: An Example of a Contemporary Comprehensive Memory Assessment

The TOMAL-2 is arguably the most comprehensive of memory batteries available and provides subtests that are exemplary of most aspects of memory that need to be assessed when a comprehensive review of a patient's memory skills is required, so it will be our example of a memory test here.

The TOMAL-2 is a comprehensive battery of 14 memory and learning tasks (8 core subtests and 6 supplementary subtests) normed for use from ages 5 years 0 months 0 days through 59 years 11 months 30 days. The eight core subtests are divided into the content domains of verbal memory and nonverbal memory that can be combined to derive a Composite Memory Index. A Verbal Delayed Recall Index that requires recall of two of the verbal subtests' stimuli 30 minutes after their first administration is also available. Learning tasks of scales such as the TOMAL-2 are those where the same stimuli are repeated over multiple trials until an examinee has recalled all of the stimuli or has reached a maximum number of trials allowed. These types of procedures also allow the plotting of learning curves for the individual relative to the average learning rate or curve of others the same age.

As stated earlier, memory may behave in unusual ways in an impaired brain and traditional content approaches to memory may not be useful. The TOMAL-2 thus provides alternative groupings of the subtests into the Supplementary Indexes of Sequential Recall, Free Recall, Associative Recall, Learning, and Attention and Concentration.

Table 13–4 summarizes the names of the subtests and summary scores, along with their metric. The TOMAL-2 subtests are scaled to the familiar metric of mean equaling 10 and a standard deviation of 3 (range 1 to 20). Composite or summary scores are scaled to a mean of 100 and standard deviation of 15.

Table 13–4	Core and Supplementary Subtests and Indexes Available for the TOMAL-2	
Core Subtests	**M**	**SD**
Verbal		
Memory for Stories	10	3
Word Selective Reminding	10	3
Object Recall	10	3
Paired Recall	10	3
Nonverbal		
Facial Memory	10	3
Abstract Visual Memory	10	3
Visual Sequential Memory	10	3
Memory for Location	10	3
Supplementary subtests		
Verbal		
Digits Forward	10	3
Letters Forward	10	3
Digits Backward	10	3
Letters Backward	10	3
Nonverbal		
Visual Selective Reminding	10	3
Manual Imitation	10	3
Summary Scores		
Core indexes		
Verbal Memory Index (VMI)	100	15
Nonverbal Memory Index (NMI)	100	15
Composite Memory Index (CMI)	100	15
Supplementary indexes		
Verbal Delayed Recall Index (VDRI)	100	15
Attention/Concentration Index (ACI)	100	15
Sequential Recall Index (SRI)	100	15
Free Recall Index (FRI)	100	15
Associative Recall Index (ARI)	100	15
Learning Index (LI)	100	15

Note: M = mean; SD = standard deviation.

Source: Reynolds, C. R. & Voress, J. (2007). *Test of Memory and Learning,* Second Edition, (TOMAL-2), Austin, TX: Pro-Ed. Reprinted with permission of Pro-Ed.

TOMAL-2 SUBTESTS. The eight core, six supplementary, and delayed recall TOMAL-2 subtests require about 45 minutes for a skilled examiner. The subtests were chosen to provide a comprehensive

Table 13–5	Description of TOMAL-2 Subtests

Core

Memory for Stories. A verbal subtest requiring recall of a short story read to the examinee. Provides a measure of meaningful and semantic recall and is also related to sequential recall in some instances.

Facial Memory. A nonverbal subtest requiring recognition and identification from a set of distractors: black-and-white photos of various ages, males and females, and various ethnic backgrounds. Assesses nonverbal meaningful memory in a practical fashion and has been extensively researched. Sequencing of responses is unimportant.

Word Selective Reminding. A verbal free-recall task in which the examinee learns a word list and repeats it only to be reminded of words left out in each trial: tests learning and immediate recall functions in verbal memory. Trials continue until mastery is achieved or until six trials have been attempted. Sequence of recall is unimportant.

Abstract Visual Memory. A nonverbal task assessing immediate recall for meaningless figures where order is unimportant. The examinee is presented with a standard stimulus and required to recognize the standard from any of six distractors.

Object Recall. The examiner presents a series of pictures, names them, has the examinee recall them, and repeats this process until mastery is achieved or until five trials have been attempted. Verbal and nonverbal stimuli are thus paired and recall is entirely verbal, creating a situation found to interfere with recall for many individuals with learning disabilities but to be neutral or facilitative for individuals without disabilities.

Visual Sequential Memory. A nonverbal task requiring recall of the sequence of a series of meaningless geometric designs. The ordered designs are shown followed by a presentation of a standard order of the stimuli and the examinee indicates the order in which they originally appeared.

Paired Recall. A verbal paired–associative task on which the examinee is required to recall a list of word pairs when the first word of each pair is provided by the examiner. Both easy and hard pairs are used.

Memory for Location. A nonverbal task that assesses spatial memory. The examinee is presented with a set of large dots distributed on a page and asked to recall the locations of the dots in any order.

Supplementary

Digits Forward. A standard verbal number recall task. Measures low-level rote recall of a sequence of numbers.

Visual Selective Reminding. A nonverbal analogue to Word Selective Reminding where examinees point to specified dots on a card, following a demonstration by the examiner, and are reminded only of dots recalled incorrectly. Trials continue until mastery is achieved or until five trials have been attempted.

Letters Forward. A language-related analogue to common digit span tasks using letters as the stimuli in place of numbers.

Manual Imitation. A psychomotor, visually-based assessment of sequential memory where the examinee is required to reproduce a set of ordered hand movements in the same sequence as presented by the examiner.

Digits Backward. This is the same basic task as Digits Forward except the examinee recalls the numbers in reverse order.

Letters Backward. A language-related analogue to the Digits Backward task using letters as the stimuli instead of numbers.

view of memory functions and, when used in toto, provide the most thorough assessment of memory available. The subtests are named and briefly described in Table 13–5.

The TOMAL-2 subtests systematically vary the mode of presentation and response so as to sample verbal, visual, motoric, and combinations of these modalities in presentation and in response formats. Multiple trials to a criterion are provided on several subtests, including selective reminding, so that learning or acquisition curves may be derived. Multiple trials (at least five are necessary) are provided on the selective reminding subtests to allow an analysis of the depth of processing. In the selective reminding format (wherein examinees are reminded only of stimuli "forgotten" or unrecalled), when items once recalled are unrecalled by the examinee on later trials, problems are revealed in the transference of stimuli from working memory and immediate memory to more long-term storage. Cueing is also provided at the end of Word Selective Reminding Delayed to add to the examiner's ability to probe depth of processing.

Subtests are included that sample sequential recall (which tends strongly to be mediated by the left hemisphere, especially temporal regions) and free recall in both verbal and visual formats to allow localization; purely spatial memory tasks are included that are very difficult to confound via verbal mediation to assess more purely right hemisphere functions.

Well-established memory tasks (e.g., recalling stories) that also correlate well with school learning are included along with tasks more common to experimental neuropsychology that have high (e.g., Facial Memory) and low (e.g., Visual Selective Reminding) ecological salience; some subtests employ highly meaningful material (e.g., Memory for Stories) whereas some use highly abstract stimuli (e.g., Abstract Visual Memory).

Aside from allowing a comprehensive review of memory function, the purpose for including such a factorial array of tasks across multiple dimensions is to allow a thorough, detailed analysis of memory function and the source of any memory deficits that may be discovered. Delayed recall tasks are routinely included in many clinical assessments of memory to evaluate forgetting as well as to distinguish organic from functional deficits in memory. Unlike many other memory tests that employ sequential recall of digits and letters in forward and backward formats, the TOMAL-2 provides separate scores for forward and backward recall because the neural substrates underlying these tasks are quite different in many respects (Ramsay & Reynolds, 1995) and should not be combined for clinical analyses (Reynolds, 1997). The task of the psychologist demands subtests with great specificity and variability of presentation and response and that sample all relevant brain functions in order to solve the complex puzzle of dysfunctional memory.

THE PROCESS OF NEUROPSYCHOLOGICAL ASSESSMENT

> *Modern clinical neuropsychologists commonly serve as an integral member of a treatment team that includes other professionals in medical settings.*

As the field of clinical neuropsychology began to emerge from a predominantly research oriented endeavor in the 1950s and 1960s, neuropsychologists were increasingly called upon to assist in determining the presence or absence of brain damage. At that time, brain pathology was generally viewed as a unitary concept, and the neuropsychologist's role was ostensibly to determine whether or not an individual had brain damage. Neuropsychologists were commonly asked to make the determination between "organic" pathology (having a structural basis) and "functional" pathology (having a psychological or other cause). This dichotomous conceptualization of pathology implied that abnormal presentations were either due to damaged neurological structures or due to other psychological, emotional, or behavioral factors. As neurology advanced, particularly with the advent and rapid progression of neuroimaging procedures, it was assumed by some that the neuropsychologist's role would inevitably be diminished and supplanted by neuroimaging. Instead, the field of clinical neuropsychology continued to expand as practitioners' scopes widened, gradually shifting away from diagnosis and toward a broader understanding of the functional implications of brain pathology. Even today, with relatively easy access to highly sophisticated and detailed neuroimaging, it is the neuropsychologist who is generally charged with making determinations regarding the functional ramifications of a brain injury or disease process. Depending on the purpose of the assessment, there may be some variations on the procedures involved in any given assessment. The next few sections will describe a general process of the assessment that is common to most purposes.

Referral

The neuropsychological assessment process inevitably begins with some referral question generated by a treatment team, agency, group, or individual. Most often, the question (or questions) revolves around suspected cognitive impairment or the functional ramifications of known brain damage, although neuropsychologists are increasingly being called upon for other purposes. Today, neuropsychologists receive referrals from an ever-increasing number of sources for a wide range of reasons. Although the bulk of referrals are due to known or suspected brain injury, evaluations are also requested for learning disabilities, vocational and occupational assessments, psychiatric and psychological disorders, treatment evaluation, disability determination, and habilitation planning. Physicians, particularly neurologists, psychiatrists, and geriatricians, are often a primary referral source for neuropsychologists. Clinical neuropsychologists commonly serve as an integral member of a treatment team that includes other professionals in medical settings. Other referral sources include schools (elementary-, secondary-, and university-level), vocational and occupational service agencies, and attorneys and judges seeking evaluations for individuals involved in forensic cases. In the case of suspected memory problems associated with aging, it is often the patient's family members who first recognize potential symptoms, prompting the patient to seek an evaluation. Special Interest Topic 13.1 describes common referrals due to brain injury.

SPECIAL INTEREST TOPIC 13.1

Common Brain Injury Referrals

Neuropsychological evaluations are requested for a wide range of brain damage and dysfunction. The type of damage or dysfunction often influences the set of referral questions that the neuropsychologist is asked to address. Communicating functional findings to medical professionals requires a basic understanding of the medical conditions for which patients are referred. This section briefly presents some of the more common referrals seen by neuropsychologists.

Traumatic Brain Injury

Tramatic brain injury (TBI) can result from any number of injury sources including motor vehicle accidents, falls, direct blows to the head, and wounds from firearms or other projectiles and missiles. TBI is typically characterized as either a *closed head injury (CHI)* or *penetrating head injury (PHI)*. In a CHI, the skull remains intact, whereas in a PHI, the skull and *dura mater* (the outermost layer of the protective tissues that cover the brain) is breached.

TBI is classified by severity. TBI may be mild, moderate, or severe, depending on several variables to include the duration of the period of *loss of consciousness*, the degree of *posttraumatic amnesia*, the severity of the structural damage, and the patient's "post-injury" functional status.

Cerebrovascular Disorders

Cerebrovascular disorders are characterized by neuronal damage resulting from any disruption of proper vascular profusion to brain tissue. These disorders range from mild occlusive events known as

(Continued on page 430)

SPECIAL INTEREST TOPIC 13.1 *(Continued)*

transient ischemic attacks (TIAs) to the more severe completed occlusive or hemorrhagic strokes with a high mortality rate. Occlusive strokes prevent oxygen and nutrients from reaching neural tissue due to a blockage in a blood vessel. Hemorrhagic strokes are the result of a blood vessel bleed, also preventing an adequate blood supply from reaching neuronal tissue. Neuropsychologists are often relied upon to measure functional capacity and preserved abilities after resolution of symptoms and stabilization of the patient.

Brain Tumors

Brain tumors can arise as either primary brain tumors or secondary brain tumors. A primary brain tumor develops from cells within the brain tissue or *meninges* (membranes that form a covering over the brain). Brain tumors developing from *glial cells* (cells providing support and nutrition to neurons) are known as *gliomas*. Brain tumors developing from the meninges are known as *menigiomas*. Secondary brain tumors arise from cancer cells that have *metastasized* (spread) from tissues outside the CNS.

If the tumor is treated through surgical intervention, radiation, or chemotherapy, the neuropsychologist is often involved in measuring posttreatment neuropsychological function. Like in the case of stroke, testing may be periodically repeated to measure progress over time. If the location of a small or slow-growing tumor prevents surgical removal, neuropsychological assessment can provide a measure of baseline function from which to periodically assess any changes of function.

Dementia

Neuropsychologists play an important role in the diagnosis and subsequent treatment of dementia. Imaging has not yet been found to be particularly helpful in the identification of many types of dementia. More important, there is little correlation between the structural changes in the brain and the functional status of the patient. As such, neuropsychologists are relied upon to quantify a patient's current functional status in various cognitive domains and to estimate the degree and type of losses from premorbid levels. Neuropsychological assessment can also provide evidence regarding the type of dementia that may be present. This type of distinction may be important with regard to treatment and prognosis. Some instruments have been found to be useful at distinguishing between the different types of dementia (e.g., the Repeatable Battery for the Assessment of Neuropsychological Status [RBANS]). Table 13–3 presents some of the differentiations between the various types of dementia.

Toxins

There is a wide range of substances that are neurotoxic, including alcohol, drugs, solvents, pesticides, and metals. Alcohol is the most common cause of brain injury due to toxins due to its wide availability and use. Heavy drinking over a period of years can result in significant damage such as alcoholic dementia and Korsakoff syndrome. In both of these progressive dementias, neuropsychological assessment is used to assist in diagnosis and in characterizing the degree and extent of damage.

Pesticides, solvents, and metals often have subtle effects on cerebral white matter producing characteristic slowness, gait and balance disturbances, and problems with attention and concentration. In all cases of possible toxicity, it is important for the neuropsychologist to gather as much information as possible from the patient, family members, and medical reports regarding the source, duration, frequency, and levels of exposure.

Review of Records

Although we often think of a neuropsychological evaluation as an administration of a series of psychometric measures, it is important to remember that these tests provide a behavioral measure at only a given time, place, and circumstance. The scores obtained in any assessment gain relevancy only when interpreted within the context of the patient's history. Much historical information can be obtained during a detailed clinical interview with the examinee, but other germane information comes from historical records, including educational records, military records, legal records, records obtained from the referring agency, medical records, previous evaluations, and standardized test scores. These types of records can be critical in attempting to establish a baseline of function prior to injury. If there is a significant event that resulted in the change in function (traumatic brain injury, stroke, toxicity, medical condition), then medical records can be critical in determining the focus of the examination. For example, a patient with a localized gunshot wound to the left temporal lobe may require a different testing focus than a patient referred by a physician due to memory complaints. Records pertaining to either individual provide a documented written record of findings that will likely have an influence over the entire evaluation process. Typically, the neuropsychologist reviews these records prior to meeting with the examinee. The pertinence of each type of record may depend on the referral question. For example, in the case of moderate or severe traumatic brain injury (TBI), the recent history of the patient's medical condition and rehabilitation progress is typically more important than the patient's early developmental history in making determinations regarding rehabilitation and prognosis. Further, in the case of TBI, it is imperative to obtain detailed information about the cause of the TBI, extent and severity of the injury, duration of loss of consciousness, posttraumatic amnesia, and so on. However, in such a case, we obviously do not have to ask the patient when his or her symptoms first occurred. In the case of a possible dementing illness, we would want to obtain as much historical information as possible regarding the genesis of early symptoms, family genetic history, substance abuse history, and family and patient reports regarding the progression of symptoms. At its core, the neuropsychological evaluation is ultimately concerned with some cognitive change and/or difference. Previous records provide a baseline from which to make inferences about current test data.

Clinical Interview

The **clinical interview** of the examinee remains a critical element of the evaluation process. The techniques and components of a general psychological clinical interview also apply within the neuropsychology context. As such, information is obtained in various domains about the person's history to include basic descriptive information, early developmental history, social history, educational, vocational, and avocational background, and psychological and psychiatric history. However, given the context of the referrals, neuropsychological interviews may be somewhat longer and more detailed, particularly in domains germane to cognitive function and/or change. For example, the examinee's apex of educational or vocational achievement provides the neuropsychologist with a gross estimate of the patient's previous or present level of functional capacity. Obtaining accurate information regarding these domains enables the neuropsychologist to make reasonable judgments regarding cognitive losses, preserved functions, and prognoses.

> *Obtaining accurate information through* clinical interviews *enables the neuropsychologist to make judgments regarding cognitive losses, preserved functions, and prognoses.*

Although it is difficult to outline all of the important historical domains of a clinical interview without knowing the specific referral question, most evaluations include aspects of the following:

1. *Information on injury or condition*—detailed accounts of accident, injury, or reason for the referral
2. *Early developmental history*—birth, developmental milestones

3. *Educational history*—elementary, secondary, university, grades, behavioral and/or academic problems, learning disabilities, academic interests, General Educational Development exam scores, standardized test scores, certifications, awards
4. *Vocational history*—present work status, work status prior to injury or condition, change in work status, highest level of vocational attainment, previous employment history, terminations
5. *Social history*—family history, marital status and history, children, present and past residences
6. *Medical history*—surgeries, hospitalizations, head injuries, current and past medications, chronic illnesses, relevant medical history of first-degree relatives
7. *Psychological and psychiatric history*—diagnoses, history of trauma, inpatient and outpatient treatment, psychotherapy
8. *Substance use and abuse*—duration, frequency, quantity, and patterns of use, periods of cessation, types of substances including alcohol, illicit drugs, nicotine, caffeine
9. *Legal history*—arrests, criminal history, incarcerations, past and present litigation

Although a clinical interview is always conducted with the patient, it is often helpful to obtain consent from the patient to also interview other individuals such as family members. Family members often provide valuable information about changes in function, including timelines and progression of the patient's functional capacity.

Test Selection

> *The purpose and intent of the assessment has great impact on the selection of tests.*

As previously discussed, the test selection is guided by a number of different factors, including the examiner's background and training, the referral question, and information obtained during interviews or observations. Typically, the examiner starts with a battery of tests to consider, partly based on the referral question. Again, the battery that one uses for an 82-year-old examinee presenting with symptoms of dementia may differ significantly from a 35-year-old physician with a mild TBI who is anticipating a return to full work status. Adjustments and modifications to the battery can be made as new information emerges from records or during the interview. If a particular deficit emerges during testing that elicits new concerns, supplemental measures can be added to further explore any particular domain. Some of the important variables that enter into the decision regarding test selection include the following.

TIME AND COST. Neuropsychological evaluations range in time from brief batteries (sometimes as short as 1 hour) to batteries sometimes lasting more than 10 hours (usually conducted over 2 days). With a gradual increase in the influence of managed care, there has been a concomitant trajectory toward the development of shorter neuropsychological batteries. However, with continuous refinement of neuropsychological techniques and improved adherence to psychometric principles, neuropsychologists have been able to reduce battery length and time without decreasing the sensitivity and specificity of their evaluation. Moreover, neuropsychologists have become increasingly sensitive to the need to avoid unnecessary testing. For example, it may not be necessary to have a test battery longer than 2 hours in order to make a general assessment regarding the presence or absence of dementia. Time and cost are often the initial determinants of the extent of the battery in conjunction with the referral question and the age and degree of impairment of the patient.

EXAMINER TRAINING. Although neuropsychologists are broadly trained in a wide range of tests and routinely undertake training with new psychometric measures, each examiner inevitably develops a set of measures with which he or she is most familiar and comfortable. This is typically a set battery that is appropriate to the referral question and patient sequelae, supplemented with additional tests that may be particularly sensitive to the condition or injury. As previously discussed, some neuropsychologists are more apt to utilize a predominantly fixed battery approach whereas others may use a flexible battery approach or process approach. However, all neuropsychologists have access to a variety of testing approaches, and some degree of flexibility in test choice is usually required.

ASSESSMENT GOALS. The purpose and intent of the assessment has great impact on the selection of tests. Sometimes, a neuropsychologist is asked to conduct a "screen" for a particular disorder. In such a case, he or she will select a short battery or a standardized screening instrument with a high sensitivity to the condition in question. This type of assessment can be very brief and focused. More often, a longer assessment will be required to adequately address the pending referral question. The injury site or specific cognitive function in question influences the battery's length and composition. For example, if there is a known injury to anterior left frontal areas, instruments that are sensitive measures of categorization and cognitive flexibility would be a necessary component to the battery (i.e., Wisconsin Card Sorting Test and the Halstead Category Test). If the nature of the assessment involved a referral of a child with ADHD symptoms, a broad battery with a preponderance of attention measures (i.e., continuous performance tests, Comprehensive Trail Making Test, Paced Auditory Serial Addition Task) would be more appropriate. In dementia assessments, the focus would center predominantly on learning and memory; instruments that are more sensitive to this cognitive domain would be required (i.e., Repeatable Battery for the Assessment of Neuropsychological Status [RBANS] or Dementia Rating Scale [DRS]). If the purpose of the assessment involves litigation or serves some other forensic requirement, it is important to consider the inclusion of validity measures. These are special instruments or indexes designed to measure the patient's level of effort. This special type of testing is discussed in more detail in Special Interest Topic 13.2.

SPECIAL INTEREST TOPIC 13.2

How Does a Neuropsychologist Measure "Effort?"

One of the most controversial issues in neuropsychological assessment is that of *effort*. Neuropsychological testing requires optimal performance in order to make valid inferences regarding cognitive function. When given a good rationale for the purpose and goals of the assessment, most patients will engage the tasks with the effort necessary to obtain a valid and representative sample of their cognitive function. However, some patients, particularly those involved in litigation, perform at suboptimal levels in order to obtain some secondary gain. Secondary gain may include some identifiable goal such as time off from work, financial compensation, or disability benefits. It may also include the perceived social and emotional advantages of assuming a sick role. At one extreme, a patient may deliberately exaggerate impairment or intentionally create neurological symptoms, known as malingering. Other causes of suboptimal effort with varying degrees of patient self-awareness include somatization, conversion, or factitious disorder. It is not incumbent upon the neuropsychologist to differentiate between the many possible presentations of suboptimal effort. However, it is critical that the examiner has a systematic and valid approach to the measurement of effort.

(Continued on page 434)

SPECIAL INTEREST TOPIC 13.2 *(Continued)*

Two types of measures have been validated for the measurement of effort. The first involves the use of an already existing neuropsychological measure. Indexes or cut-off scores are established on certain components of an existing neuropsychological test that serve as measures of effort. An example of this would be the use of the Digit Span subtest from the Wechsler intelligence scales. In this subtest, the examinee is required to repeat a series of digits in order. He or she is asked to repeat digits forward in the first portion of the subtest, followed by a task of repeating digits backwards. The relatively simple task of repeating digits forward has been found to be a relatively simple task that is quite resistant to brain damage (Reynolds, 1997; Wilson & Kaszniak, 1986), but individuals feigning poor effort are usually unaware of this finding and may therefore produce unusually poor results. Greiffenstein, Baker, and Gola (1994) have developed an effort index known as Reliable Digit Span that relies on the known expectations of Digit Span scores.

The second approach is to create a new instrument that is specifically designed as a validity test. Many of these tests are designed to appear challenging, but contain items or series of items that are rarely failed by individuals with most types of cognitive impairment. One example of this type of test is the Test of Memory Malingering (Tombaugh, 1996). Like many of these tests, it uses a forced-choice format in which the examinee is asked to choose between two items. Errors are rarely made by most individuals with documented damage, but suboptimal effort may produce profiles with very low scores, sometimes even below chance performance. Following is a list of the varied psychometric principles used in effort measures:

♦ *Cut-off scores*—some instruments and indexes use a performance cut-off score that is indicative of a high probability of suboptimal effort. This score is based on data regarding the known floor of a particular test or impairment condition, under which few scores are naturally obtained.

♦ *Atypical response patterns*—some tests examine the within-test or across-test variability. This is based on the finding that it is difficult for patients to respond suboptimally in a consistent manner.

♦ *Item analysis*—some individual items within tests are rarely, if ever, failed by individuals giving good effort. As more of these items are failed, it becomes increasingly improbable that the examinee was performing optimally.

♦ *Forced-choice format*—this format most often requires the examinee to choose between two answers. The question is designed to appear challenging, but items are rarely failed by cognitively impaired individuals. Given the two-choice format, an index of statistical probability can be established to determine to likelihood of a valid response set.

♦ *Repeated evaluation*—this format relies on the finding that it is difficult for examinees to demonstrate consistent suboptimal performance on similar tasks after a delay.

♦ *Profile analysis*—certain disorders have cognitive profiles that are fairly well established. As a simple example, it would be unlikely for an individual with pesticide exposure to consistently produce incorrect names for common objects, although this can occur in other types of brain injury. This *lack of fit* or inconsistency with expected findings can be used in making inferences regarding effort.

STAGE OF TESTING. Another aspect that has considerable impact on the test instruments chosen involves the "stage" of testing, and whether previous or subsequent testing is or will be a factor. Sometimes, the goal is to test performance changes sequentially over time and this must be considered when choosing the test battery. The model whereby the neuropsychologist conducts a single assessment to determine the extent and severity of impairment is gradually expanding into a model that is more attuned to the plasticity of functional cognitive changes. As such, the neuropsychologist must often consider the previous and/or subsequent assessment batteries when conducting the present assessment. In such cases, the neuropsychologist may be more interested in intraindividual change rather than a strict comparison to a set of norms and/or cut-off criteria. Areas of cognitive improvement are often the focus in rehabilitation settings or in serial evaluations during the implementation of school-based intervention programs. Some tests are more amenable to repeated administrations and their test characteristics have been examined with this aspect in mind (e.g., RBANS; Randolph, Tierney, Mohr, & Chase, 1998).

PSYCHOMETRICS. As with any assessment, the importance of adequate reliability and validity cannot be overstated. Neuropsychologists must take special effort to note the appropriateness of any test under the given circumstances. Thus, the patient characteristics (demographics, condition, and referral question) yield critical information about which test may be most appropriate. For example, the TOMAL-2 is established as an excellent measure of memory for a middle-aged individual, but it is not designed for measuring dementia in older adults. Likewise, other test characteristics (such as ceiling and floor effects, sensitivity and specificity, etc.) must be given high consideration when choosing a battery of tests. Understanding other test characteristics, such as the *Flynn Effect* (see Chapter 9), can have enormous influence in flexible battery approaches due to the differing standardization samples used for each measure.

INTERVIEW DATA AND BEHAVIORAL OBSERVATIONS. Information obtained by the examiner through the interview and observations may lead the neuropsychologist to augment the battery with supplemental measures or replace measures originally considered. For example, if the patient reports a motor weakness in his or her right hand, the neuropsychologist may consider additional measures designed to measure motor speed/dexterity and are more specific to left hemisphere frontal motor regions.

OBSERVATIONS MADE DURING TESTING. Neuropsychologists who are more comfortable with a process approach may sometimes consider adding additional measures to the battery as performance is observed during the assessment. This branching style of assessment in which compromised functions are given more specific attention enables the neuropsychologist to more fully investigate the observed area of deficit. Likewise, if the neuropsychologist discovers an unexpected finding that can impact the validity of some measures (e.g., a left-sided visual neglect in which the patient ignores spatial information from the left visual field), the neuropsychologist may need to give consideration to the impact of this deficit on subsequent tests as the testing proceeds.

Test Conditions

As with any psychological evaluation, test conditions can influence the ability to obtain the optimal performance necessary in neuropsychological evaluations. As such, the neuropsychologist strives to maintain a quiet environment with ample lighting and comfortable seating. Lighting conditions may be particularly important when working with patients with low vision. Neuropsychologists are more inclined than most other psychologists to be working with individuals in wheelchairs or with other specific disabilities that might require special arrangements. When working with older adults, the examiner must be particularly attentive to possible hearing and visual deficits.

> *Test conditions can influence the ability to obtain the optimal performance necessary in neuropsychological evaluations.*

It is unusual for an individual over the age of 50 to function optimally on some visually demanding tests without reading glasses, and this should be addressed prior to testing. Sometimes, a neuropsychologist is asked to conduct a "bed-side" examination, as he or she is often a member of a medical treatment team. In such cases, an optimal testing environment may not be obtainable. When this occurs, the conditions must be considered when interpreting testing results.

Neuropsychologists sometimes have to consider other factors extrinsic to the test battery that can have a profound influence on test scores. Some individuals, particularly older adults, perform suboptimally when tested later in the day or evening. Inadequate sleep the night prior to testing can also have deleterious effects on test scores. Medications, particularly in older adults, can also impact the interpretation of test scores. Special Interest Topic 13.3 presents an interesting case study involving medication effects in an older adult.

SPECIAL INTEREST TOPIC 13.3

Case Study of Medication Effects on Neuropsychological Testing

The effects of medication on neuropsychological test data have yet to be fully investigated. This is of particular concerns in older adults. Many older patients are prescribed multiple medications and the effects of these medications on test performance in clinical settings are not well known, although researchers have reported problems with cognitive efficiency in this population (e.g., Godwin-Austen & Bendall, 1990).

The following case study presents scores obtained during an actual evaluation and reveal the effects of a lorazepam (a common anxiolytic) on neuropsychological performance in an 81-year-old female. This patient was initially referred to a geriatrician by family members due to "short-term" memory loss that had been progressing for about 3 years. At the time the referral was made, the patient had been taking lorazepam for over 3 years at an approximate dose of 1 mg every 4 to 6 hours, with an average daily intake of about 6 mg.

Results of the first neuropsychological assessment appeared to be consistent with a diagnosis of dementia; however, the potential effect of her relatively high dose of lorazepam generated concerns regarding diagnosis. Given this consideration, the physician decided to titrate the patient from lorazepam and have the patient retested after titration. The patient successfully titrated from lorazepam over a 5-month period with no reported or observed difficulty. The patient was rescheduled for a second neuropsychological assessment about 6 months after the first evaluation. Scores from the two separate assessments were compared. A Reliable Change Index (RCI) was calculated for each measure in order to analyze test-retest changes.

Subject's Scores at Baseline and Follow-up

Test	Baseline	Follow-up	RCI
WTAR and RBANS (Mean of 100 and SD of 15)			
WTAR IQ	106	106	0
RBANS Immediate Memory Index	57	83	3.46[**]
RBANS Visuospatial/Constructional Index	86	102	1.70[*]
RBANS Language Index	64	80	1.74[*]
RBANS Attention Index	97	94	0.36
RBANS Delayed Memory Index	52	52	0
RBANS Total Scale Score	64	78	2.58[**]

(Continued)

Test	Baseline	Follow-up	RCI
Supplemental Measures (Reported as *T*-Scores)			
WAIS-III Vocabulary	46	—	—
WAIS-III Similarities	43	53	1.90*
WAIS-III Block Design	40	—	—
Letter Fluency	30	34	0.69
Trails A	27	31	0.66
Trails B	24	46	3.17**
Grooved Pegboard—Dominant	49	—	—
Grooved Pegboard—Nondominant	40	—	—
Smell Identification Test	37	40	0.75

Note: For Wechsler subtests, the WTAR and the RBANS RCI values were calculated using SEMs reported in their respective manuals. For other measures, RCI values were calculated using published reliability coefficients to obtain SEMs.

*Reliable change using the 90% confidence interval.
**Reliable change using the 95% confidence interval.

The table presents scores for the patient's initial assessment and follow-up. Initial scores were consistent with significant cognitive impairment, although possible medication effects were considered problematic in making a clear determination. Most scores were below expectations based on estimated premorbid ability. Impaired scores were observed in the RBANS Immediate Memory Index, Delayed Memory Index, Language Index, and Total Score. Impaired scores were also observed in verbal fluency, Trails A and B, and the bicycle drawing task (raw score of 5). Most notable was her index score of 52 on Delayed Memory, a measure of verbal and nonverbal recall of previously rehearsed information.

After titration, scores on some neuropsychological measures appeared to improve. Using a 90% confidence interval, RCI values show improvement in RBANS Total Scale score, Immediate Memory Index, Visuospatial/Constructional Index, and Language Index. Improvements were also observed in Similarities and Trails B. Despite these relative improvements, most scores remained below expected values. Most clinically notable was her equally impaired score in Delayed Memory on follow-up, which still reflected severe anterograde amnesia.

In this case study, some neuropsychological measures showed improvement after titration. This suggests the need for caution when interpreting neuropsychological profiles in older individuals taking certain medications. Nevertheless, despite some improvement after titration, the overall diagnostic picture remained similar, with the patient manifesting extremely impaired delayed recall under both conditions. This implies that neuropsychological assessment, with the RBANS as a core battery, may be robust enough to inform diagnosis, even in less than optimal test conditions.

MEASUREMENT OF DEFICITS AND STRENGTHS

As we noted, neuropsychologists are concerned with understanding the patient's current pattern of cognitive strengths and weaknesses. These patterns may have emerged acutely as the result of an injury of illness, or they may be the manifestation of longstanding cognitive patterns, such as in ADHD or a learning disability. At its essence, neuropsychological assessment inevitably boils down to a process of deficit measurement, as well as the concomitant intact neuropsychological processes in the brain. This may seem relatively straightforward when we have detailed previous test scores available. But how do we measure deficits and strengths in the absence of previous score data? At some point, present test scores must be compared against some standard by which deficits or strengths are inferred. This can be done by using a normative approach or by using an idiographic approach.

Normative Approach

> *In the* **normative approach,** *neuropsychologists compare current performance against a normative standard.*

In the **normative approach**, neuropsychologists compare current performance against a normative standard. In the early days of neuropsychological assessment, there was an emphasis on comparing presently obtained scores to raw cut-off scores presumed, based on normative databases, to indicate "brain damage." As the specialty of neuropsychology has progressed, an increased emphasis has been placed on calculating deviations from large population-based norms for any given test. For example, as with many behavioral measures, neuropsychological measures often produce scores with a normal distribution in the population. An individual's performance can be compared to population norms, thereby giving the person's scores a relative standing in the population regarding the given test domain. Clinical neuropsychologists using the normative approach typically convert raw scores to T-scores or z-scores using these population-based norms, thus providing a common metric when observing and analyzing a set of scores.

When using this approach, it is imperative that the neuropsychologist has a strong understanding of basic statistical variation. For example, in any given set of scores, a number of scores in a normal functioning individual will fall significantly below the population mean. In most cases, a preponderance of scores would have to fall below the population mean before accurate inferences can be made regarding possible damage. Additionally, these inferences must be made within the context of the individual's level of premorbid ability, a concept that is discussed in greater detail later in this chapter. For example, a prominent attorney with 18 years of education who is presently functioning in the average range on most verbal tests is more likely exhibiting signs of cognitive loss than a warehouse employee with a 9th grade education with similar scores on verbal tests.

When using population norms we must answer the question, to what population should the person's scores be compared? This seemingly simple question is not always so easily answered. While general population norms are often used, there has been an ever-increasing emphasis on demographically based norms. Demographic characteristics that typically have the most influence on neuropsychological tests include age, education, ethnicity, and gender. Some tests, for example tests of motor speed/dexterity, are most influenced by age. Tests that tap verbal fluency tend to be more influenced by level of education. Increasingly, test manuals are offering raw score transformations based on a more specifically defined demographic group with these variables in mind. Additionally, there has been an increase in the development and the use of norms manuals that provide standardized demographic scores for a wide range of neuropsychological measures. One commonly used manual, the *Revised Comprehensive Norms for an Expanded Halstead-Reitan Battery* (Heaton, Miller, Taylor, & Grant, 2004), provides demographically corrected *T*-scores for over 50 neuropsychological parameters based on the demographics of sex, education, age, and race. Using this manual, examiners may compare an individual's test score to the general population norms or to the more specific demographic group to which an individual may belong.

Idiographic Approach

In the **idiographic approach**, the examiner uses previous scores or estimates of premorbid ability as the comparison measure against which current scores are compared. **Premorbid ability** refers to an individual's cognitive status prior to the injury or condition. When detailed premorbid neuropsychological scores are available, this may seem like a relatively straightforward comparison, but there are still some challenges to making inferences about change. Sometimes, a

> *In the **idiographic approach**, the examiner uses previous scores or estimates of premorbid ability as the comparison measure against which current scores are compared.*

detailed neuropsychological evaluation existed prior to head injury and present scores can be compared to previously obtained scores. Increasingly, neuropsychologists are called upon to provide serial assessments in which present scores are compared to previous scores. However, even when previous neuropsychological scores are available, one cannot simply look at the change in scores in order to determine whether reliable and clinically important changes have occurred. Determining whether change has occurred between serial assessments is a complex issue. Although various statistical methods are available to measure change, many clinicians rely on clinical judgment in determining whether change has occurred. Psychometric formulas for evaluating change, such as the Reliable Change Index (Jacobson & Truax, 1991), will probably play a greater role in the future as neuropsychological techniques become more refined. Special Interest Topic 13.4 presents an interesting example of the use of the Reliable Change Index in a clinical setting.

SPECIAL INTEREST TOPIC 13.4

How Does a Neuropsychologist Measure Change?

Neuropsychologists are sometimes asked to compare present scores to past scores and determine whether change has occurred. For example, in the case of various types of brain injury, serial assessments are often required. But how does a neuropsychologist determine when change has actually occurred? In any given data set, there are going to be variations in scores that may not actually represent a statistical change. How do we know when sufficient change has occurred in any given measure to indicate a true change? This is complex question and some of the statistical concepts involved are beyond the scope of this text. However, the following brief synopsis presents some of the basic ideas regarding the measurement of change.

Jacobson and Truax (1991) developed a measure known as the Reliable Change Index (RCI) that can be used to calculate whether change has occurred. Based on classical test theory, the RCI is an index of the probability that a change observed in an examinee's score on the same test is due to measurement error. When this value is exceeded, there is a high probability that real change has occurred on

(Continued on page 440)

SPECIAL INTEREST TOPIC 13–4 *(Continued)*

that particular measure. The RCI is calculated using the Standard Error of the Difference (SE_D). The formula for the (SE_D) is

$$SE_D = \sqrt{2 \times (SEM)^2}$$

where SEM is the standard error of measurement. The RCI is calculated by dividing the observed amount of change by the SE_D as follows:

$$RCI = (S_2 - S_1) / SE_D$$

where S_1 = an examinee's initial test score
 S_2 = an examinee's score at retest on the same measure

As one can see from inspection of the formulae, the RCI score is critically dependent on the test's standard error of measure. As such, the test's reliability becomes paramount when giving consideration to the value of a nominal change in scores.

The examiner can choose any of several confidence intervals by which to evaluate change using the RCI, although a 95% confidence interval is routinely used. In this case, scores falling outside a range of −1.96 to 1.96 would be expected to occur less than 5% of the time as a result of measurement error alone; hence, reliable change has likely occurred. If the examiner chooses a less stringent confidence interval of 90%, scores falling outside the range of −1.64 to 1.64 would represent a reliable change.

The following is an example of the use of the RCI to determine the likelihood that change has occurred. The following score set represents theoretical scores of a patient with mild head injury. The first column contains the patient's scores 3 months postinjury. The second column contains scores obtained 3 months later using the same five tests. Using each test's SEM (third column) an RCI is calculated.

Subject's Scores at Baseline and Follow-up

Test	Baseline	Follow-up	SEM	RCI
Test 1	81	93	3.2	2.65[*]
Test 2	77	85	3.8	1.49
Test 3	106	99	3.5	−1.41
Test 4	84	90	3.8	1.12
Test 5	91	101	2.8	2.53[*]

[*]Indicates a significant change at the 95% confidence interval based on the RCI value outside the range of −1.96 and 1.96.

An initial inspection of the scores from baseline to follow-up showed nominally improved scores on four of the five tests and a lower score on one test. However, a closer perusal of the data utilizing the RCI value indicates that significant improvement occurred on only two tests. This example illustrates the importance of the relationship between a test's SEM and the RCI and the resultant effect this can have on the inferences made about such score changes.

Many neuropsychologists still rely solely on clinical judgment and experience to determine whether change has occurred. However, the use of the RCI and similar statistical analyses provides a more psychometrically sound approach to adequately answer questions regarding change of function across time. It is likely that this approach will be more widely utilized as neuropsychological assessment continues to progress.

Premorbid Ability

In order to make inferences regarding loss and/or preserved functions, some understanding of the patient's function prior to the condition or injury must be obtained. This preinjury status is often referred to as *premorbid ability* or *premorbid function,* meaning that it is a state of function prior to the disease or injury. Although this may not be an especially useful concept in all neuropsychological evaluations (e.g., a learning disability evaluation), it is a critical element when a significant change of cognitive status is suspected due to injury or possible dysfunction. If previous neuropsychological scores are not available, premorbid functioning must be inferred or estimated. All neuropsychologists view an understanding of premorbid ability as critical to the evaluation process, but there is no consensus regarding the best approach to ascertaining this. Most believe that a combination of methods probably provides the most accurate determination. In any case, any estimate of premorbid ability is primarily aimed at determining previous level of *global ability*, and is less useful at determining an individual's previous level of function on more specific functional domains.

DEMOGRAPHIC ESTIMATION.   Demographic estimation is one method used to estimate premorbid ability by producing an estimate of global ability based on an examinee's demographics. For example, age, education, and race provide strong demographic predictions of intelligence quotient (IQ). Using these and other demographic predictors, regression equations and actuarial approaches can be used to give reasonable estimates of premorbid ability. This gives us some quantitative baseline from which to compare present scores. One example of this type of actuarial approach is the Barona Index (Barona, Reynolds, & Chastain, 1984). Although this method provides a good baseline from which to draw inferences, there are two primary problems in relying too heavily on this method. The first problem entails the "fit" of the particular individual to the chosen demographic group. Actuarial data are very accurate in predicting group characteristics, but there are a number of individuals whose scores would naturally fall toward the extremes of their group or who do not conform to the group characteristic for any number of reasons. For example, some highly intelligent people fail to graduate from high school for a wide variety of noncognitive reasons, and their premorbid ability would likely be significantly underestimated when utilizing this approach in isolation. The second problem of using a demographic approach is that the band of error it produces may be too wide to be useful. For example, knowing that an individual's premorbid IQ was likely between 85 and 105 may not be especially helpful in cases of mild traumatic brain injury. Still, this method provides a "yardstick" or general range of expectations that may be helpful in making inferences about present scores.

A second approach is to use current scores to estimate premorbid ability. One method is to utilize so-called hold tests (Wechsler, 1958) to obtain an estimate of previous level of function. Some tests are more resilient to brain damage and may be helpful in providing an accurate estimate of function prior to injury. Even though Wechsler's original assumptions about the resiliency of some Wechsler subtests has been questioned (Crawford, Steward, Cochrane, & Foulds, 1989; Russell, 1972), some cognitive tasks do seem to be relatively resistant to brain damage. For example, word reading tests have been employed to estimate premorbid global ability (National Adult Reading Test—Revised [NART-R], Wechsler Test of Adult Reading [WTAR]) with some success. These tests are not designed to provide a comprehensive evaluation of reading. Rather, they test the examinee's capacity to pronounce a list of irregular words accurately. It has been found that the ability to pronounce irregular words is based on previous knowledge of the word and recognition of rules regarding their correct pronunciation. This ability is correlated with Full Scale IQ and is also usually well preserved after brain damage. These characteristics make this type of task an ideal hold measure that can be used to provide a reasonable estimate of premorbid ability.

Pattern Analysis

Another inferential model used in interpretation examines performance patterns across tasks as a means of differentiating functional from dysfunctional neural systems. In the pattern analysis model, the neuropsychologist may examine intraindividual differences or asymmetry that is symptomatic of dysfunction. This type of approach enables the neuropsychologist to identify relative strengths as well as deficits; emphasis on a strength model for intervention planning is considered more efficacious than focusing only on deficits. Again, this is usually addressed in terms of *anterior–posterior differences or left–right differences,* rather than consideration of single scores, but it also may be done by comparison of abilities or domains of function that parallel the four quadrants.

Pathognomonic Signs

*A **pathognomonic sign** is one that is highly indicative of brain damage or dysfunction.*

Another model of interpretation involves looking for, or identifying, what are called **pathognomonic signs**, in which the presence of a particular sign or symptom is highly indicative of brain damage or dysfunction (Fennell & Bauer, 2009; Kaplan, 1988). A successful architect recovering from a TBI who can no longer draw an accurate copy of a complex figure exemplifies a pathognomonic sign of cognitive loss. Pathognomonic signs are not necessarily highly *sensitive* to the condition of interest but tend to have a very high *specificity* to the condition of interest. In other words, when the pathognomonic sign is present, there is a high likelihood that the condition of interest exists. Another example of a pathognomonic sign for a specific disorder would be the relationship between the Trail Making Test and dementia. The Trail Making Test is one of the most commonly used neuropsychological tests. The second portion of the test, Trails B, consists of a connect-the-dot task whereby the patient alternatively connects numbers and letters in sequence. The vast majority of patients have no difficulty completing this task, but the speed of completion usually provides some indication about cerebral integrity. However, results of a recent study (Schmitt, Livingston, Smernoff, Reese, Hafer, & Harris, 2010) show that individuals suffering from dementia often struggled to complete the task at all. For this population, task completion may serve as a highly specific pathognomonic sign for dementia.

Summary

We reviewed key aspects and provided an introduction to neuropsychological testing. Neuropsychology is the study of brain–behavior relationships and clinical neuropsychology is the application of this knowledge to patient care. We noted that even in light of recent advances in neuroimaging (e.g., SPECT, PET, fMRI), neuropsychological testing remains the premier method of assessing brain–behavior relationships. We described the issues in fixed versus flexible battery testing in clinical neuropsychology. The Halstead-Reitan Neuropsychological Test Battery and the Luria-Nebraska Neuropsychological Battery are the two most popular standardized neuropsychological batteries. In contrast, the Boston Process Approach uses a flexible battery of developmental and psychological tests, which allows the clinician to select procedures appropriate to the specific referral question and client characteristics. We provided a review of memory assessment noting that memory complaints seem ubiquitous in nearly all cognitive disorders. We used the Test of Memory and Learning—Second Edition as an example of a comprehensive measure of memory function, and provided brief descriptions of the subtests.

We described the process of neuropsychological assessment to include the referral process, review of records, clinical interviews, test selection, and test conditions. Referral sources for neuropsychologists continue to expand and the types of different referrals were explored. The accumulation of data through a thorough review of previous records is a central aspect of assessment. The clinical interview provides the examiner with contextual information from which to draw accurate inferences. Common domains of an examinee's clinical history were presented. We explored the variables involved in test selection in detail. The importance of providing an appropriate environment for testing was discussed with a focus on the most commonly seen problems. We presented a case study of medication effects on neuropsychological assessment scores.

Clinical neuropsychological assessment is, at its essence, a process of deficit measurement in conjunction with the determination of normally functioning neuropsychological processes in the brain. Different approaches to the measurement of deficits were addressed. In the normative approach, a person's scores are compared to a normative population standard. In the idiographic approach, a person's scores are compared to some given expectation for that particular individual. This is most commonly seen when serial assessments are conducted with a patient and change is observe over time. We presented a model of change measurement known as the RCI (Jacobson & Truax, 1991). A patient's premorbid ability is a critical element in making determinations regarding change and two different approaches to estimating premorbid ability were presented. Pattern analysis and the detection of pathognomonic signs were also discussed as approaches to measuring cognitive change.

Key Terms and Concepts

Boston Process Approach (BPA), 420
Clinical interview, 431
Clinical neuropsychology, 414
Halstead-Reitan Neuropsychological
    Test Battery (HRNB), 418
Idiographic approach, 439

Normative approach, 438
Pathognomonic sign, 442
Premorbid ability, 439
Test of Memory and Learning (TOMAL), 425
Wide Range Assessment of Memory and
    Learning (WRAML), 425

Recommended Readings

Lezak, M. D., Howieson, D. B., & Loring, D. W. (2004). *Neuropsychological assessment* (4th ed.). New York: Oxford University Press.

Reynolds, C. R. (1997). Postscripts on premorbid ability estimation: Conceptual addenda and a few words on alternative and conditional approaches. *Archives of ClinicalNeuropsychology, 12*(8), 769–778.

Reynolds, C., & Fletcher-Janzen, E. (2009). *Handbook of clinical child neuropsychology* (3rd ed.). New York: Springer Science + Business Media.

Strauss, E., Sherman, E. M. S., & Spreen, O. (2006). *A compendium of neuropsychological tests: Administration, norms, and commentary* (3rd ed.). New York: University of Oxford Press.

Chapter fourteen

Forensic Applications of Psychological Assessment

The courts of our nation rely on science and the results of objective study. Psychology in the legal system has much to offer in understanding and evaluating states, traits, and extant behavior.

Learning Objectives

After reading and studying this chapter, students should be able to:

1. Define forensic psychology and describe its major applications.
2. Identify and define major terms and roles relevant to forensic psychology (e.g., expert witness, trier of fact).
3. Describe the role forensic assessments play in the court.
4. Compare and contrast forensic with clinical assessment.
5. Identify and describe major applications of forensic psychology in criminal cases.
6. Discuss the special case of mental retardation in capital sentencing.
7. Identify and describe major applications of forensic psychology in civil cases.
8. Describe and discuss the issue of third-party observers in forensic assessments.
9. Describe the issue of malingering and other forms of dissimulation in forensic assessments.
10. Discuss the issue of admissibility of testimony based on psychological test results.
11. Define and explain the importance of the *Daubert* challenge.

Psychologists and others who use psychological tests are called into courtrooms and other hearing locations frequently to give testimony regarding opinions they have that are often derived from the use of psychological testing. Because psychological tests provide objective, quantifiable data, results of psychological testing can be powerful and persuasive in an adversarial proceeding. Hence, special rules apply to the forensic use of psychological tests within the profession of psychology but also in courtrooms themselves. The federal as well as state rules of what constitutes admissible evidence in a legal proceeding, as well as established case law including rulings from the U.S. Supreme Court also speak directly to the admissibility of expert opinions based on quantifiable data such as obtained from psychological testing. In this chapter we review the application of psychological tests to a variety of forensic issues, and also discuss the special rules of the profession as well as the laws regarding admissibility of opinions derived from psychological tests as evidence.

WHAT IS FORENSIC PSYCHOLOGY?

> **Forensic psychology** *is the application of psychology to the understanding of the law and the application of psychological principles to a legal proceeding.*

Broadly conceived, **forensic psychology** is the application of psychological principles, techniques, and procedures to the understanding of the law, to legal proceedings and legislative processes, and the application of psychology to any ongoing legal proceeding such as a trial, administrative law hearing, and legal arbitration and mediation. Although some popular sources characterize forensic psychology as relating only to criminal proceedings (Wikipedia, 2009b), forensic psychology is not only practiced in both civil and criminal matters, but there are as many and likely more psychologists involved in civil proceedings. Forensic psychology has a long history in the courts of the United States as well as in other countries. The American Psychology-Law Society, which is Division 41 of the American Psychological Association, provides information for the public as well as psychologists, attorneys, and educators about forensic psychology generally as well as providing some guidelines for ethical practice in forensic psychology (*Specialty Guidelines for Forensic Psychologists,* 1991; These guidelines were under revision at the time this text was published). Although many psychologists are involved in forensic activities at some time in their career, some psychologists specialize in forensic psychology. The American Board of Forensic Psychology (ABFP), on the basis of a psychologist's education, experience, and postdoctoral training as well as through a specialized examination, grants diplomate status in forensic psychology. The primary objective of the ABFP diplomate process is to recognize, certify, and promote competence in forensic psychology and to give notice to the public of practitioners who have passed such peer review and examination. Such a specialty certification is not required to practice forensic psychology, but does serve as additional evidence of one's qualifications as well as lending credibility to the existence of forensic psychology as a professional subspecialty in the broader discipline of psychology.

Psychological tests are used by forensic psychologists to assist them in forming scientifically sound and objective opinions. Therefore, in nearly all instances of courtroom and related proceedings, psychological testing becomes useful. Entire books, longer than this textbook, have been written just on the use of psychological tests in forensic psychology (e.g., Melton, Petrila,

Poythress, & Slobogin, 2007), and this chapter will of necessity be less than comprehensive but will introduce you to the world of psychological testing applications in forensic psychology. In Special Interest Topic 14.1 a prominent forensic psychologist explains how and why she uses psychological and neuropsychological assessments in her criminal forensic practice.

> *Psychological tests are used by forensic psychologists to assist them in forming scientifically sound and objective opinions.*

EXPERT WITNESSES AND EXPERT TESTIMONY

There is much confusion in the lay public about an expert who testifies in court. Often the public thinks of an expert who testifies before a court as one who possesses very highly specialized knowledge above and beyond that of others in the same field of study or expertise—a person at the pinnacle of knowledge and skills in an area of science. This is a misconception—in fact, the ethical principles of psychologists prohibit them from making claims of specialized expertise that is unavailable to other psychologists or as having special knowledge or skills other psychologists can

---

SPECIAL INTEREST TOPIC 14.1

Why I Use Psychological and Neuropsychological Tests in Criminal Forensic Practice

Daneen Milam, PhD, ABN

Forensic psychology is a professional specialty within psychology that requires a strong ego willing to defend a position in a court of law, the willingness to spend hours with individuals who have done terrible things, and the ability to keep an open mind. At the end of the day, the third requirement is the hardest. Many professionals perform "evaluations" that are clearly just interviews. They review the facts of a crime, speak to a prisoner who "has an attitude problem" (i.e., is angry at the system that has incarcerated him, feels he is being treated unfairly or is being singled out for punishment), or a long history of skirmishes with the law, or a radically different life experience and background than the examiner, or all of the above, and make a diagnosis or arrive at other life changing opinions regarding the defendant. Research shows that these decisions are as often wrong as they are right but the mental health professional is very confident of the opinion. In fact, extremely high levels of confidence or premature closure in diagnosis or the formation of opinions have been found to be predictive of high error rates in clinical diagnosis. As of this writing, over one hundred prisoners on death row have been exonerated using new DNA analyses and evidence. Each and everyone was evaluated by a clinician who gave that prisoner a diagnosis and was very, very sure they were right—as was the sentencing jury. It is estimated that the incidence of Antisocial Personality Disorder occurs in a prison population 25% of the time, but it is diagnosed 80% of the time when the evaluation consists of a review of the records and a clinical interview. It all boils down to the concept that if the prisoner is scary looking, rude, and has a history of disrespect for the law or authority, they are ASPD and if a prisoner is ASPD, is a lost cause, beyond redemption, and probably guilty and deserving of whatever punishment is forthcoming.

Standardized testing helps us side step this "very sure but very wrong" dilemma. Standardized tests give objective estimates of a variety of cognitive and affective factors that are important to the formation of supportable opinions. They quantify behavior and compare it to known base rates of responding in the general population—base rates often misconstrued and underestimated via clinical

(Continued on page 448)

experience. After giving thousands of tests, I am often surprised by what the objective data reveal. I find supposedly mentally retarded individuals who are well within normal limits intellectually but are basically illiterate instead, which lead to their misdiagnosis. I find mentally retarded or brain injured defendants who can "pass for normal" using good street skills. I find emotionally blunted, inarticulate individuals (some with Asperger's Disorder) who have been diagnosed oppositional defiant disorder, and I find very bright, very articulate, and charming individuals who are genuinely ASPD (and are usually quite effective con artists). Stereotypes don't work; objective testing does. The clinicians who use "clinical experience" instead of hard data often mock extensive data gathering in forensic practice, but I live by the adage in the title to an article written by one of the authors of this text, Cecil Reynolds, and published in 1984: "In God we trust; all others must have data."

Note: Dr. Milam has evaluated defendants and testified at more than 30 capital murder trials, and numerous lesser crimes. She has performed more than 5,000 evaluations for Child Protective Services over her lengthy career and testifies often in these hearings. In addition, she provides risk assessments for sex offenders and performs competency to stand trial evaluations. She is a licensed psychologist and board certified in clinical neuropsychology.

not learn or master. The rules of evidence in federal and state courts define who is an expert. These rules will vary somewhat from one legal jurisdiction to another but in general a person qualified as an **expert witness** in a legal proceeding (hereafter referred to as an expert) is a person who by reason of education, training, and experience possesses knowledge and expertise necessary to assist the trier of fact in a case in understanding some important issue before the court. Generally this is an issue that requires more than common sense or logical reasoning to understand and relate to the case at bar. If it were a matter of common sense, no expert would be required. The burden of proving someone an expert is on the party that offers the testimony to the court. What is required then is that the offering party establish to the satisfaction of the presiding judge that the expert has knowledge, skill, experience, training, or education regarding the specific issue before the court that would qualify the expert to give an opinion on that specific subject. The **trier of fact** in a courtroom is the entity that makes the ultimate decision in a case and is either the judge (in a trial before the court, often referred to as a TBC) or a jury.

Expert witnesses serve a unique role and are different than fact witnesses. Expert witnesses, regardless of who hires them, have as their primary role the objective presentation of information to the court to assist the court, not a predetermined party to the case. The expert should advocate for the objective interpretation and understanding of the data on which opinions

> *An* **expert witness** *is a person who possesses knowledge and expertise necessary to assist the trier of fact in understanding some important issue before the court.*

> *A* **fact witness** *is a person with personal knowledge of the facts of a case.*

> *The* **trier of fact** *in a courtroom is the entity that makes the ultimate decision in a case (i.e., either the judge or a jury).*

are based. Given this role, it should be easy to see why psychological tests, which quantify behavior and constructs, commonly are used to provide a significant component of the expert's database and methods for reaching a particular conclusion. In practice, pure objectivity can be difficult to maintain due to client pressures and competing interests that occur during legal proceedings, which are adversarial by design. Forensic psychologists and those acting in such a role are accountable for their testimony not just to the court, however, but also to the profession. Most state licensing boards have rules of practice that deal with the practice of forensic psychology in a variety of ways and the ethical principles of psychologists espoused by state and national organizations such as the APA and the specialty guidelines for forensic psychologists noted above govern the behavior of forensic psychologists as well.

Later we will discuss some additional concepts that will aid in understanding the role and applications of psychological tests in the courtroom such as credibility of experts and also the admissibility of their testimony—which are separate issues. Three important U.S. Supreme Court cases govern the admissibility of such testimony in the federal court system and many states have similar rules.

CLINICAL ASSESSMENT VERSUS FORENSIC ASSESSMENT

Clinical assessments, designed for purposes of diagnosis, clarification of a patient's condition, and the development of appropriate treatment plans, are quite different in many respects from forensic assessments. Foremost is the circumstance of the assessment and conditions under which it is conducted. In the typical clinical assessment, someone has been referred to us or comes on his or her own to seek help with some life issue that involves a mental health diagnosis—or to rule out such an issue. The person's participation is entirely voluntary and the assessment results are confidential and can be released to no one else without the written consent of the person (or if a minor, the parent, etc.) except in very special circumstances (e.g., if during an assessment a person were to reveal the abuse of a child or an elderly person, most states have laws requiring a breach of confidentiality and mandatory reporting to law enforcement). The clinical assessment is conducted in comfortable surroundings, in a quiet setting, designed to elicit a person's best performance. The intent of the assessment is to assist the person in treatment of a condition or in resolving some important life issue.

In a **forensic assessment**, these circumstances can and most often do vary tremendously. Although some assessments in civil proceedings can come close to mimicking those of the clinical assessment, there will always remain significant differences, and in criminal proceedings, the differences are substantial in all instances. In a forensic assessment, the purpose of the assessment is to provide objective data and unbiased opinions to the court and to assist the trier-of-fact in understanding the issues before the court. As you can see, this is a very different purpose! Participation in the forensic assessment, whereas technically always voluntary, is not voluntary from a practical perspective in many instances. In a civil case related to a brain injury, for example, the plaintiffs may introduce evidence of neuropsychological injury based on a comprehensive

> *In a* **forensic assessment,** *the purpose of the assessment is to provide objective data and unbiased opinions to the court and to assist the court in understanding the issues before the court.*

assessment by their retained expert. In nearly all cases, the defense will be allowed by the court to conduct their own examination with the expert of their choice. The court lacks the authority to compel participation by the plaintiff in the defense examination, but when the court orders such an examination and the plaintiff refuses, the court will often refuse to allow the plaintiff to introduce any evidence of the injury from their own expert. So while the plaintiff's participation can be seen as voluntary—is it really? One of the authors of this text (CRR) recalls vividly a suit for damages over an alleged brain injury that was dropped by the plaintiff when she learned that her prior psychiatric history had been ordered revealed by the judge, would be the subject of testimony to the jury, and could become part of the public record of the case if it went to trial.

Consider a criminal proceeding where the defendant enters a plea of not guilty by reason of insanity and produces a report from a psychologist arguing in favor of such a finding. The prosecution is, in most states, allowed to obtain its own examination from an expert of its choosing to report to the court also. As in the civil case, the defendant may choose not to participate and the court cannot force participation, but the court may and in most cases would disallow any evidence from the defense examination to be heard by the jury. These issues of confidentiality and voluntariness hold true even in such dire forensic examinations as sentencing in death penalty cases. When the defense presents evidence of a lack of future dangerousness, for example, from an examination conducted by a defense mental health expert, the state is entitled to its own examination from an expert of its choosing. It is difficult to conceptualize such examinations as voluntary. This greatly alters the dynamic of the assessment. Nor are the results subject to the customary rules of confidentiality. Results are presented in an open courtroom to a judge or jury and often become part of a public record available to anyone (with some exceptions—under special conditions, judges can seal such records and testimony).

In criminal cases, examinations may also be conducted in jails or prison settings where the conditions are less than optimal. In some settings, examinations are conducted through a glass partition with a telephone connection between the examiner and examinee. This precludes certain types of assessments altogether. Even contact examinations are often conducted in rooms poorly designed for such exams and at times with guards observing. In the sparse, steel and concrete environment of some jail examination rooms the echoes of test items spoken by the examiner can be distracting and confounding when memory testing is being conducted and when auditory tests of attention are used. This may require modifications of the examiner's choice of measures and lessen the usefulness of the assessment. We have encountered cases personally where it was necessary to obtain court orders to force prison wardens to remove handcuffs of examinees so they could adequately participate in neuropsychological examinations.

> *It has been suspected that attorneys obtain access to various psychological tests and then coach their clients on how to answer or respond so the testing results favor their desired outcome.*

When an expert who is adverse to the position of the examinee in a forensic matter conducts an exam, it is not unusual to encounter an examinee who is hostile or curt, confrontational, guarded in responding, or who may practice dissimulation (i.e., a response set presenting a false picture of one's status). Even more insidious, in this vein, is the issue of attorney coaching of clients. Although it is clearly unethical and perhaps even illegal, it has been suspected for decades by forensic psychologists that attorneys obtain access to various psychological tests and then coach their clients on how to answer or respond so the testing results so as to favor the attorney's desired outcome. It is difficult to prove such nefarious deeds without the cooperation of the attorney's client (which is typically not in their best interest!), but nevertheless there are clear confirmations of attorney coaching in forensic settings (e.g., see Youngjohn, 1995). In contrast, in a clinical assessment in the examiner's office where someone has come for help with a significant life issue, examinees are more likely to be forthcoming and desirous of the examiner achieving an accurate and full understanding of their life, personality structure, and cognitive skills. They partner with the examiner in achieving these goals as opposed to adverse forensic assessments where the examiner may be seen as antagonistic to the goals of the examinee.

Melton et al. (1997) provided a summary table of the issues involved in clinical versus forensic assessments. Table 14–1 summarizes the major distinctions. We have not reviewed all of the issues here, nor attempted to explain all of the complexities. As you can see, there are very large texts written solely on the topic of forensic assessment.

TABLE 14-1   Dimensions Distinguishing Therapeutic From Forensic Assessment

1. **Scope.** In clinical settings, broad issues such as diagnosis, personality functioning, and treatment to effect behavior change are primary. Forensic evaluations more commonly address narrowly defined events or interactions of a nonclinical nature; clinical issues (e.g., diagnosis or treatment needs) are often background rather than foreground issues.

2. **Importance of client's perspective.** Although accuracy of information is important in both settings, the treating clinician's focus is on understanding the client's unique view of the situation or problem; a more "objective" appraisal is secondary. The forensic examiner is concerned primarily with accuracy; the client's view, although important, is secondary.

3. **Voluntariness.** Persons seeking mental health therapy commonly do so voluntarily. Persons undergoing forensic assessment commonly do so at the behest of a judge or an attorney.

4. **Autonomy.** As voluntary consumers of therapeutic services, people have greater autonomy and input regarding assessment objectives and procedures. The objectives in forensic evaluations are determined by the relevant statutes or common-law "tests" that define the legal dispute.

5. **Threats to validity.** Therapists and clients seek to develop a common agenda, based on the client's treatment needs, that will guide their interactions. Although unconscious distortion of information is a threat to validity in both contexts, the threat of conscious and intentional distortion is substantially greater in the forensic context.

6. **Relationship and dynamics.** Treatment-oriented interactions emphasize caring, trust, and empathic understanding as building blocks for a developing therapeutic alliance. Forensic examiners may not ethically nurture the client's perception that they are in a helping role; divided loyalties, limits on confidentiality, and concerns about manipulation in the adversary context dictate more emotional distance between forensic clinician and client.

7. **Pace and setting.** In the therapeutic setting, evaluations may proceed at a more leisurely pace. Diagnoses may be reconsidered over the course of treatment and revised well beyond the initial interviews. In the forensic setting, a variety of factors, including court schedules and limited resources, may limit the opportunities for contact with the client and place time constraints on getting closure on the evaluation or reconsidering formulations. At the same time, the importance of accuracy is enhanced by the finality of legal dispositions.

Source: From Melton, G., Petrila, J., Poythress, N., & Slobogin, C. (1997). *Psychological Evaluations for the Courts,* Second Edition: A Handbook for Mental Health Professionals and Lawyers. New York: Guilford Publications. Reprinted with permission of Guilford Publications.

TABLE 14-2	Examples of Types of Competency Evaluations Where Psychological Tests Are Often Used

- Competency to manage one's affairs (e.g., managing finances, making day-to-day decisions, seeking treatment, etc.).
- Testamentary capacity (i.e., competency to make and execute a will)
- Competency to make medical decisions
- Competency to consent to research
- Competency of a juvenile to be tried as an adult
- Competency to stand trial (adult)
- Competency to waive counsel at trial
- Competency to enter a plea
- Competency to waive rights (including issues such as consent to search and seizure, right to remain silent, right to an attorney, etc.)
- Competency to confess
- Competency to give testimony
- Competency to waive appeals
- Competency to be executed

APPLICATIONS IN CRIMINAL PROCEEDINGS

Forensic psychology has many applications in criminal matters and it is worth noting that the rules under which psychologists operate in the criminal arena are different in some ways from those in civil proceedings, though there are more similarities than differences. Criminal and civil proceedings overlap logically if not technically as well. For example, a person accused of a criminal act may be evaluated to determine if he or she is competent to stand trial for the alleged crime. Technically such a competency proceeding is a civil matter, but a mix of criminal and civil standards and rules end up being applied to such cases. We will discuss such competencies where they seem to fit best overall. A list of examples of the many forms of competency that can be the subject of legal decisions is given in Table 14–2. We will not discuss all of these but will review some of the more common examples. We also cannot provide a review of all criminal forensic applications of psychological tests here, but will review the major applications.

Not Guilty by Reason of Insanity: The NGRI Defense

> *One of the most widely known and likely the most controversial arenas wherein psychological tests are likely to be used in forensic settings is in the* **not guilty by reason of insanity (NGRI) defense.**

One of the most widely known and likely the most controversial arenas wherein psychological tests are likely to be used in forensic settings is in the **not guilty by reason of insanity (NGRI) defense**. This defense is controversial not only among the general public but among lawmakers, lawyers, judges, and many professionals. As we will note often in this chapter, the criteria for an NGRI verdict from a jury will differ from state to state, but the most common is that the jury must determine that at the time of the offense, the defendant, by reason of mental illness or mental defect, did not know his or her conduct was wrong. In some states, an additional clause may be added that allows a finding of NGRI if, for similar reasons, the defendant was unable to conform his or her conduct to the requirements of the law. The fundamental premise of public policy and jurisprudence on this issue is that a person who did not understand what he or she was doing or was unable to control his or her behavior because of reasons beyond the person's control should not be held culpable for a crime. Additionally, punishing such a person via criminal sanctions does not act as a deterrent to future criminal acts. It is also important to understand that the NGRI defense excludes what is commonly known as voluntary intoxication from consideration. So, if a defendant was heavily intoxicated from alcohol ingestion and committed a crime unknowingly and even has no recall of it, the state of intoxication cannot be used to form or support an NGRI defense.

The frequency with which this plea is entered by criminal defendants is grossly overestimated by the general public, and its success rate is overestimated as well. It is in fact a relatively infrequent plea and most who enter it, lose. Studies of public perception reviewed by Lilienfeld, Lynn, Ruscio, and Beyerstein (2010) indicated that the average member of the general public believes this defense is used in 37% of felony criminal trials and is successful in nearly half (44%) of these cases. Legislators, who should be more informed, estimate poorly as well, believing that 21% of cases have an NGRI defense that is successful in 40% of its attempts. The actual data show the NGRI defense is used in less than 1% of felony criminal cases and is successful in only about 25% of these cases. Some quick math indicates (0.01 × 0.25) then that less than 3 felony cases per 1,000 end in a verdict of NGRI. Most people also believe that following such a verdict, the person goes free. This is also a myth. Most are committed indefinitely to a mental facility and, in most states, if the crime involved violence, they must be committed to a mental facility. This sometimes results in a person being housed in such a mental facility longer than the maximum prison term for the charge had the person been found guilty!

Typically when a defendant notifies the court of a plea of NGRI, the defense and the prosecution each obtain independent evaluations of the defendant's mental health and related issues in the case. These are most often done by a psychologist, a psychiatrist, or both. In addition to a clinical interview and a review of records of the case and the defendant's mental health history, psychological testing is often used to obtain objective data regarding the defendant's cognitive and emotional state. Cognitive status can be important in such cases and intelligence tests and neuropsychological measures of the integrity of brain functions may be useful in some cases and personality scales are often administered, especially when defendants are thought to have a chronic mental illness such as schizophrenia that may have impaired their perceptions of reality.

Competency to Stand Trial

Competency to stand trial is one of the most common situations where a psychologist may use testing to assist in deriving an opinion within the criminal justice system. Although definitions and law vary from state-to-state and in the federal system (this caveat is true in many aspects of our discussions and not always repeated), in general persons are not competent to stand trial if by reason of mental illness or mental

> **Competency to stand trial** *is one of the most common situations where a psychologist may assist in deriving an opinion within the criminal justice system.*

defect they do not have a rational and factual understanding of the charges and proceedings against them or are unable to assist their attorney in the preparation and presentation of a defense. Defendants are assumed competent when they appear in the criminal justice system and must raise the issue with the court and then stand the burden of proof that they are in fact not competent to stand trial. In some states, only a jury can find a person incompetent to stand trial whereas in others a judge or jury can be elected to make this determination.

Simple ignorance as you can see is insufficient to make one incompetent to stand trial, because the issue is determined in part by whether you cannot do these things because of mental illness or mental defect. Following an interview in which defendants are queried and asked to explain the charges and proceedings against them as well as questions related to helping with their defense, a psychologist may reasonably conclude a defendant is competent if the answers comport with this finding and find psychological testing not to be necessary or useful. Rote recall of the charges, potential penalties, and the name of the attorney and that his or her job is to defend the defendant is not enough—defendants must evidence a reasonable understanding of the charges and proceedings. For example, such an understanding might include knowing the charges and their implications for punishment; how a plea might be arranged and function; the roles of the judge, jury, and prosecutor; the ability to understand and appraise legal advice as it applies to the specific case, to assist the attorney in choosing jurors, to follow testimony of witnesses at trial, to assess and notify defense counsel about errors in testimony and assist in developing questions, to tolerate the stress of a trial, and to maintain appropriate behavior in the courtroom. Although this may require only minimal skills in some trials, in others, such as death penalty litigation, the requirements placed on the defendant's cognitive skills may be far greater. A person competent to stand trial for shoplifting a $25 item from a store might then be found incompetent to stand trial for the death penalty in a complex robbery/murder trial in which jury selection might last more than 2 weeks and a complex trial may take several more weeks or even months.

If, however, the psychologist determines the defendant does not possess the qualities of a person competent to stand trial, then psychological testing is more likely and useful because in a legal proceeding the reason that the defendant cannot perform these functions is relevant to a legal finding of incompetency. In such determinations psychologists often will use intelligence tests or related measures of logic and reasoning, along with measures of verbal comprehension, listening comprehension, perceptual distortion, and attention and memory to look at cognitive factors that may impair one's ability to understand the charges and proceedings as well as assist one's attorney. Neuropsychological testing is common in such circumstances as well because often defendants who are raising the issue of competency have a history of central nervous system damage or illness (e.g., traumatic brain injury, stroke, seizure disorders, meningitis, or even dementias such as Alzheimer's or Korsakoff's disease—and yes, Alzheimer's patients can and do commit crimes on occasion. One of the authors served as an expert in the case of an elderly Alzheimer's patient who shot and killed a state trooper during a routine traffic stop.). When mental illnesses such as schizophrenia, schizoaffective disorder, bipolar disorder, or others are at issue, personality tests are often used as well. Clinical interviews are also used heavily, but are almost always supplemented by objective test data because these can provide an unbiased quantitative perspective on the issues before the court. There are also a variety of structured interviews for determining competency that can be scored as well, but these typically do not get at the issue of cause if the defendant is not seen as otherwise competent.

Transfer of a Juvenile to Adult Criminal Court

Here again we see overlap between criminal and civil proceedings. In many states, a juvenile who has been detained for committing an act that would be a crime for an adult is subjected to a **juvenile court** which is technically a civil, not a criminal, proceeding. The reasons for this are many but center around the lesser maturity, comprehension, and understanding of a juvenile versus an adult and the greater belief in rehabilitation at these younger ages. However, all states have means by which the state can petition the juvenile court to transfer the juvenile to the adult criminal court and thereafter be treated as would an adult in the criminal justice system. Juvenile judges have great latitude in making such decisions but nearly always request psychological evaluations to examine the cognitive, emotional, and moral maturity of the juvenile. Although the nature of the crime is usually an important deciding factor, results of psychological testing are often critical in making such a decision. Does a juvenile possess an adequate understanding of the charges, the nature of the criminal justice system, and possess the ability to assist counsel in an adult criminal proceeding? Does the juvenile in question have greater or lesser intelligence and cognitive understanding in general than other juveniles? Is the juvenile in question amenable to treatments available in the community or in the juvenile justice system or are the programs available to the adult court more appropriate?

> *All states have means by which the state can petition the* juvenile court *to transfer the juvenile to the adult criminal court system.*

In addition to a review of the juvenile's life history, school performance, and any history of mental health interventions, psychological testing can provide objective evidence of levels of intellectual functioning as well as emotional development. Responses to treatment can be predicted, though less well than many other variables, by psychological testing as well. These scores and predictions are unencumbered by the emotional pull of sympathy for adolescents that is natural to most of us and assist the court in reaching a decision that is in the best interest of the juvenile and in the best interests of society, both interests of which judges work hard to balance in such cases.

Mitigation in Sentencing

Many individuals who come before the courts for sentencing following a criminal conviction have had difficult life circumstances to encounter. This is true of most people, however, and most people do not get convicted of criminal acts. In looking for factors that a jury or a judge might consider mitigating, psychologists are often involved in reviewing the life of the individual, prior mental health records, and conducting objective examinations to determine their current mental health status. In **mitigation**, the primary concern is whether circumstances exist in the individual's life that lessen his or her moral culpability for the crime committed. So, for example, a person with a frontal lobe injury that causes him to be extremely impulsive and fail to consider the consequences of his actions who, on the spur of the moment, commits a robbery might be viewed less harshly in punishment than a person who is neuropsychologically intact, who carefully planned and carried out a robbery, and perhaps even

> *In* mitigation, *the primary concern is whether circumstances exist in the individual's life that lessen his or her moral culpability for the crime committed.*

enlisted the aid of others in doing so. In one case involving a Vietnam veteran who had suffered a brain injury in combat, who subsequently assaulted an employer he thought had cheated him on his wages, the court took into account the medical records of his injury as well as the results of a comprehensive neuropsychological examination presented during the punishment hearing in deciding to impose the minimum sentence allowed for the extant offense. We recall the case in Texas of a brain-injured teenaged girl whose drug dealer boyfriend took her with him to meet a customer and decided to rob him, and, when he resisted, killed him in the context of the drug deal. As an accomplice, she was indicted for capital murder along with her boyfriend. Her diminished mental state, documented through comprehensive psychological testing, subsequently was considered by the court as well as the prosecution, and she was subsequently charged with a lesser crime and sentenced to far fewer years in prison than the older boyfriend.

Nowhere in the criminal justice system is such evidence as important as in capital felony or death penalty cases. Although the criteria for imposing the death penalty on a person convicted of a capital felony differs across states, most require three findings from a jury in order to impose a death sentence, broadly stated here as (1) there was an intent to do harm; (2) if not executed, the defendant will represent a continuing threat of violence or harm to society; and (3) that when the defendant's life as a whole is considered, there are no circumstances that warrant mercy from the court. These criteria make the presentation of psychological expert testimony common in virtually all such cases.

Psychological tests are used along with actuarial investigations to ascertain the probability of future violence. Predicting whether someone is a continuing threat or harm to society once imprisoned for life is a precarious enterprise at best. Nevertheless, measures of moral understanding, character, personality, neuropsychological status, and the history of prior violent acts and the context in which they occurred can be informative to the jury in reaching a difficult decision. Mitigation testimony is also presented in nearly all such cases.

Mitigation testimony in sentencing hearings for capital felonies essentially recounts the life story of the defendant to the jury and notes special circumstances (i.e., out of the ordinary features) of the person's life that can be related to the crime. Such issues as abuse and neglect of the defendant as a child, use of alcohol or drugs by the mother during the pregnancy, a history of traumatic brain injury, and mental illness are all potentially relevant factors. Fetal alcohol spectrum disorders are not uncommon among capital felony defendants, but their effects on the brain and behavior are highly variable and must be determined and documented. It has been estimated that between 50 and 80% of death penalty defendants have a documented history of brain injury (Reynolds, Price, & Niland, 2004). Psychological testing is routinely used to document the effects of any potentially mitigating factors on the defendant's behavior. It is rarely enough that such factors are present—their effects on the defendant's behavior must be determined and if, and if so how, they relate to the crime must also be determined.

The U.S. Supreme Court outlawed the execution of persons with mental retardation as a violation of constitutional provisions against cruel and unusual punishment.

The Special Case of Mental Retardation in Capital Sentencing

In a landmark decision in 2002 (*Atkins v. Virginia*, 122 S. Ct. 2242), the U.S. Supreme Court outlawed the execution of persons with mental retardation as a violation of the U.S. constitutional provisions against cruel and unusual punishment, essentially declaring mental retardation a mandatory mitigating factor that excludes a defendant from eligibility for the death penalty. This decision was lauded by the mental health and mental retardation communities. Although other factors were considered important, the crux of the decision relied upon the diminished moral culpability of persons with mental retardation as related to their diminished mental capacities. Judge Stevens, writing for the majority of justices, lists the following areas in which individuals with mental retardation have diminished mental capacity to

1. understand and process information;
2. communicate;
3. abstract from mistakes and learn from experience;
4. engage in logical reasoning;
5. control impulses;
6. understand other's reactions.

This has resulted in much post hoc litigation concerning inmates on death row convicted prior to the *Atkins* decision who are raising the spectre of mental retardation in their appeals. Accurate and objective psychological testing is especially crucial in *Atkins* mental retardation claims.

Psychological and especially neuropsychological testing can assess the functional capacity or skill levels of individuals raising the *Atkins* defense to execution in each of the areas listed. Moreover, the definition of mental retardation that is most commonly applied in the United States is a psychometric one to a large extent. A diagnosis of mental retardation requires that a person score 2 or more standard deviations below the mean on an individually administered test of intelligence and evidence significant deficits in adaptive behavior, both of which must occur during the developmental period (defined somewhat arbitrarily as age 18 years). Not to be overly dramatic, but in this situation, accurate, objective psychological test results are in fact a life and death matter, and should be strongly preferred over clinical experience or anecdotal evidence. Special Interest Topic 14.2 provides information on how a correction for the "Flynn Effect" can be applied in death penalty litigation.

SPECIAL INTEREST TOPIC 14.2

The Flynn Correction in Death Penalty Litigation: An Advocacy Perspective

Since the Supreme Court's decision in *Atkins v. Virginia* (536 U.S. 304, 122 S. Ct. 2242 [2002]) that the execution of person's with mentally retardation violates the Eighth Amendment's prohibition against cruel and unusual punishment, the importance of understanding and assessing mental retardation in criminal defendants has become critical, literally a matter of life and death, in capital felony cases. Determining whether a defendant's intellectual functioning is severely limited is essential to a judgment as to whether that individual is able to act with the level of moral culpability that merits particular forms of punishment. As the most common measures of intellectual functioning, IQ tests are one of the two primary indicia of mental retardation.

IQ tests are periodically revised and renormed to keep the content appropriate to current cultural contexts, ensure the representativeness of the normative or reference group (characteristics of the target population are constantly changing), and in order to maintain an average score of 100. The findings associated with these periodic revisions led researchers to observe that scores on standardized measures of intelligence have steadily risen over the last century, a phenomenon termed the Flynn Effect, which

(Continued on page 458)

SPECIAL INTEREST TOPIC 14.2 *(Continued)*

we discussed in Chapter 3. The Flynn Effect, whatever its cause, is as real as virtually any effect can be in the social sciences. Studies have observed an increase of 0.3 point per year in average IQs; thus, in order for a test score to reflect accurately the examinee's intelligence, 0.3 point must be subtracted (the Flynn Correction) for each year since the test was standardized. Because the Flynn Effect's increased scientific acceptance in the 1990s, it has become one of the reasons why IQ tests have been revised and renormed more frequently than in the past, typically occurring on a 10- to 11-year schedule now as opposed to a 20-year or more schedule in the past. Even so, the Flynn Effect is observable in the years between revisions, and is certainly relevant where outdated test versions are used—especially where even 2 or 3 IQ points may determine whether a defendant is allowed to live or is executed.

Because of the central role IQ tests play in determining an individual's level of mental retardation, and because of the importance of mental retardation in determining a defendant's eligibility to be killed by the state, it is imperative that the Flynn Effect, if it is real, be taken into account in capital cases. IQ ranges that indicate mental retardation are determined relative to the average score (which has been set by convention, albeit arbitrarily, at 100). The so-called average score is derived from a reference group, which is a snapshot of the population at one particular point in time. The determination of the intelligence component of the diagnosis of mental retardation (we do recognize that the actual diagnosis is far more complex than looking at an IQ—but the IQ is a crucial component, and we deal only with it here) should be based on the person's standing relative to the target population at the time the person was actually tested, not the target population when the test was normed. Because it is at this time a practical impossibility to renorm tests annually to maintain a more appropriate reference group, to the extent corrections are available and valid, they should be applied to obtained scores so the most accurate estimate of standing possible is obtained. To do less is to do wrong—what possible justification could there be for issuing estimates of general intelligence in a death penalty case that are less than the most accurate estimates obtainable? The admonishments of the U.S. Supreme Court, in multiple cases over many decades, that death penalty cases require special attention to accuracy apply an even more profound legal argument to applying this correction.

In criminal proceedings, the law's primary concern is that justice is meted according to the procedures and guarantees contained in the federal and state constitutions. These constitutional concerns, as well as the need for accuracy, are at their highest when the death penalty is at issue. The highest court in this country has made the determination that executing persons with mental retardation violates the Eighth Amendment's prohibition against cruel and unusual punishment. As a generally accepted scientific theory that could potentially make the difference between a constitutional and unconstitutional execution, the Flynn Correction must be applied in the legal context. Those who oppose the Flynn Correction must dispute the scientific validity of the Flynn Effect, yet we see no such serious challenges—the remaining issue seems to be why it occurs, a debate that is irrelevant to whether it should be considered. If the Flynn Effect is real, and we believe it is, the failure to apply the Flynn Correction as we have described can have tragic outcomes. No one's life should depend on when an IQ test was normed.

This view is in fact controversial. What are your views on the issue? Should the Flynn Correction be applied in death penalty cases or other criminal proceedings where level of cognitive functioning might be relevant to mitigation of punishment? Reynolds, Niland, Wright, and Rosenn (2010) provided an example of how the Flynn Correction would be applied in individual cases.

Competency to Be Executed

Most states have laws regarding punishment of individuals convicted of a crime and allow an exception for persons not deemed competent to receive punishment. This at first seems odd, but is consistent with the moral aspects of law. To be punished, most states require that the convicted understand the reason for the punishment and the nature of the punishment. This is rarely protested in criminal cases; however, the issue is occasionally raised in individuals facing the death penalty. In 2009, for example, just hours before a death row inmate was to be executed in Texas, the federal courts issued a stay of execution and sent the case back to a state court to hear evidence regarding whether the inmate understood why he was being punished and the nature of the death sentence. As with other forms of competency, psychologists look to psychological tests to provide objective evidence of the defendant's mental state and cognitive capacities.

> *To be punished, most states require that the convicted understand the reason for the punishment and the nature of the punishment.*

APPLICATIONS IN CIVIL PROCEEDINGS

The list of applications of psychological tests in civil proceedings is even longer than in criminal proceedings. Here different rules will often apply to how and when examinations are conducted, and they are usually done in clinical settings or attorneys' offices as opposed to incarceration settings. In this section we will review some of the more common applications once again to give you an understanding of what might be involved and why psychological tests are useful.

Personal Injury Litigation

Personal injury litigation typically is an attempt to seek recovery of damages from a responsible party for injuries suffered by a person or a class of persons injured as a result of an action or lack of action by the responsible party. If the action or lack thereof is especially egregious, then punitive as well as real damages may be sought. Physical injuries are the most obvious and first thought of in such circumstances (e.g., broken

> **Personal injury litigation** *typically is an attempt to seek recovery of damages from a responsible party for injuries suffered.*

or lost limbs, being blinded, spinal injuries, etc). However, the emotional effects of brain injuries and other physical injuries that cause physical pain and suffering as well as emotional pain and suffering are compensable under our laws. Posttraumatic stress disorder (PTSD) may result from an injury or even being an eyewitness to an injury and this, too, may create compensable damages. Children who have been sexually assaulted, for example, may develop PTSD that goes unresolved and untreated into their adult years and create many emotional as well as vocational and educational problems during their lifetimes. Damages may include the loss of the ability to carry out one's job, to earn a living, to attend school successfully, to care for oneself and family (thus creating huge financial burdens that require compensation for caregivers of many types), to pay medical expenses (immediate and ongoing), to make life care plans, to plan a vocational education, to prepare for a different line of work, and the loss of consortium with a spouse in some cases.

In cases of central nervous system (CNS) damage, neuropsychologists are nearly always involved and use specialized tests to determine the degree of functional impairment to the brain, estimates that are reliably obtained only by actual testing as opposed to neuroimaging studies that can document only structural and metabolic changes to the brain. Estimates of overall loss of intellectual function and how this affects one's future educational and vocational opportunities are obtained from specialized methods of psychological testing as well. Rehabilitation plans and progress monitoring are also conducted via such testing in personal injury litigation. Using neuropsychological test data, economists and life care planners can estimate future loss of income as well as special expenses that will be incurred over the person's lifetime that are a result of the injury. All of these are considered damages that have been suffered and are recoverable in such litigation.

In the case of emotional injuries and psychic suffering, juries compensate individuals as well. The diagnosis of PTSD is often important in these cases and should be done on the basis of objective psychological testing as opposed to subjective complaints.

In both circumstances—physical and emotional injuries—it is important to quantify for the court the degree of injury and its implications for the individual's life. The implications vary tremendously across age, educational level, and occupation and each such circumstance must be considered on its on merits. Psychological tests are thus used to derive such objective estimates for the court and also to determine the extent to which the claimed injuries are real or possibly malingered—we will discuss this later in the chapter.

Divorce and Child Custody

When a divorce involves individuals with children and there is no agreement on custody of the children, psychologists and psychological testing become involved in many (but fewer than most suspect) instances. In making decisions in contested **child custody cases**, the courts are typically directed by law to consider the best interests of the children. When making this decision, the laws of various states differ in what they direct judges to consider, but primarily, judges are to consider the following matters: the wishes of the parents or custodians; the wishes of the children; the interaction of the children with the caregivers as well as siblings and other close family members; continuity of care (who has been providing routine care for the child—who takes the child to the doctor when sick, attends school conferences, attends extracurricular activities, bathes, dresses, and feeds the child—all considering the age and maturity of the child); any special needs the child may have emotionally, physically, or educationally; and the mental and physical health of the parties involved. You can see that many of these variables can be assessed via psychological tests, although clearly, as with nearly all other matters, evaluating histories and interviewing everyone will be crucial to proper interpretation of the test results.

> *In making decisions in contested* **custody cases,** *the courts are typically directed by law to consider the best interests of the children.*

However, in child custody proceedings, there are many obstacles to the clinician. Some parents are distrustful of psychologists in this process and may be hostile. Dissimulation may be common because all parents wants to appear their best emotionally and mentally at such a time, and emotions run high—very high. What is more emotional to a loving, concerned parent than who will raise his or her child? Financial considerations may also act to restrict a clinician from performing as extensive an evaluation as may be required to do a thorough job in advising the court on these matters. Also in the back of every clinician's mind who is experienced in child custody evaluations is the fact that "misconduct or bias" in child custody evaluations is the most common of all ethical complaints filed against psychologists with their state licensing boards.

In addressing these issues, parents are usually subjected to personality testing to ascertain their mental status and to determine if they have any mental health issues that would interfere with parenting. Mental health issues that do not affect parenting or the ability to build and maintain a relationship with the child are noted to be irrelevant and typically are not reported to the court. In addition to interviews with the parties, including the children, clinicians often assess the relationships of the children and the parents through the use of parenting scales such as the Parenting Relationship Questionnaire (PRQ; Kamphaus & Reynolds, 2006) as well as behavior rating scales such as the BASC-2 using methods described in Reynolds and Kamphaus (2002). Special Interest Topic 14.3 describes how the BASC-2 can be used in this context.

SPECIAL INTEREST TOPIC 14.3

Use of the BASC-2 in Custody Evaluations

Behavior rating scales have a variety of advantages in such evaluations especially when used along with self-report scales and interviews and histories. The Behavior Assessment System for Children—Second Edition (BASC-2) is an especially useful set of instruments for evaluating many of the child and relationship variables. Aside from its technical, psychometric characteristics, the BASC-2 is useful in determining the presence of emotional, behavioral, and some developmental disorders in the context of a custody dispute, just as in its general application to clinical practice. Its strong normative base also allows it to be interpreted as a measure of emotional and behavioral maturity, which interests courts in weighing not only the child's wishes but the amount of care required relative to the child's age.

In considering various aspects of the common legal instructions to the courts on variables to consider in determining custody, it is apparent the BASC-2 offers some unique and efficacious contributions. For example, the Uniform Marriage and Divorce Act instructs the court to consider "the interaction and interrelationship of the child with his [or her] parent or parents." Commonly, this is considered by child custody evaluators, including psychologists, on a subjective basis, using interview and casual (or on occasion, more structured) observations. The BASC-2 Self-Report (SRP) contains a Relations with Parents scale that provides an objective evaluation of the child's regard for the parents but also looks at the child's feelings of being esteemed by the parents. A group of experienced clinical psychologists, during early research on the development of the BASC, recommended these items as measures of overall family adjustment as well (see Reynolds & Kamphaus, 1992, p. 166). Clinically significant scores on the Relations with Parents scale among adolescents are also associated with antisocial behavior and delinquency (see Reynolds & Kamphaus, 1992, Tables 14.17 and 14.19) factors that should be considered by the evaluator as well. Although the items on this scale do not separate the parents and the child's feelings about each, they do provide an empirical measure of the relationship with the parents and the individual items are useful in direct, follow-up interviews with the child that can segregate the responses by parent.

Additionally, the SRP-C and SRP-A contain a Locus of Control (LOC) scale with many questions about how much control parents exert. A high score on LOC would alert the evaluator to query responses to such questions as "My parents blame too many of their problems on me," "My parents control my life," and "My parents expect too much from me." Melton et al. (1997) emphasized clinical inquiry into the "child's depictions and conceptualization of relationship with each parent" (p. 502). Certainly the BASC-2 and its scales should not be the sole means of such inquiry (additional interviews with collateral sources, evaluating approaches to discipline, etc., also being useful), but it does provide some objective, quantifiable data and clear suggestions for follow-up queries.

The BASC Parent Rating Scale (PRS) also offers a somewhat unique opportunity to look quantitatively at how each parent views the behavior of a child and the concordance of the views with each other and with various collateral sources. During custody evaluations, as in other evaluations, it is useful to obtain behavior rating scale data independently from each parent and from other sources who know the child well (e.g., a teacher). Once these data have been obtained and entered into either of the BASC-2 computer-scoring programs, profiles can be generated and contrasted empirically for the ratings of each parent.

(Continued on page 462)

It is particularly noteworthy to the evaluator in a custody determination when parents show disagreement over the behavior of the child. In such instances, confirmation of any negative or positive biases will be important and often can be obtained by also comparing each parent's ratings to the ratings of one or more teachers. The multiinformant report allows the contrast of a PRS with another PRS, the PRS with a TRS (Teacher Rating Scale), or a TRS with another TRS.

When children show large variations in their behavior with one parent versus the other, there are usually good reasons why and establishing why is nearly always important. Insights may be gleaned into the effectiveness of the parenting skills of each person, ability to discipline appropriately, or simply to be tolerant of the normal activity levels of children as the developmentally moving targets they represent. Overly negative views of children can be detrimental to their development and set up poor expectations while overly positive views may lead a parent to ignore real problems of behavioral and emotional development, again to the detriment of the child. Purposive distortion is virtually always seen as a negative indicator in a custody evaluation. Parties should all put the child's best interest first, and this requires honest, cooperative interaction with the evaluator and with the court. Parents who are less knowledgeable about their children may present special problems as well. Often, a lack of knowledge reveals a lack of involvement in the daily care and routine of the child, another important consideration for the court. Comparisons between TRS and PRS results will be useful in this context as well.

We have provided this level of detail to emphasize the complexity of child custody evaluations. As in other forensic contexts, the need for objectivity and a lack of bias is imperative in such evaluations. We have noted some of the ways personality scales can be used along with behavior rating scales in addressing some of these questions. Where children might have disabilities of various sorts and require specialized or more intensive care from a parent, many other types of psychological and even neuropsychological tests may be useful in determining specialized needs.

Determining Common Civil Competencies

In Table 14–2, we presented examples of some of the more common civil competencies where psychologists may be called upon to assist the court. Each of these competencies involves specific statutory requirements that must be addressed. For example, testamentary capacity (the ability to execute a will and bequeath one's assets) typically requires that persons understand the "nature of their bounty," and have knowledge of their heirs and the ability to form intent. In some cases, this can be established by an interview but at other times, psychological testing with measures of intelligence and neuropsychological function might be required. For example, an elderly stroke victim with limited or no language might have difficulty communicating these factors but neuropsychological testing could establish that the person has the intellectual wherewithal to understand and act competently in making or altering a will or to act on other financial documents. This could be true in other instances such as executing a power of attorney, agreeing to participate in medical research, or making treatment decisions in a medical setting. To be a witness in a trial, a person must understand the oath and be capable of narrating the facts they are to present to the court. Whether or not psychological testing has a contribution to make in determining such competencies is considered on an individual basis by the clinician involved, but is usually advisable and useful if the interview fails to provide clear evidence or impairments in communication exist.

Other Civil Matters

We hope we have given you an overview of how psychological tests are used in major civil actions, but there are many more applications. In child abuse investigations and in determining whether children should be removed from a home and when parental rights may be terminated, psychological testing of the parties and reports to the court are often found to be helpful. Psychological tests are often used to document the emotional and cognitive needs and any special care that might be required when adoption is a consideration to be certain the adopting parents are willing, aware, and capable of providing the needed care. Psychological tests are used in studies of the epidemiology of CNS injuries in large-scale toxic torts where exposure to neurotoxins is alleged in large members of a defined population. Virtually anytime the cognitive or emotional status and behavior of an individual in the past, present, or as predicted in the future may be informative to the court in arriving at a legal decision, objective opinions supported by psychological test results may be useful.

THIRD-PARTY OBSERVERS IN FORENSIC PSYCHOLOGICAL TESTING

In forensic settings, it is not uncommon for attorneys to ask to be present when their clients are being examined, especially by an expert retained by the other side. These requests occur in both criminal and civil matters. Requests to have their own experts present during the examinations are also common. These requests are made for a variety of reasons ranging from the legitimate interest in protecting the client's rights to the nefarious desire to learn about the tests and their content for purposes of later coaching this or another client in how to respond. Some of the issues involving **third-party observers (TPOs)** are resolved by having the expert attend in lieu of the attorney, but even this is problematic.

> **Third-party observers** *alter the standardized procedures for most individually administered psychological tests.*

The presence of a third party in the examination of psychological function is different from an observer at a purely medical examination. Having a TPO in the room is inconsistent with the provisions of the *Standards for Educational and Psychological Testing* in several ways. If not a psychologist, the security of the tests is compromised because the observer may reveal the test content in a variety of sources to individuals not qualified to purchase and use such tests. He or she introduces a variable that was not present during the standardization of most psychological tests and thus disrupts standardized testing procedures, potentially compromising the reliability of the obtained scores as well as affecting the accuracy of their interpretation in unknown ways. The presence of a TPO thus introduces an unknown variable into the testing procedure that may render the normative data, obtained under a different set of conditions, compromised and no longer appropriate as a reference standard potentially precluding valid interpretation of the test results (McCaffrey, Fisher, Gold, & Lynch, 1996). Observer effects can result in a decline in performance on complex tasks, yet enhance performance on overlearned tasks, again compromising our ability to interpret scores accurately (McCaffrey et al., 1996). TPOs are not disinterested parties and can be distracting to the examinee. Even experts in the same field can unintentionally convey approval or disapproval of answers and procedures during the exam and alter the examinee's natural responding. Having a person observe via video or one-way glass solves some but not all of the problems. The examinee's knowledge that he or she is being observed changes how the person responds to emotionally laden questions or performance tests where attention, concentration, and other skills necessary to problem solving and memory are required.

Recognizing the many issues involved, including the press by attorneys to be present when their clients are examined, the National Academy of Neuropsychology, the American Board of Clinical Neuropsychology, the Association of Test Publishers, and others have developed official position papers on the presence of TPOs in forensic examinations and all oppose such a presence. Forensic practitioners are aware of these issues and take appropriate steps to ensure the integrity of the examination process while at the same time ensuring the rights of the individual being examined. Special Interest Topic 14.4 provides additional information on presence of TPOs in forensic examinations.

SPECIAL INTEREST TOPIC 14.4

Third-Party Observers: Why You Ought Not to Watch

The realization that the presence of an observing audience could alter the performance of the individual being observed was first reported in 1898 by Norman Triplett of Indiana University who is today considered the pioneer of sports social psychology. Triplett studied racing cyclists and found that racing against other cyclists produced better times than riding alone

Subsequent researchers both supported and failed to support Triplett's findings (i.e., sometimes an audience improved performance whereas at other times it hindered performance). It was the social psychologist Zajonc (1965) who discovered that the presence of an audience enhances your performance if you are well acquainted with a task and decreases your performance if you have limited or no talent for the task.

The issue of a third-party observer (TPO) was largely ignored by clinical neuropsychologists until the publication of a seminal case study by Binder and Johnson-Greene (1995). This case study used an A-B-A-B design while testing a patient either with her mother out of the room (A) or in the room observing (B). The patient's performance was noted to decline when her mother was present in the hospital room (B) but improved when the mother was absent from the room (A). This report ignited clinical neuropsychologists' interest in the impact of TPO during neuropsychological testing, especially those conducted for forensic purposes.

Although the issue was new to clinical neuropsychologists, social psychologists had been studying the issue for several decades. These studies reported that a TPO had an impacted an examinee's performance on a wide range of tasks, several of which are of interest to clinical neuropsychologist including word generation lists, paired–associate learning, concept attainment, maze learning, letter cancellation speed and accuracy, and reaction time, as well as digit recall of numbers forward and backward (a standard component of many IQ tests).

A systematic series of research studies conducted on the issue of TPO during neuropsychological testing was begun in the late 1990s at the University at Albany, State University of New York. These studies have demonstrated that a TPO negatively impacts an examinee's performance on neuropsychological testing but especially on tests of memory. Furthermore, it does not matter whether or not the observer is a person or if the observation is via a videotape recorder or audiotape recorder.

In some professions, such as medicine, students are trained by the principle of "See One, Do One, Teach One." In fact, historically many of the skills acquired by clinical neuropsychologists involved this type of training. In a study by Yantz and McCaffrey (2005), examinee's were instructed that the student examiner's supervisor was going to be present to observe and monitor how the *examiner* administered memory tests. The examinees' memory performance was negatively impacted despite the information that the TPO was there to observe and critique the examiner. This study demonstrates that it can no longer be assumed in neuropsychological testing that the presence of a clinical supervisor as part of the "See One" style of training is benign.

The negative impact of a TPO during neuropsychological evaluations has been considered to be of such importance that both the National Academy of Neuropsychology and the American Academy of

(Continued)

Clinical Neuropsychology have published position papers opposed to the presence of a TPO. In forensic clinical neuropsychological evaluations, the presence of a TPO may have disastrous and unanticipated consequences for the examinee. Every clinical neuropsychological evaluation must contain symptom validity tests (also referred to variously as effort testing or assessment of malingering or dissimulation) to ensure that the examinee's level of effort with the testing was adequate to produce meaningful test findings. The TPO effect obtained in the Binder and Johnson-Greene (1995) case study was found on the Portland Digit Recognition Test, a symptom validity test. In a capital murder case the difference of a few IQ points could mean life or death. In a civil lawsuit, a plaintiff's performance on a symptom validity test could mean the difference between a life-changing financial verdict versus being found to be malingering brain damage by a jury.

To conduct an evaluation that will provide the clinical neuropsychologist with the best possible data on which to make a clinical diagnosis (e.g., dementia), form an opinion within a reasonable degree of clinical neuropsychological certainty, or make the most accurate diagnosis or be of maximal assistance to the trier of fact (e.g., civil or criminal matter) it is imperative to obtain the best possible data. For all of these reasons, the presence of TPO during clinical neuropsychological testing should be avoided because it is in no one's best interest, especially the examinee's.

DETECTION OF MALINGERING AND OTHER FORMS OF DISSIMULATION

In forensic settings, individuals often have motivation to present themselves as different from how they really are, to appear dissimilar from their true selves. This can result in what we call *dissimulation*—when dissimulation is done that makes the persons look far worse off than in reality they are, it is termed **malingering**. For example, a person with a mild head injury who had deficits at first but has now largely recovered may feign severe memory and learning deficits, make too many mistakes on the job, and argue he or she is no longer able to work in order to receive disability benefits or to obtain a larger settlement than is due him or her in a personal injury

> **Malingering** *is the false presentation of injury or disability for the purposes of gain.*

law suit. A person may claim to have PTSD from observing a wreck in which a child is killed when in fact he or she has recovered fully from the acute stress reaction, making the claim to obtain an insurance settlement. When such injuries are psychological and neuropsychological (and in some cases physical such as chronic pain and loss of sense of smell), psychologists evaluating the alleged injuries include assessments of malingering and other forms of dissimulation.

However, the diagnosis of malingering is fraught with conceptual, philosophical, and logistical potholes. Yet, malingering is a substantial problem in personal injury litigation, with reasonable estimates ranging from 25 to 50% incidence levels in brain injury cases alone. In criminal cases, malingering may be even more of a problem as incarcerated individuals have great motivation to be seen as less culpable for their acts and to avoid long sentences and even the death penalty. Malingering is a source of heated discussion among juries in NGRI cases, competency hearings, and mental retardation claims in capital murder cases, just to name a few examples. Considerable effort has been devoted to the evaluation of malingered responses, also sometimes referred to as *effort testing*, in the scientific literature. We are far from resolving the issues and developing a so-called gold standard indicator of malingering in clinical assessment. The nature and prevalence of the problem as well as its potential costs to society dictate that ma-

TABLE 14-3	Summary of Factors to Consider Under *Daubert* (1993) for Admissibility of Expert Testimony in Federal (and Many State) Courts

1. Is the scientific hypothesis testable?
2. Has the proposition been tested?
3. Is there a known error rate?
4. Has the hypothesis and/or technique been subjected to peer review and publication?
5. Is the theory upon which the hypotheses and/or technique is based generally accepted in the appropriate scientific community?
6. Are there non-judicial uses which have been made of the theory or technique?

These six factors are *nonexclusive* and trial courts may consider other factors in a specific case.

Source: Daubert v. Merrell Dow Pharmaceuticals, 113 S. Ct. 2786 (1993).

lingering be considered in forensic examinations. Organizations such as the National Academy of Neuropsychology have developed formal position papers noting the need for the inclusion of effort testing and assessment of malingered responses.

Assessment and diagnosis of malingering requires extensive clinical knowledge as well as very specialized psychological tests. Reynolds and Horton (2012) discussed these methods and their difficulties in a book-length treatment and there are many such books now available. In Chapter 18 of this textbook we discuss the development of scales designed to assess dissimulation. The key ideas to take from the current section is that the motivation to malinger is high in forensic settings, both civil and criminal; accurate detection of malingering is at times very difficult; specialized procedures are needed to assess malingering; and assessments of malingering should be included routinely in most forensic psychological testing batteries.

THE ADMISSIBILITY OF TESTIMONY BASED ON PSYCHOLOGICAL TESTING RESULTS

Experts render opinions and explanations to assist the trier of fact in a case. However, just because the court designates someone an expert does not mean the testimony will be allowed. The rules of evidence, guided by several U.S. Supreme Court cases, dictate criteria the judge must consider in allowing an expert to render an opinion to the court. Many state courts have adopted the federal standard, most often referred to as the *Daubert* standard after the name of the case (*Daubert v. Merrill Dow*, 509 U.S. 579, 113 S. Ct. 2786) that most recently outlined the criteria for the admissibility of scientific evidence.

> **Admissibility of testimony** *is not the same as credibility.*

Admissibility of testimony is not the same as credibility. Admitting testimony requires a threshold finding by the court that the expert's methods and reasoning are reliable and logical. The federal rules of evidence tell us that for purposes of determining whether **expert testimony** is sufficiently grounded on valid scientific principles so as to be admissible, the general acceptance of a scientific or technical theory in the scientific community is a factor to be considered; however, it is not conclusive. For purposes of determining whether expert testimony is sufficiently grounded on valid scientific principles so as to be admissible, an opinion will not be admissible merely because some part of the methodology is scientifically valid; the entire reasoning process must be valid and a credible link must be established between the reasoning and the conclusion, and, once that is accomplished, inquiry changes from one of admissibility to credibility. Table 14–3 lists the factors to be considered as outlined in the Supreme Court's *Daubert* decision regarding the admissibility of scientific testimony. Admissibility then focuses on the expert's methods—not the opinions they have derived.

The credibility of the expert's testimony accrues to the weight that is given to the expert's opinions by the trier of fact. A judge or jury may listen to an expert and decide for a variety of reasons not to give much weight to the opinions because of perceived biases of the expert, a lack of thoroughness, a failure to consider reasonable alternative interpretations of the data, and the like. Once an expert's testimony has been admitted, much of the focus of the other side of the case turns to finding fault and discrediting the testimony in the eyes of the trier of fact.

The *Daubert* challenge to the admissibility of testimony essentially makes the assertion that there is no basis or an insufficient basis for your opinions in the scientific discipline underlying your profession. As we have discussed the scientific basis and methods for developing tests throughout this text, it is easy to see that testimony based on objective methods such as psychological tests that have thorough manuals that report extensively on the psychometric characteristics of the tests and the scores derived from them is more likely to be admitted and believed than subjective judgments based on interviews and anecdotal data.

> **Expert testimony *is often subjected to the Daubert challenge.***

Nevertheless, a variety of problems can occur that cause such testimony not to be admitted. For example, in our own work we routinely rescore all tests administered by opposing experts and frequently find errors in scoring as well as in simple addition and in table lookups (e.g., reading down the wrong column, using the wrong age table, etc.) that render the underlying data unreliable. Changes in test administration procedures are found that result in a nonstandardized administration that can cause errors in the test score derivations. Not just major changes in administration, but even seemingly "minor" departures from standardized procedures have been found to lead to significant alterations in individuals' test performance. Even more problematic is the difficulty predicting what changes will have what effects. Departures from standardized administration can significantly change the psychometric properties of the tasks. Testing alteration factors interact with various examinee characteristics including disability conditions, gender, and age, providing unpredictable changes in even the direction of scoring impact. Changes in administration of tests produces changes in scores the direction of which is often counterintuitive (i.e., a change designed or thought to make a task easier may make it harder and vice versa; also see Chapter 16 of this text for discussions of how altered administrations may affect scores and their reliability and interpretation). Some clinicians use short forms of tests without investigating their psychometric characteristics. All of these issues and more may cause the results of psychological testing to be declared inadmissible. Various court decisions on the admissibility of testimony have told us that if the foundational data underlying opinion testimony are unreliable, an expert will not be permitted to present an opinion derived from the data because any opinion drawn from that data must also then be unreliable.

Summary

Psychologists and others who use psychological tests are called into courtrooms and other hearing locations frequently to give expert testimony regarding opinions they have that are often derived from the use of psychological testing. Psychological tests provide objective, quantifiable data, and the results of psychological testing can be powerful and persuasive tools in an adversarial proceeding. In this chapter we reviewed the special rules that apply to the forensic use of psychological tests within the profession of psychology but also in courtrooms themselves. We described a variety of areas of legal proceedings where psychological tests might be employed to give examples of the myriad of questions a forensic psychologist might be called upon to address using tests. The many pitfalls and challenges as well as the purposes of such testing in both criminal and civil proceedings were also described. In the context of criminal proceedings we discussed the following applications:

- Not guilty by reason of insanity: the NGRI defense
- Competency to stand trial
- Transfer of a juvenile to adult criminal court
- Mitigation in sentencing
- The special case of mental retardation in capital sentencing
- Competency to be executed

In the context of civil proceedings we described the following applications:

- Personal injury litigation
- Divorce and child custody
- Common civil competencies
- Other civil matters (e.g., child abuse investigations, epidemiology of CNS injuries)

Other important topics in the context of forensic evaluations such as the use of third-party observers in forensic examinations and the detection of dissimulation were also addressed. In closing, we briefly discussed how federal and state rules as well as established case law provide guidelines regarding the admissibility of expert opinions based on quantifiable data such as obtained from psychological testing.

Key Terms and Concepts

Admissibility of testimony, 466
Child custody cases, 460
Competency to stand trial, 453
Expert testimony, 466
Expert witnesses, 448
Forensic assessment, 449

Forensic psychology, 446
Juvenile court, 455
Malingering, 465
Mitigation, 455
Not guilty by reason of insanity
   (NGRI) defense, 452

Personal injury litigation, 459
Third-party observers (TPOs),
   463
Trier of fact, 448

Recommended Readings

Atkins v. Virginia, 122 S. Ct. 2242 (2002).

Daubert v. Merrill Dow, 509 U.S. 579, 113 S. Ct. 2786 (1993).

Wiggins v. Smith, 123 S. Ct. 2527 (2003).

Melton, G., Petrila, J., Poythress, N., & Slobogin, C. (2007). *Psychological evaluations for the courts, third edition: A handbook for mental health professionals and lawyers.* New York: Guilford.

Reynolds, C. R., Hays, J. R., & Ryan-Arredondo, K. (2001). When judges, laws, ethics, and rules of practice collide: A case study of assent and disclosure in assessment of a minor. *Journal of Forensic Neuropsychology, 2,* 41–52.

Reynolds, C. R., Price, R. J., & Niland, J. (2004). Applications of neuropsychology in capital felony (death penalty) defense. *Journal of Forensic Neuropsychology, 3,* 89–123.

Youngjohn, J. R. (1995). Confirmed attorney coaching prior to a neuropsychological evaluation. *Assessment, 2,* 279–283.

Chapter Fifteen

The Problem of Bias in Psychological Assessment

Test bias: In God we trust; all others must have data.

—REYNOLDS, 1983

Learning Objectives

After reading and studying this chapter, students should be able to:

1. Explain the cultural test bias hypothesis.
2. Describe alternative explanations for observed group differences in performance on aptitude and other standardized tests.
3. Describe the relationship between bias and reliability.
4. Describe the major objections regarding the use of standardized tests with minority students.
5. Describe what is meant by cultural loading, cultural bias, and culture-free tests.

6. Describe the mean difference definition of test bias and its current status.

7. Describe the results of research on the presence of bias in the content of educational and psychological tests.

8. Describe the results of research on the presence of bias in other internal features of educational and psychological tests.

9. Describe the results of research on bias in prediction and in relation to variables that are external to the test.

10. Explain what is implied by homogeneity of regression and describe the conditions that may result when it is not present.

Groups of people who can be defined on a qualitative basis such as gender or ethnicity (and are thus formed using a nominal scale of measurement as was discussed in Chapter 2) do not always show the same mean level of performance on various educational and psychological tests. For example, on tests of spatial skill, requiring visualization and imagery, men and boys tend to score higher than do women and girls. On tests that involve written language and tests of simple psychomotor speed (such as the rapid copying of symbols or digits), women and girls tend to score higher than men and boys (see Special Interest Topic 15.1 for additional information). Ethnic group differences in test performance also occur and are the most controversial and polemic of all nominal group differences.

There is perhaps no more controversial finding in the field of psychology than the persistent 1 standard deviation (about 15 points)

> *Much effort has been expended to determine why group differences occur on standardized aptitude tests, but we do not know for certain why.*

> *The cultural test bias hypothesis holds that differences in mean test scores across gender or ethnic groups are due to artifacts of the test or measurement process and do not reflect real differences among groups on the constructs or dimensions purported to be measured.*

difference between the intelligence test performance of black and white students taken as a group. Much effort has been expended to determine why group differences occur (there are many, many such group differences on various measures of specialized ability and achievement—and these differences go in both directions), but we do not know for certain why they exist. One major, carefully studied explanation is that the tests are biased in some way against certain groups. This is referred to as the **cultural test bias hypothesis (CTBH)**.

The CTBH represents the contention that any gender, ethnic, racial, or other nominally determined groups who perform differently on mental tests are due to inherent, artifactual biases produced within the tests through flawed psychometric methodology. Group differences are believed to stem from characteristics of the tests and to be unrelated to any actual differences in the psychological trait, skill, or ability in question. The resolution or evaluation of the validity of the cultural test bias hypothesis is one of the most crucial scientific questions facing psychology today.

SPECIAL INTEREST TOPIC 15.1

Sex Differences in Intelligence

Research has shown that although there are no significant sex differences in overall intelligence scores, substantial differences exist with regard to specific cognitive abilities. Females typically score higher on a number of verbal abilities whereas males perform better on visual–spatial and (starting in middle childhood) mathematical skills. It is believed that sex hormone levels and social factors both influence the development of these differences. As is typical of group differences in intellectual abilities, the variability in performance within groups (i.e., males and females) is much larger than the mean difference between groups (Neisser et al., 1996). Diane Halpern (1997) wrote extensively on gender differences in cognitive abilities. This table briefly summarizes some of her findings.

Selected Abilities on Which Women Obtain Higher Average Scores

Type of Ability	Examples
Rapid access and use of verbal and other information in long-term memory	Verbal fluency, synonym generation, associative memory, spelling, anagrams
Specific knowledge areas	Literature and foreign languages
Production and comprehension of prose	Writing and reading comprehension
Fine motor tasks	Matching and coding tasks, pegboard, mirror tracing
School performance	Most subjects

Selected Abilities on Which Men Obtain Higher Average Scores

Type of Ability	Examples
Transformations of visual working memory, moving objects, and aiming	Mental rotations, dynamic spatiotemporal tasks, accuracy in throwing
Specific knowledge areas	General knowledge, mathematics, science, and geography
Fluid reasoning	Proportional, mechanical, and scientific reasoning; SAT Math and GRE Quantitative

Source: This table was adapted from Halpern, 1997 (Appendix, p. 1102).

Bias in mental tests has many implications for individuals including the misplacement of students in educational programs; errors in assigning grades; unfair denial of admission to college, graduate, and professional degree programs; and the inappropriate denial of employment. The scientific implications are even more substantive. There would be dramatic implications for educational and psychological research and theory if the cultural test bias hypothesis were correct: The principal research of the past 100 years in the psychology of human differences would have to be dismissed as confounded and the results largely artifactual because much of the work is based on standard psychometric theory and testing technology. This would in turn create major upheavals in professional psychology, because the foundations of clinical, counseling, educational, industrial, and school psychology are all strongly tied to the basic academic field of individual differences.

Psychologists make diagnostic decisions daily in clinical practice that affect the lives of their patients in many ways (e.g., treatment approaches, types of psychopharmacological agents that may be applied, suitability for employment, and in forensic settings, even eligibility to receive the death penalty is affected by the results of intelligence tests!); school psychologists arrive at diagnostic and eligibility decisions that determine school placements; industrial and organizational psychologists design screening programs that test job applicants for employment skills and screen public safety officer applicants for various personality traits that predict success in law enforcement; educational psychologists conduct research using standardized tests to assess outcomes in learning environments to determine what methods and environments for learning are the most successful—these are but a few of the many uses of psychological tests in everyday practice in psychology. Typically, professionally designed tests subjected to lengthy developmental research and tryout periods and held up to the most stringent of psychometric and statistical standards are used in such decision making. If these methods turn out to be culturally biased when used with native-born American ethnic minorities, what about other alternative methods of making these decisions that are inherently more subjective (e.g., interviews, observation, review of references, performance or portfolio assessments)? If well-constructed and properly standardized tests are biased, then less standardized, more subjective approaches are almost certain to be at least as biased and probably more so. As the reliability of a test or evaluation procedure goes down, the likelihood of bias goes up, the two being inversely related. A large reliability coefficient does not eliminate the possibility of bias, but as reliability is lowered, the *probability* that bias will be present increases.

The purpose of this chapter is to address the issues and findings surrounding the cultural test bias hypothesis in a rational manner and evaluate the validity of the hypothesis, as far as possible, on the basis of existing empirical research. This will not be an easy task because of the controversial nature of the topic and its strong emotional overtones. Prior to turning to the reasons that test bias generates highly charged emotions and reviewing some of the history of these issues, it is proper to engage in a discussion of just what we mean by the term *bias*.

> *If well-constructed and properly standardized tests are biased, then interviews and other subjective evaluation procedures are almost certain to be at least as biased and probably more so.*

WHAT DO WE MEAN BY BIAS?

> *Bias carries many different connotations for the lay public and for professionals in a number of disciplines.*

Bias carries many different connotations for the lay public and for professionals in a number of disciplines. To the legal mind, bias denotes illegal discriminatory practices whereas to the lay mind it may conjure notions of prejudicial attitudes. Much of the rancor in psychology and education regarding proper definitions of *test bias* is due to the divergent uses of this term in general but especially by professionals in the same and related academic fields. Contrary to certain other opinions that more common or lay uses of the term *bias* should be employed when using *bias* in definitions or discussions of bias in educational and psychological tests, *bias* as used in the present chapter will be defined in its widely recognized, but distinct statistical sense. As defined in the *Standards* (AERA et al., 1999),

> *In terms of tests and measurements,* **bias** *is something systematic that distorts construct measurement or prediction by test scores of other important criteria.*

bias is "a systematic error in a test score" (p. 172). Therefore, a biased assessment is one that systematically underestimates or overestimates the value of the variable it is designed to measure. If the bias is a function of a nominal cultural variable (e.g., ethnicity or gender), then the test has a *cultural bias*. As an example, if an achievement test produces different mean scores for different ethnic groups, and there actually are true differences between the groups in terms of achievement, the test is not biased. However, if the observed differences in achievement scores are the result of the test underestimating the achievement of one group or overestimating the achievement of another, then the test is culturally biased.

Other uses of the term *bias* in research on the cultural test bias hypothesis or cross-group validity of tests are unacceptable from a scientific perspective for two reasons: (1) The imprecise nature of other uses of bias makes empirical investigation and rational inquiry exceedingly difficult, and (2) other uses of the term invoke specific moral value systems that are the subject of intense polemic, emotional debate without a mechanism for rational resolution. It is imperative that the evaluation of bias in tests be undertaken from the standpoint of scholarly inquiry and debate. Emotional appeals, legal-adversarial approaches, and political remedies of scientific issues appear to us to be inherently unacceptable.

PAST AND PRESENT CONCERNS: A BRIEF LOOK

Concern about cultural bias in mental testing has been a recurring issue since the beginning of the use of assessment in psychology. From Alfred Binet in the 1800s to Arthur Jensen over the last 50 years, many scientists have addressed this controversial problem, with varying, inconsistent outcomes. In the last few decades, the issue of cultural bias has come forth as a major contemporary problem far exceeding the bounds of purely academic debate and professional rhetoric. The debate over the cultural test bias hypothesis has become entangled and sometimes confused within the larger issues of individual liberties, civil rights, and social justice, becoming a focal point for psychologists, sociologists, educators, politicians, minority activists, and the lay public. The issues increasingly have become legal and political. Numerous court cases have been brought and New York State even passed "truth-in-testing" legislation that is being considered in other states and in the federal legislature. Such attempts at solutions are difficult if not impossible. Take, for example, the legal response to the question "Are intelligence tests used to diagnose mental retardation biased against cultural and ethnic minorities?" In California in 1979 (*Larry P. v. Riles*) the answer was yes but in Illinois in 1980 (*PASE v. Hannon*) the response was no. Thus two federal district courts of equivalent standing have heard nearly identical cases, with many of the same witnesses espousing much the same testimony, and reached precisely opposite conclusions. See Special Interest Topic 15.2 for more information on legal issues surrounding assessment bias.

Though current opinion on the cultural test bias hypothesis is quite divergent, ranging from those who consider it to be for the most part unresearchable (e.g., Schoenfeld, 1974) to those who considered the issue settled decades ago (e.g., Jensen, 1980), it seems clear that empirical analysis of the hypothesis should continue to be undertaken. However difficult full objectivity may be in science, we must make every attempt to view all socially, politically, and emotionally charged issues from the perspective of rational scientific inquiry. We must also be prepared to accept scientifically valid findings as real, whether we like them or not.

THE CONTROVERSY OVER BIAS IN TESTING: ITS ORIGIN, WHAT IT IS, AND WHAT IT IS NOT

Systematic group differences on standardized intelligence and aptitude tests may occur as a function of socioeconomic level, race or ethnic background, and other demographic variables. Black–White differences on IQ measures have received extensive investigation over the past 50 or 60 years. Although results occasionally differ slightly depending on the age groups under consideration, random samples of Blacks and Whites show a mean difference of about 1 standard deviation, with the mean score of the White groups consistently exceeding that of the Black groups. When a number of demographic variables are taken into account (most notably socioeconomic status, or SES), the size of the difference reduces to 0.5 to 0.7 standard deviation but remains robust in its appearance. The differences have persisted at relatively constant levels for quite some time and under a variety of methods of investigation. Some recent research suggests that the gap may be narrowing, but this has not been firmly established (Neisser et al., 1996).

Mean differences between ethnic groups are not limited to Black–White comparisons. Although not nearly as thoroughly researched as Black–White differences, Hispanic–White differences have also been documented, with Hispanic mean performance approximately 0.5 standard deviation below the mean of the White group. On average, Native Americans tend to perform lower on tests of verbal intelligence than Whites. Both Hispanics and Native Americans tend to perform better on visual–spatial tasks relative to verbal tasks. All studies of racial/ethnic group differences on ability tests do not show higher levels of performance by Whites. Asian American groups have been shown consistently to perform as well as or better than White groups. Depending on the specific aspect of intelligence under investigation, other racial/ethnic groups show performance at or above the performance level of White groups (for a readable review of this research, see Neisser et al., 1996). *It should always be kept in mind that the overlap among the distributions of intelligence test scores for different ethnic groups is much greater than the size of*

SPECIAL INTEREST TOPIC 15.2

Courtroom Controversy Over IQ Testing in the Public Schools

Largely due to overall mean differences in the performance of various ethnic groups on IQ tests, the use of intelligence tests in the public schools has been the subject of courtroom battles around the United States. Typically such lawsuits argue that the use of intelligence tests as part of the determination of eligibility for special education programs leads to overidentification of certain minorities (traditionally African American and Hispanic children). A necessary corollary to this argument is that the resultant overidentification is inappropriate because the intelligence tests in use are biased, underestimating the intelligence of minority students, and that there is in fact no greater need for special education placement among these ethnic minorities than for other ethnic groups in the population.

Attempts to resolve the controversy over IQ testing in the public schools via the courtroom have not been particularly successful. Unfortunately, but not uncharacteristically, the answer to the legal question "Are IQ tests biased in a manner that results in unlawful discrimination against minorities when used as part of the process of determining eligibility for special education placements?" depends on where you live!

There are four key court cases to consider when reviewing this question, two from California and one each from Illinois and Georgia.

The first case is *Diana v. State Board of Education* (C-70-37 RFP, N.D. Cal., 1970), heard by the same federal judge who would later hear the *Larry P.* case (see later). *Diana* was filed on behalf of Hispanic (referred to as Chicano at that time and in court documents) children classified as EMR, or educable mentally retarded (a now archaic term), based on IQ tests administered in English. However, the children involved in the suit were not native English speakers and when retested in their native language, all but one (of nine) scored above the range designated as EMR. *Diana* was resolved through multiple consent decrees (agreements by the adverse parties ordered into effect by the federal judge). Although quite detailed, the central component of interest here is that the various decrees ensured that children would be tested in their native language, that more than one measure would be used, and that adaptive behavior in nonschool settings would be assessed prior to a diagnosis of EMR.

It seems obvious to us now that whenever persons are assessed in other than their native language, the validity of the results as traditionally interpreted would not hold up, at least in the case of ability testing. This had been obvious to the measurement community for quite some time prior to *Diana,* but had not found its way into practice. Occasionally one still encounters cases of a clinician evaluating children in other than their native language and making inferences about intellectual development—clearly this is inappropriate.

Three cases involving intelligence testing of Black children related to special education placement went to trial: *Larry P. v. Riles* (343 F. Supp. 306, 1972; 495 F. Supp. 976, 1979); *PASE v. Hannon* (506 F. Supp. 831, 1980); and *Marshall v. Georgia* (CV 482-233, S.D. of Georgia, 1984). Each of these cases involved allegations of bias in IQ tests that caused the underestimation of the intelligence of Black children and subsequently led to disproportionate placement of Black children in special education programs. All three cases presented testimony by experts in education, testing, measurement, and related fields, some professing the tests to be biased and others professing they were not. That a disproportionate number of Black children were in special education was conceded in all cases—what was litigated was the reason.

In California in *Larry P. v. Riles* (Wilson Riles being superintendent of the San Francisco Unified School District), Judge Peckham ruled that IQ tests were in fact biased against Black children and resulted in discriminatory placement in special education. A reading of Peckham's decision reveals a clear condemnation of special education, which is critical to Peckham's logic. He determined that because special education placement was harmful, not helpful, to children, the use of a test (i.e., IQ) that resulted in disproportionate placement was therefore discriminatory. He prohibited (or enjoined) the use of IQ tests with Black children in the California public schools.

(Continued)

In *PASE v. Hannon* (PASE being an abbreviation for Parents in Action on Special Education), a similar case to *Larry P.* was brought against the Chicago public schools. Many of the same witnesses testified about many of the same issues. At the conclusion of the case, Judge Grady ruled in favor of the Chicago public schools, finding that although a few IQ test items might be biased, the degree of bias in the items was inconsequential.

In *Marshall v. Georgia*, the NAACP brought suit against rural Georgia school districts alleging bias in the instructional grouping and special education placement associated with IQ testing. Although some of the same individuals testified in this case, several new opinions were offered. However, the judge in *Marshall* eventually ruled in favor of the schools, finding that IQ tests were not in fact biased, and that a greater actual need for special education existed in minority populations.

In the courtroom, we are no closer to resolution of these issues today than we were in 1984 when *Marshall* was decided. However, these cases and other societal factors did foster much research that has brought us closer to a scientific resolution of the issues. They also prompted the development of new, up-to-date IQ tests and more frequent revisions or updating of older tests. Many challenges remain, especially that of understanding the continued higher failure rates (relative to the majority ethnic population of the United States) of some ethnic minorities in the public schools (whereas other ethnic minorities have a success rate that exceeds the majority population) and the disproportionate referral rates by teachers of these children for special education placement. The IQ test seems to be only one of many messengers in this crucial educational issue, and bias in the tests does not appear to be the answer.

the differences between the various groups. Put another way, there is always more within-group variability in performance on mental tests than between-group variability. Neisser et al. (1996) framed it this way:

> Group means have no direct implications for individuals. What matters for the next person you meet (to the extent that test scores matter at all) is that person's own particular score, not the mean of some reference group to which he or she happens to belong. The commitment to evaluate people on their own individual merit is central to a democratic society. It also makes quantitative sense. The distributions of different groups inevitably overlap, with the range of scores within any one group always wider than the mean differences between any two groups. In the case of intelligence test scores, the variance attributable to individual differences far exceeds the variance related to group membership. (p. 90)

Explaining Mean Group Differences

Once mean group differences are identified, it is natural to attempt to explain them. Reynolds (2000) noted that the most common explanations for these differences have typically fallen into four categories:

a. The differences primarily have a genetic basis.
b. The differences have an environmental basis (e.g., SES, education, culture).
c. The differences are due to the interactive effect of genes and environment.
d. The tests are defective and systematically underestimate the knowledge and skills of minorities.

The final explanation (i.e., category d) is embodied in the cultural test bias hypothesis (CTBH) introduced earlier in this chapter. Restated, the hypothesis represents the contention that any gender, ethnic, racial, or other nominally determined group differences on mental tests are due to inherent, artifactual biases produced within the tests through flawed psychometric methodology. Group differences are believed then to stem from characteristics of the tests and to be totally unrelated to any actual differences in the psychological trait, skill, or ability in question. Because mental tests are based largely on middle-class values and knowledge, their results are more valid for those groups and will be biased against other groups to the extent that they deviate from those values and knowledge bases. Thus, ethnic and other group differences result from flawed psychometric methodology and not from actual differences in aptitude. As will be discussed, this hypothesis reduces to one of differential validity—the hypothesis of differential validity being that tests measure intelligence and other constructs more accurately and make more valid predictions for individuals from the groups on which the tests are mainly based than for those from other groups. The practical implications of such bias have been pointed out previously and are the issues over which most of the court cases have been fought.

If the CTBH is incorrect, then group differences are not attributable to the tests and must be due to one of the other factors mentioned previously. The model emphasizing the interactive

> *The controversy over test bias should not be confused with that over etiology of any observed group differences.*

effect of genes and environment (category c, commonly referred to as Environment × Genetic Interaction Model) is dominant among contemporary professionals who reject the argument that group differences are artifacts of test bias; however, there is much debate over the relative contributions of genetic and environmental factors (Reynolds, 2000; Suzuki & Valencia, 1997). In addition to the models noted, Williams (1970), Helms (1992), and Richardson (1995) proposed other models with regard to Black–White differences on aptitude tests, raising the possibility of qualitatively different cognitive structures that require different methods of measurement.

Test Bias and Etiology

The controversy over test bias is distinct from the question of etiology. Reynolds and Ramsay (2003) noted that the need to research etiology is only relevant once it has been determined that mean score differences are real, not simply artifacts of the assessment process. Unfortunately, measured differences themselves have often been inferred to indicate genetic differences and therefore the genetically based intellectual inferiority of some groups. This inference is not defensible from a scientific perspective.

Test Bias and Fairness

Bias and fairness are related but separate concepts. As noted by Brown, Reynolds, and Whitaker (1999), fairness is a moral, philosophical, or legal issue on which reasonable people can disagree. On the other hand, bias is a statistical property of a test. Therefore, bias is a property empirically estimated from test data whereas fairness is a principle established through debate and opinion. Nevertheless, it is common to incorporate information about bias when considering the fairness of an assessment process. For example, a biased test would likely be considered unfair by essentially everyone. However, it is clearly possible that an unbiased test might be considered unfair by at least some. Special Interest Topic 15.3 summarizes the discussion of fairness in testing and test use from the *Standards* (AERA et al., 1999).

Test Bias and Offensiveness

There is also a distinction between test bias and item offensiveness. Test developers often use a minority review panel to examine each item for content that may be offensive or demeaning to

---

SPECIAL INTEREST TOPIC 15.3

Fairness and Bias—A Complex Relationship

The *Standards* (AERA et al., 1999) presented four different ways that fairness is typically used in the context of assessment.

1. *Fairness as absence of bias.* There is general consensus that for a test to be fair, it should not be biased. Bias is used here in the statistical sense: systematic error in the estimation of a value.

2. *Fairness as equitable treatment.* There is also consensus that all test takers should be treated in an equitable manner throughout the assessment process. This includes being given equal opportunities to demonstrate their abilities by being afforded equivalent opportunities to prepare for the test and standardized testing conditions. The reporting of test results should be accurate, informative, and treated in a confidential manner.

3. *Fairness as opportunity to learn.* This definition holds that test takers should all have an equal opportunity to learn the material when taking educational achievement tests.

4. *Fairness as equal outcomes.* Some hold that for a test to be fair it should produce equal performance across groups defined by race, ethnicity, gender, and so on (i.e., equal mean performance).

Many assessment professionals believe that (1) if a test is free from bias and (2) test takers received equitable treatment in the assessment process, the conditions for fairness have been achieved. The other two definitions receive less support. In reference to definition (3) requiring equal opportunity to learn, there is general agreement that adequate opportunity to learn is appropriate in some cases but irrelevant in others. However, disagreement exists in terms of the relevance of opportunity to learn in specific situations. A number of problems arise with this definition of fairness that will likely prevent it from receiving universal acceptance in the foreseeable future. The final definition (4) requiring equal outcomes has little support among assessment professionals. The *Standards* noted:

> The idea that fairness requires equality in overall passing rates for different groups has been almost entirely repudiated in the professional testing literature . . . unequal outcomes at the group level have no direct bearing on questions of test bias. (pp. 74–76)

In concluding the discussion of fairness, the *Standards* suggested:

> It is unlikely that consensus in society at large or within the measurement community is imminent on all matters of fairness in the use of tests. As noted earlier, fairness is defined in a variety of ways and is not exclusively addressed in technical terms; it is subject to different definitions and interpretations in different social and political circumstances. According to one view, the conscientious application of an unbiased test in any given situation is fair, regardless of the consequences for individuals or groups. Others would argue that fairness requires more than satisfying certain technical requirements. (p. 80)

one or more groups (e.g., see Reynolds & Kamphaus, 2003, for a practical example). This is a good procedure for identifying and eliminating offensive items, but it does not ensure that the items are not biased. Research has consistently found little evidence that one can identify, by personal inspection, which items are biased and which are not (for reviews, see Camilli & Shepard, 1994; Reynolds, Lowe, & Saenz, 1999).

Test Bias and Inappropriate Test Administration and Use

The controversy over test bias is also not about blatantly inappropriate administration and usage of mental tests. Administration of a test in English to an individual for whom English is a poor second language is inexcusable both ethically and legally, regardless of any bias in the tests themselves (unless of course, the purpose of the test is to assess English language skills). It is of obvious importance that tests be administered by skilled and sensitive professionals who are aware of the factors that may artificially lower an individual's test scores. That should go without saying, but some court cases involve just such abuses. Considering the use of tests to assign pupils to special education classes or other programs, the question needs to be asked, "What would you use instead?" Teacher recommendations alone are less reliable and valid than standardized test scores and are subject to many external influences. Whether special education programs are of adequate quality to meet the needs of children is an important educational question, but distinct from the test bias question, a distinction sometimes confused.

Bias and Extraneous Factors

The controversy over the use of mental tests is complicated further by the fact that resolution of the cultural test bias question in either direction will not resolve the problem of the role of non-intellective factors that may influence the test scores of *individuals* from any group, minority or majority. Regardless of any group differences, it is individuals who are tested and whose scores may or may not be accurate. Similarly, it is individuals who are assigned to classes and accepted or rejected for employment or college admission. Most assessment professionals acknowledge that a number of emotional and motivational factors may impact performance on intelligence tests. The extent to which these factors influence individuals as opposed to group performance is difficult to determine.

CULTURAL BIAS AND THE NATURE OF PSYCHOLOGICAL TESTING

The question of cultural bias in testing arises from and is continuously fueled by the very nature of psychological and educational processes and how we measure those processes. Psychological processes are by definition internal to the organism and not subject to direct observation and measurement but must instead be inferred from behavior. It is difficult to determine one-to-one relationships between observable events in the environment, the behavior of an organism, and hypothesized underlying mediational processes. Many classic controversies over theories of learning revolved around constructs such as expectancy, habit, and inhibition. Disputes among different camps in learning were polemical and of long duration. Indeed, there are still disputes as to the nature and number of processes such as emotion and motivation. It should be expected that intelligence, as one of the most complex psychological processes, would involve definitional and measurement disputes that prove difficult to resolve.

There are few charges of bias relating to physical measures that are on absolute scales, whether interval or ratio. Group differences in height, as an extreme example, are not attributed by anyone to any kind of cultural test bias. There is no question concerning the validity of measures of height or weight of anyone in any culture.

> *The question of bias must eventually be answered on a virtually test-by-test basis.*

Nor is there any question about one's ability to make cross-cultural comparisons of these absolute measures.

The issue of cultural bias arises because of the procedures involved in psychological testing. Psychological tests measure traits that are not directly observable, subject to differences in definition, and measurable only on a relative scale. From this perspective, the question of cultural bias in mental testing is a subset, obviously of major importance, of the problem of uncertainty and possible bias in psychological testing generally. Bias might exist not only in mental tests but in other types of psychological tests as well, including personality, vocational, and psychopathological. Making the problem of bias in mental testing even more complex, not all mental tests are of the same quality; some are certainly psychometrically superior to others. There is a tendency for critics and defenders alike to overgeneralize across tests, lumping virtually all tests together under the heading *mental tests* or *intelligence tests*. Professional opinions of mental tests vary considerably, and some of the most widely used tests are not well respected by psychometricians. Thus, unfortunately, the question of bias must eventually be answered on a virtually test-by-test basis.

OBJECTIONS TO THE USE OF EDUCATIONAL AND PSYCHOLOGICAL TESTS WITH MINORITY STUDENTS

In 1969, the Association of Black Psychologists (ABPsi) adopted the following official policy on educational and psychological testing (Williams, Dotson, Dow, & Williams, 1980):

> The Association of Black Psychologists fully supports those parents who have chosen to defend their rights by refusing to allow their children and themselves to be subjected to achievement, intelligence, aptitude and performance tests which have been and are being used to (a) label Black people as uneducable; (b) place Black children in "special" classes and schools; (c) perpetuate inferior education in Blacks; (d) assign Black children to lower educational tracks than Whites; (e) deny Black students higher educational opportunities; and (f) destroy positive intellectual growth and development of Black people.

Since 1968 the ABPsi (a group with a membership in 2008 of about 1,400) has sought a moratorium on the use of all psychological and educational tests with students from disadvantaged backgrounds. The ABPsi carried its call for a moratorium to other professional organizations in psychology and education. In direct response to the ABPsi call, the American Psychological Association's (APA) Board of Directors requested its Board of Scientific Affairs to appoint a group to study the use of psychological and educational tests with disadvantaged students. The committee report (Cleary, Humphreys, Kendrick, & Wesman, 1975) was subsequently published in the official journal of the APA, *American Psychologist*.

Subsequent to the ABPsi's policy statement, other groups adopted similarly stated policy statements on testing. These groups included the National Association for the Advancement of Colored People (NAACP), the National Education Association (NEA), the National Association of Elementary School Principals (NAESP), the American Personnel and Guidance Association (APGA), and others. The APGA called for the Association of Measurement and Evaluation in Guidance (AMEG), a sister organization, to "develop and disseminate a position paper stating the limitations of group intelligence tests particularly and generally of standardized psychological, educational, and employment testing for low socioeconomic and underprivileged and non-White individuals in educational, business, and industrial environments." It should be noted that the statements by these organizations *assumed* that psychological and educational tests are biased, and that what is needed is that the assumed bias be removed.

The request was timely and taken seriously by the profession of psychology. In 1969, there was actually very little research available to address the questions surrounding bias in psychological assessment. The efforts of ABPsi spurred the disciplines that develop and apply tests to create standards and conduct empirical inquiry into these issues. Today, we know a great deal about the problems of bias in psychological tests and assessments.

Many potentially legitimate objections to the use of educational and psychological tests with minorities have been raised by Black and other minority psychologists. Unfortunately, these objections are frequently stated, still, as facts, on rational rather than empirical grounds. The most frequently stated problems fall into one of the following categories (Reynolds, 2000; Reynolds et al., 1999; Reynolds & Ramsay, 2003).

Inappropriate Content

Black and other minority children have not been exposed to the material involved in the test questions or other stimulus materials. The tests are geared primarily toward White middle-class homes, vocabulary, knowledge, and values. As a result of inappropriate content, the tests are unsuitable for use with minority children.

Inappropriate Standardization Samples

Ethnic minorities are underrepresented in standardization samples used in the collection of normative reference data. As a result of the inappropriate standardization samples, the tests are unsuitable for use with minority children.

Examiner and Language Bias

Because most psychologists are White and speak only standard English, they may intimidate Black and other ethnic minorities and so examiner and language bias result. They are also unable accurately to communicate with minority children—to the point of being insensitive to ethnic pronunciation of words on the test. Lower test scores for minorities, then, may reflect only this intimidation and difficulty in the communication process, not lower ability.

Inequitable Social Consequences

As a result of bias in educational and psychological tests, minority group members, already at a disadvantage in the educational and vocational markets because of past discrimination, are thought to be unable to learn and are disproportionately assigned to dead-end educational tracks. This represents inequitable social consequences. Labeling effects also fall under this category.

Measurement of Different Constructs

Related to inappropriate test content mentioned earlier, this position asserts that the tests measure different constructs when used with children from other than the middle-class culture on which the tests are largely based, and thus do not measure minority intelligence validly.

> *The hypothesis of **differential validity** suggests that tests measure constructs more accurately and make more valid predictions for individuals from the groups on which the tests are mainly based than for those from other groups.*

Differential Predictive Validity

Although tests may accurately predict a variety of outcomes for middle-class children, they do not predict successfully any relevant behavior for minority group members. In other words, test usage might result in valid predictions for one group, but invalid predictions in another. This is referred to as **differential predictive validity**. Further, there are objections to the use of the standard criteria against which tests are validated with minority cultural groups. For example, scholastic or academic attainment levels in White middle-class schools are themselves considered by a variety of Black psychologists to be biased as criteria for the validation of aptitude measures.

Qualitatively Distinct Aptitude and Personality

Minority and majority groups possess aptitude and personality characteristics that are qualitatively different, and as a result test development should begin with different definitions for different groups. For example, Richardson (1995) holds that researchers have not satisfactorily settled the debate over whether intelligence tests measure general intelligence or a European cognitive style. Similarly, Helms (1992) proposed a cognitive-difference

> *The early actions of the ABPsi were most instrumental in bringing these issues into greater public and professional awareness and subsequently promoted a considerable amount of research.*

model that emphasizes differences in "European-centered" and "African-centered" values and beliefs. Helms suggested that these different styles significantly impact the way examinees respond on intelligence tests, which would then require different item sets or at least different "correct answers" from individuals of different ethnic backgrounds. Special Interest Topic 15.4 provides an introduction to a unique explanation for group differences referred to as "stereotype threat."

The early actions of the ABPsi were most instrumental in bringing forward these objections into greater public and professional awareness and subsequently prompted a considerable amount of research. When the objections were first raised, very little data existed to answer these charges. Contrary to the situation decades ago when the current controversy began, research now exists that examines many of these concerns and does so in great detail. Test developers and

SPECIAL INTEREST TOPIC 15.4

Stereotype Threat—An Emerging but Controversial Explanation of Group Differences on Various Tests of Mental Abilities

Steele and Aronson in 1995 posited a unique explanation for group differences on mental test scores. They argued that such differences were created by a variable they deemed "stereotype threat." More recently, they defined stereotype threat as follows:

> When a negative stereotype about a group that one is part of becomes relevant, usually as an interpretation of one's behavior or an experience one is having, stereotype threat is the resulting sense that one can then be judged or treated in terms of the stereotype or that one might do something that would inadvertently confirm it. (p. 389)

Although we find this explanation somewhat vague and lacking specificity for research purposes, in experimental research regarding mental testing outcomes, stereotype threat is most often operationalized as being given a test that is described as diagnostic of one's ability and/or being asked to report one's race prior to testing. Therefore we see two components to the threat—being told one's ability is to be judged on a test of mental ability, and second, being asked to report one's racial identification—or at least believing it to be relevant in some way to the evaluation of examination results (although some argue either component is sufficient to achieve the effect). Stereotype threat research goes on to argue, as one example, that if an examinee takes a test of mental ability and is told it is not for evaluating the test taker but to examine the test itself and no racial identifier is requested, then racial group differences in performance on the test will disappear.

Many studies have now been reported that demonstrate this stereotype effect, but they incorporate controversial statistical procedures that might confound the results by equating the two groups (i.e., erasing the group differences) on the basis of variables irrelevant to the effect of the stereotype threat. Sackett, Hardison, and Cullen (2004) discussed this methodological problem in detail (noting additional violations of the assumptions that underlie such analyses), and we find ourselves in essential agreement with their observations. Nomura et al. (2007) stated it succinctly when they noted from their own findings: "Equalizing the performance of racial groups in most Stereotype Threat Studies is not an effect of the manipulation of Stereotype Threat elicitors (task descriptions), but is a result of a statistical manipulation (covariance)" (p. 7). Additionally, some research that took a thorough look at the issue using multiple statistical approaches argued that stereotype threat may have just the opposite effect at times from what was originally proposed by Steele and Aronson (e.g., see Nomura et al., 2007). That is, it may enhance the performance of the majority group as opposed to denigrating the performance of the minority.

We are also bothered by the theoretical vagaries of the actual mechanism by which stereotype threat might operate as a practical matter. Steele and Aronson essentially argued that it is a process of response inhibition; that is, when an individual encounters a circumstance, event, or activity in which a stereotype of a group to which the person belongs becomes salient, anxiety or concerns about being judged according to that stereotype arise and inhibit performance. Anxiety is not named specifically as the culprit by many stereotype threat researchers, but it seems the most likely moderator of the proclaimed effect. Although the well-known inverted U-shaped anxiety–performance curve seems real enough, can this phenomenon really account for group differences in mental test scores? So far, we view the findings of racial equalization due to the neutralization of the so-called stereotype effect as a statistical artifact, but the concept remains interesting, is not yet fully understood, and we may indeed be proven wrong!

Some good readings on this issue for follow-up include:

Nomura, J. M., Stinnett, T., Castro, F., Atkins, M., Beason, S., Linden, . . . Wiechmann, K. (March, 2007). *Effects of stereotype threat on cognitive performance of African Americans.* Paper presented to the annual meeting of the National Association of School Psychologists, New York.

(Continued)

Sackett, P. R., Hardison, C. M., & Cullen, M. J. (2004). On interpreting stereotype threat as accounting for African-American differences on cognitive tests. *American Psychologist, 59*(1), 7–13.

Steele, C. M., & Aronson, J. (1995). Stereotype threat and the intellectual test performance of African Americans. *Journal of Personality and Social Psychology, 69*, 797–811.

Steele, C. M., Spencer, S. J., & Aronson, J. (2002). Contending with group image: The psychology of stereotype and social identity threat. In M. Zanna (Ed.), *Advances in experimental social psychology* (Vol. 23, pp. 379–440). New York: Academic Press.

publishers routinely examine tests for potentially biasing factors as well, prior to making tests commercially available.

THE PROBLEM OF DEFINITION IN TEST BIAS RESEARCH: DIFFERENTIAL VALIDITY

Arriving at a consensual definition of test bias has produced considerable as yet unresolved debate among many measurement professionals. Although the resulting debate has generated a number of models from which to examine bias, these models usually focus on the *decision-making system* and not on the test itself. The concept of test bias per se then resolves to a question of the validity of the proposed interpretation of performance on a test and the estimation of that performance level, that is, the test score. Test bias refers to systematic error in the estimation of some "true" value for a group of individuals. As we noted previously, differential validity is present when a test measures or estimates a construct differently for one group than for another. As stated in the *Standards* (AERA et al., 1999), bias

> is said to arise when deficiencies in a test itself or the manner in which it is used result in different meanings for scores earned by members of different identifiable subgroups. (p. 74)

As discussed in previous chapters, evidence for the validity of test score interpretations can come from sources both internal and external to the test. Bias in a test may be found to exist in any or all of these categories of validity evidence. Prior to examining the evidence on the cultural test bias hypothesis, the concept of culture-free testing and the definition of mean differences in test scores as test bias merit attention.

CULTURAL LOADING, CULTURAL BIAS, AND CULTURE-FREE TESTS

Cultural loading and *cultural bias* are not synonymous terms, though the concepts are frequently confused even in the professional literature. A test or test item can be culturally loaded without being culturally biased. **Cultural loading** refers to the degree of cultural specificity present in the test or individual items of the test. Certainly, the greater the cultural specificity of a test item, the greater the likelihood of the item being biased when used with individuals from

> **Cultural loading** *refers to the degree of cultural specificity present in the test or individual items of the test.*

other cultures. Virtually all tests in current use are bound in some way by their cultural specificity. Culture loading must be viewed on a continuum from general (defining the culture in a broad, liberal sense) to specific (defining the culture in narrow, highly distinctive terms).

A number of attempts have been made to develop a culture-free (sometimes referred to as culture fair) intelligence test. However, culture-free tests are generally inadequate from a statistical or psychometric perspective (e.g., Anastasi & Urbina, 1997). It may be that because intelligence is often defined in large part on the basis of behavior judged to be of value to the survival and improvement of the culture and the individuals within that culture, a truly culture-free test would be a poor predictor of intelligent behavior within the cultural setting. Once a test has been developed within a culture (a culture loaded test) its generalizability to other cultures or subcultures within the dominant societal framework becomes a matter for empirical investigation.

INAPPROPRIATE INDICATORS OF BIAS: MEAN DIFFERENCES AND EQUIVALENT DISTRIBUTIONS

Differences in mean levels of performance on cognitive tasks between two groups historically (and mistakenly) are believed to constitute test bias by a number of writers (e.g., Alley & Foster, 1978; Chinn, 1979; Hilliard, 1979). Those who support mean differences as an indication of test bias state correctly that there is no valid a priori scientific reason to believe that intellectual or other cognitive performance levels should differ across race. It is the inference that tests demonstrating such differences are inherently biased that is faulty. Just as there is no a priori basis for deciding that differences exist, there is no a priori basis for deciding that differences do not exist. From the standpoint of the objective methods of science, a priori or premature acceptance of either hypothesis (differences exist versus differences do not exist) is untenable. As stated in the *Standards* (AERA et al., 1999):

> Most testing professionals would probably agree that while group differences in testing outcomes should in many cases trigger heightened scrutiny for possible sources of test bias, outcome differences across groups do not in themselves indicate that a testing application is biased or unfair. (p. 75)

Some adherents to the "mean differences as bias" position also require that the *distribution* of test scores in each population or subgroup be identical prior to assuming that the test is nonbiased, regardless of its validity. Portraying a test as biased regardless of its purpose or the validity of its interpretations conveys an inadequate understanding of the psychometric construct and issues of bias. The **mean difference definition of test bias** is the most uniformly rejected of all definitions of test bias by psychometricians involved in investigating the problems of bias in assessment (e.g., Camilli & Shepard, 1994; Cleary et al., 1975; Cole & Moss, 1989; Hunter et al., 1984; Reynolds, 1982, 1995, 2000).

> *The* **mean difference definition** of test bias *is the most uniformly rejected of all definitions of test bias by psychometricians involved in investigating the problems of bias in assessment.*

Jensen (1980) discussed the mean differences as bias definition in terms of the *egalitarian fallacy*. The egalitarian fallacy contends that all human populations are in fact identical on all mental traits or abilities. Any differences with regard to any aspect of the distribution of mental test scores indicate that something is wrong with the test itself. As Jensen pointed out, such an assumption is scientifically unwarranted. There are simply too many examples of specific abilities and even sensory capacities that have been shown to differ unmistakably across human populations. The result of the egalitarian assumption then is to remove the investigation of population differences in ability from the realm of scientific inquiry, an unacceptable course of action (Reynolds, 1980).

The belief of many people in the mean differences as bias definition is quite likely related to the nature–nurture controversy at some level. Certainly data reflecting racial differences on various aptitude measures have been interpreted to indicate support for a hypothesis of genetic differences in intelligence and implicating one group as superior to another. Such interpretations understandably call for a strong emotional response and are not defensible from a scientific perspective. Although IQ and other aptitude test score differences undoubtedly occur, the differences do not indicate deficits or superiority by any group, especially in relation to the personal worth of any individual member of a given group or culture.

BIAS IN TEST CONTENT

Bias in the content of educational and psychological tests has been a popular topic of critics of testing. These criticisms typically take the form of reviewing the items, comparing them to the critics' views of minority and majority cultural environments, and then singling out specific items as biased or unfair because

> *Bias in the content of psychological and educational tests has been a popular topic of critics of testing.*

- The items ask for information that minority or disadvantaged individuals have not had equal opportunity to learn.
- The items require the child to use information in arriving at an answer that minority or disadvantaged individuals have not had equal opportunity to learn.
- The scoring of the items is improper, unfairly penalizing the minority child because the test author has a White middle-class orientation that is reflected in the scoring criterion. Thus minority children do not receive credit for answers that may be correct within their own cultures but do not conform to Anglocentric expectations—this occurs in personality tests wherein minorities may respond to various questions in ways seen as adaptive in their own subculture but as indicative of psychopathology in the mind of the test developer.
- The wording of the questions is unfamiliar to minorities and even though they may "know" the correct answer they are unable to respond because they do not understand the question.

These problems with test items cause the items to be more difficult than they should actually be when used to assess minority individuals. This, of course, results in lower test scores for minorities, a well-documented finding. Are these criticisms of test items accurate? Do problems such as these account for minority-majority group score differences on mental tests? These are questions for empirical resolution rather than armchair speculation, which is certainly abundant in the evaluation of test bias. Empirical evaluation first requires a working definition. We will define a biased test item as follows:

An item is considered to be biased when it is demonstrated to be significantly more difficult for one group than another item measuring the same ability or construct when the overall level of performance on the construct is held constant.

There are two concepts of special importance in this definition. First, the group of items must be unidimensional; that is, they must all be measuring the same factor or dimension of aptitude or personality. Second, the items identified as biased must be differentially more difficult for one group than another. The definition allows for score differences between groups of unequal standing on the dimension in question but requires that the difference be reflected on all items in the test and in an equivalent fashion across items. A number of empirical techniques are available to locate deviant test items under this definition. Many of these techniques are based on item response theory (IRT) and designed to detect differential item functioning, or DIF. The relative merits of each method are the subject of substantial debate, but in actual practice each method has led to similar general conclusions, though the specific findings of each method often differ.

With multiple-choice tests, another level of complexity can easily be added to the examination of **content bias**. With a multiple-choice question, typically three or four distracters are given in addition to the correct response. Distracters may be examined for their attractiveness (the relative frequency with which they are chosen) across groups. When distracters are found to be disproportionately attractive for members of any particular group, the item may be defined as biased.

> **Content bias** *in well-prepared standardized tests is irregular in its occurrence, and no common characteristics of items that are found to be biased can be ascertained by expert judges.*

Research that includes thousands of subjects and nearly 100 published studies consistently finds very little bias in tests at the level of the individual item. Although some biased items are nearly always found, they seldom account for more than 2 to 5% of the variance in performance and often, for every item favoring one group, there is an item favoring the other group.

Earlier in the study of item bias it was hoped that the empirical analysis of tests at the item level would result in the identification of a category of items having similar content as biased and that such items could then be avoided in future test development (Flaugher, 1978). Very little similarity among items determined to be biased has been found. No one has been able to identify those characteristics of an item that cause the item to be biased. In summarizing the research on item bias or differential item functioning (DIF), the *Standards* (AERA et al., 1999) noted:

> Although DIF procedures may hold some promise for improving test quality, there has been little progress in identifying the cause or substantive themes that characterizes items exhibiting DIF. That is, once items on a test have been statistically identified as functioning differently from one examinee group to another, it has been difficult to specify the reasons for the differential performance or to identify a common deficiency among the identified items. (p. 78)

It does seem that poorly written, sloppy, and ambiguous items tend to be identified as biased with greater frequency than those items typically encountered in a well-constructed, standardized instrument.

A common practice of test developers seeking to eliminate "bias" from their newly developed educational and psychological tests has been to arrange for a panel of expert minority group members to review all proposed test items. Any item identified as "culturally biased" by the panel of experts is then expurgated from the instrument. Because, as previously noted, no detectable pattern or common characteristic of individual items statistically shown to be biased has been observed (given reasonable care at the item writing stage), it seems reasonable to question the armchair or expert minority panel approach to determining biased items. Several researchers, using a variety of psychological and educational tests, have identified items as being disproportionately more difficult for minority group members than for members of the majority culture and subsequently compared their results with a panel of expert judges. Studies by Jensen (1976) and Sandoval and Mille (1979) are representative of the methodology and results of this line of inquiry.

After identifying the 8 most racially discriminating and 8 least racially discriminating items on the Wonderlic Personnel Test, Jensen (1976) asked panels of 5 Black psychologists and 5 White psychologists to sort out the 8 most and 8 least discriminating items when only these 16 items were presented to them. The judges sorted the items at a no better than chance level. Sandoval and Mille (1979) conducted a somewhat more extensive analysis using items from the WISC-R. These two researchers had 38 Black, 22 Hispanic, and 40 White university students from Spanish, history, and education classes identify items from the WISC-R that are more difficult for a minority child than a White child and items that are equally difficult for each group. A total of 45 WISC-R items was presented to each judge; these items included the 15 most difficult items for Blacks as compared to Whites, the 15 most difficult items for Hispanics as compared to Whites, and the 15 items showing the most nearly identical difficulty indexes for minority and White children. The judges were asked to read each question and determine whether they thought the item was (1) easier for minority than White children, (2) easier for White than minority children, or (3) of equal difficulty for White and minority children. Sandoval and Mille's (1979) results indicated that the judges were not able to differentiate between items that were more difficult for minorities and items that were of equal difficulty across groups. The effects of the judges' ethnic backgrounds on the accuracy of their item bias judgments were also considered. Minority and nonminority judges did not differ in their ability to identify accurately biased items nor did they differ with regard to the type of incorrect identification they tended to make. Sandoval and Mille's (1979) two major conclusions were that "(1) judges are not able to detect items which are more difficult for a minority child than an Anglo child, and (2) the ethnic background of the judge makes no difference in accuracy of item selection for minority children" (p. 6). Research since that time has continued to produce similar results: minority judges seldom exceed chance expectations in designating biased versus nonbiased test items in aptitude and in personality domains. Even without empirical support for its validity, the use of expert panels of minorities continues but for a different purpose. Members of various ethnic, religious, or other groups that have a cultural system in some way unique may well be able to identify items that contain material that is offensive, and the elimination of such items is proper.

How Test Publishers Commonly Identify Biased Items

Today's most recommended method for detecting item bias arises from applications of item response theory (IRT), followed by a thoughtful, logical analysis of item content (Reynolds, 2000). The goal in the use of these methods is to determine the degree of DIF, that is, that

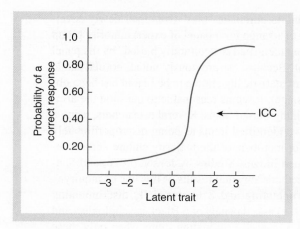

FIGURE 15–1 An Example of an Item Characteristic Curve, or ICC.

Source: Reynolds, C. R., & Lowe, P. A. (1999). *The problem of bias in psychological assessment.* In T. B. Gutkin & C. R. Reynolds (Eds.), The handbook of school psychology, Fourth edition (pp. 332–374). New York: Wiley. Reprinted with permission of Wiley.

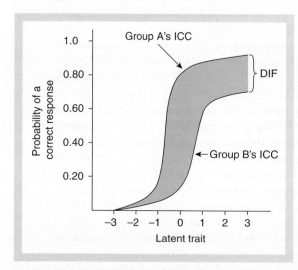

FIGURE 15–2 A Visual Representation of DIF is the Shaded Region Between Group A's and Group B's characteristic curves (ICCs).

Source: Reynolds, C. R., & Lowe, P. A. (1999). *The problem of bias in psychological assessment.* In T. B. Gutkin & C. R. Reynolds (Eds.), The handbook of school psychology, Fourth edition (pp. 332–374). New York: Wiley. Reprinted with permission of Wiley.

items (as indicated by model parameters associated with the items) function differently across groups. Embretson and Reise (2000) presented an excellent overview of the theory and applications of item response theory, including a highly readable chapter on detecting DIF. Statistically significant DIF, coupled with a logical analysis of item content that suggests the item may measure construct irrelevant differences across groups, provides a basis for rejecting items from tests.

IRT is concerned fundamentally with creating a mathematical model of item difficulty—or more technically, the probability of occurrence of a particular response to a test item as a function of an examinee's relative position on a latent trait. Such models specify various parameters that describe the behavior of the item within the model; most IRT models include one, two, or three parameters, which may be graphically represented in an item characteristic curve (ICC). The three parameters in the three-parameter (3P) model are *a* (discrimination power of the item, or slope of the ICC), *b* (item difficulty, located at the point on the difficulty level of the latent trait at which the examinee has a 50% chance of correctly answering the item), and *c* (guessing parameter). Figure 15–1 demonstrates a one-parameter ICC (also known as the Rasch model after its originator) unidimensional model which is widely used in aptitude testing. Its appropriateness depends on the context, and particularly for multiple-choice items, the other ICC models may be more appropriate. The greater complexity that can be modeled with the 3P model comes with a price: One generally requires a much larger sample to develop a good (valid, reliable) 3P model. Two computer programs widely used to estimate item and latent parameters are LOGIST and BILOG, respectively using the joint maximum likelihood (JML) and marginal maximum likelihood (MML) methods.

In using IRT to determine DIF, one compares the ICCs of two different groups, yielding a DIF "index." Various statistical methods have been developed for measuring the gaps between ICCs across groups of examinees. Figure 15–2 demonstrates this DIF gap across two hypothetical groups.

Another method used by test publishers is a partial correlation approach. Using partial correlations, one may test for differences between groups on the degree to which there exists significant or meaningful variation in observed scores on individual test items not attributable to the total test score. It provides a simpler method than either the ICC or IRT models, and it is readily accessible through major statistical programs. In this method, the partial correlation between item score and the nominal variable of interest (e.g., sex) is calculated, partialing the correlation between total test score and the nominal variable. This method essentially holds total score constant across the groups, and resulting differences (if significant and particularly if meaningful, the latter determination commonly based on effect size) may be used to identify problematic items (see Reynolds, Willson, & Chatman, 1984, for information on the development of this method). (One may obtain a measure of effect size simply by squaring the partial r value.) The main risk of using this method is that it may overidentify differences between groups, so it is necessary to calculate experiment-wise error rates. However, this also makes the partial correlation method more sensitive to potentially biased items.

Reynolds and Kamphaus (2003) used the partial correlation method to detect potential bias items in their development of the Reynolds Intellectual Assessment Scales (RIAS). They computed the partial r of item subtest total score partialing the total score correlation with each nominal variable of interest (gender and ethnicity) one variable at a time and separately by age group. One advantage of the partial correlation in such studies is that it can be used successfully with much smaller sample sizes than the ICC and most other techniques. Thus analyses can be run at smaller age intervals and any developmental interaction can be detected more readily. The partial r and subsequently its effect size stabilize at smaller Ns compared to the IRT approach.

From a large number of studies employing a wide range of methodology a relatively clear picture emerges. Content bias in well-prepared standardized tests is irregular in its occurrence, and no common characteristics of items that are found to be biased can be ascertained by expert judges (minority or nonminority). The variance in group score differences on mental tests associated with ethnic group membership when content bias has been found is relatively small (typically ranging from 2 to 5%). Although the search for common biased item characteristics will continue, cultural bias in aptitude tests has found no consistent empirical support in a large number of actuarial studies contrasting the performance of a variety of ethnic and gender groups on items of the most widely employed intelligence scales in the United States. Most major test publishing companies do an adequate job of reviewing their assessments for the presence of content bias. Nevertheless, certain standardized tests have not been examined for the presence of content bias, and research with these tests should continue regarding potential content bias with different ethnic groups (Reynolds & Ramsay, 2003).

BIAS IN OTHER INTERNAL FEATURES OF TESTS

There is no single method for the accurate determination of the degree to which educational and psychological tests measure a distinct construct. The defining of bias in construct measurement then requires a general statement that can be researched from a variety of viewpoints with a broad range of methodology. The following rather parsimonious definition is proffered:

> Bias exists in regard to construct measurement when a test is shown to measure different hypothetical traits (psychological constructs) for one group than another or to measure the same trait but with differing degrees of accuracy. (after Reynolds, 1982)

As is befitting the concept of construct measurement, many different methods have been employed to examine existing psychological tests and batteries of tests for potential bias. One of the more popular and necessary empirical approaches to investigating construct measurement is *factor analysis*. Factor analysis, as a procedure, identifies clusters of test items or clusters of subtests of psychological or educational tests that correlate highly with one another, and less so or not at all with other subtests or items. Factor analysis allows one to determine patterns of interrelationships of performance among groups of individuals. For example, if several subtests of an intelligence scale load highly on (are members of) the same factor, then if a group of individuals score high on one of these subtests, they would be expected to score at a high level on other subtests that load highly on that factor. Psychometricians attempt to determine through a review of the test content and correlates of performance on the factor in question what psychological trait underlies performance; or, in a more hypothesis testing approach, they will make predictions concerning the pattern of factor loadings. Hilliard (1979), one of the more vocal critics of IQ tests on the basis of cultural bias, pointed out early in test bias research that one of the potential ways of studying bias involves the comparison of factor analytic results of test studies across race.

> If the IQ test is a valid and reliable test of "innate" ability or abilities, then the factors which emerge on a given test should be the same from one population to another, since "intelligence" is asserted to be a set of *mental* processes. Therefore, while the configuration of scores of a particular group on the factor profile would be expected to differ, logic would dictate that the factors themselves would remain the same. (p. 53)

Although not agreeing that identical factor analyses of an instrument speak to the "innateness" of the abilities being measured, consistent factor analytic results across populations do provide strong evidence that whatever is being measured by the instrument is being measured in the same manner and is in fact the same construct within each group. The information derived from comparative factor analysis across populations is directly relevant to the use of educational and psychological tests in diagnosis and other decision-making functions. Psychologists, in order to make consistent interpretations of test score data, must be certain that the test (or tests) measures the same variable across populations.

A number of studies of factorial similarity of tests' latent structures have appeared over the past three decades, dealing with a number of different tasks. These studies have for the most part focused on aptitude or intelligence tests, the most controversial of all techniques of measurement. Numerous studies of the similarity of factor analysis outcomes for children of different ethnic groups, across gender, and even diagnostic groupings have been reported over the past 30 years. Results reported are highly consistent in revealing that the internal structure of most standardized tests varies quite little across groups. Comparisons of the factor structure of the Wechsler intelligence scales (e.g., WISC-III, WAIS-III) and the Reynolds Intellectual Assessment Scales (RIAS; Reynolds & Kamphaus, 2003) in particular and other intelligence tests find the tests to be highly factorially similar across gender and ethnicity for Blacks, Whites, and Hispanics. The structure of ability tests for other groups has been researched less extensively, but evidence thus far with the Chinese, Japanese, and Native Americans does not show substantially different factor structures for these groups.

As is appropriate for studies of construct measurement, comparative factor analysis has not been the only method of determining whether bias exists. Another method of investigation involves the comparison of internal consistency reliability estimates across groups. As described in Chapter 4, internal consistency reliability is determined by the degree to which the items are all measuring a similar construct. The internal consistency reliability coefficient reflects the accuracy of measurement of the construct. To be unbiased with regard to construct validity, internal consistency estimates should be approximately equal across race. This characteristic of tests has been investigated for a number of popular aptitude tests for Blacks, Whites, and Hispanics with results similar to those already noted.

How Test Publishers Commonly Identify Bias in Construct Measurement

Factor analysis across groups is the most common method in use by various commercial test developers to assess for bias in construct measurement. However, many other methods of comparing construct measurement across groups have been used to investigate bias in tests. These methods include the correlation of raw scores with age, comparison of item-total correlations across groups, comparisons of alternate form and test-retest correlations, evaluation of kinship correlation and differences, and others (see Reynolds, 2002, for a discussion of these methods). A more recently proposed method for assessing test bias is comparative item selection (Reynolds, 1998). This method involves the use of the same method of selecting items for inclusion in a test repeated across the groups of interest; one is free to use item selection methods based on either classical test theory or IRT. Unbiased tests will generally obtain about a 90% rate of overlap between selected items. The technique will yield substantially lower rate of overlap with biased tests, as well as tests with poor item reliabilities. This method also requires large samples for stable results. Reynolds (1998) provided a full discussion of this approach and demonstrated its application to several personality measures. The general results of research with all of these methods have been supportive of the consistency of construct measurement of tests across ethnicity and gender.

Construct measurement of a large number of popular psychometric assessment instruments has been investigated across ethnicity and gender with a divergent set of methodologies. No consistent evidence of bias in construct measurement has been found in the many prominent standardized tests investigated. This leads to the conclusion that these psychological tests function in essentially the same manner across ethnicity and gender, the test materials are perceived and reacted to in a similar manner, and the tests are measuring the same construct with equivalent accuracy for Blacks, Whites, Hispanic, and other American minorities for both sexes. Differential validity or single-group validity has not been found and likely is not an existing phenomenon with regard to well-constructed standardized psychological and educational tests. These tests appear to be reasonably unbiased for the groups investigated, and mean score differences do not appear to be an artifact of test bias (Reynolds & Ramsay, 2003).

> *No consistent evidence of bias in construct measurement has been found in the many prominent standardized tests investigated.*

BIAS IN PREDICTION AND IN RELATION TO VARIABLES EXTERNAL TO THE TEST

Internal analyses of bias (such as with item content and construct measurement) are less confounded than analyses of bias in prediction due to the potential problems of bias in the criterion measure. Prediction is also strongly influenced by the reliability of criterion measures, which frequently is poor. (The degree of relation between a predictor and a criterion is restricted as a function of the square root of the product of the reliabilities of the two variables.) Arriving at a consensual definition of bias in prediction is also a difficult task. Yet, from the standpoint of the traditional practical applications of aptitude and intelligence tests in forecasting probabilities of future performance levels, prediction is the most crucial use of test scores to examine.

> *From the standpoint of traditional practical applications on aptitude and intelligence tests in forecasting probabilities of future performance levels, prediction is the most crucial use of test scores to examine.*

Looking directly at bias as a characteristic of a test and not a selection model, Cleary et al.'s (1975) definition of test fairness, as restated here in modern terms, is a clear direct statement of test bias with regard to prediction bias:

> A test is considered biased with respect to prediction when the inference drawn from the test score is not made with the smallest feasible random error or if there is constant error in an inference or prediction as a function of membership in a particular group. (after Reynolds, 1982, p. 201)

The evaluation of bias in prediction under the Cleary et al. (1975) definition (known as the regression definition) is quite straightforward. With simple regressions, predictions take the form $Y = a + bX$, where a is a constant and b is the regression coefficient. When the equation is graphed (forming a regression line), a is the Y-intercept and b the slope of the regression line. Given our definition of bias in prediction validity, nonbias requires errors in prediction to be independent of group membership, and the regression line formed for any pair of variables must be the same for each group for whom predictions are to be made. Whenever the slope or the intercept differs significantly across groups, there is bias in prediction if one attempts to use a regression equation based on the combined groups. When the regression equations for two (or more) groups are equivalent, prediction is the same for those groups. This condition is referred to variously as homogeneity of re-

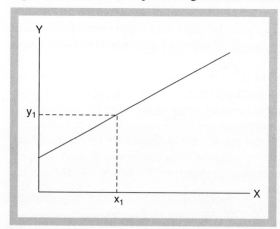

FIGURE 15–3 Equal Slopes and Intercepts.
Note: Equal slopes and intercepts result in homogeneity of regression where the regression lines for different groups are the same.

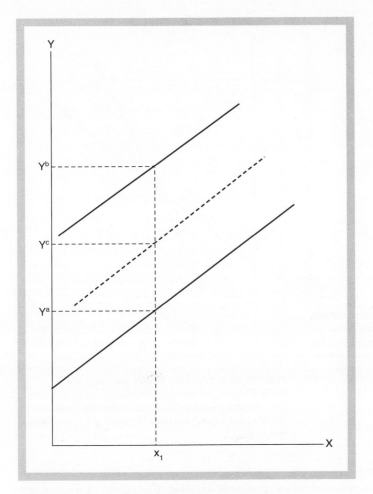

FIGURE 15–4 Equal Slopes With Differing Intercepts.
Note: Equal slopes with differing intercepts result in parallel regression lines that produce a constant bias in prediction.

gression across groups, simultaneous regression, or fairness in prediction. Homogeneity of regression is illustrated in Figure 15–3, in which the regression line shown is equally appropriate for making predictions for all groups. Whenever homogeneity of regression across groups does not occur, then separate regression equations should be used for each group concerned.

> *When the regression equations are the same for two or more groups, prediction is the same for those groups.*

In actual clinical practice, regression equations are seldom generated for the prediction of future performance. Rather, some arbitrary, or perhaps statistically derived, cutoff score is determined, below which failure is predicted. For school performance, a score of 2 or more standard

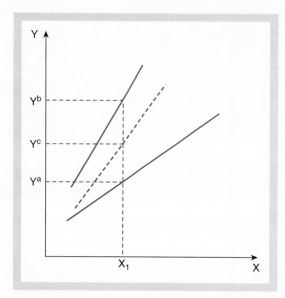

FIGURE 15–5 Equal Intercepts and Differing Slopes.
Note: Equal intercepts and differing slopes result in nonparallel regression lines, with the degree of bias depending on the distance of the individual's score from the origin.

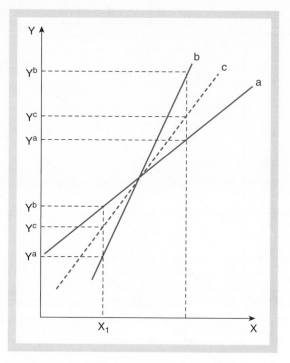

FIGURE 15–6 Differing Slopes and Intercepts.
Note: Differing slopes and intercepts result in a complex situation where the amount and the direction of the bias are a function of an individual's score from the origin.

deviations below the test mean is used to infer a high probability of failure in the regular classroom if special assistance is not provided for the student in question. Essentially then, clinicians are establishing prediction equations about mental aptitude that are *assumed* to be equivalent across race, sex, and so on. Although these mental equations cannot be readily tested across groups, the actual form of criterion prediction can be compared across groups in several ways. Errors in prediction must be independent of group membership. If regression equations are equal, this condition is met. To test the hypothesis of simultaneous regression, regression slopes and regression intercepts must both be compared.

When homogeneity of regression does not occur, three basic conditions can result: (a) intercept constants differ, (b) regression coefficients (slopes) differ, or (c) slopes and intercepts differ. These conditions are illustrated in Figures 15–4, 15–5, and 15–6, respectively.

When intercept constants differ, the resulting bias in prediction is constant across the range of scores. That is, regardless of the level of performance on the independent variable, the direction and degree of error in the estimation of the criterion (systematic over- or underprediction) will remain the same. When regression coefficients differ and intercepts are equivalent, the direction of the bias in prediction will remain constant, but the amount of error in prediction will vary directly as a function of the distance of the score on the independent variable from the origin. With regression coefficient differences, then, the higher the score on the predictor variable, the greater the error of prediction for the criterion. When both slopes and intercepts differ, the situation becomes even more complex: Both the degree of error in prediction and the direction of the "bias" will vary as a function of level of performance on the independent variable.

A considerable body of literature has developed over the last 30 years regarding differential prediction of tests across ethnicity for employment selection, college admissions, and school or academic performance generally. In an impressive review of 866 Black–White prediction comparisons from 39 studies of test bias in personnel selection, Hunter, Schmidt, and Hunter (1979) concluded that there was no evidence to substantiate hypotheses of differential or single-group validity with regard to the prediction of the job performance across race for Blacks and Whites. A similar conclusion has been reached by other independent researchers (e.g., Reynolds, 1995). A number of studies have also focused on differential validity of the Scholastic Assessment Test (SAT) in the prediction of college performance (typically measured by grade point average). In general these studies have found either no difference in the prediction of criterion performance for Blacks and Whites or a bias (underprediction of the criterion) against Whites. When bias against Whites has been found, the differences between actual and predicted criterion scores, while statistically significant, have generally been quite small.

A number of studies have investigated bias in the prediction of school performance for children. Studies of the prediction of future performance based on IQ tests for children have covered a variety of populations including normal as well as referred children; high-poverty, inner-city children; rural Black; and Native American groups. Studies of preschool as well as school-age children have been carried out. Almost without exception, those studies have produced results that can be adequately depicted by Figure 15–1, that is, equivalent prediction for all groups. When this has not been found, intercepts have generally differed resulting in a constant bias in prediction. Yet, the resulting bias has not been in the popularly conceived direction. The bias identified has tended to *overpredict* how well minority children will perform in academic areas and to underpredict how well White children will perform. Reynolds (1995) provided a thorough review of studies investigating the prediction of school performance in children.

With regard to bias in prediction, the empirical evidence suggests conclusions similar to those regarding bias in test content and other internal characteristics. There is no strong evidence to support contentions of differential or single-group validity. Bias occurs infrequently and with no apparently observable pattern, except with regard to instruments of poor reliability and high specificity of test content. When bias occurs, it usually takes the form of small overpredictions for low-SES, disadvantaged ethnic minority children, or other low-scoring groups. These overpredictions are unlikely to account for adverse placement or diagnosis in these groups (Reynolds & Ramsay, 2003).

> *Single-group or differential validity has not been found and likely is not an existing phenomenon with regard to well-constructed standardized psychological tests.*

SPECIAL INTEREST TOPIC 15.5

Why is the Cultural Test Bias Hypothesis So Robust in the Profession— and Why Do So Many Hold the Mean Differences Equals Bias Ideology?

Since the late 1960s, a substantial body of content and methodological research on bias has been conducted. Much of this research has been conducted by psychometricians and published in major psychometric journals not often read by those in other psychological specialties. However, much of what has been learned is summarized in book chapters and entire books easily accessible to mainstream psychologists and some of the empirical and methodological research has appeared in the most widely subscribed journals of the American Psychological Association. Nevertheless, certain myths persist in the writings and actions of many professional psychologists who are either unaware of this research or choose to ignore it. Following are some thoughts of this seeming conundrum.

With regard to the media, Herrnstein (1982) provided an account of his own media encounters that leads one to believe that bias in the media is responsible for their selective reporting (see also Brown et al., 1999, for additional examples). Perhaps this is the case, but with specific regard to race and ethnic differences on measures of IQ, aptitude, and achievement, a broader explanation—and one that captures the biases of psychologists—seems required. Whatever this explanation may be, it is likely related to the phenomenon that leads some in our profession to believe in miraculous cures for mental retardation and the dramatic resistance to the discrediting of the Milwaukee Project (Reynolds, 1987). (The Milwaukee Project's initial results supported the hypothesis that early, intensive interventions with children at risk for mental retardation could dramatically increase intelligence and future academic achievement. However, subsequent research found little or no support for the hypothesis that early interventions could result in lasting changes in IQ or achievement.)

Particularly for health providers, but for most of the lay public as well, it is our concern, our hope, and our belief in our fellow humans that leads to ready acceptance of the cultural test bias hypothesis and to the idea that any mean difference in scores or performance levels on psychological tests confirms that tests are biased. We want everyone to be created equal not just in the sense of worth as a human being as acknowledged in our Constitution, but in the sense of level of aptitude or ability. We find it anathema that ethnic differences in aptitude or ability might be real; we simply do not want it to be so. So, we search for reasons for why these differences are not true. The cultural test bias hypothesis seems far more palatable than the alternative, as it argues that racial and ethnic group differences on mental tests result from problems with the tests themselves—tests also being something for which we all have some, though varying degrees of dislike anyway. The emotional and political appeal of the hypothesis is strong but dangerous. It is also the appeal of the egalitarian fallacy.

Some who do read the psychometric research dismiss it in favor of political arguments. Gould (1995, 1996) acknowledged that tests are not statistically biased and do not show differential predictive validity. He argued, however, that defining cultural bias statistically is confusing: The public is concerned not with statistical bias, but with whether minority–White IQ differences occur because society treats ethnic minorities unfairly. That is, the public considers tests biased if they record biases originating elsewhere in society (Gould, 1995). In this context we interpret the tests as the messengers—the Gould approach is the "kill the messenger" approach and does not lead to solutions; rather, it leads to ignorance.

A related issue that is also likely involved in the profession's reluctance to abandon the cultural test bias hypothesis is a failure to separate the cultural test bias hypothesis from questions of etiology. Data reflecting ethnic differences on aptitude measures have been interpreted as supporting the hypothesis of genetic differences in intelligence and implicating one group as superior to another. Such interpretations understandably call for an emotional response and are not defensible from a scientific perspective.

The task of science and rational inquiry is to understand the source of these differences, to pit alternative theories boldly against one another, to analyze and consider our data and its complexities again and again, and to do so without the emotional overpull of our compassion and our beliefs. Particularly with regard to such sensitive and polemic topics as racial and ethnic differences on mental tests, we must stay especially close to our empirical research, perhaps adopting an old but articulate rubric, the one with which we opened this chapter: In God we trust; all others must have data.

How Test Publishers Commonly Identify Bias in Prediction

Commercial test developers seldom demonstrate the presence or absence of bias in prediction prior to test publication. Unfortunately the economics of the test development industry as well as that for researchers developing tools for specific research projects prohibit such desirable work prepublication. Most such work occurs postpublication and by independent researchers with interests in such questions.

Summary

A considerable body of literature currently exists failing to substantiate cultural bias against native-born American ethnic minorities with regard to the use of well-constructed, adequately standardized intelligence and aptitude tests. With respect to personality scales, the evidence is promising yet far more preliminary and thus considerably less conclusive. Despite the existing evidence, we do not expect the furor over the cultural test bias hypothesis to be resolved soon. Bias in psychological testing will remain a torrid issue for some time. Psychologists and educators will need to keep abreast of new findings in the area. As new techniques and better methodology are developed and more specific populations examined, the findings of bias now seen as random and infrequent may become better understood and seen to indeed display a correctable pattern.

In the meantime, however, one cannot ethnically fall prey to the sociopoliticolegal *Zeitgeist* of the times and infer bias where none exists (see Special Interest Topic 15.5 for further thoughts on this issue). Psychologists and educators cannot justifiably ignore the fact that low IQ, ethnic, disadvantaged children are just as likely to fail academically as are their White, middle-class counterparts. Black adolescent delinquents with deviant personality scale scores and exhibiting aggressive behavior need treatment environments as much as their White peers. The potential outcome for score interpretation (e.g., therapy versus prison, special education versus regular education) cannot dictate the psychological meaning of test performance. We must practice *intelligent testing* (Kaufman, 1994). We must remember that it is the purpose of the assessment *process* to beat the prediction made by the test, to provide insight into hypotheses for environmental interventions that prevent the predicted failure or subvert the occurrence of future maladaptive behavior.

Test developers are also going to have to be sensitive to the issues of bias, performing appropriate checks for bias prior to test publication. Progress is being made in all of these areas. However, we must hold to the data even if we do not like them. At present, only scattered and inconsistent evidence for bias exists. The few findings of bias do suggest two guidelines to follow in order to ensure nonbiased assessment: (1) Assessment should be conducted with the most reliable instrumentation available, and (2) multiple abilities should be assessed. In other words, educators and psychologists need to view multiple sources of accurately derived data prior to making decisions concerning individuals. One hopes that this is what has actually been occurring in the practice of assessment, although one continues to hear isolated stories of grossly incompetent placement decisions being made. This is not to say educators or psychologists should be blind to an individual's cultural or environmental background. Information concerning the home, community, and school environment must all be evaluated in individual decisions. As we noted, it is the *purpose* of the assessment process to beat the prediction and to provide insight into hypotheses for environmental interventions that prevent the predicted failure.

Without question, scholars have not conducted all the research that needs to be done to test the cultural test bias hypothesis and its alternatives. A number and variety of criteria need to be explored further before the question of bias is empirically resolved. Many different achievement tests and teacher-made, classroom-specific tests need to be employed in future studies of predictive bias. The entire area of differential validity of tests in the affective domain is in need of greater exploration. A variety of views toward bias have been expressed in many sources; many with differing opinions offer scholarly, nonpolemical attempts directed toward a resolution of the issue. Obviously, the fact that such different views are still held indicates resolution lies in the future. As far as the present situation is concerned, clearly all the evidence is not in. With regard to a resolution of bias, we believe that were a scholarly trial to be held, with a charge of cultural bias brought against mental tests, the jury would likely return the verdict other than guilty or not guilty that is allowed in British law—"not proven." Until such time as a true resolution of the issues can take place, we believe the evidence and positions taken in this chapter accurately reflect the state of our empirical knowledge concerning bias in mental tests.

Key Terms and Concepts

Bias, 474
Content bias, 488
Cultural loading, 485

Cultural test bias hypothesis (CTBH), 471
Differential predictive validity, 483
Mean difference definition of test bias, 486

Recommended Readings

Cleary, T. A., Humphreys, L. G., Kendrick, S. A., & Wesman, A. (1975). *American Psychologist, 30,* 15–41. This is the report of a group appointed by the APA's Board of Scientific Affairs to study the use of psychological and educational tests with disadvantaged students—an early and influential article.

Embretson, S., & Reise, S. (2000). *Item response theory for psychologists.* London: Taylor & Francis. An excellent overview of the theory and applications of IRT.

Halpern, D. F. (1997). Sex differences in intelligence: Implications for education. *American Psychologist, 52,* 1091–1102. A good article that summarizes the literature on sex differences with an emphasis on educational implications.

Neisser, U., BooDoo, G., Bouchard, T., Boykin, A., Brody, N., Ceci, S., . . . Urbina, S. (1996). Intelligence: Knowns and unknowns. *American Psychologist, 51,* 77–101. This report of an APA task force provides an excellent review of the research literature on intelligence.

Reynolds, C. R. (1995). Test bias in the assessment of intelligence and personality. In D. Saklofsky & M. Zeidner (Eds.), *International handbook of personality and intelligence* (pp. 545–573). New York: Plenum Press. This chapter provides a thorough review of the literature.

Reynolds, C. R. (2000). Why is psychometric research on bias in mental testing so often ignored? *Psychology, Public Policy, and Law, 6,* 144–150. This article provides a particularly good discussion of test bias in terms of public policy issues.

Reynolds, C. R., & Ramsay, M. C. (2003). Bias in psychological assessment: An empirical review and recommendations. In J. R. Graham & J. A. Naglieri (Eds.), *Handbook of psychology: Assessment psychology* (pp. 67–93). New York: Wiley. This chapter also provides an excellent review of the literature.

Suzuki, L. A., & Valencia, R. R. (1997). Race-ethnicity and measured intelligence: Educational implications. *American Psychologist, 52,* 1103–1114. A good discussion of the topic with special emphasis on educational implications and alternative assessment methods.

Assessment Accommodations

Assessment accommodations help students show what they know without being placed at a disadvantage by their disability.

— U.S. Department of Education, 2001, p. 8

Chapter Outline

Accommodations Versus Modifications

The Rationale for Accommodations

When Are Accommodations *Not* Appropriate or
   Necessary?

Strategies for Accommodations

Determining What Accommodations to Provide

Assessment of English Language Learners (ELLs)

Reporting Results of Modified Assessments

Summary

Learning Objectives

After reading and studying this chapter, students should be able to:

1. Explain the rationale for making modifications in assessment procedures for examinees with disabilities.

2. Distinguish between appropriate and inappropriate assessment accommodations and give examples of both.

3. Identify situations where assessment accommodations are inappropriate or unnecessary.

4. Identify major legislation that has impacted the provision of educational services to examinees with disabilities.

5. Identify and give examples of modifications of presentation format that might be appropriate for examinees with disabilities.

6. Identify and give examples of modifications of response format that might be appropriate for examinees with disabilities.

7. Identify and give examples of modifications of timing that might be appropriate for examinees with disabilities.

8. Identify and give examples of modifications of setting that might be appropriate for examinees with disabilities.

9. Identify and give examples of adaptive devices and supports that might be appropriate for examinees with disabilities.

10. Describe and give examples illustrating the use of limited portions of an assessment or an alternate assessment with an examinee with a disability.

11. Briefly describe the current status of research on the selection of assessment accommodations.

12. Identify and give examples of strategies for assessing examinees with limited English proficiency.

   So far in this text we have emphasized the importance of strictly adhering to standard assessment procedures when administering tests and other assessments. This is necessary to maintain the reliability of test scores and the validity of score interpretations. However, there are times when it is appropriate to deviate from these standard procedures. Standard assessment procedures may not be appropriate for an examinee with a disability if the assessment requires him or her to use some ability (e.g., sensory, motor, language, etc.) that is affected by a disability *but is irrelevant to the construct being measured.* To address this, psychologists and others involved in assessment may need to modify standard assessment procedures to accommodate the special needs of examinees with disabilities. In this context, the *Standards* (AERA et al., 1999) noted that **assessment accommodations** are changes in the standard assessment procedures that are implemented to minimize the impact of examinee characteristics that are irrelevant to the construct being measured by the assessment that would alter obtained scores if the test was administered under standardized conditions. The *Standards* stated that the goal of accommodations is to provide the most valid and accurate measurement of the construct of interest for each examinee. An important consideration when selecting accommodations is that we only want to implement accommodations that preserve the reliability of test scores and the validity of their interpretations. As an example, consider an achievement test designed to measure an examinee's knowledge of biology. A blind examinee would not be able to read the material in its standard printed format, but if he or she can read Braille, an appropriate accommodation would be to convert the test to the Braille format. In this example, it is important to recognize that reading standard print is

> *The goal of* **assessment accommodations** *is to provide the most valid and accurate measurement of the construct of interest for every examinee.*

incidental to the construct being measured. That is, the test was designed to measure the examinee's knowledge of biology, not his or her ability to read standard print. On several versions of the Wechsler intelligence scales, the construct of processing speed is assessed, but the methods of assessing this construct rely heavily on rapid motor movements. For examinees with motor impairments then, this method of assessment would not be appropriate as a measure of processing speed and accommodations that would make it appropriate are difficult to imagine. So, in some cases, accommodations cannot be made and different methods altogether must be sought.

In addition to professional standards, there are laws related to the issue of assessment accommodations. For example, in our public schools the Individuals with Disabilities Education Act of 2004 (IDEA 2004) requires that students with disabilities be included in state/district high-stakes assessments and sanctions the use of testing accommodations when necessary. Special Interest Topic 16.1 provides more information on major laws that impact the assessment of students with disabilities. In forensic settings, there are legal guidelines (discussed in Chapter 14) that hold that if data used by an expert witness to form an opinion are unreliable or invalid, any opinions based on the data are not admissible. As a result, when assessment procedures are changed to accommodate an examinee's disability, this can call into question the reliability of the test data and result in it being inadmissible as evidence (Lee et al., 2003).

SPECIAL INTEREST TOPIC 16.1

Major Legislation that Guides the Assessment of Students with Disabilities

A number of federal laws mandate assessment accommodations for students with disabilities in our public schools. The Individuals with Disabilities Education Act (IDEA) and Section 504 of the Rehabilitation Act of 1973 are the laws most often applied in the schools. IDEA requires that public schools provide students with disabilities a free appropriate public education (FAPE) and identifies a number of disability categories. These include learning disabilities, communication disorders, mental retardation, emotional disturbance, other health impaired (OHI), hearing impairment, visual impairment, multiple disabilities, orthopedic impairments, autism, traumatic brain injury, and developmental delay. A key factor in the provision of services to students with disabilities is the individualized educational program (IEP). The IEP is a written document developed by a committee that specifies a number of factors, including the examinees' instructional arrangement, the special services they will receive, and any assessment accommodations they will receive.

Section 504 of the Rehabilitation Act of 1973, often referred to as Section 504 or simply 504, prohibits discrimination against individuals with disabilities in any agency or school that receives federal funds. In the public schools, Section 504 requires that schools provide examinees with disabilities reasonable accommodations to meet their educational needs. Section 504 provides a broad standard of eligibility, simply stating that an individual with a disability is anyone with a physical or mental disability that limits one or more life activities. Because Section 504 is broader than IDEA, it is possible for an examinee to qualify under Section 504 and not qualify under IDEA. This is sometimes referred to as "504 only."

The issue of assessment accommodations is relevant to practically all psychologists. For example, school psychologists often work with children and adolescents who have disabilities and are receiving special education services. Neuropsychologists frequently work with individuals who have experienced brain or other central nervous system injuries or have other disabilities that might limit their performance on standard assessments. In fact, every psychologist who conducts assessments needs to be sensitive to the possibility that physical and mental disabilities might compromise the validity of their assessment results. Knowledge about assessment accommodations is important not only to psychologists and professional psychometricians. For example, teachers in all grades regularly develop and administer tests in their classrooms, and these tests may also need to be modified to accommodate the needs of students with disabilities. In addition to disabilities, one must also be sensitive to the fact that examinees with limited English proficiency may need assessment accommodations to ensure a valid assessment. In this chapter we will review a wide range of assessment accommodations that might facilitate the assessment of individuals with disabilities or limited English proficiency.

ACCOMMODATIONS VERSUS MODIFICATIONS

The *Standards* (AERA et al., 1999) noted that the terms *accommodation* and *modification* are used differently by professionals. For some, *accommodation* implies that the construct measured by the test is not altered whereas *modification* implies a potential change in the construct being measured. The *Standards* do not adopt this interpretation and use the terms interchangeably. This is also the interpretation we use in this text, but when reading other literature, you should take care to note how the author or authors use these terms.

THE RATIONALE FOR ASSESSMENT ACCOMMODATIONS

As we noted earlier, standard assessment procedures may not be appropriate for an examinee with a disability if the assessment requires the examinee to use some ability that is affected by his or her disability, but is irrelevant to the construct being measured. Assessment accommodations are modifications to standard assessment procedures that are granted in an effort to minimize the impact of examinee characteristics that are irrelevant to the construct being measured. If this is accomplished the assessment will provide a more valid and accurate measurement of the examinee's true standing on the construct (AERA et al., 1999). The goal is not to simply allow the examinee to obtain a higher score; the goal is to

> *Standard assessment procedures may not be appropriate for a client with a disability if the assessment requires the client to use some ability that is affected by the disability, but is irrelevant to the construct being measured.*

obtain more valid score interpretations. Assessment accommodations should increase the validity of the score interpretations so they more accurately reflect the examinee's true standing on the construct being measured.

Whereas some physical, cognitive, sensory, or motor deficits may be readily apparent to professionals (e.g., vision or hearing impairment and physical disability) other deficits that might undermine examinees' performance are not as obvious. For example, an examinee with a learning disability might not appear outwardly to have any deficits that would impair performance on a test, but in fact have significant cognitive processing deficits that limit his or her ability to complete standard assessments. In some situations the examinee may have readily observable deficits, but have associated characteristics that also need to be considered. For example, an examinee with a physical disability (e.g., partial paralysis) may be easily fatigued when engaging in standard assessment activities. Because some tests require fairly lengthy testing sessions, the examinee's susceptibility to fatigue needs to be considered when planning assessment accommodations, not only the more obvious physical limitations (AERA et al., 1999).

> *Fairness to all parties is a central issue when considering assessment accommodations.*

Fairness to all parties is a central issue when considering assessment accommodations. For examinees with disabilities, fairness requires that they not be penalized as the result of disability-related characteristics that are irrelevant to the construct being measured by the assessment. For examinees without disabilities, fairness requires that those receiving accommodations not be given an unjust advantage over those being tested under standard conditions. As you can see, these are serious issues that deserve careful consideration.

WHEN ARE ACCOMMODATIONS *NOT* APPROPRIATE OR NECESSARY?

The *Standards* (AERA et al., 1999) specified three situations where accommodations should not be provided or are not necessary:

1. *Accommodations are not appropriate if the affected ability is directly relevant to the construct being measured.* For example, it would not be appropriate to give an examinee with a visual impairment a magnification device if the test is designed to measure visual acuity. Similarly, it would not be appropriate to give an examinee with a reading disability the use of a "reader" on a test designed to measure reading ability. Even if the test is designed as a measure of reading comprehension (as opposed to decoding or reading fluency), having someone else read the material turns the test into one of listening comprehension, not reading comprehension (Fuchs, 2002). In other words, if the testing accommodation changes the construct being measured, the accommodation is inappropriate. Again the essential question is, does the assessment require the use of some ability that is affected by the disability, but is *irrelevant* to the construct being measured?

2. *Accommodations are not appropriate for an assessment if the purpose of the test is to assess the presence and degree of the disability.* For example, it would not be appropriate to give an examinee with attention deficit hyperactivity disorder (ADHD) extra time on a test designed to diagnose the presence of attention problems. Likewise, it would not be appropriate to modify a test of dexterity for an examinee with impaired fine-motor skills.

3. *Accommodations are not necessary for all examinees with disabilities.* All examinees with disabilities do not need accommodations. Even when an examinee with a disability requires accommodations on one test, this does not necessarily mean accommodations will be needed on all tests. As we will discuss in more detail later, assessment accommodations should be individualized to meet the specific needs of each examinee with a disability. There is no specific accommodation that is appropriate, necessary, or adequate for all examinees with a given disability. As an example, consider examinees with learning disabilities. Learning disabilities are a heterogeneous group of disabilities

> *Assessment accommodations should be individualized to meet the specific needs of each examinee with a disability.*

that can impact an individual in a multitude of ways. One examinee with a learning disability may require extended time whereas this accommodation may not be necessary for another examinee with the same diagnosis.

STRATEGIES FOR ACCOMMODATIONS

A variety of assessment accommodations have been proposed and implemented to meet the needs of individuals with disabilities. Below is a brief description of some of the most widely used accommodations compiled from a number of sources (AERA et al., 1999; King, Baker, & Jarrow, 1995; Mastergeorge & Miyoshi, 1999; Northeast Technical Assistance Center, 1999; U.S. Department of Education, 2001). To facilitate our presentation we divided these accommodations into major categories. However, these categories are not mutually exclusive and some accommodations may be classified accurately into more than one category.

Modifications of Presentation Format

Modifications of presentation format involve modifying or changing the medium or format used to present the directions, items, or tasks to the examinee. An example would be the use of braille or large-print editions for examinees with visual impairments (which can be supplemented with large-print or braille figures). Closed-circuit television (CCTV) is an adaptive device that enlarges text and other

> **Modifications of presentation format** *involve modifying the medium or format used to present the directions, items, or tasks to the examinee.*

materials and magnifies them onto a screen (see http://www.visionaid.com/cctvpage/cctvdeal. htm). For computer-administered tests, ZoomText Magnifier/ScreenReader allows examinees to enlarge the image on a computer screen and has a screen reader that reads the text on the screen. In some cases the use of oversized monitors may be appropriate. Reader services, which involve listening to the test being read aloud, may also be employed. Here the reader can read directions and questions and describe diagrams, graphs, and other visual material. For examinees with hearing impairments verbal material may be presented through the use of sign communication or in writing. Other common modifications to the presentation format include increasing the spacing between items; reducing the number of items per page; using raised line drawings; using language-simplified directions and questions; changing from a written to oral format (or vice versa); defining words; providing additional examples; and helping examinees understand directions, questions, and tasks. Table 16–1 provides a listing of these and related accommodations.

Modifications of Response Format

Modifications of response format allow examinees to respond with their preferred method of communication. For example, if an examinee is unable to write due to a physical disability you can allow him or her to take the exam orally or provide access to a scribe to write down responses. In such cases, recorders should have training in verbatim transcription and write exactly what was

> **Modifications of response format** *allow examinees to respond with their preferred method of communication.*

Table 16–1	Accommodations Involving Modifications of Presentation Format

- ❖ Braille format
- ❖ Large-print editions
- ❖ Large-print figure supplements
- ❖ Braille figure supplements
- ❖ CCTV to magnify text and materials
- ❖ For computer-administered tests, devices such as ZoomText Magnifier/ScreenReader to magnify material on the screen or read text on the screen
- ❖ Reader services (read directions and questions, describe visual material)
- ❖ Sign language
- ❖ Audiotaped administration
- ❖ Videotaped administration
- ❖ Written exams converted to oral exams and oral exams to written format
- ❖ Alternative background and foreground colors
- ❖ Increased spacing between items
- ❖ Reduced number of items per page
- ❖ Raised line drawings
- ❖ Language-simplified questions
- ❖ Defined words
- ❖ Additional examples
- ❖ Clarification and help for examinees to understand directions, questions, and tasks
- ❖ Highlighted key words or phrases
- ❖ Cues (e.g., bullets, stop signs) on test booklet
- ❖ Rephrased or restated directions and questions
- ❖ Simplified or clarified language
- ❖ Templates to limit amount of print visible at one time

said and not interpret what was said. An examinee whose preferred method of communication is sign language could respond in sign language and his or her responses subsequently could be translated for grading. However, interpreting the signs is a potential issue in standardized testing and specialized training is often required. Other common modifications to the response format include allowing the examinee to point to the correct response; having an aide mark the answers; using a tape recorder to record responses; using a computer or braillewriter to record responses; using voice-activated computer software; providing increased spacing between lines on answer sheets; using graph paper for math problems; and allowing the examinee to mark responses in the test booklet rather than on a computer answer sheet. Table 16–2 provides a summary listing of these and related accommodations.

Modifications of Timing

Modifications of timing are probably the most frequent accommodation provided. Extended time is appropriate for any examinee who may be slowed down due to reduced processing speed, reading speed, or writing speed. It is also appropriate for examinees who use other accommodations such as a scribe or some form of adaptive equipment because these often re-

Table 16–2	Accommodations Involving Modifications of Response Format

- ❖ Oral examinations
- ❖ Scribe services (examinee dictates response to scribe who creates written response)
- ❖ Examinee allowed to respond in sign language
- ❖ Examinee allowed to point to the correct response
- ❖ Aide to mark answers
- ❖ Tape-recorder to record responses
- ❖ Computer with read-back capability to record responses
- ❖ Braillewriter to record responses
- ❖ Voice-activated computer software
- ❖ Increased spacing between lines on the answer sheet
- ❖ Graph paper for math problems
- ❖ Examinee allowed to mark responses in the test booklet rather than on a computer answer sheet (e.g., Scantron forms)
- ❖ Ruler for visual tracking

Table 16–3	Accommodations Involving Modifications of Timing

- ❖ Extended time
- ❖ More frequent breaks
- ❖ Administration in sections
- ❖ Testing spread over several days
- ❖ Time of day the test is administered changed

quire more time. Determining how much time to allow is a complex consideration. Research suggests that 50% additional time is adequate for most examinees with disabilities (Northeast Technical Assistance Center, 1999). Whereas this is probably a good rule-of-thumb, be sensitive to special conditions that might demand extra time. Nevertheless, most assessment professionals do not recommend "unlimited time" as an accommodation. It is not necessary, can complicate the scheduling of assessments, and can be seen as "unreasonable" and undermine the credibility of the accommodation process. Other time-related modifications include providing more frequent breaks or administering the test in sections, possibly spread over several days. Extra testing time is the most commonly requested accommodation on college and professional school admission tests such as the SAT and GRE as well as professional licensing examinations. The CEEB, ETS, and various licensing boards have specific requirements for evaluating the need for this and other accommodations that you can read about on their websites. For some examinees it may be beneficial to change the time of day the test is administered to accommodate their medication schedule or fluctuations in their energy levels. Table 16–3 provides a summary listing of these and related accommodations.

Modifications of Setting

Modifications of setting allow examinees to be tested in a setting that will allow them to perform at their best. For example, on group-administered tests examinees who are highly distractible may be given the test individually or in a small-group setting. For other examinees preferential

Table 16–4	Accommodations Involving Modifications of Setting
❖ Individual test administration	
❖ Administration in a small-group setting	
❖ Preferential seating	
❖ Space or accessibility considerations	
❖ Avoidance of extraneous noise/distractions	
❖ Special lighting	
❖ Special acoustics	
❖ Study carrel to minimize distractions	
❖ Alternate sitting and standing	

seating in a standard assessment center may be sufficient. Some examinees will have special needs based on space and accessibility requirements (e.g., a room that is wheelchair accessible). Other examinees may need special accommodations such as a room free from extraneous noise/distractions, special lighting, special acoustics, or the use of a study carrel to minimize distractions. Table 16–4 provides a summary listing of these and related accommodations.

> **Modifications of setting** *allow examinees to be tested in a setting that will allow them to perform their best.*

Adaptive Devices and Supports

There is a multitude of **adaptive devices and supports** that may be useful when testing examinees with disabilities. These can range from sophisticated high-technology solutions to fairly simple low-technology supports. For individuals with visual impairments, a number of companies produce products ranging from handheld magnification devices to systems that automatically enlarge the size of print viewed on a computer screen (e.g., ZoomText Magnifier/ScreenReader, ClearView, Optelec, and Visualtek). There are voice recognition computer programs that allow examinees to dictate their responses and print out a document containing their text (e.g., Dragon Dictate). A number of adaptive keyboards and trackball devices are available as well (e.g., Intellikeys keyboard, Kensington Trackball mouse, HeadMaster Plus mouse). Auditory amplification devices in addition to audiotape and videotape players and recorders may be appropriate accommodations. On the low-tech side, examinees may benefit from special chairs and large-surface desks; earplugs/earphones; colored templates; markers to maintain place; paper secured to the desk with tape; and dark, heavy, or raised lines of pencil grips. It may be appropriate to provide an abacus, math tables, or calculators to facilitate math calculations. Accordingly,

> *A multitude of* **adaptive devices and supports** *exist that may be useful when testing examinees with disabilities.*

in some situations it may be appropriate to provide reference materials such as a dictionary or thesaurus. In many situations the use of aids such as calculators, spell check, and reference materials have become so common they are being made available to examinees without disabilities. Table 16–5 provides a summary listing of these and related accommodations.

Table 16–5	Accommodations Involving Adaptive Devices and Supports

❖ Handheld magnification devices and CCTV

❖ Systems that enlarge print (e.g., ZoomText Magnifier/ScreenReader, ClearView, Optelec, and Visualtek)

❖ Systems that read text on the screen (ZoomText Magnifier/ScreenReader)

❖ Voice recognition computer programs that allow examinees to dictate their responses and print out a document containing the text (e.g., Dragon Dictate)

❖ Adaptive keyboards and trackball devices (e.g., HeadMaster Plus mouse, Intellikeys keyboard, Kensington Trackball mouse)

❖ Auditory amplification devices

❖ Audiotape and videotape players and recorders

❖ Special chairs and large-surface desks

❖ Earplugs/earphones

❖ Colored templates or transparencies

❖ Markers to maintain place, highlighters

❖ Paper secured to desk with tape

❖ Dark, heavy, or raised lines of pencil grips

❖ Abacus, math tables, or calculators (or talking calculators)

❖ Reference materials such as a dictionary or thesaurus, spell checkers

❖ Watches or clocks with reminder alarms

Using Only Portions of a Test

In some situations it may be appropriate to use limited portions of an assessment with an examinee with a disability. In clinical settings clinicians might delete certain subtests of a test battery that are deemed inappropriate for an individual with a disability. For example, when testing an examinee with a severe visual impairment a psychologist administering the WISC-IV (see Chapter 9) might delete subtests that require vision (e.g., Block Design, Matrix Reasoning, Picture Concepts) and use only subtests that are presented and responded to orally (e.g., Vocabulary, Information, Similarities). The same principle can be applied to classroom achievement tests. That is, a teacher might decide to delete certain items that are deemed inappropriate for certain examinees with disabilities. Along the same lines, in some situations items will be deleted simply to reduce the length of the test (e.g., to accommodate an examinee who is easily fatigued). These may be acceptable accommodations in some situations, but it is also possible that using only portions of an assessment will significantly alter the nature of the construct being measured (AERA et al., 1999). As a result, this approach should be used with considerable caution.

> *The use of* alternate assessments *may be an appealing accommodation because, with careful planning and development they can produce reliable and valid results.*

Using Alternate Assessments

A final category of accommodations involves using **alternate assessments**, or replacing the standard test with one that has been specifically developed for examinees with a disability

(AERA et al., 1999). This accommodation is often appropriate for examinees with severe disabilities that prevent them from participating in the standard assessments, even with the use of more common accommodations. The use of alternate assessments may be an appealing accommodation because, with careful planning and development they can produce reliable and valid results. The major limitation with this approach is that it may be difficult to find satisfactory alternate assessments that measure the same construct as the standard assessment (AERA et al., 1999).

DETERMINING WHAT ACCOMMODATIONS TO PROVIDE

> *Relatively little research exists on assessment accommodations, and what is available has often produced contradictory results.*

Determining if an examinee needs assessment accommodations and which accommodations are appropriate is not an easy decision. In terms of making this decision, the *Standards* (AERA et al., 1999) stated, "the overarching concern is the validity of the inference made from the score on the modified test: fairness to all parties is best served by a decision about test modification that results in the most accurate measure of the construct of interest" (p. 102). The *Standards* emphasized the importance of professional judgment in making this decision. There is relatively little research on assessment accommodations, and what is available has often produced contradictory findings (AERA et al., 1999; Fuchs, 2002). Special Interest Topic 16.2 presents more on this topic. As a result, there are few universally accepted guidelines about determining what assessment accommodations

---

SPECIAL INTEREST TOPIC 16.2

Differential Effects and Assessment Accommodations

Fuchs (2002) noted that one of the prominent strategies for examining the validity of assessment accommodations is to look for differential effects of the accommodation between examinees with and without disabilities. In these studies, the validity of an accommodation is supported when it increases the performance of examinees with disabilities substantially more than it increases the performance of examinees without disabilities. For example, consider the use of the Braille format for examinees with a visual impairment who can read Braille. It is reasonable to expect that the Braille format will allow examinees with visual impairments to increase their performance on a test of reading comprehension. However, the use of the Braille format would not result in an increase in performance of examinees without visual impairments (in fact it would severely hamper their performance). Differential effects are evident and this supports the validity of this assessment accommodation with examinees with visual impairments.

As we noted, there is relatively little research on the validity of assessment accommodations. To complicate the situation, the research has produced conflicting results. Consider these examples. Runyan (1991) examined the effects of extended time on a reading test among college students. Her results showed that for examinees with learning disabilities the extra time significantly improved their performance. In contrast, for the examinees without a disability the extra time did not result in a significant increase in their performance. In other words, her results demonstrate differential effects and support the validity of extended time as an accommodation with these students. In contrast, Fuchs, Fuchs, Eaton, Hamlett, Binkley, and Crouch (2000) examined the effects of extended time for fourth-grade examinees with and without disabilities on a reading test. This research did not find evidence of differential effects

(Continued)

between examinees with learning disabilities and examinees without disabilities. In fact, there was some evidence that examinees without disabilities benefited more from the extra time relative to examinees with disabilities. In other words, this research suggests extended time on reading tests benefits all students, not just those with learning disabilities. How do you explain these contradictory results? At this time we don't have enough research to explain these discrepancies. The explanation that appears most promising involves the difference in age. Runyan (1991) examined college examinees whereas Fuchs, Fuchs, Eaton, Hamlett, Binkley, and Crouch (2000) studied fourth-grade students.

On the positive side, educators and researchers are developing strategies that might help resolve many of these issues. For example, Fuchs and colleagues (Fuchs, 2002; Fuchs, Fuchs, Eaton, Hamlett, & Karns, 2000; Fuchs, Fuchs, Eaton, Hamlett, Binkley, & Crouch, 2000) developed and studied a system called the Dynamic Assessment of Test Accommodations (DATA). When using DATA, teachers administer alternate forms of brief math and reading tests and determine which accommodations produce differential effects relative to normative data obtained from examinees without disabilities. If the increase an examinee with a disability receives using a specific accommodation (e.g., extended time) substantially exceeds that observed for examinees without disabilities, DATA recommends that accommodation for classroom and standardized assessments. If the increase obtained with an accommodation is similar to that observed with examinees without disabilities, DATA does not recommend that accommodation. The results of preliminary studies of the DATA system are very encouraging and this system may soon help teachers and other educators make objective decisions about assessment accommodations.

should be provided. For example, Fuchs (2002) noted that the accommodations that some states recommend for their statewide assessments in public schools are actually prohibited by other states. Nevertheless, there are a few principles that are generally accepted by experts working with examinees with disabilities. These are listed in the following sections.

MODIFICATIONS SHOULD BE TAILORED TO MEET THE SPECIFIC NEEDS OF THE INDIVIDUAL EXAMINEES. Don't try to apply a "one-size-fits-all" set of accommodations to examinees with disabilities, even when they have the same disability. Not all examinees with any specific type of disability need the same set of accommodations. For example, examinees with learning disabilities are a heterogeneous group and vary in terms of the nature and severity of their disability. As a result, it would be inappropriate to provide the same set of assessment accommodations to all examinees with learning disabilities. The *Standards* (AERA et al., 1999) gave the example of providing a test in Braille format to all examinees with visual impairments. This might be an appropriate accommodation for some examinees with visual impairments, but for others it might be more appropriate to provide large-print testing materials whereas for others it might be preferable to provide a reader or an audiotape with the questions. Look at each examinee individually and determine what his or her specific needs are. This information should serve as the basis for decisions about assessment accommodations.

ACCOMMODATIONS THAT STUDENTS ROUTINELY RECEIVE IN CLASSROOM INSTRUCTION ARE GENERALLY APPROPRIATE FOR ASSESSMENTS. In public schools, if an accommodation is seen as being appropriate and necessary for promoting learning during classroom instruction it is likely that the same accommodation will be appropriate and necessary for assessments. This applies to both classroom assessments and state and district assessment programs. For example, if a student with a visual impairment receives large-print instructional materials in class (e.g., large-print textbook, handouts, and other class materials), it would be logical to provide large-print versions of classroom assessments as well as standardized assessments. Mastergeorge and Miyoshi (1999) suggested three questions to ask: (1) What type of instructional accommodations are being provided in the classroom? (2) Are these same accommodations appropriate and necessary to allow the examinee to demonstrate his or her knowledge and skills on assessments? (3) Are any additional assessment accommodations indicated?

TO THE EXTENT POSSIBLE, SELECT ACCOMMODATIONS THAT PROMOTE INDEPENDENT FUNCTIONING. Although you want to provide assessment accommodations that minimize the impact of irrelevant examinee characteristics, it is also good educational practice to promote the independent functioning of examinees (King et al., 1995). For example, if an examinee with a visual impairment can read large-print text this accommodation likely would be preferable to providing a reader. Similarly, you might want to provide tape-recorded directions/items versus a reader or a word processor with a read-back function versus a scribe. You want to provide the accommodations that are needed to produce valid and reliable results, but this can often be accomplished while also promoting examinee independence.

FOLLOW THE PUBLISHER'S GUIDELINES WHEN MODIFYING STANDARDIZED ASSESSMENTS. Many authors and publishers provide guidelines regarding what accommodations are appropriate for their tests. When these guidelines are available they should be followed strictly. This applies to both individually and group-administered tests. Increasingly authors of individually administered tests are providing guidance about which accommodations are appropriate for their tests and which are inappropriate. For example, the *Interpretive Manual for the Stanford-Binet Intelligence Scale—Fifth Edition* (SB5; Roid, 2003) specified appropriate accommodations and inappropriate modifications for each subtest in the battery (adopting the terminology that modifications imply changes that alter the construct being measured). As an example, on the Memory for Sentences subtest, which measures working auditory memory and language development, the author indicated that it is appropriate to allow responses in writing or signs and to allow additional time for the examinee to respond, but it is inappropriate to present the items in writing, to repeat items, or suggest memory strategies. Publishers of many group-administered assessments have also developed guidelines for determining which accommodations are appropriate. For example, the College Board has a special division that handles requests for assessments accommodations and determines which accommodations are appropriate. Applicants must provide documentation that they have a disability and their need for special assessment accommodations (http://professionals.collegeboard.com/testing/ssd/accommodations). Special Interest Topic 16.3 illustrates the assessment accommodations that are allowed on one statewide assessment.

> *Many publishers provide guidelines regarding what accommodations are appropriate for their tests.*

PERIODICALLY REEVALUATE THE NEEDS OF THE EXAMINEE. Over time the needs of an examinee may change. In some cases, clients will mature and develop new skills and abilities. In other situations there may be a loss of some abilities due to a progressive disorder. As a result, it is necessary to periodically reexamine the needs of the examinee and determine if the existing accommodations are still necessary and if any new modifications need to be added.

We want to reemphasize that when determining which accommodations to provide you must ensure that the reliability and validity of the assessment results are maintained. As professionals, we don't always have well-developed research-based information to help us make these

SPECIAL INTEREST TOPIC 16.3

Allowable Accommodations in a Statewide Assessment Program

The Texas Student Assessment Program includes a number of assessments, the most widely administered being the Texas Assessment of Knowledge and Skills (TAKS). The TAKS manual (Texas Education Agency, 2003) noted that accommodations that do not compromise the validity of the test results may be provided. Decisions about what accommodations to provide should be based on the individual needs of the student and consideration whether the student regularly receives the accommodation in the classroom. For students receiving special education services, the requested accommodations must be noted on their IEP. The manual identifies the following as *allowable* accommodations:

- Signed or translated oral instructions
- Signed prompt on the writing test
- Oral administration of selected tests (e.g., math, social studies, and science)
- Colored transparencies or place markers
- Small-group or individual administration
- Braille or large-print tests
- Modified methods of response
  - ✓ Respond orally.
  - ✓ Mark responses in test booklet (vs. machine-scorable response form).
  - ✓ Type responses.
  - ✓ Tape-record essays, then play back to a scribe while spelling, capitalizing, and punctuating it; the examinee is then allowed to read the essay and indicate any desired corrections.
- Reference materials (English dictionaries are allowed during certain tests)
- Calculators (allowed during certain tests)

Naturally, the testing program allows individuals to request accommodations that are not included on this list, and these will be evaluated on a one-by-one basis. However, the manual identifies the following as *nonallowable* accommodations:

- Reading assistance on the writing, reading, and language arts tests
- Use of foreign-language reference materials
- Use of calculators on certain tests
- Translation of test items
- Clarified or rephrased test questions, passages, prompts, or answer choices
- Any other accommodation that would invalidate the results

In addition to the TAKS, there is the State-Developed Alternative Assessment (SDAA). It is designed for students who are receiving instruction in the state-specified curriculum but for whom the IEP committee has decided the TAKS is inappropriate. Although the TAKS is administered based on the student's assigned grade level, the SDAA is based on the student's instructional level as specified by the IEP committee. The goal of the SDAA is to provide accurate information about the student's annual growth in the areas of reading, writing, and math. In terms of allowable accommodations, the manual (Texas Education Agency, 2003) simply specifies the following:

With the exception of the nonallowable accommodations listed below, accommodations documented in the individual education plan (IEP) that are necessary to address the student's

(Continued on page 516)

SPECIAL INTEREST TOPIC 16.3 *(Continued)*

instructional needs based on his or her disability may be used for this assessment. Any accommodation made MUST be documented in the student's IEP and must not invalidate the tests. (p. 111)

The following accommodations are *not allowed* on the SDAA:

- ◆ Direct or indirect assistance that identifies or helps identify the correct answer
- ◆ Clarified or rephrased test questions, passages, prompts, or answer choices
- ◆ Reduced number of answer choices for an item
- ◆ Oral administration of reading and writing tests (with exception of specific prompts)

Table 16–6   Determining Which Accommodations to Provide

- ❖ Tailor the modifications to meet the specific needs of the individual examinee (i.e., no "one-size-fits-all" accommodations).
- ❖ If an examinee routinely receives an accommodation in classroom instruction, that accommodation is usually appropriate for assessments.
- ❖ When possible, select accommodations that will promote independent functioning.
- ❖ Follow the publisher's guidelines when modifying standardized assessments.
- ❖ Periodically reevaluate the needs of the examinee (e.g., Does he or she still need the accommodation? Does he or she need additional accommodations?).

---

decisions, and often we have to base them on professional judgment. In other words, you will have to carefully examine the needs of the examinee and the intended use of the assessment and make a decision about which accommodations are needed and appropriate. As an example, reading the test items to an examinee would clearly invalidate an assessment of reading comprehension. In contrast, administering the assessment in a quiet setting would not undermine the validity of the results (U.S. Department of Education, 2001). Table 16–6 provides a summary of factors to consider when selecting assessment accommodations for examinees.

ASSESSMENT OF ENGLISH LANGUAGE LEARNERS (ELLs)

> *When assessing examinees with limited English proficiency, psychologists should ensure that they are actually assessing the examinees' knowledge and skills and not their proficiency in English.*

The *Standards* (AERA et al., 1999) noted that "any test that employs language is, in part, a measure of language skills. This is of particular concern for test takers whose first language is not the language of the test" (p. 91). Accordingly, both IDEA and NCLB hold that when assessing students with limited English proficiency, educators should ensure that they are actually assessing the students' knowledge and skills and not their proficiency in English. For example, if a bilingual examinee with limited English proficiency is unable to correctly answer a mathematics word problem that is presented in English, one must question if the examinee's failure reflects inadequate mathematical reasoning and computation skills, or insufficient proficiency in English. If the goal is to assess the examinee's English proficiency, it is appropriate to test an English language learner (ELL) examinee in English. However, if the goal is to assess his or her achievement in an area other than English, you need to carefully consider the type of assessment or set of accommodations that are needed to ensure a valid assessment. This often requires testing examinees in their primary or native language.

A number of factors need to be considered when assessing ELL examinees. First, when working with examinees with diverse linguistic backgrounds it is important to carefully assess their level of acculturation, language dominance, and language proficiency before initiating the formal assessment (Jacob & Hartshorne, 2007). For example, you must determine the examinee's dominant language (i.e., the preferred language) and his or her proficiency in both dominant and nondominant languages. It is also important to distinguish between conversational and cognitive/academic language skills. For example, conversational skills may develop in about 2 years, but cognitive/academic language skills may take 5 or more years to emerge (e.g., Cummins, 1984). The implication is that psychologists and teachers should not rely on their subjective impression of an ELL examinee's English proficiency based on subjective observations of daily conversations, but should employ objective measures of written and spoken English proficiency. The *Standards* (AERA et al., 1999) provided excellent guidance in language proficiency assessment.

> *A number of strategies exist for assessing examinees with limited English proficiency.*

A number of strategies exist for assessing examinees with limited English proficiency. These include:

- Locating tests with directions and materials in the examinee's native language. A number of commercial tests are available in languages other than English. However, these tests vary considerably in quality depending on how they were developed. For example, a simple translation of a test from one language to another does not ensure test equivalence. In this context, equivalence means it is possible to make comparable inferences based on test performance (AERA et al., 1999). The question is, does the translated test produce results that are comparable to the original test in terms of validity and reliability?
- It may be possible to use a nonverbal test. A number of nonverbal tests were designed to reduce the influence of cultural and language factors. However, keep in mind that even though these assessments reduce the influence of language and culture, they do not eliminate them. It is also possible they are not measuring the same construct as verbal tests designed for similar purposes.
- If it is not possible to locate a suitable translated test or a nonverbal test, a qualified bilingual examiner may conduct the assessment, administering the tests in the examinee's native language. When a qualified bilingual examiner is not available, an interpreter may be used. Whereas this is a common practice, there are a number of inherent problems in the use of translators that may compromise the validity of the test results (AERA et al., 1999). Also, the difficulty level of the vocabulary used may vary tremendously across languages and may give the examinee undue advantage or create undue difficulty for the examinee— and, it is not at all intuitive as to which situation has been created by using a translation. Translators typically have been trained to interpret, not only translate, which creates additional problem in determining scores accurately and in generalization of validity evidence. It is recommended that anyone considering this option consult the *Standards* (AERA et al., 1999) for additional information on the use of interpreters in assessing individuals with limited English proficiency.

Salvia, Ysseldyke, and Bolt (2007) provided suggestions for assessing students with limited English proficiency in terms of classroom achievement. First, they encouraged teachers to ensure that they assess what is actually taught in class, not related content that relies on incidental learning. Students with different cultural and language backgrounds might not have had the same opportunities for incidental learning as native English speakers. Second, ELL students should be given extra time to process their responses. The authors noted that for a variety of reasons, students with limited English proficiency may require additional time to process information and formulate a response. Finally, they suggested that teachers provide ELL students with opportunities to demonstrate achievement in ways that do not rely exclusively on language.

REPORTING RESULTS OF MODIFIED ASSESSMENTS

> *Some professionals support the use of "flags" to denote scores resulting from nonstandard assessments, whereas others feel this practice is unfair to examinees with disabilities and may place them at a disadvantage.*

When psychologists modify an individually administered standardized test to accommodate the needs of an examinee with a disability, they typically document this in the psychological or educational assessment report. This is standard practice and is not the focus of serious debate. In contrast, the way that scores of examinees receiving accommodations on large-scale standardized tests are reported has been the focus of considerable debate. Some assessment organizations use an asterisk or some other **"flag"** to denote a score resulting from a nonstandard administration. The *Standards* (AERA et al., 1999) indicated that this practice is promoted by some but seen as discriminatory by others. Proponents of the practice argue that without flags denoting nonstandard administrations the scores may be misleading to those interpreting assessment results. That is, they will assume no accommodations were made when they actually were. Opponents of the practice hold that it unfairly labels and stigmatizes examinees with disabilities and potentially puts them at a disadvantage—it may also convey they have a disability without having obtained consent to release such information. The *Standards* suggested that two principles apply: (1) important information necessary to interpret scores accurately should be provided, and (2) extraneous information that is not necessary to interpret scores accurately should be withheld. Based on this guidance, if there is adequate evidence demonstrating that scores are comparable both with and without accommodations, flagging is not necessary. When there is insufficient evidence regarding the comparability of test scores, flagging may be indicated. However, a simple flag denoting the use of accommodations is rather imprecise and when permissible by law it is better to provide specific information about the accommodations that were provided.

Different agencies providing professional assessment services handle this issue differently. The Educational Testing Service (ETS) indicates that when an approved assessment accommodation is thought to affect the construct being measured, it includes a statement indicating that the assessment was taken under nonstandard testing conditions. However, if only minor accommodations are required the administration can be considered standard and the scores are not flagged. Minor accommodations include providing wheelchair access, using a sign language interpreter, or providing large-print test material. For more information about the testing accommodations ETS provides, go to the website www.ets.org/disability/info.html. Special Interest Topic 16.4 provides a brief review of selected legal cases involving the provision of assessment accommodations.

SPECIAL INTEREST TOPIC 16.4

Assessment of Students with Disabilities—Selected Legal Issues

[A]n otherwise qualified student who is unable to disclose the degree of learning he actually possesses because of the test format or environment would be the object of discrimination solely on the basis of his handicap.

> —Chief Justice Cummings, U.S. Seventh Circuit Court of Appeals[1]

Section 504 imposes no requirement upon an educational institution to lower or to effect substantial modifications of standards to accommodate a handicapped person.

> —Justice Powell, U.S. Supreme Court[2]

Phillips (1993) selected these quotes to illustrate the diversity in legal opinions that have been rendered regarding the provision of assessment accommodations for students with disabilities. Phillips wrote extensively in this area (e.g., 1993, 1994, 1996) and her writings provide some guidelines regarding the assessment of students with disabilities. Some of these guidelines are most directly applicable to high-stakes assessment programs, but they also have implications for other educational assessments.

Notice

Students should be given adequate notice when they will be required to engage in a high-stakes testing program (e.g., assessments required for graduation). This requirement applies to all students, but it is particularly important for students with disabilities to have adequate notice of any testing requirements because it may take them longer to prepare for the assessment. What constitutes "adequate notice"? With regard to a test required for graduation from high school, one court found 1½ years to be inadequate (*Brookhart v. Illinois State Board of Education*). Another court agreed, finding that approximately 1 year was inadequate, but suggested that 3 years were adequate (*Northport v. Ambach*).

Curricular Validity of the Test

If a state is going to implement a high-stakes assessment, it must be able to show that students had adequate opportunities to acquire the knowledge and skills assessed by the assessment (*Debra P. v. Turlington*). This includes students with disabilities. One way to address this is to include the learning objectives measured by the assessment in the student's individualized educational plan (IEP). One court ruled that parents and educators could decide not to include the skills and knowledge assessed by a mandatory graduation test on a student's IEP, but only if there was adequate time for the parents to evaluate the consequences of their child receiving a certificate or completion in lieu of a high school diploma (*Brookhart*).

Accommodations Must Be Individualized

Both IDEA and Section 504 require that educational programs and assessment accommodations be tailored to meet the unique needs of the individual student. For example, it is not acceptable for educators to decide that all students with a specific disability (e.g., learning disability) will receive the same assessment accommodations. Rulings by the federal Office for Civil Rights (OCR) maintain that decisions to provide specific assessment accommodations must be made on a case-by-case basis.

Invalid Accommodations

Courts have ruled that test administrators are not required to grant assessment accommodations that "substantially modify" a test or that "pervert" the purpose of the test (*Brookhart*). In psychometric

---

[1]*Brookhart v. Illinois State Board of Education*, 1983.

[2]*Southeastern Community College v. Davis*, 1979.

(Continued on page 520)

SPECIAL INTEREST TOPIC 16.4 *(Continued)*

terms, the accommodations should not invalidate the interpretation of test scores. Phillips (1994) suggested the following questions should be asked when considering a given accommodation:

1. Will format changes or accommodations in testing conditions change the skills being measured?
2. Will the scores of examinees tested under standard conditions have a different meaning than scores for examinees tested with the requested accommodation?
3. Would examinees without disabilities benefit if allowed the same accommodation?
4. Does the examinee with disabilities have the capability of adapting to standard test administration conditions?
5. Is the disability evidence or testing accommodation policy based on procedures with doubtful validity and reliability? (p. 104)

If the answer to any of these questions is yes, Phillips suggested the accommodations are likely not appropriate.

Flagging

"Flagging" refers to administrators adding notations on score reports, transcripts, or diplomas indicating that assessment accommodations were provided (and in some cases what the accommodations were). Proponents of flagging hold that it protects the users of assessment information from making inaccurate interpretations of the results. Opponents of flagging hold that it unfairly labels and stigmatizes students with disabilities, breaches their confidentiality, and potentially puts them at a disadvantage. If there is substantial evidence that the accommodation does not detract from the validity of the interpretation of scores, flagging is not necessary. However, flagging may be indicated when there is incomplete evidence regarding the comparability of test scores. Phillips (1994) described a process labeled "Self-Selection with Informed Disclosure." Here administrators grant essentially any reasonable accommodation that is requested, even if it might invalidate the assessment results. Then, to protect users of assessment results, they add notations specifying what accommodations were provided. An essential element is that the examinee requesting the accommodations must be adequately informed that the assessment reports will contain information regarding any accommodations provided and the potential advantages and disadvantages of taking the test with accommodations. However, even when administrators get informed consent, disclosure of assessment accommodations may result in legal action.

Phillips (1993) noted that at times the goal of promoting valid and comparable test results and the legal and political goal of protecting the individual rights of students with disabilities may be at odds. She recommended that educators develop detailed policies and procedures regarding the provision of assessment accommodations, decide each case on an individual basis, and provide expeditious appeals when requested accommodations are denied. She noted:

> To protect the rights of both the public and individuals in a testing program, it will be necessary to balance the policy goal of maximum participation by the disabled against the need to provide valid and interpretable students test scores. (p. 32)

Summary

In this chapter we focused on the use of assessment accommodations with examinees with disabilities. We noted that standard assessment procedures might not be appropriate for an examinee with a disability if the assessment requires the examinee to use an ability that is affected by his or her disability but is irrelevant to the construct being measured. In these situations it may be necessary to modify the standard assessment procedures. We gave the example of an examinee with a visual impairment taking a written test of world history. Although the examinee cannot read the material in its standard format, if he or she can read Braille an appropriate accommodation would be to convert the test to the braille format. Because the test is designed to measure knowledge of world history, not the ability to read standard print, this would be an appropriate accommodation. The goal of assessment accommodations is not simply to allow the examinee to obtain a higher score, but to provide the most reliable and valid assessment of the construct of interest. To this end, assessment accommodations should always increase the validity of the score interpretations so they more accurately reflect the examinee's true standing on the construct being measured.

We noted three situations when assessment accommodations are not appropriate or necessary (AERA et al., 1999). These are (1) when the affected ability is directly relevant to the construct being measured, (2) when the purpose of the assessment is to assess the presence and degree of the disability, and (3) when the examinee does not actually need the accommodation.

A number of assessment accommodations have been developed to meet the needs of examinees with disabilities. These include:

- Modifications of presentation format (e.g., use of Braille or large print to replace standard text)
- Modifications of response format (e.g., allow an examinee to respond using sign language)
- Modifications of timing (e.g., extended time)
- Modifications of setting (e.g., preferential seating, study carrel to minimize distractions)
- Adaptive devices and supports (e.g., magnification and amplification devices)
- Use of only a portion of a test (e.g., reducing test length)
- Use of alternate assessments (e.g., tests specifically developed for examinees with disabilities)

We noted that there is relatively little research on assessment accommodations and what is available has produced inconsistent results. As a result, only a few principles about providing assessment accommodations are widely accepted. These include:

- Accommodations should be tailored to meet the specific needs of the individual examinee.
- Accommodations that examinees routinely receive in their classroom instruction are generally appropriate for assessments.
- To the extent possible, accommodations that promote independent functioning should be selected.
- Publisher's guidelines should be followed when modifying standardized assessments.
- The needs of the examinee should be periodically reevaluated.

In addition to examinees with disabilities, it may be appropriate to make assessment accommodations for English language learners (ELLs). Both IDEA and NCLB require that when assessing examinees with limited English proficiency, we must ensure that we are actually assessing the examinee's knowledge and skills and not their proficiency in English. The same principle applies to assessments outside the public schools. In terms of standardized assessments, typical accommodations include locating tests with directions and materials in the examinee's native language, substituting a nonverbal test designed to reduce the influence of cultural and language factors, and using a bilingual examiner or interpreter.

The final topic we addressed concerns reporting the results of modified assessments. In the context of individual psychological and educational assessments it is common for the clinician to report any modifications to the standardized assessment procedures. However, in the context of large-scale standardized assessments there is considerable debate. Some experts recommend the use of "flags" to denote a score resulting from a modified administration of a test. Proponents of this practice suggest that without the use of flags, individuals interpreting the assessment results will assume that there was a standard administration and interpret the scores accordingly. Opponents of the practice feel that it unfairly labels and stigmatizes examinees with disabilities and may put them at a disadvantage.

Key Terms and Concepts

Adaptive devices and supports, 510

Alternate assessments, 511

Assessment accommodations, 503

Modifications of presentation format, 507

Modifications of response format, 507

Modifications of setting, 509

"flags", 518

Recommended Readings

American Educational Research Association, American Psychological Association, & National Council on Measurement in Education. (1999). *Standards for educational and psychological testing*. Washington, DC: AERA. The *Standards* provide an excellent discussion of assessment accommodations.

Mastergeorge, A. M., & Miyoshi, J. N. (1999). *Accommodations for students with disabilities: A teacher's guide* (CSE Technical Report 508). Los Angeles: National Center for Research on Evaluation, Standards, and Student Testing. This guide provides some useful information on assessment accommodations specifically aimed toward teachers.

Phillips, S. E. (1994). High-stakes testing accommodations: Validity versus disabled rights. *Applied Measurement in Education*, 7(2), 93–120. An excellent discussion of legal cases involving assessment accommodations for students with disabilities.

Thurnlow, M., Hurley, C., Spicuzza, R., & El Sawaf, H. (1996). *A review of the literature on testing accommodations for students with disabilities* (Minnesota Report No. 9). Minneapolis: University of Minnesota, National Center on Educational Outcomes. Retrieved from http://education.umn.edu/NCEO/OnlinePubs/MnReport9.html.

Turnbull, R., Turnbull, A., Shank, M., Smith, S., & Leal, D. (2002). *Exceptional lives: Special education in today's schools*. Upper Saddle River, NJ: Merrill Prentice Hall. This is an excellent text that provides valuable information regarding the education of students with disabilities.

17

Best Practices:
Legal and Ethical Issues

With power comes responsibility!

Learning Objectives

After reading and studying this chapter, students should be able to:

1. Explain why the assessment practices of psychologists are held to high professional standards.
2. Identify major professional organizations that have written guidelines addressing psychological assessment issues.
3. Describe and give examples of the principles to consider when developing psychological and educational assessments.
4. Describe and give examples of the principles to consider when selecting psychological assessments.

5. Identify major resources that provide information about published tests and describe the type of information each one provides.
6. Describe and give examples of the principles to consider when administering psychological and educational assessments.
7. Describe and give examples of the principles to consider when interpreting, using, and communicating test results.
8. Describe and give examples of the primary responsibilities of test takers.
9. Describe 10 assessment-related activities that psychologists should avoid.

523

Although psychologists might not always be aware of it, their positions bestow them with considerable power. Psychologists make decisions in their professional roles that often significantly impact their clients, and many of these decisions involve information garnered from psychological assessments. Measurement devices are also used in research that affects science, public policy, law, and how groups of people and their behaviors are viewed and understood. As a result, it is our responsibility as psychologists to ensure that the assessments we use are developed, administered, scored, and interpreted in a technically, ethically, and legally sound manner regardless of where they are employed. This chapter provides some guidelines that will help you ensure that your assessment practices are sound.

Much of the information discussed in this chapter has been introduced in previous chapters. We will also incorporate guidelines that are presented in existing professional codes of ethics and standards of professional practice. The following guidelines reflect a compilation of principles presented in the *Standards for Educational and Psychological Testing* (AERA et al., 1999), the *Ethical Principles of Psychologists and Code of Conduct* (APA, 2002—hereafter referred to as the APA Ethics Code), and the *Rights and Responsibilities of Test Takers: Guidelines and Expectations* (JCTP, 1998).

GUIDELINES FOR DEVELOPING ASSESSMENTS

The Joint Committee on Testing Practices (JCTP; 1998) noted that the most fundamental right of test takers is to be evaluated with assessments that meet high professional standards and that are valid for the intended purposes. Accordingly, psychologists who are involved in developing tests have a professional responsibility to develop instruments that meet or exceed all applicable technical, ethical, and legal standards. The most explicit and comprehensive guidelines for developing and evaluating tests are the *Standards for Educational and Psychological Testing* (AERA et al., 1999). Whereas these standards apply most directly to professionally developed, standardized tests, they may be applied appropriately to less formal assessment procedures like those designed for research studies or to be used in classrooms. Following are some brief guidelines for the development of assessments that meet professional standards. For a more detailed discussion of test development principles, refer to Chapter 18.

> *The most fundamental right of test takers is to be evaluated with assessments that meet high professional standards and that are valid for the intended purposes.*

CLEARLY SPECIFY YOUR ASSESSMENT OBJECTIVES AND DEVELOP A TABLE OF SPECIFICATIONS (TOS). When developing any test, the first step is to specify the purpose of the test and the construct or domain to be measured. To this end, psychologists should begin by explicitly specifying the construct to be measured and developing a table of specifications. The **table of specifications (TOS)** or *test blueprint* should clearly define the content and format of the test and be directly linked to the construct being assessed (see Chapter 18 for more information and examples of tables of specifications). Although the importance of this process should be obvious, in real-world situations it may be tempting to skip these steps and simply start writing the test. However, this is actually one of the most important steps in developing high-quality tests. If you have not specified exactly what you want to measure, you are not likely to do a very effective job.

DEVELOP ASSESSMENT PROCEDURES THAT ARE APPROPRIATE FOR MEASURING THE SPECIFIED CONSTRUCT. Once the TOS is developed, it should be used to guide the development of items and scoring procedures. Guidelines for developing items of different types were present-ed in Chapter 6. Selected-response and constructed-response items have their own specific strengths and weaknesses, and are appropriate for assessing some constructs and inappropriate for assessing others. It is the test developer's responsibility to determine which procedures are most appropriate for the test he or she is developing.

> *The development of items and the scoring criteria should be an integrated process guided by the* **table of specifications (TOS)** *or test blueprint.*

DEVELOP EXPLICIT SCORING CRITERIA. Practically all types of assessments require clearly stated criteria for scoring the items. These can range from fairly straightforward scoring keys for selected-response and short-answer items to detailed scoring rubrics for evaluating constructed-response items. Whatever the format, developing the items and the scoring criteria should be an integrated process guided by the TOS. Scoring procedures should be consistent with the purpose of the test and facilitate valid score interpretations (AERA et al., 1999).

SPECIFY A SAMPLING PLAN FOR STANDARDIZATION AND COLLECT NORMATIVE DATA. It is important to clearly specify the target population and collect standardization data based on an appropriate sample. This is discussed in more detail in Chapter 18.

DEVELOP CLEAR GUIDELINES FOR TEST ADMINISTRATION. All aspects of test administration should be clearly specified. This includes instructions to examinees taking the test, time limits, testing conditions (e.g., classroom or laboratory), and any equipment that will be utilized. Psy-chologists should develop administration instructions in sufficient detail so that others will be able to administer the test in a standardized manner.

PLAN ACCOMMODATIONS FOR TEST TAKERS WITH DISABILITIES AND OTHER SPECIAL NEEDS. As discussed in Chapter 16, it is becoming more common for tests to be modified to ac-commodate the needs of individuals with disabilities or those with limited English proficiency. When developing assessments, some thought should be given to what types of accommodations may be necessary for these examinees.

CAREFULLY REVIEW THE ASSESSMENT PRIOR TO ADMINISTRATION. Psychologists who devel-op tests should carefully review their tests to ensure technical accuracy. To this end it is beneficial to have a trusted colleague familiar with the measured construct review the test and scoring criteria prior to administration. In addition to reviewing for technical accuracy, assessments should be reviewed for potentially insensitive content or language and evidence of bias due to race, gender, or ethnic background. Bias in psychological assessment is discussed in detail in Chapter 15.

EVALUATE THE PSYCHOMETRIC PROPERTIES OF ASSESSMENTS. After administering the test, psychologists should use quantitative and qualitative item analysis procedures to evaluate and re-fine their assessments (discussed in Chapter 7). Psychologists should also perform analyses that will allow them to assess the reliability and validity of their measurements. Reliability and validity

TABLE 17–1 Checklist for Developing Assessments
1. Have the test objectives been clearly specified and a table of specifications developed?
2. Are the assessment procedures appropriate for measuring the specified construct?
3. Have explicit scoring criteria been developed?
4. Was a sampling plan for standardization developed and were appropriate data collected?
5. Have clear guidelines for test administration been developed?
6. Have accommodations for test takers with disabilities and other special needs been planned?
7. Has the assessment been reviewed for technical accuracy and potentially insensitive or biased content?
8. Have the technical properties of the assessment been evaluated?

were discussed in Chapters 4 and 5. The extent of the reliability and validity studies depends on the application of the test. That is, tests being developed for commercial publication must have extensive evidence regarding the reliability of scores and validity of score interpretations. Less formal tests like those developed for research studies and classroom applications will require less extensive studies. Although it might be difficult for psychologists working independently to perform some of the more complex reliability and validity analyses, at a minimum they should use some of the simplified procedures outlined in the appropriate chapters. These guidelines are summarized in Table 17–1.

GUIDELINES FOR SELECTING PUBLISHED ASSESSMENTS

As we noted in Chapter 1, most psychologists will not specialize in test development. However, most psychologists who work in applied clinical or research settings will select published tests to administer to their clients or research participants. In selecting these tests, as when developing assessments, it is imperative to ensure that the assessments meet high professional standards and are valid for the intended purposes. Following are a few guidelines for selecting assessments that meet professional standards.

Most psychologists who work in applied clinical or research settings will select published tests to administer to their clients or research participants.

SELECT ASSESSMENTS THAT HAVE BEEN VALIDATED FOR THE INTENDED PURPOSE. As we have emphasized throughout this text, validity is a fundamental consideration when developing or selecting a test (see Chapter 5). Professionally developed assessments should clearly specify the recommended interpretations of test scores and provide a summary of the validity evidence supporting each interpretation. However, in the end it is the person selecting the test who is responsible for determining if the assessment is appropriate for use in a particular setting (AERA et al., 1999). The essential questions are, how will the assessment information be used and have the proposed interpretations of the results of the test been validated for those uses?

SELECT ASSESSMENTS WITH NORMATIVE DATA THAT ARE REPRESENTATIVE OF THE TARGET POPULATION. The validity of norm-referenced interpretations is dependent on the how representative the normative or standardization group is to the target population (see Chapter 3) or another reference group with whom examinees are to be compared. The fundamental question is, does the normative sample adequately represent the type of examinees the test will be used with or alternatively a different reference sample to whom the examinees are to be compared? It is also important to consider how current the norms are because their usefulness diminishes over time (AERA et al., 1999).

SELECT ASSESSMENTS THAT PRODUCE RELIABLE SCORES. It is important to select assessment procedures that produce reliable results. In Chapter 4 we presented guidelines regarding the levels of reliability recommended for different applications or uses. For example, when making high-stakes decisions it is important to use assessment results (i.e., test scores) that are highly reliable (e.g., $r_{xx} > 0.95$).

SELECT TESTS THAT ARE FAIR. Even though no assessment procedure is absolutely free from bias, efforts should be made to select assessments that have been shown to be relatively free from bias due to race, gender, or ethnic background. Bias in psychological assessment is discussed in detail in Chapter 15. It is important to note, however, that even when research demonstrates that reliability and validity evidence is generalizable across groups, a biased user can alter interpretations of test scores in ways that bias an otherwise fair and appropriate assessment.

SELECT ASSESSMENTS BASED ON A THOROUGH REVIEW OF THE AVAILABLE LITERATURE. The selection of assessment procedures can have significant consequences for a large number of individuals. As a result, the decision should be based on a careful and thorough review of the available information. It is appropriate to begin this review by examining information and material provided by the test publishers. This can include catalogs, test manuals, specimen test sets, score reports, and other supporting documentation. However, the search should not stop here and you should seek out independent evaluations and reviews of the tests you are considering. A natural question is, where can I access information about assessments? Four of the most use-

> *Psychologists should select assessments based on a thorough review of the available literature.*

ful references are the *Mental Measurements Yearbook, Tests in Print, Tests,* and *Test Critiques.* These resources can be located in the reference section of most university and larger public libraries. The Testing Office of the American Psychological Association Science Directorate provides the following description of these resources.

Mental Measurements Yearbook (MMY). The *Mental Measurements Yearbook (MMY)* is published by the Buros Institute for Mental Measurements. *MMY* lists tests alphabetically by title and is an invaluable resource for researching published assessments. Each listing provides descriptive information about the test, including test author, publication dates, intended population, forms, prices, and publisher. It also contains additional information regarding the availability of reliability, validity, and normative data, as well as scoring and reporting services. Most listings include one or more critical reviews by qualified assessment experts.

Tests in Print (TIP). *Tests in Print (TIP)* is also published by the Buros Institute for Mental Measurements. TIP is a bibliographic encyclopedia of information on practically every published test in psychology and education. Each listing includes the test title, intended population, publication date, author, publisher, and references. *TIP* does not contain critical reviews or psychometric information, but it does serve as a master index to the Buros Institute reference series on tests. In *TIP* the tests are listed alphabetically, within subjects (e.g., achievement tests, intelligence tests). There are also indexes that can help you locate specific tests. After locating a test that meets your criteria, you can turn to *MMY* for more detailed information on the test.

Tests. *Tests* is published by Pro-Ed, Inc. and is a bibliographic encyclopedia covering thousands of assessments in psychology and education. It provides a brief description of the tests, including information on the author, purpose, intended population, administration time, scoring method, cost, and the publisher. *Tests* does not contain critical reviews or information on reliability, validity, or other technical aspects of the tests.

Test Critiques. *Test Critiques* is also published by Pro-Ed, Inc. and is designed to be a companion to *Tests*. *Test Critiques* contains a tripart listing for each test that includes these sections: Introduction (e.g., information on the author, publisher, and purposes), Practical Applications/Uses (e.g., intended population, administration, scoring, and interpretation guidelines), and Technical Aspects (e.g., information on reliability, validity), followed by a critical review of the test. The reference is written in a user-friendly style that makes it appropriate for individuals with limited training in psychometrics.

In addition to these traditional references, Test Reviews Online is a web-based service of the Buros Institute of Mental Measurements (http://www.unl.edu/buros). This service makes test reviews available online to individuals precisely as they appear in *MMY*. For a relatively small fee (i.e., currently $15), users can download information on any of over 2,000 tests that include specifics on test purpose, population, publication date, administration time, and descriptive test critiques. You should also search the scientific literature for reviews of tests published in refereed journals in addition to research on the use of specific tests that will almost always be more current than information contained in test reviews or test manuals. For more detailed information on these and other resources, the Testing Office of the American Psychological Association Science Directorate has numerous resources available at its website: http://www.apa.org/science/programs/testing.

SELECT AND USE ONLY ASSESSMENTS THAT YOU ARE QUALIFIED TO ADMINISTER, SCORE, AND INTERPRET. Because the administration, scoring, and interpretation of many psychological tests require advanced training, it is important to select and use only tests that you are qualified to administer as a result of your education and training. For example, the administration of an individual intelligence test such as the Wechsler Intelligence Scale for Children—Fourth Edition (WISC-IV) requires extensive training and supervision that is typically acquired in graduate psychology and education programs. Most test publication firms have established procedures that allow individuals and organizations to qualify to purchase tests based on specific criteria. For example, Psychological Assessment Resources (2003) has a three-tier system that classifies assessment products according to qualification requirements. In this system, Level A products require no special qualifications whereas Level C products require an advanced professional degree or license based on advanced training and experience in psychological and educational assessment practices. Before purchasing restricted tests,

> *It is important to select and use only tests that you are qualified to use as a result of your education and training.*

the potential buyer must provide documentation that he or she meets the necessary requirements. In some situations psychologists use what are referred to as technicians or psychological assistants to administer and score psychological tests under their supervision. In this context psychologists select the tests to be administered, interpret the results, and write the reports while the technicians actually administer and score the tests under the supervision of the psychologists. There are professional standards for the education and training of technicians, such as those published by the National Academy of Neuropsychology.

GUARD AGAINST POTENTIAL MISUSES AND MISINTERPRETATIONS. When selecting assessments, avoid selecting those that are likely to be used or interpreted in an invalid or biased manner. This is a difficult responsibility to discharge and requires continual vigilance. Nitko (2001) suggested that to meet this responsibility you must have a broad knowledge of how assessments are being used in your professional setting and any potential misuses or misinterpretations.

MAINTAIN TEST SECURITY. For assessments to be valid, it is important that test security be maintained. Individuals selecting, purchasing, and using standardized assessments have a professional and legal responsibility to maintain the security of assessments instruments. For example, the Psychological Corporation (2003) included the following principles in its security agreement: (a) test takers should not have access to testing material or answers before taking the test; (b) assessment materials cannot be reproduced or paraphrased; (c) assessment materials and results can only be released to qualified individuals; (d) if test takers or their parents/guardians ask to examine test responses or results, this review must be monitored by a qualified representative of the organization conducting the assessment; and (e) any request to copy materials must be approved in writing. Examples of breaches in the security of standardized tests include allowing clients to examine the test before taking it, using actual items from a test for preparation purposes, making and distributing copies of a test, and allowing test takers to take the test outside a controlled environment (e.g., allowing them to take the test home to complete it).

BEFORE USING TESTS AS PART OF AN ASSESSMENT OR OTHER DECISION-MAKING PROCESS, CONSIDER THE CONSEQUENCES OF TESTING AND NOT TESTING. Are objective data needed to improve the decision-making process? In most cases the answer is yes, but a cost–benefit analysis may be necessary when in doubt. These guidelines are summarized in Table 17–2. Special Interest Topic 17.1 provides information on the controversial release of sensitive information about a popular projective technique

---

TABLE 17–2 Checklist for Selecting Published Assessments

1. Have the desired interpretations of performance on the selected assessments been validated for the intended purpose?
2. Do the selected assessments have normative data that are representative of the target population?
3. Do selected assessments produce reliable results?
4. Are interpretations of the selected assessments fair?
5. Was the selection process based on a thorough review of the available literature?
6. Are you qualified to administer, score, and interpret the selected assessments?
7. Have you screened assessments for likely misuses and misinterpretations?
8. Have steps been taken to maintain test security?

SPECIAL INTEREST TOPIC 17.1

Wikipedia and the Rorschach Inkblot Test

If you are not familiar with Wikipedia, it is self-described as a web-based, free-content encyclopedia. It is open to editing by the public and is written in a collaborative manner by over 85,000 volunteers around the world. In 2009 it was visited by approximately 65,000,000 visitors a month (Wikipedia, 2009a).

A controversy emerged in 2009 when the 10 Rorschach color plates were published in the Wikipedia article on the Rorschach. Additionally the article contained information on the scoring and interpretation of the test along with information about popular responses. Although detailed technical information on the scoring and interpretation of the Rorschach can be obtained in numerous psychological textbooks that are available for purchase by the public, we are not aware of the actual plates ever being reproduced and made available to the public. For example, we include inkblots similar to those used in the Rorschach in this textbook, but they were specifically created as examples and are not actual Rorschach inkblots.

On one side of the substantial debate are psychologists noting that the publication of these pictures undermines the utility of the Rorschach and is a clear violation of the ethics codes of major professional psychological associations such as the American Psychological Association (APA). On the other side it is argued that the Rorschach plates are in the public domain because they were initially published over 70 years ago, which exceeds the copyright term in many countries. Even though legal action against Wikipedia has been threatened to force removal of the plates, as this text goes to press, the Wikipedia article still contains the reproduced plates!

It might not be illegal to reproduce these pictures and post them in the public domain, but it is clearly unethical! We will never know with certainty how much damage was been done to the clinical utility of the test. It is possible that clients might access this article prior to taking the Rorschach and exposure to the plates and accompanying information most certainly will impact their responses. Additionally, this makes "coaching" of clients by attorneys in forensic settings even more likely.

We see this as a clear example of an unethical breach of test security! It is not clear who posted the plates or if he or she is a psychologist, but in consideration of the public welfare we hope that in the future organizations like Wikipedia will respect and honor the ethical codes of major professions when it comes to publishing potentially damaging images and/or information!

GUIDELINES FOR ADMINISTERING ASSESSMENTS

So far we have discussed your professional responsibilities related to developing and selecting tests. Clearly, your professional responsibilities do not stop there. Every step of the assessment process has its own important responsibilities, and now we turn to those associated with the administration of assessments. Subsequently we will address responsibilities related to the scoring, interpreting, using, and communicating assessment results. The following guidelines involve your responsibilities when administering assessments.

PROVIDE INFORMATION TO EXAMINEES AND OBTAIN INFORMED CONSENT BEFORE ADMINISTERING ANY ASSESSMENTS. In most situations, psychologists are ethically and legally required to obtain informed consent before providing professional services, including assessments. Informed consent is obtained when a psychologist (or other health professional) provides information to a prospective client about the services (i.e., assessment and/or treatment) to be provided. The client then has the opportunity to carefully consider that

> *In most situations, psychologists are ethically and legally required to obtain* **informed consent** *before providing professional services, including assessments.*

information and decide if he or she wants to receive the services. In terms of assessments, this information includes (1) when and under what conditions the assessment will be administered, (2) the abilities and characteristics that will be assessed, (3) how the assessments will be scored and interpreted, (4) how the results will used, (5) confidentiality issues and who will have access to the results, and (6) how the results are likely to impact the client (APA, 2002; JCTP, 1998; Nitko, 2001). An excellent resource for all test takers is *Rights and Responsibilities of Tests Takers: Guidelines and Expectations* developed by the Joint Committee on Testing Practices (1998). Informed consent is mandated in both clinical (i.e., working with clients) and research (i.e., working with research participants) settings.

WHEN ASSESSING MINORS, HAVE LEGAL WRITTEN CONSENT FROM THE PARENT OR LEGAL GUARDIAN. Minors should be asked to assent to the testing procedures; however, a minor can not give consent for participation—this is true when conducting testing or survey research just

---

SPECIAL INTEREST TOPIC 17.2

Aspects of Informed Consent

As discussed earlier, psychologists must secure informed consent prior to providing professional services such as assessments or counseling. Most authorities on informed consent highlight the following four legal aspects:

Capacity

It is necessary that the individual providing consent to treatment have the mental capacity to understand all relevant information and what they are agreeing to. This implies the individual is competent and rational. If the potential client does not have the mental capacity to provide the consent, other options must be pursued. For example, it may be necessary to have a custodian appointed by a court to make health care decisions for the individual. When the client is a minor, the parents are typically given the right to provide informed consent because minors are usually not considered to have the capacity to consent to psychological services. Many states allow minors to provide consent to psychological services in certain situations. For example, in the state of Texas minors may provide consent when there is suicide potential, when they have been abused, and when the treatment is for substance abuse or dependency.

Sufficient Information Provided

It is necessary that potential clients be given adequate information about the services to be provided to allow them to make an informed decision. That is, do they want these services? As we noted, clients need to know what assessments and interventions they are agreeing to and the potential consequences of these actions. This information must be provided in sufficient detail and in a manner that is easily understandable to the client.

Voluntary

Consent to treatment must be provided in a voluntary manner; there should be no coercion. In certain situations this is not as clear as it might initially appear. As described in Chapter 14, in some situations failing to provide consent might be prejudicial to the client, so subtle pressure might be present even though his or her consent is technically voluntary.

Documentation

As our lawyer friends are fond of saying, "If it is not documented—it didn't happen!" In other words, the informed consent process should include a document that details the process and the client's agreement. This should be signed by the client signifying his or her acceptance of the arrangement. The client should be given a copy of the documents for the record and the original retained in his or her file.

TABLE 17–3	Checklist for Administering Assessments
1. Did you provide information on the assessment and obtain informed consent before administering it?	
2. Are you qualified by education and training to administer the assessments?	
3. Was the assessment administered in a standardized and fair manner?	
4. When appropriate, was the assessment modified to accommodate the needs of test takers with disabilities?	
5. Were proper test security measures followed?	

as much as it is in clinical settings. For minors, assent and consent are both ethical, and in many cases, legal requirements of participation.

ADMINISTER ONLY THOSE ASSESSMENTS FOR WHICH YOU ARE QUALIFIED BY EDUCATION AND TRAINING. As noted previously, it is important to select and use only tests that you are qualified to administer as a result of your education and training. Some assessments require extensive training and supervision before you are able to administer them independently.

ADMINISTER THE ASSESSMENTS IN A STANDARDIZED MANNER. Assessments should be administered in the standardized manner specified in the test manual. This ensures fairness and promotes the reliability of scores and validity of their interpretations. Except in rare situations (see the next guideline), this requires that all examinees take the assessment under the same conditions. For example, all examinees receive the same materials and have access to the same resources (e.g., the use of calculators), receive the same instructions, and have the same time limits. Efforts should be made to ensure that the assessment environment is comfortable, quiet, and relatively free from distractions. Examinees should be given opportunities to ask reasonable questions.

MODIFY ASSESSMENT ADMINISTRATION TO MEET THE NEEDS OF EXAMINEES WITH DISABILITIES. As discussed in Chapter 16, when assessing examinees with disabilities it is often necessary and appropriate to modify the standard administration procedures to address the special needs of these examinees. Assessment accommodations are granted to minimize the impact of examinee characteristics that are irrelevant to the construct being measured by the assessment. A major consideration when selecting accommodations is to select only accommodations that do not undermine the reliability or validity of the assessment results. Many test publishers provide guidelines regarding what accommodations are permissible under specific conditions.

MAINTAIN TEST SECURITY. As we noted previously it is important to maintain test security throughout the assessment process. Obviously test administration is a time when security can be breached. For example, it would be unethical to allow examinees to take the test outside a controlled environment (e.g., allowing them to take the test home to complete it). These guidelines are summarized in Table 17–3.

GUIDELINES FOR SCORING ASSESSMENTS

MAKE SURE ASSESSMENTS ARE SCORED PROPERLY AND RECORDED ACCURATELY. It is a psychologist's professional responsibility to ensure the assessments are scored in an accurate manner. This applies to both commercial and personally developed assessments. With selected-response

TABLE 17–4	Checklist for Scoring Assessments

1. Are procedures in place to ensure that assessments are scored and the results are recorded accurately?
2. Are procedures in place to ensure the scoring is fair?
3. Are assessment results kept confidential?

items this will involve carefully applying scoring keys and double-checking errors. Better yet—use computer scoring when possible! With constructed-response items and performance assessments this involves the careful application of scoring rubrics. The importance of double-checking your calculations cannot be over-emphasized. In Chapter 14 we mentioned that it is not uncommon to discover scoring and clerical errors in assessments submitted to the courts.

> *It is a psychologist's professional responsibility to ensure their assessments are scored in an accurate manner.*

MAKE SURE THE SCORING IS FAIR. An aspect of the previous guideline that deserves special attention involves fairness or the absence of bias in scoring. Whenever scoring involves subjective judgment, it is also important to take steps to ensure that the scoring is based solely on performance or content, and is not contaminated by *expectancy effects* related to examinees. That is, you don't want your personal impression of the examinee to influence your evaluation of his or her performance, in either a positive or negative manner. For example, in some situations it may be possible to score assessments without being aware of the examinee's identification.

KEEP ASSESSMENT RESULTS CONFIDENTIAL. It is the responsibility of psychologists and others who score assessments to keep the results confidential. Although different standards of confidentiality and privacy exist in different settings, it is the psychologist's professional, ethical, and legal responsibility to be aware of the laws and policies applicable in the settings where they provide services. For example, there are both state and federal laws that govern the confidentiality of psychological and medical test results. At the federal level the Health Information Portability and Accountability Act (HIPAA) and the Family Educational Rights and Privacy Act (FERPA) specify guidelines for maintaining the confidentiality of psychological test results in health and school settings, respectively. In summary, only in a limited number of situations (e.g., court order) can the results of a client's assessments be disclosed without his or her permission.

> *It is the responsibility of psychologists and others who score assessments to keep the results confidential.*

As noted, information on the confidentiality of assessment results should be discussed with the client when obtaining informed consent. These guidelines are summarized in Table 17–4.

GUIDELINES FOR INTERPRETING ASSESSMENT RESULTS, MAKING CLINICAL DECISIONS, AND REPORTING RESULTS

In Chapter 1 we stated that we advocate a model of assessment that incorporates psychometric sophistication, clinical insight, knowledge of psychological theory, and thoughtful reasoning. In this model, assessment involves a dynamic evaluation and synthesis of information that is obtained in a reliable and valid manner from multiple sources using multiple procedures. We noted that a psychologist conducting an assessment should assume the role of a "detective" that collects, evaluates, and synthesizes information and integrates that information with a thorough understanding of psychological theories of development, psychopathology, and individual differences (Kaufman, 1994). Following are some more specific guidelines.

USE ASSESSMENT RESULTS ONLY FOR PURPOSES FOR WHICH THEY HAVE BEEN VALIDATED. When interpreting assessment results, the issue of validity is the overriding concern. A primary consideration when interpreting and using assessment results is to determine if there is sufficient validity evidence to support the proposed interpretations and uses. When psychologists use assessment results it is their responsibility to promote valid interpretations and guard against invalid interpretations. Do not attach meaning to test scores or other indications of test performance for which there is no scientific support. We have encountered psychologists who have made unique interpretations of test performance and justified them (erroneously) by arguing there was no research to say the interpretation was not correct—validation of test score interpretations is an affirmative requirement.

> *Use assessment results only for purposes for which they have been validated.*

USE MULTIPLE SOURCES AND TYPES OF ASSESSMENT INFORMATION. In this text we have described a wide variety of assessment procedures: cognitive tests (e.g., intelligence, achievement, and neuropsychological tests), self-report personality measures, behavior rating scales, interviews, and behavioral observations. All of these have a role to play in psychological assessment. Different assessment procedures have different strengths and weaknesses, and psychologists are encouraged to use the results of multiple assessments when making important decisions that impact their clients. It is not appropriate to base important decisions on the result of one assessment, particularly when it is difficult to take corrective action when mistakes occur.

STAY CLOSE TO THE DATA. This guideline holds that psychologists should remain evidence-based in their test interpretations and not "overweight" their clinical judgment. There is a substantial amount of research demonstrating that an actuarial or statistical approach to interpreting assessment information is superior to a clinical or impressionistic approach. In the clinical/impressionistic approach, the clinician uses personal judgment and subjective processes to interpret the assessment information and make decisions. Often, such alterations in test score interpretation are based on faulty recollection of anecdotal data from years of "clinical experience." Although we will not review this research here, there is much evidence to indicate that clinicians and others tend to have selective recall of "facts" and cases that support a particular view and fail to recall as well or as accurately anecdotal data that disagree with their predispositions. In an actuarial/statistical approach, human judgment is eliminated entirely and the interpretation is based solely on empirically established relationships (Dawes, Faust, & Meehl, 1989). Examples of these empirically based models include the use of regression equations, actuarial tables, and nomograms to facilitate clinical diagnosis and decision making. Grove and Meehl (1996) concluded that reliance on the least efficient of two decision-making models "is not only unscientific and irrational, it is unethical" (p. 320). Actuarial models are not available to address many of the decisions professional psychologists are asked to make, but when they are available, we encourage their careful application. See Special Interest Topic 17.3 for more information on the actuarial versus clinical debate.

SPECIAL INTEREST TOPIC 17.3

Accuracy of the Clinical Versus Actuarial Approach to Interpreting Assessment Results

Almost 70 years ago, Sarbin (1943, as reported in Grove & Meehl, 1996) compared the accuracy of two very different approaches to interpreting assessment results. One approach involved a two-variable regression equation to predict college grade point average (GPA). The two variables were those most commonly used for predicting success in college: a college aptitude test score and high school GPA. The second approach was considerably more elaborate. In addition to the aptitude scores and high school GPA used in the linear equation, the counselor also had

- Notes from an interviewer who had completed preliminary interviews
- Results of the Strong Vocational Interest Blank (i.e., an interest inventory)
- Results of a four-factor personality inventory
- Information from an eight-page questionnaire completed by the students
- Results of additional aptitude and achievement tests
- A personal interview with the students

The research question was—which approach is the most accurate? Can the counselor, with the benefit of all this additional information, make better predictions about student academic success than the two-variable equation? The answer might surprise you!

For female students, the two approaches were approximately equal. However, for male students the two-variable regression equation was significantly more accurate than those of the counselor. If this was an isolated finding it would be easy to dismiss it as a chance happening. However, a significant amount of research done in the last 70 years essentially supports these results—actuarial or statistical approaches to interpreting assessment data are more accurate than clinical or impressionistic approaches. Youngstrom, Freeman, and Jenkins (2009) recently noted that "The superiority of statistical approaches has been demonstrated more than 130 times in disciplines spanning economics and education as well as clinical decision making" (p. 363).

Two questions seem to jump to mind when considering these results: (1) Why are clinicians inferior to simple actuarial methods when interpreting assessment information? and (2) Why do most clinicians continue to rely on subjective impressionistic approaches in light of these findings? Although it is beyond the scope of this text to review all of the research addressing these questions, we can give you two quick responses:

- **Why are clinicians inferior to simple actuarial methods when interpreting assessment information?** From the beginning of this text we have emphasized that people are not very good at making subjective judgments about other people. This is behind our vigorous promotion of the use of objective assessment data to drive clinical decision making. The basis for our failure to accurately make judgments and predictions based on subjective impressions is likely the result of internal biases (e.g., halo effect, self-fulfilling prophecy) and heuristics (i.e., mental shortcuts people use to rapidly process information). For those of you interested in learning more about this topic, examine the research in cognitive psychology regarding human judgment. Grove and Meehl (1996) is a good article to start with.

- **Why do most clinicians continue to rely on subjective impressionistic approaches in light of these findings?** Grove and Meehl (1996) identified a number of reasons why clinicians have not adopted actuarial approaches for interpreting assessment information. These include:

(Continued on page 536)

SPECIAL INTEREST TOPIC 17.3 *(Continued)*

Reason 1. Fear of being replaced by a computer

Reason 2. Threat to self-concept if one acknowledges a simple regression equation is superior

Reason 3. Attachment to specific psychological theories

Reason 4. Belief that actuarial approaches dehumanize clients

Reason 5. Aversion to the idea of computers competing with humans on cognitive tasks

Reason 6. An education that did not instill a preference for scientific inquiry over subjective reasoning

The authors suggest that reason 6 is probably the major culprit! We agree this is a major contributing factor, but believe reason 1 and reason 2 are also prominent. However, this is an empirical question that should be addressed using a well-designed research design!

BE AWARE OF THE LIMITATIONS OF THE ASSESSMENT RESULTS. All assessments contain error, and some have more error than others. It is the responsibility of psychologists and other users of assessment results to be aware of the limitations of assessments and to take these limitations into consideration when interpreting and using assessment results.

CONSIDER PERSONAL FACTORS OR EXTRANEOUS EVENTS THAT MIGHT HAVE INFLUENCED TEST PERFORMANCE. This guideline holds that psychologists should be sensitive to factors that might have negatively influenced a student's performance. For example, was the examinee feeling ill or upset on the day of the assessment? Is the examinee prone to high levels of test anxiety? This guideline also extends to administrative and environmental events that might have impacted the examinee. For example, were there errors in administration that might have impacted the examinee's performance? Did any events occur during the administration that might have distracted the examinee or otherwise undermined performance? If it appears any factors compromised the examinee's performance, this should be considered when interpreting assessment results.

CONSIDER ANY DIFFERENCES BETWEEN THE NORMATIVE GROUP AND EXAMINEES OR BETWEEN THE NORMATIVE SAMPLE AND THE POPULATION TO WHICH EXAMINEES ARE COMPARED. If there are meaningful differences between the normative groups and the actual examinees, this must be taken into consideration when interpreting and using the assessment results. Likewise, if comparison to a specific population is necessary, to which the examinee might not belong, be sure the standardization sample of the test adequately reflects the population parameters on important variables.

> *It is the responsibility of psychologists to present assessments results in a timely and understandable manner.*

DISCUSS ASSESSMENT RESULTS WITH EXAMINEES IN AN EASILY UNDERSTANDABLE MANNER. In most situations, examinees have the right to receive comprehensive information about assessment results that is presented in an understandable and timely manner. Additionally, it is the psychologist's responsibility to explain to examinees any likely consequences of the

TABLE 17–5	Checklist for Interpreting, Using, and Communicating Assessment Results

1. Are assessment results used only for purposes for which they have been validated?
2. Were multiple sources and types of assessment information used when making high-stakes educational decisions?
3. Did you "stay close to the data" and minimize subjective inferences?
4. Did you take into consideration the limitations of the assessment results?
5. Have you considered personal factors or extraneous events that might have influenced test performance?
6. Are there any differences between the normative group and actual test takers that need to be considered?
7. Were results communicated in an easily understandable and timely manner?

assessments, both positive and negative. Special situations that may preclude the explanation of tests results include forensic evaluations and security screenings. In these situations psychologists must clearly explain the arrangements prior to obtaining informed consent and conducting the assessment (APA, 2002). These guidelines are summarized in Table 17–5.

RESPONSIBILITIES OF TEST TAKERS

So far we have emphasized the rights of clients and other examinees and the responsibilities of psychologists and other assessment professionals. However, the *Standards* (AERA et al., 1999) stated that test takers also have responsibilities. These responsibilities include:

EXAMINEES ARE RESPONSIBLE FOR PREPARING FOR THE ASSESSMENT. Examinees have the right to have adequate information about the nature and use of assessments. In turn, examinees are responsible for preparing for the assessment.

EXAMINEES ARE RESPONSIBLE FOR FOLLOWING THE DIRECTIONS OF THE INDIVIDUAL ADMINISTERING THE ASSESSMENT. Examinees are expected to follow the instructions provided by the individual administering the test or assessment. This includes behaviors such as showing up on time for the assessment, starting and stopping when instructed to do so, and recording responses as requested.

EXAMINEES ARE RESPONSIBLE FOR RESPONDING IN A MANNER THAT ACCURATELY REFLECTS THEIR CHARACTERISTICS AND ABILITIES. Examinees should not misrepresent themselves in an effort to look more socially acceptable or to look more pathological. In other words, they should not engage in dissimulation.

Cheating on tests is a related issue that is particularly problematic in academic settings. Cheating includes copying from another examinee, using prohibited resources (e.g., notes or other unsanctioned aids), securing stolen copies of tests, or having someone else take the test for you. Any form of dissimulation or cheating reduces the validity of the test results. Special Interest Topic 17.4 provides guidelines for teachers to help prevent cheating in their classrooms, and Special

> *Examinees should not misrepresent themselves in an effort to look more socially acceptable or to look more pathological.*

Interest Topic 17.5 alerts us that cheating is not limited to students alone, but that at times those responsible for administering tests have been guilty of compromising the assessment process.

SPECIAL INTEREST TOPIC 17.4

Steps to Prevent Student Cheating

Linn and Gronlund (2000) provided the following suggestions for teachers to help prevent cheating in their classrooms:

1. Take steps to keep the test secure before the testing date.
2. Prior to taking the test, have students clear off the top of their desks.
3. If students are allowed to use scratch paper, have them turn it in with their tests.
4. Carefully monitor the students during the test administration.
5. When possible, provide an empty row of seats between students.
6. Use two forms of the test and alternate forms when distributing (you can use the same test items, just arranged in a different order).
7. Design your tests to have good face validity (i.e., so it appears relevant and fair).
8. Foster a positive attitude toward tests by emphasizing how assessments benefit students (e.g., students learn what they have and have not mastered—a fair way of assigning grades).

IN GROUP TESTING SITUATIONS, EXAMINEES ARE RESPONSIBLE FOR NOT INTERFERING WITH THE PERFORMANCE OF OTHER EXAMINEES. Examinees should refrain from any activity that might be distracting to other examinees.

EXAMINEES ARE RESPONSIBLE FOR INFORMING THE PSYCHOLOGIST OR OTHER PROFESSIONAL IF THEY BELIEVE THE ASSESSMENT RESULTS DO NOT ADEQUATELY REPRESENT THEIR TRUE ABILITIES. If, for any reason an examinee feels that the assessment results do not adequately represent their actual abilities, they should inform the psychologist. This should be done as soon as possible so the psychologist can take appropriate actions.

EXAMINEES SHOULD RESPECT THE COPYRIGHT RIGHTS OF TEST PUBLISHERS. Examinees should not be allowed to make copies or in any other way reproduce assessment materials.

EXAMINEES SHOULD NOT DISCLOSE INFORMATION ABOUT THE CONTENTS OF A TEST. In addition to not making copies of an assessment, psychologists should refrain from divulging in any other manner information about the contents of a test. For example, they should not give other examinees information about what to expect on a test. Again, this is an issue of test security! These guidelines are summarized in Table 17–6.

TABLE 17–6 Responsibilities of Test Takers

1. Examinees are responsible for preparing for the assessment.
2. Examinees are responsible for following the directions of the individual administering the assessment.
3. Examinees are responsible for responding in a manner that accurately reflects their characteristics and abilities.
4. In group testing situations, examinees are responsible for not interfering with the performance of other test takers.
5. Examinees are responsible for informing the psychologist if they believe the assessment results do not adequately represent their true abilities.
6. Examinees should respect the copyright rights of test publishers.
7. Examinees should not disclose information about the contents of a test.

SPECIAL INTEREST TOPIC 17.5

Teachers Cheating?

Over 50 New York City educators may lose their job after an independent auditor produced evidence that they helped students cheat on state tests.
—Hoff, 1999

State officials charge that 71 Michigan schools might have cheated on state tests.
—Keller, 2001

Georgia education officials suspend state tests after 270 actual test questions were posted on an Internet site that was accessible to students, teachers, and parents.
—Olson, 2003

Cizek (1998) noted that the abuse of standardized assessments by educators has become a national scandal. With the advent of high-stakes assessments it should not be surprising that some educators would be inclined to cheat. With one's salary and possibly one's future employment riding on how students perform on state-mandated achievement tests, the pressure to ensure that those students perform well may override ethical and legal concerns for some people. Cannell (1988, 1989) was among the first to bring abusive test practices to the attention on the public. Cannell revealed that by using outdated versions of norm-referenced assessments, being lax with test security, and engaging in inappropriate test preparation practices all 50 states were able to report that their students were above the national average (this came to be referred to as the Lake Wobegon phenomenon). Other common "tricks" that have been employed by educators to inflate scores include using the same form of a test for a long period of time so that teachers could become familiar with the content; encouraging low-achieving students to skip school on the day of the test; selectively removing answer sheets of low-performing students; and excluding limited English proficiency and special education students from assessments (Cizek, 1998).

Don't be fooled into thinking that these unethical practices are limited to top administrators trying to make their schools look good; they also involve classroom teachers. Cizek (1998) reported that there are a number of recent cases where principals or other administrators have encouraged teachers to cheat by having students practice on the actual test items, and in some cases even erasing and correcting wrong responses on answer sheets. Other unethical assessment practices engaged in by teachers included providing hints to the correct answer, reading questions that the students are supposed to read, answering questions about test content, rephrasing test questions, and sometimes simply giving the students the answers to items. Gay (1990) reported that 35% of the teachers responding to a survey had either witnessed or engaged in unethical assessment practices. The unethical behaviors included changing incorrect answers, revealing the correct answer, providing extra time, allowing the use of inappropriate aids (e.g., dictionaries), and using the actual test items when preparing students for the test.

Just because other professionals are engaging in unethical behavior does not make it right. Cheating by administrators, teachers, or students undermines the validity of the assessment results. If you need any additional incentive to avoid unethical test practices, be warned that the test publishers are watching! The states and other publishers of standardized tests have a vested interest in maintaining the validity of their assessments. As a result, they are continually scanning the results for evidence of cheating. For example, Cizek (1998) stated that unethical educators have been identified as the result of fairly obvious clues such as ordering an excessive number of blank answer sheets or a disproportionate number of erasures, to more subtle clues such as unusual patterns of increased scores. The fact is, educators who cheat are being caught and punished, and the punishment may include the loss of one's job and license to teach!

Summary and Top 10 Assessment-Related Behaviors to Avoid

In this chapter we discussed psychologists' responsibility to ensure that the assessments they use are developed, administered, scored, and interpreted in a technically, ethically, and legally sound manner. We are sometimes asked, "Now that you have told us what we should do, what are the most important things we should avoid?" To that end, here is our list of 10 assessment-related behaviors that should be avoided.

1. Don't use assessments that produce poor-quality data or scores (e.g., unreliable data, data that lack relevant validity evidence, inadequate normative data).

2. Don't use assessments that you are not qualified to administer, score, and interpret.

3. Don't base high-stakes decisions on the results of a single assessment.

4. Don't let your personal preferences and biases impact the scoring of assessments.

5. Don't breach confidentiality regarding assessment information.

6. Don't use technical jargon without a clear, commonsense explanation when reporting the results of assessments.

7. Don't ignore the special assessment needs of persons with disabilities or diverse linguistic/cultural backgrounds.

8. Don't breach test security.

9. Don't make changes to standardized materials or to administration procedures without validation work indicating how these changes affect performance.

10. Don't assume that because an "expert" (you included) made up a set of test questions, they will work as intended—always collect evidence to support test applications.

Key Terms and Concepts

Informed consent, 530   Table of specifications (TOS),   524

Recommended Reading

American Educational Research Association, American Psychological Association, & National Council on Measurement in Education (1999). *Standards for educational and psychological testing.* Washington, DC: AERA. This is *the* source for technical information on the development and use of tests in educational and psychological settings.

Internet Sites of Interest

In addition to the Standards (AERA et al., 1999), the following resources are useful references:

http://www.nanonline.org/NAN/home/home.aspx
(1) The use, education, training and supervision of neuropsychological test technicians (psychometrists) in clinical practice. This site provides access to the Official Statement of the National Academy of Neuropsychology.

http://www.apa.org/
This site of the American Psychological Association includes a link to the Rights and Responsibilities of Test Takers: Guidelines and Expectations.

Chapter Eighteen

How to Develop a Psychological Test
A Practical Approach

We have oft heard it said there are 3 things you should not watch being made: Laws, sausage, and psychological tests!

Learning Objectives

After reading and studying this chapter, students should be able to:

1. Describe the process of developing a psychological test.
2. Understand the sequence of steps in designing and developing a psychological test.
3. Describe the importance of construct definition.
4. Explain the difference between conceptual and operational definitions of constructs.
5. Describe different types of common dissimulation scales and the purpose of each.
6. Design a table of specifications or blueprint for test content.
7. Describe the factors to consider in choosing a normative or standardization sample for a test.
8. Describe the factors to consider when choosing a type of score for a test.
9. Describe necessary reliability and validity studies for a new measure.
10. Draft a proposal for the development of a psychological test.
11. Carry out the plan for developing a new psychological test.

541

This chapter presents a practical approach to developing tests in the context of a general model that will apply to most types of tests. Some tests, such as those for employment, will have a few extra steps involved to satisfy certain legal criteria regarding their usage; however, you can learn about these if you go forward in the field of psychology as you begin to specialize. The chapter emphasizes the development of a strategic plan for test development over the day-to-day nuts and bolts of actually carrying out the plan—implementation of your plan will vary greatly depending on the setting and the level of support you have available. However, our experience is that a strong, detailed plan leads to successful development. After all, would you expect a contactor to build a skyscraper without a blueprint? A careful plan must come first.

The validity of test score interpretations is ultimately the crux of quality of any test, and ensuring the validity of those interpretations begins when you begin the process of test development. This approach to test development is derived from the experiences of the authors of this text in actual commercial test development and from the practices of multiple test publishers of various sizes around the world and does not reflect a pure model of any one company's approach. Neither is this approach purely psychometric nor idealized, but stems from our desire for you to understand how psychological tests are typically developed, when done well. We have chosen to focus on how commercial products are designed and implemented because commercial tests are by far the most likely tests you will encounter beyond classroom, teacher-made tests. However, this model also serves well those desiring to develop a test for limited research applications, but on a smaller scale of implementation.

To facilitate our presentation of this model we have separated the steps into four broad phases or stages: (1) test conceptualization, (2) specification of test structure and format, (3) planning standardization and psychometric studies, and (4) plan implementation. The first phase, test conceptualization, is designed to give you and others who may be working with you (test development is always a team effort) as much clarity as possible as to the nature of the test and what it is intended to measure as well as why and how it might be used. This knowledge will drive many of the later aspects of the design, as you will see. Table 18–1 provides an outline for this first phase of the test development process. For a practical guide to the day-to-day aspects of carrying out such a plan, we recommend a chapter by Gary Robertson (2003), who was for many years in charge of developing and carrying out such plans for several major publishers and who generously has shared his expertise and experiences with the profession.

PHASE I: TEST CONCEPTUALIZATION

Conduct a Review of Literature and Develop a Statement of Need for the Test

In developing a psychological or educational test, one first begins by identifying a need. This should include specifying the construct you want to measure and establishing that there is a need

TABLE 18–1	Phase I: Steps in Test Conceptualization
1.	Conduct a review of literature and develop a statement of need for the test.
2.	Describe the proposed uses and interpretations of results from the test.
3.	Decide who will use the test and why (including a statement of user qualifications).
4.	Develop conceptual and operational definitions of constructs you intend to measure.
5.	Determine whether measures of dissimulation are needed and, if so, what kind.

for a new way to measure it. There are literally thousands of psychological and educational tests available commercially. As many or more (no one is sure how many) measures are published in journal articles or on the Internet and designed for narrow or highly specific

> *Test development begins with defining a need in the profession.*

applications. Therefore the first task of the test developer is to identify a need in the field. As psychology and education progress as sciences, new constructs are specified and old constructs are modified. For example, intelligence was once measured via simple reaction time and measurements of sensory acuity. Next, knowledge became more important in the definitions of intelligence and informational items became more prominent among intelligence tests. Now, most intelligence tests emphasize problem solving, and do so in two domains (some more): crystallized intelligence, which is the application of knowledge to problem solving, and fluid intelligence, which is the ability to solve problems that are novel wherein no prior knowledge is required. So even though each era has seen the development and promulgation of many intelligence tests, the tests have changed as our thinking about intelligence has changed—some tests were revised and made modern in this sense whereas others simply could not be updated to current thinking and were put out of print. Entirely new tests of intelligence also were developed along the way to coincide with modern theories of intelligence. This same process occurs in areas such as personality, psychopathology, and even academic achievement as the curricula of schools change as well and tests must be created to follow curricula requirements.

At times, a clinician or researcher will have a need to measure a variable that is well defined and for which tests are available, but the quality of the available tests is suspect or the psychometric qualities of the test are simply outdated as reported in the test manual or relevant literature. In such instances, a test developer may decide to pursue the development of "a better mousetrap." As technology and theory advance in psychology, we also develop better or more exacting methods of measuring a construct via different methods or approaches or even items that were not available or feasible in earlier years, again leading one to devise an improved means of measuring a variable of interest. Measures of reaction time were once done via human observation and recording with a stopwatch. This is certainly crude compared to computer-controlled stimulus presentation and very accurate electronic measurement in milliseconds that are now commonplace in such research.

Tests may assess clinically useful constructs as well but be impractical for real-world clinical application. The concept of sensation-seeking is a good example. Known in the research literature for many decades and believed to be of clinical interest with adolescents as well as with adult offender populations in particular, the early measures of sensation-seeking were quite long and cumbersome although they measured the construct well. However, sensation-seeking was not widely assessed in clinical practice until the 1990s when Reynolds and Kamphaus (1992, 2004) devised a rapid, reliable measure of sensation-seeking that made the construct practical for application in clinical work with adolescents.

Standardization samples also may become dated and inapplicable to current examinees, and a test author or developer may have lost interest in updating and revising such a test, creating another opportunity for test development if there remains a need for measuring the constructs in question.

> *Measurement is a set of rules for assigning numbers to objects, events, or behaviors.*

New constructs are sometimes defined in the fields of psychology and education as well. When this happens, the constructs are usually derived from theoretical observations and then must be studied and manipulated to be understood. To be studied, such constructs must be measured. And, measurement requires a set of rules for assigning numerical values to some observation—as you recall, that is essentially our definition of a test as a tool, a means of deriving numerical values to assign to observations of a construct or activity. Thus there are always needs for new testing instruments in our field, whether it is to modernize existing instruments or to measure new constructs. Test developers and researchers can conduct very detailed and comprehensive electronic literature searches for research on almost any psychological construct and easily determine what instruments, if any, may be available for assessing a construct. These instruments can then be gathered and reviewed for quality and applicability. Only after such a review can need truly be determined. In addressing the question of need, we always like to ask: (1) Will the test I am considering developing improve practice or research in some area? (2) Will it enhance the human condition or our understanding of it?

Describe the Proposed Uses and Interpretations of Results From the Test

Once you have identified the need for a new test to measure a construct, you should describe the proposed uses and interpretations of the results. That is, assuming the test is well developed, how would it be used? In what settings and for what purposes would this instrument be employed? Once a user has the results of the test in hand, what purposes will have been served and what interpretations of these results are likely to be made?

The answers to these questions should flow logically from the preceding step. If you find them difficult to answer, there is a very good chance your conceptualization of the test and very likely the constructs you intend to measure are too vague at this point and you should return to step 1 and develop your ideas and conceptualization in more detail before proceeding.

Knowing how and in what setting a test may be used is crucial to many aspects of its development. For example, there are many omnibus personality tests available but they tend to emphasize different aspects of personality, emotion, and affect. Some emphasize normal personality and some emphasize psychopathological states. The setting (e.g., a psychiatric hospital vs. employee selection) and intended use of the results will dictate different content as well as interpretive schemes.

It is common now for many public and private agencies, including the U.S. military, to conduct some form of personality screening for the hiring of public safety officers such as police, armed security forces, or even loss prevention specialists in department stores (who often dress as shoppers and simply roam the store watching for shoplifters and alerting security when thefts are observed). Tests designed specifically to assist in the selection of people who are likely to be happy and successful in such jobs and to work well with the public when in positions of authority appear on the surface to be highly similar to tests designed to diagnose psychopathology. However, during the development process, such tests are carefully scrutinized for items that are illegal to ask in preemployment screening and they emphasize normal range variations in personality traits over psychopathology in an attempt to match the responses of job applicants to those of prior employees who were very successful in the same job. Knowing the setting and purpose to which a test will be put, then, influences the proper response to all the remaining factors in the chapter—from who is the likely user of the test, to the proper normative sample, to the types of validity studies that must be done to validate the proposed interpretations of the scores.

Determine Who Will Use the Test and Why

Tests should be designed with specific users in mind. Here we refer to individuals who perform specific functions that are facilitated by the use of psychological and/or educational tests as well as to the types of formal academic training and supervised experiences

> *Know whom you expect to use a test before it is developed.*

(if any) that might be required of users to apply test results appropriately. For most clinical tests, licensure and certification requirements are in place in various state laws restricting the use of tests to certain classes of professionals such as psychologists. However, these requirements vary a great deal from state to state. Many test manuals will devote a brief section to the description of test user qualifications. Table 18–2 presents an example of the user qualifications statement for the Behavior Assessment System for Children—Second Edition (BASC-2; Reynolds & Kamphaus, 2004). You will see how the authors dealt with the variability in licensure and certification issues in this statement by relying more on formal academic training and supervised experience for use of the BASC-2, both of which are considered crucial because the test is used so widely in clinical diagnosis and in eligibility determination. The authors relied more on competencies expected of individuals with such training than job titles. We think the inclusion of such a section that explains the expectations of the test makers (the authors and the publisher) for training those who would use the test should be included in all test manuals.

It is also helpful at this stage to determine which individuals in what settings are most likely to find the proposed test helpful in their roles. Hopefully this flows directly from the purpose of the test and the proposed interpretations of the results of the test. If the purpose of the test is to diagnose the presence of a clinical condition such as pediatric bipolar disorder, the targeted user will most likely be a clinical or pediatric psychologist or perhaps even a psychiatrist. However, a test being designed to screen large numbers of children to see if they have elevated risk levels for

TABLE 18–2	Example of a Test Manual's User Qualifications Section

Individuals using the Behavior Assessment System for Children-2 (BASC-2) interpret its various components and use them in the evaluation, diagnosis, and treatment of developmental, learning, and behavioral disorders. Users are expected to have completed a recognized graduate-level training program in psychology; to have received formal academic training in the administration, scoring, and interpretation of behavior rating scales and personality scales; and to have received supervised experience with such instruments. Most clinical, school, pediatric, counseling, neuro-, and applied developmental psychologists will have received such training. Administration and scoring of the various BASC-2 components may, with appropriate training and supervision, be completed by clerical staff.

Because of the wide variability across jurisdictions in certification requirements and the use of professional titles, it is not possible to determine solely by title, licensure, or certification who is qualified to use the BASC-2. Consistent with the principles presented in the *Standards for Educational and Psychological Testing* (American Educational Research Association [AERA], American Psychological Association [APA], & National Council on Measurement in Education [NCME], 1999), each individual practitioner must decide whether his or her formal academic training and supervised experience provide the necessary background and knowledge to use and interpret the BASC-2 appropriately. A variety of other professionally trained or certified staff (e.g., psychometrists, educational diagnosticians, clinical social workers, psychiatrists, and pediatricians) might have received the necessary formal academic training and supervised experience to use instruments such as the BASC-2.

Source: Behavior Assessment System for Children, Second Edition (BASC-2). Copyright © 2004 NCS Pearson, Inc. Reproduced with permission. All rights reserved. "BASC" is a trademark, in the US and/or other countries, of Pearson Education, Inc. or its affiliates(s).

emotional and behavior disorders and to determine whether a follow-up evaluation of their mental health or behavioral or emotional status is warranted, might be designed so that it can be administered and scored by a teacher or a mental health aide or even a nurse. Knowing the anticipated user will result in design changes, particularly related to the complexity of the test's administration, scoring, and interpretation because different classes of test users will have different skill levels.

Develop Conceptual and Operational Definitions of Constructs You Intend to Measure

Often we think we understand the meaning of constructs such as depression, anxiety, crystallized intelligence, fluid intelligence, aggression, agreeableness, and the like until we try to put them into words and realize we are not as clear as we thought. Putting them into words ensures we understand them and that others can see our intended meaning—which is very important to measurement because, often, people understand or interpret construct names differently. Frequently we find our first attempts at writing a definition of a construct we think we understand quite well to be awkward, and several rewrites are usually necessary. Writing a clear description of what we intend to measure also forces us to clarify to ourselves what we intend to measure so that we can explain it more clearly to others. Having such definitions in mind and on documents to which we can refer throughout the test development process also helps us in item writing and in item selection as well as in test score interpretation later in the process. We recommend writing two types of definitions—a *conceptual* one and an *operational* one.

A conceptual definition explains our construct at a theoretical level and may use many interpretive words. An operational definition tells others exactly how our test will define or measure the construct. This is better illustrated through example. Let's consider the common psychological term *depression.*

> *A possible conceptual definition might read:* Depression is a state of melancholy, sadness, and low energy levels that leads to anhedonia, feelings of worthlessness, and chronic fatigue.

> *An operational definition might read:* On the Student's Rating Scale of Depression, depression will be assessed by summing ratings in the scored direction on observations of behavior such as expressions of feelings of sadness, feelings of loneliness, of being misunderstood, and being not liked, a lack of engagement in pleasurable activities, too much or too little sleep, teariness at inappropriate times, and complaints of fatigue.

So, a conceptual definition tells what it is you want to measure in the abstract, and the operational definition tells more directly and specifically how the construct score will be derived. Some may find these efforts tedious for scales that have many constructs; however, the more constructs that are present on a test, the more we find such a process useful.

Determine Whether Measures of Dissimulation Are Needed and, If So, What Kind

Dissimulation is the presentation of oneself in a manner that is different from how you really are—presenting yourself though a disguise of sorts or under pretense. Persons who engage in dissimulation present themselves in ways that are dissimilar from how they really are. For example, if you are feeling very sad but do not want to admit it to others, you might respond falsely to a personality test question such as "I feel sad" to conceal your feelings from others. It is also possible for you to engage in dissimulation of others if you are completing a rating scale about another person such as your child, spouse, or an elderly parent.

> ***Dissimulation means presenting oneself in a disguise or under pretense.***

Why do people engage in dissimulation? There are many reasons. People will deny symptoms on an assessment of personality or psychopathology because they do not want to be seen as having what they consider to be undesirable traits, or do not want to admit to behaviors others may find unacceptable. This phenomenon occurs even among people seeking treatment! In employment settings, it is not uncommon for job applicants to try and answer the questions in the way they think is most likely to get them the job they are seeking.

People will also endorse the presence of symptoms they do not have to make themselves look far more impaired than is actually the case. This occurs for a variety of reasons and is termed *malingering*, when they have something to gain by making such a false presentation. For example, people may fake personality and behavior problems as well as cognitive deficits to obtain disability benefits, to enhance damage rewards in lawsuits over a personal injury, or to avoid punishments such as prosecution for crimes they may have committed. In the case of cognitive assessments, the evaluation of the possibility of dissimulation is often accomplished through effort testing—that is, giving tests that are easily accomplished by nearly anyone as long as the person tries to complete the task accurately. Effort testing is recommended in nearly all forensic matters and whenever a patient has something to gain by feigning cognitive deficits (Bush et al., 2005).

Exaggerated endorsement of problems may occur at times when a person actually is experiencing a great deal of intrapsychic pain as well and wants to be sure to get the clinician's attention. Teachers sometimes endorse emotional and behavioral problems in more extreme ways than are present in a student when completing behavior rating scales to get the attention of the school psychologist and to obtain help as soon as possible in managing the student's behavior.

Dissimulation can take many forms and sometimes you will see more specific definitions of certain types of dissimulation. For example, Bush and colleagues (2005, p. 420) offered the following definitions of terms, all of which can come under the more general umbrella of dissimulation:

Symptom validity: the accuracy or truthfulness of the examinee's behavioral presentation (signs), self-reported symptoms (including cause and course), or performance.

Response bias: an attempt to mislead the examiner through inaccurate or incomplete responses or effort.

Effort: investment in performing at capacity levels. Although often not specified in discussions of *effort testing*, this term refers to the examinee's effort to perform well—that is, to *pass* an effort test is to do well on the test.

Malingering: the intentional production of false or exaggerated symptoms, motivated by external incentives. Although symptom validity tests are commonly referred to as *malingering tests*, malingering is just one possible cause of invalid performance.

Dissimulation: the intentional misrepresentation or falsification of symptoms, by overrepresentation or underrepresentation of a true set of symptoms in an attempt to appear dissimilar from one's true state.

If you understand the purpose of your test as well as who will be using it and in what circumstances, you will then know if you need to include scales to detect dissimulation of various types. The field of psychology has expended great effort over the years to develop sophisticated means of detecting dissimulation, and we will now turn to an explanation of the most common methods.

SCALES FOR DETECTING DISSIMULATION ON ASSESSMENTS OF PERSONALITY AND BEHAVIOR. The most common scales of dissimulation (also known commonly as validity scales) on measures of personality and behavior are F-scales, L-scales, and inconsistency indexes. These are briefly described here:

> *Dissimulation scales are often referred to as validity scales.*

F-Scales. F-scales are also known as Infrequency scales and are sometimes referred to as "Fake Bad" scales. The latter usage is because F-scales are designed to detect exaggerated symptom presentation. Infrequency or F-scales are designed by including special items or taking extreme responses to traditional items that are very seldom endorsed as present even in persons with significant levels of psychopathology (hence the name Infrequency Scale) and that do not cluster together well enough to form a coherent construct. F-scales then consist of infrequently endorsed symptom levels (even among patient populations) that have a low average intercorrelation (i.e., they are poorly associated with one another so that when an examinee indicates the presence of a large number of unrelated symptoms, it indicates an exaggerated presentation of psychopathology). The responses of the standardization sample are then evaluated and the distribution of the total item score across a set of infrequently endorsed items is examined to set a cutoff level that indicates a high probability of a false presentation that is negative in nature.

L-Scales. L-scales are often termed Social Desirability scales. They are also referred to as "Fake Good" scales. The name L-scale comes from the original name of these scales—Lie scales, a term now seen as pejorative and considered archaic. L-scales are designed to detect the inaccurate denial of symptoms that are really present, detecting the opposite response bias of the F-scale. L-scales typically are determined by including special items along with extreme responses to traditional items that reflect commonplace flaws that nearly everyone experiences at some time. For example, on an item that reads "I have feelings of sadness," a person who wants to deny symptoms might respond with *Never*. Because at least occasional feelings of sadness are a common human experience, such a response would earn the examinee a point on the L-scale. No single item response will get someone tagged as engaging in dissimulation; rather it is the cumulative response pattern that is examined just as with the F-scale.

Inconsistency Scales. Inconsistency scales are designed to detect inconsistencies in responses to item stems on personality and behavior scales. When a respondent is not consistent in responding to similar items, the results are not considered to be reliable. One reason for inconsistent responding may be dissimulation, but other reasons are plausible in many cases as well. For example, a respondent who is having difficulty understanding or reading the questions may produce an elevated score on an Inconsistency scale. Inconsistency scales are derived by examining first the correlation matrix of all the items on a test to see which items are the most similar in terms of their response patterns—that is, if we know the answer to one item, does it predict well the answer to another item? Items are then chosen in pairs for the Inconsistency scale by choosing items that correlate highly with one another and that have similar content. Once the item pairs are chosen, the scores on each item in the pairs are subtracted to create a difference score for each pair of items. These difference scores are converted to their absolute values and then summed. Next, the standardization sample data are examined to find the distribution of the difference in scores between each item in each pair to establish a cutoff for inconsistency in responding.

For certain types of tests, it may be useful to derive other dissimulation scales for special purposes. It is common when developing measures for selection of public safety personnel, for example, to include more advanced and subtle indicators of response biases because this applicant pool tends to deny most common problems and to minimize any emotional discord they may experience when responding to personality tests.

Although not measures of dissimulation, test authors sometimes also include scales that look at the comprehension of the items and cooperation level of the examinee on self-report and rating scales. These scales go by various names and are sometimes simply referred to as a V-scale or Validity Scale. These scales typically contain nonsensical items where the answer is the same for everyone who takes the test seriously, cooperates with the exam process, and can comprehend the items. For example, one of the items on a V-scale might be "I drink at least 100 glasses of water every day." Of course, no one does this, so anyone who answers yes or true to such an item most likely is either not cooperating with the evaluation process or cannot comprehend the items on the test. A V-scale will contain multiple items to ensure against false positives because anyone can mark one item incorrectly by mistake. Such scales might be considered "effort testing" for personality and behavior rating scales.

SCALES FOR DETECTING DISSIMULATION ON ASSESSMENTS OF APTITUDE AND ACHIEVEMENT. As we have noted, some individuals will not make an effort to do well on tests of aptitude or achievement for reasons of gain and such a lack of effort is commonly seen as malingering, though other reasons are plausible. For example, individuals with a traumatic injury to certain locations in the frontal regions of the brain may have as a symptom of their injury amotivational syndrome—a disorder that causes them to have difficulty putting forth good effort and recognizing when effort is needed to succeed.

Few cognitive measures have built-in measures of dissimulation or lack of effort. (We do not worry about people faking good on such performance measures because you cannot be smarter than you really are!) However, some do build in scales or items to detect lack of effort. Most often, malingering on cognitive measures is evaluated by assessing the following (Bush et al., 2005):

- Performance patterns on ability measures indicative of invalid responding
- Inconsistencies between test results and known patterns of brain functioning
- Inconsistencies between test results and observed behavior
- Inconsistencies between test results and reliable collateral reports
- Inconsistency between test results and documented background information

Built-in scales for detecting effort can also be useful when they have been demonstrated empirically to reflect a lack of effort. For example, on the Test of Memory and Learning—Second edition (Reynolds & Voress, 2007) one of the subtests contains sets of word pairs an examinee has to recall. The examiner reads a list of word pairs and then gives the examinee one of the words from the pair, and the examinee is to recall the other word in the pair. Half of the word pairs on the list are extremely easy, however, and it is rare for anyone, even very young children, to respond incorrectly on the "easy pairs." On some measures, such as parts of the Halstead-Reitan Neuropsychological Test Battery, an early item set is presented to teach the examinee how to respond to the test in question. It is rare for anyone, even those with significant brain injuries, to respond incorrectly to more than one or two of these types of items if the person is truly attempting to do them accurately.

Often in the cognitive domains, however, there are entire tests devoted to detection of lack of effort or malingering. The two most popular such methods are Symptom Validity Tests and Forced-Choice Tests. These types of tasks also may be built in to a larger test battery.

Symptom Validity Tests (SVTs). Symptom validity tests (SVTs) are tests that are designed to look very difficult but are in fact very easy and on which most people who put forth effort to succeed do so. The instructions for such tests are also important on occasion as they will tell the examinee that the task is going to be quite hard and not to be upset if he or she cannot perform well. For example, one such test presents an examinee with 15 items to memorize in only 10 seconds. As part of the instructions, the examinee is told he or she is about to take a memory test that is very difficult because he or she will be asked to memorize 15 things on a page but will have only 10 seconds to do so. However, the items for memorization are logically related in such a way they are very easy to memorize in even less than the allotted time, and it is rare that anyone putting forth reasonable effort does not recall 10 or 11 of the stimuli, and most people recall all 15 correctly. On such SVTs, performance below established cut-off scores (on one or more well-validated tests designed to measure exaggeration or fabrication of cognitive deficits) suggests insufficient effort to do well.

> *Symptom validity tests are tests designed to look very difficult but that are in fact very easy.*

Forced-Choice Tests. Forced-choice tests as measures of malingering are simply multiple-choice tests that may be true–false, yes–no, or with more possible responses. If we know the number of choices per item and the number of items, we can calculate the chance level of responding. For example, on a 40-item 4-choice multiple-choice test, a person who knew none of the answers should get about 10 items correct. We know how often such a person would get 5, 6, 7, or other numbers correct purely by chance alone. If the number correct deviates below chance at a significant level on forced-choice tests we know that either the person is extremely unlucky or he or she actually knew the correct answers and responded incorrectly to look impaired. One of the authors of this text (CRR) in a forensic examination some years ago gave such a test to an examinee claiming a particular brain injury—on this 40-item, 4-choice multiple-choice test, the examinee earned a raw score of zero. The odds of this happening are extremely low on a chance basis and the best explanation of this low level of performance was that the examinee did in fact know the answers but chose to respond incorrectly. Performance on one or more forced-choice measures of cognitive functioning that falls below chance to a statistically significant degree typically is interpreted to indicate biased responding.

PHASE II: SPECIFICATION OF TEST STRUCTURE AND FORMAT

During this phase of test development the author should prepare a detailed description of the proposed test and the testing materials. Table 18–3 provides an outline of the numerous steps to be completed during this phase.

TABLE 18–3	Phase II: Specification of Test Structure and Format

During this phase the goal is to clearly describe the proposed test, including information on the following:

1. Age range appropriate for this measure
2. Testing format (e.g., individual or group; print or computerized); who will complete the test (e.g., the examiner, the examinee, or some other informant)
3. The structure of the test (e.g., subscales, composite scores, etc.) and how the items and subscales (if any) will be organized
4. Written table of specifications
5. Item formats (given by subtests or subscales if any, with sample items illustrating ideal items) and a summary of instructions for administration and scoring
   a. Indicate the likely number of items required for each subtest or scale.
   b. Indicate the type of medium required for each test (e.g., verbal cue, visual cue, physically manipulated objects or puzzle parts, etc.).
6. Written explanation of methods for item development (how items will be determined—will you need content experts to help write or review items?), tryout, and final item selection

Designate the Age Range Appropriate for the Measure

Be sure to determine the appropriate age range for the assessment at the very beginning of the test description. The age of the examinees for whom the test is intended will also dictate a variety of design features. Young children, for example, cannot perform some tasks that older children can perform and need more interaction with an examiner. Tests that require the child to read and respond to test items (unless it is a test of reading) do not work very well before the age of 8 or 9 years. Tests for elderly individuals that require rapid motor responses or good coordination skills (unless measuring these factors is the purpose of the test) usually are not a good idea and will confound the interpretation of the test results. Younger as well as older examinees also may require more time for testing, and bonus points for quick performance are often a poor idea for tests with these populations.

Determine and Describe the Testing Format

The first key consideration here is to determine whether the test will be administered only to individuals by an examiner or whether groups of people can be tested with minimal examiner interaction. (A test designed for group administration typically can be administered to individuals as well.) Will the test be presented in a print or computerized format? Who will actually complete the test or answer sheet? Will it be the examiner, the examinee, or some other third-party informant such as occurs with behavior rating scales?

Describe the Structure of the Test

Will the test yield only one score as a sum of all of the item responses or will it need to be broken into subscales? The structure of the test most often is dictated by the constructs you intend to measure, so the definitions you have written are quite important to consult in making this determination. If there are subscales or subtests then will there also be composite scores that provide summary indexes of the subtest groupings? Explain how the items and subscales (if any) will be organized and if it is not clearly apparent from your rationale for the test and discussion of the underlying constructs, it is important to address why this specific organization of the items and subtests is the most appropriate (recognizing, of course, that research you conduct during the test development process may result in alterations to your intended structure if dictated by the actual data).

Develop a Table of Specifications (TOS)

The content of tests should emphasize what was emphasized in the definitions of constructs. The method of ensuring congruence among the construct definitions, operational definitions, and test content is the development and application of a table of specifications (TOS), which is also referred to as a test blueprint. Traditionally a TOS is developed for measures of achievement to ensure congruence with a curriculum or field of study in which academic accomplishment is to be assessed. An example is given in Table 18–4. The column on the left, labeled "Content Areas," lists the major content areas to be covered in the test. These content areas are derived by carefully reviewing the educational objectives and selecting major content areas to be included in the test. Across the top of the two-way table we list the levels of Bloom's cognitive taxonomy (see Special Interest Topic 18.1 for a brief description of Bloom's Taxonomy). The inclusion of this section encourages us to consider the complexity of the cognitive processes we want to measure. There is a tendency for authors to rely heavily on lower level processes (e.g., rote memory) in achievement tests in particular and to underemphasize higher level cognitive processes. By incorporating these categories in our TOS we are reminded to incorporate a wider range of cognitive processes into our tests.

> *A table of specifications is a blueprint to the content of the test.*

The numbers in the body of the table reflect the number of items to be devoted to assessing each content area at each cognitive taxonomic level. Table 18–4 depicts specifications for a 30-item test. If you examine the first content area (Scales of measurement) you see that two knowledge-level items, two comprehension-level items, and two analysis-level items will be devoted to assessing this content area. The next content area (Measures of central tendency) will be assessed by three knowledge-level items and three comprehension-level items. The number of items dedicated to assessing each objective should reflect the importance of the objective in the curriculum and how much instructional time was devoted to it. In our TOS, we determined

TABLE 18–4	Table of Specifications for a Test on a Chapter on Basic Statistics (Number of Items by Content Area and Level of Objective)						
Content Areas	**Level of Objective**						
	Knowledge	**Comprehension**	**Application**	**Analysis**	**Synthesis**	**Evaluation**	**Total**
Scales of measurement	2	2		2			6
Measures of central tendency	3	3					6
Measures of variability	3	3	3				9
Correlation and regression	2	3		2	2		9

SPECIAL INTEREST TOPIC 18.1

Bloom's Taxonomy of Cognitive Objectives

Bloom, Englehart, Furst, Hill, and Krathwohl (1956) developed a taxonomy of cognitive objectives that is commonly referred to as "Bloom's Taxonomy." This taxonomy provides a useful way of describing the complexity of an objective by classifying it into one of six hierarchical categories ranging from the most simple to the most complex. These categories are briefly described as follows.

Knowledge

The simplest level of the taxonomy is *knowledge.* Objectives at the knowledge level involve learning or memorizing specific facts, terms, names, dates, and so on. Examples of educational objectives in the knowledge category include:

- *The student will be able to name each state capital.*
- *The student will be able to list U.S. presidents in the order they served.*

Comprehension

Objectives at the comprehension level require understanding, not simply rote memorization. Objectives at this level often use verbs such as *interpret, translate, explain,* or *summarize.* Examples of educational objectives at the comprehension level include:

- *The student will be able to describe the use of each symbol on a U.S. Geographical Survey map.*
- *The student will be able to explain how interest rates affect unemployment.*

Application

Objectives at the application level involve the use of general rules, principles, or abstract concepts to solve a problem not previously encountered. Examples of objectives at the application level include:

- *The student will be able to write directions for traveling by numbered roads from any city on a map to any other city.*
- *The student will be able to apply multiplication and division of double digits in applied math problems.*

Analysis

Objectives at the analysis level require the student to reduce or break down a complex concept into its basic parts or elements in a manner that illustrates the relationship of parts to whole. Examples of educational objectives at this level include:

- *The student will describe maps in terms of function and form.*
- *The student will distinguish the different approaches to establishing validity and illustrate their relationship to each other.*

Synthesis

Objectives at the synthesis level require the student to blend existing elements in such a way that they form new structures or patterns. Examples of objectives at the synthesis level include:

- *The student will construct a map of a hypothetical country with given characteristics.*
- *The student will propose a viable plan for establishing the validity of an assessment instrument following the guidelines presented in the Standards for Psychological and Educational Testing (AERA et al., 1999).*

(Continued on page 554)

SPECIAL INTEREST TOPIC 18.1 *(Continued)*

Evaluation

Objectives at the evaluation level require the student to make evaluative judgments regarding the quality, value, or worth of something for a stated purpose. Examples of objectives at the evaluation level include:

- *The student will evaluate the usefulness of a map to enable him/her to travel from one place to another.*
- *The student will judge the quality of validity evidence for a specified assessment instrument.*

Although somewhat dated, we believe Bloom's Taxonomy is helpful because it presents a framework that reminds test developers to include items reflecting more complex educational objectives in their tests. This is not to imply that lower level objectives are trivial and should be ignored. For each objective in your curriculum you must decide at what level you expect students to perform. In a brief introduction to a topic it may be sufficient to expect only knowledge and comprehension of major concepts. In a more detailed study of a topic higher, more complex levels of mastery will typically be required. However, it is often not possible to master high-level objectives without first having mastered low-level objectives. We strongly encourage the development of higher level objectives, but it is not realistic to require high-level mastery of everything. Education is a pragmatic process of choosing what is most important to emphasize in a limited amount of instructional time. Our culture helps us make some of these choices, as do legislative bodies, school boards, administrators, and even occasionally parents and students. In some school districts the cognitive objectives are provided in great detail, whereas in others they are practically nonexistent. As noted earlier, the current trend is for federal and state lawmakers to exert more and more control over curriculum content.

---

the number of items dedicated to each content area/objective by examining how much material was devoted to each topic in the text, how much time we typically spend on each topic in class lectures, and the relative importance we give the topic.

Some experts recommend using percentages instead of the number of items when developing a TOS, because the final number of test items might vary from your initial estimates. To do this, simply replace the number of items in each cell with the percentage of items you wish to fall into each category. When done this way, it also becomes apparent how your items will weight the test in any particular direction. For example, you might determine that approximately 20% of your instruction involved the different scales of measurement. You would like to reflect this weighting in your test so you devote 20% of the test to this content area. If you are developing a 30-item test this means you will write 6 items to assess objectives related to scales of measurement ($0.20 \times 30 = 6$). If you are developing a 40-item test this will mean you write 8 items to assess objectives related to scales of measurement ($0.20 \times 40 = 8$).

Although TOSs traditionally are built for tests of achievement and aptitude, they are also immensely helpful with tests of personality and behavior. For example, depression is a multifaceted problem. If I want to develop a measure of depression, I must be sure my test items sample the broad domain of depressive symptoms accurately and that different facets of depression are covered in reasonable percentages. Otherwise, I may overemphasize some aspects of depression to the exclusion of others. Table 18–5 gives an example of what a TOS for a measure of depression might look like. The areas or facets of depressive symptoms appear horizontally across the top of the table, and the types of behaviors—overt (those easily observable by others) and covert (those usually known only to the individual)—appear vertically along the left side of the table.

Table 18–5	Table of Specifications for a Measure of Depression						
	Facets of Depression (%)						
Types of behavior	**Melancholy**	**Physiological Symptoms**	**Isolationism**	**Anhedonia**	**Cognitive Issues (Attention, Concentration, Decision Making)**	**Thoughts of Death or Self-harm**	**Totals**
Overt behaviors associated with depression	10%	10%	5%	10%	10%	5%	50%
Covert behaviors associated with depression	10%	10%	5%	10%	10%	5%	50%
Total	**20%**	**20%**	**10%**	**20%**	**20%**	**10%**	**100%**

Because depression has both overt behaviors that are recognized by others as well as internal thoughts and feelings that are considered important to diagnosis, I want to be sure to cover both areas in each facet or dimension of depression. My TOS helps me write items that reflect all of these cells in the table—it is my blueprint to content coverage!

Determine and Describe the Item Formats and Write Instructions for Administration and Scoring

Different types of items are useful in different circumstances and can be used to measure different characteristics in different ways. For example, assessment of feelings, thoughts, self-talk, and other covert behaviors is usually best accomplished via self-report. This is clear, but even in the self-report domain we

> *Different item formats serve different purposes and are not always interchangeable.*

can use items in different formats. Many self-report scales use a simple true–false or yes–no response option. However, self-report scales can also use rating scales. Take the item "I feel sad," for instance. By altering the response format, we change the intent and interpretation of the item responses with changes in response formats.

I feel sad.	True	False			
I feel sad.	Never	Sometimes	Often	Almost always	
I feel sad.	Daily	Weekly	Monthly	Once a year or less	Never

   The first option asks more about a current state (i.e., how I feel right now), whereas the other options look at longer-term trends in feelings. So even on a self-report scale, changes in item formats will influence how well we have implemented our operational definitions. It is crucial to consider how the item format will impact factors such as administration and scoring, but even more so, how the chosen item formats may affect the validity of our proposed test score interpretations as well as the degree of construct consistency between our item formats and our conceptual and operational definitions of constructs.

We have reviewed and discussed item formats and item types in several other areas of this book, so we will not focus on them here. However, it is crucial to a successful test development project that item formats be specified no later than this stage of the planning process and that they are evaluated logically for construct consistency. Item formats should be chosen first for construct consistency and next for efficiency of the test-taking process, including ease and accuracy of administration and scoring. It is important to be aware of the psychometric characteristics of different item formats as well. For example, for rating scales, either four or five response options seem to be optimal in developing reliability without unduly lengthening the time required of the person completing the ratings. Rating scales with more than four or five options rarely improve reliability or validity of test score interpretation and take longer for examinees to complete. Unnecessary length is always an undesirable attribute for a test.

In developing item formats, it is also important to address several other questions. The testing medium must be specified for each item format. Will visual cues be provided such as pictures? Will the items require the examinee to manipulate objects physically as in puzzle-solving tasks or tests of dexterity? Will verbal cues be the item format and, if so, will the examinee read the cue or will the examiner read it? If the latter case, will the examinee read along with the examiner? Is the item format appropriate for the construct within the target population? For example, individuals with autism spectrum disorders often have language difficulties, so items that are verbal and require good oral or expressive language that are intended to measure anything other than expressive language will be poor choices for such a population. Take a measure developed to assess intelligence in autistic children and consider whether a test question that asked the child to "Explain why it is important for everyone to follow the rules when playing a game" is useful in assessing intelligence with such a child, or whether it is too confounded with the ability to express the answer verbally to assess intelligence (i.e., the ability to solve the question and deduce the answer).

Once you have chosen the proper item formats, write sample items for each format you plan to use on your test. In writing items, it is important to follow solid principles of item writing such as those outlined in Chapter 6. In writing your items, also write what you believe will be the correctly keyed response according to what you are attempting to measure and the direction of scoring of the test (i.e., will a high score be positively or negatively valued by the recipient of the scores)? Some tests score errors so that a high score means poor performance, whereas others score numbers correct so that a high score means good performance.

Next, you are ready to write the instructions for administration and scoring of the test items. Begin this process by drafting the instructions for the examiner to follow in administering the test followed by the instructions to be conveyed to the examinee. Our experience is that initial drafts of such instructions, no matter how hard we try or how many times we have done this, are not very good! They tend to be overly long and detailed or too short and leave out crucial information. Once you draft the instructions, sit with them and the test materials you have drafted so far, and attempt to both administer and to take the test. You will almost certainly find problems within this first draft. Redraft the instructions at this point and then give the materials to someone unfamiliar with the test and see if he or she can administer the test to you without making mistakes. Following this exercise, continue to revise the directions for administration and scoring until someone unfamiliar with the test can

> *When writing items for a new test, always draft at least twice as many items as you think will be necessary to measure the construct reliably.*

administer and score it accurately. To assess the scoring accuracy, have more than one person score the responses of several examinees and calculate the interscorer reliability coefficients—this likely will have to wait until a tryout version of all the items is available, but will be worthwhile to complete.

This is also a good time to estimate the number of items you think will be required to assess the construct(s) reliably. Keep in mind the rule-of-thumb that has been verified repeatedly over decades of test development experience—you should initially write a minimum of twice as many items as you expect to end up needing on the test. For constructs that are lesser known or difficult to measure, three times the final targeted number of items is a reasonable goal for the first draft. This will not be wasteful of anyone's time. Many items will drop out due to poor item statistics, item bias issues, and ambiguity, just to name a few of the issues you will encounter. This rule is followed by very experienced item writers. Having an advance estimate of the number of items is useful for a variety of reasons. The number of items obviously relates to the length of time it takes to administer and score the test as well as the time it takes the examinee to complete it. Some target populations for tests are far more sensitive to the time a test takes to complete than others, especially younger and older examinees. Individuals with certain disorders such ADHD and many of the pervasive developmental disorders among others, have limited attention spans (e.g., see Reynolds & Kamphaus, 2004) and unless the items are intended to measure attention, lengthy scales may be confounded by the attentional problems inherent to such populations.

Develop an Explanation of Methods for Item Development, Tryout, and Final Item Selection

Now you are ready to build your plan for actually writing the test items that form the foundation for the test proper. In preparing this plan, determine what theory if any you will be following, so refer back once again to your initial conceptualization and definitions to be sure you are on target and keep your TOS handy! The next real issue is to determine who will be writing the item drafts and what kind of background and training he or she will need as well as supplying the item writer(s) with all of the information you have written so far.

For virtually any test except those of very narrow constructs where you are the leading researcher, content area experts will be needed to help write effective items. Although this is most obvious for academic achievement tests, we have found it to be true in every category of test we have developed. No clinician, for example, no matter how good can be an expert in writing test items in all aspects of psychopathology, for all aspects of aptitude and intelligence and related cognitive processes, or personnel selection or interest measures. Also, as we noted indirectly in the previous section, item writers need to have knowledge of the target population as well because some groups of individuals will be unable or ill equipped to respond appropriately to certain item types, thus introducing confounds into the assessment of the construct you want to measure.

This is also the time to set down the methods for choosing items for the test. A series of procedures will be necessary in determining the final items for any test. We recommend the following:

1. *Have a panel of content-area experts from different ethnic, religious, and gender groups review the items for cultural ambiguity and offensiveness.* Although some advocate this procedure for detecting culturally biased items, research (see Chapter 15) indicates that expert reviewers are no better than chance at such tasks. However, such experts are necessary to determine whether an item contains content that might be seen ambiguously or with different meanings in other cultures or might contain material that is acceptable in one cultural setting but considered offensive in others.

2. *Designate a plan for an item tryout.* Choose a small sample of the target population and have the test administered and scored so you can receive feedback on all aspects of the test including the item content and formats, instructions, scoring, and the stimulus materials. Apply statistical methods for item analysis to detect any items that perform poorly at this stage and either rewrite or eliminate these items before going forward.

3. *Designate the statistical methods you will employ for item selection.* There are multiple approaches to item selection such as determining the correlation of each item with total score on the measure, reviewing the item score distributions and percentage of responses in the keyed direction, comparing the mean item scores of different groups predicted to differ on the items, and so on. Each of these methods will select many of the same items, but it is rare that the methods overlap completely in their selection of items. Different item selection criteria are most appropriate for different types of tests with different purposes, so be sure to match your item selection procedure to your purpose and target population.

4. *Designate the statistical methods you will use to assess items for differential item function (DIF) across ethnicity and gender (i.e., what statistical assessments of item bias you will perform).* Methods for detecting item bias are discussed in more detail in Chapter 15; however, a priori planning for item bias studies is important for several reasons. The first has to do with sample size. Certain methods (e.g., models based in item response theory) require larger samples to stabilize than do other approaches. Disproportional sample sizes across the groups being compared (e.g., comparing responses of White and Black samples) adversely affect some statistical procedures whereas others are robust to such issues if they are not too extreme. Knowing what methods you are going to employ in advance ensures adequate sampling to carry out the analyses.

As we have noted throughout this chapter, planning each step in advance is far more likely to produce tests with reliable scores and interpretations that are consistent with the initial intent of developing the measure.

PHASE III: PLANNING STANDARDIZATION AND PSYCHOMETRIC STUDIES

In the next phase of test development the author should describe the standardization procedures that will be used, describe the reliability and validity studies that will be pursued, and describe any special studies that might be needed to support the test interpretations. Table 18–6 provides an outline of these steps.

Table 18–6	Phase III: Planning Standardization and Psychometric Studies

1. Describe the reference or norm group and sampling plan for standardization.
2. Describe your choice of scaling methods and the rationale for this choice.
3. Outline the reliability studies to be performed and their rationale.
4. Outline the validity studies to be performed and their rationale.
5. Include any special studies that may be needed for development of this test or to support proposed interpretations of performance.
6. List the components of the test (e.g., manual, record forms, any test booklets or stimulus materials, etc.).

Specify a Sampling Plan for Standardization

Describing the target population for the test is the first step in deciding on a sampling plan. The standardization sample for a test determines the normative scores, also known as norms, and forms the reference group to whom examinees are compared in a norm-referenced test. In other types of tests (e.g., criterion-referenced

> *Describing the target population for the test is the first step in deciding on a sampling plan.*

tests) the performance of target populations will also be important in designating cut scores and related decision making concerning performance on the measure. Once you have defined the target population, that is, the reference group for each person who takes the test, you are ready to develop a sampling plan.

It would be best to always obtain a true random sample of the target population for the test, but this is a near impossibility. We typically cannot know all members of the population and even if we could, we could not force all randomly selected members of the population to take our test! Anyone we choose to take the test as part of our sample has the right to refuse. Nevertheless, we need to ensure that our sample is representative of the targeted population. The current best method for doing so is to write out a population proportionate stratified random sampling plan. To do this, we first determine what characteristics (strata) of our population are salient for ensuring the representativeness of the sample. Then we determine what percentages of people with each of those characteristics are needed to make our sample representative. This is best understood with an example.

On most measures of general aptitude or general intelligence, the target reference group is "persons living in the United States and who are fluent in English." We know the United States is composed of people from many different ethnic backgrounds, different levels of socioeconomic status, different regions of the country, and different levels of population density. Because these variables are relevant to establishing how well our sample mimics the population, we will want to sample people from all of these groups according to their relative proportions in the population at large. If 1% of our target population is African American women living in the northeast region of the United States in cities with a population of more than 100,000 and with an educational level of high school graduate, we would want 1% of our sample to include people who match this description. Statistics on population demographics are gathered and maintained by the U.S. Bureau of the Census and are typically available for numerous demographic characteristics on the bureau's website. In the measurement of constructs that are affected by aging or human

TABLE 18–7	Demographic Characteristics of School-Age and Adult Normative Samples for the Comprehensive Trail-Making Test (Reynolds, 2002)			
Characteristics	**Percentages of School-Age Sample**	**Percentages of U.S. School-Age Population**		
Geographic Area				
Northeast	17%	18%	19%	20%
Midwest	29	24	28	23
South	35	35	34	35
West	19	23	19	22
Gender				
Male	50%	51%	45%	48%
Female	50	49	55	52
Race				
White	79%	79%	85%	84%
Black	15	16	11	12
Other	6	5	4	4
Ethnicity				
Native American	1%	1%	1%	1%
Hispanic American	10	13	8	9
Asian American	2	4	2	3
African American	15	15	12	11
Other	72	67	77	76
Disability Status				
No Disability	92%	90%	92%	90%
Learning Disability	5	6	1	6
Speech-Language Disorder	1	2	1	2
Other Disability	2	2	6	2
Family Income				
Under $15,000	9%	14%	8%	13%
$15,000–$24,999	8	13	8	13
$25,000–$34,999	17	14	16	13
$35,000–$49,999	21	18	20	18
$50,000–$74,999	23	21	24	22
$75,000 and over	22	20	24	21
Educational Attainment of Parents or Adults				
Less than bachelor's degree	81%	74%	76%	74%
Bachelor's degree	12	18	16	18
Master's, professional, doctorate degrees	7	8	8	8

Source: Reynolds, C. R. (2002). *Comprehensive Trail-Making Test: Examiner's Manual.* Austin, TX: PRO-ED. Reprinted with permission of PRO-ED.

development, we also need to decide if age-corrected scores are to be provided and, if so, include age as a variable in our stratification table.

Table 18–7 shows an example of demographic characteristics of school-age and adult normative samples for a test standardized just after the 2000 U.S. Census data were available. This is a real-world example, and you can see that the sample is not a perfect match to the U. S. population on the variables chosen, but it is very close in terms of the percentages of persons in each demographic category. This still does not ensure the people who agreed to participate are a true random sample of the population within each cell. However, having a standardization plan like this one and then comparing the actual outcomes to the idealized outcomes provides us with evidence of a reasonable effort to create such a sample, and makes users aware of any discrepancies between our sample of the population and the ideal sample.

Next, you will need to determine the appropriate size of the sample overall. This is determined by many different factors including the item statistics and other statistical analyses you will be conducting. Some require larger samples for stability than do others, as well as very practical matters such as the costs to obtain the samples in both time and money. The relative precision required of the normative data will also be a factor. For example, tests designed for applications in clinical diagnosis, personnel selection, and other instances that strongly affect people's lives require larger, more accurate samples than might a scale designated purely for research purposes.

Determine Your Choice of Scaling Methods and Rationale

Many different types of scores can be determined for a test and they are not all the same—they have different purposes, answer different types of questions about the examinees, and have different psychometric characteristics. So, what scores should you use? Just as different reference groups or standardization samples provide us with different kinds of information, allowing us to answer different questions, different types of test scores answer different questions. Prior to being able to answer our question of which scores we should use, we need to know what it is we want the test score to tell us. Following are some brief descriptions of major types of scores:

> *Just as different standardization samples provide us with different kinds of information, different types of test scores answer different questions.*

- *Raw scores* tell us the number of points accumulated by a person on a measure and can tell us his or her relative rank among test takers, assuming we know everyone's raw score, but typically provide us only with ordinal scale measurement.
- Traditional *standard scores* address the general question of how this person's performance compares to the performance of some specified reference group and typically reflect interval scale measurement.
- *Rasch* or *IRT-based scores* are on an equal-interval scale that reflects position on some underlying or latent trait. These scores are particularly useful in evaluating the degree of change in scores over time and in comparing scores across tests of a common latent trait.
- *Criterion-referenced scores* tell us whether or not or to what extent a person's performance has approached a desired level of proficiency.

To illustrate how the use of different types of test scores might address different questions, consider the issue of whether or not a student's performance in reading has changed following the introduction of specialized teaching methods after it was discovered the student was having great difficulty acquiring reading skills. In such a circumstance, a student, John, would be administered a reading test prior to initiating an intervention or specialized reading methods to obtain a baseline level of performance. After some period of specialized instruction, John would be tested a second time to determine whether or not his skills in reading had changed. If the test used provided one of the four types of scores noted previously, what would each of these scores tell us about John's change in reading skill?

- Common standard scores that are norm-referenced by age group would answer the following question: *How has John's reading performance changed relative to the average rate of change of other children the same age?*
- Rasch-type scores would answer the question: *How has John's reading performance changed relative to the starting point of his specialized instruction?*
- Raw scores would answer this question as well, but are not on an equal-interval scale and make it difficult to estimate by how much John's reading performance has changed. The advantage of a Rasch-type score in this circumstance is that the distance between each score point is the same throughout the entire range of scores.
- Criterion-referenced scores answer a different question. Criterion-referenced scores address the question: *Has John's performance in reading reached a predetermined level of proficiency or a set goal for his instructional progress?*

All of these questions may be important, but they are in fact quite different and different types of scores are required to answer each of these questions. To understand the difference in the types of information provided, consider if John were running a race instead of learning to read. Norm-referenced standard scores would reflect John's position in the race relative to all other runners at any given time. Rasch-type scores would indicate accurately his distance from the starting point (or any other designated point) but would not allow us to assess his progress relative to other runners without also knowing their Rasch score. Raw scores would indicate distance from the starting point as well, but unlike being measured in feet or meters in a race, when used with psychological or educational variables they would not indicate the distance accurately at each point of progress. A criterion-referenced score would let us know when John had passed specific points on the racetrack or had reached the finish line. So here we see that each type of score provides us with a different type of information. Which score we should use is dependent on the type of information we desire.

For purposes of evaluating change, in some circumstances standard scores that are age corrected are the most appropriate but in other circumstances, criterion-referenced scores or even Rasch scores may be more appropriate. In an educational environment where we are looking to assess improvement in academic achievement levels of an individual student, the question of acquisition of academic skills relative to an age-appropriate peer group would be the most appropriate question to address in nearly all instances. That is, it is important to know if a student is making progress or keeping pace relative to other students the same age and not relative to only the starting point. If we considered progress relative to only a starting point and thus looked solely at changes in raw scores or some other form of growth score such as reflected in a Rasch scale, we could certainly determine if a student was making progress;

however, the student may be progressing at a rate that is less than that of classmates and so is falling further and further behind. By using age-corrected standard scores, we see easily whether the student is progressing at a lesser rate, the same pace, or more quickly than other students the same age.

In a therapeutic environment, we have very different concerns. A person who is in psychotherapy and being treated for depressive symptoms may be making progress; however, we would not want to discontinue therapy until a specific criterion point had been reached. In such cases, we would be more interested in the absolute level of symptomatology present or absolute level of distress experienced by the patient as opposed to his or her relative level of change compared to some peer group, and tests designed for this purpose may require a different scaling option.

Once we know what type of score we want to use, in the case of norm-referenced scores, we need to address whether to use normalized (a type of nonlinear score transformation) scores or linear transformations of these scores. The choice of linear scaling versus nonlinear scaling may be made after data have been collected. The rationale for each choice is discussed in Chapter 3 of this text and also in Reynolds and Kamphaus (2004).

Briefly Outline the Reliability Studies to Be Performed and Their Rationale

Tests designed for different purposes as well as tests of different types (most notably speeded vs. nonspeeded tests) produce scores that should be evaluated differently for relative reliability. For most tests, the relative accuracy of the domain sampling of the items and coherency of the items with one another should be examined. Most often this is done

> *Tests designed for different purposes produce scores that should be evaluated differently for relative reliability.*

through the calculation of internal consistency reliability coefficients, the most popular and widely applicable being Cronbach's alpha (also see Chapter 4 for details on reliability estimation). If alternate forms of a test are being developed, that is, two or more versions of a test intended to measure the same constructs, then the correlation between the two forms can serve as an estimate of the internal consistency reliability of the scores yielded by the different forms of the test. However, this is true only if the different forms actually measure the same construct. The stability of the scores over time should also be assessed except in unusual circumstances. Assessment of the stability of the scores over time is typically termed *test-retest reliability*, and tells us the extent to which scores on the test change or remain the same over a specified period. Whether this is due to issues with the test or reflects true change in the construct is an important distinction to be made in the interpretation of test-retest or stability coefficients as well. Test-retest studies also afford the opportunity to assess practice or testing effects—that is, the effects on future scores of having taken the test on a previous occasion. Such information is quite valuable when interpreting scores for the same person taken on more than one occasion. In planning test-retest studies, these issues need to be considered when determining the appropriate time interval between the initial and follow-up testing. Are practice or testing effects anticipated and should the underlying construct being measured be expected to change in this time period? As mentioned previously, when scoring involves subjective judgment, it is also important to evaluate inter-rater reliability. If the test requires someone to time responses with a high degree of accuracy, it is useful to establish the inter-rater reliability of the timing of responses as well.

Briefly Outline the Validity Studies to Be Performed and Their Rationale

Be certain the validity studies target the proposed interpretations of the scores as well as their intended application

As with reliability studies, it is crucial to plan validity studies in advance. Also, it is vital to the success of the project that the validity studies be conceptualized and designed in a way that allows the assessment of the appropriateness of the proposed interpretations of the test once it has been completed. We discussed five basic categories or classifications of validity evidence in Chapter 5. Each area will need to be addressed; however, the emphasis and level of detail of the validity evidence will (or should) vary depending on the constructs assessed, the proposed interpretations of the test scores, and the purposes for which the scores will be applied. As an example, with an intelligence test intended for use as a predictor of academic success, predictive studies of the criterion of academic success intended to be predicted should receive the highest priority and be emphasized in the validity studies determined to be necessary. Similarly, tests for personnel selection should undergo studies of the predictive accuracy of the scores with regard to job success (however the user defines this—which should be on an a priori basis) over some specified period. Job success can have many definitions, by the way, so criterion definitions also must be specified. Some users might define job success as number of years with one employer, some according to supervisor ratings of job performance, some according to number of items produced on an assembly line, or in the case of sales workers, the number of dollars in sales generated over a quarter, year, or longer. Different tests might be necessary to predict each outcome variable, although all might be called job success.

A measure of developmental psychopathology that is intended to result in enhanced diagnostic accuracy among the various autism spectrum disorders would receive a different emphasis. Here, validity studies should emphasize the ability of the test scores to discriminate among groups of individuals diagnosed (independently of the test) with each of the relevant disorders. Often, journal editors see "validity studies" of tests designed to assist in the diagnosis of clinical disorders that look only at the ability of the test scores to distinguish diagnosed groups from nondiagnosed or normal samples. This type of research is seldom helpful and almost any test will distinguish normal from nonnormal given good test score reliability and large samples. The real issue is distinguishing among the correct diagnoses within a referral sample—seldom do clinicians attempt to determine if a person who has not been referred has one specific disorder such as depression versus an absence of any disorder.

The bottom line is to be certain the validity studies target the proposed interpretations of the scores as well as their intended application. There is no limit to what can be designed as validity studies. Some legal requirements exist for certain types of tests such as personnel selection or classification measure, but for the most part, validity studies are limited only by the creativity of the researcher and their knowledge of the construct and relevant theories that embody the construct intended for measurement.

Determine If There Are Any Special Studies That May Be Needed for Development of This Test or to Support Proposed Interpretations of Performance

Depending on the uniqueness of the measure or the construct targeted for measurement, there may be some very specialized studies required that do not routinely appear in test manuals. Reconsider the proposed applications of the test at this point and try to think of at least one such study that would enhance the application of the measure. You may decide there is nothing unusual required, but this is the time to think outside traditional validity evidence to see if there is anything you can do uniquely to support applications of your proposed measure.

List the Components of the Test

Before implementing any part of the testing or tryouts of the materials, items, instructions, and the like, make a complete list of all the physical components of the test and review it carefully to be sure you have all the necessary parts. This also gives you a better idea of the potential cumbersomeness of the proposed test and a preview of its costs! At this point you should also note if there are any special manufacturing needs for the proposed test or any special software considerations.

PHASE IV: PLAN IMPLEMENTATION

Reevaluate the Test Content and Structure

The final phase of the test development process is where the author actually implements the test plan. At this point, we might paraphrase a famous old English story and remind you that "the best laid plans of mice and men oft go astray." As you implement your developmental plan, you will undoubtedly note changes that need to be made in the items and per-

> *As a great piece of literature stated, "the best laid plans of mice and men oft go astray."*

haps even the structure of the test. As you carry out the necessary developmental research, you will find the data do not support all of your assumptions about the test 100%. It is a wise and more likely successful test developer and author who after each phase of the project reevaluates the remaining steps to see if any modifications are necessary to produce the desired end product. Never be afraid to make changes dictated by the data or the feedback received from those involved in administering tryout versions of the test. In the end, it will make for a better test. Flexible development plans and flexibility in implementation guided by the ongoing data collection process are necessary to success.

Prepare the Test Manual

Once the test development process is complete, it is time to prepare the manual for the test. Test manuals should contain a description of the test development process that is sufficient to allow others to replicate what has been accomplished and for users to make accurate determinations as to the usefulness of the test for their purposes. Generally, a test manual should contain chapters that introduce and describe the measure and its conceptual and theoretical foundations, detailed instructions for administration and scoring of the test, an interpretive schema that is supported by validity evidence developed during the test development process, detailed information on the item development process and the standardization and related psychometric characteristics of the test, its score, and its interpretation, including information on test score reliability and evidence for the proposed interpretations of performance on the test. Limitations and cautions in using the measure as well as any special applications of the measure in the field should also be noted. The *Standards* (AERA et al., 1999) provided additional and, in some cases, more detailed guidance concerning the information that should be included in the professional manual for psychological and educational tests. The preceding sentences are a general outline of the content of the manual and the specific contents will vary according to the type of test and its applications, and some measures (e.g., tests for personnel selection) may have special legal requirements for information that must be available prior to their usage.

Submit a Test Proposal

If you want to have your test published, you will need to submit a test proposal to an appropriate publisher. The major test publishers have slightly different guidelines for developing and submitting a test proposal or prospectus. Table 18–8 provides an example of the test proposal guide used by Psychological Assessment Resources (PAR). Although there is variation among publishers in the information and format required for their proposals, this is a fairly representative example.

TABLE 18–8	Example of a New Test Proposal Guide From Psychological Assessment Resources

Product Proposals for Submission to Psychological Assessment Resources

The following questions are designed to help you prepare your product submission. Each applicable question should be addressed in your proposal.

Purpose and Rationale for the Test

1. What does the test measure?
2. What are the concepts or theories underlying the development of this test?
3. What demonstrated need does this test serve?

Description of the Test

1. What is the structure of the instrument: How many subtests does the test contain? What does each subtest measure? How many items does the test contain? What type(s) of scores are generated?
2. What is the format of the test: Group or individual administration? Multiple-choice, open ended, or other type(s) of item(s)?
3. What are the required response modes of the test: Oral, paper-and-pencil, pointing to the correct answer, motoric, computerized, and so on?
4. What is the total estimated time required for administration?
5. What is the proposed scoring procedure? How long will it take to score the test?
6. Describe the proposed normative standard and procedures. How long will it take for the user to obtain normative scores?

(Continued)

Components

1. What nonconsumable (i.e., reusable) components do you anticipate will be required for administering, scoring, and interpreting the test (e.g., test manuals, scoring keys, test plates, booklets, manipulatives)? Describe each of these components in terms of the anticipated production characteristics: page size, number of pages, color(s) of ink, special forms (e.g., multiforms, self-carboning), extraordinary use of graphical images, line drawings, or other illustrations, and so forth.

Primary Markets

1. What is the target population for the test (i.e., demographic characteristics such as age, gender, etc.)?
2. What professional discipline(s) would be potential purchasers and users of this test?
3. Which settings would be appropriate for use of this test (e.g., schools, private clinics, hospitals, private practice, etc.)?

Market Competition and Special Features of the Test

1. What other tests are currently available that serve a similar function?
2. If other similar tests are available, what features would set this test apart from its competitors? Why would an examiner want to use this test instead of other similar tests?

Empirical Research

Note: If these studies are yet to be done, provide methodological details of planned studies (i.e., sample size, sampling strategies, where will the data come from, statistics to be used, timeframe for completion, etc.).

1. Describe how the test items were/will be developed (e.g., item writing, bias panel review, alpha item tryout, and revision of the item pool).
2. Describe the reliability of the test (e.g., internal consistency, alternate-form reliability, interrater reliability, and test-retest reliability/temporal stability) or how the reliability will be examined.
3. Describe the validity of the test (e.g., content, construct, and criterion-related validity) or how the validity will be established.
4. Describe the normative comparison group(s) and the procedures used (or the procedures that will be used) to collect these data.
5. Describe future/other research and development work that should be completed prior to publication of the test. Discuss anticipated completion date, funding needs, and research responsibilities. Describe your idea of the role PAR can/will play in the remaining research and development.

Source: Reprinted with permission of PAR.

Summary

In this chapter we described what we have experienced and many others have recommended as the necessary steps and components of the test development process from a practical perspective. Throughout this textbook we have introduced or provided details on certain constructs such as dissimulation scales and how to determine their necessity. The chapter emphasized the early conceptual phases of test development as critical to a successful project, especially determining the need for a new test and developing conceptual and operational definitions of constructs you intend to measure. We also emphasized the necessity of describing in advance of initiating the development of a new measure the intended uses and interpretations of results from the test as well as who will use the test and why.

The largest section of the chapter was devoted to instructions for preparing a detailed description of the test, including a table of specifications, or test blueprint. We gave examples of a publisher's requirements for submission of proposals for new commercial psychological tests. Last, we gave a general description of the content to be covered in typical test manuals noting that some specialized tests may have additional requirements for information that must be available prior to their legal and ethical application in practice.

Careful review of all these materials as well as the preceding chapters of this text will prepare you well to embark on what can be a truly interesting but, at times, trying endeavor of psychological and educational test development.

Recommended Readings

Bush, S., Ruff, R., Troster, A., Barth, J., Koffler, S., Pliskin, N., . . . Silver, C. (2005). Symptom validity assessment: Practice issues and medical necessity. *Archives of Clinical Neuropsychology, 20,* 419–426. This paper states the official position of the National Academy of Neuropsychology on the assessment of dissimulation in clinical assessment procedures.

Kaufman, A. S., & Kaufman, N. L. (1983). *Kaufman Assessment Battery for Children: Examiner manual and technical manual.* Circle Pines, MN: American Guidance Service. The Kaufman's were one of the first to provide detailed development information on an intelligence test in the professional Manual, including information on the theoretical underpinnings of the test.

Reynolds, C. R., & Kamphaus, R. W. (2003). *Reynolds Intellectual Assessment Scales and Reynolds Intellectual Screening Test: Professional manual.* Lutz, FL: Psychological Assessment Resources. This Manual contains one of the more detailed descriptions of the total test development process relative to most test manuals.

Robertson, G. J. (2003). A practical model for test development. In C. R. Reynolds & R. W. Kamphaus (Eds.), *Handbook of psychological and educational assessment of children, Vol. 1: Intelligence, aptitude, and achievement* (2nd ed., pp. 24–57). New York: Guilford. This chapter gives the perspectives of a seasoned professional who was in charge of developing numerous commercial tests for several of the largest test publishers in the United States.

PROPORTIONS OF AREA UNDER THE NORMAL CURVE

TABLE A.1 Proportions of Area under the Normal Curve

(a) Value of +z / −z	(b)	(c)	(a) Value of +z / −z	(b)	(c)	(a) Value of +z / −z	(b)	(c)
.00	.0000	.5000	.28	.1103	.3897	.56	.2123	.2877
.01	.0040	.4960	.29	.1141	.3859	.57	.2157	.2843
.02	.0080	.4920	.30	.1179	.3821	.58	.2190	.2810
.03	.0120	.4880	.31	.1217	.3783	.59	.2224	.2776
.04	.0160	.4840	.32	.1255	.3745	.60	.2257	.2743
.05	.0199	.4801	.33	.1293	.3707	.61	.2291	.2709
.06	.0239	.4761	.34	.1331	.3669	.62	.2324	.2676
.07	.0279	.4721	.35	.1368	.3632	.63	.2357	.2643
.08	.0319	.4681	.36	.1406	.3594	.64	.2389	.2611
.09	.0359	.4641	.37	.1443	.3557	.65	.2422	.2578
.10	.0398	.4602	.38	.1480	.3520	.66	.2454	.2546
.11	.0438	.4562	.39	.1517	.3483	.67	.2486	.2514
.12	.0478	.4522	.40	.1554	.3446	.68	.2517	.2483
.13	.0517	.4483	.41	.1591	.3409	.69	.2549	.2451
.14	.0557	.4443	.42	.1628	.3372	.70	.2580	.2420
.15	.0596	.4404	.43	.1664	.3336	.71	.2611	.2389
.16	.0636	.4364	.44	.1700	.3300	.72	.2642	.2358
.17	.0675	.4325	.45	.1736	.3264	.73	.2673	.2327

(continued)

TABLE A.1 Continued

(a) Value of +z	(b)	(c)	(a) Value of +z	(b)	(c)	(a) Value of +z	(b)	(c)
.18	.0714	.4286	.46	.1772	.3228	.74	.2704	.2296
.19	.0753	.4247	.47	.1808	.3192	.75	.2734	.2266
.20	.0793	.4207	.48	.1844	.3156	.76	.2764	.2236
.21	.0832	.4168	.49	.1879	.3121	.77	.2794	.2206
.22	.0871	.4129	.50	.1915	.3085	.78	.2823	.2177
.23	.0910	.4090	.51	.1950	.3050	.79	.2852	.2148
.24	.0948	.4052	.52	.1985	.3015	.80	.2881	.2119
.25	.0987	.4013	.53	.2019	.2981	.81	.2910	.2090
.26	.1026	.3974	.54	.2054	.2946	.82	.2939	.2061
.27	.1064	.3936	.55	.2088	.2912	.83	.2967	.2033
.84	.2995	.2005	1.53	.4370	.0630	2.22	.4868	.0132
.85	.3023	.1977	1.54	.4382	.0618	2.23	.4871	.0129
.86	.3051	.1949	1.55	.4394	.0606	2.24	.4875	.0125
.87	.3078	.1922	1.56	.4406	.0594	2.25	.4878	.0122
.88	.3106	.1894	1.57	.4418	.0582	2.26	.4881	.0119
.89	.3133	.1867	1.58	.4429	.0571	2.27	.4884	.0116
.90	.3159	.1841	1.59	.4441	.0559	2.28	.4887	.0113
.91	.3186	.1814	1.60	.4452	.0548	2.29	.4890	.0110
.92	.3212	.1788	1.61	.4463	.0537	2.30	.4893	.0107
.93	.3238	.1762	1.62	.4474	.0526	2.31	.4896	.0104

.94	.3264	.1736	1.63	.4484	.0516	2.32	.4898	.0102
.95	.3289	.1711	1.64	.4495	.0505	2.33	.4901	.0099
.96	.3315	.1685	1.65	.4505	.0495	2.34	.4904	.0096
.97	.3340	.1660	1.66	.4515	.0485	2.35	.4906	.0094
.98	.3365	.1635	1.67	.4525	.0475	2.36	.4909	.0091
.99	.3389	.1611	1.68	.4535	.0465	2.37	.4911	.0089
1.00	.3413	.1587	1.69	.4545	.0455	2.38	.4913	.0087
1.01	.3438	.1562	1.70	.4554	.0446	2.39	.4916	.0084
1.02	.3461	.1539	1.71	.4564	.0436	2.40	.4918	.0082
1.03	.3485	.1515	1.72	.4573	.0427	2.41	.4920	.0080
1.04	.3508	.1492	1.73	.4582	.0418	2.42	.4922	.0078
1.05	.3531	.1469	1.74	.4591	.0409	2.43	.4925	.0075
1.06	.3554	.1446	1.75	.4599	.0401	2.44	.4927	.0073
1.07	.3577	.1423	1.76	.4608	.0392	2.45	.4929	.0071
1.08	.3599	.1401	1.77	.4616	.0384	2.46	.4931	.0069
1.09	.3621	.1379	1.78	.4625	.0375	2.47	.4932	.0068
1.10	.3643	.1357	1.79	.4633	.0367	2.48	.4934	.0066
1.11	.3665	.1335	1.80	.4641	.0359	2.49	.4936	.0064
1.12	.3686	.1314	1.81	.4649	.0351	2.50	.4938	.0062
1.13	.3708	.1292	1.82	.4656	.0344	2.51	.4940	.0060
1.14	.3729	.1271	1.83	.4664	.0336	2.52	.4941	.0059
1.15	.3749	.1251	1.84	.4671	.0329	2.53	.4943	.0057
1.16	.3770	.1230	1.85	.4678	.0322	2.54	.4945	.0055
1.17	.3790	.1210	1.86	.4686	.0314	2.55	.4946	.0054
1.18	.3810	.1190	1.87	.4693	.0307	2.56	.4948	.0052
1.19	.3830	.1170	1.88	.4699	.0301	2.57	.4949	.0051
1.20	.3849	.1151	1.89	.4706	.0294	2.58	.4951	.0049

(continued)

TABLE A.1 Continued

(a) Value of +z	(b)	(c)	(a) Value of +z	(b)	(c)	(a) Value of +z	(b)	(c)
1.21	.3869	.1131	1.90	.4713	.0287	2.59	.4952	.0048
1.22	.3888	.1112	1.91	.4719	.0281	2.60	.4953	.0047
1.23	.3907	.1093	1.92	.4726	.0274	2.61	.4955	.0045
1.24	.3925	.1075	1.93	.4732	.0268	2.62	.4956	.0044
1.25	.3944	.1056	1.94	.4738	.0262	2.63	.4957	.0043
1.26	.3962	.1038	1.95	.4744	.0256	2.64	.4959	.0041
1.27	.3980	.1020	1.96	.4750	.0250	2.65	.4960	.0040
1.28	.3997	.1003	1.97	.4756	.0244	2.66	.4961	.0039
1.29	.4015	.0985	1.98	.4761	.0239	2.67	.4962	.0038
1.30	.4032	.0968	1.99	.4767	.0233	2.68	.4963	.0037
1.31	.4049	.0951	2.00	.4772	.0228	2.69	.4964	.0036
1.32	.4066	.0934	2.01	.4778	.0222	2.70	.4965	.0035
1.33	.4082	.0918	2.02	.4783	.0217	2.71	.4966	.0034
1.34	.4099	.0901	2.03	.4788	.0212	2.72	.4967	.0033
1.35	.4115	.0885	2.04	.4793	.0207	2.73	.4968	.0032
1.36	.4131	.0869	2.05	.4798	.0202	2.74	.4969	.0031
1.37	.4147	.0853	2.06	.4803	.0197	2.75	.4970	.0030
1.38	.4162	.0838	2.07	.4808	.0192	2.76	.4971	.0029
1.39	.4177	.0823	2.08	.4812	.0188	2.77	.4972	.0028

z			z			z		
1.40	.4192	.0808	2.09	.4817	.0183	2.78	.4973	.0027
1.41	.4207	.0793	2.10	.4821	.0179	2.79	.4974	.0026
1.42	.4222	.0778	2.11	.4826	.0174	2.80	.4974	.0026
1.43	.4236	.0764	2.12	.4830	.0170	2.81	.4975	.0025
1.44	.4251	.0749	2.13	.4834	.0166	2.82	.4976	.0024
1.45	.4265	.0735	2.14	.4838	.0162	2.83	.4977	.0023
1.46	.4279	.0721	2.15	.4842	.0158	2.84	.4977	.0023
1.47	.4292	.0708	2.16	.4846	.0154	2.85	.4978	.0022
1.48	.4306	.0694	2.17	.4850	.0150	2.86	.4979	.0021
1.49	.4319	.0681	2.18	.4854	.0146	2.87	.4979	.0021
1.50	.4332	.0668	2.19	.4857	.0143	2.88	.4980	.0020
1.51	.4345	.0655	2.20	.4861	.0139	2.89	.4981	.0019
1.52	.4357	.0643	2.21	.4864	.0136	2.90	.4981	.0019
2.91	.4982	.0018	3.18	.4993	.0007	3.45	.4997	.0003
2.92	.4982	.0018	3.19	.4993	.0007	3.46	.4997	.0003
2.93	.4983	.0017	3.20	.4993	.0007	3.47	.4997	.0003
2.94	.4984	.0016	3.21	.4993	.0007	3.48	.4997	.0003
2.95	.4984	.0016	3.22	.4994	.0006	3.49	.4998	.0002
2.96	.4985	.0015	3.23	.4994	.0006	3.50	.4998	.0002
2.97	.4985	.0015	3.24	.4994	.0006	3.51	.4998	.0002
2.98	.4986	.0014	3.25	.4994	.0006	3.52	.4998	.0002
2.99	.4986	.0014	3.26	.4994	.0006	3.53	.4998	.0002
3.00	.4987	.0013	3.27	.4995	.0005	3.54	.4998	.0002
3.01	.4987	.0013	3.28	.4995	.0005	3.55	.4998	.0002
3.02	.4987	.0013	3.29	.4995	.0005	3.56	.4998	.0002
3.03	.4988	.0012	3.30	.4995	.0005	3.57	.4998	.0002
3.04	.4988	.0012	3.31	.4995	.0005	3.58	.4998	.0002

(continued)

TABLE A.1 Continued

(a) Value of +z / −z	(b)	(c)	(a) Value of +z / −z	(b)	(c)	(a) Value of +z / −z	(b)	(c)
3.05	.4989	.0011	3.32	.4995	.0005	3.59	.4998	.0002
3.06	.4989	.0011	3.33	.4996	.0004	3.60	.4998	.0002
3.07	.4989	.0011	3.34	.4996	.0004	3.61	.4998	.0002
3.08	.4990	.0010	3.35	.4996	.0004	3.62	.4999	.0001
3.09	.4990	.0010	3.36	.4996	.0004	3.63	.4999	.0001
3.10	.4990	.0010	3.37	.4996	.0004	3.64	.4999	.0001
3.11	.4991	.0009	3.38	.4996	.0004	3.65	.4999	.0001
3.12	.4991	.0009	3.39	.4997	.0003	3.66	.4999	.0001
3.13	.4991	.0009	3.40	.4997	.0003	3.67	.4999	.0001
3.14	.4992	.0008	3.41	.4997	.0003	3.68	.4999	.0001
3.15	.4992	.0008	3.42	.4997	.0003	3.69	.4999	.0001
3.16	.4992	.0008	3.43	.4997	.0003	3.70	.4999	.0001
3.17	.4992	.0008	3.44	.4997	.0003			

APPENDIX B

INTERPRETIVE REPORT: CLINICAL SETTINGS

This appendix contains a detailed computer-generated MMPI-2-RF interpretation report for a 34-year-old woman who was tested on admission to an inpatient psychiatric facility. The report includes annotation (with endnotes) that links each of the statements in the report to specific MMPI-2-RF findings. The client's scores on the Validity scales (page 2 of the report) indicate that she attempted to portray herself in an overly favorable light by denying minor faults and shortcomings that most individuals readily acknowledge. Her scores on the Higher-Order scales (page 3 of the report) indicate that she is likely experiencing a significant thought disorder, and her scores on the RC scales indicate that her thought dysfunction symptoms include persecutory beliefs and unusual thoughts and perceptions. Together, these findings raise the possibility that she would meet diagnostic criteria for Schizophrenia, Paranoid Type. The remaining scales indicate that she also experiences anxiety and fears that could reflect an associated anxiety disorder, vague somatic complaints that focus primarily on unusual neurological symptoms, significant family conflict, and a lack of interest in socializing with others. Although there are no indications of acting-out behaviors in these results, this cannot be ruled out because of her tendency to deny character flaws.

MMPI-2-RF®
Minnesota Multiphasic Personality Inventory-2-Restructured Form™
Yossef S. Ben-Porath, PhD, & Auke Tellegen, PhD

ID Number:	001
Age:	34
Gender:	Female
Marital Status:	Divorced
Years of Education:	12
Date Assessed:	06/05/2009

PEARSON   *PsychCorp*

Trade Secret InformHlation

MMPI-2-RF Validity Scales

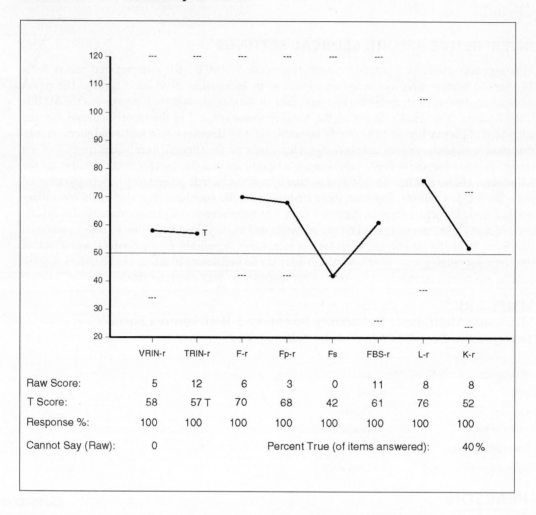

	VRIN-r	TRIN-r	F-r	Fp-r	Fs	FBS-r	L-r	K-r
Raw Score:	5	12	6	3	0	11	8	8
T Score:	58	57 T	70	68	42	61	76	52
Response %:	100	100	100	100	100	100	100	100

Cannot Say (Raw):   0   Percent True (of items answered):   40%

The highest and lowest T scores possible on each scale are indicated by a "---"; MMPI-2-RF T scores are non-gendered.

VRIN-r	Variable Response Inconsistency	Fs	Infrequent Somatic Responses
TRIN-r	True Response Inconsistency	FBS-r	Symptom Validity
F-r	Infrequent Responses	L-r	Uncommon Virtues
Fp-r	Infrequent Psychopathology Responses	K-r	Adjustment Validity

MMPI-2-RF Higher-Order (H-O) and Restructured Clinical (RC) Scales

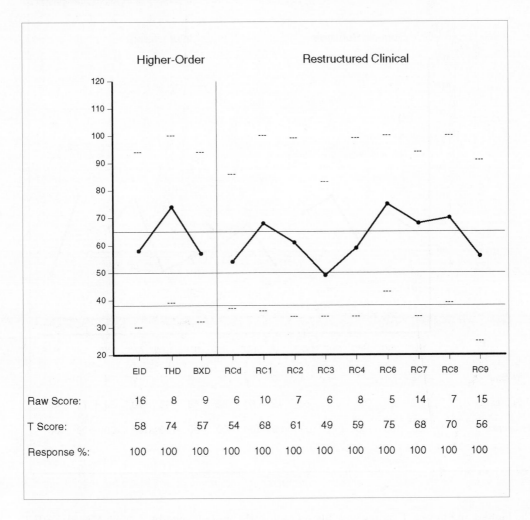

	EID	THD	BXD	RCd	RC1	RC2	RC3	RC4	RC6	RC7	RC8	RC9
Raw Score:	16	8	9	6	10	7	6	8	5	14	7	15
T Score:	58	74	57	54	68	61	49	59	75	68	70	56
Response %:	100	100	100	100	100	100	100	100	100	100	100	100

The highest and lowest T scores possible on each scale are indicated by a "---"; MMPI-2-RF T scores are non-gendered.

EID	Emotional/Internalizing Dysfunction	RC3	Cynicism
THD	Thought Dysfunction	RC4	Antisocial Behavior
BXD	Behavioral/Externalizing Dysfunction	RC6	Ideas of Persecution
RCd	Demoralization	RC7	Dysfunctional Negative Emotions
RC1	Somatic Complaints	RC8	Aberrant Experiences
RC2	Low Positive Emotions	RC9	Hypomanic Activation

MMPI-2-RF Somatic/Cognitive and Internalizing Scales

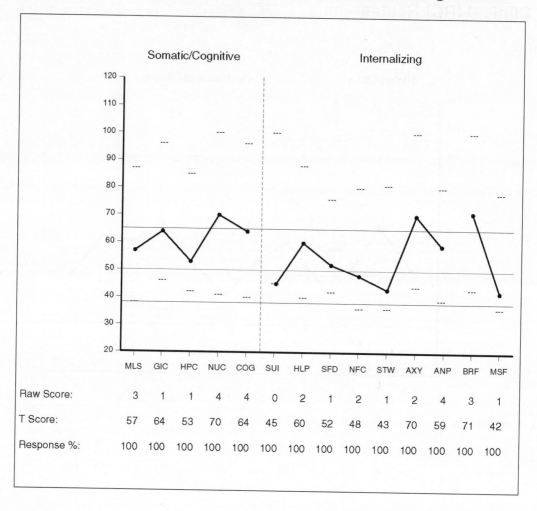

The highest and lowest T scores possible on each scale are indicated by a "---"; MMPI-2-RF T scores are non-gendered.

MLS	Malaise	SFD	Self-Doubt
GIC	Gastrointestinal Complaints	NFC	Inefficacy
HPC	Head Pain Complaints	STW	Stress/Worry
NUC	Neurological Complaints	AXY	Anxiety
COG	Cognitive Complaints	ANP	Anger Proneness
SUI	Suicidal/Death Ideation	BRF	Behavior-Restricting Fears
HLP	Helplessness/Hopelessness	MSF	Multiple Specific Fears

MMPI-2-RF Externalizing, Interpersonal, and Interest Scales

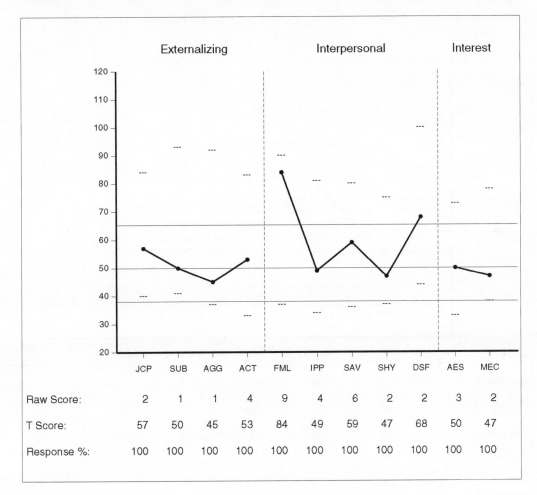

The highest and lowest T scores possible on each scale are indicated by a "---"; MMPI-2-RF T scores are non-gendered.

JCP	Juvenile Conduct Problems		SAV	Social Avoidance
SUB	Substance Abuse		SHY	Shyness
AGG	Aggression		DSF	Disaffiliativeness
ACT	Activation		AES	Aesthetic-Literary Interests
FML	Family Problems		MEC	Mechanical-Physical Interests
IPP	Interpersonal Passivity			

MMPI-2-RF PSY-5 Scales

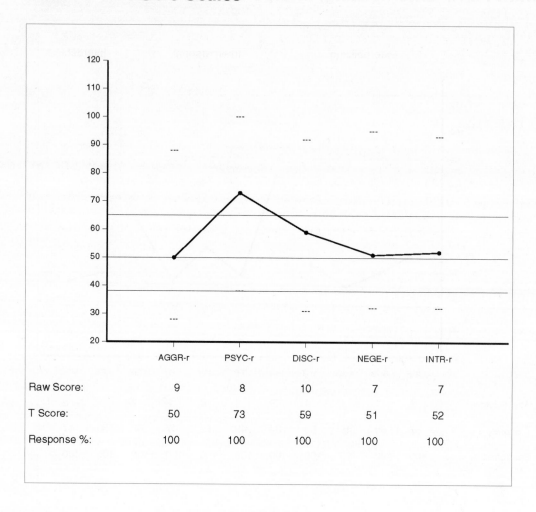

	AGGR-r	PSYC-r	DISC-r	NEGE-r	INTR-r
Raw Score:	9	8	10	7	7
T Score:	50	73	59	51	52
Response %:	100	100	100	100	100

The highest and lowest T scores possible on each scale are indicated by a "---"; MMPI-2-RF T scores are non-gendered.

AGGR-r Aggressiveness-Revised
PSYC-r Psychoticism-Revised
DISC-r Disconstraint-Revised
NEGE-r Negative Emotionality/Neuroticism-Revised
INTR-r Introversion/Low Positive Emotionality-Revised

This interpretive report is intended for use by a professional qualified to interpret the MMPI-2-RF. The information it contains should be considered in the context of the test taker's background, the circumstances of the assessment, and other available information.

SYNOPSIS

Scores on the MMPI-2-RF validity scales raise concerns about the possible impact of under-reporting on the validity of this protocol. With that caution noted, scores on the substantive scales indicate somatic complaints and emotional, thought, and interpersonal dysfunction. Somatic complaints include preoccupation with poor health and neurological symptoms. Emotional-internalizing findings include anxiety and fears. Dysfunctional thinking includes ideas of persecution and aberrant perceptions and thoughts. Interpersonal difficulties include family problems and a dislike of people and being around them.

PROTOCOL VALIDITY

Content Non-Responsiveness

There are no problems with unscorable items in this protocol. The test taker responded relevantly to the items on the basis of their content.

Over-Reporting

There are no indications of over-reporting in this protocol.

Under-Reporting

The test taker presented herself in a very positive light by denying several minor faults and shortcomings that most people acknowledge. This level of virtuous self-presentation is uncommon, but may, to some extent, reflect a background stressing traditional values. Any absence of elevation on the substantive scales should be interpreted with caution. Elevated scores on the substantive scales may underestimate the problems assessed by those scales[1].

SUBSTANTIVE SCALE INTERPRETATION

Clinical symptoms, personality characteristics, and behavioral tendencies of the test taker are described in this section and organized according to an empirically guided framework. Statements containing the word "reports" are based on the item content of MMPI-2-RF scales, whereas statements that include the word "likely" are based on empirical correlates of scale scores. Specific sources for each statement can be viewed with the annotation features of this report.

The following interpretation needs to be considered in light of cautions noted about the possible impact of under-reporting on the validity of this protocol.

Somatic/Cognitive Dysfunction

The test taker reports multiple somatic complaints[2] including vague neurological complaints[3]. She is likely to complain of fatigue[4]. She is also likely to be preoccupied with physical health concerns[5] and to be prone to developing physical symptoms in response to stress[6].

Emotional Dysfunction

The test taker reports various negative emotional experiences[7] and is likely to be inhibited behaviorally by these emotions[8]. She is also likely to be self-critical and guilt-prone[9]. She also reports feeling anxious[10] and is likely to experience significant anxiety and anxiety-related problems[11], intrusive ideation, and nightmares[12]. In addition, she reports multiple fears that significantly restrict normal activity in and outside the home[13].

Thought Dysfunction

The test taker's responses indicate significant and pervasive thought dysfunction[14]. More specifically, she reports significant persecutory ideation such as believing that others seek to harm her[15]. She is likely to be suspicious of and alienated from others[16], to experience interpersonal difficulties as a result of suspiciousness[17], and to lack insight[17].

She reports unusual thought processes[18]. She is likely to engage in unrealistic thinking[19] and to believe she has unusual sensory-perceptual abilities[20]. Her aberrant experiences may include somatic delusions[21].

Behavioral Dysfunction

There are no indications of maladaptive externalizing behavior in this protocol. However, because of indications of under-reporting described earlier, such problems cannot be ruled out.

Interpersonal Functioning Scales

The test taker reports conflictual family relationships and lack of support from family members. Negative family attitudes and experiences include frequent quarrels, dislike of family members, feeling unappreciated by family members, and feeling that family members cannot be counted upon in time of need[22]. She is indeed very likely to have family conflicts and to experience poor family functioning[23], to have strong negative feelings about family members[23], and to blame family members for her difficulties[23].

She reports disliking people and being around them[24], and is likely to be asocial[25] and socially introverted[25], but her asocial behavior is not associated with social anxiety[26].

Interest Scales

The test taker reports an average number of interests in activities or occupations of an aesthetic or literary nature (e.g., writing, music, the theater)[27]. She also reports an average number of interests in activities or occupations of a mechanical or physical nature (e.g., fixing and building things, the outdoors, sports)[28].

Diagnostic Considerations*This section provides recommendations for psychodiagnostic assessment based on the test taker's MMPI-2-RF results. It is recommended that she be evaluated for the following:*

Emotional-Internalizing Disorders

- Somatoform disorder and/or conditions involving somatic delusions, if physical origin for neurological complaints has been ruled out[29]
- Anxiety-related disorders including PTSD[30]
- Agoraphobia and specific phobias[31]

Thought Disorders

- Disorders involving persecutory ideation[17]
- Disorders manifesting psychotic symptoms[32]
- Personality disorders manifesting unusual thoughts and perceptions[33]

Treatment Considerations*This section provides inferential treatment-related recommendations based on the test taker's MMPI-2-RF scores.*

Areas for Further Evaluation

- May require inpatient treatment due to thought dysfunction[34].
- Extent to which genuine physical health problems contribute to the scores on the Somatic Complaints (RC1) and Neurological Complaints (NUC) scales[21].

Psychotherapy Process Issues

- Likely to reject psychological interpretations of somatic complaints[21].
- Emotional difficulties may motivate her for treatment[35].
- Persecutory ideation may interfere with forming a therapeutic relationship and treatment compliance[36].
- Impaired thinking may disrupt treatment[37].
- Her aversive response to close relationships may make it difficult to form a therapeutic alliance and achieve progress in treatment[38].

Possible Targets for Treatment

- Dysfunctional negative emotions[35]
- Anxiety[39]
- Behavior-restricting fears[31]
- Persecutory ideation[36]
- Family problems[40]

ITEM-LEVEL INFORMATION

Unscorable Responses

The test taker produced scorable responses to all the MMPI-2-RF items.

Critical Responses

Seven MMPI-2-RF scales--Suicidal/Death Ideation (SUI), Helplessness/Hopelessness (HLP), Anxiety (AXY), Ideas of Persecution (RC6), Aberrant Experiences (RC8), Substance Abuse (SUB), and Aggression (AGG)--have been designated by the test authors as having critical item content that may require immediate attention and follow-up. Items answered by the individual in the keyed direction (True or False) on a critical scale are listed below if her T score on that scale is 65 or higher. The percentage of the MMPI-2-RF normative sample that answered each item in the keyed direction is provided in parentheses following the item content.

Anxiety (AXY, T Score = 70)
      228. Item content removed. (True, 17.3%)
      275. Item content removed. (True, 5.0%)

Ideas of Persecution (RC6, T Score = 75)
      34. Item content removed. (True, 10.6%)
      71. Item content removed. (True, 2.0%)
      194. Item content removed. (True, 17.1%)
      212. Item content removed. (False, 9.1%)
      233. Item content removed. (True, 5.5%)

Aberrant Experiences (RC8, T Score = 70)
      12. Item content removed. (True, 22.2%)
      32. Item content removed. (True, 21.1%)
      46. Item content removed. (True, 2.2%)
      85. Item content removed. (False, 17.1%)
      179. Item content removed. (True, 12.6%)
      311. Item content removed. (True, 32.4%)
      330. Item content removed. (True, 15.2%)

ENDNOTES

This section lists for each statement in the report the MMPI-2-RF score(s) that triggered it. In addition, each statement is identified as a Test Response, if based on item content, a Correlate, if based on empirical correlates, or an Inference, if based on the report authors' judgment. (This information can also be accessed on-screen by placing the cursor on a given statement.) For correlate-based statements, research references (Ref. No.) are provided, keyed to the consecutively numbered reference list following the endnotes.

1 Correlate: L-r = 76, Ref. 7, 13
2 Test Response: RC1 = 68
3 Test Response: NUC = 70
4 Correlate: RC1 = 68, Ref. 13
5 Correlate: RC1 = 68, Ref. 3, 4, 5, 10, 11, 13; NUC = 70, Ref. 13
6 Correlate: RC1 = 68, Ref. 4, 13; NUC = 70, Ref. 13
7 Test Response: RC7 = 68
8 Correlate: RC7 = 68, Ref. 13, 14; BRF = 71, Ref. 13
9 Correlate: RC7 = 68, Ref. 13
10 Test Response: AXY = 70
11 Correlate: RC7 = 68, Ref. 2, 9, 10, 11, 13, 14; AXY = 70, Ref. 13
12 Correlate: RC7 = 68, Ref. 6, 13, 15; AXY = 70, Ref. 13
13 Test Response: BRF = 71
14 Correlate: THD = 74, Ref. 13; PSYC-r = 73, Ref. 13
15 Test Response: RC6 = 75
16 Correlate: RC6 = 75, Ref. 1, 5, 8, 11, 13
17 Correlate: RC6 = 75, Ref. 13
18 Test Response: RC8 = 70; PSYC-r = 73
19 Correlate: RC8 = 70, Ref. 2, 4, 13; PSYC-r = 73, Ref. 13
20 Correlate: RC8 = 70, Ref. 2, 4, 12, 13; PSYC-r = 73, Ref. 13
21 Inference: RC1 = 68; NUC = 70
22 Test Response: FML = 84
23 Correlate: FML = 84, Ref. 13
24 Test Response: DSF = 68
25 Correlate: DSF = 68, Ref. 13
26 Inference: SAV > 65 and SHY > 65
27 Test Response: AES = 50
28 Test Response: MEC = 47
29 Inference: RC1 = 68; RC8 = 70; NUC = 70
30 Correlate: RC7 = 68, Ref. 6, 9, 14, 15; AXY = 70, Ref. 13
31 Inference: BRF = 71
32 Correlate: RC8 = 70, Ref. 13
33 Inference: RC8 = 70; PSYC-r = 73
34 Inference: THD = 74; PSYC-r = 73
35 Inference: RC7 = 68
36 Inference: RC6 = 75
37 Inference: RC8 = 70
38 Inference: DSF = 68
39 Inference: AXY = 70
40 Inference: FML = 84

RESEARCH REFERENCE LIST

1. Arbisi, P. A., Sellbom, M., & Ben-Porath, Y. S. (2008). Empirical correlates of the MMPI-2 Restructured Clinical (RC) Scales in psychiatric inpatients. *Journal of Personality Assessment, 90,* 122-128.

2. Forbey, J. D., & Ben-Porath, Y. S. (2007). A comparison of the MMPI-2 Restructured Clinical (RC) and Clinical Scales in a substance abuse treatment sample. *Psychological Services, 4,* 46-58.

3. Forbey, J. D., & Ben-Porath, Y. S. (2008). Empirical correlates of the MMPI-2 Restructured Clinical (RC) Scales in a non-clinical setting. *Journal of Personality Assessment, 90,* 136-141.

4. Forbey, J. D., Ben-Porath, Y. S., & Gartland, D. (in press). Validation of the MMPI-2 computerized adaptive version (MMPI-2-CA) in a correctional intake facility. *Psychological Services.*

5. Handel, R. W., & Archer, R. P. (2008). An investigation of the psychometric properties of the MMPI-2 Restructured Clinical (RC) Scales with mental health inpatients. *Journal of Personality Assessment, 90,* 239-249.

6. McDevitt-Murphy, M. E., Weathers, F. W., Flood, A. M., Eakin, D. E., & Benson, T. A. (2007). The utility of the PAI and the MMPI-2 for discriminating PTSD, depression, and social phobia in trauma-exposed college students. *Assessment, 14,* 181-195.

7. Sellbom, M., & Bagby, R. M. (2008). The validity of the MMPI-2-RF (Restructured Form) L-r and K-r scales in detecting under-reporting in clinical and non-clinical samples. *Psychological Assessment, 20,* 370-376.

8. Sellbom, M., & Ben-Porath, Y. S. (2005). Mapping the MMPI-2 Restructured Clinical (RC) Scales onto normal personality traits: Evidence of construct validity. *Journal of Personality Assessment, 85,* 179-187.

9. Sellbom, M., Ben-Porath, Y. S., & Bagby, R. M. (2008a). On the hierarchical structure of mood and anxiety disorders: Confirmatory evidence and elaboration of a model of temperament markers. *Journal of Abnormal Psychology, 117,* 576-590.

10. Sellbom, M., Ben-Porath, Y. S., & Graham, J. R. (2006). Correlates of the MMPI-2 Restructured Clinical (RC) Scales in a college counseling setting. *Journal of Personality Assessment, 86,* 89-99.

11. Sellbom, M., Graham, J. R., & Schenk, P. (2006). Incremental validity of the MMPI-2 Restructured Clinical (RC) Scales in a private practice sample. *Journal of Personality Assessment, 86,* 196-205.

12. Simms, L. J., Casillas, A., Clark, L. A., Watson, D., & Doebbeling, B. I. (2005). Psychometric evaluation of the Restructured Clinical Scales of the MMPI-2. *Psychological Assessment, 17,* 345-358.

13. Tellegen, A., & Ben-Porath, Y. S. (2008). *The Minnesota Multiphasic Personality Inventory-2-Restructured Form (MMPI-2-RF): Technical manual.* Minneapolis: University of Minnesota Press.
14. Tellegen, A., Ben-Porath, Y. S., Sellbom, M., Arbisi, P. A., McNulty, J. L., & Graham, J. R. (2006). Further evidence on the validity of the MMPI-2 Restructured Clinical (RC) Scales: Addressing questions raised by Rogers et al. and Nichols. *Journal of Personality Assessment, 87,* 148-171.
15. Wolf, E. J., Miller, M. W., Orazem, R. J., Weierich, M. R., Castillo, D. T., Milford, J., Kaloupek, D. G., & Keane, T. M. (2008). The MMPI-2 Restructured Clinical Scales in the assessment of posttraumatic stress disorder and comorbid disorders. *Psychological Assessment, 20,* 327-340.

End of Report

ITEM RESPONSES

1: 2	2: 1	3: 2	4: 1	5: 2	6: 2	7: 1	8: 1	9: 1	10: 2
11: 1	12: 1	13: 2	14: 2	15: 2	16: 2	17: 2	18: 2	19: 2	20: 2
21: 1	22: 1	23: 2	24: 2	25: 1	26: 2	27: 2	28: 1	29: 2	30: 2
31: 1	32: 1	33: 2	34: 1	35: 2	36: 2	37: 1	38: 1	39: 1	40: 2
41: 2	42: 2	43: 2	44: 2	45: 2	46: 1	47: 2	48: 2	49: 2	50: 2
51: 1	52: 2	53: 1	54: 2	55: 1	56: 2	57: 1	58: 1	59: 1	60: 2
61: 2	62: 2	63: 1	64: 1	65: 2	66: 2	67: 1	68: 1	69: 2	70: 2
71: 1	72: 2	73: 1	74: 2	75: 2	76: 2	77: 1	78: 1	79: 2	80: 2
81: 2	82: 1	83: 1	84: 2	85: 2	86: 2	87: 2	88: 1	89: 2	90: 1
91: 2	92: 2	93: 2	94: 2	95: 2	96: 2	97: 2	98: 2	99: 2	100: 1
101: 2	102: 2	103: 1	104: 1	105: 2	106: 2	107: 2	108: 2	109: 1	110: 2
111: 2	112: 2	113: 2	114: 1	115: 1	116: 1	117: 2	118: 1	119: 1	120: 2
121: 1	122: 2	123: 2	124: 2	125: 2	126: 2	127: 1	128: 1	129: 2	130: 1
131: 1	132: 1	133: 2	134: 1	135: 2	136: 1	137: 2	138: 1	139: 2	140: 1
141: 2	142: 2	143: 1	144: 2	145: 2	146: 2	147: 1	148: 2	149: 2	150: 2
151: 2	152: 2	153: 2	154: 2	155: 1	156: 1	157: 1	158: 2	159: 2	160: 1
161: 1	162: 1	163: 1	164: 2	165: 1	166: 2	167: 2	168: 2	169: 2	170: 2
171: 1	172: 2	173: 2	174: 1	175: 2	176: 2	177: 2	178: 1	179: 1	180: 2
181: 1	182: 2	183: 2	184: 2	185: 1	186: 1	187: 2	188: 1	189: 1	190: 2
191: 2	192: 2	193: 2	194: 1	195: 2	196: 1	197: 1	198: 2	199: 2	200: 1
201: 2	202: 2	203: 2	204: 1	205: 1	206: 2	207: 1	208: 2	209: 1	210: 1
211: 1	212: 2	213: 2	214: 2	215: 1	216: 2	217: 1	218: 2	219: 1	220: 1
221: 1	222: 1	223: 2	224: 2	225: 2	226: 2	227: 1	228: 1	229: 2	230: 2
231: 2	232: 2	233: 1	234: 2	235: 1	236: 2	237: 2	238: 1	239: 1	240: 2
241: 1	242: 1	243: 2	244: 1	245: 1	246: 1	247: 1	248: 2	249: 1	250: 1
251: 2	252: 2	253: 2	254: 2	255: 2	256: 1	257: 2	258: 2	259: 2	260: 2
261: 2	262: 2	263: 2	264: 2	265: 1	266: 2	267: 1	268: 1	269: 2	270: 2
271: 1	272: 1	273: 2	274: 1	275: 1	276: 2	277: 2	278: 1	279: 1	280: 2
281: 1	282: 2	283: 2	284: 1	285: 2	286: 1	287: 2	288: 1	289: 2	290: 2
291: 1	292: 1	293: 2	294: 2	295: 1	296: 2	297: 2	298: 2	299: 2	300: 1
301: 2	302: 2	303: 1	304: 2	305: 1	306: 2	307: 1	308: 2	309: 2	310: 2
311: 1	312: 2	313: 2	314: 2	315: 2	316: 1	317: 2	318: 2	319: 1	320: 2
321: 1	322: 1	323: 1	324: 2	325: 1	326: 2	327: 2	328: 1	329: 2	330: 1
331: 2	332: 2	333: 2	334: 2	335: 1	336: 1	337: 2	338: 1		

APPENDIX C

ANSWERS TO PRACTICE PROBLEMS

Chapter 2

1. Calculate the mean, variance, and standard deviation for the following score distributions.

Distribution 1	Distribution 2	Distribution 3
Mean = 7.267	Mean = 5.467	Mean = 5.20
Variance = 3.3956	Variance = 5.182	Variance = 4.427
SD = 1.8427	SD = 2.276	SD = 2.104

2. Calculate the Pearson Correlation Coefficient for the following pairs of scores.

Sample 1: r = 0.631

Sample 2: r = 0.886

Sample 3: r = 0.26

Chapter 3

1. Transform the following raw scores to the specified standard score formats. The raw score distribution has a mean of 70 and standard deviation of 10.

a Raw score = 85	z-score = 1.5	T-score = 65
b Raw score = 60	z-score = −1.0	T-score = 40
c Raw score = 55	z-score = −1.5	T-score = 35
d Raw score = 95	z-score = 2.5	T-score = 75
e Raw score = 75	z-score = 0.5	T-score = 55

2 Convert the following z-scores to T-scores and CEEB scores.

a z-score = 1.5	T-score = 65	CEEB score = 650
b z-score = −1.5	T-score = 35	CEEB score = 350
c z-score = 2.5	T-score = 75	CEEB score = 750
d z-score = −2.0	T-score = 30	CEEB score = 300
e z-score = −1.70	T-score = 33	CEEB score = 330

Chapter 4

1. Calculating KR-20:

	Item 1	Item 2	Item 3	Item 4	Item 5	Total Score
Student 1	0	1	1	0	1	3
Student 2	1	1	1	1	1	5
Student 3	1	0	1	0	0	2
Student 4	0	0	0	1	0	1
Student 5	1	1	1	1	1	5
Student 6	1	1	0	1	0	3
pi	0.6667	0.6667	0.6667	0.6667	0.5	SD *2 = 2.1389
qi	0.3333	0.3333	0.3333	0.3333	0.5	
pi *qi	0.2222	0.2222	0.2222	0.2222	0.25	

SUM p_i*q_i = 0.2222 + 0.2222 + 0.2222 + 0.2222 + 0.25

SUM p_i*q_i = 1.1388

KR-20 = 5/4*(2.1389 − 1.1388/2.139)

= 1.25*(1.0001/2.1389)

= 1.25*(0.4675)

= 0.58

2. Calculating Coefficient Alpha:

	Item 1	Item 2	Item 3	Item 4	Item 5	Total Score
Student 1	4	5	4	5	5	23
Student 2	3	3	2	3	2	13
Student 3	2	3	1	2	1	9
Student 4	4	4	5	5	4	22
Student 5	2	3	2	2	3	12
Student 6	1	2	2	1	3	9
SD_i^2	1.2222	0.8889	1.8889	2.3333	1.6667	SD² = 32.89

$$\text{Coefficient Alpha} = 5/4*\left(1 - \frac{1.2222 + 0.8889 + 1.8889 + 2.3333 + 1.6667}{32.89}\right)$$

= 1.25*(1 − 8/32.89)

= 1.25*(1 − 0.2432)

= 1.25*(0.7568)

= 0.946

REFERENCES

Achenbach, T. M. (1991a). *Manual for the Child Behavior Checklists/4–18 and 1991 profile*. Burlington: University of Vermont, Department of Psychiatry.

Achenbach, T. M. (1991b). *Manual for the Teacher's Report Form and 1991 profile*. Burlington: University of Vermont, Department of Psychiatry.

Aiken, L. R. (2000). *Psychological testing and assessment*. Boston: Allyn & Bacon.

Aiken, L. R. (2002). *Psychological testing and assessment*. New York: Allyn & Bacon.

Alley, G., & Foster, C. (1978). Nondiscriminatory testing of minority and exceptional children. *Focus on Exceptional Children, 9,* 1–14.

American Educational Research Association. (2000). *AERA position statement concerning high-stakes testing in PreK–12 education*. Retrieved April 12, 2011, from http://www.aera.net/policyandprograms/?id=378

American Educational Research Association, American Psychological Association, & National Council on Measurement in Education. (1999). *Standards for educational and psychological testing*. Washington, DC: American Educational Research Association.

American Psychiatric Association. (2000). *Diagnostic and statistical manual of mental disorders* (4th ed., text rev.). Washington, DC: Author.

American Psychological Association. (1954). Technical recommendations for psychological tests and diagnostic techniques. *Psychological Bulletin, 51* (2, pt. 2).

American Psychological Association. (1966). *Standards for educational and psychological tests and manuals*. Washington, DC: Author.

American Psychological Association. (1993, January). Call for book proposals for test instruments. *APA Monitor, 24,* 12.

American Psychological Association. (2002). Ethical principles of psychologists and code of conduct. *American Psychologist, 57,* 1060–1073.

American Psychological Association, American Educational Research Association, & National Council on Measurement in Education. (1974). *Standards for educational and psychological testing*. Washington, DC: Author.

American Psychological Association, American Educational Research Association, & National Council on Measurement in Education. (1985). *Standards for educational and psychological testing*. Washington, DC: Author.

Amrein, A. L., & Berliner, D. C. (2002). High-stakes testing, uncertainty, and student learning. *Education Policy Analysis Archives, 10*(18). Retrieved from http://epaa.asu.edu/epaa/v10n18/

Anastasi, A., & Urbina, S. (1997). *Psychological testing* (7th ed.). Upper Saddle River, NJ: Prentice Hall.

Anderson, N., & Witvliet, C. (2008). Fairness reactions to personnel selection methods: An international comparison between the Netherlands, the United States, France, Spain, Portugal, and Singapore. *International Journal of Selection and Assessment, 16*(1), 1–13.

Arthur, W., Day, E. A., McNelly, T. L., & Edens, P. S. (2003). A meta-analysis of the criterion-related validity of assessment center dimensions. *Personnel Psychology, 56,* 125–154.

Arvey, R. D., & Faley, R. H. (1992). *Fairness in selecting employees*. New York: Addison-Wesley.

Asher, J. J., & Sciarrino, J. A. (1974). Realistic work sample tests: A review. *Personnel Psychology, 27,* 519–533.

Austin, J. T., & Villanova, P. (1992). The criterion problem: 1917–1992. *Journal of Applied Psychology, 77*(6), 836–874.

Bakker, D. J., Fisk, J. L., & Strang, J. D. (1983). *Child neuropsychology.* New York: Guilford Press.

Baron, I., Fennell, E., & Voeller, K. (1995). *Pediatric neuropsychology in the medical setting.* New York: Oxford University Press.

Barona, A., Reynolds, C., & Chastain, R. (1984). A demographically based index of premorbid intelligence for the WAIS-R. *Journal of Consulting and Clinical Psychology, 52*(5), 885–887.

Barrick, M. R., & Mount, M. K. (1991). The big five personality dimensions and job performance: A meta-analysis. *Personnel Psychology, 44,* 1–26.

Beck, A. T., Steer, R. A., & Brown, G. K. (1996). *Manual for the Beck Depression Inventory—Second Edition.* San Antonio, TX: Psychological Corporation.

Becker, T. E., & Klimoski, R. J. (1989). A field study of the relationship between the organizational feedback environment and performance. *Personnel Psychology, 42,* 343–358.

Benjamin, L. T. (1997). Organized industrial psychology before division 14: The ACP and the AAAP (1930–1945). *Journal of Applied Psychology, 82*(4), 459–466.

Ben-Porath, Y. S., & Tellegen, A. (2008). *MMPI-2-RF (Minnesota Multiphasic Personality Inventory—Second Edition): Manual for administration, scoring, and interpretation.* Minneapolis: University of Minnesota Press.

Berry, C. M., Sackett, P. R., & Wiemann, S. (2007). A review of recent developments in integrity test research. *Personnel Psychology, 60,* 271–301.

Binder, L. M., & Johnson-Greene, D. (1995). Observer effects on neuropsychological performance: A case report. *The Clinical Neuropsychologist, 9,* 74–78.

Bloom, B. S., Engelhart, M. D., Furst, E. J., Hill, W. H., & Krathwohl, D. R. (1956). *Taxonomy of educational objectives: The classification of educational goals: Handbook. Cognitive domain.* White Plains, NY: Longman.

Bommer, W. H., Johnson, J. L., Rich, G. A., Podsakoff, P. M., & Mackenzie, S. B. (1995). On the interchangeability of objective and subjective measures of employee performance: A meta-analysis. *Personnel Psychology, 48,* 587–605.

Borman, W. C. (1991). Job behavior, performance, and effectiveness. In M. D. Dunnette & L. M. Hough (Eds.), *Handbook of industrial and organizational psychology* (pp. 271–326). Palo Alto, CA: Consulting Psychologists Press.

Boser, U. (1999). Study finds mismatch between California standards and assessments. *Education Week, 18,* 10.

Braden, J. P. (1997). The practical impact of intellectual assessment issues. *School Psychology Review, 26,* 242–248.

Brookhart, S. M. (2004). *Grading.* Upper Saddle River, NJ: Pearson Merrill Prentice Hall.

Brown, R. T., Reynolds, C. R., & Whitaker, J. S. (1999). Bias in mental testing since "Bias in Mental Testing." *School Psychology Quarterly, 14,* 208–238.

Bush, S., Ruff, R., Troster, A., Barth, J., Koffler, S., Pliskin, N., . . . Silver, C. (2005). Symptom validity assessment: Practice issues and medical necessity. *Archives of Clinical Neuropsychology, 20,* 419–426.

Butcher, J. N., Dahlstrom, W. G., Graham, J. R., Tellegen, A., & Kaemmer, B. (1989). MMPI-2: Manual for administration and scoring. Minneapolis: University of Minnesota Press.

Byham, W. C. (1970). Assessment center for spotting future managers. *Harvard Business Review, 48,* 150–160.

Camilli, G., & Shepard, L. A. (1994). *Methods for identifying biased test items.* Thousand Oaks, CA: Sage.

Campbell, D. T., & Fiske, D. W. (1959). Convergent and discriminant validation by the multitrait-multimethod matrix. *Psychological Bulletin, 56*(2), 546–553.

Campion, M., Pursell, E., & Brown, B. (1988). Structured interviewing: Raising the psychometric properties of the employment interview. *Personnel Psychology, 41,* 25–42.

Cannell, J. J. (1988). Nationally normed elementary achievement testing in America's public schools: How all 50 states are above average. *Educational Measurement: Issues and Practice, 7,* 5–9.

Cannell, J. J. (1989). *The "Lake Wobegon" report: How public educators cheat on standardized achievement tests.* Albuquerque, NM: Friends for Education.

Canter, A. S. (1997). The future of intelligence testing in the schools. *School Psychology Review, 26,* 255–261.

Carroll, J. B. (1993). *Human cognitive abilities: A survey of factor-analytic studies.* New York: Cambridge University Press.

Cascio, W. F. (1991). *Applied Psychology in Personnel Management.* Upper Saddle River, NJ: Prentice Hall.

Case, J. C., & Blackwell, T. L. (2008). Test review: Strong Interest Inventory, Revised Edition. *Rehabilitation Counseling Bulletin, 51*(2), 122–126.

Cattell, R. (1966). *Handbook of multivariate experimental psychology.* Chicago: Rand McNally.

Cederblom, D., & Lounsbury, J. W. (1980). An investigation of user acceptance of peer evaluations. *Personnel Psychology, 33,* 567–579.

Ceperley, P. E., & Reel, K. (1997). The impetus for the Tennessee value-added accountability system. In J. Millman (Ed.), *Grading teachers, grading schools* (pp. 133–136). Thousand Oaks, CA: Corwin Press.

Chan, D., Schmitt, N., DeShon, R. P., Clause, C. S., & Delbridge, K. (1997). Reaction to cognitive ability tests: The relationship between race, test performance, face validity, and test-taking motivation. *Journal of Applied Psychology, 82,* 300–310.

Chandler, L. A. (1990). The projective hypothesis and the development of projective techniques for children. In C. R. Reynolds & R. Kamphaus (Eds.), *Handbook of psychological and educational assessment of children: Personality, behavior, & context* (pp. 55–69). New York: Guilford Press.

Chinn, P. C. (1979). The exceptional minority child: Issues and some answers. *Exceptional Children, 46,* 532–536.

Christ, T. J., Burns, M. K., & Ysseldyke, J. E. (2005). Conceptual confusion within response-to-intervention vernacular: Clarifying meaningful differences. *Communiqué, 34*(3), 1–2.

Cizek, G. J. (1998). Filling in the blanks: Putting standardized tests to the test. *Fordham Report, 2*(11).

Cleary, T. A., Humphreys, L. G., Kendrick, S. A., & Wesman, A. (1975). Educational uses of tests with disadvantaged students. *American Psychologist, 30,* 15–41.

Cohen, R. C., & Swerdlik, M. E. (2002). Psychological testing and assessment: An introduction to tests and measurement. New York: McGraw-Hill.

Cole, N. S., & Moss, P. A. (1989). Bias in test use. In R. L. Linn (Ed.), *Educational measurement* (3rd ed., pp. 201–219). New York: Macmillan.

Cooper, W. H. (1981). Ubiquitous halo. *Psychological Bulletin, 90*(2), 218–244.

Costa, P. T., & McCrae, R. R. (1992). *Professional manual: Revised NEO Personality Inventory (NEO PI-R) and NEO Five-Factor Inventory (NEO-FFI).* Odessa, FL: Psychological Assessment Resources.

Costin, F. (1970). The optimal number of alternatives in multiple-choice achievement tests: Some empirical evidence for a mathematical proof. *Educational & Psychological Measurement, 30,* 353–358.

Crawford, J., Stewart, L., Cochrane, R., & Foulds, J. (1989). Estimating premorbid IQ from demographic variables: Regression equations derived from a UK sample. *British Journal of Clinical Psychology, 28*(3), 275–278.

Crocker, L., & Algina, J. (1986). *Introduction to classical and modern test theory.* Belmont, CA: Wadsworth.

Cronbach, L., Rajaratnam, N., & Gleser, G. (1963). Theory of generalizability: A liberalization of reliability theory. *British Journal of Statistical Psychology, 16*(2), 137–163.

Cronbach, L. J. (1951). Coefficient alpha and the internal structure of tests. *Psychometrika, 16,* 297–334.

Cronbach, L. J. (1990). *Essentials of psychological testing* (5th ed.). New York: HarperCollins.

Cronbach, L. J., & Gleser, G. C. (1965). *Psychological tests and personnel decisions* (2nd ed.). Champaign: University of Illinois Press.

CTB/Macmillan/McGraw-Hill. (1993). *California Achievement Test/5.* Monterey, CA: Author.

Cullum, M. (1998). Neuropsychological assessment of adults. In C. R. Reynolds (Ed.), Assessment, Vol. 4 of A. Bellack & M. Hersen (Eds.), *Comprehensive clinical psychology* (pp. 303–348). Oxford, England: Elsevier Science.

Cummins, J. (1984). *Bilingualism and special education: Issues in assessment and pedagogy.* Clevedon, England: Multilingual Matters.

Dahlstrom, W. G. (1993). Tests: Small samples, large consequences. *American Psychologist, 48,* 393–399.

Dawes, R. M., Faust, D., & Meehl, P. E. (1989). Clinical versus actuarial judgment. *Science, 243,* 1668–1774.

Deiderich, P. B. (1973). *Short-cut statistics for teacher-made tests.* Princeton, NJ: Educational Testing Service.

DeNisi, A .S., & Mitchell, J. L. (1978). An analysis of peer ratings as predictors & criterion measures and a proposed new application. *Academy of Management Review, 3,* 369–374.

Derogatis, L. R. (1994). *Symptom Checklist–90-R: Administration, scoring, and procedures manual* (3rd ed.). Minneapolis, MN: National Computer Systems.

Doherty, K. M. (2002). Education issues: Assessment. *Education Week.* Retrieved from http://www.edweek.org/context/topics/issuespage.cfm?id=41

Donnay, D., Morris, M., Schaubhut, N., & Thompson, R. (2004). *Strong Interest Inventory* (Rev. ed.). Mountain View, CA: Consulting Psychologists Press.

Dudek, F. (1979). The continuing misinterpretation of the standard error of measurement. *Psychological Bulletin, 86*(2), 335–337.

Embretson, S., & Reise, S. (2000). *Item response theory for psychologists.* London: Taylor & Francis.

Engelhart, M. D. (1965). A comparison of several item discrimination indices. *Journal of Educational Measurement, 2,* 69–76.

Exner, J. E. (1974). *The Rorschach: A comprehensive system, I.* New York: Wiley.

Exner, J. E., Jr. (1991). *The Rorschach: A comprehensive system: Vol. 2. Interpretation* (2nd ed.). New York: Wiley.

Exner, J. E., Jr. (1993). *The Rorschach: A comprehensive system: Vol. 1. Basic foundations* (3rd ed.). New York: Wiley.

Exner, J. E., Jr., & Weiner, I. B. (1995). *The Rorschach: A comprehensive system: Vol. 3. Assessment of children and adolescents* (2nd ed.). New York: Wiley.

Fancher, R. E. (1985). *The intelligence men: Makers of the IQ controversy.* New York: Norton.

Farmer, W. L. (2006). *A brief review of biodata history, research, and applications.* Retrieved from http://www.dtic.mil/cgi-bin/

GetTRDoc?AD=ADA460872&Location= U2&doc=GetTRDoc.pdf

Feifer, S. G., & Della Toffalo, D. (2007). *Integrating RTI with cognitive neuropsychology: A scientific approach to reading*. Middletown, MD: School Neuropsych Press.

Fennell, E., & Bauer, R. (2009). Models of inference in evaluating brain–behavior relationships in children. In E. Fletcher-Janzen & C. R. Reynolds (Eds.), *Handbook of clinical child neuropsychology* (3rd ed., pp. 231–243). New York: Springer Science + Business Media.

Finch, A. J., & Belter, R. W. (1993). Projective techniques. In T. H. Ollendick & M. Hersen (Eds.), *Handbook of child and adolescent assessment* (pp. 224–238). Boston: Allyn & Bacon.

Fiske, D. (1949). Consistency of the factorial structures of personality ratings from different sources. *Journal of Abnormal and Social Psychology, 44*(3), 329–344.

Flaugher, R. (1978). The many definitions of test bias. *American Psychologist, 33*(7), 671–679.

Fletcher, J. M., Foorman, B. R., Boudousquie, A., Barnes, M. A., Schatschneider, C., & Francis, D. J. (2002). Assessment of reading and learning disabilities: A research based intervention-oriented approach. *Journal of School Psychology, 40,* 27–63.

Flynn, J. R. (1998). IQ gains over time: Toward finding the cause. In U. Neisser (Ed.), *The rising curve: Long-term gains in IQ and related measures* (pp. 25–66). Washington, DC: American Psychological Association.

Forer, B. (1949). The fallacy of personal validation: A classroom demonstration of gullibility. *Journal of Abnormal and Social Psychology, 44,* 118–123.

Friedenberg, L. (1995). *Psychological testing: Design, analysis, and use*. Boston: Allyn & Bacon.

Fuchs, D., Mock, D., Morgan, P., & Young, C. (2003). Responsiveness-to-intervention: Definitions, evidence, and implications for the learning disabilities construct. *Learning Disabilities Research & Practice* (Blackwell Publishing Limited), *18*(3), 157–171.

Fuchs, L. S. (2002). Best practices in providing accommodations for assessment. In A. Thomas & J. Grimes (Eds.), *Best practices in school psychology IV* (pp. 899–909). Bethesda, MD: NASP.

Fuchs, L. S., Fuchs, D., Eaton, S. B., Hamlett, C., Binkley, E., & Crouch, R. (2000). Using objective data sources to enhance teacher judgments about test accommodations. *Exceptional Children, 67,* 67–81.

Fuchs, L. S., Fuchs, D., Eaton, S. B., Hamlett, C. L., & Karns, K. M. (2000). Supplemental teacher judgments of mathematics test accommodations with objective data sources. *School Psychology Review, 29,* 65–85.

Galton, F. (1884). Measurement of character. *Fortnightly Review, 42,* 179–185. (Reprinted in L. D. Goodstein & R. I. Lanyon (Eds.), *Readings in personality assessment.* New York: Wiley.)

Gatewood, R. D., & Feild, H. S. (1998). *Human resource selection*. Fort Worth, TX: Dryden Press.

Gaugler, B. B., Rosenthal, D. B., Thornton, G. C., & Bentson, C. (1987). Meta-analysis of assessment center validity. *Journal of Applied Psychology, 72*(3), 493–511.

Gay, G. H. (1990). Standardized tests: Irregularities in administering the test effects test results. *Journal of Instructional Psychology, 17,* 93–103.

Ghiselli, E. E., Campbell, J. P., & Zedeck, S. (1981). *Measurement theory for the behavioral sciences*. San Francisco: W.H. Freeman.

Gillberg, C. (1995). The prevalence of autism and autism spectrum disorders. In H. M. Koot & F. C. Verhulst (Eds.), *The epidemiology of child and adolescent psychopathology* (pp. 227–257). New York: Oxford University Press.

Glutting, J., McDermott, P., & Stanley, J. (1987). Resolving differences among methods of establishing confidence limits for test scores. *Educational and Psychological Measurement, 47*(3), 607–614.

Godwin-Austen, R., & Bendall, J. (1990). *The neurology of the elderly*. New York: Springer-Verlag.

Goldberg, L. (1993). The structure of phenotypic personality traits. *American Psychologist, 48*(1), 26–34.

Golden, C. J. (1997). The Luria-Nebraska Neuropsychological Battery—Children's Revision. In C. R. Reynolds & E. Fletcher-Janzen (Eds.), *Handbook of clinical child neuropsychology* (2nd ed., pp. 237–251). New York: Plenum Press.

Golden, C. J., Purisch, A. D., & Hammeke, T. A. (1991). *Luria-Nebraska Neuropsychological Battery: Forms I and II (manual)*. Los Angeles: Western Psychological Services.

Gottfredson, L. (1986). Societal consequences of the *g* factor in employment. *Journal of Vocational Behavior, 29,* 379–410.

Gould, S. J. (1995). Curveball. In S. Fraser (Ed.), *The bell curve wars: Race, intelligence, and the future of America* (pp. 11–22). New York: Basic Books.

Gould, S. J. (1996). *The mismeasure of man* (rev. ed.). New York: Norton

Graham, J. R. (1993). *MMPI-2: Assessing personality and psychopathology* (2nd ed.). New York: Oxford University Press.

Graham, J. R. (2000). *MMPI-2: Assessing personality and psychopathology* (3rd ed.). New York: Oxford University Press.

Gray, P. (1999). *Psychology*. New York: Worth.

Gregory, R. (2004). *Psychological testing: History, principles, and applications*. Needham Heights, MA: Allyn & Bacon.

Greiffenstein, M., Baker, W., & Gola, T. (1994). Validation of malingered amnesia measures with a large clinical sample. *Psychological Assessment, 6*(3), 218–224.

Gresham, F. M., & Witt, J. C. (1997). Utility of intelligence tests for treatment planning, classification, and placement decisions. Recent empirical findings and future directions. *School Psychology Quarterly, 12,* 146–154.

Grier, J. (1975). The number of alternatives for optimum test reliability. *Journal of Educational Measurement, 12*(2), 109–113.

Gronlund, N. E. (2003). *Assessment of student achievement* (7th ed.). Boston: Allyn & Bacon.

Grove, W. M., & Meehl, P. E. (1996). Comparative efficiency of informal (subjective, impressionistic) and formal (mechanical, algorithmic) prediction procedures: The clinical-statistical controversy. *Psychology, Public Policy, and Law, 2,* 293–323.

Guilford, J. (1936). *Psychometric methods*. New York: McGraw-Hill.

Guilliksen, H. (1950). *Theory of mental tests*. New York: Wiley.

Guion, R. (1998). Some virtues of dissatisfaction in the science and practice of personnel selection. *Human Resource Management Review, 8*(4), 351–365.

Guion, R. M. (1991). Personnel assessment, selection, and placement. In M. D. Dunnette & L. M. Hough (Eds.), *Handbook of industrial and organizational psychology* (pp. 327–397). Palo Alto, CA: Consulting Psychologists Press.

Guion, R. M., & Gottier, R. F. (1965). Validity of personality measures in personnel selection. *Personnel Psychology, 8,* 135–164.

Halpern, D. F. (1997). Sex differences in intelligence: Implications for education. *American Psychologist, 52,* 1091–1102.

Halstead, W. (1947). *Brain and intelligence: A quantitative study of the frontal lobes*. Chicago: University of Chicago Press.

Hammer, E. (1985). The House-Tree-Person Test. In C. Newmark (Ed.), *Major psychological assessment instruments* (pp. 135–164). Boston: Allyn & Bacon.

Handler, L. (1985). The clinical use of the Draw-A-Person (DAP) Test. In C. Newmark (Ed.), *Major psychological assessment instruments* (pp. 165–216). Boston: Allyn & Bacon.

Harkness, A. R., & McNulty, J. L. (1994). The Personality Psychopathology Five (PSY-5): Issues from the pages of a diagnostic manual instead of a dictionary. In *Differentiating normal and abnormal personality* (pp. 291–315). New York: Springer.

Harrington, T. F., & O'Shea, A. J. (2000). *Career Decision-Making System—Revised.* Circle Pines, MN: American Guidance Service.

Harris, M. M., & Schaubroeck, J. (1988). A meta-analysis of self-supervisor, self-peer, and peer-supervisor ratings. *Personnel Psychology, 41,* 43–62.

Harvey, R. J. (1991). Job analysis. In M. D. Dunnette & L. M. Hough (Eds.), *Handbook of industrial and organizational psychology* (pp. 71–163). Palo Alto, CA: Consulting Psychologists Press.

Hathaway, S. R. (1960). Forward. In W. G. Dahlstrom, & G. S. Welsh, *An MMPI handbook: A guide to use in clinical practice and research.* Minneapolis: University of Minnesota Press.

Hathaway, S. R. (1972). Forward. In W. G. Dahlstrom, G. S. Welsh, & L. E. Dahlstrom, *An MMPI handbook: Vol. 1. Clinical interpretation.* Minneapolis: University of Minnesota Press.

Hathaway, S. R., & McKinley, J. C. (1940). A Multiphasic Personality Schedule: I. Construction of the schedule. *Journal of Psychology, 10,* 249–254.

Hathaway, S. R., & McKinley, J. C. (1943). *The Minnesota Multiphasic Personality Inventory* (Rev. ed.). Minneapolis: University of Minnesota Press.

Hathaway, S. R., & McKinley, J. C. (1989). *Manual for the Minnesota Multiphasic Personality Inventory-2 (MMPI-2).* Minneapolis: University of Minnesota Press.

Hausknecht, J. P., Day, D. V., & Thomas, S. C. (2004). Applicant reactions to selection procedures: An updated model and meta-analysis. *Personnel Psychology, 57,* 639–683.

Hays, W. (1994). *Statistics* (5th ed.). New York: Harcourt Brace.

Heaton, R. K., Miller, S. W., Taylor, M. J., & Grant, I. (2004). *Revised comprehensive norms for an expanded Halstead–Reitan battery (norms, manual and computer program).* Odessa, FL: Psychological Assessment Resources.

Helms, J. E. (1992). Why is there no study of cultural equivalence in standardized cognitive ability testing? *American Psychologist, 47,* 1083–1101.

Hermelin, E., Lievens, F., & Robertson, I. T. (2007). The validity of assessment centres for the prediction of supervisory performance ratings: A meta-analysis. *International Journal of Selection and Assessment, 15*(4), 405–411.

Herrnstein, R. J. (1982, August). IQ testing and the media. *Atlantic Monthly, 250,* 68–74.

Herszenhorn, D. M. (2006, May 5). As test-taking grows, test-makers grow rarer. *The New York Times.* Retrieved from http://www.noca.org/portals/0/nytimes-psychometrics.pdf

Hilliard, A. G. (1979). Standardization and cultural bias as impediments to the scientific study and validation of "intelligence." *Journal of Research and Development in Education, 12,* 47–58.

Hilliard, A. G. (1989). Back to Binet: The case against the use of IQ tests in the schools. *Diagnostique, 14,* 125–135.

Hoff, D. J. (1999). N.Y.C. probe levels test-cheating charges. *Education Week, 19,* 3.

Hoffman, C. C., Nathan, B. R., & Holden, L. M. (1991). A comparison of validation criteria: Objective versus subjective performance measures and self-versus supervisor ratings. *Personnel Psychology, 44,* 601–619.

Hogan, R., & Hogan, J. (1995). *Hogan Personality Inventory manual.* Tulsa, OK: Hogan Assessment Systems.

Holland, J. L. (1997). *Self-Directed Search* (4th ed.). Tampa Bay, FL: Psychological Assessment Resources.

Hopkins, K. D. (1998). *Educational and psychological measurement and evaluation* (8th ed.). Boston: Allyn & Bacon.

Horn, J. L. (1989). Measurement of intellectual capabilities: A review of theory. In K. S. McGrew, J. K. Werder, & R. W. Woodcock (Eds.), *WJ-R technical manual* (pp. 197–245). Chicago: Riverside.

Horn, J. L., & Noll, J. (1997). Human cognitive capabilities: *Gf-Gc* theory. In D. P. Flanagan, J. L. Genshaft, & P. L. Harrison (Eds.), *Contemporary intellectual assessment: Theories, tests and issues* (pp. 53–91). New York: Guilford Press.

Huffcutt, A. I., & Arthur, W., Jr. (1994). Hunter and Hunter (1984) revisited: Interview validity for entry-level jobs. *Journal of Applied Psychology, 79,* 184–190.

Hunter, J. E., & Hunter, R. F. (1984). Validity and utility of alternative predictors of job performance. *Psychological Bulletin, 96,* 72–98.

Hunter, J. E., Schmidt, F. L., & Hunter, R. (1979). Differential validity of employment tests by race: A comprehensive review and analysis. *Psychological Bulletin, 86,* 721–735.

Hunter, J. E., Schmidt, F. L., & Rauschenberger, L. (1984). Methodological, statistical, and ethical issues in the study of bias in psychological tests. In C. R. Reynolds & R. T. Brown (Eds.), *Perspectives on bias in mental testing* (pp. 41–100). New York: Plenum Press.

Hynd, G., & Obrzut, J. (1981). *Neuropsychological assessment of the school-aged child: Issues and procedures.* New York: Grune & Stratton.

International Task Force on Assessment Center Guidelines. (2000). *Guidelines and ethical considerations for assessment center operations.* Retrieved from http://www.assessmentcenters.org/pdf/00guidelines.pdf

Isquith, P., Roth, R., & Gioia, G. (2010). *Tasks of executive control: Professional manual.* Lutz, FL: Psychological Assessment Resources.

Jacob, S., & Hartshorne, T. (2007). *Ethics and law for school psychologists* (5th ed.). Hoboken, NJ: Wiley.

Jacobson, N., & Truax, P. (1991). Clinical significance: A statistical approach to defining meaningful change in psychotherapy research. *Journal of Consulting and Clinical Psychology, 59*(1), 12–19.

Janda, L. (1998). *Psychological testing: Theory and applications.* Needham Heights, MA: Allyn & Bacon.

Jensen, A. R. (1976). Test bias and construct validity. *Phi Delta Kappan, 58,* 340–346.

Jensen, A. R. (1980). *Bias in mental testing.* New York: Free Press.

Johnson, A. P. (1951). Notes on a suggested index of item validity: The U-L index. *Journal of Educational Measurement, 42,* 499–504.

Joint Committee on Testing Practices. (1998). *Rights and responsibilities of test takers: Guidelines and expectations.* Washington, DC: American Psychological Association.

Kamphaus, R., & Campbell, J. (Eds.). (2006). *Psychodiagnostic assessment of children: Dimensional and categorical approaches.* New York: Wiley.

Kamphaus, R. W. (1993). *Clinical assessment of children's intelligence: A handbook for professional practice.* Boston: Allyn & Bacon.

Kamphaus, R. W. (2001). *Clinical assessment of child and adolescent intelligence.* Boston: Allyn & Bacon.

Kamphaus, R. W., & Frick, P. J. (2002). *Clinical assessment of child and adolescent personality and behavior*. Boston: Allyn & Bacon.

Kamphaus, R. W., & Reynolds, C. R. (1998). BASC Monitor for ADHD. Circle Pines, MN: American Guidance Service.

Kamphaus, R. W., & Reynolds, C. R. (2006). *Parenting relationship questionnaire*. Bloomington, MN: Pearson Assessments.

Kaplan, E. (1988). A process approach to neuropsychological assessment. In T. Boll & B. K. Bryant (Eds.), *Clinical neuropsychology and brain function: Research, measurement, and practice*. Washington, DC: American Psychological Association.

Kaplan, E. (1990). The process approach to neuropsychological assessment of psychiatric patients. *Journal of Neuropsychiatry, 2*(1), 72–87.

Katzell, R. A., & Austin, J. T. (1992). From then to now: The development of industrial-organizational psychology in the United States. *Journal of Applied Psychology, 77*(6), 803–835.

Kaufman, A. S. (1994). *Intelligent testing with the WISC-III*. New York: Wiley.

Kaufman, A. S. (2009). *IQ testing 101*. New York: Springer.

Kaufman, A. S., & Lichtenberger, E. O. (1999). *Essentials of WAIS-III assessment*. New York: Wiley.

Keith, T. Z., & Reynolds, C. R. (1990). Measurement and design issues in child assessment research. In C. R. Reynolds & R. W. Kamphaus (Eds.), *Handbook of psychological and educational assessment of children: Intelligence and achievement* (pp. 29–62). New York: Guilford Press.

Keller, B. (2001). Dozens of Michigan schools under suspicion of cheating. *Education Week, 20,* 18, 30.

Kelley, T. L. (1939). The selection of upper and lower groups for the validation of test items. *Journal of Educational Psychology, 30,* 17–24.

King, W. L., Baker, J., & Jarrow, J. E. (1995). *Testing accommodations for students with disabilities*. Columbus, OH: Association on Higher Education and Disability.

Kober, N. (2002). Teaching to the test: The good, the bad, and who's responsible. *Test Talk for Leaders* (Issue 1). Washington, DC: Center on Education Policy. Retrieved from http://www.cep-dc.org/testing/testtalkjune2002.htm

Koppes, L. L. (1997). American female pioneers of industrial and organizational psychology during the early years. *Journal of Applied Psychology, 82*(4), 500–515.

Koppitz, E. M. (1977). *The visual aural digit span test*. New York: Grune & Stratton.

Kovacs, M. (1991). *The children's depression inventory* (CDI). North Tonawanda, NY: Multi-Health Systems.

Kranzler, J. H. (1997). Educational and policy issues related to the use and interpretation of intelligence tests in the schools. *School Psychology Review, 26,* 50–63.

Kubiszyn, T., & Borich, G. (2003). *Educational testing and measurement: Classroom application and practice* (7th ed.). New York: Wiley.

Kuder, G. F., & Richardson, M. W. (1937). The theory of the estimation of reliability. *Psychometrika, 2,* 151–160.

Lamb, K. (1994). Genetics and Spearmans's "g" factor. *Mankind Quarterly, 34*(4), 379–391.

Lance, C. (2008). Why assessment centers do not work the way they are supposed to. *Industrial and Organizational Psychology: Perspectives on Science and Practice, 1*(1), 84–97.

Landy, F. J. (1997). Early influences on the development of I/O psychology. *Journal of Applied Psychology, 82*(4), 467–477.

Latané, B. (1981). The psychology of social impact. *American Psychologist, 36*(4), 343–356.

Lawshe, C. H. (1975). A quantitative approach to content validity. *Personnel Psychology, 28,* 563–575.

Lee, D., Reynolds, C., & Willson, V. (2003). Standardized test administration: Why bother? *Journal of Forensic Neuropsychology, 3*(3), 55.

Likert, R. (1932). A technique for the measurement of attitudes. *Archives of Psychology, 22*(140), 55.

Lilienfeld, S. Lynn, S., Ruscio, J., & Beyerstein, B. (2010). *50 great myths of popular psychology.* Oxford, England: Wiley.

Linn, R. L., & Gronlund, N. E. (2000). *Measurement and assessment in teaching* (8th ed.). Upper Saddle River, NJ: Prentice Hall.

Livingston, R. B., Eglsaer, R., Dickson, T., & Harvey-Livingston, K. (2003). *Psychological assessment practices with children and adolescents.* Presentation at the 23rd Annual National Academy of Neuropsychology Conference, Dallas, TX.

Lord, F. M. (1952). The relation of the reliability of multiple-choice tests to the distribution of item difficulties. *Psychometrika, 17,* 181–194.

Lord, F. M., & Novick, M. R. (1968). *Statistical theories of mental test scores.* Reading, MA: Addison-Wesley.

Love, K. G. (1981). Comparison of peer assessment methods: Reliability, validity, friendship bias, and user reaction. *Journal of Applied Psychology, 66,* 451–457.

Luria, A. (1966). *Higher cortical functions in man* (B. Haigh, Trans.). New York: Basic Books.

Mael, F. A. (1991). A conceptual rationale for the domain and attributes of biodata items. *Personnel Psychology, 44,* 763–792.

Magnusson, D. (1967). *Test theory.* Reading, MA: Addison-Wesley.

Marshall, R., & Wilkinson, B. (2008). *Pediatric Behavior Rating Scale.* Lutz, FL: Psychological Assessment Services.

Maruish, M. E. (2004). Introduction. In M. Maruish (Ed.), *The use of psychological testing for treatment planning and outcomes assessment: Volume 1. General considerations* (3rd ed., pp. 1–64). Mahwah, NJ: Erlbaum.

Mastergeorge, A. M., & Miyoshi, J. N. (1999). *Accommodations for students with disabilities: A teacher's guide* (CSE Technical Report 508). Los Angeles: National Center for Research on Evaluation, Standards, and Student Testing.

McCaffrey, R. J., Fisher, J. M., Gold, B. A., & Lynch, J. K. (1996). Presence of third parties during neuropsychological evaluations: Who is evaluating whom? *The Clinical Neuropsychologist, 10,* 435–449.

McCarthy, D. (1972). *McCarthy Scales of Children's Abilities.* San Antonio, TX: Psychological Corporation.

McDaniel, M. A., Whetzel, D. L., Schmidt, F. L., & Maurer, S. D. (1994). The validity of employment interviews: A comprehensive review and meta-analysis. *Journal of Applied Psychology, 79*(4), 599–616.

McEvoy, G. M., & Buller, P. F. (1987). User acceptance of peer appraisals in an industrial setting. *Personnel Psychology, 40,* 785–797.

McFall, R. M., & Treat, T. T. (1999). Quantifying the information value of clinical assessment with signal detection theory. *Annual Review of Psychology, 50,* 215–241.

McGrew, K. (2009). Editorial: CHC theory and the human cognitive abilities project: Standing on the shoulders of the giants of psychometric intelligence research. *Intelligence, 37,* 1–10.

McGrew, K. S. (1997). Analysis of the major intelligence batteries according to a proposed comprehensive *Gf-Gc* framework. In D. P. Flanagan, J. L. Genshaft, & P. L. Harrison (Eds.), *Contemporary intellectual assessment: Theories, tests, and issues* (pp. 151–179). New York: Guilford Press.

McGrew, K. S. (2005). The Cattell-Horn-Carroll theory of cognitive abilities. In D. P. Flanagan & P. L. Harrison (Eds.), *Contemporary intellectual assessment: Theories, tests, and issues* (2nd ed., pp. 136–181). New York: Guilford Press.

Melton, G., Petrila, J., Poythress, N., & Slobogin, C. (1997). *Psychological evaluations for the courts: A handbook for mental health professionals and lawyers* (2nd ed.). New York: Guilford Press.

Melton, G., Petrila, J., Poythress, N., & Slobogin, C. (2007). *Psychological evaluations for the courts: A handbook for mental health professionals and lawyers* (3rd ed.). New York: Guilford Press.

Meriac, J. P., Hoffman, B. J., Woehr, D. J., & Fleisher, M. S. (2008). Further evidence for the validity of assessment center dimensions: A meta-analysis of the incremental criterion-related validity of dimension ratings. *Journal of Applied Psychology, 93*(5), 1042–1052.

Messick, S. (1989). Validity. In R. L. Linn (Ed.), *Educational measurement* (3rd ed., pp. 13–103). Upper Saddle River, NJ: Merrill Prentice Hall.

Messick, S. (1994). The interplay of evidence and consequences in the validation of performance assessments. *Educational Researcher, 23,* 13–23.

Meyer, G. J., Finn, S. E., Eyde, L. D., Kay, G. G., Moreland, K. L., Dies, R. R., . . . Reed, G. M. (2001). Psychological testing and psychological assessment: A review of evidence and issues. *American Psychologist, 56,* 128–165.

Millon, T., & Davis, R. (1996). An evolutionary theory of personality disorders. In J. F. Clarkin & M. F. Lenzenweger (Eds.), *Major theories of personality disorder* (pp. 221–346). New York: Guilford Press.

Millon, T., Millon, C., & Davis, R. D. (1994). *Manual for the Millon Clinical Multiaxial Inventory-III (MCMI-III).* Minneapolis, MN: National Computer Systems.

Morgeson, F. P, Campion, M. A., Dipboye, R. L., Hollenbeck, J. R., Murphy, K. & Schmitt, N. (2007). Reconsidering the use of personality tests in personnel selection contexts. *Personnel Psychology, 60,* 683–729.

Morgeson, F. P., Mumford, T. V., & Campion, M. A. (2005). Coming full circle using research and practice to address 27 questions about 360-degree feedback programs. *Consulting Psychology Journal: Practice and Research, 57*(3), 196–209.

Mount, M. K. (1984). Psychometric properties of subordinate ratings of managerial performance. *Personnel Psychology, 37,* 687–701.

Murphy, K. R., Cronin, B. E., & Tam, A. P. (2003). Controversy and consensus regarding the use of cognitive ability testing in organizations. *Journal of Applied Psychology, 88*(4), 660–671.

Murray, H. A. et al. (1943). *Thematic Apperception Test: Manual.* Cambridge, MA: Harvard University Press.

Myers, I. B., & McCaulley, M. H. (1985). *Manual: A guide to the development and use of the Myers-Briggs Type Indicator.* Palo Alto, CA: Consulting Psychologists Press.

Myers, I. B., McCaulley, M. H., Quenk, N. L., & Hammer, A. L. (1998). *MBTI Manual: A guide to the development and use of the Myers Briggs Type Indicator* (3rd ed). Palo Alto, CA: Consulting Psychologists Press.

Nathan, B. R., & Alexander, R. A. (1988). A comparison of criteria for test validation: A meta-analytic investigation. *Personnel Psychology, 41,* 517–535.

National Council on Measurement in Education. (1995). *Code of professional responsibilities in educational measurement.* Washington, DC: Author.

Neisser, U., BooDoo, G., Bouchard, T., Boykin, A., Brody, N., Ceci, S., . . . Urbina, S. (1996). Intelligence: Knowns and unknowns. *American Psychologist, 51,* 77–101.

Nitko, A. J. (2001). *Educational assessment of students.* Upper Saddle River, NJ: Merrill Prentice Hall.

Nitko, A. J. (Ed.). (1990). *Educational measurement: Issues and practice, 9*(4), 3–32.

Norcross, J. C. (2000). Clinical versus counseling psychology: What's the diff? *Eye on Psi Chi, 5*(1), 20–22.

Norcross, J. C., Karg, R. S., & Prochaska, J. O. (1997). Clinical psychologists in the 1990s: Part II. *Clinical Psychologist, 50,* 4–11.

Northeast Technical Assistance Center. (1999). Providing test accommodations. *NETAC Teacher Tipsheet.* Rochester, NY: Author.

Nunnally, J. C. (1978). *Psychometric theory* (2nd ed.). New York: McGraw-Hill.

Nunnally, J. C., & Bernstein, I. H. (1994). *Psychometric theory* (3rd ed.). New York: McGraw-Hill.

Olson, L. (2003). Georgia suspends testing plans in key grades. *Education Week, 22,* 1, 15.

Olson, R., Verley, J., Santos, L., & Salas, C. (2004). What we teach students about the Hawthorne studies: A review of content within a sample of introductory I-O and OB textbooks. *The Industrial-Organizational Psychologist, 41*(3), 23–39.

Ones, D. S., Dilchert, S., Viswesvaran, C., & Judge, T. A. (2007). In support of personality assessment in organizational settings. *Personnel Psychology, 60,* 995–1027.

Ones, D. S., Viswesvaran, C., & Schmidt, F. L. (1993). Comprehensive meta-analysis of integrity test validities: Findings and implications for personnel selection and theories of job performance. *Journal of Applied Psychology, 78*(4), 679–703.

Oosterhof, A. C. (1976).Similarity of various item discrimination indices. *Journal of Educational Measurement, 13,* 145–150.

Osterlind, S. J. (2006). *Modern measurement: Theory, principles, and applications of mental appraisal.* Upper Saddle River, NJ: Pearson.

Phelps, R., Eisman, E. J., & Kohout, J. (1998). Psychological practice and managed care: Results of the CAPP practitioner survey. *Professional Psychology: Research and Practice, 29,* 31–36.

Phillips, S. E. (1993). Testing accommodations for disabled students. *Education Law Reporter, 80,* 9–32.

Phillips, S. E. (1994). High-stakes testing accommodations: Validity versus disabled rights. *Applied Measurement in Education, 7*(2), 93–120.

Phillips, S. E. (1996). Legal defensibility of standards: Issues and policy perspectives. *Educational Measurement: Issues and Practice, 15*(2), 5–19.

Piacentini, J. (1993). Checklists and rating scales. In T. H. Ollendick & M. Hersen (Eds.), *Handbook of child and adolescent assessment* (pp. 82–97). Boston: Allyn & Bacon.

Pike, L. W. (1979). *Short-term instruction, testwiseness, and the Scholastic Aptitude Test: A literature review with research recommendations.* Princeton, NJ: Educational Testing Service.

Popham, W. J. (1999). *Classroom assessment: What teachers need to know.* Boston: Allyn & Bacon.

Popham, W. J. (2000). *Modern educational measurement: Practical guidelines for educational leaders.* Boston: Allyn & Bacon.

Powers, D. E., & Kaufman, J. C. (2002). *Do standardized multiple-choice tests penalize deep-thinking or creative students?* (RR-02-15). Princeton, NJ: Educational Testing Service.

Psychological Assessment Resources. (2003). *Catalog of professional testing resources* (p. 26). Lutz, FL: Author.

Psychological Corporation. (2002). *WIAT-II: Examiners manual.* San Antonio, TX: Author.

Psychological Corporation. (2003). *The catalog for psychological assessment products.* San Antonio, TX: Author.

Pulakos, E. D., & Schmitt, N. (1996). An evaluation of two strategies for reducing adverse impact and their effects on criterion-related validity. *Human Performance, 9,* 241–258.

Ramsay, M., Reynolds, C., & Kamphaus, R. (2002). *Essentials of behavioral assessment.* New York: Wiley.

Ramsay, M. C., & Reynolds, C. R. (1995). Separate digits tests: A brief history, a literature review, and re-examination of the factor structure of the Tests of Memory and Learning (TOMAL). *Neuropsychology Review, 5,* 151–171.

Randolph, C., Tierney, M. C., Mohr, E., & Chase, T. N. (1998). The Repeatable Battery for the Assessment of Neuropsychological Status (RBANS): Preliminary clinical validity. *Journal of Clinical and Experimental Neuropsychology, 20,* 310–319.

Reitan, R. M., & Wolfson, D. (1985). *The Halstead-Reitan Neuropsychological Test Battery.* Tucson, AZ: Neuropsychology Press.

Reitan, R. M., & Wolfson, D. (1993). *The Halstead-Reitan Neuropsychological Test Battery: Theory and clinical interpretation* (2nd ed.). Tucson, AZ: Neuropsychology Press.

Reynolds, C. (1997). Forward and backward memory span should not be combined for clinical analysis. *Archives of Clinical Neuropsychology, 12,* 29–40.

Reynolds, C., & Mayfield, J. (2005). Neuropsychological assessment in genetically linked neurodevelopmental disorders. In S. Goldstein & C. R. Reynolds (Eds.), *Handbook of neurodevelopmental and genetic disorders in adults* (pp. 9–28). New York: Guilford Press.

Reynolds, C., & Shaywitz, S. (2009). Response to Intervention: Ready or not? Or, from wait-to-fail to watch-them-fail. *School Psychology Quarterly, 24*(2), 130–145.

Reynolds, C., Willson, V., & Chatman, S. (1984). Item bias on the 1981 revision of the Peabody Picture Vocabulary Test using a new method of detecting bias. *Journal of Psychoeducational Assessment, 2*(3), 219–224.

Reynolds, C. R. (1980). In support of "Bias in Mental Testing" and scientific inquiry. *Behavioral and Brain Sciences, 3,* 352.

Reynolds, C. R. (1982). The problem of bias in psychological assessment. In C. R. Reynolds & T. B. Gutkin (Eds.), *The handbook of school psychology* (pp. 178–208). New York: Wiley.

Reynolds, C. R. (1983). Test bias: In God we trust; all others must have data. *Journal of Special Education, 17,* 241–260.

Reynolds, C. R. (1985). Critical measurement issues in learning disabilities. *Journal of Special Education, 18,* 451–476.

Reynolds, C. R. (1987). Raising intelligence: Clever Hans, Candides, and the Miracle in Milwaukee. *Journal of School Psychology, 25,* 309–312.

Reynolds, C. R. (1990). Conceptual and technical problems in learning disability diagnosis. In C. R. Reynolds & R. W. Kamphaus (Eds.), *Handbook of psychological and educational assessment of children: Intelligence and achievement* (pp. 571–592). New York: Guilford Press.

Reynolds, C. R. (1995). Test bias in the assessment of intelligence and personality. In D. Saklofsky & M. Zeidner (Eds.), *International handbook of personality and intelligence* (pp. 545–576). New York: Plenum Press.

Reynolds, C. R. (1998). Fundamentals of measurement and assessment in psychology. In A. Bellack & M. Hersen (Eds.), *Comprehensive clinical psychology* (pp. 33–55). New York: Elsevier.

Reynolds, C. R. (1999). Inferring causality from relational data and design: Historical and contemporary lessons for research and clinical practice. *The Clinical Neuropsychologist, 13,* 386–395.

Reynolds, C. R. (2000). Why is psychometric research on bias in mental testing so often ignored? *Psychology, Public Policy, and Law, 6,* 144–150.

Reynolds, C. R. (2002). *Comprehensive Trail-Making Test: Examiner's manual.* Austin, TX: Pro-Ed.

Reynolds, C. R. (August, 2005). *Considerations in RTI as a method of diagnosis of learning disabilities.* Paper presented to the Annual Institute for Psychology in the Schools of the American Psychological Association, Washington, DC.

Reynolds, C. R. (2007). Koppitz Developmental Scoring System for the Bender Geslalt Test (KOPPITZ-2). Austin, TX: Pro-Ed.

Reynolds, C. R. (2008). RTI, neuroscience, and sense: Chaos in the diagnosis and treatment of learning disabilities. In E. Fletcher-Janzen & C. R. Reynolds (Eds.), *Neuropsychological perspectives on learning disabilities in the era of RTI* (pp. 14–27). New York: Wiley.

Reynolds, C. R. (2009). *Determining the R in RTI: Which score is the best score?* Miniskills workshop presented at the annual meeting of the National Association of School Psychologists, February, Boston.

Reynolds, C. R., & Bigler, E. D. (1994). *Test of Memory and Learning.* Austin, TX: Pro-Ed.

Reynolds, C. R., & Bigler, E. D. (2001). Clinical Assessment Scales for the Elderly. Odessa, FL: Psychological Assessment Resources.

Reynolds, C. R., & Fletcher-Janzen, E. (2002). Intelligent testing. In C. R. Reynolds & E. Fletcher-Janzen (Eds.), *Concise encyclopedia of special education* (2nd ed., pp. 522–523). New York: Wiley.

Reynolds, C. R., & Fletcher-Janzen, E. (Eds.). (1997). *Handbook of clinical child neuropsychology* (2nd ed.). New York: Plenum Press.

Reynolds, C. R., Hays, J. R., & Ryan-Arredondo, K. (2001). When judges, laws, ethics, and rules of practice collide: A case study of assent and disclosure in assessment of a minor. *Journal of Forensic Neuropsychology, 2,* 41–52.

Reynolds, C. R., & Horton, A. M. (2010). *Detection of malingering in head injury litigation* (2nd ed.) New York: Springer.

Reynolds, C. R., & Kamphaus, R. W. (1992). *Behavior Assessment System for Children: Manual.* Circle Pines, MN: American Guidance Service.

Reynolds, C. R., & Kamphaus, R. W. (1998). *Behavior Assessment System for Children: Manual.* Circle Pines, MN: American Guidance Service.

Reynolds, C. R., & Kamphaus, R. W. (2002). *Clinical and research applications of the BASC.* New York: Guilford Press.

Reynolds, C. R., & Kamphaus, R. W. (2003). Reynolds Intellectual Assessment Scales. Lutz, FL: Psychological Assessment Resources.

Reynolds, C. R., & Kamphaus, R. W. (2004). Behavior Assessment System for Children (2nd ed.). Circle Pines, MN: American Guidance Service.

Reynolds, C. R., & Kamphaus, R. W. (2007). *Reynolds Intellectual Assessment Scales/ Wide Range Achievement Test 4 Discrepancy Interpretive Report professional manual supplement.* Lutz, FL: Psychological Assessment Resources.

Reynolds, C. R., & Kaufman, A. S. (1990). Assessment of children's intelligence with the Wechsler Intelligence Scale for Children—Revised (WISC-R). In C. R. Reynolds & R. W. Kamphaus (Eds.), *Handbook of psychological and educational assessment of children: Intelligence and achievement* (pp. 127–165). New York: Guilford Press.

Reynolds, C. R., Livingston, R. B., & Willson, V. (2009). *Measurement and assessment in education.* Boston: Allyn & Bacon.

Reynolds, C. R., Lowe, P. A., & Saenz, A. (1999). The problem of bias in psychological assessment. In T. B. Gutkin & C. R. Reynolds (Eds.), *The handbook of school psychology* (3rd ed., pp. 549–595). New York: Wiley.

Reynolds, C. R., Price, R. J., & Niland, J. (2004). Applications of neuropsychology in capital felony (death penalty) defense. *Journal of Forensic Neuropsychology, 3,* 89–123.

Reynolds, C. R., & Ramsay, M. C. (2003). Bias in psychological assessment: An empirical review and recommendations. In J. R. Graham & J. A. Naglieri (Eds.), *Handbook of psychology: Assessment psychology* (pp. 67–93). New York: Wiley.

Reynolds, C. R., & Voress, J. (2007). *Test of Memory and Learning—Second Edition (TOMAL-2).* Austin, TX: Pro-Ed.

Richardson, T. Q. (1995). The window dressing behind the bell curve. *School Psychology Review, 24,* 42–44.

Riverside Publishing. (2002). *Cognitive Abilities Test, Form 6: A short guide for teachers.* Itasca, IL: Author.

Riverside Publishing. (2003). *Clinical and Special Needs Assessment Catalog.* Itasca, IL: Author.

Roberts, G. E., & Gruber, C. (2005). *Roberts-2.* Los Angeles: Western Psychological Services.

Robertson, G. J. (2003). A practical model for test development. In C. R. Reynolds & R. W. Kamphaus (Eds.), *Handbook of psychological and educational assessment of children: Vol. 1. Intelligence, aptitude, and achievement* (2nd ed., pp. 24–57). New York: Guilford Press.

Roid, G. H. (2003). *Stanford-Binet Intelligence Scale—Fifth Edition.* Itasca, IL: Riverside.

Rorschach, H. (1921). *Psychodiagnostics: A diagnostic test based on perception* (3rd ed. rev.). Oxford, England: Grune & Stratton.

Rosvold, H., Mirsky, A., Sarason, I., Bransome, E., & Beck, L. (1956). A continuous performance test of brain damage. *Journal of Consulting Psychology, 20*(5), 343–350.

Roth, P. L., Bobko, P., & McFarland, L. A. (2005). A meta-analysis of work sample test validity: Updating and integrating some classic literature. *Personnel Psychology, 58,* 1009–1037.

Roth, P. L., Bobko, P., McFarland, L. A., & Buster, M. (2008). Work sample tests in personnel selection: A meta-analysis of Black–White differences in overall and exercise scores. *Personnel Psychology, 61,* 637–662.

Rothstein, H. R., Schmidt, F. L., Erwin, F. W., Owens, W. A., & Sparks, C. P. (1990). Biographical data in employment selection: Can validities be made generalizable? *Journal of Applied Psychology, 75*(2), 175–184.

Rourke, B. P., Bakker, D. I., Fisk, J. L., & Strang, J. D. (1983). *Child neuropsychology: An introduction to theory, research, and clinical practice.* New York: Guilford Press.

Runyan, M. K. (1991). The effect of extra time on reading comprehension scores for university students with and without learning disabilities. *Journal of Learning Disabilities, 24,* 104–108.

Russell, E. (1972). WAIS factor analysis with brain-damaged subjects using criterion measures. *Journal of Consulting and Clinical Psychology, 39*(1), 133–139.

Rutland-Brown, W., Langlois, J. A., Thomas, K. E., & Xi, Y. L. (2006) Incidence of traumatic brain injury in the United States, 2003. *The Journal of Head Trauma Rehabilitation, 21,* 544–548.

Sackett, P. R., Burris, L. R., & Callahan, C. (1989). Integrity testing for personnel selection: An update. *Personnel Psychology, 42,* 491–529.

Sackett, P. R., & Decker, P. J. (1979). Detection of deception in the employment context: A review and critique. *Personnel Psychology, 32,* 487–506.

Sackett, P. R., & Ellingson, J. E. (1997). The effects of forming multi-predictor composites on group differences and adverse impact. *Personnel Psychology, 50,* 707–722.

Sackett, P. R., Schmitt, N., Ellingson, J. E., and Kabin, M. B. (2001). High stakes testing in employment, credentialing, and higher education: Prospects in a post-affirmative action world. *American Psychologist, 56,* 302–318.

Sackett, P. R., & Wanek, J. E. (1996). New developments in the use of measures of honesty, integrity, conscientiousness, dependability, trustworthiness, and reliability for personnel selection. *Personnel Psychology, 49,* 787–829.

Salvia, T., Ysseldyke, T. E., & Bolt, S. (2007). *Assessment in special and inclusive education* (10th ed). Boston: Houghton Mifflin.

Sanders, W. L., Saxton, A. M., & Horn, S. P. (1997). The Tennessee value-added assessment system: A quantitative, outcomes-based approach to educational assessment. In J. Millman (Ed.), *Grading teachers, grading schools* (pp. 137–162). Thousand Oaks, CA: Corwin Press.

Sandoval, J., & Mille, M. P. W. (1979). *Accuracy judgments of WISC-R item difficulty for minority groups.* Paper presented at the annual meeting of the American Psychological Association, New York.

Sarbin, T. R. (1943). A contribution to the study of actuarial and individual methods of prediction. *American Journal of Sociology, 48,* 593–602.

Sarnacki, R. E. (1979, Spring). An examination of test-wiseness in the cognitive domain. *Review of Educational Research, 49,* 252–279.

Sattler, J. M. (1992). *Assessment of children* (3rd ed., rev.). San Diego, CA: Author.

Saupe, J. L. (1961). Some useful estimates of the Kuder-Richardson formula number 20 reliability coefficient. *Educational and Psychological Measurement, 2,* 63–72.

Schmidt, F., & Hunter, J. (2004). General mental ability in the world of work: Occupational attainment and job performance. *Journal of Personality and Social Psychology, 86*(1), 162–173.

Schmidt, F. L., & Hunter, J. (1998). The validity and utility of selection methods in personnel psychology: Practical and theoretical implications of 85 years of research findings. *Psychological Bulletin, 124*(2), 262–274.

Schmidt, F. L., & Zimmerman, R. D. (2004). A counterintuitive hypothesis about employment interview validity and some supporting evidence. *Journal of Applied Psychology, 89*(3), 553–561.

Schmitt, A., Livingston, R., Smernoff, E., Reese, E., Hafer, D., & Harris, J. (2010). Factor analysis of the Repeatable Battery for the Assessment of Neuropsychological Status (RBANS) in a large sample of patients suspected of dementia. *Applied Neuropsychology, 17*(1), 8–17.

Schoenfeld, W. N. (1974). Notes on a bit of psychological nonsense: "Race differences in intelligence." *Psychological Record, 24,* 17–32.

Schopler, E., Reichler, R., & Renner, B. (1988). *The Childhood Autism Rating Scale (CARS).* Los Angeles: Western Psychological Services.

Sheslow, D., & Adams, W. (1990). *Wide Range Assessment of Memory and Learning.* Wilmington, DE: Jastak Associates.

Sidick, J. T., Barrett, G. V. & Doverspike, D. (1994). Three-alternative multiple choice tests: An attractive option. *Personnel Psychology, 47,* 829–835.

Sireci, S. G. (1998). Gathering and analyzing content validity data. *Educational Assessment, 5,* 299–321.

Sireci, S. G., Thissen, D., & Wainer, H. (1991). On the reliability of testlet-based tests. *Journal of Educational Measurement, 28,* 237–247.

Slick, D., Hopp, G., Strauss, E., & Fox, D. (1996). Effects of prior testing with the WAIS-R NI on subsequent retest with the WAIS-R. *Archives of Clinical Neuropsychology, 11*(2), 123–130.

Smith, P. C., & Kendall, L. M. (1963). Retranslation of expectations: An approach to the construction of unambiguous anchors for rating scales. *Journal of Applied Psychology, 47,* 149–155.

Snyderman, M., & Rothman, S. (1987). Survey of expert opinion on intelligence and aptitude testing. *American Psychologist, 42,* 137–144.

Society for Industrial and Organizational Psychology, Inc. (2003). *Principles for the validationand use of personnel selection procedures.* (3rd ed.). College Park, MD: Author.

Spearman, C. (1904). "General intelligence," objectively determined and measured. *The American Journal of Psychology, 15*(2), 201–293.

Spearman, C. (1907). Demonstration of formulae for true measurement of correlation. *The American Journal of Psychology, 18*(2), 161–169.

Spearman, C. (1913). Correlations of sums or differences. *British Journal of Psychology, 5,* 417–426.

Specialty guidelines for forensic psychologists. (1991). *Law & Human Behavior, 15*(6), 665–666.

Sternberg, R. J. (1990). *Metaphors of mind: Conceptions of the nature of intelligence.* Cambridge, England: Cambridge University Press.

Stevens, S. S. (1946). On the theory of scales of measurement. *Science, 103,* 677–680.

Stiggins, R. J., & Conklin, N. F. (1992). *In teachers' hands: Investigating the practices of classroom assessment.* Albany: State University of New York Press.

Stroud, K. C., & Reynolds, C. R. (2006). *School Motivation and Learning Strategies Inventory (SMALSI).* Los Angeles: Western Psychological Services.

Suzuki, L. A., & Valencia, R. R. (1997). Race-ethnicity and measured intelligence: Educational implications. *American Psychologist, 52,* 1103–1114.

Teglasi, H. (1998). Assessment of schema and problem-solving strategies with projective techniques. In C. R. Reynolds (Ed.), Assessment, Vol. 4 of A. Bellack & M. Hersen (Eds.), *Comprehensive Clinical Psychology* (pp. 459–500). Oxford, England: Elsevier Science.

Tellegen, A., & Ben-Porath, Y. S. (2008). *MMPI-2-RF (Minnesota Multiphasic Personality Inventory-2): Technical manual.* Minneapolis: University of Minnesota Press.

Tellegen, A., Ben-Porath, Y. S., McNulty, J. L., Arbisi, P. A., Graham, J. R., & Kaemmer, B. (2003). *MMPI-2 Restructured Clinical (RC) Scales: Development, validation, and interpretation.* Minneapolis: University of Minnesota Press.

Tett, R. P., & Christiansen, N. D. (2007). Personality tests at the crossroads: A response to Morgeson, Campion, Dipboye, Hollenbeck, Murphy, and Schmitt. *Personnel Psychology, 60,* 967–993.

Tett, R. P., Jackson, D. N., & Rothstein, M. (1991). Personality measures as predictors of job performance: A meta-analytic review. *Personnel Psychology, 44,* 703–742.

Texas Education Agency. (2003). *2003 district and campus coordinator manual.* Austin, TX: Author.

Thorndike, R. (1949). *Personnel selection: Test and measurement techniques.* Oxford, England: Wiley.

Thorndike, R. M. (2005). *Measurement and evaluation in psychology and education.* Upper Saddle River, NJ: Pearson.

Thurstone, L. (1931). *The reliability and validity of tests: Derivation and interpretation of fundamental formulae concerned with reliability and validity of tests and illustrative problems.* Ann Arbor, MI: Edwards Brothers.

Tombaugh, T. N. (1996). *The Test of Memory Malingering.* Toronto, Canada: Multi-Health Systems.

Triplett, N. (1898). The dynamogenic factors in pacemaking and competition. *American Journal of Psychology, 9,* 507–533.

Uniform guidelines on employee selection procedures. (1978). Federal Register, 43 (166), 38296–38309.

U.S. Department of Education. (2001). *Guidance on standards, assessments, and accountability—II. Assessments.* Retrieved from http://www.ed.gov/offices/OESE/StandardsAssessments/assess.html

Valleley, R. J. (2009). Review of the Roberts-2. In *Mental Measurements Yearbook* (Vol. 18). Lincoln, NE: Buros Institute of Mental Measurementst.

Vannest, K., Reynolds, C. R., & Kamphaus, R. W. (2009). *Intervention guide for behavioral and emotional issues.* Bloomington, MN: Pearson Assessments.

Wagner, R. K. (1997). Intelligence, training, and employment. *American Psychologist, 52*(10), 1059–1069.

Webster, W. J., & Mendro, R. L. (1997). The Dallas value-added accountability system. In J. Millman (Ed.), *Grading teachers, grading schools* (pp. 81–99). Thousand Oaks, CA: Corwin Press.

Wechsler, D. (1958). *The measurement and appraisal of adult intelligence* (4th ed.). Baltimore, MD: Williams & Wilkins.

Wechsler, D. (1997). *Wechsler Adult Intelligence Scale—Third Edition.* San Antonio, TX: Psychological Corporation.

Wechsler, D. W. (2003). *Wechsler Intelligence Scale for Children—Fourth Edition: Technical and interpretive manual.* San Antonio, TX: Psychological Corporation.

Weiss, D. J. (1982). Improving measurement quality and efficiency with adaptive theory. *Applied Psychological Measurement, 6,* 473–492.

Weiss, D. J. (1985). Adaptive testing by computer. *Journal of Consulting and Clinical Psychology, 53,* 774–789.

Weiss, D. J. (1995). Improving individual difference measurement with item response theory and computerized adaptive testing. In D. Lubinski & R. Dawis (Eds.), *Assessing individual differences in human behavior: New concepts, methods, and findings* (pp. 49–79). Palo Alto, CA: Davies-Black.

White, R., & Rose, F. (1997). The Boston process approach: A brief history and current practice. In G. Goldstein & T. M. Incagnoli (Eds.), *Contemporary approaches to neuropsychological assessment* (pp. 171–211). New York: Plenum Press.

Wigdor, A. K., & Garner, W. K. (1982). *Ability testing: Uses, consequences, and controversy.* Washington, DC: National Academy Press.

Wikipedia. (2009a). About. Retrieved from http://en.wikipedia.org/wiki/Wikipedia:about

Wikipedia. (2009b). Forensic psychology. Retrieved from http://en.wikipedia.org/wiki/Forensic-psychology

Wilk, S., & Cappelli, P. (2003). Determinants and outcomes of employee selection procedures. *Personnel Psychology, 56*(1), 103–125.

Wilkinson, L., & Task Force on Statistical Inferences. (1999). Statistical methods in psychology journals: Guidelines and explanations. *American Psychologist, 54*(8), 594–604.

Williams, R. L. (1970). Danger: Testing and dehumanizing Black children. *Clinical Child Psychology Newsletter, 9,* 5–6.

Williams, R. L., Dotson, W., Dow, P., & Williams, W. S. (1980). The war against testing: A current status report. *Journal of Negro Education, 49,* 263–273.

Wilson, R. S., & Kaszniak, A. W. (1986). Longitudinal changes: Progressive idiopathic dementia. In L.W. Poon, T. Crook, K. L. Davis, C. Eisdorfer, & B. J. Gurland (Eds.), *Handbook for clinical memory assessment of older adults* (pp. 285–293). Washington, DC: American Psychological Association.

Witt, J., Heffer, R., & Pfeiffer, J. (1990). Structured rating scales: A review of self-report and informant rating processes, procedures, and issues. In C. R. Reynolds & R. Kamphaus (Eds.), *Handbook of psychological and educational assessment of children: Personality, behavior, and context* (pp. 364–394). New York: Guilford Press.

Woodcock, R. W. (1978). Development and standardization of the *Woodcock-Johnson Psycho-Educational Battery.* Rolling Meadows, IL: Riverside.

Woodcock, R. W. (1999). What can Rasch-based scores convey about a person's test performance? In S. E. Embretson & S. L. Hershberger (Eds.), *The new rules of measurement: What every psychologist and educator should know* (pp. 105–127). Mahwah, NJ: Erlbaum.

Woodcock, R. W., McGrew, K. S., & Mather, N. (2001a). *Woodcock-Johnson III (WJ III) Complete Battery.* Itasca, IL: Riverside.

Woodcock, R. W., McGrew, K. S., & Mather, N. (2001b). *Woodcock-Johnson III (WJ III) Tests of Achievement.* Itasca, IL: Riverside.

Woodcock, R. W., McGrew, K. S., & Mather, N. (2001c). *Woodcock-Johnson III (WJ III) Tests of Cognitive Abilities.* Itasca, IL: Riverside.

Yantz, C. L., & McCaffrey, R. J., (2005). Effects of a supervisor's observation on memory test performance of the examinee: Third party observer effect confirmed. *Journal of Forensic Neuropsychology, 4,* 27–38.

Youngjohn, J. R. (1995). Confirmed attorney coaching prior to a neuropsychological evaluation. *Assessment, 2,* 279–283.

Youngstrom, E. A., Freeman, A. J., & Jenkins, M. M. (2009). The assessment of children and adolescents with bipolar disorder. *Child and Adolescent Psychiatry Clinics of North America, 18*(2), 353–390.

Zajonc, R. B. (1965). Social facilitation. *Science, 149,* 269–274.

INDEX

vs. Nonstandardized test, 14–15

Standards for Educational and Psychological Testing, 97, 143, 155-156, 159, 160–161, 164, 173, 177, 179–180, 463, 474, 485, 486, 488, 503, 506–507, 513, 516, 517, 518, 524

  Description, 27

Stanford Achievement Test Series – Tenth Edition (Stanford 10), 253, 294

Stanford-Binet Intelligence Scale, 7, 280, 285–286, 300–301, 306, 421, 514

  Reliability of, 130

Strong Interest Inventory – Revised Edition (SII-R), 408–410

Summative evaluation, 24–25, 271

T

TerraNova CTBS, 252

TerraNova – the Second Edition, 253, 293

Test

  Benefits of using, 21–23

  Defined, 8–9

  Major categories, 11–15

  Objective vs. Subjective, 12

Test bias

  and etiology, 478

  and extraneous factors, 480

  and fairness, 478–479

  Inappropriate indicators of, 486–487

  and inappropriate test administration and use, 480

  Mean difference definition of, 486–487

  and offensiveness, 479–480

  Problem of definition in research Differential validity, 485

Test of Memory and Learning – 2nd edition (TOMAL-2), 421, 425-428, 435

Tests, 255, 528

Tests Critique, 255, 528

Tests of Cognitive Skills – 2nd edition (TCS/2), 280, 293

Tests in Print, 255, 527–528

Test takers, responsibilities of, 537–538

Texas Assessment of Knowledge and Skills (TAKS), 257

  Accommodations, 515–516

Therapeutic assessment, 324–326

Thurstone scales, 215-216

Time sampling error, 114

Trier of fact

  Defined, 448

Typical response items, 210–218

  Formats, 211–214

  Guidelines, 214–218

  Percent endorsement statistic, 224–225

Typical response test, 327

  Defined, 13

U

Uniform Guidelines on Employee Selection Procedures (1978) 407

United States Medical Licensing Examination (USMLE) 275–276

  Item discrimination, 230–231

Universal Nonverbal Intelligence Test (UNIT), 287

V

Validity

  Coefficients

    Interpreting, 167–168

  Construct, 159

  Content, 159

  Convergent evidence, 170–172

  Criterion-related, 159

  Defined, 11, 155

ABNORMAL PSYCHOLOGY
Beidel, Bulik & Stanley *Abnormal Psychology*, 2/e ©2012, 9780205205011/ 0205205011
Oltmanns & Emery *Abnormal Psychology*, 7/e ©2012, 9780205037438 / 0205037437
Meyer *Case Studies in Abnormal Behavior*, 9/e ©2012, 9780205036998 / 0205036996

ADJUSTMENT
Duffy, Kirsh & Atwater *Psychology for Living: Adjustment, Growth and Behavior*, 10/e ©2011, 9780205790364 / 0205790364

ADOLESCENT DEVELOPMENT
Arnett *Adolescence and Emerging Adulthood: A Cultural Approach,* 4/e ©2010, 9780138144586 / 0138144583
Dolgin *The Adolescent,* 13e ©2011, 9780205731367 / 0205731368
Garrod, Smulyan, Powers & Kilkenny *Adolescent Portraits: Identity, Relationships, and Challenges,* 7/e ©2012, 9780205036233 / 0205036236

ADULTHOOD & AGING
Bjorklund *Journey of Adulthood,* 7/e ©2011, 9780205018055 / 020501805X
Mason *Adulthood and Aging* ©2011, 9780205433513 / 0205433510

BEHAVIOR MODIFICATION
Martin & Pear *Behavior Modification,* 9/e ©2011, 9780205792726 / 0205792723

BIOPSYCHOLOGY / BEHAVIORAL NEUROSCIENCE
Pinel *Biopsychology,* 8e ©2011, 9780205832569 / 0205832563

CHILD DEVELOPMENT (Chronological Approach)
Berk *Infants, Children, and Adolescents,* 7/e ©2011, 9780205718160 / 0205718167

CHILD DEVELOPMENT (Topical Approach)
Kail *Children and Their Development,* 6/e ©2012, 9780205034949 / 0205034942

CLINICAL PSYCHOLOGY
Lilienfeld & O'Donohue *Great Readings In Clinical Science* ©2012, 9780205698035 / 0205698034
Linden & Hewitt *Clinical Psychology,* 1/e ©2012, 9780132397278 / 0132397277

CLOSE RELATIONSHIPS / INTERPERSONAL
Erber & Erber *Intimate Relationships: Issues, Theories, and Research,* 2/e ©2011, 9780205454464 / 0205454461

COGNITION
Levitin *Foundations of Cognitive Psychology* ©2011, 9780205711475 / 0205711472
Robinson-Riegler *Cognitive Psychology: Applying The Science of the Mind,* 3/e ©2012, 9780205033645 / 0205033644

CROSS-CULTURAL / MULTICULTURAL PSYCHOLOGY
White, Parham & Ajamu *Psychology of Blacks,* 4/e ©2011, 9780131827738 / 0131827731

DRUGS AND BEHAVIOR
Ettinger *Psychopharmacology* ©2011, 9780136013068 / 0136013066
Levinthal *Drugs, Behavior, and Modern Society,* 7/e ©2012, 9780205037261 / 0205037267
Grilly *Drugs and Human Behavior,* 6e ©2012, 9780205750528 / 0205750524

GENDER
Helgeson *Psychology of Gender,* 4/e ©2012, 9780205050185 / 0205050182

HEALTH PSYCHOLOGY
Ragin *Health Psychology* ©2011, 9780131962972 / 0131962973

HUMAN SEXUALITY
King *Human Sexuality Today,* 7/e ©2012, 9780205015672 / 0205015670

INFANT DEVELOPMENT
Gross *Infancy: From Birth to Age 3,* 2/e ©2011, 9780205734191 / 0205734197

INTRODUCTORY PSYCHOLOGY
Ciccarelli & White *Psychology,* 3/e ©2012, 9780205832576 / 0205832571